KEYS USED IN FORM

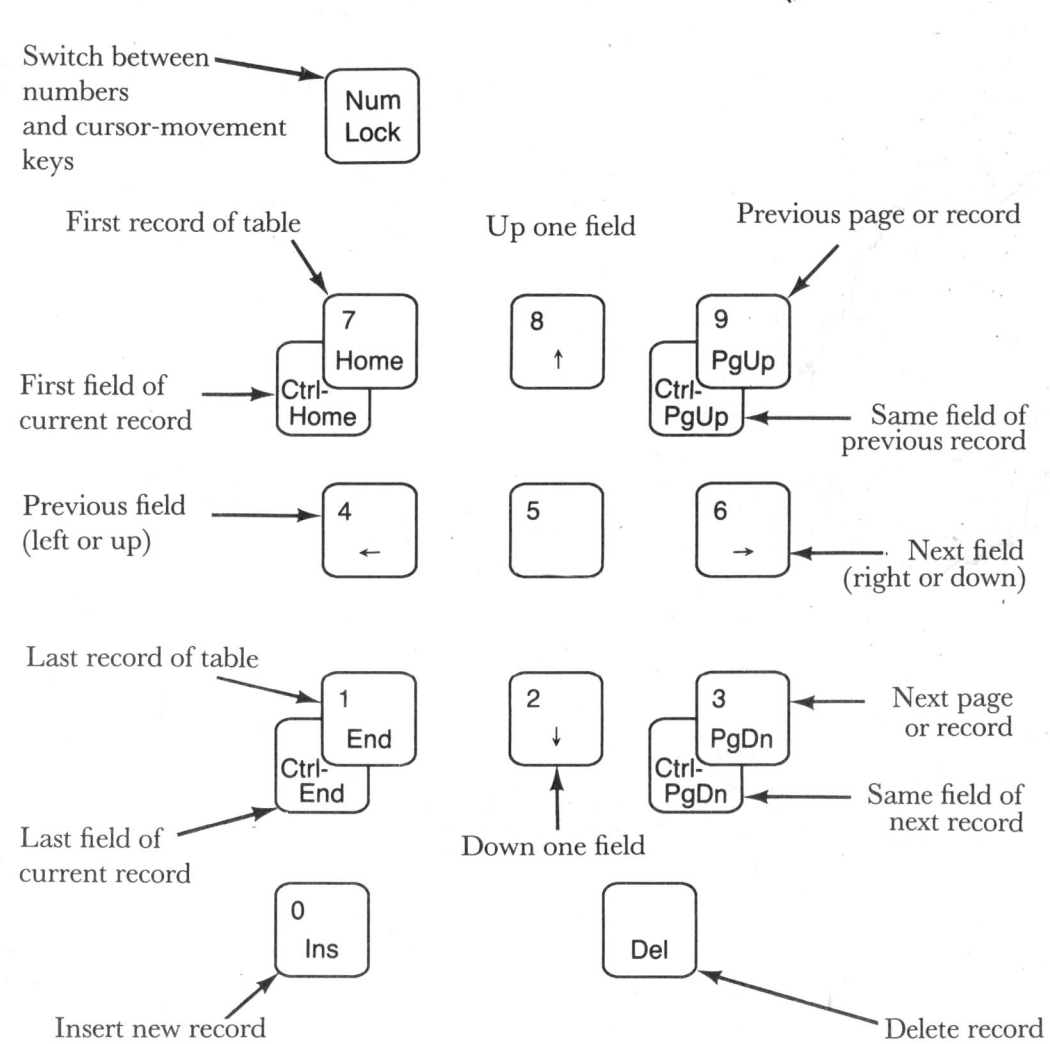

- Switch between numbers and cursor-movement keys → **Num Lock**
- First record of table → **7 Home**
- First field of current record → **Ctrl-Home**
- Up one field → **8 ↑**
- Previous page or record → **9 PgUp**
- Same field of previous record → **Ctrl-PgUp**
- Previous field (left or up) → **4 ←**
- **5**
- Next field (right or down) → **6 →**
- Last record of table → **1 End**
- Last field of current record → **Ctrl-End**
- Down one field → **2 ↓**
- Next page or record → **3 PgDn**
- Same field of next record → **Ctrl-PgDn**
- Insert new record → **0 Ins**
- Delete record → **Del**

MASTERING PARADOX 3.5

MASTERING PARADOX® 3.5

Fifth Editon

ALAN SIMPSON

SYBEX ®

San Francisco • Paris • Düsseldorf • Soest

Acquisitions Editor: Dianne King
Copy Editors: Christian T.S. Crumlish, Brendan Fletcher
Technical Editors: Lin Beacom, Bob Campbell
Word Processors: Lisa Mitchell, Chris Mockel, Bob Myren
Book Designer: Charlotte Carter
Screen Graphics: Cuong Le, Sonja Schenk
Typesetters: Len Gilbert, Winnie Kelly
Proofreaders: Eddie Lin, Dina F. Quan
Indexer: Julie Kawabata
Cover Designer: Thomas Ingalls + Associates
Cover Photographer: Michael Lamotte
Some screen reproductions produced by XenoFont.

SYBEX is a registered trademark of SYBEX, Inc.

TRADEMARKS: SYBEX has attempted throughout this book to distinguish proprietary trademarks from descriptive terms by following the capitalization style used by the manufacturer.

SYBEX is not affiliated with any manufacturer.

Every effort has been made to supply complete and accurate information. However, SYBEX assumes no responsibility for its use, nor for any infringement of the intellectual property rights of third parties which would result from such use.

The text of this book is printed on recycled paper.

First edition copyright ©1986 SYBEX Inc.
Second edition copyright ©1986 SYBEX Inc.
Third edition copyright ©1988 SYBEX Inc.
Fourth edition copyright ©1989 SYBEX Inc.

Copyright ©1990 SYBEX Inc., 2021 Challenger Drive, Alameda, CA 94501. World rights reserved. No part of this publication may be stored in a retrieval system, transmitted, or reproduced in any way, including but not limited to photocopy, photograph, magnetic or other record, without the prior agreement and written permission of the publisher.

Library of Congress Card Number: 90-71326

ISBN: 0-89588-677-4

Manufactured in the United States of America

10 9 8 7 6 5 4 3

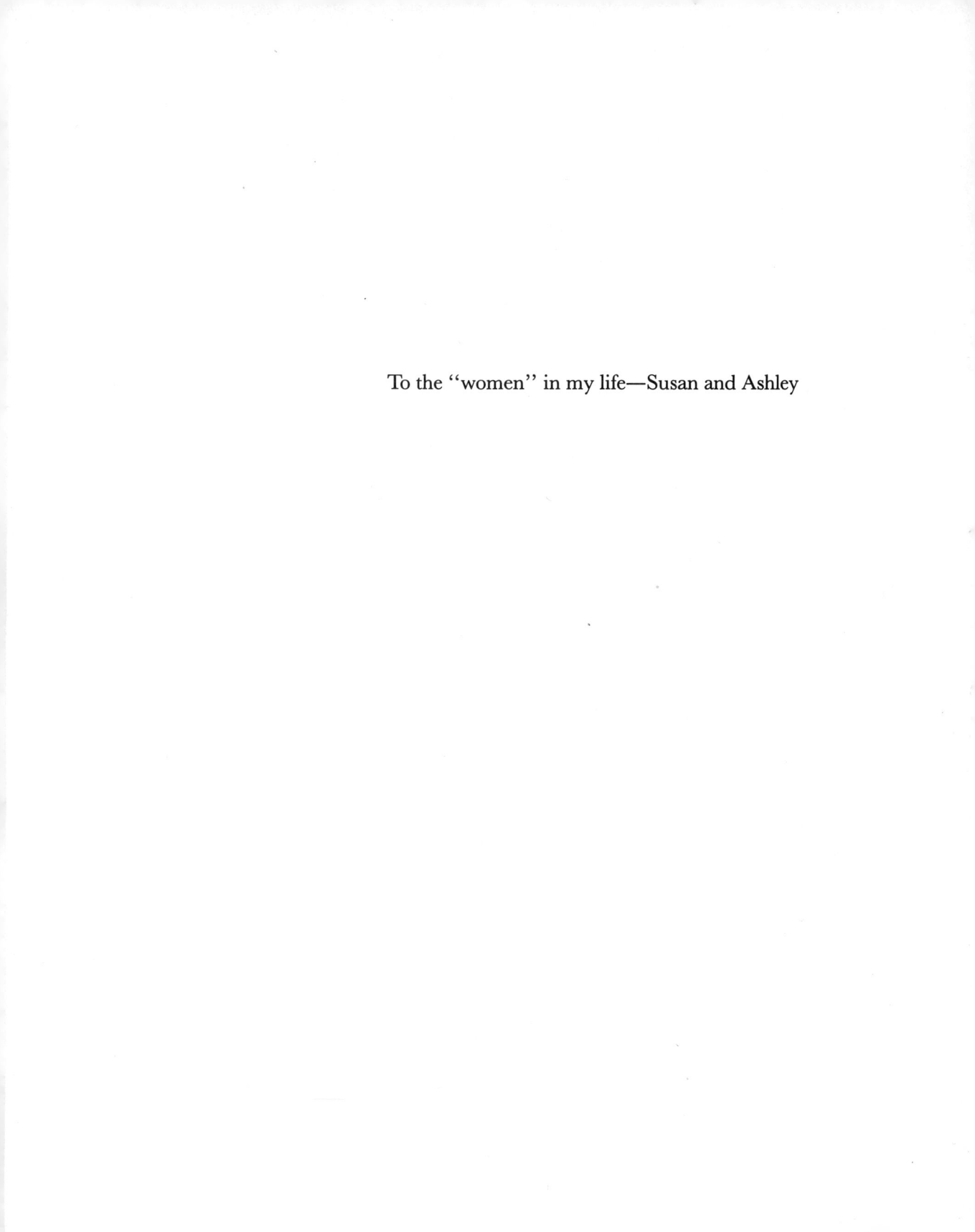

To the "women" in my life—Susan and Ashley

ACKNOWLEDGMENTS

Many thanks to John Calderas of Salient Seven Technologies and the Southern California Paradox User's Group (LAPALS) for his precise edits and many contributions to this book. Also from LAPALS, many thanks to Rod Walsh for his valuable suggestions.

Many thanks to all of the people at SYBEX who contributed to the production of this book.

Thanks to Bill and Cynthia Gladstone; friends, family, and literary agents, for keeping my writing career alive and well.

And of course, many thanks to Susan and Ashley, for being patient and supportive while Daddy stays locked away in the office.

CONTENTS AT A GLANCE

	Introduction	*xxv*
PART 1:	***The Basics***	***1***
Chapter 1:	Databases	2
Chapter 2:	Creating a Table	10
Chapter 3:	Adding Data to a Table	26
Chapter 4:	Viewing Table Data	48
Chapter 5:	Editing and Validating Data	64
Chapter 6:	Sorting	82
Chapter 7:	Searching the Database	100
Chapter 8:	Printing Formatted Reports	132
Chapter 9:	Custom Forms	180
Chapter 10:	Graphics	200
Chapter 11:	Scripts	254
PART 2:	***Multiple Tables in a Database***	***263***
Chapter 12:	Database Design with Multiple Tables	264
Chapter 13:	Advanced Queries and Calculations	294
Chapter 14:	Advanced Report and Form Techniques	330
Chapter 15:	Automatic Updating	408
Chapter 16:	Managing Files	422
PART 3:	***The Paradox Application Language***	***457***
Chapter 17:	Introduction to PAL Programming	458
Chapter 18:	A Sample PAL Application	492
Chapter 19:	Handy Tips and Scripts	522
Chapter 20:	The Paradox Personal Programmer	560
Appendix A:	*Installing Paradox*	620
Appendix B:	*Networks, SQL Link, and Memory Management*	628
Appendix C:	*Customizing Paradox*	664
	Index	*690*

TABLE OF CONTENTS

INTRODUCTION — xxv

PART 1 — *The Basics*

Chapter 1: DATABASES — 2
- What Is a Database? — 3
- Field Names — 5
- Managing a Database — 7
- Paradox Limitations — 7
- Summary — 8

Chapter 2: CREATING A TABLE — 10
- Installation — 11
- Starting Paradox — 11
- The Main Menu — 12
  - Selecting Menu Items — 13
  - Unselecting Menu Items — 14
  - Calling Up the Menu — 14
- Getting Help — 14
- Creating a Table — 16
  - Field Names — 18
  - Data Types — 18
- Entering the Table Structure — 19
- Saving the Table Structure — 22
- Exiting Paradox — 23
- Changing a Table Structure — 23
- Key Fields — 24
- Summary — 24

Chapter 3: ADDING DATA TO A TABLE — 26
- Paradox Data Entry — 27
  - Field View Editing — 33
  - The Ditto Key — 35

Using Form View	35
Data Entry Shortcuts	38
Numeric Fields	38
Date Fields	38
Saving Your Work	41
Entering New Records in the Edit Mode	42
Inserting Records	43
A Few Cautions	44
Summary	45

Chapter 4: VIEWING TABLE DATA — 48

Viewing a Table	49
The Image Menu	50
Changing the Table Size	51
Changing the Column Width	52
Formatting Numeric and Date Fields	54
Large Moves through the Image	56
Moving Columns	58
Quick Moves with the Rotate Command	60
Switching to Form View	60
Saving Image Settings	61
Printing an Image Quickly	62
Clearing an Image	62
Summary	63

Chapter 5: EDITING AND VALIDATING DATA — 64

The Edit Mode	65
Simple Edits	65
Field View Editing	66
Saving Edits	66
Undoing Edits	66
Deleting a Record	68
Undeleting a Record	68
Locating the Record to Edit	68
An Exercise in Editing	69
Inserting a Record	71
When the Data Doesn't Fit	71
The Edit Menu	71

	Checking the Validity of Data	72
	Defining the Lowest Acceptable Value	72
	Defining the Highest Acceptable Value	73
	Entering Default Values	73
	Entering Picture Formats	74
	Defining Required Values	77
	TableLookup	77
	Clearing Validity Checks	77
	Saving Validity Checks	78
	Sample Validity Checks	78
	Getting Unstuck	79
	Summary	80
Chapter 6:	***SORTING***	*82*
	Sorting by a Single Field	83
	Descending Sorts	84
	Sorting by Several Fields	87
	Examples	92
	The Sort Menu	98
	Summary	98
Chapter 7:	***SEARCHING THE DATABASE***	*100*
	Query Forms	101
	Selecting Fields to View	102
	Printing the Answer	102
	Clearing the Answer Table	103
	Seeing Unique Items	103
	Controlling the Sort Order	104
	Finding a Particular Group of Records	105
	Searching for Values	107
	Searching for Nonmatches	110
	Searching for Ranges	110
	Performing And/Or Searches	112
	Pattern-Matching Searches	116
	Queries as an Editing Tool	122
	Global Edits	122
	Global Deletions	125
	Limitations	126

Sample Queries 127
Summary 130

Chapter 8: PRINTING FORMATTED REPORTS — 132

Designing a Report 134
    Placing Fields 138
    Adding the Record Number 143
    A Trial Run 145
    Squeezing Out the Blanks 146
Saving a Report Format 147
Canceling a Report Format 147
Printing the Sorted Directory 148
    Presorting the Table 148
    Printing a Report from the Main Menu 149
Fine-Tuning Your Report 150
    Changing an Existing Report Format 150
    Changing Heading and Footing Margins 151
    Adjusting Page Length 152
    Adjusting Page Width 153
    Changing the Margin Setting 153
Mailing Labels 155
    Copying a Report Format 155
    Formatting Labels 156
    Deleting a Field from a Report 157
    Continuous-Feed Paper 159
    Multiple Label Columns 160
    Fine-Tuning the Labels 160
    Printing the Mailing Labels 161
Form Letters 162
    Page Breaks 164
    Single-Sheet Printing 165
    Formatting the Letter 165
    A Trial Run with Your Form Letter 166
Printing Groups of Pages 167
Using Query Forms with Reports 167
Other Report Options 170
    Dates and Times 170
    Page Numbers 171
    Formatted Numbers 172
    Condensed and Expanded Print 173

Temporary Printer Redirection	177
More Control over Page Lengths	178
Additional Report Capabilities	178
Summary	178

Chapter 9: CUSTOM FORMS — 180

Creating a Custom Form	182
Managing the Form Cursor	184
Placing Text on the Form	184
Placing Fields on the Screen	185
Borders	189
Moving Items on the Form	190
Adding Help to a Form	191
Coloring a Form	193
Saving a Form	195
Using a Form	196
Changing a Form	196
Reformatting Fields on a Form	197
Erasing Parts of the Form	197
Erasing a Field	197
Erasing a Border	197
Erasing an Area	198
Summary	198

Chapter 10: GRAPHICS — 200

A Quick Tour of Graphs	201
Viewing an Instant Graph	201
How Paradox Designs an Instant Graph	203
Exploring Graph Types	204
General Techniques for Displaying Sample Graphs	204
Stacked Bar	206
Standard Bar	206
Rotated Bar	206
3-D Bar	206
X-Y Graph	209
Area Graph	209
Line Graph	210

Markers Graph	211
Combined Lines and Markers	211
Pie Chart	213
Combined Graphs	213
Customizing Graphs	214
Selecting the Graph Type	215
Customizing the Titles	215
Quick View of Changes	216
Saving Custom Graph Titles	218
Using Custom Graphs in the Future	219
Modifying a Custom Graph	220
Using One Custom Graph to Create Another	220
Refining Graphs	221
Refining Overall Settings	221
The Graph Settings Overall Submenu	222
Modifying Graph Colors	222
Matching Screen Colors to Printer Colors	224
Modifying Graph Axes	224
Modifying Graph Grids	229
Customizing Graph Series	230
Modifying Legends and Labels	230
Modifying Markers and Fill Patterns	231
Special Techniques for Pie Charts	233
Modifying the Label Format	235
Customizing Pie Slices	236
Printing Graphs	236
Preparing the Printer for Graphs	237
Printing a Graph	238
Customizing the Printed Graph Layout	238
Selecting a Temporary Printer	239
Saving Graphs for Printing Later	241
Limiting the Duration of a Graph	242
Cross Tabulations	242
Creating a Sample Table	243
Using CrossTab	243
Generating a Crosstab	245
Graphing a Crosstab Table	245
Arranging Fields for Crosstabs	248
A Shortcut Method for Crosstabs	250
Summary	251

Chapter 11:	**SCRIPTS**	**254**
	Your First Script	255
	Viewing a Recorded Script	257
	The Scripts Menu	258
	Instant Scripts	260
	The PAL Menu	260
	Autoexecute Scripts	261
	Being Creative	261
	Summary	261

PART 2 *Multiple Tables in a Database*

Chapter 12:	**DATABASE DESIGN WITH MULTIPLE TABLES**	**264**
	The One-to-One Database Design	265
	The One-to-Many Database Design	265
	Using a Common Field to Relate Tables	267
	Guidelines for Creating a Common Field	269
	The Master-Table/Transaction-Table Structure	271
	The Many-to-Many Database Design	272
	A Scheduling Database	272
	An Exploded Inventory Database	275
	Normalizing a Database	278
	Remove Redundant Data	278
	Remove All Partial Dependencies	278
	Remove Transitive Dependencies	279
	The Fully Normalized Database	280
	A Working Inventory Example	280
	Master Inventory Table	280
	Rejecting Duplicate Entries	280
	The Sales Table	283
	Automatic Validation and Fill-In	284
	Refining the Sales Table	286
	Experimenting with Help and Fill-In	287
	The Purchase Table	291
	Summary	292

Chapter 13: ADVANCED QUERIES AND CALCULATIONS — 294

- Querying Multiple Tables — 295
  - Entering Examples — 296
- Searches with Multiple Tables — 299
  - And and Or Queries with Multiple Tables — 302
- Displaying Non-Matching Records — 304
- Using Queries to Calculate Results — 305
  - Calculations on Groups of Records — 307
  - Frequency Distributions — 308
- Calculations with Examples — 309
- Performing Queries in a Many-to-Many Design — 312
- Calculations in a Many-to-Many Design — 314
- Asking About Sets of Records — 319
  - Creating Set Queries — 320
  - Comparing Records to Summary Tables — 324
  - The Groupby Operator — 325
- Handling Blanks in Query Calculations — 326
- Saving Queries — 327
- Query Speed-Up — 328
- Summary — 329

Chapter 14: ADVANCED REPORT AND FORM TECHNIQUES — 330

- Tabular Reports — 331
- The Tabular Report Menu — 332
- Managing Report Columns — 333
  - Inserting Columns — 333
  - Erasing Columns — 334
  - Resizing Columns — 334
  - Moving Columns — 335
  - Copying Columns — 336
- Managing Fields — 336
  - General Techniques for Placing and Formatting Fields — 337
  - Placing Regular Fields — 340
  - Placing Calculated Fields — 340
  - Placing Summary Fields — 349
  - Placing the Date Field — 350
  - Placing the Time Field — 351
  - Placing the Page Field — 351
  - Placing the #Record Field — 352

Column Alignment	352
Word-Wrap	353
Grouping	356
A Note on Report Bands	356
Placing Group Bands in the Report	357
The Group Menu	361
Inserting Groups	361
Group Headers, Footers, and Blank Lines	366
Removing Grouping Values from the Table Band	369
Deleting Groups	370
Group Headings	370
Sorting Groups	371
Changing Groups	371
Tabular Report Settings	371
Summary Reports	375
Printing Reports from Multiple Tables	376
Using Summary Operators in Reports	379
Multiple-Page Forms	382
Display-Only Fields	383
Calculated Fields	386
Combining Multiple Forms for Multiple Tables	387
Tables Used in the Sample Form	390
Designing a Subform	396
Developing a Multirecord Form	397
Developing the Master Form	398
A Few Finishing Touches	401
Using the Multitable Form	403
Using the Cursor on a Multitable Form	404
How Paradox Manages Multitable Forms	405
Summary	405

Chapter 15: AUTOMATIC UPDATING 408

History Tables	410
Automating an Update Procedure	410
Recording the Script	411
Summarizing the Sales Transactions	411
Subtracting Sales from Master Quantities	412
Moving Records to the History Table	414
Summarizing the Purchase Transactions	414
Adding Purchases to Master Quantities	415

Moving Purchase Transactions to the Purhist Table	417
Completing the Script	417
Verifying the Update	417
Developing a Schedule	418
Correcting Update Transactions	419
A Master Inventory Report	419
Summary	420

Chapter 16: MANAGING FILES 422

Renaming Objects	423
Copying Objects	424
Deleting Objects	425
Copying Records from One Table to Another	425
Removing Records from a Table	426
Emptying a Table	427
Protecting Data	428
Password Protection	429
Reactivating Passwords	431
Write Protection	431
Setting a Directory	432
General File Information	432
Viewing Table Structures	433
Viewing the File Inventory	434
Viewing Families	435
Restructuring a Table	435
Adding a New Field	436
Saving the New Structure	436
Changing Your Mind	437
Deleting a Field	437
Renaming a Field	437
Rearranging Fields	437
Changing the Length of a Field	438
Changing the Type of a Field	438
Speeding Up Queries	439
Interfacing with Other Software Systems	440
Quattro	440
1-2-3 and Symphony	441
dBASE II, III, and IV	442
Framework	443
Reflex	443

PFS	443
VisiCalc	443
ASCII	444
Interfacing with Word Processors	446
Exporting a Report	446
Mailmerge Files for Form Letters	447
WordPerfect Form-Letter Files	448
Running External Programs	453
Summary	454

PART 3 *The Paradox Application Language*

Chapter 17: **INTRODUCTION TO PAL PROGRAMMING**	*458*
Creating a PAL Program	459
Saving a PAL Program	460
Running a PAL Program	461
The PAL Canvas	462
Canceling a PAL Script	462
Debugging	462
Editing a PAL Program	463
Interacting with the User	463
Looping	468
Avoiding the Infamous Infinite Loop	471
Making Decisions	472
IF...THEN...ELSE...ENDIF	472
SWITCH...CASE...OTHERWISE...ENDSWITCH	474
Custom Menus	477
Script Conventions	480
Menu Selections	481
Literal Keystrokes	481
Special Keys	482
Commands and Functions	484
Field Names	485
Variables	485
Structured Programming	488
Summary	489

Chapter 18: A SAMPLE PAL APPLICATION — 492

The Main Menu	493
Adding New Records	498
Printing Reports	502
Editing the Mailing List	513
Speeding Up Mail	519
Summary	520

Chapter 19: HANDY TIPS AND SCRIPTS — 522

Tips on Scripts	523
Running Scripts from DOS	523
Automatic Scripts	523
Protecting Scripts	524
Printing Scripts	524
Using External Word Processors to Edit Scripts	524
Running External Programs from Scripts	525
Keyboard Macros	526
A Keyboard Macro to Type a Name	528
A Macro to Eject a Page	528
A Macro to Display Script Inventory	529
Activating the SETKEY Command	529
Keyboard Macro Limitations	530
Canceling Keyboard Macros	531
Debugging PAL Scripts	531
The Value Option	532
The Step Option	534
The Next Option	535
The Go Option	535
The Miniscript Option	535
The Where? Option	536
The Pop Option	536
The Editor Option	537
The Quit Option	537
Using Record Numbers in Tables	537
Translating Numbers into Words	541
Preparsed Procedure Libraries	545
Procedure to Create a Library	546
Using the Procedure Library	549

	Modifying Procedure Libraries	551
	Check-Printing Revisited	551
	Looking into Procedures	557
	Summary	558

Chapter 20: THE PARADOX PERSONAL PROGRAMMER 560

Requirements and Limitations	562
Hardware Requirements	562
Experience Requirements	562
Planning an Application	563
An Inventory Management System	563
The Inventory System Tables	564
The Application Menu Tree	564
Creating a Directory for the Application	567
Copying Objects	567
Starting the Personal Programmer	568
Creating the Application	570
Selecting Tables for the Application	571
Defining the Main Menu	574
Assigning Actions to Menu Items	576
The Master Inventory Submenu	577
Inventory Sales Submenu	584
The Sales Submenu	585
The Purchases Submenu	594
Testing Our Progress	598
Custom Scripts for the Inventory System	600
The Reorder Report	600
Inventory System Update Scripts	603
Attaching Custom Scripts	604
Running the Inventory Application	605
Managing the Master Inventory Table	606
Managing the Sales Table	607
Managing the Purchase Table	608
Entering Adjustment Transactions	608
Updating	609
Leaving the Inventory System	609
Modifying an Application	609
More Personal Programmer Features	611
Adding Custom Help Screens	611
Slash Screens	612

Summarizing an Application	612
Testing the Menu Structure	615
General Application Management	615
Summary	616

APPENDIX A: Installing Paradox — 620

APPENDIX B: Networks, SQL Link, and Memory Management — 628

APPENDIX C: Customizing Paradox — 664

INDEX — 690

INTRODUCTION

Quite simply, Paradox is a powerful database-management system that anyone can use. Historically, database-management systems have been "programming-language" oriented and thus best used as tools by programmers and sophisticated computer users. The need to remember numerous commands, functions, data types, syntax rules, file structures, and so on made the older database-management systems unwieldy for the neophyte and occasional computer user.

Enter Paradox—a new approach to database management that frees the user from having to memorize complex commands. With Paradox, even the occasional user can effectively manage large amounts of data with no programming whatsoever. You can store, retrieve, sort, print, change, and ask questions about your data by selecting options from menus and filling in standardized forms.

So what is so paradoxical about Paradox? The paradox is that even though the program is so easy to use, it does not compromise on power or flexibility. You can ask complex questions about several interrelated tables of data without any programming. On the other hand, if you like to program or you want to develop sophisticated custom applications, Paradox allows you to do so, using a sophisticated programming language named PAL.

WHO THIS BOOK IS FOR

This book is designed for a true database novice—one who has never used Paradox or any other database-management system. In fact, if you can turn a computer on and off, you're off to a good start. If you don't know what a database-management system is, don't worry about it—you will after the first chapter.

This book will also help those who already have experience with Paradox or some other database-management system. By working through the basics using common, practical examples and then building on acquired skills, this book can help anyone gain full mastery over Paradox's more advanced features, including techniques for designing and managing systems with multiple tables.

Those who are already accomplished Paradox users and want to learn programming techniques in PAL may find that this book is too introductory. While this book does touch on the subject and presents examples of more common programming techniques, a complete tutorial on advanced database-management techniques is simply beyond its scope.

This book is designed to be a tutorial, not a reference guide. Of course, you can use the book as a reference simply by referring to the index, but the book is designed to be read from beginning to end. Concepts are taught in order of complexity, from the simple to the more abstract. Such an approach facilitates learning and understanding. Once you've learned how to use Paradox effectively and understand what Paradox is all about, you'll find more technical information, in a form that is easier to assimilate, in the *Paradox User's Guide* that comes with the program.

HELPFUL TOOLS

Before embarking on your work with Paradox, you should familiarize yourself with some helpful tools included in the Paradox package. To begin with, there is a plastic template that shows the effects of the various function keys on your keyboard. Put this template over the function keys for quick reference.

In Chapter 2 of the *Paradox User's Guide*, there is a fold-out diagram of special keys you can use while working in various modes of Paradox. The inside covers of this book also show keys that you can use in Paradox's various modes.

The other manuals that come with the Paradox package are, of course, also valuable tools. These manuals, though difficult to learn from, present all the capabilities of Paradox and are useful reference books. This book does not duplicate all of the material found in those manuals, so you should refer to them for more technical information when necessary.

STRUCTURE OF THE BOOK

This book starts with the basics and builds on acquired skills to help you gain total mastery. In the first ten chapters you will learn how to create, edit, store, retrieve, sort, search, print, and graph data. Chapter 11 touches on the concept of *scripts*, which allow you to record and play back long keystroke sequences.

Chapters 12 through 15 deal with more advanced techniques involving multiple tables of information. Chapter 16 discusses general techniques that you can use to manage information, as well as techniques for interfacing with other software systems such as Quattro Pro, Lotus 1-2-3, Symphony, dBASE, WordStar, and WordPerfect.

Chapter 17 introduces PAL, the Paradox Applications Language, and demonstrates numerous PAL commands and programming techniques that you can use in developing custom applications. Chapter 18 presents a complete application, written with PAL, to manage a mailing list or customer list. Chapter 20 demonstrates the Paradox Personal Programmer, a tool that comes with your Paradox package to help you develop custom applications, even if you have little or no programming experience.

WHICH VERSION OF PARADOX?

This book is written for versions 3 and 3.5 of Paradox, which are nearly identical except for some "behind the scenes" ways of doing things. Features that are unique to version 3.5 are summarized below:

- Paradox 3.5 uses Borland's new VROOMM (Virtual Runtime Object-Oriented Memory Manager) technology. In nontechnical terms this simply means that Paradox 3.5 can do more, and do it faster, than earlier versions of Paradox.

- Paradox 3.5 takes advantage of the high performance features of 286-, 386-, and 486-based computers, thus allowing you to use up to 16Mb of extended memory. Previously only Paradox 386 could do this. You no longer need to buy a special version of Paradox to get the most out of higher-powered machines.

- Paradox 3.5 can be run with Borland's Paradox SQL Link package, a program that lets Paradox run faster and more efficiently on a network.

If you are new to Paradox or computers, all of this may just seem like a bunch of meaningless techno-babble. Don't worry—it's not necessary to understand all of these advanced topics to use Paradox. You can, however, learn more about them in Appendix B of this book.

CONVENTIONS USED IN THIS BOOK

Several typographical conventions used throughout this book are summarized here:

Crtl-, Alt-, Shift-	Indicates that you must hold down the Ctrl, Alt, or Shift key (respectively) while typing the character that follows. For example, Ctrl-Z means, "Hold down the Ctrl key and press the letter Z."
F keys	Function keys labeled F1 through F10 (or F12) on your keyboard are displayed in text as they are on the keyboard. For example, "Press F1" means, "Press the F1 key", *not* "Press the two separate keys F and 1."
Ins	The Ins key is labeled Insert on some keyboards.
Del	The Del key is labeled Delete on some keyboards.
Enter	The Enter key is labeled ↵ on some keyboards and Return on others.
Esc	The Escape key is labeled Esc, Escape, or Cancel on different keyboards.

A GOOD TIP FOR TYROS

If you are an absolute beginner on computers, a simple saying to keep in mind is

If in doubt...
Escape key out!

This means that if you ever find yourself lost in the Paradox menus, and want to get back to more familiar territory, you can usually press the Esc key (labeled Esc, Escape, or Cancel on your keyboard) to move back up the menu system until you are in more familiar territory. The key is named "Escape" because it usually lets you do just that!

PART I

THE BASICS

DATABASES

CHAPTER 1

IF YOU ARE NEW TO THE DATABASE-MANAGEMENT game, you'll need to understand a few basic concepts, as well as the buzzwords that go along with them. In this chapter, we'll discuss all the basics to get you started in the direction of total mastery, beginning with a definition of the term *database management*.

WHAT IS A DATABASE?

A database is simply a collection of information or *data,* like a Rolodex file, file cabinet, or shoe box filled with names and addresses on index cards. Whenever you access a database, whether it be to add new information, get information, change information, or sort the information into some meaningful order, you are *managing* your database.

A computer *database-management system,* like Paradox, performs these same types of operations on a database that is stored on a computer disk. It allows you to add, change, delete, look up, and sort information. However, tasks that may take several minutes, hours, or even days to perform manually usually take the computer only a few seconds to perform.

We often refer to our paper databases as files. A computer database is also called a *file,* or a *table.* The term table stems from the unique structure that all databases use. Every file, or table, in a database is neatly organized into *columns* and *rows.* Let's look at an example.

Suppose you have a Rolodex file, and each card in the Rolodex file contains the name and address of an individual, as in Figure 1.1. The Rolodex card has four lines of information on it: (1) name, (2) address, (3) city, state, zip, and (4) phone number.

This one Rolodex card represents 1 row, or *record,* on a database table. Each unique item of information (name, address, city, state, zip code) represents roughly 1 column, or *field,* of information on a table. Figure 1.2 shows how information from a Rolodex file might look on a database table.

Note in Figure 1.2 that the table consists of three records (rows): one each for Smith, Jones, and Zeepers. Each record contains seven fields (columns): Last Name, First Name, Address, City, State, Zip Code, and Phone. As you've probably guessed by now, the terms *record* and *row* are synonymous, as are the terms *fields* and *column.*

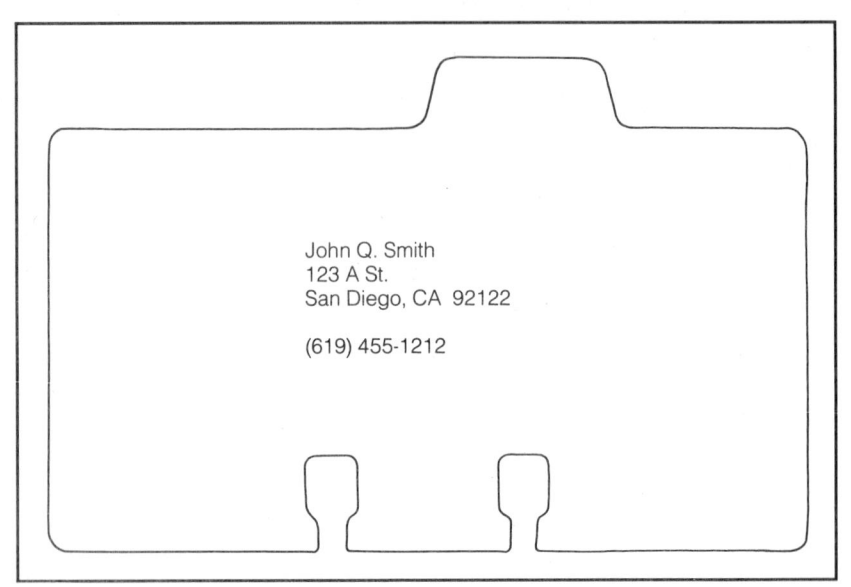

```
John Q. Smith
123 A St.
San Diego, CA  92122

(619) 455-1212
```

Figure 1.1: A sample Rolodex card

```
Last Name    First Name    Address      City         State  Zip Code   Phone
=============================================================================
Smith        John Q.       123 A St.    San Diego    CA     92122      (619)455-1212
Jones        Alma          234 B St.    Berkeley     CA     94710      (415)555-4141
Zeepers      Zeke          Box 1234     Ashland      OR     98765      (123)555-1010
```

Figure 1.2: A sample database table with three records

Do keep in mind that this is only a simple example. A table can be used to store and manage any kind of information—inventory, bookkeeping, accounts payable, receivables . . . just about anything that comes to mind. However, regardless of the *type* of information you plan on managing, that information will be stored in tables consisting of rows and columns (that is, records and fields). Some types of information might be spread across several tables, but we need not concern ourselves with that issue just yet.

FIELD NAMES

One important difference between human database managers and computers is the issue of *context*. Humans can often tell what a piece of information is just by its context. For example, it does not take a genius to figure out that on a Rolodex card, Smith is probably someone's last name, and (619) 455-1212 is probably a phone number. This seems pretty obvious.

Nothing is obvious to a computer. Therefore, each column in a database must have a name. Notice that in Figure 1.2, field names were listed across the top of the table, as below:

Last Name	First Name	Address	City	State	Zip Code	Phone

When storing data on a database table, each unique item of information must have a unique *field name* associated with it. With that in mind, we need to discuss just what constitutes a *unique* item of information.

In the sample Rolodex card we discussed a while ago, each card contained the following information:

Name
Address
City, State   Zip code
Phone number

Hastily, one might set up a table with four fields of information to resemble the format of the Rolodex card, as below:

Name	Address	CityStateZip	Phone

But to set up a database table in this way would be a mistake, simply because the table is not broken down into enough unique items of information. For example, if you wanted to sort the data in this table into zip code order to do a bulk mailing, you would not be able to. Because the zip code is embedded in the same field as the city and state, there is no way to tell Paradox to sort by zip code. Zip code would have to be a unique field in order to sort on it.

And what about the Name field? Suppose you had a list of names as below:

   Andy Zeepers
   Melba Miller
   Zanda Adams

If you asked Paradox to sort these names into alphabetical order, they would stay in their current order, rather than being ordered alphabetically by last name. To properly sort by last name, the Name field would need to be divided into at least two fields—Last Name and First Name. That way, you could tell Paradox specifically to sort into last name order.

Finally, suppose you wanted a listing of only California residents. Again, the hasty table structure would not allow you to obtain such a list, because the state is embedded in the same field as the city and zip code.

With a bit of experience (which you'll gain while using this book) and forethought, you would probably structure a table of names and addresses for the Rolodex data with at least seven fields, as below:

Last Name	First Name	Address	City	State	Zip Code	Phone

Now, each *meaningful* item of data is placed in a separate field, which will give you complete freedom in managing your data. (If you've never used a computer before, don't worry. You'll find out soon enough what I mean by "complete freedom" in managing your data.)

Once you've broken your information down into meaningful units of information (which we've just done) and structured a database table with Paradox (which we'll do in the next chapter), you can begin *managing* your data. Let's discuss this term in more detail.

MANAGING A DATABASE

Managing a database primarily involves the following tasks:

- *Adding* new data to the database
- *Sorting* the database into some meaningful order
- *Searching* the database for types of information
- *Printing* data from the database onto formatted reports and graphs
- *Editing* data in the database
- *Deleting* data from the database

Looking back at our Rolodex example, occasionally we may need to *add* some new cards. We may want to *sort* the cards into some meaningful order (say, alphabetically or by zip code) for easy access. We might want to *search* through them and find all the people who live in Los Angeles, or all the people in the 92123 zip code area, or perhaps just find out where Clark Kenney lives. If Clark Kenney moves, we may want to change (*edit*) his card to reflect his new address and phone number. Then again, if Clark Kenney stops paying his dues, we may want to *delete* him altogether from the Rolodex. We might want to use these data to *print* various other documents, such as mailing labels, form letters, or a directory.

Paradox can easily handle all of these basic database-management tasks. In fact, these tasks represent only a small sample of Paradox's full capabilities. Paradox can do all kinds of additional tasks, such as calculate totals and subtotals, access and combine data from multiple tables, and import and export data from other software systems. However, the big difference between managing a database by hand and doing so with Paradox is speed. As mentioned earlier, what might take hours with a typewriter and Rolodex cards will probably take only seconds or minutes with Paradox.

PARADOX LIMITATIONS

Now that you know what records and fields are, you may be curious about just how much information Paradox can handle. Paradox limitations are listed below. Keep in mind that one *character* of information is equal to one alphabetic letter. For example, "Dog" consists of three characters, and "My House" consists of eight characters (spaces count as characters). Furthermore, the term *byte* also refers to one character, hence "My House" contains eight bytes. In Paradox, a single table can contain the following quantities of information, in these combinations:

- 2 billion rows (records)
- 4,000 characters on a single record
- 255 fields in a single record
- 255 characters within a single field

There is no limit to the number of tables that you can manage with Paradox, other than the sheer amount of disk storage capacity that you have.

Let's review the basics of database management with Paradox before we move on to Chapter 2 and start putting Paradox to work.

SUMMARY

- A *database* is a collection of information, like a file cabinet or a Rolodex file.
- Paradox stores information in *tables*.
- A *table* consists of *rows* (*records*) and *columns* (*fields*).
- Each *column* or *field* in a database contains a unique item of information, such as a last name, address, or zip code.
- Each field in a table must have a unique *field name*.

CREATING A TABLE

CHAPTER 2

NOW THAT YOU HAVE A BASIC IDEA OF WHAT DATAbase management is all about, it's time to get Paradox "up and running" on your computer, and get a feel for the way it works. You'll also create your first database table in this chapter.

INSTALLATION

Before you can use Paradox, it needs to be *installed* on your computer. You only need to install Paradox once; not each time you wish to use it. If you or a co-worker has already installed Paradox, you can move on to the next section. If Paradox has never been installed on your computer, refer to the Appendix in this book for instructions on installing Paradox. When you've completed the installation process, proceed with the next section in this chapter.

STARTING PARADOX

To start Paradox on your computer, follow the steps below:

If you are using Paradox version 3, substitute **PARADOX3** for PDOX35 and PARADOX in steps 2 and 3. If you are using Paradox on a network, refer to Appendix B for additional information.

1. Start your computer in the usual manner so that the DOS command prompt (usually **C>**) appears.

2. Switch to the Paradox35 directory by typing the command

   CD \PDOX35

   next to the DOS prompt. Then press the Enter key (the one with the ⏎ symbol on it).

3. Next, type in the command:

   PARADOX

   and then press the Enter key.

You'll see a screen that includes the program title, serial number, and copyright information appear first; the Paradox Main menu then appears.

(Note that if Paradox did not start after you followed the steps above, then it is either not installed on the computer or not installed in the standard way. If you share a computer with co-workers, you may need to ask the person in charge of the company computer for specific instructions on how to start Paradox.)

THE MAIN MENU

Once you've started Paradox, you'll see the Main menu as shown in Figure 2.1. The top two lines of the screen represent the *menu area*. The empty space below the menu area is called the *workspace*. The first menu item, View, is highlighted with the *menu highlight*. In addition, some messages will occasionally be displayed in the lower-right corner of the screen in an area called the *message window*.

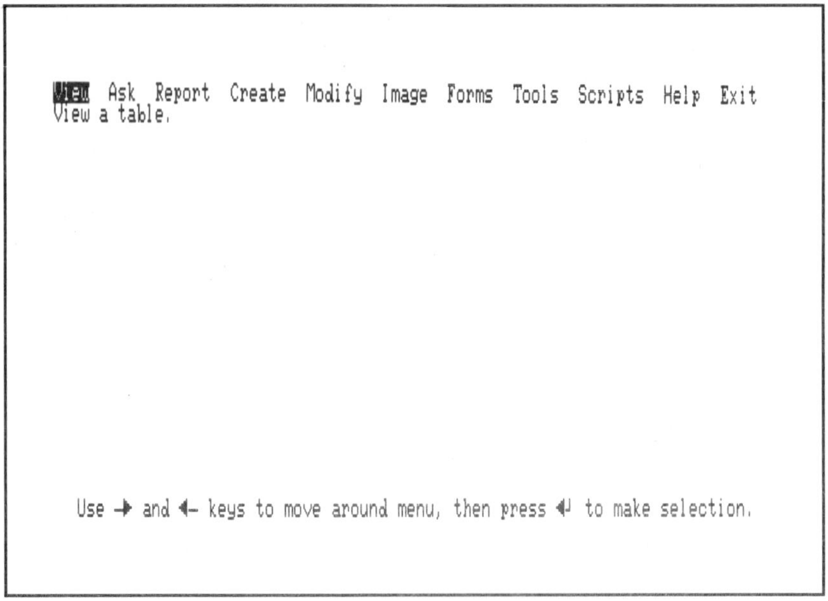

```
View  Ask  Report  Create  Modify  Image  Forms  Tools  Scripts  Help  Exit
View a table.




















Use → and ← keys to move around menu, then press ↵ to make selection.
```

Figure 2.1: The Paradox Main menu

You can move the menu highlight from one menu item to the next using these keys:

KEY	EFFECT
←	Move highlight to the left one item
→	Move highlight to the right one item
Home	Move highlight to the first menu item
End	Move highlight to the last menu item
Enter	Select the currently highlighted item
Esc	Unselect an item: return to previous menu

To try out the keys, try pressing the ← and → keys a few times. (Notice that if you hold one of these keys down, the highlight moves quickly through the options.) As you highlight each menu option, a brief description of what the menu option does appears below the menu. For example, when the View option is highlighted, the message

View a table.

appears just below the menu.

Pressing the Home key moves the highlight to the first menu item; pressing End moves the highlight to the last menu item. If these arrow keys do not work, and instead produce only beeps, press the NumLock key above the number pad on your keyboard. This will switch from ''Numbers'' to ''Arrow'' mode.

SELECTING MENU ITEMS

There are two ways to select items from the menu:

1. Highlight the option you wish to select, using the arrow keys, then press Enter.

2. Type the first letter of the menu option. For example, to select View, type V.

UNSELECTING MENU ITEMS

Occasionally, particularly as a beginner, you might get lost in the series of menus that Paradox will display. In that case, simply press the Escape key (labeled Esc or CANCEL on most keyboards) to return to the previous menu. The rule of thumb on navigating menus is

> If in doubt . . .
> Escape key out

To try out the Escape key, select the Tools option, either by moving the highlight to the option and pressing Enter or by typing the letter T. The Tools menu will appear, as below:

Rename QuerySpeed ExportImport Copy Delete Info Net More

Since probably none of these items means much to you right now, you can "back out" of this menu by pressing the Escape key. Do so now to return to the Main menu.

CALLING UP THE MENU

In some situations the Paradox Main menu will disappear, to be replaced by other information. To bring the menu back to the screen, simply press the Menu (F10) key. This is an important key to remember, because most Paradox operations begin by selecting an item from a menu.

> Some menus that appear as a single line across the top of your screen are broken into two lines in this book, simply because your screen is 80 columns across, and these printed pages are about 60 columns across.

GETTING HELP

Paradox has an elaborate system of help screens, which you can access at any time by pressing the Help (F1) key. For example, if you press the Help (F1) key while the View option on the Main menu is highlighted, you'll see the help screen shown in Figure 2.2.

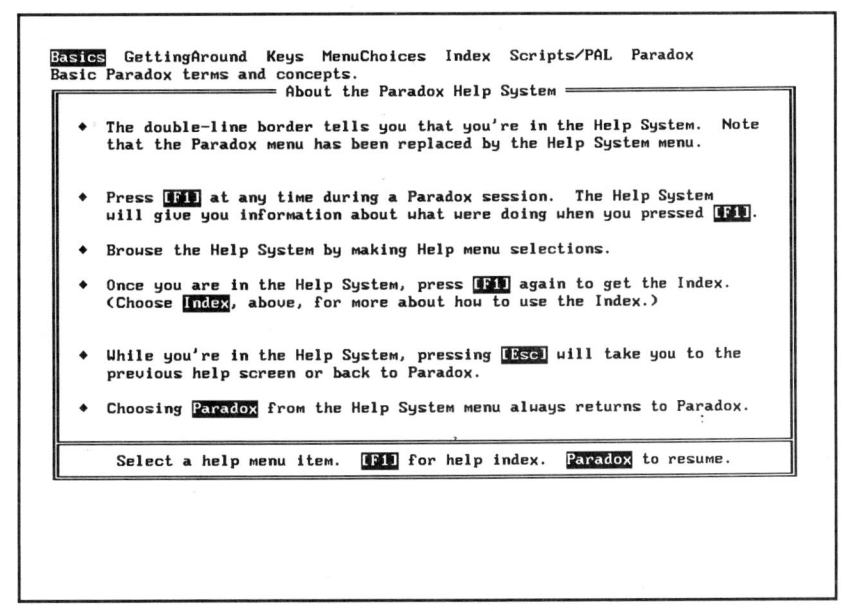

```
   Basics  GettingAround  Keys  MenuChoices  Index  Scripts/PAL  Paradox
   Basic Paradox terms and concepts.
   ═══════════════════ About the Paradox Help System ═══════════════════
   ♦ The double-line border tells you that you're in the Help System. Note
     that the Paradox menu has been replaced by the Help System menu.

   ♦ Press [F1] at any time during a Paradox session. The Help System
     will give you information about what were doing when you pressed [F1].

   ♦ Browse the Help System by making Help menu selections.

   ♦ Once you are in the Help System, press [F1] again to get the Index.
     (Choose Index, above, for more about how to use the Index.)

   ♦ While you're in the Help System, pressing [Esc] will take you to the
     previous help screen or back to Paradox.

   ♦ Choosing Paradox from the Help System menu always returns to Paradox.

   ─────────── Select a help menu item. [F1] for help index. Paradox to resume. ──────────
```

Figure 2.2: A Paradox help screen

Notice that there is a menu above the help screen. Like all menus in Paradox, you can move the highlight with the arrow keys. You select an option either by pressing Enter when the option is highlighted or by typing in the first letter of the menu option.

You might want to take a moment now to explore the help screens. Paradox's help system is *context sensitive,* which means that if you press Help while creating a table, you'll receive help in creating a table. If you press Help while sorting a table, you'll see a help screen with information about sorting.

Pressing the Help key while you are viewing any help screen brings you to the highest-level help screen (the one shown in Figure 2.2). Selecting the Paradox option (or typing P) while you are viewing a help screen always returns you to the place where you left off before pressing the Help key. Take a moment to read the contents of the help screen in Figure 2.2 and experiment with some of its options. When you are done, select the Paradox option to return to the Main menu, so we can create our first table.

CH. 2

CREATING A TABLE

> If you are using Paradox on a network, see "Creating a Table on a Network" in Appendix B.

For our first example, we'll create a table to manage a basic mailing list, or customer list. We'll put the following fields of information on it:

FIELD NAME	CONTENTS
Mr/Mrs	A title such as Mr., Mrs., Ms., or Dr.
Last Name	An individual's last name
First Name	An individual's first name
M.I.	A middle initial and period (for example, M.)
Company	A company name
Department	A department name
Address	A street address or mailing address
City	A city name
State	A two-letter state abbreviation
Zip	A zip code up to 10 digits (for example, 12345-1234)
Start Date	The date the record was entered into the computer
Credit Limit	A dollar amount

I've included the Credit Limit field only to demonstrate techniques used in managing numbers. A basic mailing-list system might not need such a field, but we will need it for examples and exercises later in the book.

In later chapters, we'll develop some more complex, interrelated tables. But to get a good foundation in the basics, we'll start with this fairly simple example.

The first step in creating a table is to select the Create option from the Main menu. Do so now. Paradox will ask for the name of the new table, as shown below:

```
Table:
Enter new table name
```

CREATING A TABLE 17

A table name must adhere to a few simple rules, listed below:

- It can be no more than eight characters in length.
- It can contain letters, numbers, and underline characters (_), but the name must begin with a letter or number.
- It should not contain any blank spaces—that is, it must be a single word.
- Though not essential, the table name should describe its contents, such as "Mail" for a mailing-list table, or "Invoices" for an invoice table.

For this example, enter the table name Custlist by typing in the name Custlist and pressing Enter. This brings up a screen for entering the table structure, as shown in Figure 2.3. Notice that the word "STRUCT" appears in the upper-left corner of the box on the screen. This is short for "structure."

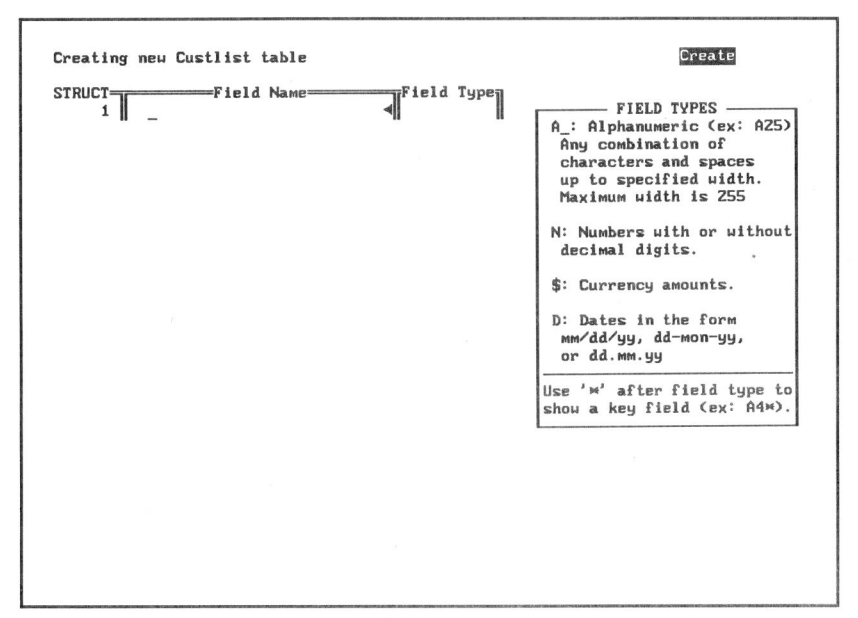

```
Creating new Custlist table                                    Create
STRUCT      Field Name            Field Type
   1    _                                      ── FIELD TYPES ──
                                              A_: Alphanumeric (ex: A25)
                                              Any combination of
                                              characters and spaces
                                              up to specified width.
                                              Maximum width is 255

                                              N: Numbers with or without
                                                 decimal digits.

                                              $: Currency amounts.

                                              D: Dates in the form
                                                 mm/dd/yy, dd-mon-yy,
                                                 or dd.mm.yy

                                              Use 'ж' after field type to
                                              show a key field (ex: A4ж).
```

Figure 2.3: A screen for creating a new table

FIELD NAMES

The Field Name area on the screen is where you enter the name of each field to be used in the table. Rules for entering field names are listed below:

- Each can be no more than 25 characters in length.
- Each field name can contain letters, numbers, spaces, and other symbols, but it must begin with a letter.
- Each must be unique within the table: a single table cannot have two fields with the same name.

Now, keep in mind that you may assign any name you like to a field. For example, you could actually assign the field names "hamburger" or "termite lips" to a field that contains zip codes. Neither Paradox, nor your computer, would object, since neither knows the difference between a zip code, a hamburger, or a pair of termite lips. However, for the sake of convenience it is best to assign field names that describe the contents of the fields. Therefore, you should use descriptive field names, such as Zip or Zip Code, when creating table structures for a field containing zip codes.

DATA TYPES

The Field Type column is where you define the type of data to be stored in a field. Your options, as displayed on the screen, are listed below:

SYMBOL	DATA TYPE
A	Alphanumeric data: These fields can contain letters, numeric characters, spaces, and other symbols. Alphanumeric data consists of "textual" information such as names, addresses, titles, or any other information for which you will not be performing math. A field length must be included with this data type. For example, A25 defines an alphanumeric

field with a fixed length of 25 characters. The maximum length you can define is 255 characters.

N Numeric data: These fields store "real" numbers, such as quantities, and allow for mathematical operations such as addition, subtraction, multiplication, and division. They can accept only numeric characters (0–9), decimal points, commas, and negative signs. Alphabetic characters are not allowed.

$ Currency data: These fields store numeric data representing dollar amounts. Currency data is like numeric data, except that all numbers are automatically rounded to two decimal places of accuracy, and negative values are enclosed in parentheses.

D Date: This data type is used to store dates in either MM/DD/YY or DD-Mon-YY format. Paradox automatically validates any entry, rejecting a date like 02/31/90, and allows for "date arithmetic."

Armed with this knowledge of data types, we can begin structuring our table.

ENTERING THE TABLE STRUCTURE

To enter a table structure, simply type in field names and data types. Finish each entry by pressing the Enter key. For example, to enter the first field, "Mr/Mrs", type **Mr/Mrs** and press Enter. This field will contain alphanumeric data, with a maximum (fixed) length of four characters, so enter the data type as A4 (by typing A4), then press the Enter key. Your screen should now look like Figure 2.4.

Before entering any more field definitions, take a look at the key commands listed in Table 2.1. These keys, as you'll discover later, are almost universal in Paradox. That is, they are used in the same manner to perform several different tasks. Take a moment to study them now. Be advised that the Backspace key is the one with the large, dark, left arrow, which is usually on the upper-right corner of the main typing keys on your keyboard.

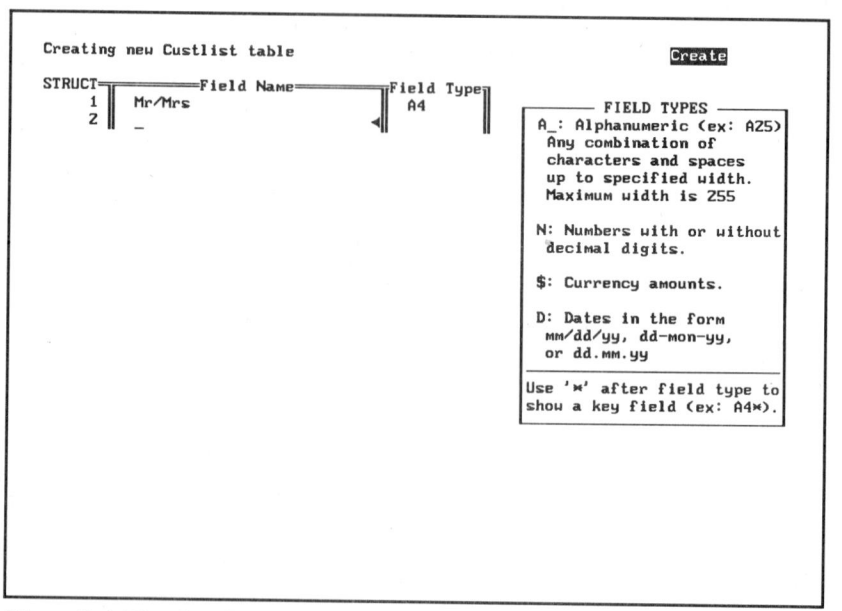

```
Creating new Custlist table                              Create
STRUCT      Field Name         Field Type
   1    Mr/Mrs                   A4              FIELD TYPES
   2                                       A_: Alphanumeric (ex: A25)
                                            Any combination of
                                            characters and spaces
                                            up to specified width.
                                            Maximum width is 255

                                           N: Numbers with or without
                                            decimal digits.

                                           $: Currency amounts.

                                           D: Dates in the form
                                            mm/dd/yy, dd-mon-yy,
                                            or dd.mm.yy

                                           Use '*' after field type to
                                           show a key field (ex: A4*).
```

Figure 2.4: The first field defined for the Custlist table

Table 2.1: Keys used when defining a table structure

Key	Effect
Backspace	Moves cursor to the left, and erase as moving
→	Moves cursor to the right
←	Moves cursor to the left
↑	Moves cursor up a row
↓	Moves cursor down a row
Enter	Completes entry of a field definition
Ins	Inserts a blank at this field position
Del	Deletes this field definition
DO-IT! (F2)	Saves table structure
Help (F1)	Provides help defining a table structure

Enter the remaining field definitions as shown in Figure 2.5. If you make a mistake while entering the table structure, try using the key commands shown in Table 2.1 to make corrections.

Let's discuss the rationale for the structure for our table. First of all, the customer name is actually divided into four separate fields: a title (Mr/Mrs), last name, first name, and middle initial (M.I.). As we'll see later, it is easier to manage the database when the name is broken into this many meaningful pieces of information. We've made each of these fields the alphanumeric data type, since none has any numeric value. The fixed (maximum) length for the title is four characters ("Miss" is the longest title), both Last Name and First Name have maximum lengths of 15 characters, and M.I. (middle initial) has a length of two characters.

When determining a length for a field, keep in mind that the longer the maximum length assigned, the more memory will be required to store the information. (For example, even the last name "Nye" will be stored as 15 characters of information if the field definition allows 15 characters.) Therefore, be conservative, though realistic, when defining lengths.

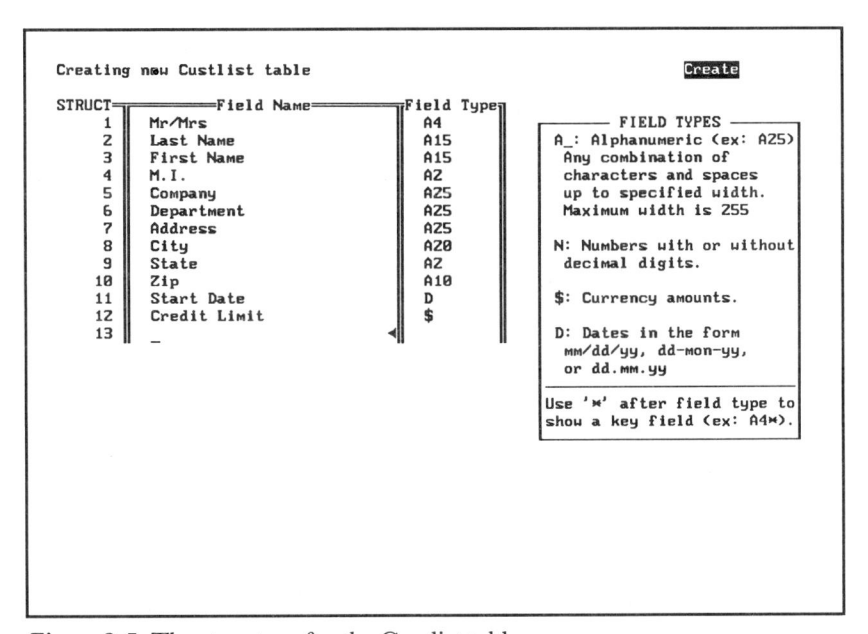

```
Creating new Custlist table                                    Create
STRUCT      Field Name            Field Type
   1     Mr/Mrs                   A4              ──── FIELD TYPES ────
   2     Last Name                A15         A_: Alphanumeric (ex: A25)
   3     First Name               A15            Any combination of
   4     M.I.                     A2             characters and spaces
   5     Company                  A25            up to specified width.
   6     Department               A25            Maximum width is 255
   7     Address                  A25
   8     City                     A20         N: Numbers with or without
   9     State                    A2             decimal digits.
  10     Zip                      A10
  11     Start Date               D           $: Currency amounts.
  12     Credit Limit             $
  13      _                                   D: Dates in the form
                                                 mm/dd/yy, dd-mon-yy,
                                                 or dd.mm.yy

                                              Use '*' after field type to
                                              show a key field (ex: A4*).
```

Figure 2.5: The structure for the Custlist table

The Company, Department, Address, City, State, and Zip Code fields are also alphanumeric data. They have lengths of 25, 25, 25, 20, 2, and 10, respectively.

Now you may be wondering why the zip code is not stored as a number. After all, isn't 92122 a number? The answer to that is both yes and no. While it is true that 92122 is a number, some zip codes, such as 92038-2802, or 00341, or A0341J11, are not. If the Zip Code field were defined as a real number (N), the following problems would occur with the "oddball" zip codes:

1. Hyphenated zip codes might eventually be treated as equations. For instance, 92038-2802 might result in 89236, which is the difference of 92,038 minus 2,802.

2. Leading zeroes are always eliminated from real numbers; hence the zip code 00341 would appear as 341 on a mailing label or envelope.

3. A foreign zip code such as A0341J11 would not be allowed in the table, since real numbers cannot contain alphabetic characters.

In view of these constraints, a zip code is clearly not a real number. (The same holds true for phone numbers, for similar reasons.) Hence we've defined Zip Code as alphanumeric data. (Don't worry, they will still sort into proper order later.)

The Start Date field is defined as the date data type. No length is specified, because only alphanumeric fields require a length specification. The Credit Limit field is defined as the currency data type, since it reflects a dollar amount.

SAVING THE TABLE STRUCTURE

Once you've defined your table structure as shown in Figure 2.5, save it by pressing the DO-IT! (F2) key. You will see the message

Creating Custlist

momentarily on the screen, and then you will be returned to the Main menu.

At this point you could begin entering data into the table. But first let's discuss the important aspect of exiting Paradox.

EXITING PARADOX

Before you turn off your computer, or even before you remove any disks from their drives (except in special cases when the screen tells you to do so), you should *always* exit Paradox first. This ensures that any new data or changes to existing data will be properly stored on disk.

To exit Paradox, select the Exit option from the Main menu. Remember, if the Main menu is not displayed, press the Menu (F10) key to bring up the menu. Selecting the Exit option displays this prompt:

```
No   Yes
Do not leave Paradox
```

Because the highlight is already on the No option, if you change your mind and decide to stay in Paradox, just press Enter. Otherwise, type the letter Y to answer Yes, and you'll be returned to the DOS prompt. All of your work will be saved on your hard disk. When the DOS prompt is on the screen, it is safe to remove the floppy disks and turn off the computer.

CHANGING A TABLE STRUCTURE

Don't worry too much about getting your table structure exactly right the first time. Just try to break the information into as many meaningful fields as possible. If you decide to add new fields later, or delete fields, you can do so using the Modify option from the Main menu (as discussed in Chapter 16). Paradox is very flexible, so corrections and changes are easy to make.

KEY FIELDS

You may have noticed this message near the bottom of the screen when creating your first table:

Use "*" after field type to
show a key field (ex: A4*).

Key fields are not relevant to this table, so don't worry about this. We'll use this option in a later example.

In the next chapter, we'll call our Custlist table back into Paradox and add some data to it. But first, we'll take a moment to review some of the basic commands and techniques discussed in this chapter.

SUMMARY

- Before you can use Paradox, it needs to be installed on your computer.
- To start Paradox from the DOS prompt, first switch to the Paradox35 directory by typing the command **CD\PDOX35** and pressing the ⏎ key. Then, type the command **PARADOX** and press ⏎.
- To perform operations in Paradox, select options from the Main menu. You can select menu options by highlighting the option and pressing the Enter key, or by typing in the first letter of the menu option.
- To unselect previous menu selections, press the Escape key to move back to the previous menu.
- To call up a menu at any time, press the Menu (F10) key.
- To get help at any time, press the Help (F1) key.
- To create a new table, select the Create option from the Main menu.
- Table names can contain a maximum of eight characters, with no spaces.

- Field names can be up to 25 characters in length.
- Fields can be any one of four data types: alphanumeric (A), numeric (N), currency ($), or date (D).
- To save a table structure, press the DO-IT! (F2) key.
- To exit Paradox before removing disks or turning off the computer, select the Exit option from the Main menu.

ADDING DATA TO A TABLE

CHAPTER 3

NOW THAT YOU'VE CREATED A TABLE, YOU NEED TO learn how to add data to it. In the last chapter, we left off by exiting Paradox back to the DOS prompt. So in this chapter, you first need to get Paradox "up and running" on your computer, as we discussed in the last chapter.

PARADOX DATA ENTRY

If you are using Paradox on a network, see "Data Entry on a Network" in Appendix B.

There are several techniques that you can use to add data to a table. In most situations, you'll want to use the DataEntry option from the Modify option on the Main menu. Let's try it now.

Select the Modify option from the Main menu. This will bring up a submenu, as below:

    Sort Edit CoEdit DataEntry MultiEntry Restructure

Select the DataEntry option. The screen will then ask for the name of the table to add data to, as below:

    Table:
    Enter name of table to add records to, or press ↵ for a list

You can either type in the table name, Custlist, or press Enter to see a list of table names. Press the Enter key now. You'll see the Custlist table name (and perhaps some other table names, as in the example below):

    Struct Custlist Orders

If there are more table names than will fit across the screen, some will run off the right edge of the screen. The following keys will help you find a table name:

End	Move to end of table name list
Home	Move to beginning of table name list
→	Move highlighter right one table name
←	Move highlighter left one table name
Ctrl-→	Move right one "screen"
Ctrl-←	Move left one "screen"
Any letter	Display tables starting with that letter

If there are many table names on your screen, you can narrow down the display by typing the first letter of the table name you are interested in. In this example, you would type the letter C to view table names that begin with C. (Note: If only one table name begins with the letter you enter, that table will be selected automatically.)

Now, move the highlighter to the CustList table name (if necessary) and press Enter, just as you would select a menu item. A screen for entering data will appear, as in Figure 3.1.

Notice that only a portion of the table appears on the screen—as much as will fit. As you enter data, the screen will scroll to the left, so you can fill in other fields.

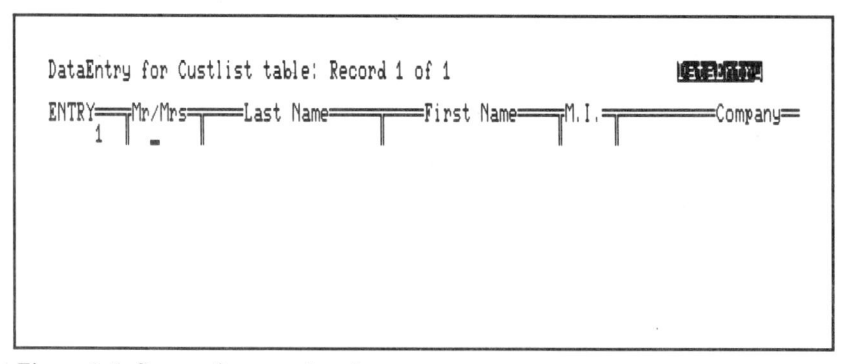

```
DataEntry for Custlist table: Record 1 of 1                DataEntry
ENTRY══╤══Mr/Mrs══╤══Last Name══╤══First Name══╤══M.I.══╤══════Company══
   1   │          │             │              │        │
```

Figure 3.1: Screen for entering data

Let's enter the following data into our first record:

Ms. Janet J. Jackson
Zeerox, Inc.
Accounts Payable
1234 Corporate Hwy.
Los Angeles, CA   91234

Start Date: January 1, 1990
Credit Limit: 10,000.00

The cursor is in the Mr/Mrs field, so type

>   **Ms.**

and press Enter. (Remember, you can use the Backspace and ← keys to correct errors.) The cursor moves to the Last Name field. Type

>   **Jackson**

and press Enter. Then type

>   **Janet**

and press Enter; then type

>   **J.**

and press Enter. At this point, the screen scrolls to the left so that you can enter data into the Company field. Type

>   **Zeerox, Inc.**

and press Enter. For the Department field, type

>   **Accounts Payable**

and press Enter. For the Address field, type

>   **1234 Corporate Hwy.**

and press Enter. For the City field, type

> **Los Angeles**

and press Enter. Type

> **CA**

as the state and press Enter. Type

> **91234**

as the zip code and press Enter.

When entering dates, you can use either a MM/DD/YY format or a DD-Mon-YY format. So you can enter January 1, 1990 as either

> **1/1/90**

or

> **1-Jan-90**

If you enter an invalid date, such as 2/29/90, Paradox will reject the entry and ask that you reenter it (Paradox knows all about leap years and leap centuries). Press the Backspace key, reenter the date, and then press Enter.

Finally, enter the credit limit. When entering dollar amounts, you need not type ".00" at the end if you are entering an even dollar amount. You can enter commas between thousands (such as 10,000), or you can leave them out (like 10000). For this example, type

> **10,000**

At this point, you've entered data for one record. Your screen will look like Figure 3.2.

When you press the Enter key, the screen will scroll to the right so that you can enter another record, as shown in Figure 3.3. Note that the display resembles a table, with rows and columns. For this reason, this type of display is called the *Table View* in Paradox. (Later, we'll look at another way of displaying data.)

ADDING DATA TO A TABLE **31**

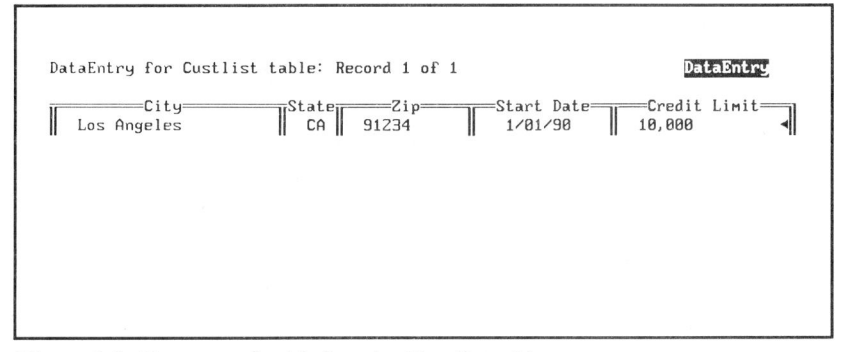

```
DataEntry for Custlist table: Record 1 of 1                    DataEntry
┌──────City──────┬─State─┬──Zip──┬─Start Date─┬─Credit Limit─┐
│  Los Angeles   │  CA   │ 91234 │   1/01/90  │    10,000    │◄
```

Figure 3.2: One record added to the Custlist table

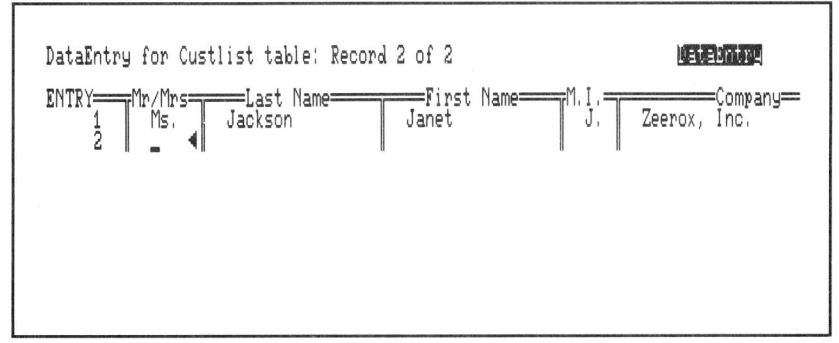

```
DataEntry for Custlist table: Record 2 of 2                    DataEntry
ENTRY═╤═Mr/Mrs═╤═Last Name═╤═First Name═╤═M.I.═╤═Company═
  1   │  Ms.   │  Jackson  │   Janet    │  J.  │ Zeerox, Inc.
  2   │   _   ◄│           │            │      │
```

Figure 3.3: Paradox ready to accept a second record

> Look inside the front cover of this book for a quick reference to keys used in Table view.

When entering new data into a table, you can use the keys shown in Table 3.1 to help you make changes and corrections as you type. Note that Ctrl-Backspace (hold down the Ctrl key and press the Backspace key) deletes the entire contents of a field. (Throughout the book, we'll use a hyphen to indicate when two keys should be held down together. For example, Ctrl-Y will mean "hold down the Ctrl key and type **Y**.")

Table 3.1: Basic keys for entering and editing data

KEY	EFFECT
←	Moves cursor to the left one field
→	Moves cursor to the right one field

Table 3.1: Basic keys for entering and editing data (continued)

KEY	EFFECT
↑	Moves up one record
↓	Moves down one record
Backspace	Moves back one character and erases
Ctrl-Backspace	Deletes entire field entry
Home	Moves to first record
Ctrl-Home	Moves to first field
End	Moves to last record
Ctrl-End	Moves to last field
Ins	Inserts a new record
Del	Deletes a record
Ctrl-→	Moves to the right one screen
Ctrl-←	Moves to the left one screen

Now we want to enter the following data for the second record:

Mr. Andy A. Adams
23 Ocean View Dr.
San Diego, CA   92038

Start Date: January 15, 1990
Credit Limit: $2,500.00

Before you type in these data, read along to learn a few new tricks. Begin by typing

Mr.

into the Mr/Mrs field, and press Enter. Then type

Adams

in the Last Name field, and press Enter. Then type

   Andy

into the First Name field and press Enter; then type

   A.

into the M.I. field and press Enter.
   Since Andy has no company affiliation, press Enter to leave the Company field empty. Press Enter again to leave the Department field empty. This brings you to the Address field. Type in the address

   23 Ocean View Dr.

and press Enter.
   Now let's try a little experiment. Suppose you suddenly realize that Andy's address should have been 234 Ocean View Dr. Press the ← key to move back to the Address field. You have two options for making the correction. The more laborious option is to press the Backspace key and erase everything but the "23", then type "4 Ocean View Dr." Let's look at an alternative.

FIELD VIEW EDITING

   A more elegant way to make this correction is to enter the *Field View* mode by typing Alt-F5 (hold down the Alt key while pressing the F5 key). (The term Field View is based upon the fact that the arrow keys are reduced to operating within a single field. For example, pressing ← moves the cursor to the left one character within the field, rather than all the way to the next field.) The cursor will change from an underline to a block (and turn grey on a color screen). Now press the ← key until the cursor is between "23" and "Ocean", as below:

   23_Ocean View Dr.

Type the number 4. You'll see it inserted into the current position, as below:

234_Ocean View Dr.

Press Enter when you're done editing. The cursor will shrink back to an underline, and you'll be in normal Edit mode.

Table 3.2 shows the keys that you can use to perform edits in the Field View mode. Also, pressing Help (the F1 key) provides some helpful information.

> Look inside the back cover of this book for a quick reference to keys used in Field View.

Table 3.2: Keys used in Field View

KEY	EFFECT
Alt-F5	Enters Field View mode
←	Moves cursor one character to the left
→	Moves cursor one character to the right
Home	Moves cursor to first character in the field
End	Moves cursor to last character in the field
Del	Deletes character at cursor
Backspace	Moves back one character and erases
Ctrl-Backspace	Deletes entire field entry
Ins	Turns Insert mode on/off
Enter	Ends Field View mode

You can enter Field View at any time, so it is possible to move the cursor to any field, in any record, and make changes using Field View. Pressing Enter always indicates that you are done editing, and returns you to the normal cursor and editing mode.

Now press Enter to put the cursor in the City field and type

San Diego

Press Enter.

THE DITTO KEY

Now we can learn another trick to simplify data entry. Since both this record and the record above have "CA" as the state, you can use the Ditto command to copy the contents of the field in the previous record to this field. The Ditto command is Ctrl-D (hold down the Ctrl key while typing D). You'll see CA inserted into the State field. The Ditto command works at any time, in any field, so you might want to use it later as you add more records. Keep in mind that it always duplicates the field from the record directly above.

To finish Andy's data, press Enter and type **92038** into the Zip Code field, **1/15/90** into the Start Date field, and **2,500** into the Credit Limit field. Press Enter and you're ready to enter data for the third record.

Before continuing, let's discuss another technique for entering data which you may (or may not) prefer.

USING FORM VIEW

There is another technique that you can use to enter records into a table. By simply pressing the Form Toggle (F7) key, you can switch from the current Table View, where the data are displayed in a tabular format, to a *Form View,* where only one record at a time is displayed on a screen resembling a paper form. If you press Form Toggle (F7) now, you'll see the Form View for the Custlist table, as in Figure 3.4.

The same basic editing keys are used for making changes as you type in the Form View as in the Table View. That is, the arrow keys, Backspace, Enter, and Field View (Alt-F5) all perform the same tasks as before except that PgUp and PgDn move up and down through records, and ↑ and ↓ move up and down through fields.

Now enter another record into the table, as below, by typing the data into the form. As usual, be sure to get the right data in the right field, and press Enter after entering data into each field:

    Dr. Ruth Zastrow
    Scripts Clinic
    Internal Medicine

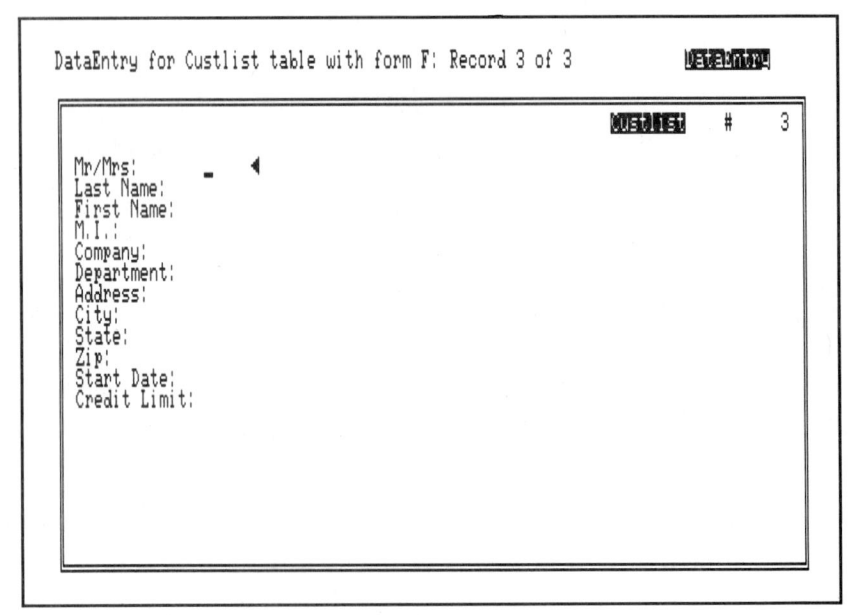

```
DataEntry for Custlist table with form F: Record 3 of 3        DataEntry

                                                      CUSTLIST   #    3
Mr/Mrs:       ─ ◄
Last Name:
First Name:
M.I.:
Company:
Department:
Address:
City:
State:
Zip:
Start Date:
Credit Limit:
```

Figure 3.4: The Custlist table in Form View

    4331 La Jolla Scenic Dr.
    La Jolla, CA   92037

    Start Date: 1/1/90
    Credit Limit: 10,000

When you have entered this record, your screen should look like Figure 3.5.

In Form View, several other keys can be used to scroll through records in a table. You might want to try some of these out. Table 3.3 shows additional keys that work in the Form View.

> Look inside the front cover of this book for a quick reference to keys used in Form view.

Table 3.3: Keys used in Form View

KEY	EFFECT
←	Previous field (left or up)
→	Next field (right or down)
↑	Up one field

ADDING DATA TO A TABLE   37

```
DataEntry for Custlist table with form F: Record 3 of 3        DataEntry

                                                          Custlist   #    3
   Mr/Mrs:        Dr.
   Last Name:    Zastrow
   First Name:   Ruth
   M.I.:
   Company:      Scripts Clinic
   Department:   Internal Medicine
   Address:      4331 La Jolla Scenic Dr.
   City:         La Jolla
   State:        CA
   Zip:          92037
   Start Date:    1/01/90
   Credit Limit: 10,000                            ◄
```

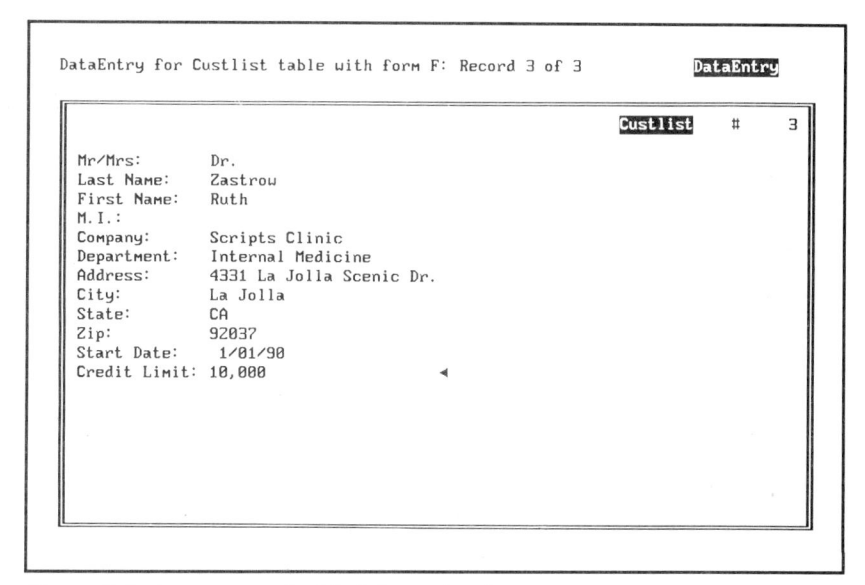

Figure 3.5: A new record added through a form

Table 3.3: Keys used in Form View (continued)

Key	Effect
↓	Down one field
PgUp	Up one record (or screen)
Ctrl-PgUp	Same field of previous record
PgDn	Down one record (or screen)
Ctrl-PgDn	Same field of next record
Home	First record of table
Ctrl-Home	First field of current record
End	Last record of table
Ctrl-End	Last field of record
Del	Deletes record
Backspace	Erases character to left
Ctrl-Backspace	Erases field contents
Alt-F5	Switches to Field View

To switch back and forth between Table View and Form View, just press the F7 key. Try it—you'll see that it is very easy to do.

DATA ENTRY SHORTCUTS

There are a few shortcuts that you can use when entering data into numeric, currency, or date fields. These are summarized below.

NUMERIC FIELDS

When entering data into currency or numeric fields, the following shortcuts might help speed your work:

- You can press the Space bar in lieu of the period (or comma in international format) to enter a decimal point.
- Negative numbers may be entered with either a leading minus sign (hyphen) or enclosed in parentheses.
- If you omit the ".00" portion of a currency amount, Paradox will automatically fill it in for you.
- You may separate thousands places with a comma (or period in international format) when entering large numbers, so long as the punctuators are in the correct places. For example, you may enter 7654321 or 7,654,321 or 7.654.321 but not 76,543,21, because the punctuators (commas in this case) are in the wrong place.

DATE FIELDS

When entering dates into a field of the Date data type, use the following shortcuts to speed your work:

- As mentioned earlier, you may enter dates in the MM/DD/YY or DD-Mon-YY format, and you may also use the international format, DD.MM.YY. For example, you may enter January 31, 1990 as 1/31/90, 31-Jan-90, or 31.1.90. Regardless of the format you enter dates in, you can later select any format for displaying those dates using the Image Format options from the Main menu (discussed in the next chapter).

- To place the current month, day, or year into a date, just press the Space bar. (You must make sure, of course, that DOS knows what the correct date is.) For example, if the current date is March 31, 1990, pressing the space bar three times will enter the date 03/31/90. You can enter any individual component into the date field by pressing the Space bar once. In the example above, you could type 5, Space bar, 89 to have Paradox enter the date 5/31/89.

- To enter the month name in a date, you can enter the first letter only, followed by a couple of presses on the space bar. In cases where more than one month begins with a given letter (such as January, June, and July), Paradox enters the earlier date. Hence, typing 31, then J, then the Space bar twice, enters 31-Jan into the Date field.

Remember that Paradox will reject invalid dates such as June 31 (June has only 30 days). In your zeal to use shortcuts, you might occasionally enter an invalid date and have to reenter without using a shortcut technique.

You may want to experiment with some of these shortcut techniques while entering new data. To build up this database to help with future exercises, add the following records to the table. Use whichever method you prefer, Form View or Table View. Be sure to put the right data in the right field. For example, don't put "Richard" in the Last Name field when entering the data below:

Dr. Richard L. Rosiello
Raydontic Labs
Accounts Payable
P.O. Box 77112
Newark, NJ   00123

Start Date: 3/15/90
Credit Limit: 7,500

On the record below, enter **Tara Rose** as the first name, and leave the M.I. field blank.

> Miss Tara Rose Gladstone
> Waterside, Inc.
> Acquisitions
> P.O. Box 121
> New York, NY   12345
>
> Start Date: 2/28/90
> Credit Limit: 15,000
>
> Mrs. Susita M. Simpson
> SMS Publishing
> Software Division
> P.O. Box 2802
> Philadelphia, PA   23456
>
> Start Date: 1/1/90
> Credit Limit: 15,000

Careful, the next one has a Company field, but no Department field:

> Mr. Clark E. Kenney
> Legal Aid
> 371 Ave. of the Americas
> New York, NY   12345
>
> Start Date: 1/31/90
> Credit Limit: 5,000

This next record has no Middle Initial, Company, or Department fields:

> Ms. Randi Davis
> 371 Oceanic Way
> Manhattan Beach, CA   90001

Start Date: 3/1/90
Credit Limit: 7,500

SAVING YOUR WORK

Once you've finished adding new records to your table, you need to save them by pressing the DO-IT! (F2) key. Don't worry about getting everything perfect before pressing DO-IT!. It's simple to make changes later. When you press the DO-IT! key, all the data you entered will be stored on disk under the file name Custlist.DB (DB stands for database). Paradox automatically assigns the ''.DB'' file name extension whenever you save the data with the DO-IT! key. Then you'll be returned to the Main menu, and the new records will appear on the workspace, as in Figure 3.6.

You can always tell when you are in the ''Viewing'' mode because the top of the screen displays

    Viewing (table name) table: Record X of Y

Let's take a look at an alternative method of adding new records to a table.

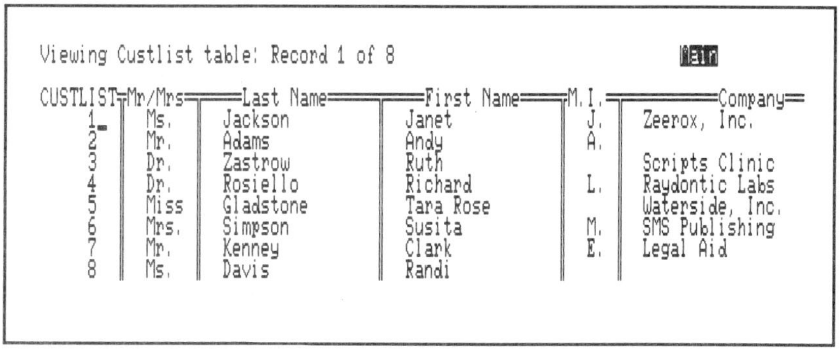

```
Viewing Custlist table: Record 1 of 8                    Main
CUSTLIST=Mr/Mrs====Last Name=======First Name====M.I.=======Company==
     1    Ms.     Jackson         Janet          J.      Zeerox, Inc.
     2    Mr.     Adams           Andy           A.
     3    Dr.     Zastrow         Ruth                   Scripts Clinic
     4    Dr.     Rosiello        Richard        L.      Raydontic Labs
     5    Miss    Gladstone       Tara Rose              Waterside, Inc.
     6    Mrs.    Simpson         Susita         M.      SMS Publishing
     7    Mr.     Kenney          Clark          E.      Legal Aid
     8    Ms.     Davis           Randi
```

Figure 3.6: New records displayed in the workspace

ENTERING NEW RECORDS IN THE EDIT MODE

You can also add new records to a table in the Paradox Edit mode. To enter the Edit mode, just press the Edit (F9) key while viewing records. The message at the top of the screen will change to

> Editing Custlist table: Record 1 of 8   EDIT

To add new records in this Edit mode, press the End key to move the cursor to the last record in the table. Then press ↓. The screen will make room for record number 9, as shown in Figure 3.7.

Type in the data below as record number 9, using the same techniques you used for entering the previous records in this chapter. (The arrow keys, Backspace, and Field View options all work the same as they do when entering data through the DataEntry mode.)

    Mr. Mark S. Macallister
    BBC Publishing
    Foreign Sales
    121 Revelation Dr.
    Bangor, ME   00001

    Start Date: 3/15/90
    Credit Limit: 7,500

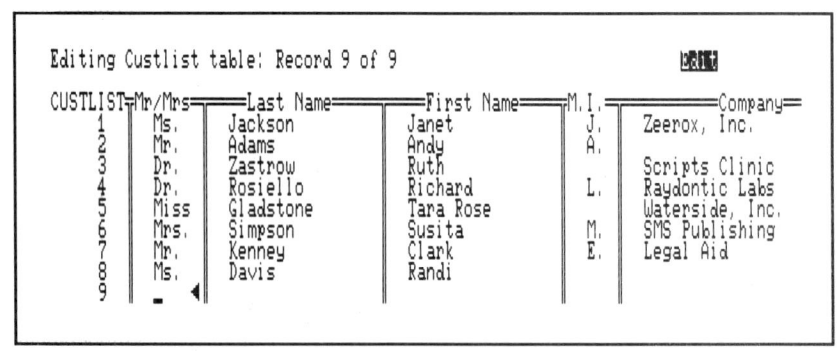

```
Editing Custlist table: Record 9 of 9                          EDIT
CUSTLIST=Mr/Mrs====Last Name======First Name====M.I.======Company==
       1   Ms.     Jackson        Janet         J.    Zeerox, Inc.
       2   Mr.     Adams          Andy          A.
       3   Dr.     Zastrow        Ruth                Scripts Clinic
       4   Dr.     Rosiello       Richard       L.    Raydontic Labs
       5   Miss    Gladstone      Tara Rose           Waterside, Inc.
       6   Mrs.    Simpson        Susita        M.    SMS Publishing
       7   Mr.     Kenney         Clark         E.    Legal Aid
       8   Ms.     Davis          Randi
       9   _
```

Figure 3.7: Space for a new record in the Edit mode

ADDING DATA TO A TABLE **43**

When you are done, press Enter. The screen will make room for another new record. Enter the information below, which you will note includes no Company or Department fields:

Miss Ann Z. Abzug
301 Crest Dr.
Encinitas, CA   92024

Start Date: 3/1/90
Credit Limit: 7,500

Press Enter after typing in the new record.

INSERTING RECORDS

Any time that you are in the Edit mode, you can add new records to the table by inserting them between existing records. Try this example: press the ↑ key six times to move the cursor to "Gladstone". To insert a blank record, press the Ins (or Insert) key. The screen will make space for the new record, as shown in Figure 3.8.

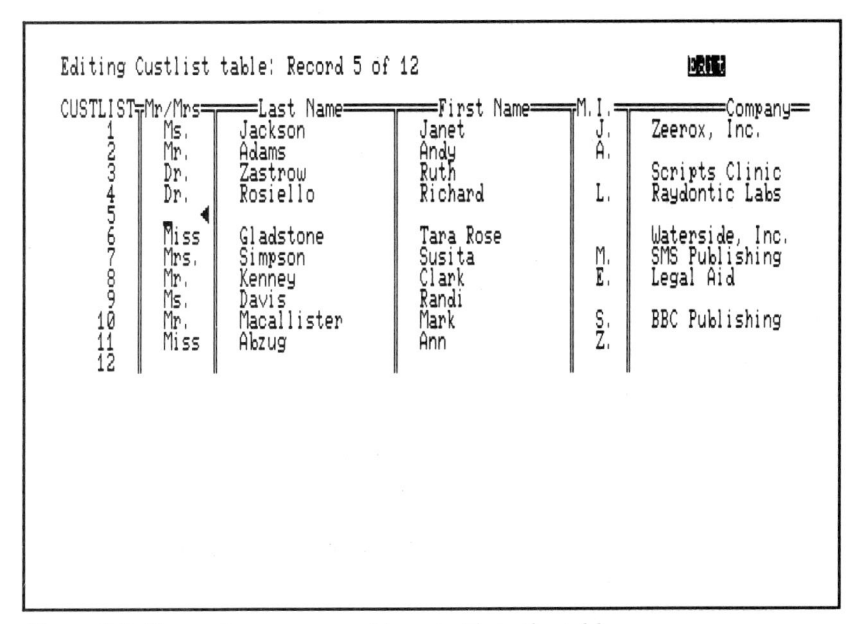

```
Editing Custlist table: Record 5 of 12                    EDIT
CUSTLIST=Mr/Mrs====Last Name======First Name====M.I.=========Company=
    1       Ms.    Jackson        Janet          J.    Zeerox, Inc.
    2       Mr.    Adams          Andy           A.
    3       Dr.    Zastrow        Ruth                 Scripts Clinic
    4       Dr.    Rosiello       Richard        L.    Raydontic Labs
    5     ◄
    6       Miss   Gladstone      Tara Rose            Waterside, Inc.
    7       Mrs.   Simpson        Susita         M.    SMS Publishing
    8       Mr.    Kenney         Clark          E.    Legal Aid
    9       Ms.    Davis          Randi
   10       Mr.    Macallister    Mark           S.    BBC Publishing
   11       Miss   Abzug          Ann            Z.
   12
```

Figure 3.8: Room for new record inserted into the table

At this point, you could type in a new record. Or you could change your mind and press the Del (or Delete) key to delete the record. Press the Del key now and watch the table "close up" again. The table will appear as it did before you entered the new, blank record.

(*Note:* Though you can insert records, it is not necessary to do so just to maintain a sorted order. Paradox can quickly and easily re-sort your table into any order you wish, as we'll discuss later.)

When done entering new records in the Edit mode, press DO-IT! (F2) to save your changes. You'll be returned to the View mode, and will see your new records at the bottom of the table, as in Figure 3.9.

We'll discuss the Edit mode and editing techniques in more detail in a later chapter.

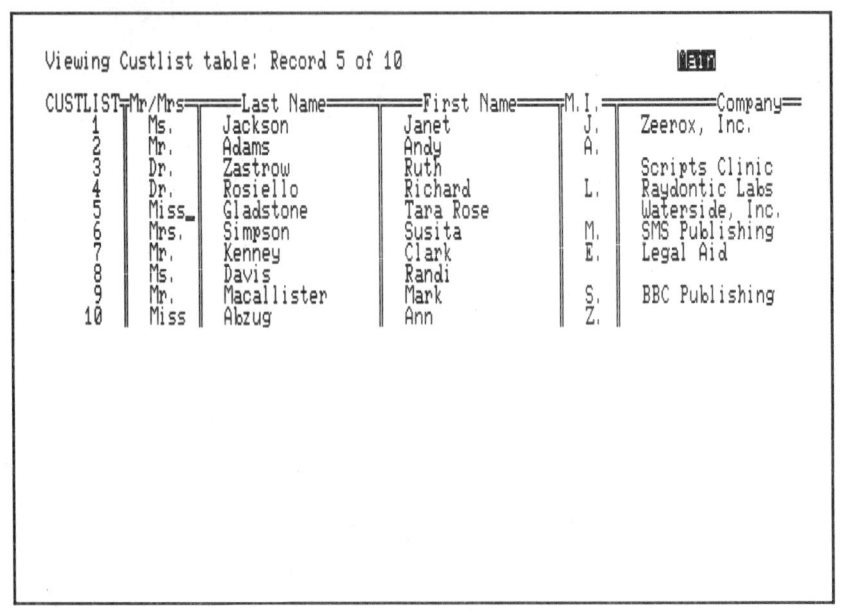

```
Viewing Custlist table: Record 5 of 10                    Main
CUSTLIST=Mr/Mrs======Last Name======First Name======M.I.======Company=
    1  |  Ms.   | Jackson    | Janet      | J. | Zeerox, Inc.
    2  |  Mr.   | Adams      | Andy       | A. |
    3  |  Dr.   | Zastrow    | Ruth       |    | Scripts Clinic
    4  |  Dr.   | Rosiello   | Richard    | L. | Raydontic Labs
    5  |  Miss_ | Gladstone  | Tara Rose  |    | Waterside, Inc.
    6  |  Mrs.  | Simpson    | Susita     | M. | SMS Publishing
    7  |  Mr.   | Kenney     | Clark      | E. | Legal Aid
    8  |  Ms.   | Davis      | Randi      |    |
    9  |  Mr.   | Macallister| Mark       | S. | BBC Publishing
   10  |  Miss  | Abzug      | Ann        | Z. |
```

Figure 3.9: New records added to the Custlist table

A FEW CAUTIONS

Keep in mind that whenever you add new records to a table through DataEntry, the first record is always number 1, even though there may already be other records in the table. Don't worry about this. DataEntry always starts adding new records at record number

1, then adds the new records to the existing table after you press the DO-IT! key.

Whenever you enter or change data in a table, the changes are not permanent until you press the DO-IT! (F2) key. Therefore, if you are adding a great deal of data to a table, you should occasionally press the DO-IT! key to save your work. Then you can select the Modify and DataEntry options from the menu or press the Edit (F9) key to continue adding new records.

Only an accidental cancellation, a power failure, or some other unlikely hazard will destroy your work, so you need not press DO-IT! after every new record or modification. However, if you plan on entering hundreds of records to a table, you might want to press DO-IT! after every 25 or so new records. It would be a real pity to be on your 999th record and have a friendly cohort trip over a wire and unplug your computer by accident. You could lose quite a bit of your work (as well as a friendly cohort).

You may be ready to take a break now, so you can just exit Paradox in the usual fashion. Select Exit from the Main menu. Remember, if the Main menu is not displayed, press Menu (F10) to call up the Main menu. If you are in the middle of some other task, such as data entry, press DO-IT! (F2) to finish that task, then select Exit from the Main menu.

SUMMARY

In this chapter, you've learned a great deal about adding new records to a table. However, you've also learned a number of techniques for managing the cursor and making corrections, which will come in handy in future chapters. Take a moment now to review some of the basic techniques we've discussed in this chapter.

- To add new data to a table, select the Modify option from the Main menu and the DataEntry option from the submenu.
- Enter dates in either MM/DD/YY format or DD-Mon-YY format. Invalid dates will be rejected, and you'll need to reenter using the Backspace key.

- When entering dollar amounts it is not necessary to type in ".00" if you are entering a whole dollar amount.
- To make a simple change when entering data in a table, use the arrow and Backspace keys.
- To make a more refined change while entering data, change to Field View (press Alt-F5) while the cursor is in the field that you want to edit. Press Enter when you are done editing.
- To duplicate data from the previous record in a field, use the Ditto command (Ctrl-D).
- To switch from Table View to Form View when entering records, press the Form Toggle (F7) key.
- To save all new records added to a table, press the DO-IT! (F2) key.
- As an alternative, you can add records to a table through the Edit mode. When viewing a table, just press the Edit (F9) key. Use the arrow, Backspace, Field View, Ins, and Del keys to help with data entry. Press DO-IT! (F2) when you are done entering new records.
- If you are entering large amounts of data into a table, press the DO-IT! (F2) key occasionally to save your work. Then select the Modify and DataEntry options from the menus, or press the Edit (F9) key, to continue entering new records.

VIEWING TABLE DATA

CHAPTER 4

BECAUSE THE DATA YOU ENTER INTO A TABLE ARE always stored on disk, the copy of the records that you see on the screen is often referred to as an *image*. In this chapter, we'll discuss basic techniques for calling up an image of the data, as well as techniques for modifying the image on the screen. In later chapters, we'll discuss techniques for developing formatted reports, such as a directory, mailing labels, and form letters.

VIEWING A TABLE

> If you are using Paradox on a network, see "Viewing Data on a Network" in Appendix B.

> For a quick reminder of keys used in managing the cursor, look inside the front cover of this book.

To see a portion of the data stored in a table, first get Paradox up and running, of course, and select the View option from the Main menu. Paradox will ask for the name of the table to view. As before, you can type in the table name, Custlist, and press Enter. Or you can press Enter to view the names of existing tables, then highlight the name of the Custlist table and press Enter. A portion of the table data will appear on the screen, in Table View format, as in Figure 4.1.

You can use the same keys we discussed in the last chapter to move the cursor and scroll the screen. You can exaggerate the movements of the arrow keys by holding down the Ctrl key while pressing an arrow key. (The Paradox manual sometimes refers to the Ctrl key as the *Turbo* key, because it exaggerates movements.) For example, pressing Ctrl-→ moves the cursor an entire screen to the right, displaying fields that were previously hidden. Since the current table is about three screens wide, pressing Ctrl-→ three times will scroll all the way to the right end of the table. Pressing Ctrl-← three times will scroll all the way back to the first field.

The ↑ and ↓ keys do not work in the same way with the Ctrl key. Instead, you use the PgUp key to scroll up a page and PgDn to scroll down a page. (The Custlist table is too small to fully demonstrate these keys, but trying them will give you an idea of how they work.)

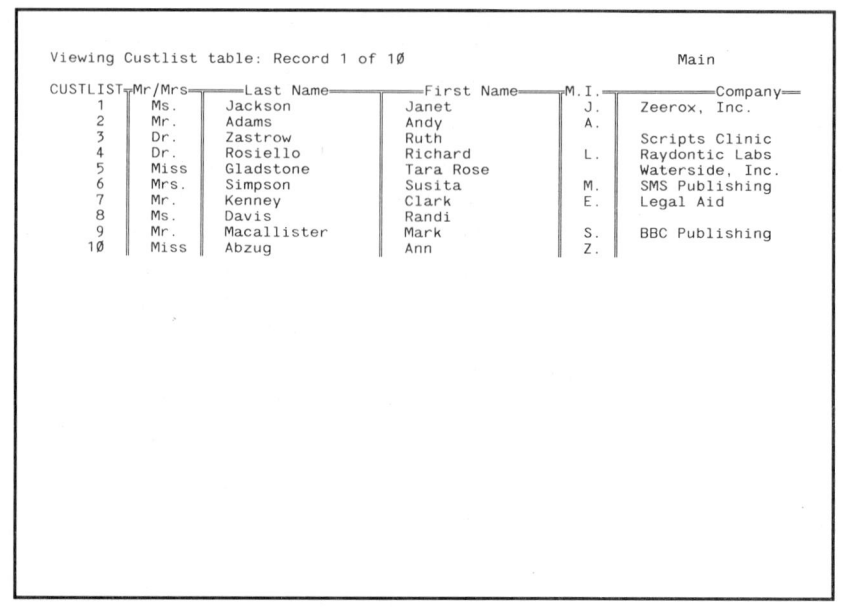

```
Viewing Custlist table: Record 1 of 10                    Main
CUSTLIST=Mr/Mrs====—Last Name====—First Name====M.I.====Company===
    1    Ms.      Jackson         Janet           J.    Zeerox, Inc.
    2    Mr.      Adams           Andy            A.
    3    Dr.      Zastrow         Ruth                  Scripts Clinic
    4    Dr.      Rosiello        Richard         L.    Raydontic Labs
    5    Miss     Gladstone       Tara Rose             Waterside, Inc.
    6    Mrs.     Simpson         Susita          M.    SMS Publishing
    7    Mr.      Kenney          Clark           E.    Legal Aid
    8    Ms.      Davis           Randi
    9    Mr.      Macallister     Mark            S.    BBC Publishing
   10    Miss     Abzug           Ann             Z.
```

Figure 4.1: Viewing data on the workspace

The Home key always takes you to the first record in a table. Ctrl-Home takes you to the first field in a record. The End key moves the cursor to the last record in a table, and Ctrl-End to the last field in a record. Table 4.1 lists these keys.

THE IMAGE MENU

There are a number of things you can do to alter the image you see on the screen without affecting the actual contents of the table. All of these options are under the Image selection on the Main menu. (If the Main menu is not displayed, just press the Menu (F10) key.) When you highlight the Image option, this sentence appears below the menu:

Resize or reformat images; go to records or values; pick forms; specify graphs.

Table 4.1: Keys used when viewing records in Table View

KEY	EFFECT
↑	Up one record
PgUp	Up one screen
↓	Down one record
PgDn	Down one screen
←	Left one field
Ctrl-←	Left one screen
→	Right one field
Ctrl-→	Right one screen
Home	First record in table
Ctrl-Home	First field in record
End	Last record in table
Ctrl-End	Last field in record

Selecting the Image option displays the following submenu:

TableSize   ColumnSize   Format   Zoom   Move
PickForm   KeepSet   Graph

We'll discuss each of these options in the remaining sections.

CHANGING THE TABLE SIZE

When several tables are displayed simultaneously on the screen, you may want to alter the sizes of some of them. Though it is not necessary to do so with the small Custlist table, we'll discuss this option now for use later in the book.

To alter the table size, select the TableSize option. The screen will display these instructions:

> Use ↑ to decrease the table by one row; ↓ to increase by one row . . . then press ⏎ when finished.

Pressing the ↑ key shortens the table display; pressing the ↓ key lengthens it. Increasing or decreasing the table display does not affect the number of records in the table. For example, if you shorten the display to two records, only two records at a time will appear on the screen. However, you can still use the arrow or PgUp and PgDn keys to scroll through all the records in the table. After altering the table size with the arrow keys, press Enter.

CHANGING THE COLUMN WIDTH

You can change the width of any column on the screen by selecting the Image option from the Main menu and the ColumnSize option from the submenu. Doing so brings up these instructions:

> Use ← and → to move to the column you want to resize . . . then press ⏎ to select it.

For this example, press the → key twice to move the cursor to the Last Name field, then press the Enter key. The instructions on the screen will then read

> Now use → to increase column width, ← to decrease . . . press ⏎ when finished.

You can narrow the Last Name field by pressing the ← key four times. Press Enter when you're done.

Let's do the same for the First Name field. Call up the Main menu, and select the Image and then the ColumnSize options. Move the cursor to the First Name field and press Enter. Press the ← key six times, and press Enter. Now both the Last Name and First Name field are smaller, leaving more room for the Company field, as shown in Figure 4.2.

VIEWING TABLE DATA 53

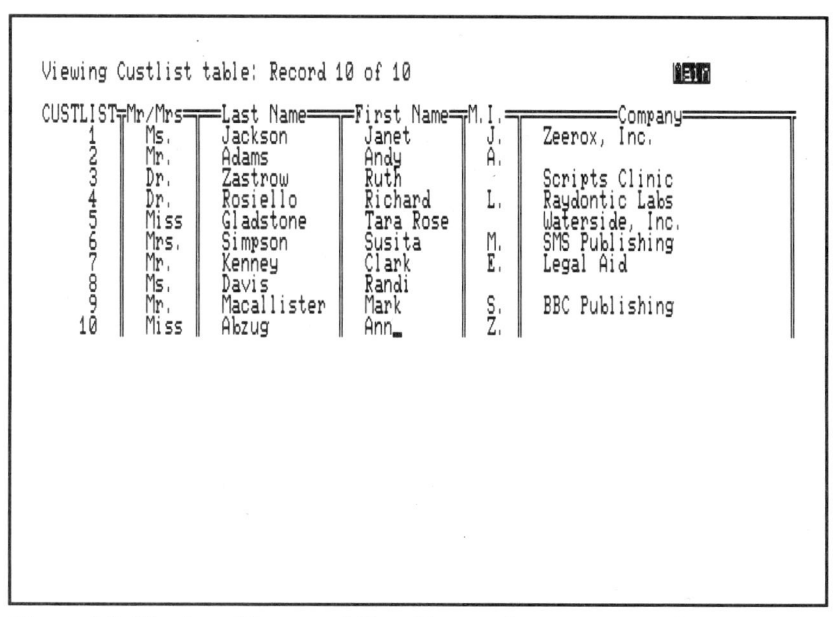

```
┌─────────────────────────────────────────────────────────────────────┐
│ Viewing Custlist table: Record 10 of 10                      Main   │
│ CUSTLIST╤Mr/Mrs══╤══Last Name═══╤═First Name═╤M.I.╤═════Company════ │
│    1  │  Ms.   │  Jackson      │  Janet      │ J. │ Zeerox, Inc.   │
│    2  │  Mr.   │  Adams        │  Andy       │ A. │                │
│    3  │  Dr.   │  Zastrow      │  Ruth       │    │ Scripts Clinic │
│    4  │  Dr.   │  Rosiello     │  Richard    │ L. │ Raydontic Labs │
│    5  │  Miss  │  Gladstone    │  Tara Rose  │    │ Waterside, Inc.│
│    6  │  Mrs.  │  Simpson      │  Susita     │ M. │ SMS Publishing │
│    7  │  Mr.   │  Kenney       │  Clark      │ E. │ Legal Aid      │
│    8  │  Ms.   │  Davis        │  Randi      │    │                │
│    9  │  Mr.   │  Macallister  │  Mark       │ S. │ BBC Publishing │
│   10  │  Miss  │  Abzug        │  Ann_       │ Z. │                │
│                                                                     │
└─────────────────────────────────────────────────────────────────────┘
```

Figure 4.2: The Last Name and First Name columns narrowed

Besides the ← and → keys, you can use the following keys when changing the column size:

KEY	EFFECT
Home	Quickly resizes to the minimum width of 1 character
End	Quickly resizes to the maximum width as set in the table structure
Escape	Cancels the resizing for the current column
Enter	Finishes the resizing for the current column

Keep in mind that these changes affect only the image on the screen; they have no effect on the structure of the table. Also, unless you specifically save these changed sizes (as discussed in a moment), they will last only during your current work section; they will be reset back to their original value as soon as you exit Paradox.

There are a few limitations to changing column sizes, as listed below:

- The minimum width of a column is one character.

> If you make a numeric or currency column too narrow, some numbers will be displayed as a row of asterisks (until you widen the column).

- A numeric or currency field can be no more than 25 characters wide.
- A date field can be no more than 14 characters wide, unless the field name is longer.
- An alphanumeric field can be no wider than the width defined in the table structure, or 76 characters, whichever is less.

When resizing a field, Paradox will beep when you reach the maximum width.

FORMATTING NUMERIC AND DATE FIELDS

You can modify the way in which numeric and date data are displayed in the image by selecting the Image and Format options from the Main menu. Let's give it a whirl. Choose the Image and Format options from the Main menu. The screen will display these instructions:

    Use → and ← to move to the field you want to reformat . . .
    then press ↵ to select it.

Move the cursor to the Start Date field and press Enter.
Next, the screen displays the following options:

    MM/DD/YY   DD-Mon-YY   DD.MM.YY

Move the cursor to the right to select the DD-Mon-YY option, and press Enter. The dates convert to the new format, as shown in Figure 4.3.

If, during the formatting process, you select a numeric field to reformat, you'll be given the following menu of choices:

    General   Fixed   Comma   Scientific

When you select an option, the screen will display this prompt:

    Number of decimal places: 2
    Enter the number of digits to show after the decimal point
    (Range: 0–15)

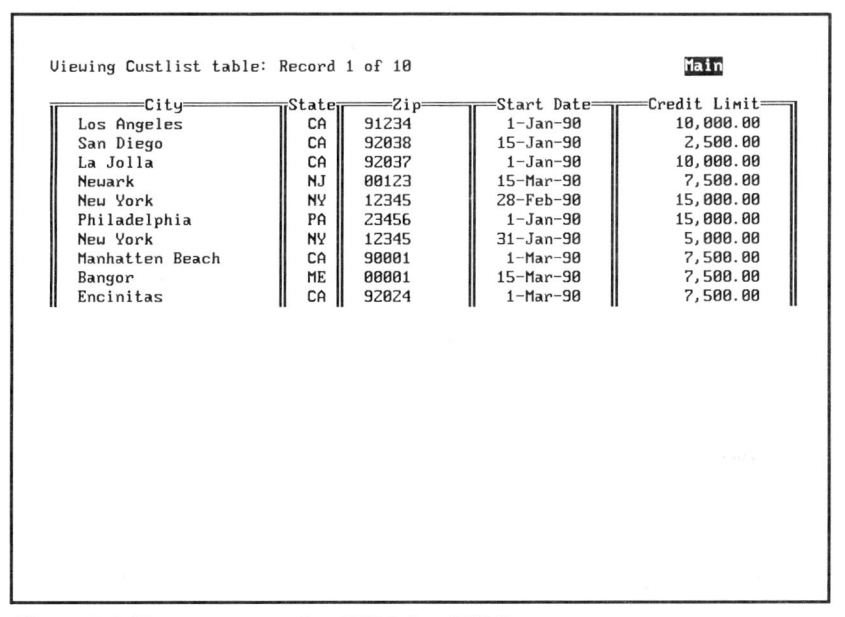

```
Viewing Custlist table: Record 1 of 10                              Main
┌─────City──────┬─State─┬──Zip──┬──Start Date──┬──Credit Limit──┐
│ Los Angeles   │  CA   │ 91234 │   1-Jan-90   │    10,000.00   │
│ San Diego     │  CA   │ 92038 │  15-Jan-90   │     2,500.00   │
│ La Jolla      │  CA   │ 92037 │   1-Jan-90   │    10,000.00   │
│ Newark        │  NJ   │ 00123 │  15-Mar-90   │     7,500.00   │
│ New York      │  NY   │ 12345 │  28-Feb-90   │    15,000.00   │
│ Philadelphia  │  PA   │ 23456 │   1-Jan-90   │    15,000.00   │
│ New York      │  NY   │ 12345 │  31-Jan-90   │     5,000.00   │
│ Manhatten Beach│  CA  │ 90001 │   1-Mar-90   │     7,500.00   │
│ Bangor        │  ME   │ 00001 │  15-Mar-90   │     7,500.00   │
│ Encinitas     │  CA   │ 92024 │   1-Mar-90   │     7,500.00   │
└───────────────┴───────┴───────┴──────────────┴────────────────┘
```

Figure 4.3: Dates converted to DD-Mon-YY format

Type in a number between 0 and 15 (inclusive) to specify the number of decimal places to display. (In most situations, 2 is adequate.)

The various formats for displaying numbers are discussed below:

FORMAT   *DISPLAY*

General   Each number in the column is displayed with as many decimal places as accuracy requires, within the limits you specified in the first prompt. Hence, 1234.00 is displayed as 1234, and 1234.567000 is displayed as 1234.567.

Fixed   Sets a fixed number of decimal places for the numbers in the column. If you specify 3 decimal places of accuracy, the number 1234 is displayed as 1234.000. The number 1234.123456789 is displayed as 1234.123.

Comma   Commas separate thousands, and negative numbers are displayed in parentheses. Hence, the value 1234 is displayed as 1,234.00, and the number –1234.56 is displayed as (1,234.56).

Scientific   Generally used only in scientific applications where very large numbers are involved, this option displays numbers in exponential format. Hence, 123456 is displayed as 1.23E+05.

Paradox can store very large numbers in the range of 10^{-307} to 10^{308}, with up to 15 significant digits. Note that if a column is too narrow to display a number, the number will appear as a series of asterisks (for example, *****). To remedy this, select the Image and ColumnSize options from the Main menu, and widen the column. A number might also be displayed as asterisks if a portion of it is off the edge of the screen. Scrolling the screen will remedy that situation.

Numbers that are too large to display in Paradox's General format will automatically be converted to Scientific format.

LARGE MOVES THROUGH THE IMAGE

When a table becomes very large, it is unwieldy to move through records and fields by scrolling. The Zoom option under the Image menu allows you to jump directly to a particular record or field.

To try this out, call up the Main menu and select the Image option, then select the Zoom option. The screen will display three options:

Field   Record   Value

If you select the Field option, the screen displays a menu of possible fields to jump to, as below:

Mr/Mrs   Last Name   First Name   M.I.   Company
Department   Address

Use the arrow keys to highlight the name of the field you want to jump to, then press Enter. The cursor will jump to the appropriate field within the current record.

Selecting the Record option from the Zoom submenu displays this prompt:

Record Number:
Enter record number you want.

You type in the record number and press Enter. For example, if you type in 6 and press ENTER, the cursor will jump to record number 6.

The Value option from the Zoom submenu lets you locate a particular value within a field. For example, if you select Image from the Main menu, Zoom from the submenu, and Value from the Zoom submenu, the screen displays the prompt

> Use → and ← to move to the column you want to search in...then press ↵ to select it.

Use the → key to move the cursor to the Zip field, and press Enter to select this field. Next the screen prompts:

> Value: Enter value or pattern to search for.

Type in a zip code to look for (such as 12345) and press Enter. The cursor will immediately jump to the first record that has 12345 in the zip-code field.

A shortcut technique for accessing the Value option on the Zoom menu is to use the Zoom (Ctrl-Z) key. To use the Zoom key, first position the cursor in the field (column) you wish to search. Then press Ctrl-Z, and you'll immediately be presented with the prompt to enter a value to search for. Fill in a value and press Enter. The cursor will move to the first record that contains that value. To move the cursor to the *next* record that has the same value, press the Zoom Next key (Alt-Z). You can continue using Zoom Next to locate the next matching record until there are no more records in the database that match the search value.

When you search for a value using the Zoom menu option, or Zoom key, character strings must match in case in order for the search to be successful. For example, if you attempt to locate the string *adams*, the screen will display the message

> Match not found

and the cursor will stay at its current position. The reason for the search's failure is that the name is stored as *Adams*, not *adams*.

> The Zoom (Ctrl-Z) key works only when no menu is displayed at the top of the screen.

You may use the *wild-card characters*

>   ..

and

>   @

in search values using Zoom. The @ wild-card character matches any other character, and .. matches any group of characters. For example, a search for the value

>   Sm@th

will match Smith, Smyth, Smath, and so forth. A search for a value such as

>   J..n

would match Johnson, Jan, Jordan, Jackson, and any other word beginning with *J* and ending with *n*. These wild-card characters are discussed in more detail in Chapter 7.

Note that when you use Zoom a second time, it displays the value entered from the previous search. To remove this old value quickly, press Ctrl-Backspace. To modify the displayed value quickly, you can use Field View (Alt-F5).

Zoom offers only a rudimentary technique for positioning the cursor in a particular field or record. In larger databases you'll need more advanced search, or *query*, techniques to look up information quickly. These powerful techniques are discussed in Chapter 7.

MOVING COLUMNS

You can also rearrange the order of the columns displayed on the screen. Let's give it a try by moving the Last Name field to the right of the M.I. field. Call up the Main menu (F10), and select the Image option. From the submenu, select the Move option. Paradox displays this prompt:

> Name of field to move:
> Mr/Mrs   Last Name   First Name   M.I.   Company
>   Department   Address

Use the → key to highlight the Last Name field, then press Enter to select that field. Paradox displays this message:

> Now use → and ← to show the new position for the field . . .
> then press ↵ to move it.

Press the → key to move the cursor to the M.I. field, then press Enter. The Last Name field is inserted in the position indicated by the cursor, as shown in Figure 4.4.

Keep in mind that this affects only the current display, not the structure of the table. Also, unless you specifically save these changes to the image (through a procedure we'll discuss in a moment), they will be lost when you exit Paradox.

```
Viewing Custlist table: Record 6 of 10                          Main
CUSTLIST=Mr/Mrs==First Name==M.I.==Last Name======Company========
    1  │ Ms.   │ Janet      │ J.  │ Jackson    │ Zeerox, Inc.
    2  │ Mr.   │ Andy       │ A.  │ Adams      │
    3  │ Dr.   │ Ruth       │     │ Zastrow    │ Scripts Clinic
    4  │ Dr.   │ Richard    │ L.  │ Rosiello   │ Raydontic Labs
    5  │ Miss  │ Tara Rose  │     │ Gladstone  │ Waterside, Inc.
    6  │ Mrs.  │ Susita     │ M.  │ Simpson_   │ SMS Publishing
    7  │ Mr.   │ Clark      │ E.  │ Kenney     │ Legal Aid
    8  │ Ms.   │ Randi      │     │ Davis      │
    9  │ Mr.   │ Mark       │ S.  │ Macallister│ BBC Publishing
   10  │ Miss  │ Ann        │ Z.  │ Abzug      │
```

Figure 4.4: The Last Name field moved to a new position

QUICK MOVES WITH THE ROTATE COMMAND

You can move a field quickly from any position on the image to the far-right column position by moving the cursor to that field, using the usual arrow keys, and issuing the Rotate command (Ctrl-R). For example, if you place the cursor in the Mr/Mrs field and press Ctrl-R, the Mr/Mrs field will disappear off the right edge of the screen, and all fields to the right will rotate to the left. Each time you press Ctrl-R, the fields will rotate to the left. If you press Ctrl-R a total of 12 times (once for each field in the table), the Mr/Mrs field will rotate back to its original position.

SWITCHING TO FORM VIEW

As we have already learned, you can switch quickly from Table View to Form View, and vice versa, by pressing the Form Toggle (F7) key. Figure 4.5 shows a record from the Custlist table in Form View.

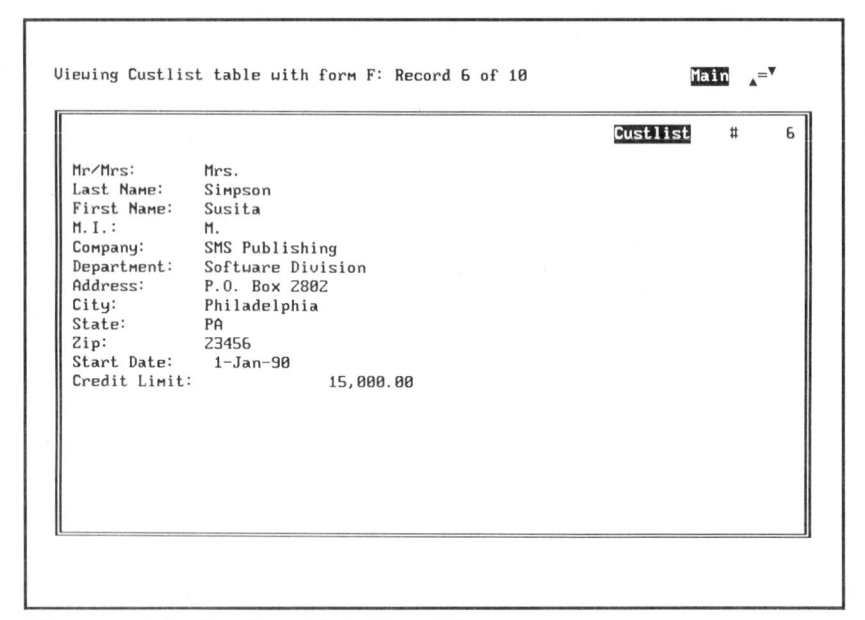

```
Viewing Custlist table with form F: Record 6 of 10          Main

                                                        Custlist   #   6

    Mr/Mrs:         Mrs.
    Last Name:      Simpson
    First Name:     Susita
    M.I.:           M.
    Company:        SMS Publishing
    Department:     Software Division
    Address:        P.O. Box 2802
    City:           Philadelphia
    State:          PA
    Zip:            23456
    Start Date:     1-Jan-90
    Credit Limit:             15,000.00
```

Figure 4.5: The Custlist table in Form View

The Image menu also presents the option Graph, which lets you create graphs from table data. Graphs are discussed in Chapter 10.

You can also switch to Form View by selecting the PickForm option from the Image menu and F from the submenu. As we'll see in later chapters, Paradox allows you to develop your own custom forms in addition to this standard form. The PickForm option, in turn, will allow you to select the particular form (standard or one of your custom forms) you want to display. The Form Toggle (F7) key switches back to Table View, even if you used the PickForm option to switch to Form View.

SAVING IMAGE SETTINGS

As mentioned throughout this chapter, any changes that you make to the image are only active during the current session. There is no need to save the image settings we used in this chapter. But for general information, in order to save image settings, you select the Image option from the Main menu, and then select the KeepSet option from the submenu.

If you change image settings and select the KeepSet option, the new settings will overwrite the old settings. (The actual table structure, of course, remains unchanged.)

To erase previously saved settings and return to the original image display, call up the Main menu and select the Tools option. From the submenu select the Delete option and then the KeepSet option. Specify the name of the table (Custlist in this example), and press Enter. If the current image does not change, clear the screen by pressing the Clear Image (F8) key, and select the View option from the Main menu. Then specify the name of the table to view.

Those of you familiar with file names and DOS commands might be interested to know that the image settings are stored on a file with the same name as the table, but with the extension .SET (for instance, Custlist.SET). Therefore, you can also erase settings by using the command

ERASE Custlist.SET

from the DOS prompt, outside of Paradox.

PRINTING AN IMAGE QUICKLY

If you want a quick printed copy of your table, make sure your printer is on and on-line, ready to accept the output. Then just press the Instant Report (Alt-F7) key combination. The data will be displayed in Table Format, as on the screen. (This printed display is indeed a rudimentary one. I'll discuss techniques for printing much fancier, formatted reports in Chapter 8.)

If you wish to stop printing before the entire table is printed, press Ctrl-Break (hold down the Ctrl key and press the ScrollLock key). You'll be returned to the View mode.

Now, let me digress for a moment and give you a little lesson on managing pages in a printer. Before you turn on your printer, you should always make sure there is a page perforation just above the print head. That way, Paradox "knows" where the top of a page is and can properly place margins at the top and bottom of each page. If you "hand crank" the paper in the printer, Paradox will no longer "know" where page breaks are, and you'll likely get future reports spread randomly across page perforations.

If at any time you are not sure that the pages are properly aligned in the printer, first turn the printer off, manually crank the paper through to the top of the next page, then turn the printer back on. Many printers have a Form Feed button to move the paper to the top of the next page. If you have such a printer, use the Form Feed button, rather than hand cranking, to move pages through the printer.

CLEARING AN IMAGE

If you wish to remove an image from the screen (for example, if you want to clear one image to view another), just press the Clear Image (F8) key. The workspace will clear and you'll see only the Main menu. To view another table, select the View option and enter the name of the table.

SUMMARY

- To view a table, call up the Main menu (F10) and select the View option. Specify the name of the table to view when requested.

- To change the size of the table on the screen, select the Image option from the Main menu and the TableSize option from the submenu.

- To change the width of a column on the screen, select the Image option from the Main menu and the ColumnSize option from the submenu.

- To change the format of numbers or dates, select the Image option from the Main menu and the Format option from the submenu.

- To jump the cursor to a particular field or record, select the Image option from the Main menu and the Zoom option from the submenu. You can also press the Zoom key (Ctrl-Z) to enter a value to search for, without using the menus.

- To change the order of columns on the screen, select the Image option from the Main menu and the Move option from the submenu. To move a column quickly to the far right of the table, move the cursor to the column and issue the Rotate command (Ctrl-R).

- To switch between Table View and Form View, press the Form Toggle (F7) key.

- To save image settings, select the Image option from the Main menu and the KeepSet option from the submenu.

- For a printed copy of your data, press the Instant Report (Alt-F7) key combination.

- To clear an image from the screen, press the Clear Image (F8) key.

EDITING AND VALIDATING DATA

CHAPTER 5

WHEN WORKING WITH COMPUTERS, THE TERM *EDIT* refers to any type of modification to the data on a table, whether it is a change of address, correction of a misspelling, deletion of a record, or any other change. Editing data with Paradox is easy. In fact, you already know quite a bit about it, as you'll see.

Before you can edit a table, it needs to be on the workspace. If the workspace on your screen is empty, select the View option from the Main menu, and specify Custlist as the table to use.

THE EDIT MODE

If you are using Paradox on a network, see "Editing on a Network" in Appendix B.

To begin editing the Custlist table, just press the Edit (F9) key. The top portion of the screen will read as follows:

    Editing Custlist table: Record 1 of 10   Edit

You can edit data in Table View, Form View (by pressing the Form Toggle (F7) key), or Field View (by pressing Alt-F5). In any of these cases, the arrow keys have their usual effects as described earlier (and shown inside the covers of this book).

SIMPLE EDITS

Simple edits in the Edit mode are identical to those discussed when we were adding new data to the table. The following keys have the following effects:

- Any character typed into a field will just be added to the field. For example, if the cursor is in the Last Name field for Adams and you type the letters "on", the Last Name field will contain "Adamson".

- Backspace: Pressing the Backspace key erases the character to the left of the cursor and moves the cursor to the left one space.
- Ctrl-Backspace: Pressing Ctrl-Backspace erases the entire current contents of the field.
- Typing Ctrl-U "undoes" an edit.
- Arrow keys: The arrow keys move the cursor up, down, left, and right, without changing any data.

FIELD VIEW EDITING

As we discussed in Chapter 3, pressing Field View (Alt-F5) narrows the effects of the arrow keys to the current field. Review Table 3.2 or the chart inside the back cover if you need to be reminded of the effects of the editing keys in Field View.

SAVING EDITS

You can move the cursor around the table and make whatever changes you wish as long as you are in the Edit mode. To save your changes and return to the View mode, press the DO-IT! (F2) key. To reenter the Edit mode, just press the Edit (F9) key again.

You can also save your edits by calling up the Edit menu while in the Edit mode. To do so, press F10 and select the DO-IT! option from the menu that appears on the screen. All of your changes will be saved, and you'll be returned to the View mode.

UNDOING EDITS

Occasionally, you may feel a little lost while editing records in a table and want to *undo* some of your changes. There are a few techniques that you can use to undo recent changes to a table. The quickest method is simply to press Ctrl-U. Doing so undoes the most recent edit *transaction* that occurred. (A single edit *transaction* is all changes made to a single record while the cursor was still within the record.) Hence, if you were to move the cursor to record 2 and change the name Adams to Adamson and the zip code to 99999, then pressing Ctrl-U would undo both of those edits.

Ctrl-U works in a reverse, incremental order. If you repeatedly press Ctrl-U, Paradox will undo edit transactions in the reverse order of that in which they occurred. For example, suppose you make two changes to record number 2 in a table and three changes to record number 6. The first time you press Ctrl-U, Paradox will undo the three changes made to record number 6. If you press Ctrl-U again right away, Paradox will undo both changes made to record number 2.

You can also use the Edit menu to undo changes made to a table. To call up the Edit menu while in the Edit mode, just press the F10 key. You'll be given the options

    Image   Undo   ValCheck   Help   DO-IT!   Cancel

The Undo option under the Edit menu works in exactly the same manner that the Ctrl-U keys do, except that the menu option gives you a second chance to change your mind. When you select UnDo from the Edit menu, you'll be presented with the options

    No   Yes
    Do not undo the last change made to current image.

Selecting Yes undoes the most recent edit transaction and returns you to the Edit mode. Selecting No retains the most recent edit and returns to the Edit submenu. (To resume editing from this point, just press the Esc key.)

To abandon *all* the edits made in the current editing session, select Cancel from the Edit menu. You'll see the submenu

    No   Yes
    Do not undo changes made to the current image.

If you select Yes, Paradox will undo *all* recent edits (since the last DO-IT! command) and return to the View mode. (To edit more records, you'll need to press the F9 key again.) If you select No, Paradox will not undo recent edits and will return to the previous menu. To continue editing, press the Esc key.

We'll experiment with edits and undos in a moment. However, you may want to experiment now with some of these editing features to get a feel for how they operate. When you are done experimenting, call up the Edit menu (by pressing F10) and select Cancel and Yes to undo all your experimental edits and bring the table back to its previous form.

DELETING A RECORD

To delete a record while in Edit mode, move the cursor to the record and press the Del key. All the records following the deleted record will move up one notch. For example, press F9 now to begin editing, then move the cursor to the record for Clark Kenney in the Custlist table and press the Del key. The record will disappear, and all those beneath will move up a row, as in Figure 5.1.

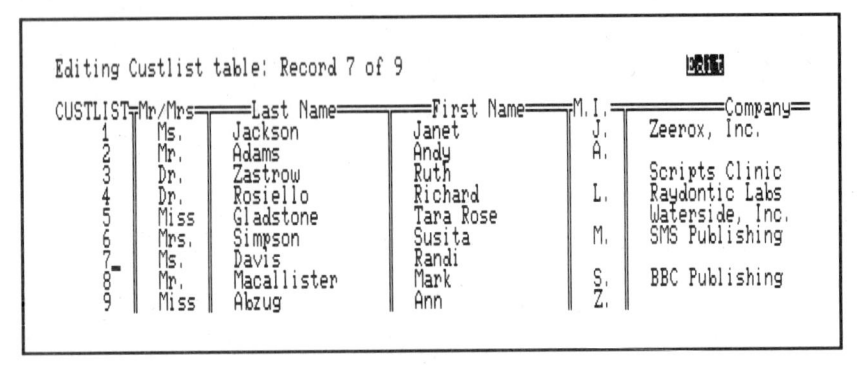

```
Editing Custlist table: Record 7 of 9                         Edit
CUSTLIST=Mr/Mrs===Last Name====First Name===M.I.====Company===
   1       Ms.      Jackson       Janet        J.     Zeerox, Inc.
   2       Mr.      Adams         Andy         A.
   3       Dr.      Zastrow       Ruth                Scripts Clinic
   4       Dr.      Rosiello      Richard      L.     Raydontic Labs
   5       Miss     Gladstone     Tara Rose           Waterside, Inc.
   6       Mrs.     Simpson       Susita       M.     SMS Publishing
   7       Ms.      Davis         Randi
   8       Mr.      Macallister   Mark         S.     BBC Publishing
   9       Miss     Abzug         Ann          Z.
```

Figure 5.1: Kenney deleted from the Custlist table

UNDELETING A RECORD

If you delete a record by accident, or change your mind, you can retrieve the record by pressing Ctrl-U or by calling up the menu (press F10) and selecting the Undo and Yes options. The record will reappear, as in Figure 5.2.

LOCATING THE RECORD TO EDIT

As discussed in the previous chapter, you can use Zoom (Ctrl-Z) to locate a particular record quickly for editing, based on a value in a field. For example, if you wanted to edit the record for a person

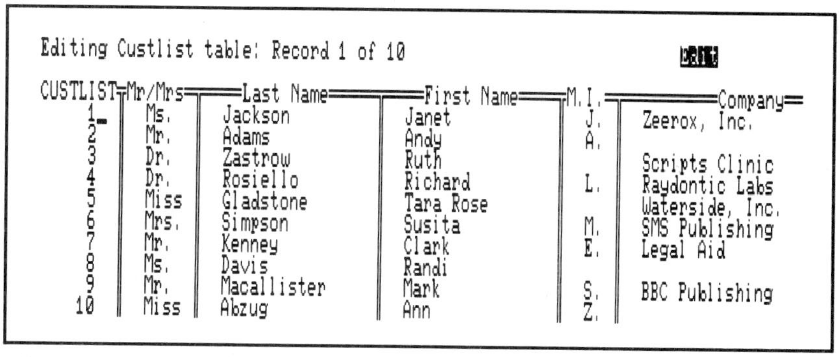

```
Editing Custlist table: Record 1 of 10                    EDIT
CUSTLIST┬Mr/Mrs────┬────Last Name────┬────First Name────┬M.I.┬────Company────┐
   1─   │ Ms.      │ Jackson         │ Janet            │ J. │ Zeerox, Inc.  │
   2    │ Mr.      │ Adams           │ Andy             │ A. │               │
   3    │ Dr.      │ Zastrow         │ Ruth             │    │ Scripts Clinic│
   4    │ Dr.      │ Rosiello        │ Richard          │ L. │ Raydontic Labs│
   5    │ Miss     │ Gladstone       │ Tara Rose        │    │ Waterside, Inc.│
   6    │ Mrs.     │ Simpson         │ Susita           │ M. │ SMS Publishing│
   7    │ Mr.      │ Kenney          │ Clark            │ E. │ Legal Aid     │
   8    │ Ms.      │ Davis           │ Randi            │    │               │
   9    │ Mr.      │ Macallister     │ Mark             │ S. │ BBC Publishing│
  10    │ Miss     │ Abzug           │ Ann              │ Z. │               │
```

Figure 5.2: A record recalled from deletion

named Smith in a large table, you would move the cursor to the Last Name field, press Ctrl-Z, and enter **Smith** as the name to search for. If the first Smith that the cursor located was not the correct Smith, you could press Zoom Next (Alt-Z) to locate the next Smith until the cursor was positioned at the appropriate record.

AN EXERCISE IN EDITING

To test some of the editing techniques discussed so far, you might want to try the following rather simple exercise. Suppose you wish to change the name Susita to Susan in the sixth record. One way to do so would be to put the cursor in the First Name field, press Ctrl-Z, and enter **Susita** as the value to search for. (Then, of course, press Enter.)

Press F9 to go into the Edit mode. With the cursor to the right of Susita, you can enter Field View by pressing Alt-F5. As usual, the cursor changes from an underline to a box. Next, press the ← key three times so that the box is over the letter *i*, as in the example below (which shows an underline where the box would be located):

    Sus<u>i</u>ta

Type the letters

    an

so the name now reads

    Susan_ita

To delete the unnecessary *ita* press the Del key three times, leaving only the name *Susan:*

    Susan –

Press Enter to finish the edit and leave Field View. The cursor once again appears as an underline, and you are back in normal editing.

    Now, suppose you also wish to delete the record for Rosiello. You could either position the cursor to the Last Name field and use Zoom to locate the record, or just press ↑ twice (in this simple example) to get the cursor to the appropriate record. Press the Del key, and the entire record will disappear, as shown in Figure 5.3.

```
Editing Custlist table: Record 4 of 9                        Edit
CUSTLIST┬Mr/Mrs═════Last Name══════First Name═══M.I.═══════Company═
    1  │ Ms.   │ Jackson     │ Janet     │ J. │ Zeerox, Inc.
    2  │ Mr.   │ Adams       │ Andy      │ A. │
    3  │ Dr.   │ Zastrow     │ Ruth      │    │ Scripts Clinic
    4  │ Miss  │ Gladstone   │ Tara Rose_│    │ Waterside, Inc.
    5  │ Mrs.  │ Simpson     │ Susan     │ M. │ SMS Publishing
    6  │ Mr.   │ Kenney      │ Clark     │ E. │ Legal Aid
    7  │ Ms.   │ Davis       │ Randi     │    │
    8  │ Mr.   │ Macallister │ Mark      │ S. │ BBC Publishing
    9  │ Miss  │ Abzug       │ Ann       │ Z. │
```

Figure 5.3: Rosiello deleted from the table

    For the sake of example, suppose you change your mind about the record you just deleted. To recall the record, just press Ctrl-U. Rosiello's record instantly reappears on the screen. If you now wish to go ahead and save the change to Susan Simpson's name, press DO-IT!. Note that Paradox returns to the View mode (as indicated in the upper-left corner of the screen), and the change to Susan's name remains. (To resume editing, press F9 again.)

INSERTING A RECORD

As discussed in Chapter 3, you can insert a new record into the table at any time while in Edit mode. Just move the cursor to the place where you want the new record to appear and press Ins. (Optionally, move the cursor to the last record and press ↓.) A blank record will be added to the table, and you can fill in the fields with new data.

WHEN THE DATA DOESN'T FIT

Occasionally, the data in a field won't fit into a column on the screen (most likely because the column was narrowed manually using the Image and ColumnSize options). You will see either a group of asterisks (✶✶✶) or only a portion of a field with the rest off the screen.

When that situation occurs, the cursor will land at the start of the field, rather than at the end, when editing. To view the entire field so you can see what you're editing, switch to Field View (press Alt-F5).

THE EDIT MENU

As discussed earlier, pressing the Menu (F10) key when in the Edit mode brings up the following menu:

    Image Undo ValCheck Help DO-IT! Cancel

The Image option allows you to perform the same tasks as the Image option from the Main menu. You can resize a column or a table, format numeric and date fields, move a field, switch to Form View (or a graph), or go to a specified field or record.

The Undo option, as discussed earlier, undoes edit transactions incrementally in reverse order.

The Help option displays help screens, as does pressing the Help (F1) key.

The DO-IT! option saves all edits and returns to the View mode, as does pressing the DO-IT! (F2) key.

The Cancel command, as discussed, undoes all edits since the last DO-IT! command and returns to the View mode.

The ValCheck command allows you to set up "validity checks" that limit the types of data entered into fields. We'll discuss this menu option in more detail in the next section.

CHECKING THE VALIDITY OF DATA

Paradox automatically makes some checks on data that you enter into a table, such as ensuring that dates are proper and that numeric fields contain only numeric values. The ValCheck option from the Edit menu (as well as under the DataEntry option from the Modify menu) lets you set up additional checks on data entered into a table. This helps keep erroneous data from being stored in the table, which in turn reduces the need to edit and make corrections later on.

To enter validity checks, first make sure you are in the Edit mode and then press F10 to call up the Edit menu. Select Valcheck, and you'll see the submenu below:

    Define   Clear

Selecting the Define option displays these instructions:

    Use → and ← to move to field for which you want to set check . . .
    then press ↵ to select.

Once you select the field for which you want to define validity checks and press Enter, the following submenu of options appears on the screen:

    LowValue   HighValue   Default   TableLookup   Picture
    Required

Each of these options is discussed below in general terms. We'll try out some later in the chapter.

DEFINING THE LOWEST ACCEPTABLE VALUE

Selecting the LowValue option from the Define submenu allows you to set the minimum acceptable value for a field. When selected, this option displays the following instructions:

Value:
Enter the lowest acceptable value for this field.

This option is most often used with numeric or currency fields. For example, if you wanted the minimum credit limit entered into the Custlist table to be $500, typing in 500 and pressing Enter would ensure that values smaller than $500 are rejected from entry when adding or editing data.

The LowValue option can also ensure that numbers are not inadvertently added to alphanumeric fields. For example, if you define the letter A as the LowValue for the Last Name and First Name fields, it would be impossible to inadvertently enter a number into either of these fields.

DEFINING THE HIGHEST ACCEPTABLE VALUE

The HighValue option allows you to define the highest acceptable value for a field. The HighValue option displays these instructions:

Value:
Enter the highest acceptable value for this field.

For example, if you wanted to ensure that nobody on the Custlist table was assigned a credit limit greater than $15,000, you would enter 15000 as the HighValue and press Enter.

ENTERING DEFAULT VALUES

Default values are those that will automatically appear in a field if the field is left blank. For example, suppose that the vast majority of entries on the Custlist table were California residents. You could set up a default value that automatically filled in the State field with the letters CA. Simply highlight the State field and select the Default option from the menu. The screen displays the following instructions:

Value:
Enter the value to insert if field is left blank.

Type in CA and press Enter. And that's all there is to it!

ENTERING PICTURE FORMATS

A Picture format is a template that ensures a consistency in the format of the data being entered. The most common uses of Picture formats are for social security numbers and telephone numbers. For example, the Picture format ###-##-#### ensures that a social security number will be entered with hyphens in the appropriate places. The Picture format (###)###-#### is good for telephone numbers with area codes.

Other characters used in Picture formats act as default values that are automatically added to typed-in data. For example, the Picture template (###)###-#### accepts only numeric digits and automatically inserts the parentheses and the hyphen.

Paradox provides a number of symbols that you can use in Picture formats to restrict data entry in different parts of the format in different ways.

SYMBOL	ACCEPTS
#	Numeric digits
?	Any letter A–Z or a–z
&	Any letter, but automatically converts it to uppercase
@	Any character (no exclusions)
!	Any character, converting all letters to uppercase
*	Repeats the next symbol either indefinitely or the number of times specified by the number following the *
;	Take following symbol as a literal character
[ ]	Optional item, but must be complete
{ }	Specifies a group of acceptable entries
,	Separates acceptable values within a group

When you select the Picture option, the screen displays the following prompt:

Picture:
Enter a PAL picture format, (e.g. ###-##-####)

(PAL stands for Paradox Application Language; but don't worry about this just yet.) Type in your Picture template and press Enter.

Let's look at some sample picture formats and the types of data that they allow (and exclude). Later, we'll create some examples that can be used within the sample Custlist table.

The template #####-#### would allow only a 9-digit numeric value (such as an extended zip code) into a field. However, if you used the picture format #####[-####], the last four digits would be optional, so either a 5-digit zip code or extended 9-digit zip code would be acceptable.

The picture format &??????????????????? would require a 20-character string to be entered into the field. Every character entered must be a letter. The first character would be converted to uppercase.

The picture format &*@ would allow an entry of any length and convert the first letter to uppercase. The picture format &*19? would convert the first letter to uppercase and require 19 additional letters to be entered into the field.

If you want to include a symbol as a *literal* character in a field, use the semicolon character to change the symbol to a literal. For example, suppose you have an inventory system that uses the # symbol in part codes, as in the part number ABC-#1234. If you tried using the picture &&&-#@@@@, then an entry such as ABC-1234 would be considered incomplete, because Paradox interprets -#@@@@ as requiring five characters to the right of the hyphen. However, if you enter the picture as &&&-;#@@@@, Paradox "knows" that the # symbol is to be placed into the entry, so when you typed in ABC-1234 Paradox would display

ABC-#1234

The template

{Yes,No,Maybe}

would allow only the letter *Y*, *N*, or *M* to be entered into an alphanumeric field, and would immediately convert the entry to Yes, No, or Maybe. Note the use of the curly braces to enclose the alternative acceptable entries and the use of commas to separate them within the curly braces.

The pictures that support alternative choices can be *nested* to allow multiple choices with the same first letter. For example, if you wanted to present the alternatives

{Mon,Tue,Wed,Thu,Fri}

entering the letter *T* would automatically fill in the field as *Tue* because *Tue* comes before *Thu* in the list of alternatives. To provide the choice *ue* or *hu* within the common *T* entry, nest these choices within the T alternative:

{Mon,T{ue,hu},Wed,Fri}

In English, the above picture reads, "Accept M, T, W, or F entries. If a T is entered, accept either *u* or *h* before filling in the rest of the field."

From the above example, you see how the following example would allow Saturday or Sunday to be entered into the field as well, again allowing the letter *S*, but asking for *at* or *un* before completing the entry:

{Mon,T{ue,hu},Wed,Fri,S{at,un}}

Notice in the above example that there are exactly as many open curly braces as closed curly braces. Make sure when entering your own pictures that yours also have an equal number of open and closed curly braces.

Note that curly braces can also be used to force entry of a particular character instead of automatically filling in the character. For example, if you use the picture ###-##-#### for a social security field, Paradox will automatically fill in the two hyphens when you later enter the number. If you prefer to type in the hyphens yourself (but still want Paradox to reject any other character), you can enter the picture in the format ###{-}##{-}####. In a sense, {-} means, "The only option allowed here is a hyphen."

When experimenting with pictures of your own, remember to avoid using symbols that conflict with the data type of the field. For example, you would not want to use the ? or @ symbol in a Numeric or Currency field since these symbols require alphabetic characters and Numeric and Currency fields allow only numbers! Also keep in mind that for *formatting* the display of numbers and dates (rather than performing validity checks), you can use the Image Format options from the Main menu.

DEFINING REQUIRED VALUES

A field that is assigned the Required validity check *must* have data entered into it; it cannot be left blank. For example, you could ensure that no record in the Custlist table is inadvertently entered without a last name by assigning the Required validity check to the Last Name field.

When you select this option, the screen displays these options:

```
No   Yes
Field may be left blank.
```

Select the Yes option to disallow blank entries into the field.

TABLELOOKUP

TableLookup is a special type of validity check, by which the value entered into a table is compared against that in another table. We'll discuss this option when we get to the chapters on managing multiple tables.

CLEARING VALIDITY CHECKS

The Clear option from the ValCheck submenu lets you eliminate previously defined validity checks. When selected, this option displays the submenu below:

> On a network, you may need to know a password to clear or change a validity check.

```
Field   All
Remove Validity checks from one field.
```

If you select the Field option, you are given the opportunity to move the cursor to the field from which you want to clear validity check(s). Do so, and then press Enter to clear the validity check(s). If you select the All option, validity checks are removed from all fields in the table.

SAVING VALIDITY CHECKS

When you've defined validity checks for a table, you must select DO-IT! from the Edit menu (or press F2) to save those validity checks. Otherwise, the validity checks you defined will be erased when you exit Paradox and will not be activated the next time that you use the table. (Those of you who are familiar with DOS might be interested to know that Paradox stores all validity checks on disk in a file with the same name as the table combined with the extension .VAL.)

SAMPLE VALIDITY CHECKS

If you'd like to try some validity checks, first make sure the Custlist table is on the screen and you are in Edit mode. (Press the Edit (F9) key if you are in View mode.)

Let's first add an upper limit of $15,000 to the Credit Limit field. Press the Menu (F10) key, and select the ValCheck option. From the submenu, select Define. Then use → or ← to move the cursor to the Credit Limit field, and press Enter to select the field. Select the HighValue option, and type in 15000 when the screen asks for a value. Then press Enter. A brief message informs you that the entry has been recorded.

Let's now make CA the default value for the State field. Call up the menu (F10), and select the ValCheck option. Select the Define option, move the cursor to the State field, and press Enter. Select the Default option. Enter CA as the Default value, and press Enter.

Let's now make Last Name a required field. Call up the menu and select the ValCheck and Define options. Move the cursor to the Last Name field and press Enter. Select the Required option, and answer Yes to the prompt.

Here's a tricky one. Let's add a Picture template to the Last Name field that ensures that the last name always begins with a capital letter. Call up the menu and select the ValCheck and Define options. Move the cursor to the Last Name field (if it isn't already there), and press Enter. Select the Picture option. Enter the picture as

&*@

and press Enter. This picture translates as "capitalize the first letter and accept any character in the rest of the field." The asterisk indicates that the @ symbol should be repeated an indefinite number of times. That is, the name can be any length. If you had entered the picture as

&*4@

the last name could contain only five characters—the first letter and four others. Now let's try out the validity checks we've made.

Press the End key to move to the last record in the table, then the ↓ key to add a new blank record. Type in **Mrs.** in the Mr/Mrs field and press Enter.

Now try leaving the Last Name field blank by just pressing Enter. Note that Paradox displays this message:

A value must be provided in this field; press [F1] for help.

Now try typing in the last name **smith** (no capitals), then press Enter. Notice that the first letter is automatically capitalized because of the Picture format.

Type in **Stan** as the first name, and press Enter several times to skip over the Company, Department, Address, and City fields. Notice that the State field is empty. If you press Enter to skip over this field, it is automatically filled with CA as the state.

Press Enter twice to move over to the Credit Limit field. Try entering a limit of **100,000**. Notice that Paradox displays the message

Value no greater than 15000.00 is expected.

Use the Backspace key to change the entry to 15,000, and press Enter again. Paradox will accept the new value.

For now, delete the new record but save the validity checks. To do so, press Ctrl-U and then press F2.

GETTING UNSTUCK

If you ever get stuck in a field and can't get out because of an error message, there are several techniques you can use to get unstuck.

First, try using the Backspace key to edit the value to an acceptable value. If you have trouble with that, use Ctrl-Backspace to delete the entire entry. Then either leave the field by pressing Enter or enter a new value.

If all else fails, press the Del key or Ctrl-U to delete the entire record. If it is necessary to delete an entire record, there may be something wrong with your validity check. Call up the menu, select ValCheck, and either clear or replace the validity check with a new one.

SUMMARY

Thus far in this book, you've learned techniques for creating a table, adding data to it, and changing those data. In addition, you've learned some valuable techniques for validating data as they are entered into the table, which will help prevent mistakes from being entered in the first place. By now you're probably ready to learn features of Paradox with more power, such as sorting, querying, formatting reports, custom screens, and more. These are discussed in the next few chapters. But before moving ahead, take a moment to review the rich array of editing features we've discussed in this chapter.

- To edit data in a table, press the Edit (F9) key.
- To switch between Table View and Form View, press the Form Toggle (F7) key.
- To switch to Field View for editing, press Alt-F5. Press Enter when you are done editing in Field View to return to normal Edit mode.
- To save edits, press the DO-IT! (F2) key or call up the menu (F10) and select the DO-IT! option.
- To delete a record, move the cursor to the record and press the Del key.
- To undo current edits, call up the menu (F10) and select the Undo or Cancel option or just press Ctrl-U.
- To set validity checks for a table while in Edit mode, call up the menu and select the ValCheck option.

- There are six types of validity checks: HighValue (highest acceptable value), LowValue (lowest acceptable value), Default (automatic values), TableLookup, Picture (format templates), and Required (fields for which data *must* be entered).
- To clear validity checks, select the Clear option from the ValCheck menu.

SORTING

CHAPTER 6

SORTING INVOLVES PUTTING ALL THE DATA IN A table into some kind of order, such as zip code order for producing bulk mailings or alphabetical order by last name for a printed directory. Sorting is very easy in Paradox, and quite fast. For example, on an IBM XT, it takes only about a minute to sort a table with 1,000 records on it. Sorting is handled by the Sort option under the Modify option from the Main menu.

SORTING BY A SINGLE FIELD

Query forms, discussed in the next chapter, also help you sort data in a table.

To sort a table, you need merely specify the field (or fields) you wish to sort by, using a simple form that Paradox displays. Let's try sorting the Custlist table. First, make sure the Custlist table is on the screen. (If not, select the View option from the Main menu and specify the Custlist table.) You'll see it in its original, unsorted order, as in Figure 6.1.

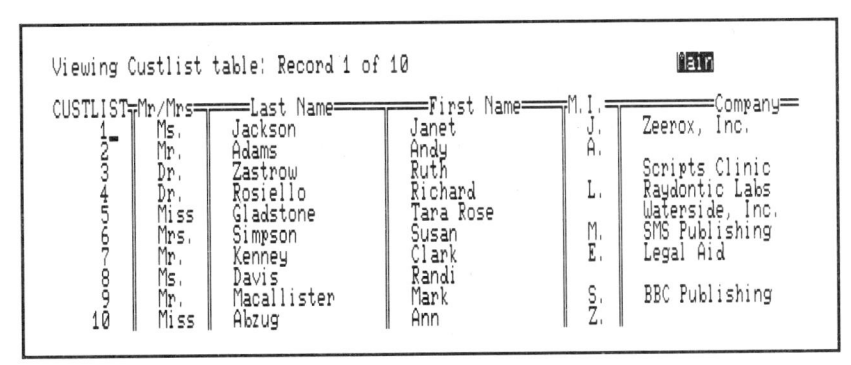

```
Viewing Custlist table: Record 1 of 10                              Main
CUSTLIST=Mr/Mrs======Last Name=======First Name======M.I.=========Company==
      1-    Ms.      Jackson          Janet            J.    Zeerox, Inc.
      2     Mr.      Adams            Andy             A.
      3     Dr.      Zastrow          Ruth                   Scripts Clinic
      4     Dr.      Rosiello         Richard          L.    Raydontic Labs
      5     Miss     Gladstone        Tara Rose              Waterside, Inc.
      6     Mrs.     Simpson          Susan            M.    SMS Publishing
      7     Mr.      Kenney           Clark            E.    Legal Aid
      8     Ms.      Davis            Randi
      9     Mr.      Macallister      Mark             S.    BBC Publishing
     10     Miss     Abzug            Ann              Z.
```

Figure 6.1: The Custlist table in its original order

To sort this table, call up the Main menu (F10) and select the Modify option. This brings up the following submenu:

Sort   Edit   CoEdit   DataEntry   MultiEntry   Restructure

Select the Sort option. The screen displays this prompt:

Table:
Enter name of table to sort, or press ⏎ to see a list of tables.

Either type in or highlight the table name Custlist and press Enter. Next, Paradox displays two more options:

Same   New
Place results of sort in the same table.

> If you are using Paradox on a network, see "Sorting on a Network" in Appendix B.

If you select the Same option, the data will be reordered in the Custlist table. If you select the New option, the sorted records will be placed in a new table with the name you specify, and the records in the Custlist table will remain in their original order. Unless there is some reason why you want to retain the original unsorted order in the Custlist table, select the Same option. (Do so now.) Paradox then displays a screen for specifying fields to sort by (which we'll refer to hereafter as the sort form), as shown in Figure 6.2.

To sort by a single field, simply type the number 1 in front of the field name, press Enter, and then press the DO-IT! key. In this example, we'll sort by last name. So use the arrow keys to move the cursor to the Last Name field. Type 1 and press Enter, so your screen looks like Figure 6.3.

Press the DO-IT! (F2) key and wait a couple of seconds. In a moment you'll see the Custlist table sorted by last name, as in Figure 6.4.

You can sort on any field in a table, regardless of the type of information the field contains.

DESCENDING SORTS

Unless you specify otherwise, Paradox always sorts data in ascending (smallest to largest) order. To specify descending order, simply

Figure 6.2: Screen for specifying sort orders

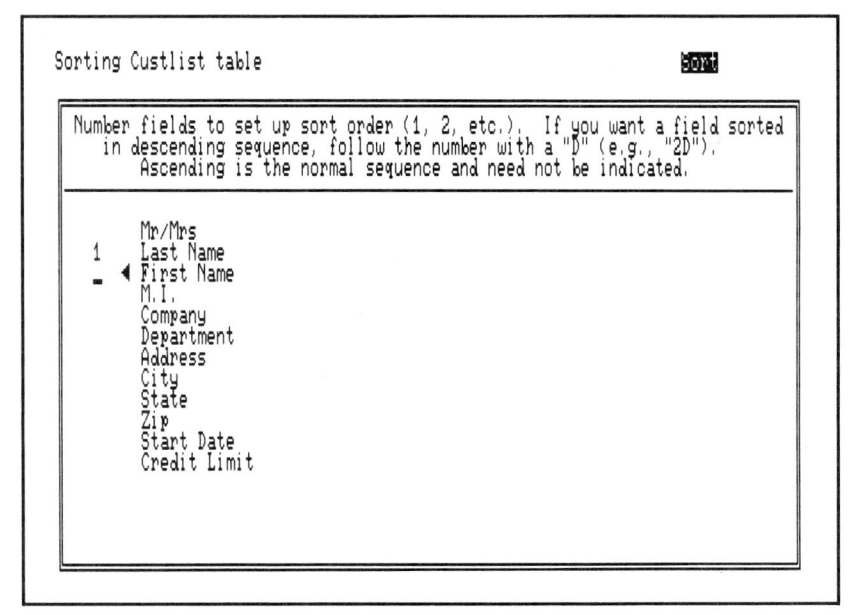

Figure 6.3: Last Name field selected for sorting

place the letter D next to the number when specifying a field. Let's try it out.

Call up the Main menu, and select the Modify and Sort options once again. Enter Custlist as the name of the table, and select the Same option from the submenu. When the menu of fields appears, move the cursor to the Zip field and type in 1D, then press Enter. Your screen should look like Figure 6.5.

```
Viewing Custlist table: Record 1 of 10                    Main
CUSTLIST⊤Mr/Mrs════Last Name═══════First Name══M.I.═══════Company═══
     1▬   Miss     Abzug           Ann          Z.
     2    Mr.      Adams           Andy         A.
     3    Ms.      Davis           Randi
     4    Miss     Gladstone       Tara Rose              Waterside, Inc.
     5    Ms.      Jackson         Janet        J.        Zeerox, Inc.
     6    Mr.      Kenney          Clark        E.        Legal Aid
     7    Mr.      Macallister     Mark         S.        BBC Publishing
     8    Dr.      Rosiello        Richard      L.        Raydontic Labs
     9    Mrs.     Simpson         Susan        M.        SMS Publishing
    10    Dr.      Zastrow         Ruth                   Scripts Clinic
```

Figure 6.4: Custlist table sorted by last name

```
Sorting Custlist table                                    Sort
┌─────────────────────────────────────────────────────────────┐
│ Number fields to set up sort order (1, 2, etc.). If you want a field sorted │
│    in descending sequence, follow the number with a "D" (e.g., "2D").       │
│         Ascending is the normal sequence and need not be indicated.         │
├─────────────────────────────────────────────────────────────┤
│         Mr/Mrs                                              │
│         Last Name                                           │
│         First Name                                          │
│         M.I.                                                │
│         Company                                             │
│         Department                                          │
│         Address                                             │
│         City                                                │
│         State                                               │
│     1D  Zip                                                 │
│     ▬ ◀ Start Date                                          │
│         Credit Limit                                        │
│                                                             │
└─────────────────────────────────────────────────────────────┘
```

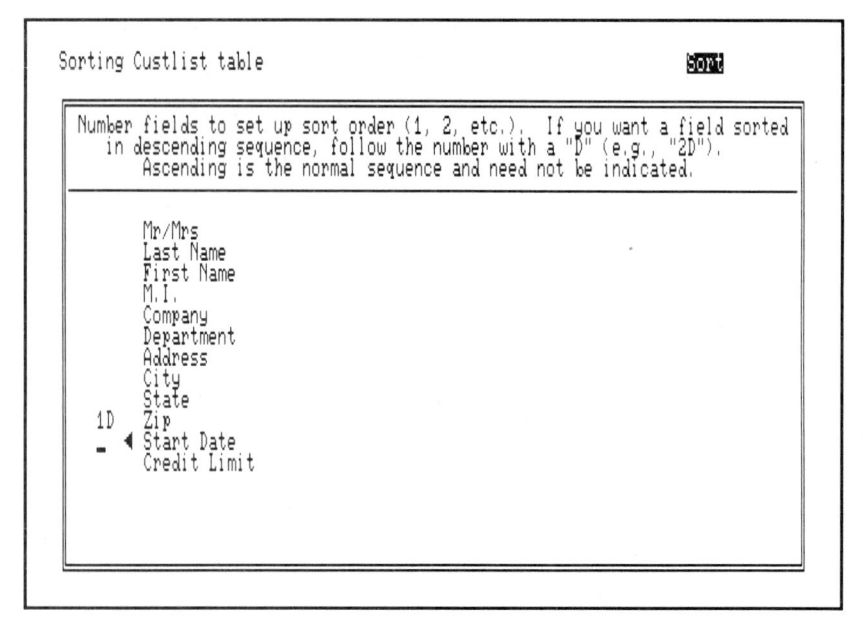

Figure 6.5: Sorting records into descending zip code order

Press the DO-IT! key and wait a couple of seconds. When the table reappears, you'll need to scroll over to the Zip field to see the results. (Press Ctrl-→ twice.) You'll see that the table has been sorted into descending zip code order, as shown in Figure 6.6.

```
Viewing Custlist table: Record 1 of 10                    Main
┌─────Address─────────┬──────City────────┬─State┬──Zip──┬─Star
│ 234 Ocean View Dr._ │ San Diego        │ CA   │ 92038 │ 1/1
│ 4331 La Jolla Scenic Dr. │ La Jolla    │ CA   │ 92037 │ 1/0
│ 301 Crest Dr.       │ Encinitas        │ CA   │ 92024 │ 3/0
│ 1234 Corporate Hwy. │ Los Angeles      │ CA   │ 91234 │ 1/0
│ 371 Oceanic Way     │ Manhattan Beach  │ CA   │ 90001 │ 3/0
│ P.O. Box 2802       │ Philadelphia     │ PA   │ 23456 │ 1/0
│ P.O. Box 121        │ New York         │ NY   │ 12345 │ 2/2
│ 371 Ave. of the Americas │ New York    │ NY   │ 12345 │ 1/3
│ P.O. Box 77112      │ Newark           │ NJ   │ 00123 │ 3/1
│ 121 Revelation Dr.  │ Bangor           │ ME   │ 00001 │ 3/1
```

Figure 6.6: Table sorted into descending order by zip code

SORTING BY SEVERAL FIELDS

On a large table, sorting by a single field may be inadequate. Though our Custlist table is much too small to demonstrate the full power of sorting by several fields, a general example will demonstrate the usefulness of this capability.

Suppose you had a table with 10,000 names and addresses. On that table, there happened to be about 200 Smiths. If you sorted the table by last name, all the Smiths would be grouped together, but they would be in random order by first name, as shown below:

Smith   Michael   K.

Smith   Anton   A.

Smith   Jennifer   J.

Smith   Wally   P.

Smith   Anita   R.

Smith   Michael   D.

Smith   Antonio   L.
Smith   Vera
Smith   Susan   M.

.

.

.

However, if you specified Last Name as the first (1) sort field and First Name as the second (2) sort field, the records would be sorted alphabetically by first name within a common last name, as below:

Smith   Anita   R.
Smith   Anton   A.
Smith   Antonio   L.
Smith   Jennifer J.
Smith   Michael   K.
Smith   Michael   D.
Smith   Susan   M.
Smith   Vera
Smith   Wally   P.

.

.

.

This order makes it much easier to look up a particular Smith in a printed copy of the table.

Notice that the second sort field acts as a "tie breaker." That is, when two individuals have the same last name, the secondary sort order is used to break the tie, enforcing a sort order within the major sort order.

You can specify as many fields as you wish when sorting. For example, if you made Last Name the first sort field, First Name the second sort field, and Middle Initial the third sort field, the order would be refined even more. (Notice, in the list below, that Michael D. is now listed before Michael K.)

Smith	Anita	R.
Smith	Anton	A.
Smith	Antonio	L.
Smith	Jennifer	J.
Smith	Michael	D.
Smith	Michael	K.
Smith	Susan	M.
Smith	Vera	
Smith	Wally	P.

.

.

.

Now let's try out an example on our small Custlist table. Call up the Main menu, and select the Modify and Sort options. Enter Custlist as the table name, and select Same from the submenu. On the sort form, specify Last Name as the second sort field and Start Date as the first sort field, as in Figure 6.7.

Press the DO-IT! (F2) key to perform the sort. The records in the table will be sorted into chronological order by start date. Within common start dates, the records will be in alphabetical order by last name. You can see this better if you move the Start Date column over to the left. (To do so, call up the menu, and select the Image and Move options. Highlight the Start Date field and press Enter. Move the cursor to the Last Name field, and press Enter.)

With the Start Date field placed next to the Last Name field, you can see that within identical dates the records are sorted by last name, as in Figure 6.8.

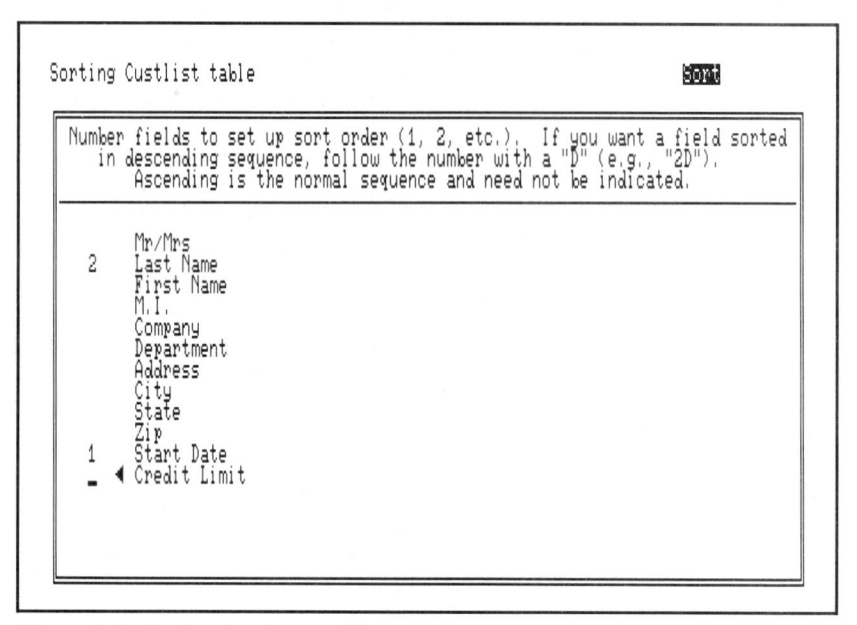

```
Sorting Custlist table                                    Sort
┌──────────────────────────────────────────────────────────────┐
│ Number fields to set up sort order (1, 2, etc.).  If you want a field sorted │
│    in descending sequence, follow the number with a "D" (e.g., "2D").         │
│           Ascending is the normal sequence and need not be indicated.         │
└──────────────────────────────────────────────────────────────┘

        Mr/Mrs
    2   Last Name
        First Name
        M.I.
        Company
        Department
        Address
        City
        State
        Zip
    1   Start Date
    _ ◄ Credit Limit
```

Figure 6.7: Sorting by date and last name

```
Viewing Custlist table: Record 1 of 10                    Main
CUSTLIST  Start Date   Last Name       First Name    M.I.      Co
    1      1/01/90     Jackson         Janet         J.        Zeerox, In
    2      1/01/90     Simpson         Susan         M.        SMS Publis
    3      1/01/90     Zastrou         Ruth                    Scripts Cl
    4      1/15/90     Adams           Andy          A.
    5      1/31/90     Kenney          Clark         E.        Legal Aid
    6      2/28/90     Gladstone       Tara Rose               Waterside,
    7      3/01/90     Abzug           Ann           Z.
    8      3/01/90     Davis           Randi
    9      3/15/90     Macallister     Mark          S.        BBC Publis
   10      3/15/90     Rosiello        Richard       L.        Raydontic
```

Figure 6.8: Records in chronological and alphabetical order

You can even combine ascending and descending sort orders. Let's try an example, and at the same time we'll try sorting records to a new table. Call up the Main menu and select the Modify and Sort options. Specify Custlist as the table to sort, and select the New option when

Paradox asks whether you want to sort to the same or a new table. Paradox displays this prompt:

Table:
Enter name for new sorted table.

You can enter any valid table name (remember, no spaces or punctuation). In this example, enter the name Tempsort as the table to store the sorted records in. (If the Cancel/Replace options appear, select Replace.)

On the sort form, specify Start Date as the first sort field, in descending order (1D), and Last Name as the second sort field (2), as shown in Figure 6.9.

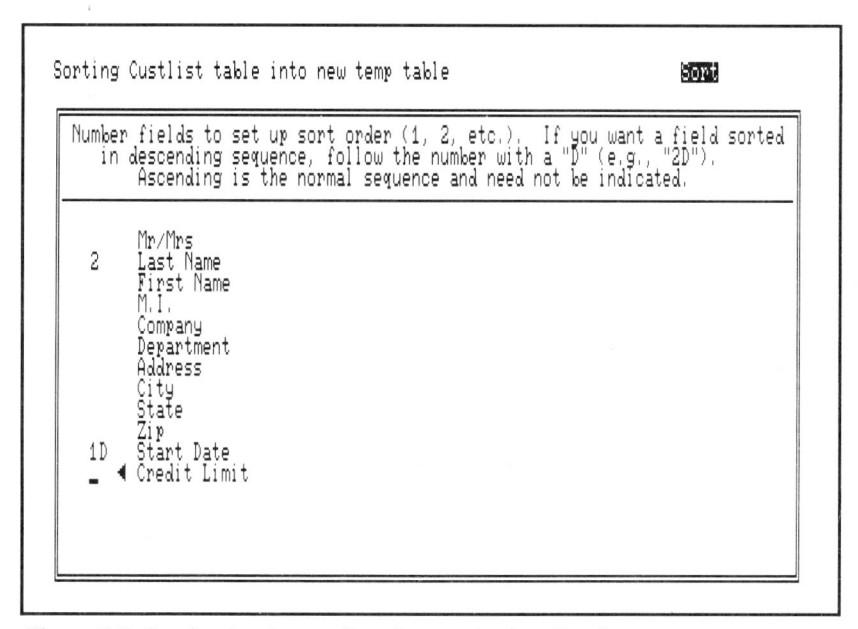

```
Sorting Custlist table into new temp table                    Sort
┌─────────────────────────────────────────────────────────────────┐
│ Number fields to set up sort order (1, 2, etc.). If you want a field sorted
│   in descending sequence, follow the number with a "D" (e.g., "2D").
│       Ascending is the normal sequence and need not be indicated.
├─────────────────────────────────────────────────────────────────┤
│        Mr/Mrs
│    2   Last Name
│        First Name
│        M.I.
│        Company
│        Department
│        Address
│        City
│        State
│        Zip
│   1D   Start Date
│    _ ◄ Credit Limit
│
└─────────────────────────────────────────────────────────────────┘
```

Figure 6.9: Sorting by descending date and ascending last name

Press the DO-IT! key. The records will be sorted in a new table named Tempsort and displayed on the screen, as in Figure 6.10. Notice that in the Tempsort table the dates are in descending order, and last names within common dates are in ascending alphabetical order.

```
Viewing Tempsort table: Record 1 of 10                          Main
CUSTLIST  Start Date    Last Name      First Name    M. I.         Co
     2    1/01/90       Simpson        Susan         M.       SMS Publis
     3    1/01/90       Zastrou        Ruth                   Scripts Cl
     4    1/15/90       Adams          Andy          A.
     5    1/31/90       Kenney         Clark         E.       Legal Aid
     6    2/28/90       Gladstone      Tara Rose              Waterside,
     7    3/01/90       Abzug          Ann           Z.
     8    3/01/90       Davis          Randi
     9    3/15/90       Macallister    Mark          S.       BBC Publis
    10    3/15/90       Rosiello       Richard       L.       Raydontic

TEMPSORT  Start Date    Last Name      First Name    M. I.         Co
     1    3/15/90       Macallister    Mark          S.       BBC Publis
     2    3/15/90       Rosiello       Richard       L.       Raydontic
     3    3/01/90       Abzug          Ann           Z.
     4    3/01/90       Davis          Randi
     5    2/28/90       Gladstone      Tara Rose              Waterside,
     6    1/31/90       Kenney         Clark         E.       Legal Aid
     7    1/15/90       Adams          Andy          A.
     8    1/01/90       Jackson        Janet         J.       Zeerox, In
     9    1/01/90       Simpson        Susan         M.       SMS Publis
    10    1/01/90       Zastrou        Ruth                   Scripts Cl
```

Figure 6.10: Records in descending date and ascending last name order

You'll notice that both the Custlist table and the new Tempsort table are displayed on the screen. Tempsort contains the records in their latest sort order. (Once again, I've moved the Start Date column to the left of the Last Name column to better display the sort order.) The Custlist table still has records in the previous sort order.

We don't really need this Tempsort table for anything just now, so you can press Clear Image (F8) to erase it from the screen.

EXAMPLES

Sorting is very easy in Paradox, and with a little practice you'll be able to sort any table into any order you wish. As mentioned, our small Custlist table cannot demonstrate the full potential of Paradox's sorting abilities. But take a look at the examples below to see how various sorting options would affect the order of a Custlist table with many records on it.

The sort form in Figure 6.11 specifies that records be sorted in ascending Credit Limit order (1). Within identical credit limits, records are sorted by last name (2), first name (3), and middle initial (4).

On a very large table, a portion of this sort order might appear as below:

5,000	Adams	Andy	A.
5,000	Adams	Andy	Z.
5,000	Adams	Barbara	Z.
5,000	Miller	Mike	M.
5,000	Zastrow	Ruth	R.
7,500	Aardvark	Annie	A.
7,500	Smith	Bob	
7,500	Smith	Sandy	S.

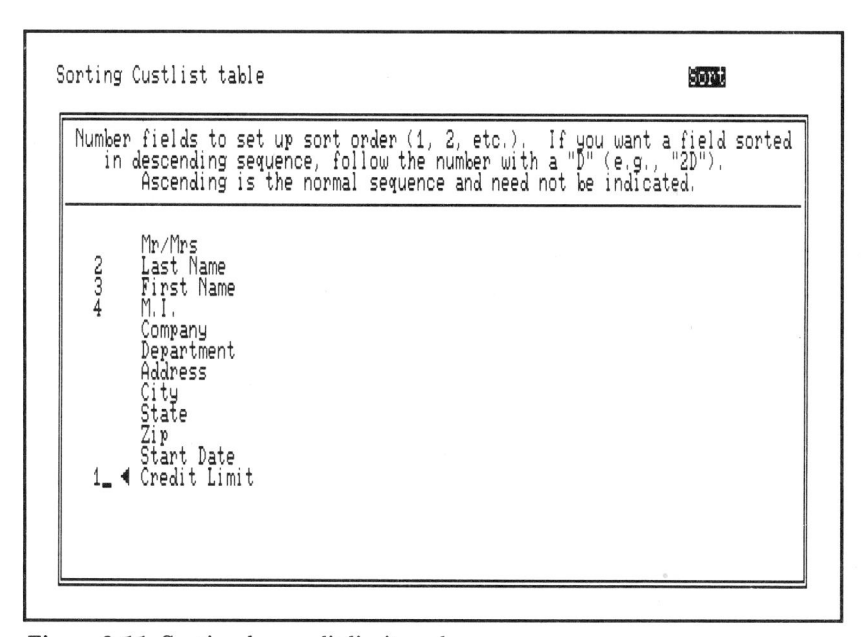

```
Sorting Custlist table                                    Sort

  Number fields to set up sort order (1, 2, etc.).  If you want a field sorted
     in descending sequence, follow the number with a "D" (e.g., "2D").
           Ascending is the normal sequence and need not be indicated.

         Mr/Mrs
    2    Last Name
    3    First Name
    4    M.I.
         Company
         Department
         Address
         City
         State
         Zip
         Start Date
    1_ ◄ Credit Limit
```

Figure 6.11: Sorting by credit limit and name

7,500	Zeepers	Zeppo	Z.
10,000	Baker	Babs	T.
10,000	Baker	Mary	J.
10,000	Miller	Andy	A.

.

.

.

Figure 6.12 shows a similar order specified on the sort form, but here the Credit Limit field is specified as descending order. The other sort fields are still in ascending order.

The resulting sort on a hypothetical table might appear as below:

15,000	Aronson	Aaron	A.
15,000	Aronson	Aaron	T.
15,000	Baker	Billy	
15,000	Miller	Mary	M.
15,000	Miller	Mary	N.
15,000	Miller	Nancy	A.
15,000	Young	Yolanda	Z.
10,000	Abraham	Arthur	T.
10,000	Carlson	Carla	J.
10,000	Carlson	Manny	
10,000	Mason	Tara	
10,000	Watson	Wilbur	A.
7,500	Askey	Albert	J.
7,500	Byte	Robert	B.
7,500	Miller	Mandy	L.

.

.

.

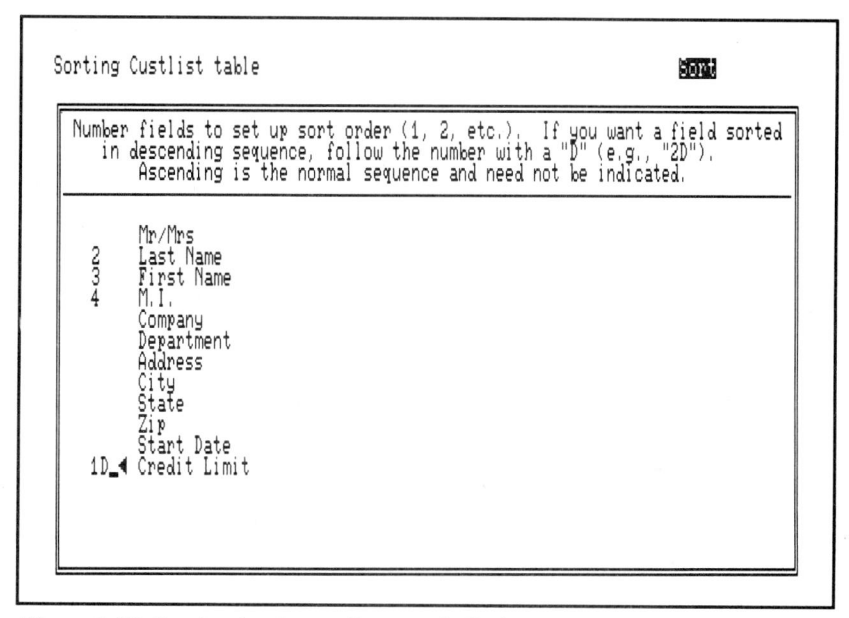

```
Sorting Custlist table                               SORT
┌─────────────────────────────────────────────────────────┐
│ Number fields to set up sort order (1, 2, etc.). If you want a field sorted │
│ in descending sequence, follow the number with a "D" (e.g., "2D").          │
│         Ascending is the normal sequence and need not be indicated.         │
├─────────────────────────────────────────────────────────┤
│          Mr/Mrs                                         │
│       2  Last Name                                      │
│       3  First Name                                     │
│       4  M.I.                                           │
│          Company                                        │
│          Department                                     │
│          Address                                        │
│          City                                           │
│          State                                          │
│          Zip                                            │
│          Start Date                                     │
│      1D◄ Credit Limit                                   │
│                                                         │
└─────────────────────────────────────────────────────────┘
```

Figure 6.12: Sorting by descending credit limit and ascending name

Figure 6.13 displays a request to sort records alphabetically by company name (1) and, within each company, alphabetically by department (2).

The resulting sort order on a hypothetical table might appear as below. Notice that the names are in random order within the departments. Had we specified Last Name as the third sort field and First Name as the fourth sort field, the names would have been alphabetized within each department in each company.

ABC Co.	Accounts Payable	Albertson	Steve
ABC Co.	Accounts Receivable	Miller	Mikey
ABC Co.	Accounts Receivable	Brookes	Alvin
ABC Co.	Accounts Receivable	Peterson	Anne
ABC Co.	Insurance Division	Root	Quincy
ABC Co.	Insurance Division	Parker	Carl
ABC Co.	Training Division	Davies	Tina

Baker Int.	Bookkeeping	Starlight	Stella
Baker Int.	Training Division	Adams	Arthur
Cable View	Installation Dep't	Mason	Maggie
Cable View	Installation Dep't	Andrews	Mick
Cable View	Special Projects	Targa	Ferry

.
.
.

Figure 6.14 shows a sort form with State specified as the first sort field, City as the second sort field, and Address as the third sort field.

The resulting sort would put all records in alphabetical order by state. Within each state, cities would be in alphabetical order. Within

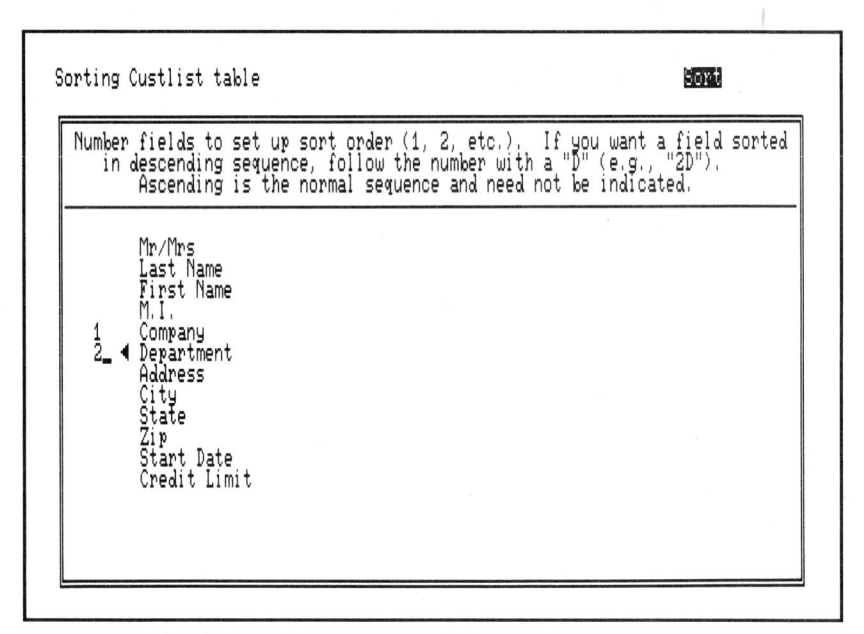

```
Sorting Custlist table                                    Sort

┌──────────────────────────────────────────────────────────────┐
│ Number fields to set up sort order (1, 2, etc.). If you want a field sorted │
│    in descending sequence, follow the number with a "D" (e.g., "2D").       │
│         Ascending is the normal sequence and need not be indicated.         │
├──────────────────────────────────────────────────────────────┤
│         Mr/Mrs
│         Last Name
│         First Name
│         M.I.
│      1_ Company
│      2_◀Department
│         Address
│         City
│         State
│         Zip
│         Start Date
│         Credit Limit
└──────────────────────────────────────────────────────────────┘
```

Figure 6.13: Sorting by company and department

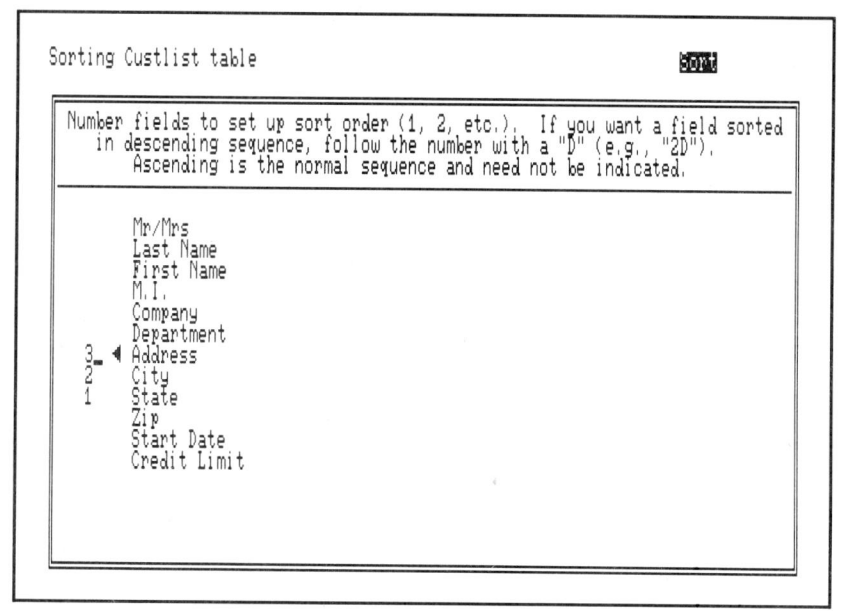

```
┌──────────────────────────────────────────────────────────────────┐
│  Sorting Custlist table                              [Sort]      │
│  ┌────────────────────────────────────────────────────────────┐  │
│  │ Number fields to set up sort order (1, 2, etc.). If you want a field sorted │
│  │   in descending sequence, follow the number with a "D" (e.g., "2D").        │
│  │       Ascending is the normal sequence and need not be indicated.           │
│  └────────────────────────────────────────────────────────────┘  │
│              Mr/Mrs                                              │
│              Last Name                                           │
│              First Name                                          │
│              M.I.                                                │
│              Company                                             │
│              Department                                          │
│         3_ ◄ Address                                             │
│         2    City                                                │
│         1    State                                               │
│              Zip                                                 │
│              Start Date                                          │
│              Credit Limit                                        │
│                                                                  │
└──────────────────────────────────────────────────────────────────┘
```

Figure 6.14: Sorting by state, city, and address

each city, addresses would be in order, as below:

Alabama	Arken	455 Elm Rd.
Alabama	Bakerville	999 Oak St.
Alaska	Akron	100 A St.
Alaska	Akron	100 B St.
Alaska	Akron	101 Grape Drive
Alaska	Akron	102 Village Square
Alaska	Akron	200 A St.
Alaska	Akron	201 B St.
Alaska	Briton	999 First St.
Alaska	Cavern City	344 Ashton Way

.
.
.

Learning to master Paradox's sorting capabilities is basically a matter of trying things out and practicing. Experiment freely; you cannot possibly do any harm to Paradox or your computer.

THE SORT MENU

While the sort form is displayed on the screen, you can press the Menu (F10) key to bring up the menu shown below:

    Help DO-IT! Cancel

The Help option displays a help screen for sorting (as does pressing the F1 key). The DO-IT! option performs the requested sort, as does pressing the F2 key. The Cancel option terminates the sort request and returns you to View mode without sorting the records.

SUMMARY

- To sort a database on a single field, select the Modify and Sort options from the menus. You can sort the existing table by selecting Same, or you can make a sorted copy of the existing table by selecting New from the submenu.

- To specify a field to sort by, place a 1 next to the field name on the sort form that Paradox displays.

- To sort in descending (largest to smallest) order, place a D next to the number on the sort menu (for example, 1D).

- To perform sorts within sorts, specify fields in order of importance (1, 2, 3, and so forth) on the sort form.

SEARCHING THE DATABASE

CHAPTER 7

TO SEARCH (OR *QUERY*) A DATABASE MEANS TO PULL out all records that meet some criterion. For example, you might want to view only New York residents, or individuals in California with credit limits over $10,000. Perhaps you'll want to send a form letter to individuals whose starting date was one year ago, or maybe you just want to look up Clark Kenney's address. In this chapter, we'll discuss several techniques for searching a database through *query forms*.

QUERY FORMS

You can call up the query form at any time by selecting the Ask option from the Main menu. It's a little easier to work with query forms if the workspace is clear on the screen. If you are currently viewing the Custlist table, press Clear All (Alt-F8) to clear the screen. Then select the Ask option from the Main menu. When prompted, specify Custlist as the table to ask about. You'll see a query form as in Figure 7.1.

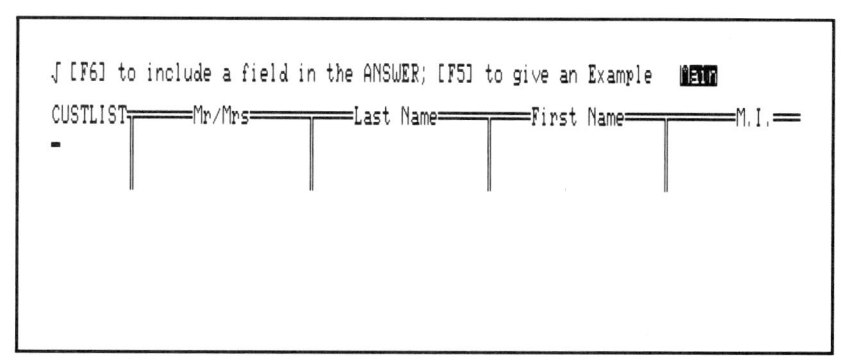

```
√ [F6] to include a field in the ANSWER; [F5] to give an Example  Main
CUSTLIST    Mr/Mrs       Last Name      First Name       M.I.
```

Figure 7.1: The query form for the Custlist table

You can enter and change data on the query form as you do with tables. That is, the arrow keys move the cursor, the Backspace key erases characters that you've typed, and Field View (Alt-F5) allows you to make more refined edits.

SELECTING FIELDS TO VIEW

You may not want to see all the fields in a table when querying. You can specify which fields to display by putting check marks in those fields. Pressing the Checkmark (F6) key toggles the check-mark symbol. That is, pressing Checkmark once puts a check mark into a field. If you change your mind, just press Checkmark again to erase the check mark.

You can quickly enter check marks into all the fields on the query form by pressing the Checkmark (F6) key while the cursor is in the leftmost column. Pressing the Checkmark key a second time erases all the check marks.

Suppose you wish to view only the names from the Custlist table. Using the arrow keys and Checkmark (F6) key, place a check mark in the Last Name, First Name, and M.I. fields, as shown in the top half of Figure 7.2. Press DO-IT! (F2) after entering the check marks, and you'll see the three fields from the Custlist table displayed on the screen, as in the bottom half of Figure 7.2.

Notice that the table displaying the data is named Answer. This is NOT the same table as Custlist; it is only an image of the data from the Custlist table, displaying the fields that you requested. Note also that the record numbers on the Answer table may not correspond to those on the Custlist table. You shouldn't do any editing on the Answer table because it will not be reflected in the original Custlist table. (However, we'll see a way around this later in the chapter.)

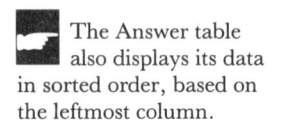

The Answer table also displays its data in sorted order, based on the leftmost column.

PRINTING THE ANSWER

To create a printed copy of the answer to your query, make sure the printer is ready, then press Instant Report (Alt-F7).

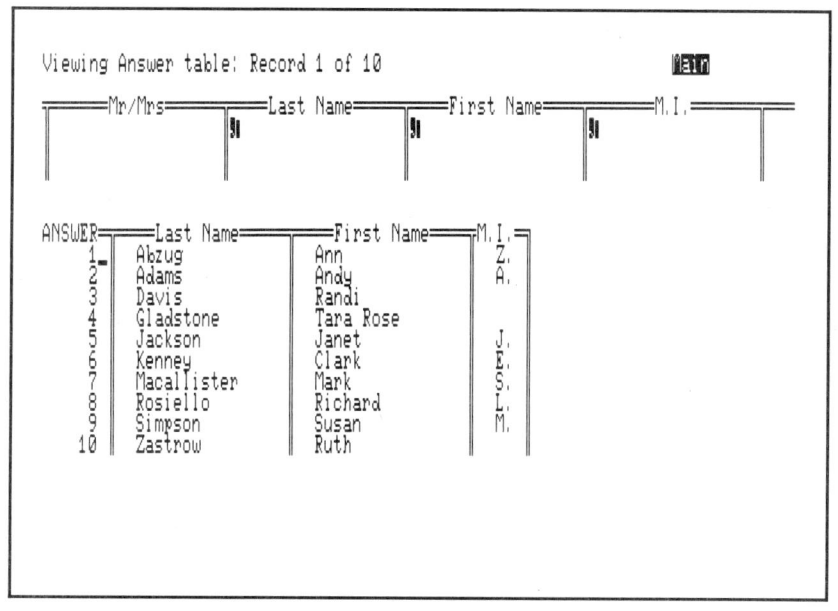

```
Viewing Answer table: Record 1 of 10                    Main
   ╔═Mr/Mrs═╗ ╔═Last Name═╗ ╔═First Name═╗ ╔═M.I.═╗
                   │¶│          │¶│            │¶│


  ANSWER══╤══Last Name═══╤══First Name══╤═M.I.═╗
      1_  │ Abzug        │ Ann          │ Z.
      2   │ Adams        │ Andy         │ A.
      3   │ Davis        │ Randi        │
      4   │ Gladstone    │ Tara Rose    │
      5   │ Jackson      │ Janet        │ J.
      6   │ Kenney       │ Clark        │ E.
      7   │ Macallister  │ Mark         │ S.
      8   │ Rosiello     │ Richard      │ L.
      9   │ Simpson      │ Susan        │ M.
     10   │ Zastrow      │ Ruth         │
```

Figure 7.2: Selecting three fields from the Custlist table

CLEARING THE ANSWER TABLE

Once you've viewed your answer, simply press the Clear Image (F8) key. This will bring you back to the query form. You can change the query form and perform another query, or press Clear Image (F8) to clear the query form and return to the Main menu.

SEEING UNIQUE ITEMS

Normally, Paradox will not display duplicates when you select fields to display. Duplicate entries are those whose fields are identical as far as the terms of the query are concerned. For example, if you place a check mark in only the Start Date field on the query form and press DO-IT!, you'll see only the unique dates, as in Figure 7.3.

If you prefer that all records including duplicates be displayed, use the check-plus symbol in the query form. Do this by pressing Check Plus

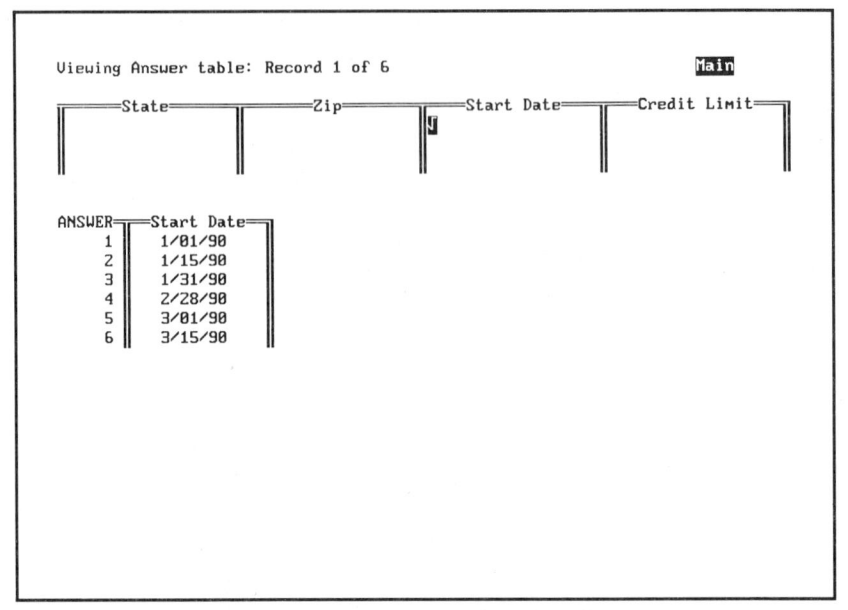

```
Viewing Answer table: Record 1 of 6                    Main
    ┌═State═══╤═══Zip═══╤═Start Date═╤═Credit Limit═┐
    │         │         │█           │              │
    │         │         │            │              │


  ANSWER══╤══Start Date══
     1   │   1/01/90
     2   │   1/15/90
     3   │   1/31/90
     4   │   2/28/90
     5   │   3/01/90
     6   │   3/15/90
```

Figure 7.3: Viewing unique dates from the Custlist table

(Alt-F6). Placing a check plus in the Start Date field on the query form and pressing DO-IT! displays all the dates, as in Figure 7.4.

If several fields are selected with check marks, records that have identical data in all fields will be listed only once. For example, if you place check marks in the Zip and State fields, all records with unique zip codes and states will be displayed. If you place check-plus symbols in the Zip and State fields, all zip codes and dates will be displayed, including those that duplicate one another.

CONTROLLING THE SORT ORDER

As you've seen in preceding examples, Paradox automatically displays data in the Answer table sorted in ascending (smallest-to-largest) order. If several columns are included in the Answer table, the leftmost column determines the sort order. (You can rotate the fields in the Query Form, using the Ctrl-R key.)

You can have Paradox display data in the resulting Answer table in descending (largest-to-smallest) order quite easily. When placing

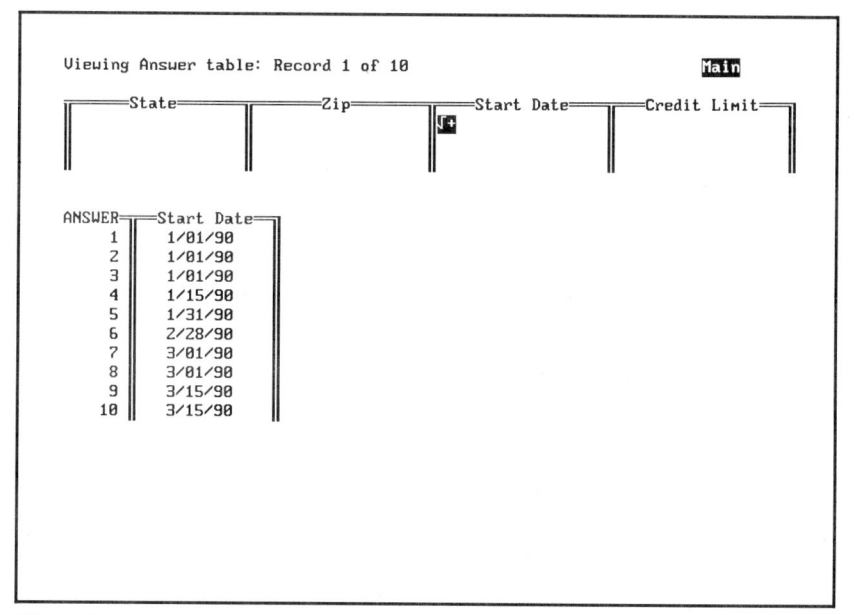

```
Viewing Answer table: Record 1 of 10                          Main
┌────State────┬─────Zip─────┬─Start Date─┬─Credit Limit─┐
│             │             │ √+         │              │
└             ┴             ┴            ┴              ┘

ANSWER ┬─Start Date─┐
   1   │   1/01/90  │
   2   │   1/01/90  │
   3   │   1/01/90  │
   4   │   1/15/90  │
   5   │   1/31/90  │
   6   │   2/28/90  │
   7   │   3/01/90  │
   8   │   3/01/90  │
   9   │   3/15/90  │
  10   │   3/15/90  │
```

Figure 7.4: Viewing all start dates from the Custlist table

check marks in the query form, use Ctrl-F6 rather than F6 or Alt-F6. Pressing Ctrl-F6 displays a check mark followed by a down-pointing triangle in the query form.

For example, if you create a query like the one in Figure 7.3, but press Ctrl-F6 to place the check mark in the Start Date field, the resulting dates will be displayed in descending (latest-to-earliest) rather than ascending (earliest-to-latest) order.

FINDING A PARTICULAR GROUP OF RECORDS

Besides placing check marks in the query form, you can enter *criteria* that define the types of records you want to display. For example, let's say that you want to see the name and city of all individuals who live in California. First, let's start with a fresh query screen. Press Clear Image (F8) until only the Main menu appears on the screen. Select the Ask option, and then specify Custlist as the table to query.

Place a check mark in the Last Name, First Name, City, and State

I've used the Rotate key (Ctrl-R) in several examples in this chapter to better fit the query form on the screen and page. You need not rearrange or alter your own query form to perform these queries. Just be sure to place the check marks and search criteria in the appropriate fields.

fields, using the usual arrow and Checkmark (F6) keys. Now, to specify that only California residents be displayed, type the letters CA next to the check mark in the State field, as shown at the top of Figure 7.5.

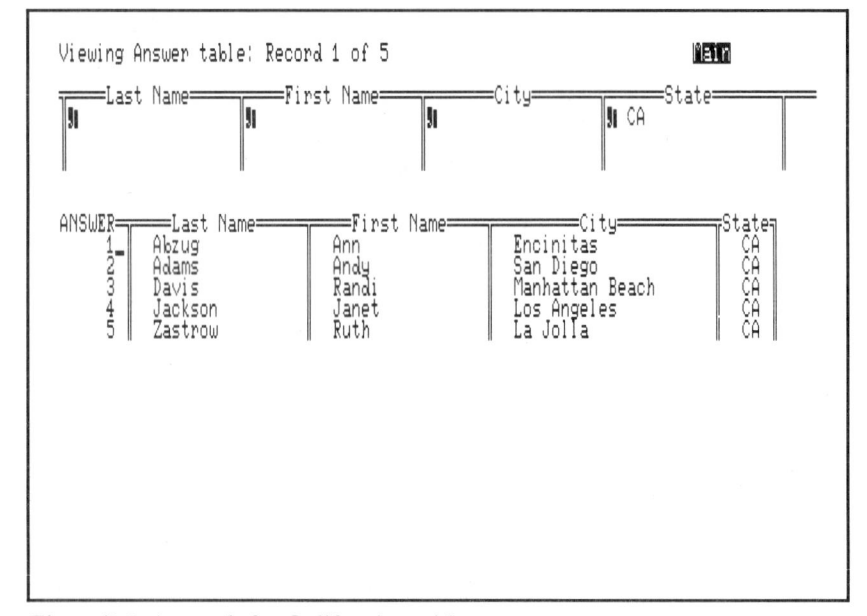

```
Viewing Answer table: Record 1 of 5                          Main
 ====Last Name======First Name======City======State====
 |√|             |√|             |√|           |√| CA

 ANSWER===Last Name======First Name======City======State=
    1_  Abzug          Ann             Encinitas         CA
    2   Adams          Andy            San Diego         CA
    3   Davis          Randi           Manhattan Beach   CA
    4   Jackson        Janet           Los Angeles       CA
    5   Zastrow        Ruth            La Jolla          CA
```

Figure 7.5: A search for California residents

Press DO-IT! to perform the search. The Answer table will display only California residents, and only those fields you've checked, as shown in the bottom half of Figure 7.5.

This same technique will work with any field. To see only people whose last name is Jackson, first press Clear Image (F8) twice to clear the screen and the query form. Then select the Ask option from the Main menu and Custlist as the table. Enter Jackson into the Last Name field on the query form. Use check marks to mark the fields you want to see in the image, and then press DO-IT! to see the records. The screen will display only people with the last name Jackson, as shown in Figure 7.6.

When searching for letters and words, you must match the case you used in the original table. For example, a search for "ca" or "jackson" (instead of "CA" or "Jackson") would produce nothing, because the cases don't match. (However, we'll see a way around this later in the chapter.)

To see the records of customers whose Start Date is 3/1/90, call up the query form, check-mark the fields you want to see displayed in the answer, type 3/1/90 into the Start Date field of the query form, and press DO-IT!. The records containing the date March 1, 1990, will be displayed, as in Figure 7.7.

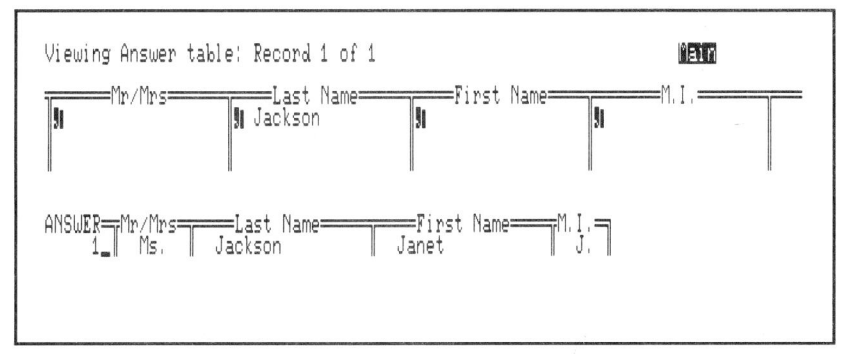

Figure 7.6: A search for records with the last name Jackson

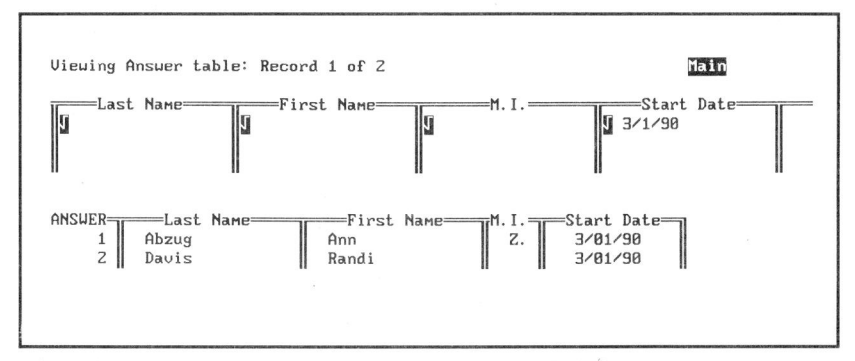

Figure 7.7: A search for records with start dates of 3/1/90

SEARCHING FOR VALUES

Often, you'll want to view records that have some value that is less than or greater than some constant. For example, you might want to view records for people who have credit limits of $10,000 or more. You can use *range operators* to perform such searches. Paradox's range operators are listed below:

OPERATOR	MEANING
=	Equal to
<	Less than
>	Greater than
<=	Less than or equal to
>=	Greater than or equal to

To try this, start with a blank query screen and put check marks in the Last Name, First Name, and Credit Limit fields. Next to the check mark in the Credit Limit field, type

>= 10000

(*Note:* You cannot use commas in numbers on the query form. That is, 10000 cannot be entered as 10,000. Commas are used for something else in query forms, as we'll see.) Press the DO-IT! key to see the answer, which is shown in Figure 7.8.

You can use range operators with date and alphanumeric data as well. For example, if you type

>= M

in the Last Name field of the query form, the Answer table will display records for individuals with last names beginning with the letters M through Z, as shown in Figure 7.9. (Remember to erase the >= 10000 in the Credit Limit field before pressing F2!)

If you wanted to see all individuals whose start dates were on or before March 1, 1990, you would enter the following criterion into the Start Date field of the query form:

<= 3/1/90

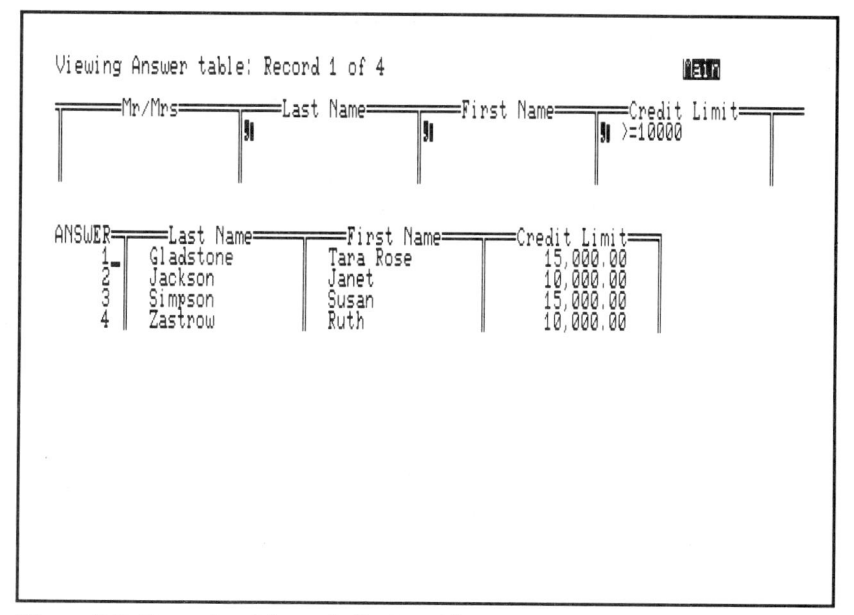

```
Viewing Answer table: Record 1 of 4                    Main
   ═Mr/Mrs══════Last Name═══════First Name══════Credit Limit═
           |             |               |    >=10000

ANSWER═══════Last Name══════First Name══════Credit Limit═
    1      Gladstone      Tara Rose         15,000.00
    2      Jackson        Janet             10,000.00
    3      Simpson        Susan             15,000.00
    4      Zastrow        Ruth              10,000.00
```

Figure 7.8: Records with credit limits of $10,000 or more

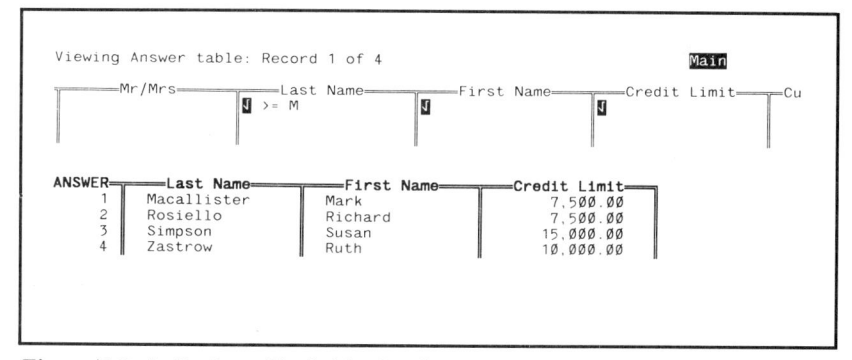

```
Viewing Answer table: Record 1 of 4                    Main
   ═Mr/Mrs══════Last Name═══════First Name══════Credit Limit═══Cu
           |   >= M     |               |

ANSWER═══════Last Name══════First Name══════Credit Limit═
    1      Macallister    Mark               7,500.00
    2      Rosiello       Richard            7,500.00
    3      Simpson        Susan             15,000.00
    4      Zastrow        Ruth              10,000.00
```

Figure 7.9: A display of individuals whose last names begin with letters M–Z

The resulting Answer table would display records for individuals whose Start Date field contained a date on or before March 1, 1990, as shown in Figure 7.10. (Again, you'll need to erase any previous query conditions before pressing F2 to perform the query.)

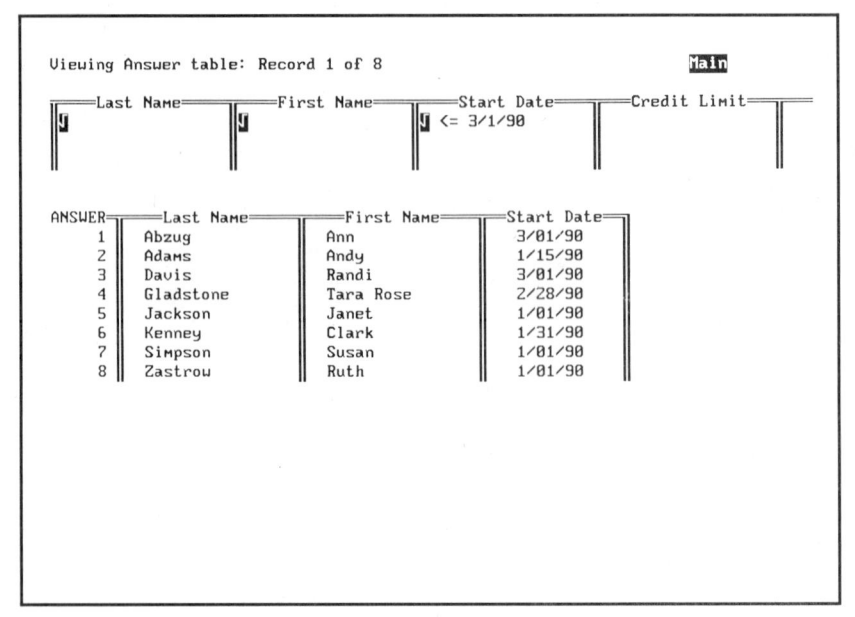

```
Viewing Answer table: Record 1 of 8                          Main
┌──Last Name──┐┌──First Name──┐┌──Start Date──┐┌──Credit Limit──┐
│ y           ││ y            ││ y <= 3/1/90  ││                │


ANSWER──┬──Last Name────┬──First Name───┬──Start Date──
   1    │  Abzug        │  Ann          │  3/01/90
   2    │  Adams        │  Andy         │  1/15/90
   3    │  Davis        │  Randi        │  3/01/90
   4    │  Gladstone    │  Tara Rose    │  2/28/90
   5    │  Jackson      │  Janet        │  1/01/90
   6    │  Kenney       │  Clark        │  1/31/90
   7    │  Simpson      │  Susan        │  1/01/90
   8    │  Zastrow      │  Ruth         │  1/01/90
```

Figure 7.10: A search for records with start dates on or before 3/1/90

SEARCHING FOR NONMATCHES

Suppose you wanted to view records for everyone in the table except California residents. You would use the *not* operator in that case. For example, placing the criterion

    not CA

in the State field, as shown in the top portion of Figure 7.11, results in an Answer table of non-California residents, as shown in the bottom half of the figure.

SEARCHING FOR RANGES

You can pull out records based on a range of values, for example all records with start dates between 1/1/90 and 3/1/90, or records with credit limits from $7,500 to $10,000. To do so, you need to place

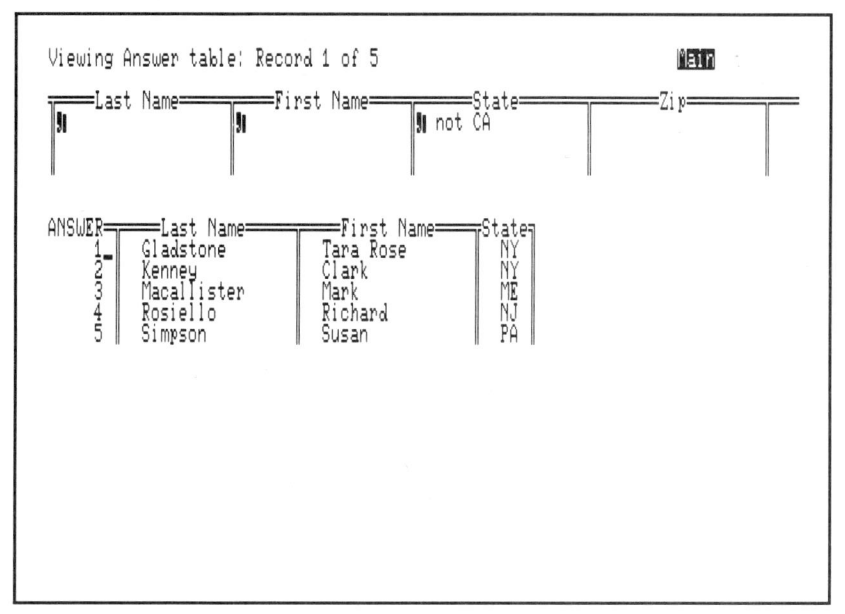

```
Viewing Answer table: Record 1 of 5                    Main
   ==Last Name==     ==First Name==    ==State==        ==Zip==
  |              |                  | not CA        |

ANSWER==    ==Last Name==      ==First Name==    ==State==
   1        Gladstone          Tara Rose         NY
   2        Kenney             Clark             NY
   3        Macallister        Mark              ME
   4        Rosiello           Richard           NJ
   5        Simpson            Susan             PA
```

Figure 7.11: The Answer table of non-California residents

two search criteria, separated by a comma, in the appropriate field of the query form. For example, Figure 7.12 shows a search for records with dates between 1/1/90 and 2/28/90 on the query form, and the results of the query. Figure 7.13 shows a query for records with credit limits from $7,500 to $10,000, and the results of the query.

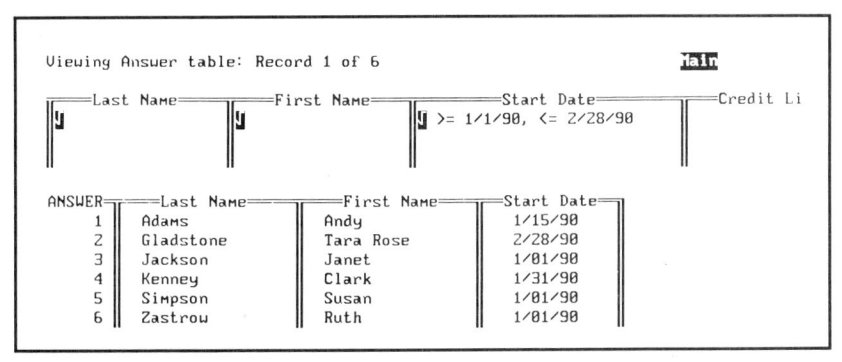

```
Viewing Answer table: Record 1 of 6                    Main
   ==Last Name==    ==First Name==    ==Start Date==        ==Credit Li
  |              |                  | >= 1/1/90, <= 2/28/90

ANSWER==    ==Last Name==      ==First Name==    ==Start Date==
   1        Adams              Andy              1/15/90
   2        Gladstone          Tara Rose         2/28/90
   3        Jackson            Janet             1/01/90
   4        Kenney             Clark             1/31/90
   5        Simpson            Susan             1/01/90
   6        Zastrou            Ruth              1/01/90
```

Figure 7.12: A search for records with start dates between 1/1/90 and 2/28/90

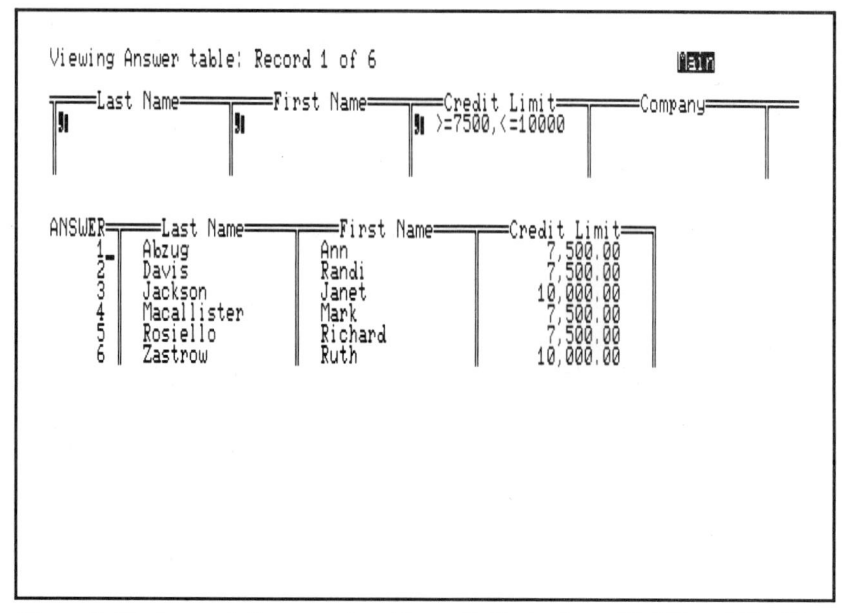

```
Viewing Answer table: Record 1 of 6                         Main
 ═Last Name═══    ═First Name═══   ═Credit Limit═   ═Company═
|9|              |9|              |9| >=7500,<=10000


ANSWER══  ═Last Name═══   ═First Name═══   ═Credit Limit═
  1-      Abzug           Ann                    7,500.00
  2       Davis           Randi                  7,500.00
  3       Jackson         Janet                 10,000.00
  4       Macallister     Mark                   7,500.00
  5       Rosiello        Richard                7,500.00
  6       Zastrow         Ruth                  10,000.00
```

Figure 7.13: A search for records with credit limits from $7,500 to $10,000

Range searches also work with alphanumeric data. For example, the criteria

>=M, <=S

in the Last Name field of the query form would display individuals whose last names begin with the letters M through S, as shown in Figure 7.14. Note that two search criteria are used, separated by a comma, which translate to "greater than or equal to M, *and* less than or equal to S." Using multiple criteria allows you to perform interesting And and Or searches, as we'll see in the next section.

PERFORMING AND/OR SEARCHES

Some of your queries might become a little more complicated than those we've discussed so far. For example, you might want to see a list of all California residents whose credit limits are over $10,000 and whose start dates are in January, or you might want a list consisting

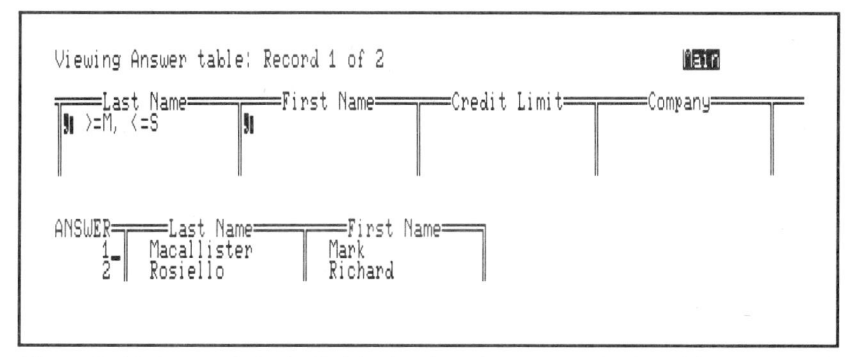

```
Viewing Answer table: Record 1 of 2                          Main
    ====Last Name====   ====First Name====  ====Credit Limit====  ====Company====
    |✓ >=M, <=S     |   |✓              |   |               |   |            |



ANSWER====Last Name========First Name====
    1 |  Macallister    | Mark           |
    2 |  Rosiello       | Richard        |
```

Figure 7.14: A search for individuals whose last names begin with letters M-S

only of residents of New York or California. For these kinds of searches, you need to specify *And* or *Or* relationships in your queries.

And relationships are specified by simply filling in more than one criterion on a single line of the query form. Figure 7.15 shows a query for California residents whose start dates are in the month of January and whose credit limits are equal to or greater than $10,000. The Answer table shows the results of the query.

Notice that the criteria in the State, Start Date, and Credit Limit fields are on the same line of the query form. Placing the criteria on the same line specifies that an And relationship is to be used with the criteria. In an And query, only records that meet *all* criteria will be displayed.

For an *Or* search, you need to place the criteria on separate lines of the query form. Furthermore, be sure to place check marks in the fields on

```
Viewing Answer table: Record 1 of 2                          Main
CUSTLIST====State====  ====Start Date====       ====Credit Limit====   ====Mr/
        |✓ CA       |  |✓ >=1/1/90, <=1/31/90|  |✓ >= 10000        |   |


ANSWER====Last Name====  ====First Name====  ====State====  ====Start Date====  ====Credit Lim
    1 |  Jackson      |  | Janet          |  |  CA       |  |  1/01/90       |  | 10,000.00
    2 |  Zastrou      |  | Ruth           |  |  CA       |  |  1/01/90       |  | 10,000.00
```

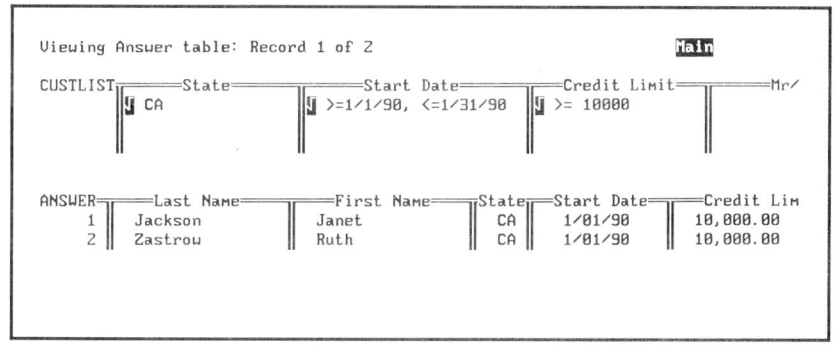

Figure 7.15: A search for California residents with start dates in 1/90 and credit limits of $10,000 or more

both lines. Figure 7.16 shows a search for all people who live in either California or New York. Notice that check marks for displaying last name and first name are also specified in both lines of the query form. The resulting Answer table is also displayed in the figure. In answer to an Or query, a record will be displayed if it matches any one or all criteria.

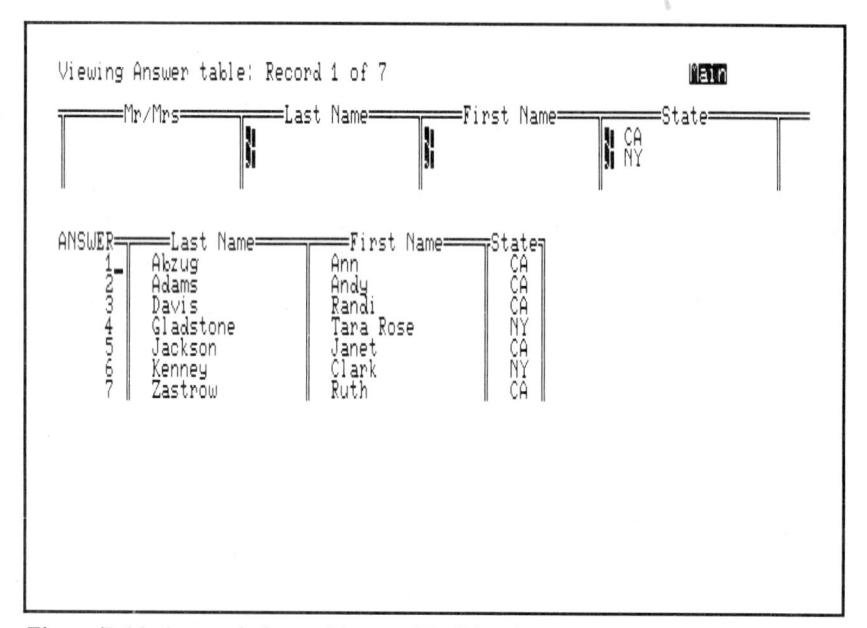

```
Viewing Answer table: Record 1 of 7                          Main
   ┌────Mr/Mrs────┬────Last Name────┬────First Name────┬────State────┐
   │              │ ✓               │ ✓                │ CA          │
   │              │                 │                  │ NY          │
   └──────────────┴─────────────────┴──────────────────┴─────────────┘

   ANSWER──┬──Last Name──┬──First Name──┬──State─┐
        1  │ Abzug       │ Ann          │ CA     │
        2  │ Adams       │ Andy         │ CA     │
        3  │ Davis       │ Randi        │ CA     │
        4  │ Gladstone   │ Tara Rose    │ NY     │
        5  │ Jackson     │ Janet        │ CA     │
        6  │ Kenney      │ Clark        │ NY     │
        7  │ Zastrow     │ Ruth         │ CA     │
```

Figure 7.16: A search for residents of California or New York

When filling out query forms, remember that Paradox compares values in the table with what you enter into the query form. It does not attempt to guess at what you mean in English. For example, take a look at the query in Figure 7.17. Notice that no records were selected as matching the search criterion, so the Answer table is empty. That's because it is impossible for any record in the Custlist table to have both CA and NY in the State field at the same time.

The query we performed in Figure 7.16 showed the correct form for displaying all residents of either California and New York by placing the criteria on separate lines, thereby specifying records that have CA in the State field *or* have NY in the state field.

SEARCHING THE DATABASE 115

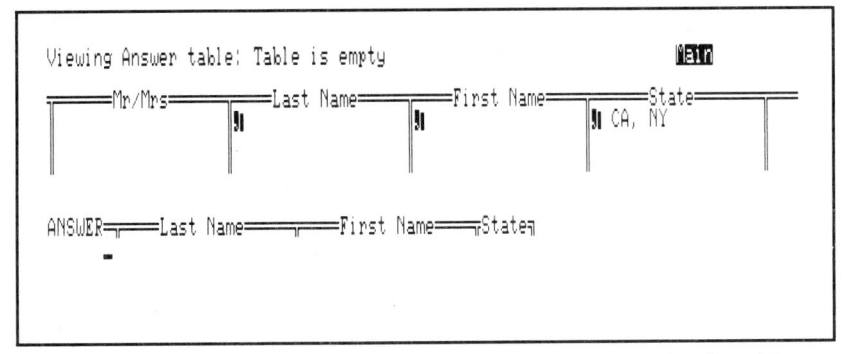

```
Viewing Answer table: Table is empty                    Main
    ╤═Mr/Mrs══╤    ╤═Last Name══╤    ╤═First Name══╤    ╤═State══╤
              │                 │                 │    │ CA, NY │


ANSWER╤══Last Name══╤══First Name══╤═State╤
```

Figure 7.17: An incorrect attempt to list California and New York residents

Or searches can be a little tricky and usually require a little thought. For example, look at the query and results shown in Figure 7.18.

Notice that California and New York residents are displayed, as well as a Pennsylvania resident with a credit of $10,000 or more. Furthermore, several California and New York residents whose credit limits are below $10,000 are displayed. That's because the query criteria ask for "records with CA in the State field, *or* NY in the State

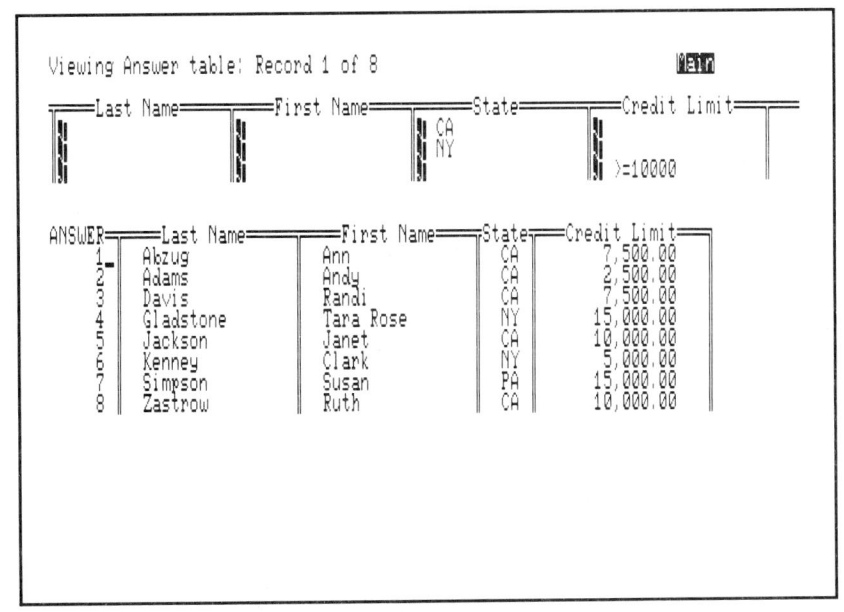

```
Viewing Answer table: Record 1 of 8                     Main
  ╤═Last Name══╤  ╤═First Name══╤  ╤═State═╤  ╤═Credit Limit══╤
                                   │ CA    │
                                   │ NY    │  │ >=10000       │

ANSWER╤══Last Name══╤══First Name══╤═State═╤══Credit Limit══╤
   1    Abzug          Ann            CA          7,500.00
   2    Adams          Andy           CA          2,500.00
   3    Davis          Randi          CA          7,500.00
   4    Gladstone      Tara Rose      NY         15,000.00
   5    Jackson        Janet          CA         10,000.00
   6    Kenney         Clark          NY          5,000.00
   7    Simpson        Susan          PA         15,000.00
   8    Zastrow        Ruth           CA         10,000.00
```

Figure 7.18: Three Or criteria in the query form

field, *or* credit limits of $10,000 or more." (In other words, people with credit limits over $10,000 are displayed, regardless of what state they live in.)

Now take a look at the query criteria and results in Figure 7.19. Notice that only California and New York residents with credit limits of $10,000 or more are displayed.

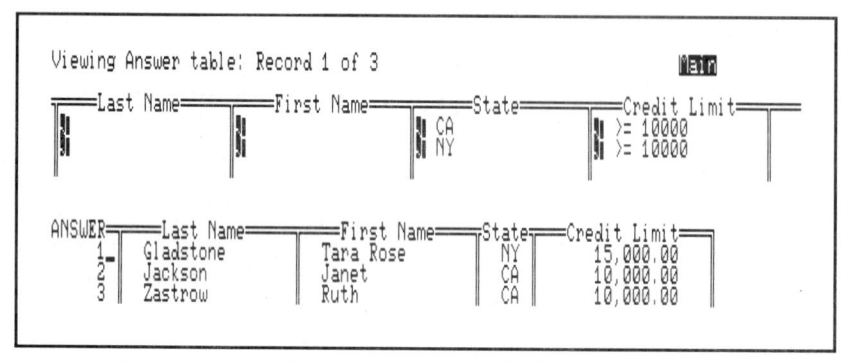

```
Viewing Answer table: Record 1 of 3                           Main
 ╔═Last Name═╤═First Name═╤═State═╤═Credit Limit═╗
 ║           │            │ CA    │ >= 10000     ║
 ║           │            │ NY    │ >= 10000     ║

 ANSWER═╤═Last Name═══╤═First Name═══╤═State═╤═Credit Limit═╗
   1    │ Gladstone   │ Tara Rose    │ NY    │ 15,000.00    
   2    │ Jackson     │ Janet        │ CA    │ 10,000.00    
   3    │ Zastrow     │ Ruth         │ CA    │ 10,000.00    
```

Figure 7.19: A search for California and New York residents with credit limits of $10,000 or more

Chapter 13 discusses advanced querying techniques, including an alternative method for performing *Or* searches.

The results are different, because these criteria translate as "Display records that have CA in the State field *and* a credit limit of at least $10,000, *or* NY in the State field *and* a credit limit of at least $10,000."

PATTERN-MATCHING SEARCHES

Sometimes, you might want to view records that match some pattern or contain a certain sequence of characters. For example, in an inventory system, you might want to view all records that have the letter J2 embedded in the part number (assuming this is some meaningful code). If you want to look up an individual named Smith but are not sure of the spelling, you might wish to view records that are spelled like Smith (though not exactly). The operators that you can use for these types of searches are listed below:

OPERATOR	MEANING
..	Stands for any series of characters, numbers, spaces, and so on
@	Stands for any single character
like	Matches items similar to the criterion
blank	Matches items that have no data in the field
today	Used to compare items against today's date
not	Preceding the criterion, matches items that do not match the criterion

Let's look at some examples. Suppose you want to list all individuals who live on a particular street. You can't ask for all records that contain a street name, such as Ocean, because the word Ocean will be embedded somewhere in the middle of the address (for example, 1234 Ocean St.). However, you could use the .. operator to indicate the numbers preceding the street name, followed by the word Ocean, followed by .. again to indicate any other characters. Figure 7.20 shows such a query and its results. Notice that records with the word Ocean embedded in the Address field are displayed.

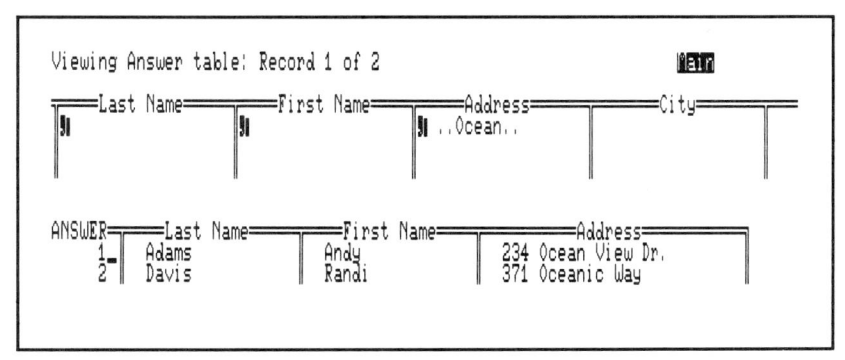

```
Viewing Answer table: Record 1 of 2                    Main
┌═Last Name══╤═First Name══╤═Address══════╤═City══════
│ ✓          │ ✓           │ ✓ ..Ocean..  │

ANSWER═╤═Last Name══╤═First Name══╤═Address═════════
   1   │ Adams      │ Andy        │ 234 Ocean View Dr.
   2   │ Davis      │ Randi       │ 371 Oceanic Way
```

Figure 7.20: A search for records with Ocean embedded in the Address field

You could, of course, be more specific in your query for residents on Ocean. For example, a query such as

..Ocean Blvd

would list any records with addresses that start with any characters and end with Ocean Blvd (thereby excluding Ocean View, Ocean Ave, Ocean Way, and so forth). In addition, you could set up an And condition on the search to find only residents on Ocean Blvd in a certain city, by specifying

..Ocean Blvd

in the Address field and a particular city name (Malibu, for instance) in the City field.

You can also use the .. operator to pull out records for a particular month. Notice the query and results in Figure 7.21. Since a particular day was not specified in the 1/../90 query, all records with start dates in the month of January are listed.

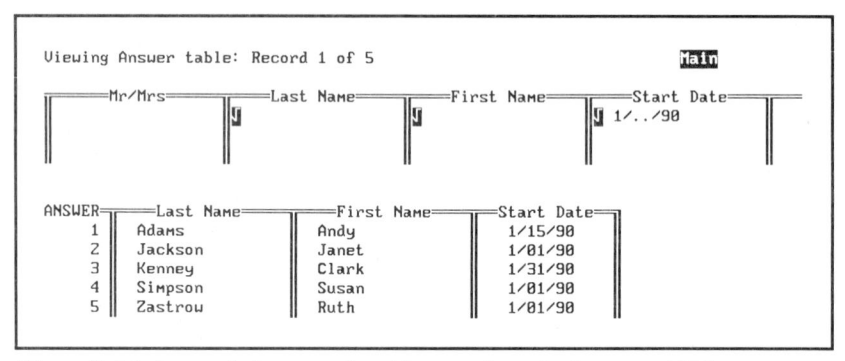

```
Viewing Answer table: Record 1 of 5                    Main
       ┌─Mr/Mrs─┐  ┌─Last Name─┐  ┌─First Name─┐  ┌─Start Date─┐
       │       y│  │          y│  │           y│  │y 1/../90   │



ANSWER┬─Last Name─┬─First Name─┬─Start Date─┐
   1  │  Adams    │  Andy      │  1/15/90   │
   2  │  Jackson  │  Janet     │  1/01/90   │
   3  │  Kenney   │  Clark     │  1/31/90   │
   4  │  Simpson  │  Susan     │  1/01/90   │
   5  │  Zastrou  │  Ruth      │  1/01/90   │
```

Figure 7.21: A search for records with start dates in January 1990

The @ operator is used to match a single character, as opposed to any series of characters. For example, a search for Sm@th would find names such as Smith and Smyth. A search for Sm@th.. would find Smith, Smythe, Smithsonian, Smathers, and others that have a single letter embedded between the m and the t, with or without any characters following the h.

The use of upper- and lowercase letters will sometimes mislead a query. As mentioned earlier in the chapter, a query for all "ca" residents would display nothing, since CA is stored in uppercase in all records. This could be a problem if you were not absolutely certain of the case in all records. But using the *like* operator takes care of the problem. Notice that the query in Figure 7.22 asks for all records that have states like ca. Paradox displays all California residents. (Had there been some records with the state stored as CA or Ca, these too would have been displayed.)

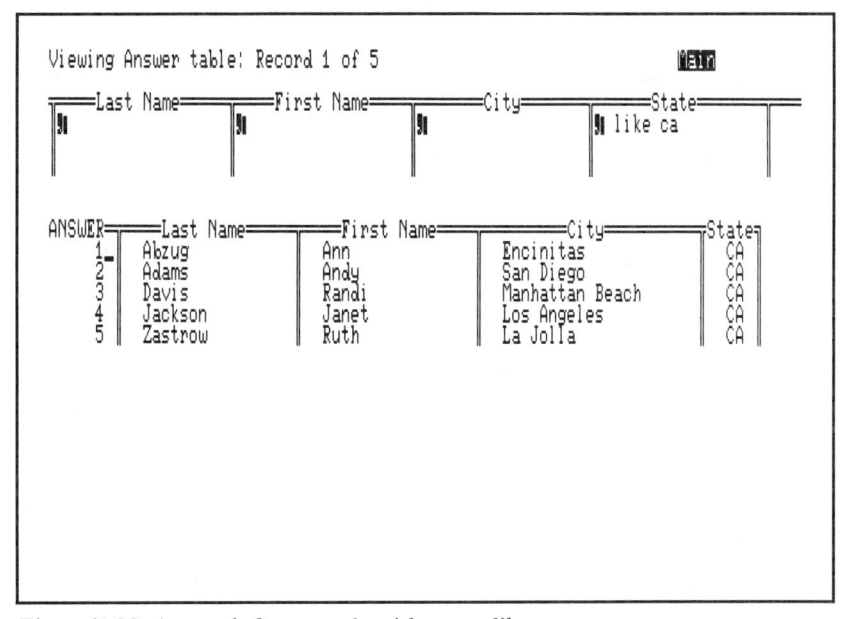

```
Viewing Answer table: Record 1 of 5                          MAIN
   ╒══Last Name══╤══First Name══╤═════City═════╤═════State═════
   │¶            │¶             │¶             │¶ like ca      │


   ANSWER╤══Last Name══╤══First Name══╤═════City═════╤═State═
      1  │ Abzug       │ Ann          │ Encinitas    │ CA
      2  │ Adams       │ Andy         │ San Diego    │ CA
      3  │ Davis       │ Randi        │ Manhattan Beach│ CA
      4  │ Jackson     │ Janet        │ Los Angeles  │ CA
      5  │ Zastrow     │ Ruth         │ La Jolla     │ CA
```

Figure 7.22: A search for records with states like ca

You should use the *like* operator liberally, since it may find records with slight misspellings that might otherwise have gone unnoticed. Similarly, if you are not absolutely sure of the spelling of something you are trying to find, try using the like operator. Note the query in Figure 7.23, which asks for records with last names like Abzig. The results display a record for Abzug, which would not have been found without the like operator.

The *blank* operator finds records that have no data in a field. For example, the query in Figure 7.24 asks to see the last name and first name of individuals who do not have a company affiliation (that is, the Company field is blank). The results of the query show the appropriate records.

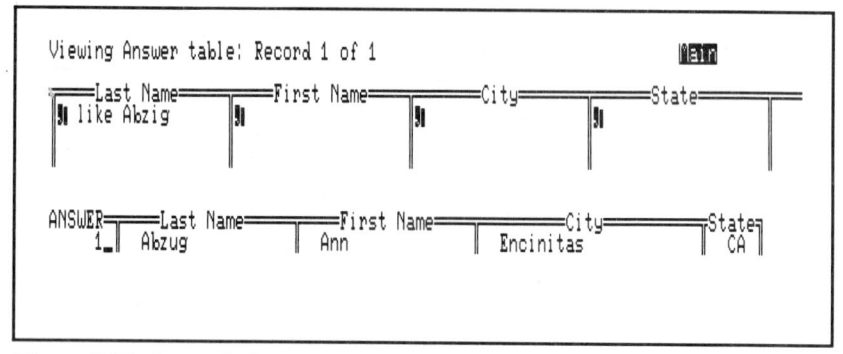

Figure 7.23: A search for records with last names like Abzig

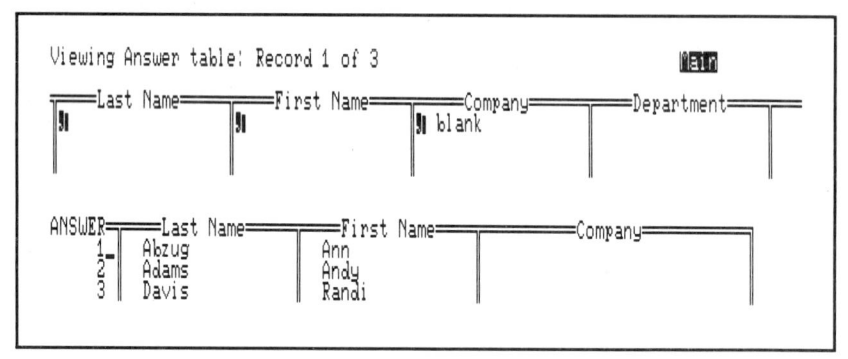

Figure 7.24: Records with blank Company fields

Records can be compared against the current date (the date you type in when you first boot up your computer) by using the *today* operator. For example, if the current date were 3/1/90 and you entered the query shown in Figure 7.25, you'd see records whose start dates match today's date.

You can use the usual $<$, $>$, $<=$, $>=$, and the arithmetic operators listed below when working with dates:

OPERATOR MEANS

+   Add a number of days to the date

–   Subtract a number of days from the date

Once again, assuming today's date is 3/1/90, the query in Figure 7.26 requests all records with start dates that are 30 or more days earlier than today's date.

The *not* operator reverses the meaning of any query criterion. For example, the criterion *not blank* displays records that do not contain a

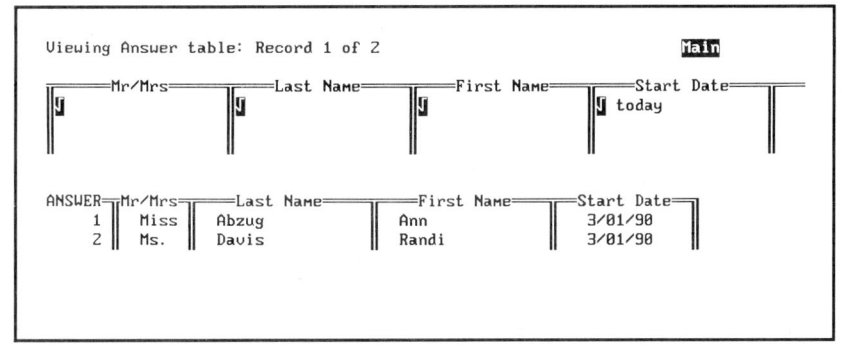

```
Viewing Answer table: Record 1 of 2                          Main
     ┌─Mr/Mrs─┐  ┌─Last Name─┐  ┌─First Name─┐  ┌─Start Date─┐
     │y       │  │y          │  │y           │  │y today     │


ANSWER┬─Mr/Mrs─┬─Last Name─┬─First Name─┬─Start Date─┐
   1  │ Miss   │ Abzug     │ Ann        │ 3/01/90    │
   2  │ Ms.    │ Davis     │ Randi      │ 3/01/90    │
```

Figure 7.25: Records that match today's date

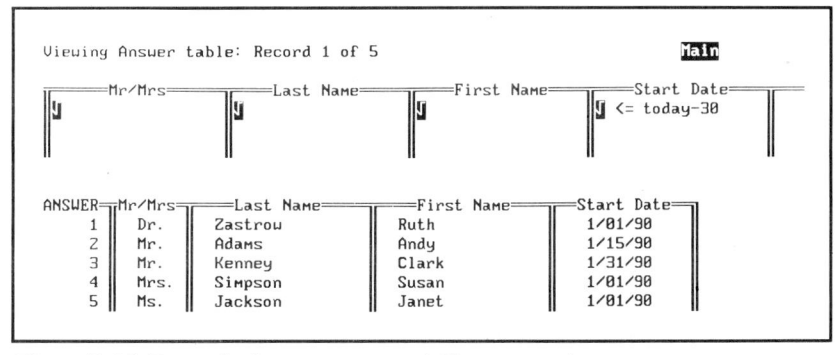

```
Viewing Answer table: Record 1 of 5                          Main
     ┌─Mr/Mrs─┐  ┌─Last Name─┐  ┌─First Name─┐  ┌─Start Date──┐
     │y       │  │y          │  │y           │  │y <= today-30│


ANSWER┬─Mr/Mrs─┬─Last Name─┬─First Name─┬─Start Date─┐
   1  │ Dr.    │ Zastrow   │ Ruth       │ 1/01/90    │
   2  │ Mr.    │ Adams     │ Andy       │ 1/15/90    │
   3  │ Mr.    │ Kenney    │ Clark      │ 1/31/90    │
   4  │ Mrs.   │ Simpson   │ Susan      │ 1/01/90    │
   5  │ Ms.    │ Jackson   │ Janet      │ 1/01/90    │
```

Figure 7.26: Records that were entered 30 or more days ago

blank in a field. The criterion *not CA* displays records that do not have CA in a field. The criterion *not ..Ocean Blvd..* displays records that do not have Ocean Blvd in the address. The criterion *not ../../89* displays records that do not have the year 1989 in a date.

QUERIES AS AN EDITING TOOL

On a very large table, editing can become laborious. You might spend a good deal more time looking for items that you want to change than you spend making the changes. With the use of the *find* operator, you can make the query form into a great tool for looking up and editing quickly. When you use the word *find* in the leftmost column of the query form, Paradox displays the actual table, which you can edit, rather than the Answer table. (Since the find operator always displays the actual table, you cannot use check marks to display only certain fields.) Let's try an example.

First, let's pretend that there are 1,000 records on the database, and you need to make a change to Kenney's record. To make matters a little more interesting, let's assume that you're not even sure how to spell Kenney.

Rather than using the arrow keys to scroll around searching, you can call up the query screen and enter the word *find* into the leftmost column. In the Last Name column, enter the criterion

    like Kenny

Press the DO-IT! (F2) key and, lo and behold, the cursor is right on Kenney's record in the Custlist table, as shown in Figure 7.27. To edit, just press the Edit (F9) key as usual, and the DO-IT! key when finished editing.

GLOBAL EDITS

Here is a technique that may someday save you many hours of tedious work. Through a process known as *global editing,* you can automatically change the contents of a field to a new value in records

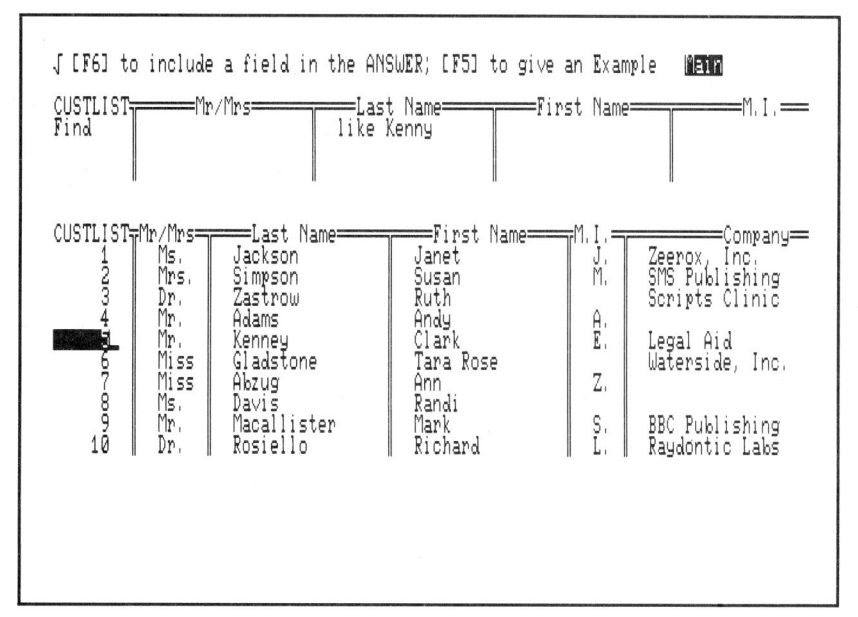

```
  √ [F6] to include a field in the ANSWER; [F5] to give an Example   Main
  CUSTLIST==Mr/Mrs=======Last Name======First Name=========M.I.==
  Find                  like Kenny


  CUSTLIST┬Mr/Mrs====┬====Last Name=====┬===First Name===┬M.I.┬=====Company==
     1   │ Ms.      │ Jackson          │ Janet          │ J. │ Zeerox, Inc.
     2   │ Mrs.     │ Simpson          │ Susan          │ M. │ SMS Publishing
     3   │ Dr.      │ Zastrow          │ Ruth           │    │ Scripts Clinic
     4   │ Mr.      │ Adams            │ Andy           │ A. │
     5   │ Mr.      │ Kenney           │ Clark          │ E. │ Legal Aid
     6   │ Miss     │ Gladstone        │ Tara Rose      │    │ Waterside, Inc.
     7   │ Miss     │ Abzug            │ Ann            │ Z. │
     8   │ Ms.      │ Davis            │ Randi          │    │
     9   │ Mr.      │ Macallister      │ Mark           │ S. │ BBC Publishing
    10   │ Dr.      │ Rosiello         │ Richard        │ L. │ Raydontic Labs
```

Figure 7.27: A query to find and edit a record for Kenney

that meet a certain criterion. For example, suppose you have two different people entering data into your database. One types in *Los Angeles* for all Los Angeles residents, and the other types in *L.A.*. This ends up creating problems, because queries that search for Los Angeles records miss those with L.A. and vice versa. (Even though an Or search could take care of this, it would still be better to have a consistent entry.)

Another use of global editing would be to increase credit limits. For instance, you might want to raise all credit limits by 25 percent, as long as the current limit is less than $10,000.

You use the *changeto* operator in your queries to perform such global changes. We can try a global change with even the small Custlist table. We'll make a simple global edit of changing all records that have CA in the state field to ca. First, clear any images from the screen with the Clear Image (F8) key, so only the Main menu is displayed. Then select the Ask option and specify the Custlist table. Fill in the query screen as shown at the top of Figure 7.28.

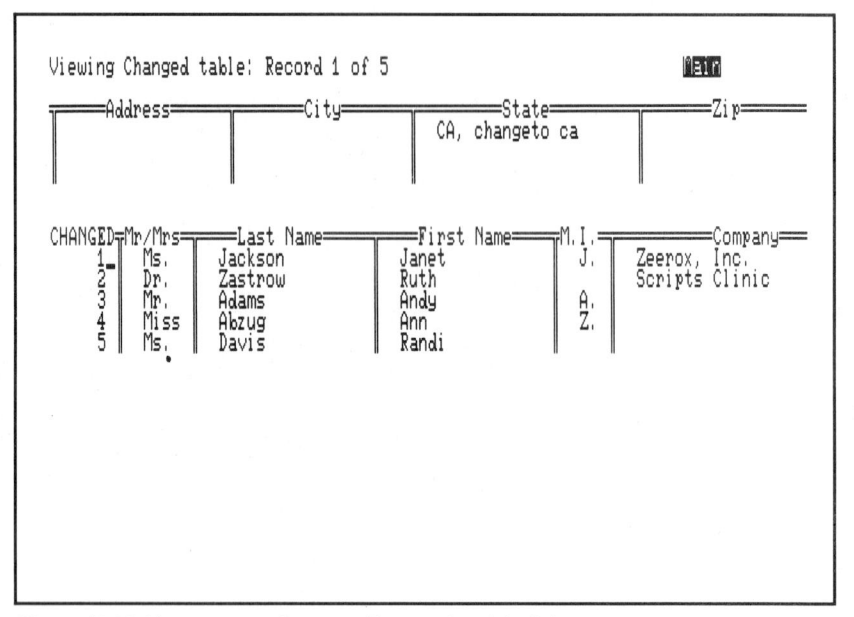

```
Viewing Changed table: Record 1 of 5                    MAIN
┌════Address════╤════City════╤════State════╤════Zip════┐
│               │            │ CA, changeto ca          │
│               │            │             │           │
│                                                      │
│                                                      │
│ CHANGED╤Mr/Mrs╤═Last Name═╤═First Name═╤M.I.╤═Company═│
│    1-    Ms.   Jackson      Janet        J.   Zeerox, Inc.
│    2     Dr.   Zastrow      Ruth              Scripts Clinic
│    3     Mr.   Adams        Andy        A.
│    4     Miss  Abzug        Ann         Z.
│    5     Ms.   Davis        Randi
│                                                      │
└──────────────────────────────────────────────────────┘
```

Figure 7.28: A query to change all records with CA to ca

Notice how the query is set up. CA in the State field indicates that CA is the value we're searching for. The comma separates the query (CA) from the command

changeto ca

When you press DO-IT! (F2), Paradox displays the records that have been changed in a special table called Changed, as shown in the bottom half of Figure 7.28. (Like the find operator, changeto always displays all the fields in a table. Hence, check marks cannot be used on the query form.)

The changes themselves do not actually show up in the Changed table. To see the new values in the Custlist table, first clear the Changed image and the query form from the screen by pressing Clear Image (F8) twice. Then select the View option from the Main menu and specify Custlist as the table to work with. Scroll over to the State field to view the changes. Notice all the ca entries are in lowercase, as Figure 7.29 shows.

```
Viewing Custlist table: Record 1 of 10                    Main
CUSTLIST       City            State    Zip      Start Date    Credit Lim
      1    Los Angeles          ca     91234       1/01/90      10,000.00
      2    Philadelphia         PA     23456       1/01/90      15,000.00
      3    La Jolla             ca     92037       1/01/90      10,000.00
      4    San Diego            ca     92038       1/15/90       2,500.00
      5    New York             NY     12345       1/31/90       5,000.00
      6    New York             NY     12345       2/28/90      15,000.00
      7    Encinitas            ca     92024       3/01/90       7,500.00
      8    Manhatten Beach      ca     90001       3/01/90       7,500.00
      9    Bangor               ME     00001       3/15/90       7,500.00
     10    Newark               NJ     00123       3/15/90       7,500.00
```

Figure 7.29: The results of a global edit to the State field in the Custlist table

To restore the original values, clear the image (press F8). Select the Ask option from the menu and specify the Custlist table. Enter the criterion

ca, changeto CA

in the State field, and press DO-IT!. Press Clear All (Alt-F8) to clear the screen. Select the View option and specify the Custlist table. Scroll over to the State field to see that all CA entries are back in uppercase.

In our hypothetical example of changing the L.A. entries to Los Angeles, you would enter the following criterion into the City field of the query form:

L.A., changeto Los Angeles

This would globally change the L.A. entries to Los Angeles.

We'll discuss global changes that increase or decrease numbers in a later chapter on managing numbers. For now, just keep in mind that you can use the changeto operator to alter records in a table globally. We'll see more uses for this type of query throughout this book.

GLOBAL DELETIONS

By placing the word *delete* in the leftmost column of the query form, you can globally delete a group of records that meet a certain criterion.

This is not a particularly safe technique to try out right now, because we do not have enough skill to undo a global deletion. However, we can try a hypothetical and safe example with our Custlist table.

Select the Ask option from the Main menu and specify the Custlist table. In the leftmost column of the query form, type in the word *delete*. In the State column, enter the letters TX and press DO-IT! (F2). The effect of this query is to delete all records that have TX in the State field.

The records that have been deleted will be displayed in a table named Deleted, as shown in Figure 7.30. In this example, there were no records with TX in the State field, so no records were deleted. This is just as well, since the table need not be any smaller. Nonetheless, this little example should give you an idea of how this capability works.

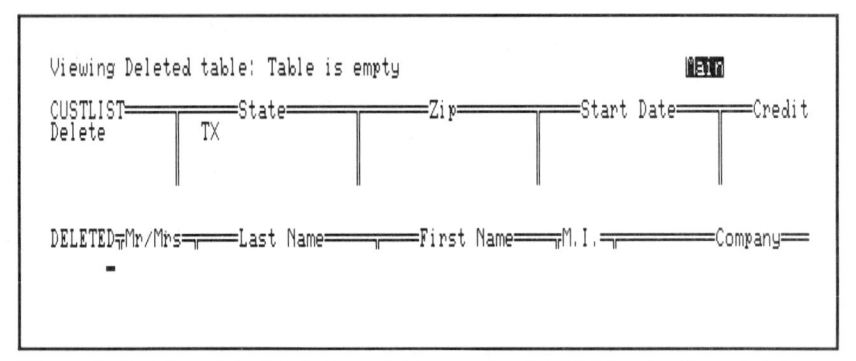

Figure 7.30: The global deletion of all records with TX in the State field

LIMITATIONS

Basically, there is no limit to the number of ways in which you can combine the various searching techniques we've discussed here. The only limitation is that the query form can contain only 22 rows of information (22 Or conditions), which are probably far more than you'll ever need.

However, one must exercise caution in the use of certain keywords and symbols in queries. For example, suppose you wish to find a record for someone with the last name Davis, Jr. If you enter the query by typing

    Davis, Jr.

into the Last Name field, Paradox will separate Davis and Jr. as two separate queries (as in an And search). Hence, the query will attempt to find records that contain only the name Davis, and only the name Jr. No records will meet such a criterion. Therefore, to state that you literally are looking for the name *Davis, Jr.,* enclose the query in quotation marks, as below:

    "Davis, Jr."

Similarly, suppose there were a city named Blank, and you wished to view records of everyone who lived there. If you enter the query

    Blank

in the city field, you'll get all the records that have no data in the City field (since Blank has special meaning in Paradox queries). To specify that you literally are looking for a city named Blank, enclose the name in quotation marks, as below:

    "Blank"

Using quotation marks in queries keeps Paradox from converting special symbols and words (such as the comma and the words *blank, not,* and *today*) into commands, and instead treats them as items to look up.

SAMPLE QUERIES

Before ending this chapter, let's look at a few more examples that combine the many techniques we've discussed. Since the Custlist table is too small to demonstrate the full query capability of Paradox, we'll just present some examples and the types of data they would display.

The query in Figure 7.31 requests all records of individuals who live in Red Rock, Arizona (that is, records with Red Rock in the City field and AZ in the State field).

The query in Figure 7.32 would locate all individuals whose title is Dr. and whose zip code is in the 90000 to 99999 area.

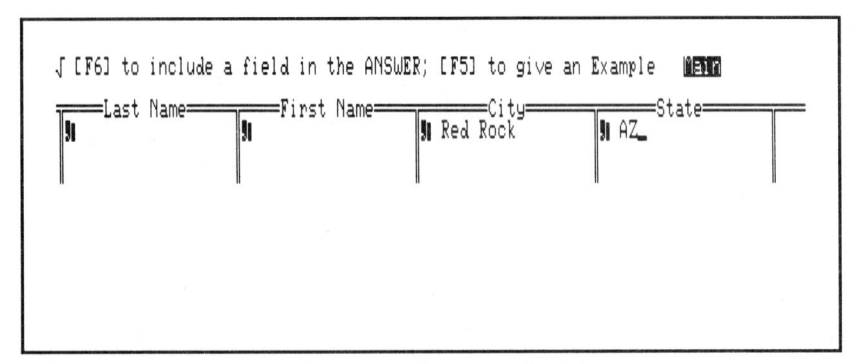

Figure 7.31: A search for residents of Red Rock, Arizona

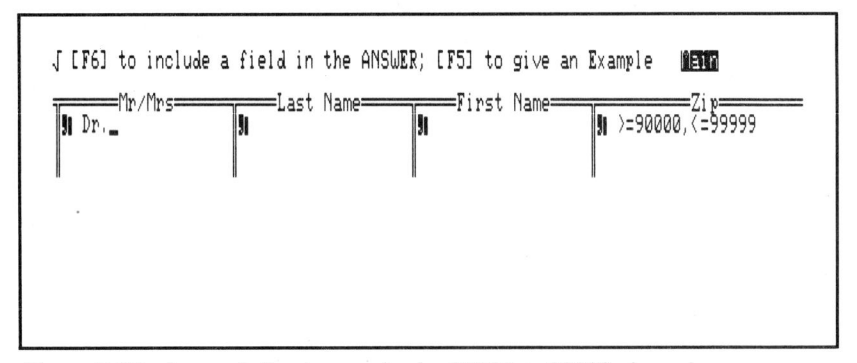

Figure 7.32: A search for doctors in the 90000 to 99999 zip code area

The query in Figure 7.33 requests all records that have the letter *s* embedded in either the Last Name, First Name, or M.I. (middle initial) field. This may seem a bit odd as a query, but you may be surprised. Someday you may have a database with three different part numbers per record, and you need to find records that have some code embedded in any of the three part numbers. It would be the same type of query, but with different fields.

The query in Figure 7.34 would display all San Diego residents whose credit limits were in the range of 5,000 to 10,000. Note the three And conditions. In English, this query finds "all records that have San Diego in the City field, *and* have Credit Limits greater than or equal to $5000, *and* Credit Limits less than or equal to $10000."

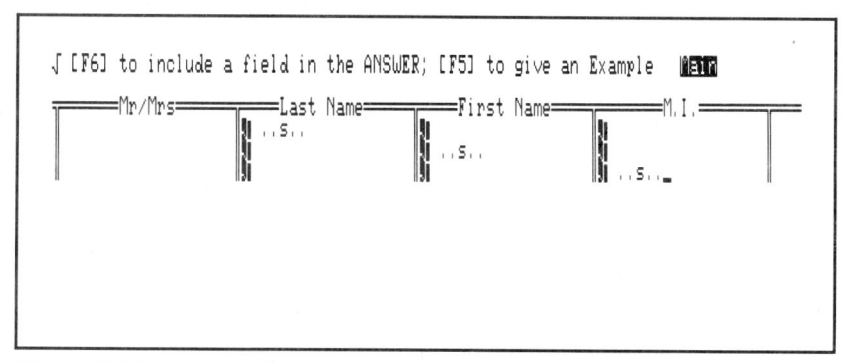

Figure 7.33: A query for records with the letter *s* in the Last Name, First Name, or M.I. fields

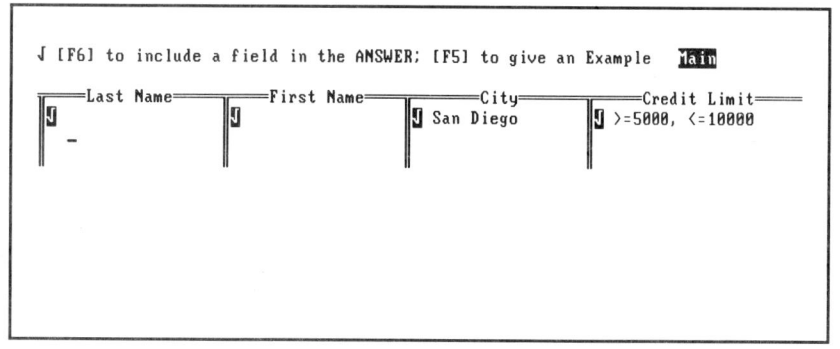

Figure 7.34: A search for San Diego residents with a credit limit of $5,000 to $10,000

The query in Figure 7.35 asks for the records of all people who have credit limits in the range of $5,000 to $10,000 and who have zip codes in the range of 80000 to 85000.

The best way to fully master the query form is to experiment. Again, don't be worried about doing any harm. You cannot possibly

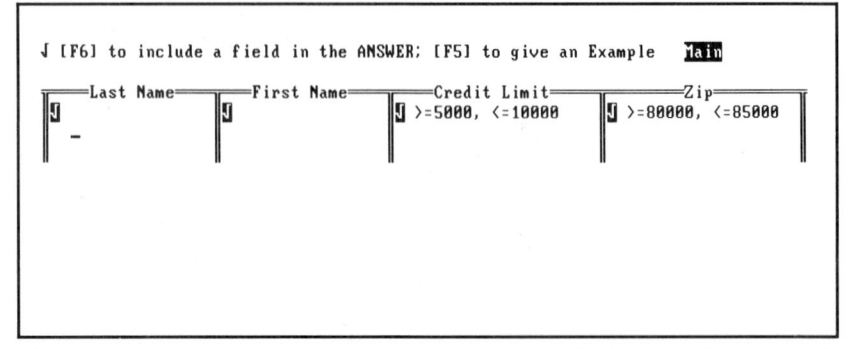

```
┌─────────────────────────────────────────────────────────────────┐
│ √ [F6] to include a field in the ANSWER; [F5] to give an Example   Main │
│ ┌──Last Name──┬──First Name──┬──Credit Limit──┬──────Zip──────┐ │
│ │ √           │ √            │ √ >=5000, <=10000 │ √ >=80000, <=85000 │ │
│ │             │              │                │               │ │
│ └─────────────┴──────────────┴────────────────┴───────────────┘ │
└─────────────────────────────────────────────────────────────────┘
```

Figure 7.35: A search for residents in the 80000–85000 zip code area with credit limits of $5,000 to $10,000

damage anything by using queries. Experiment and enjoy. Later, we'll do more queries with bigger tables, as well as with several tables simultaneously.

SUMMARY

- To search (or query) a table, select the Ask option from the Main menu and specify a table name.
- Press Checkmark (F6) to place a check mark in each field of the query form that you want to see displayed.
- Place a check plus (press Alt-F6) in each field if you wish to include duplicates in a display.
- To display records in descending order in the Answer table, mark the leftmost displayed column by pressing Ctrl-F6.
- To search for particular records, put the data that you want to search for in the appropriate field in the query form.
- To search for values, use the <, >, < =, and > = operators in your query forms.
- To search for nonmatches, use the not operator in your criterion.
- To search for ranges, place two values (with < or < =, and > or > = operators) in a single field, separated by a comma.

- To specify an And relationship among several criteria, place all items in the same row on the query form.
- To specify an Or relationship among criteria in the query form, place the criteria on different rows.
- For trickier searches, you can use the .., @, *like, blank,* and *today* operators.
- To edit data using queries, use the *find* operator in the leftmost column of the query form and the criteria you wish to search for in the appropriate column(s).
- To globally change a table, use the *changeto* operator in your criterion.
- To globally delete records on a table, use the *delete* operator in the leftmost column of the query form.

PRINTING FORMATTED REPORTS

CHAPTER 8

> If you are using Paradox on a network, see "Reports on a Network" in Appendix B.

IN COMPUTER JARGON, A *REPORT* IS ANY FORMATTED display of data. In this chapter we'll explore techniques for displaying table data in a variety of formats, including a printed directory, mailing labels, and form letters. We'll use the Paradox *report generator* to design and develop these reports.

The Paradox report generator is very powerful, very flexible, and also a bit overwhelming at first glance. In this chapter, we'll cover the basics and develop some reports for our Custlist table. Later, we'll deal with more complicated issues such as subtotals and grouping.

Now let's jump right in and develop a printed directory that displays data from the Custlist table in the format shown in Figure 8.1. Notice that the report is formatted, as well as sorted into alphabetical order.

```
   3/31/90              Directory of Customers           Page   1

   Abzug, Miss Ann Z.
           301 Crest Dr.
           Encinitas, CA   92024     (1)
           Start Date: 3/01/90        Credit Limit:7,500.00
   Adams, Mr. Andy A.
           234 Ocean View Dr.
           San Diego, CA   92038     (2)
           Start Date: 1/15/90        Credit Limit:2,500.00
   Davis, Ms. Randi
           371 Oceanic Way
           Manhattan Beach, CA   90001    (3)
           Start Date: 3/01/90        Credit Limit:7,500.00
   Gladstone, Miss Tara Rose
           Waterside, Inc.
           Acquisitions
           P.O. Box 121
           New York, NY   12345      (4)
           Start Date: 2/28/90        Credit Limit:15,000.00
```

Figure 8.1: A printed directory from the Custlist table

DESIGNING A REPORT

To design a report format for the directory shown in Figure 8.1, select the Report option from the Main menu. You'll be given five options:

Output   Design   Change   RangeOutput   SetPrinter

To create a new report, select the Design option. When Paradox asks for the name of the table to use, enter Custlist as the table name. Paradox will show another menu:

R   1   2   3   4   5   6   7   8   9

"R" is the standard report format Paradox automatically creates for every table; it is the format used when you press Instant Report (Alt-F7) to print a report. Additional reports used with a table can be assigned to the numbers 1 through 14. Select option 1 to assign report number 1 to the directory report. Paradox then displays all report options that begin with the number 1, as below:

1   10   11   12   13   14
Unused report

Note that option 1 is highlighted, and the prompt *Unused report* informs you that no report format has been assigned to this number yet. Press Enter to select number 1. (Optionally, you can use the arrow keys to highlight another number, and then press Enter to select that number. However, for simplicity, it makes sense to number our first report as 1.)

Paradox will now ask for a description of the report:

Report description:
Enter report description.

You can enter any description up to 40 characters long. For this example, type

Directory of Customers

and press Enter. (This description can also be used as a title in the report, as we'll see in a moment.)

Next, Paradox asks which type of report you want, as below:

Tabular   Free-form

The Tabular option displays data in much the same way that Table View does on the screen. Each field of information is placed in a single column. The Free-form option allows you to display data in any format you wish. All the sample reports in this chapter will use the Free-form option, so go ahead and select Free-form now.

A suggested report format will appear on the screen, which looks like the standard form you see on the screen when you display data in Form View. This screen, shown in Figure 8.2, is called the *report specification,* because it allows you to specify a format for the report.

Notice that the report specification shows lines for a *page band* and a *form band* (indicated by down-pointing triangles next to the words *page* and *form*). The page band shows what will appear at the top and bottom of each printed page of the report. In this example, the current date

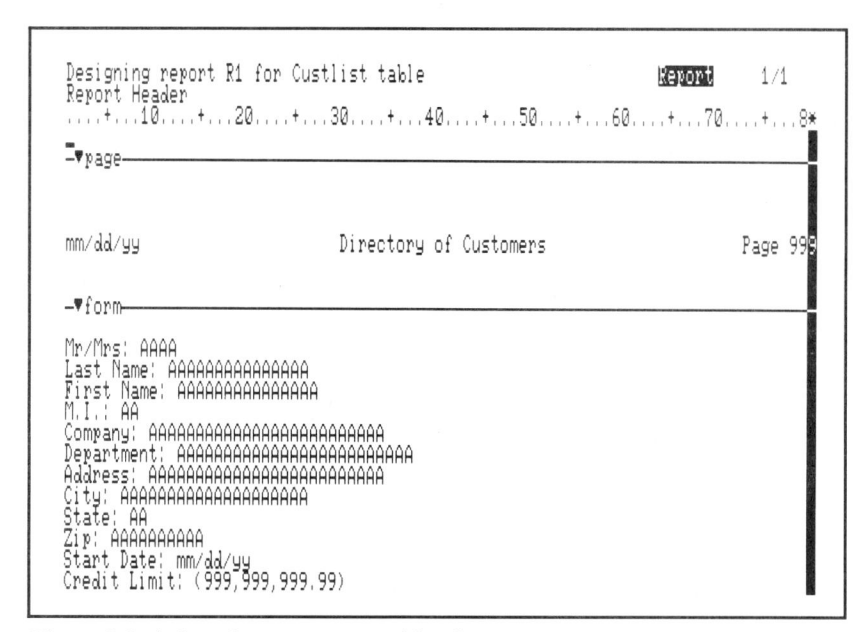

Figure 8.2: A free-form report specification

(mm/dd/yy), title (Directory of Customers), and page number will be displayed at the top of each page (unless we make changes).

Within the page band is the form band. The form band shows what will be printed for each record in the table. The contents of the form band will be printed as many times as necessary to fill a single page. In other words, while the heading will appear only at the top of each page, the contents of the form band may be repeated several times on a page.

To get the exact format we want for the directory, we'll need to modify this suggested format on the report specification. As usual, you can use the arrow keys to move the cursor up, down, left, and right, and Backspace and Ctrl-Backspace to delete items and make corrections. In addition, you can use the keys listed in Table 8.1 to help design a report format.

Table 8.1: Keys used for designing report formats

KEY	EFFECT
Ctrl-←	Moves left half a screen
Ctrl-→	Moves right half a screen
PgUp	Moves up one screen
PgDn	Moves down one screen
Home	Moves to first line of screen
Ctrl-Home	Moves to beginning of line
End	Moves to last line
Ctrl-End	Moves to last character of line
Ins	Turns Insert mode on/off
Del	Deletes character at cursor
Ctrl-Y	Deletes all characters to right of cursor
Ctrl-V	Turns vertical ruler line on/off
Enter	If Insert mode is on, inserts a blank line

Note that the Ctrl-Y key combination deletes all characters to the right of the cursor. If the cursor is in the leftmost column, Ctrl-Y deletes the entire line.

The Ins key toggles the Insert mode on and off. When Insert mode is on, newly typed characters are inserted between existing characters, and pressing the Enter key inserts a whole new line. When Insert mode is off, newly typed characters overwrite existing characters, and pressing Enter merely moves the cursor to the next line. We'll get a little practice with these keys in this chapter.

Now let's get to work. Use the arrow keys to move the cursor to the start of the Mr/Mrs field, as below:

Mr/Mrs: AAAA

Type Ctrl-Y to delete the entire line.

Next, press the Del key 11 times to erase the words *Last Name* and the colon, so that the form band looks like this:

```
AAAAAAAAAAAAAAA
First Name: AAAAAAAAAAAAAAA
M.I.: AA
Company: AAAAAAAAAAAAAAAAAAAAAAAAA
Address: AAAAAAAAAAAAAAAAAAAAAAAAA
City: AAAAAAAAAAAAAAAAAAAA
State: AA
Zip: AAAAAAAAA
Start Date: mm/dd/yy
Credit Limit: (999,999,999.99)
```

Notice that most fields have *templates,* consisting of the letter A or the number 9, next to them. These act as markers that tell you where a field's contents will appear on the printed report and how much room they'll take up. (The size and configuration come from the original table structure.) You can tell which template goes with which field by moving the cursor into the template and looking at the upper-right corner of the screen. For example, when the cursor is in the current template, the upper-right corner of the screen shows the words *Last Name.*

Now type Ctrl-End to move the cursor to the last character of this template, and type in a comma. Then press the Space bar, so the top line looks like this:

AAAAAAAAAAAAAAA, –

PLACING FIELDS

Now let's put the Mr/Mrs title next to the last name, after the comma. With the cursor in its current position, press Menu (F10) to call up the Report menu. Note that you are given several new options, as below:

Field Group Output Setting Help DO-IT! Cancel

To place a field on the report specification, select the Field option. Another submenu appears, as below:

Place Erase Reformat Justify CalcEdit WordWrap Lookup

We want to place a field, so select the Place option. Now another submenu appears:

Regular Summary Calculated Date Time Page #Record

Mr/Mrs is a regular table field, so select the Regular option.

At this point Paradox displays a menu of field names. Press Enter to select the Mr/Mrs option. The screen displays these instructions:

Use ↑↓ → ← to indicate where field should begin . . .
then press ⏎ to place it . . .

The cursor is already at the position we want to display the Mr/Mrs field, so just press Enter.

Next, Paradox instructs you as follows:

Now use → and ← to indicate how many characters to show . . .
press ⏎ when finished.

We want to show all the characters in the Mr/Mrs field, so just press the Enter key.

You'll notice that when the cursor is in the new AAAA template, the upper-right corner of the screen displays the name of the field, Mr/Mrs. Again, this is just to help you keep track of which template goes with which field.

Now let's place the First Name field next to the Mr/Mrs field. Press the → key twice so there is a space between the last A in the Mr/Mrs template and the cursor, as below:

AAAAAAAAAAAAAA, AAAA   –

Place the First Name field here by following these steps:

1. Press the Menu (F10) key.
2. Select Field.
3. Select Place.
4. Select Regular.
5. Select First Name.

Once again, Paradox will ask that you place the cursor and then specify a size. Just press Enter in response to both these prompts.

Now, to place the middle initial, press the → key twice to move the cursor to the right. Again, call up the menu (press F10) and select the Field, Place, and Regular options; then select the M.I. option from the menu. Press Enter twice to bypass the two questions about placement and size.

Now the report specification has the entire name in a single row, with a comma after the last name:

Last Name, Mr/Mrs First Name M.I.

(For example, *Smith, Dr. Albert T.*) We no longer need the First Name and M.I. fields from the lines below, so use ↓ and Ctrl-← to move the cursor down a line and to the leftmost column. Then type Ctrl-Y twice to erase the original suggested First Name and M.I. rows. Your screen should look like Figure 8.3.

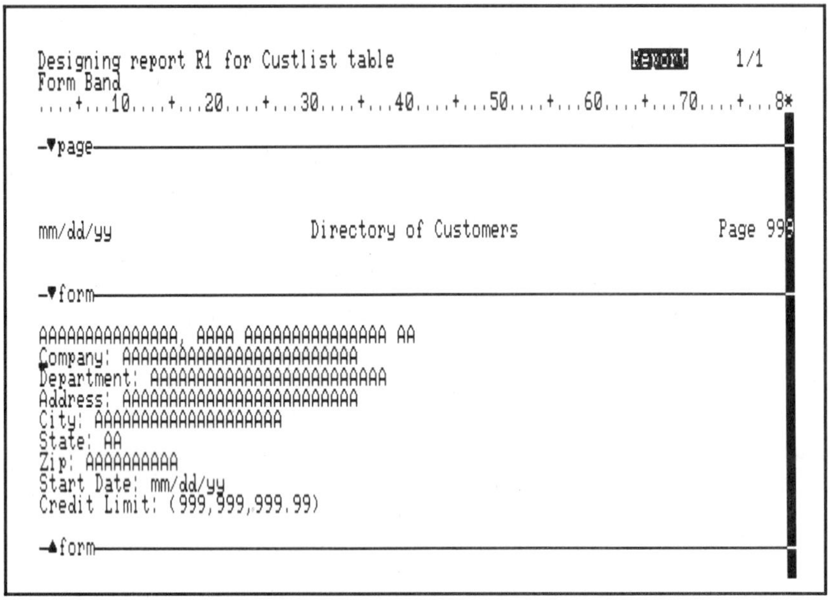

```
Designing report R1 for Custlist table                    Report    1/1
Form Band
....+...10....+...20....+...30....+...40....+...50....+...60....+...70....+...8*
 -▼page─────────────────────────────────────────────────────────────────


   mm/dd/yy                  Directory of Customers              Page 999
 -▼form─────────────────────────────────────────────────────────────────
   AAAAAAAAAAAAAA, AAAA AAAAAAAAAAAAAA AA
   Company: AAAAAAAAAAAAAAAAAAAAAAAA
   Department: AAAAAAAAAAAAAAAAAAAAAAAA
   Address: AAAAAAAAAAAAAAAAAAAAAAAA
   City: AAAAAAAAAAAAAAAAAAAA
   State: AA
   Zip: AAAAAAAAA
   Start Date: mm/dd/yy
   Credit Limit: (999,999,999.99)
 -▲form─────────────────────────────────────────────────────────────────
```

Figure 8.3: The name portion of the directory defined

Now let's erase the title *Company:* but leave the contents of the field indented. First, make sure the Insert mode is off. (Press the Ins key repeatedly, and watch for the Ins message to appear and disappear at the upper-right corner of the screen. Stop pressing when the Ins message does *not* appear on the screen.) Now, overwrite *Company:* with spaces by pressing the Space bar eight times. Your form band should now look something like this:

```
          AAAAAAAAAAAAAA, AAAA AAAAAAAAAAAAAA AA
                   AAAAAAAAAAAAAAAAAAAAAAAA
Department: AAAAAAAAAAAAAAAAAAAAAAAA
Address: AAAAAAAAAAAAAAAAAAAAAAAA
City: AAAAAAAAAAAAAAAAAAAA
State: AA
Zip: AAAAAAAAA
Start Date: mm/dd/yy
Credit Limit: (999,999,999.99)
```

Let's take care of the Department field now. Press ↓, then Ctrl-←. Press the Space bar nine times to overwrite most of the word

Department:, then press Del three times to delete the rest of the word and line up the Department template with the Company template, as follows:

AAAAAAAAAAAAAA, AAAA AAAAAAAAAAAAAA AA
              AAAAAAAAAAAAAAAAAAAAAAAA
              AAAAAAAAAAAAAAAAAAAAAAAA
Address: AAAAAAAAAAAAAAAAAAAAAAAAA
City: AAAAAAAAAAAAAAAAAAA
State: AA
Zip: AAAAAAAAA
Start Date: mm/dd/yy
Credit Limit: (999,999,999.99)

For the Address field, press ↓, then Ctrl-←. Press the Space bar eight times to erase the *Address:* heading.

For the City field, press ↓, Ctrl-←, and then the Space bar five times to erase the *City:* heading. To get the City template aligned with the others, press the Ins key so that the Insert mode is on. (The word Ins appears in the upper-right corner of the screen.) Press the Space bar three times to move the template to the right. Your screen should look like this:

AAAAAAAAAAAAAA, AAAA AAAAAAAAAAAAAA AA
              AAAAAAAAAAAAAAAAAAAAAAAA
              AAAAAAAAAAAAAAAAAAAAAAAA
              AAAAAAAAAAAAAAAAAAAAAAAAA
              AAAAAAAAAAAAAAAAAAA
State: AA
Zip: AAAAAAAAA
Start Date: mm/dd/yy
Credit Limit: (999,999,999.99)

Now we want to place a comma after the city and tack on the State and Zip fields. Press Ctrl-End to move the cursor to the last character of the City template. Then type in a comma and press the Space bar, so the line looks like this:

        AAAAAAAAAAAAAAAAAAA, –

Call up the menu and select the Field, Place, and Regular options. Select State from the menu of field names, and press Enter twice to bypass the prompts about position and size.

Now press the → key four times. Place the Zip field by pressing Menu (F10) and selecting the usual Field, Place, and Regular options. Select Zip from the menu of field names, and press Enter twice to bypass the position and size prompts.

We don't need the original suggested City and State fields anymore, so press ↓, Ctrl-←, then Ctrl-Y twice to erase the original fields. Now your screen should look like Figure 8.4.

```
Designing report R1 for Custlist table              Report  Ins 1/1
Form Band
....+...10....+...20....+...30....+...40....+...50....+...60....+...70....+...8*
-▼page─────────────────────────────────────────────────────────────────────────


  mm/dd/yy                   Directory of Customers                  Page 999

-▼form─────────────────────────────────────────────────────────────────────────

  AAAAAAAAAAAAAA, AAAA AAAAAAAAAAAAAA AA
               AAAAAAAAAAAAAAAAAAAAAAAA
               AAAAAAAAAAAAAAAAAAAAAAAA
               AAAAAAAAAAAAAAAAAAAAAAAA
               AAAAAAAAAAAAAAAAAA, AA     AAAAAAAAA
  Start Date: mm/dd/yy
  Credit Limit: (999,999,999.99)

-▲form─────────────────────────────────────────────────────────────────────────

```

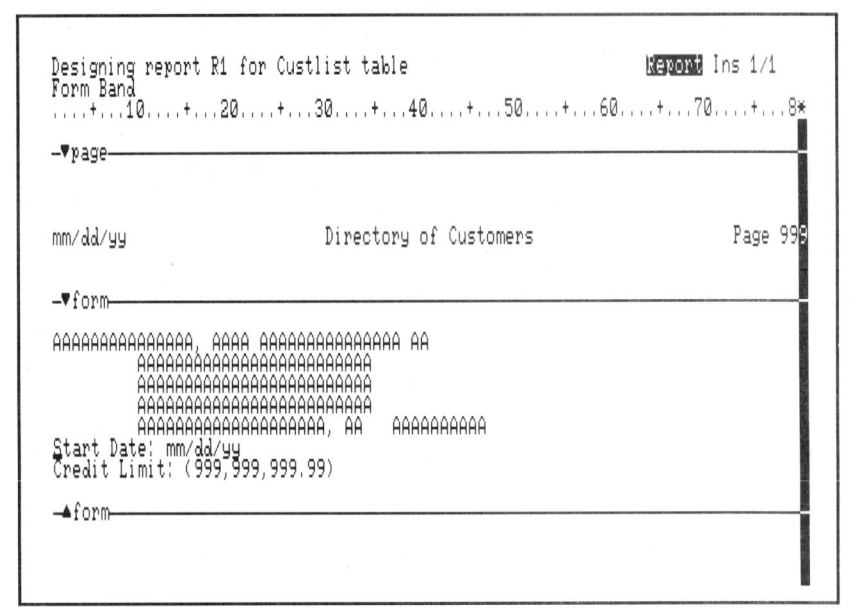

Figure 8.4: The Name and Address portions of the directory defined

Let's take care of the Start Date and Credit Limit fields now. First, press the Space bar nine times (the Insert mode is still on) to move the Start Date field to the right nine places. Next, press Ctrl-End, then the → key seven times so that the cursor is to the right of the Start Date template, aligned with the Zip template, as below:

```
AAAAAAAAAAAAAA, AAAA AAAAAAAAAAAAAA AA
         AAAAAAAAAAAAAAAAAAAAAAAA
         AAAAAAAAAAAAAAAAAAAAAAAA
         AAAAAAAAAAAAAAAAAAAAAAAA
         AAAAAAAAAAAAAAAAAA,  AA    AAAAAAAAA
         Start Date: mm/dd/yy              _
```

Now, type

Credit Limit:

(including the colon and a space). Place the Credit Limit field by using the usual method. (Press Menu (F10), select the Field, Place, and Regular options, and select the Credit Limit field.) Because Credit Limit is a currency field, Paradox will ask about the position, size, and number of decimal places to display. Once again, you can just press Enter in response to these prompts, because the default values are adequate.

We don't need the Credit Limit field down below anymore, so press ↓ and Ctrl-←, then Ctrl-Y to delete the line. Now your screen should look like Figure 8.5.

ADDING THE RECORD NUMBER

It's always nice (though not necessary) to have a record number on a printed report to simplify looking up table data from a printed

```
Designing report R1 for Custlist table                    Report  Ins 1/1
Form Band
....+...10....+...20....+...30....+...40....+...50....+...60....+...70....+...8*
—▼page—————————————————————————————————————————————————————

mm/dd/yy                    Directory of Customers              Page 999

—▼form—————————————————————————————————————————————————————
AAAAAAAAAAAAAAA, AAAA AAAAAAAAAAAAAAA AA
         AAAAAAAAAAAAAAAAAAAAAAAAAA
         AAAAAAAAAAAAAAAAAAAAAAAAAA
         AAAAAAAAAAAAAAAAAAAAAAAAAA
         AAAAAAAAAAAAAAAAAAAA, AA    AAAAAAAAA
         Start Date: mm/dd/yy        Credit Limit:(999,999,999.99)
—▲form—————————————————————————————————————————————————————
```

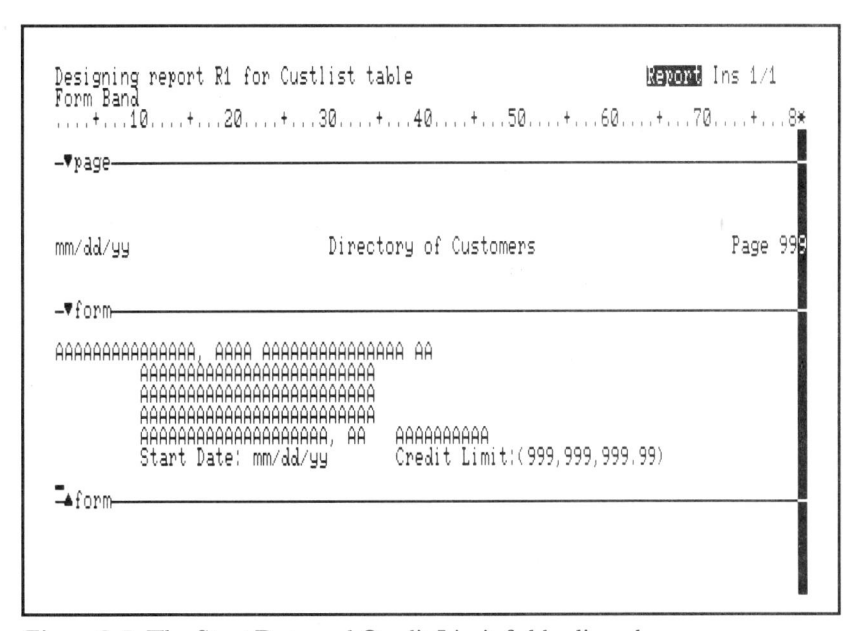

Figure 8.5: The Start Date and Credit Limit fields aligned

directory. We can add the record number to the directory by following these steps. First, press ↑ twice to move the cursor to the City-State-Zip line. Position the cursor somewhere to the right of the Zip template, and type an open parenthesis, as below:

AAAAAAAAAAAAAAAAAAAA,   AA   AAAAAAAAAA   (

To the right of this parenthesis, we'll put the record number. Call up the menu (press F10) and select the Field and Place options. From the submenu, select the #Record option (which always displays the current record number). Next, select the Overall option (since this report uses no grouping), and press Enter twice to bypass the position and size prompts. (Grouping is a technique used most often in reports that contain subtotals. We'll discuss such reports in a later chapter.)

Press → until the cursor is to the right of the last 9 on the 999 template. Type a closing parenthesis to surround the record-number template. That should just about do it. Your screen should now look like Figure 8.6.

```
Designing report R1 for Custlist table                    Report Ins 1/1
Form Band
....+...10....+...20....+...30....+...40....+...50....+...60....+...70....+...8*
—▼page——————————————————————————————————————————————————————————


 mm/dd/yy                    Directory of Customers                 Page 999
—▼form——————————————————————————————————————————————————————————

AAAAAAAAAAAAAAA, AAAA AAAAAAAAAAAAAAA AA
              AAAAAAAAAAAAAAAAAAAAAAAAA
              AAAAAAAAAAAAAAAAAAAAAAAAA
              AAAAAAAAAAAAAAAAAAAAAAAAA
              AAAAAAAAAAAAAAAAAAAAA, AA    AAAAAAAAAA  (999)
              Start Date: mm/dd/yy         Credit Limit:(999,999,999.99)
—▲form——————————————————————————————————————————————————————————
```

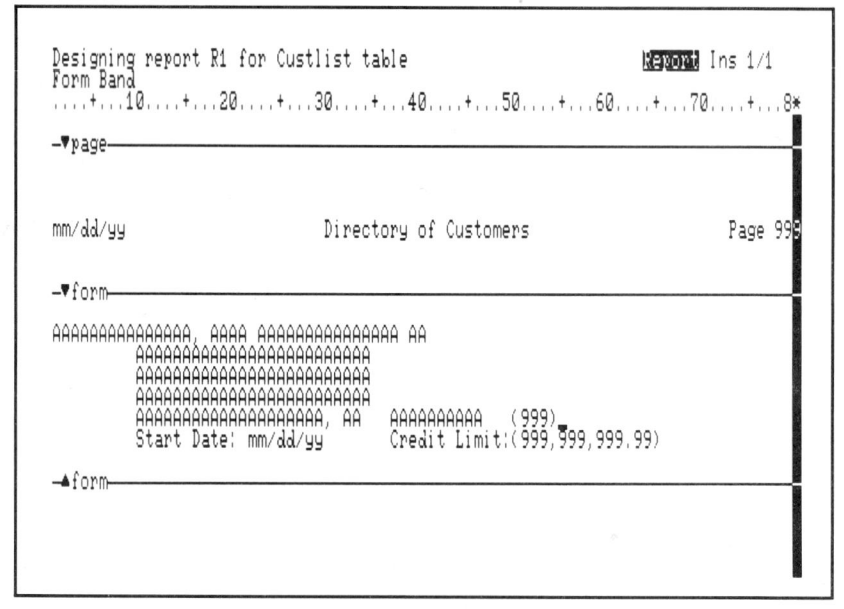

Figure 8.6: The completed report format for the directory

You might want to take a moment now to compare the report format that appears on the screen (and in Figure 8.6) to the actual printed report shown in Figure 8.1. Notice how the A's show the placement of various alphanumeric fields on the report, the 9's show the placement of numbers (including Currency values), and the mm/dd/yy shows where the date is displayed. In addition, the actual words Start Date and Credit Limit, and the parentheses surrounding the record number, appear directly on the report format.

Note also that we've used the basic editing keys listed in Table 8.1 to move, insert, and delete information from the original "suggested" format to create the format we want. In addition, we've used a few basic menu selections to place fields directly on the report format. (If you're feeling like this went a bit too quickly, don't worry. You'll get more practice in this chapter.)

A TRIAL RUN

Before we save this report format, let's take a look at an actual report that it will produce. To do so, call up the menu (press F10) and select Output. For our trial run, we'll just take a look at the report on the screen, so select the Screen option from the displayed submenu. You'll see the report go by on the screen in pages, as in Figure 8.7.

The basic format is right, but as you can see, the report is not quite in tip-top shape. As you press any key to scroll from page to page, you'll see that the fields include the blank spaces allocated for the field in the table structure. Also, people who have no company or department data have blank lines in their records. It looks like the directory still needs a little work.

To finish viewing the report, keep pressing any key until you see the prompt

>**End of Report**
>**Press any key to continue...**

Then press any key to view the report format once again. Now let's get to work on taking out all those extraneous blank spaces and blank lines.

```
Now Viewing Page 1 of Page Width 1
Press any key to continue...


    3/31/90                Directory of Customers              Page    1


   Abzug            , Miss Ann              Z.

            301 Crest Dr.
            Encinitas           , CA   92024           (   1)
            Start Date:  3/01/90      Credit Limit:     7,500.00

   Adams            , Mr.  Andy             A.

            234 Ocean View Dr.
            San Diego           , CA   92038           (   2)
            Start Date:  1/15/90      Credit Limit:     2,500.00
```

Figure 8.7: The directory report still in need of a little work

SQUEEZING OUT THE BLANKS

To delete extraneous blanks from the printed report format, press F10 while the report format is displayed on the screen to call up the Report menu. Select the Setting option, which displays the following submenu of options:

    RemoveBlanks   PageLayout   Margin   Setup   Wait   Labels

Right now, we'll be concerned only with the RemoveBlanks option. Select it, and you'll see this submenu:

    LineSqueeze   FieldSqueeze

To squeeze out blank lines (like empty Company and Department fields on some records), select the LineSqueeze option, and answer Yes to the ensuing prompt. Do so now.

The next submenu displays the options and prompt

**Fixed   Variable
Forms are the same length; blank lines moved to the bottom.**

If you select Fixed, blank lines will be squeezed out of individual records, but added to the bottom of each page so that the same number of records appear on each page. If you highlight the Variable option (by pressing →), the prompt displays

Forms are variable length; blank lines deleted.

which means that any blank lines will be deleted entirely, and thus not carried to the bottom of the page. Since it is not necessary to include exactly the same number of records on each page in this report format, press Enter while the Variable option is highlighted to select that option.

We also need to squeeze out all those blank spaces from people's names. So call up the menu (F10) again and select the Setting and RemoveBlanks options. Then select FieldSqueeze and answer Yes to the next prompt to squeeze out trailing blanks from individual fields.

Let's take another look at the report. Call up the menu (press F10) and select the Output and Screen options. You'll see a much-improved version of the directory, as shown in Figure 8.8. Keep pressing any key to scroll through the pages of the report, until you see the report specification again.

SAVING A REPORT FORMAT

We certainly do not want to go through all these steps each time we want to print a directory, so let's save this format for future use. To do so, just press the DO-IT! (F2) key. You'll be returned to the Main menu.

CANCELING A REPORT FORMAT

If by some chance you really make a mess of your report and want to start all over from scratch, you can cancel and abandon your work

```
Now Viewing Page 1 of Page Width 1
Press any key to continue...


    3/31/90              Directory of Customers              Page   1


    Abzug, Miss Ann Z.
          301 Crest Dr.
          Encinitas, CA   92024     (1)
          Start Date: 3/01/90       Credit Limit: 7,500.00

    Adams, Mr. Andy A.
          234 Ocean View Dr.
          San Diego, CA   92038     (2)
          Start Date: 1/15/90       Credit Limit: 2,500.00

    Davis, Ms. Randi
          371 Oceanic Way
          Manhattan Beach, CA   90001     (3)
```

Figure 8.8: The directory report with extra blanks removed

by calling up the Report menu (F10) and selecting the Cancel option. Paradox will double-check for permission before abandoning the report format. (*Note:* You can always change a report format after it is saved, so you need not cancel every time you make a small mistake.) You'll be returned to the Main menu.

PRINTING THE SORTED DIRECTORY

Let's now make a nice printed copy of our directory. If you haven't saved the report format yet, do so now by pressing DO-IT!.

PRESORTING THE TABLE

Before you print the directory, you might as well sort it into alphabetical order by name. Select the Modify option from the Main menu and the Sort option from the submenu. Specify the Custlist table, and select Same when asked how to sort the table. Make Last

Name the first sort field, First Name the second sort field, and M.I. the third sort field on the sort form, as shown below:

```
  Mr/Mrs
1 Last Name
2 First Name
3 M.I.
  Company
  Address
  City
  State
  Zip
  Start Date
  Credit Limit
```

Press the DO-IT! (F2) key. After a brief delay, the data will appear on the screen in the appropriate sort order.

PRINTING A REPORT FROM THE MAIN MENU

To print a report from the Main menu (F10), select the Report option. This will bring up the submenu

Output   Design   Change   RangeOutput   SetPrinter

Select the Output option to print the report. When Paradox asks for the name of the table to use, enter or select Custlist. Next, Paradox asks which report you want to print, as below:

R   1

R is the standard tabular report that Paradox prints by default. If you move the highlight to the 1, you'll see the description associated with report #1, as shown below:

R   1
Directory of Customers

Press Enter to select this report.

Finally, Paradox gives you three options for displaying the report, as below:

Printer   Screen   File

Selecting the Printer option will print the report. Selecting Screen displays the report on the screen only. Selecting File allows you to assign a file name, and then the report is stored on disk under the file name you assign. (This option is sometimes used to pass reports to word processed documents, as we'll discuss in Chapter 16.)

For now, select the Printer option. (Make sure your printer is hooked up, turned on, and on line.) You'll see the printed report, with the first page looking something like Figure 8.9.

FINE-TUNING YOUR REPORT

After printing your report, you may find that some more changes are needed in the general format, such as a change in page length, width, or margins. Let's discuss general techniques for formatting a report on the printed page.

CHANGING AN EXISTING REPORT FORMAT

To modify an existing report, select the Report option from the Main menu and the Change option from the submenu. Paradox will prompt you for the name of the associated table (enter Custlist in this example) and then display a menu of existing reports, as below:

R   1

Select the 1 option to modify the Directory of Customers report. Paradox will display the report description and allow you to modify it. To retain the original report description, just press Enter. The report format appears on the screen, ready for editing.

The keys you use to modify the report at this point are identical to those used when creating it. So you can easily move the cursor around, place fields, and so forth, just as we did when first creating the report. Now we'll look at other ways to change the appearance of the report.

```
3/31/90           Directory of Customers          Page    1


Abzug, Miss Ann Z.
        301 Crest Dr.
        Encinitas, CA    92024    (1)
        Start Date: 3/01/90          Credit Limit:7,500.00




Adams, Mr. Andy A.
        234 Ocean View Dr.
        San Diego, CA    92038    (2)
        Start Date: 1/15/90          Credit Limit:2,500.00



Davis, Ms. Randi
        371 Oceanic Way
        Manhattan Beach, CA    90001    (3)
        Start Date: 3/01/90          Credit Limit:7,500.00




Gladstone, Miss Tara Rose
        Waterside, Inc.
        Acquisitions
        P.O. Box 121
        New York, NY    12345    (4)
        Start Date: 2/28/90          Credit Limit:15,000.00


Jackson, Ms. Janet J.
        Zeerox, Inc.
        Accounts Payable
        1234 Corporate Hwy.
        Los Angeles, CA    91234    (5)
        Start Date: 1/01/90          Credit Limit:10,000.00


Kenney, Mr. Clark E.
        Legal Aid
        371 Ave. of the Americas
        New York, NY    12345    (6)
        Start Date: 1/31/90          Credit Limit:5,000.00
```

Figure 8.9: The first page of the printed Directory of Customers

CHANGING HEADING AND FOOTING MARGINS

You can change the size of the margins at the top and bottom of each printed page by changing the gap between the page band and the form band. For example, if you move the cursor down to near the bottom of the screen (under the bottom form band marker and above the bottom page band marker), you can type Ctrl-Y a few times to narrow the gap between the two bands. Figure 8.10 shows the directory report format with a smaller margin at the bottom of each page. Note how close the bottom form band and page band are.

```
Changing report R1 for Custlist table                    Report    1/1
Page Footer
....+...10....+...20....+...30....+...40....+...50....+...60....+...70....+...8*
-▼page─────────────────────────────────────────────────────────────


mm/dd/yy                     Directory of Customers              Page 999
-▼form─────────────────────────────────────────────────────────────
AAAAAAAAAAAAAAA, AAAA AAAAAAAAAAAAAAA AA
          AAAAAAAAAAAAAAAAAAAAAAAAA
          AAAAAAAAAAAAAAAAAAAAAAAAA
          AAAAAAAAAAAAAAAAAAAAAAAAA
          AAAAAAAAAAAAAAAAAAAAAA, AA    AAAAAAAAAA  (999)
          Start Date: mm/dd/yy          Credit Limit:(999,999,999.99)
-▲form─────────────────────────────────────────────────────────────
-▲page─────────────────────────────────────────────────────────────
```

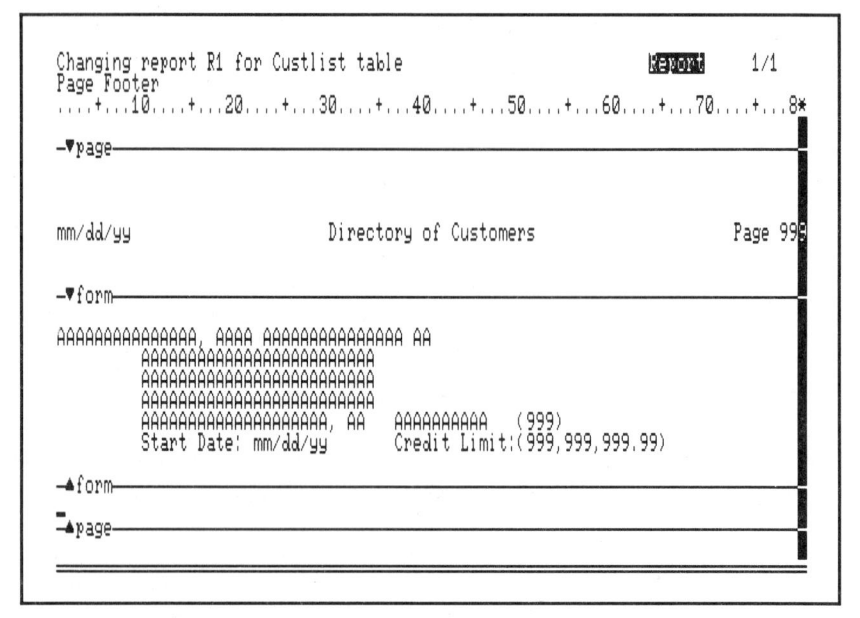

Figure 8.10: The page footer size reduced on the Directory report

You can change the size of the heading margin in the same manner. Put the cursor between the page band and form band lines near the top of the screen, and use Ctrl-Y to delete blank lines. To increase the size of the margin, make sure Insert mode is on and press Enter a few times.

Deleting blank lines between the form bands and page bands reduces the white space at the top and bottom of each printed page. You may want to experiment with this on your own.

ADJUSTING PAGE LENGTH

Most often, you will probably be using 8½ by 11-inch paper in your printer, so there won't be any need to change the page length. However, if you do need to adjust the page length, simply call up the Report menu, select the Setting option, and then select the PageLayout option. The PageLayout submenu will appear as follows:

    Length   Width   Insert   Delete

Select the Length option. The screen will display

> New page length: 66
> Enter number of lines per page.

To leave the setting at the usual 66 lines per page, just press Enter. Otherwise, enter a new page length and then press Enter. (For now, 66 lines per page is fine.)

ADJUSTING PAGE WIDTH

The default page width for reports is 80 characters, which is good for the screen but leaves little room for margins on an 8½ by 11-inch sheet of paper. To change the page width, select Setting from the Report menu, and PageLayout and then Width from the submenus. Paradox will display

> Enter new page width: 80
> Enter the new width for report pages, or press ← to leave unchanged.

Press the Backspace key twice to erase the 80, then type in 75 and press Enter. You'll notice that the bar marking the right edge of the page moves to the left five spaces on the report specification. This causes the page number to extend beyond the right margin, which we'll have to rectify. But before doing so, let's add a left margin. First, so you can better see the report specification, press Ctrl-Home to scroll to the left.

CHANGING THE MARGIN SETTING

To change or add a margin, select the Setting option from the Report menu and the Margin setting from the submenu. Paradox displays this prompt:

> Margin size: 0
> Enter the new width for the left margin, or press ← to leave unchanged.

For now, enter the number 5 and press Enter.

When the report specification reappears, you'll see that everything has been shifted to the right. Now the heading extends well beyond the right margin (which will cause part of it to be displayed on a separate page). To rectify this situation, simply move the cursor to the heading line, somewhere between the date and the title (with spaces to the right of the cursor). Press the Del key to delete a few blank spaces so that the title moves in closer to the center of the report.

Next, move the cursor to the right of the title, but leave space in front of the page number. Again, press the Del key to pull the page number in from the right. You may have to experiment a little bit to get everything within the margins and reasonably centered, as in Figure 8.11.

When you've made these changes in the format, save them by pressing the DO-IT! (F2) key. You may want to print a copy of the report again by selecting the Report and Output options from the Main and Report menus.

As you can see from this exercise, designing a report is an iterative process. You can "rough out" a report by placing fields within the

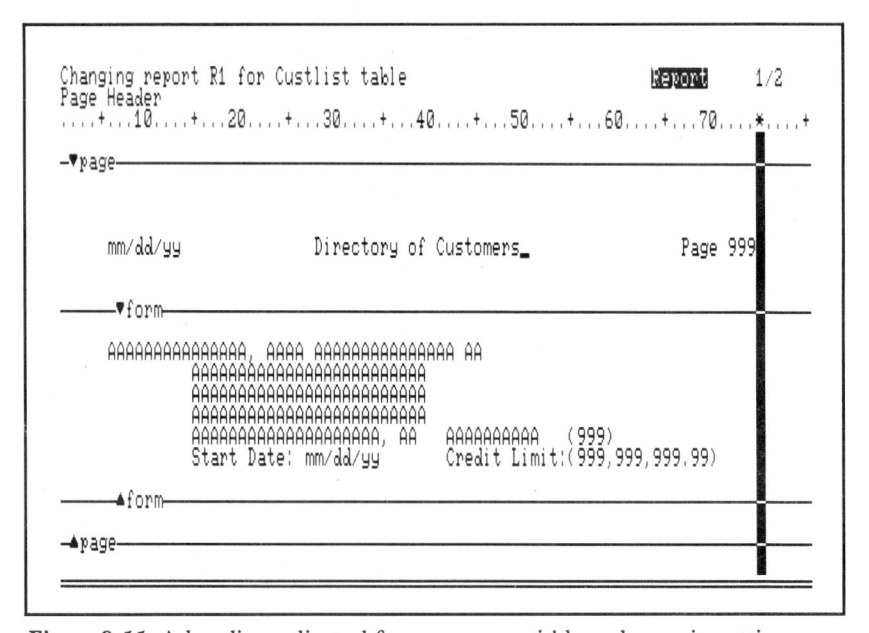

```
Changing report R1 for Custlist table                    Report    1/2
Page Header
....+...10....+...20....+...30....+...40....+...50....+...60....+...70....*....+
 -▼page─────────────────────────────────────────────────────────────────

         mm/dd/yy              Directory of Customers_           Page 999
     ─▼form─────────────────────────────────────────────────────────────

        AAAAAAAAAAAAAAA, AAAA AAAAAAAAAAAAAAA AA
               AAAAAAAAAAAAAAAAAAAAAAAAAA
               AAAAAAAAAAAAAAAAAAAAAAAAAA
               AAAAAAAAAAAAAAAAAAAAAAAAAA
               AAAAAAAAAAAAAAAAAA, AA    AAAAAAAAA  (999)
               Start Date: mm/dd/yy     Credit Limit:(999,999,999.99)
     ─▲form─────────────────────────────────────────────────────────────
 ─▲page─────────────────────────────────────────────────────────────────
```

Figure 8.11: A heading adjusted for new page width and margin setting

form band and printing a copy. If what you get is not quite what you had in mind, simply return to the report specification and make changes. Just remember to press the DO-IT! key after creating or modifying a report format to save your work.

MAILING LABELS

The same techniques we used to develop a report format for printing a directory will help us print mailing labels. In fact, rather than develop a report format from scratch, we'll borrow the report format from our Directory of Customers report, since its format already resembles the address portion of a letter and will therefore require relatively little modification.

COPYING A REPORT FORMAT

Paradox has the ability to copy anything, although we will not discuss this topic in depth until Chapter 16. For now, we need to make a copy of the Directory report format to simplify the development of a mailing-labels report format. Select the Tools option from the Main menu and the Copy option from the submenu. Next, select the Report option.

Paradox presents the options SameTable and DifferentTable. You use SameTable to copy a report that's associated with a certain table to another number for that table. You use DifferentTable to copy a report that's associated with one table and to have the copy associated with another table. In this case, you want to make a copy of the Directory of Customers report for the current table, so select SameTable. When Paradox asks for the name of the table containing the report to copy, press Enter, and select CustList.

Paradox will display a list of existing report formats, as below:

   R   1

To copy the Directory format, select option 1. Paradox will then display a list of other report formats that you can copy to. Select 2 in this example, since it is the next unused option in the list. You'll see this message:

    Copying R1 report for Custlist to R2

indicating that copying is in progress.

Now, we need to change report 2 from an identical copy of the Directory report into a format for mailing labels. Select the Report option from the Main menu and the Change option from the submenu. Specify the Custlist table and report 2 (select 2 from the submenu).

Paradox will display the description of the report as Directory of Customers. Type Ctrl-Backspace to erase this description, and enter the description

    Mailing Labels

FORMATTING LABELS

Now you'll see the report specification on the screen. First of all, it's pretty obvious that mailing labels do not need a report heading. So delete the heading by placing the cursor just below and inside the page band (press ↓ twice). Then type Ctrl-Y until there is no heading at all, as in Figure 8.12.

Next, we need to reorganize the name portion of the label. Move the cursor to the line where the name currently appears. Make sure the cursor is in the leftmost column (type Ctrl-← if it is not). Make sure you are in the Insert mode (press the Ins key if not), then press the Space bar about 15 times to make room for the data we will be moving. Type Ctrl-← once again to move the cursor to the left column.

Place the Mr/Mrs field in the leftmost column by calling up the menu and selecting the Field, Place, and Regular options. Select the Mr/Mrs field from the menu, and press Enter twice to use the suggested position and size provided. Press → twice to make some space. Now place the First Name field by selecting the Field, Place, and Regular options from the menus provided and the First Name field from the menu of field names, and pressing Enter twice. Place the M.I. field by pressing → twice, then selecting the usual Field, Place, and Regular options from the menus, and M.I. from the field-name menu. Again, press Enter twice.

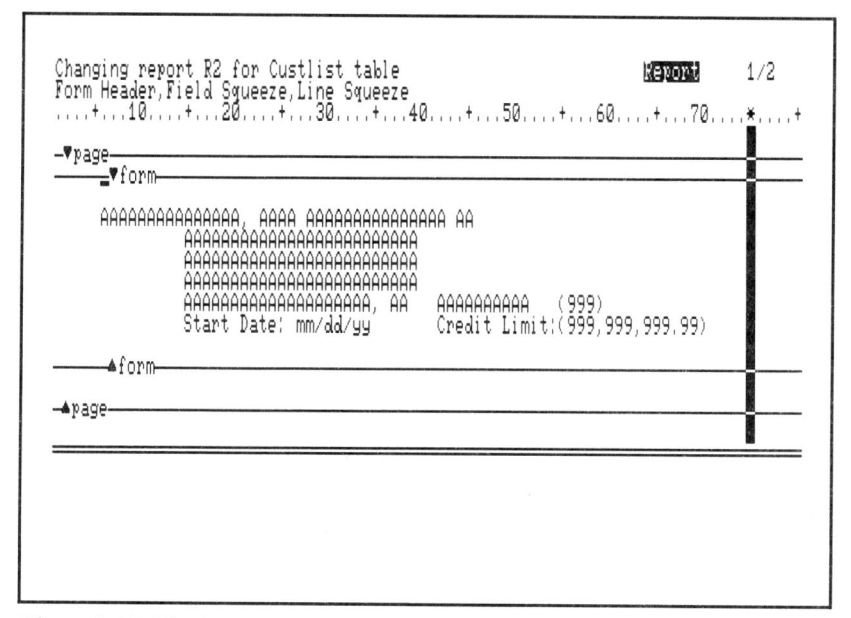

```
Changing report R2 for Custlist table                    Report    1/2
Form Header,Field Squeeze,Line Squeeze
....+...10....+...20....+...30....+...40....+...50....+...60....+...70....*....+
─▼page──────────────────────────────────────────────────────────
   ─▼form────────────────────────────────────────────────────
        AAAAAAAAAAAAAA, AAAA AAAAAAAAAAAAAA AA
                AAAAAAAAAAAAAAAAAAAAAAAAAA
                AAAAAAAAAAAAAAAAAAAAAAAAAA
                AAAAAAAAAAAAAAAAAAAAAAAAAA
                AAAAAAAAAAAAAAAAAAAA, AA   AAAAAAAAA  (999)
                Start Date: mm/dd/yy       Credit Limit:(999,999,999.99)
   ─▲form────────────────────────────────────────────────────
─▲page──────────────────────────────────────────────────────────
```

Figure 8.12: The heading removed for mailing labels

Now press → twice, and the Del key 12 times to bring the Last Name field template over to the M.I. field, leaving a blank space between. Move the cursor to the comma trailing the Last Name template, and type Ctrl-Y to delete everything to the right of the cursor. Your screen should now look something like Figure 8.13.

We no longer want the remaining fields to be indented. So press ↓ and Ctrl-← to move the cursor to the leftmost position on the screen. Press the Del key nine times to align the Company field template with the name field. Do the same for the Department, Address, and City-state-zip lines, so the screen looks like Figure 8.14.

DELETING A FIELD FROM A REPORT

We might as well get rid of the record number, since it won't do much good on a mailing label. To remove a field from a report specification, call up the Report menu and select the Field and the Erase options. As instructed, use the arrow keys to move the cursor to the field you wish to delete (999 on this screen), and press Enter. After

CH. 8

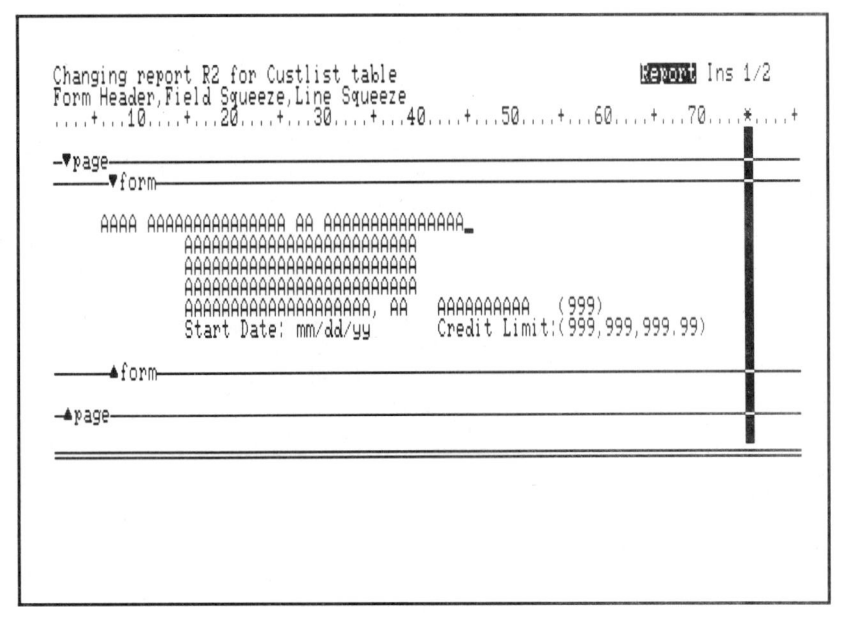

```
Changing report R2 for Custlist table              Report Ins 1/2
Form Header,Field Squeeze,Line Squeeze
....+...10....+...20....+...30....+...40....+...50....+...60....+...70....*....+
 ▼page
    ▼form
     AAAA AAAAAAAAAAAAAAA AA AAAAAAAAAAAAAA_
             AAAAAAAAAAAAAAAAAAAAAAAA
             AAAAAAAAAAAAAAAAAAAAAAAA
             AAAAAAAAAAAAAAAAAAAAAAAA
             AAAAAAAAAAAAAAAAAAAAAA, AA    AAAAAAAAA  (999)
             Start Date: mm/dd/yy     Credit Limit:(999,999,999.99)

    ▲form
 ▲page
```

Figure 8.13: The Name portion of mailing label modified

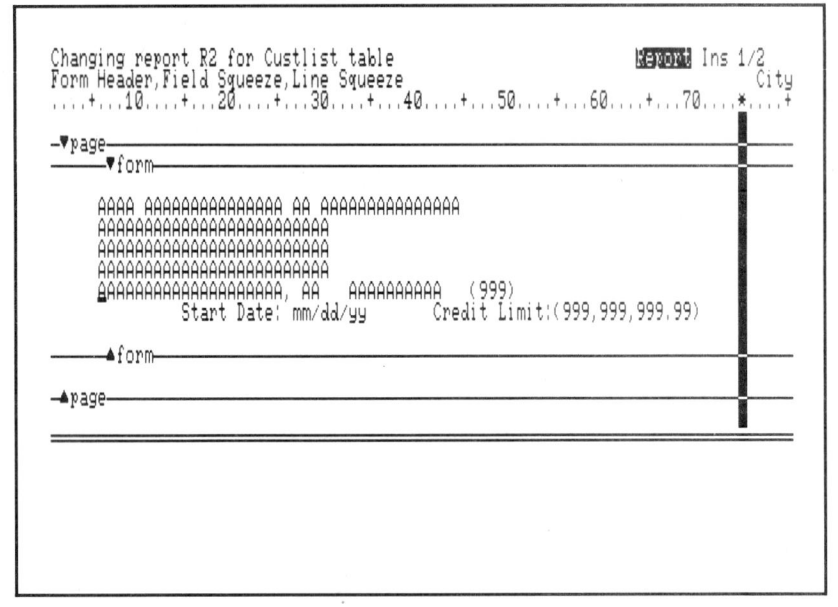

```
Changing report R2 for Custlist table              Report Ins 1/2
Form Header,Field Squeeze,Line Squeeze                          City
....+...10....+...20....+...30....+...40....+...50....+...60....+...70....*....+
 ▼page
    ▼form
     AAAA AAAAAAAAAAAAAAA AA AAAAAAAAAAAAAA
     AAAAAAAAAAAAAAAAAAAAAAAA
     AAAAAAAAAAAAAAAAAAAAAAAA
     AAAAAAAAAAAAAAAAAAAAAAAA
     AAAAAAAAAAAAAAAAAAAAAA, AA    AAAAAAAAA  (999)
             Start Date: mm/dd/yy     Credit Limit:(999,999,999.99)

    ▲form
 ▲page
```

Figure 8.14: The mailing-labels specification with name and address aligned

removing the field, you can get rid of the parentheses by using the Del key.

We won't need the Start Date and Credit Limit fields on mailing labels, so press ↓, Ctrl-←, and Ctrl-Y to delete this line from the screen.

Now we have to think a little about the way the address will fit on the labels. Most mailing labels are one inch tall, and most printers print six lines to the inch. Because the addresses are five lines long, we need to ensure that six lines are printed for each label so that each address will be placed on a separate label. To do this, leave one blank line inside the form band on the screen, and no blank lines between the form bands and page bands. Use Ctrl-Y to delete the blank line just above the bottom form band. Figure 8.15 shows how the screen looks when set up like this.

CONTINUOUS-FEED PAPER

Now all we need to do is tell Paradox to exclude *form feeds* between pages when printing labels. (Form feeds leave margins at the top and bottom of each printed page.) You do so by setting the page length to C (for continuous). Call up the Report menu and select the Setting,

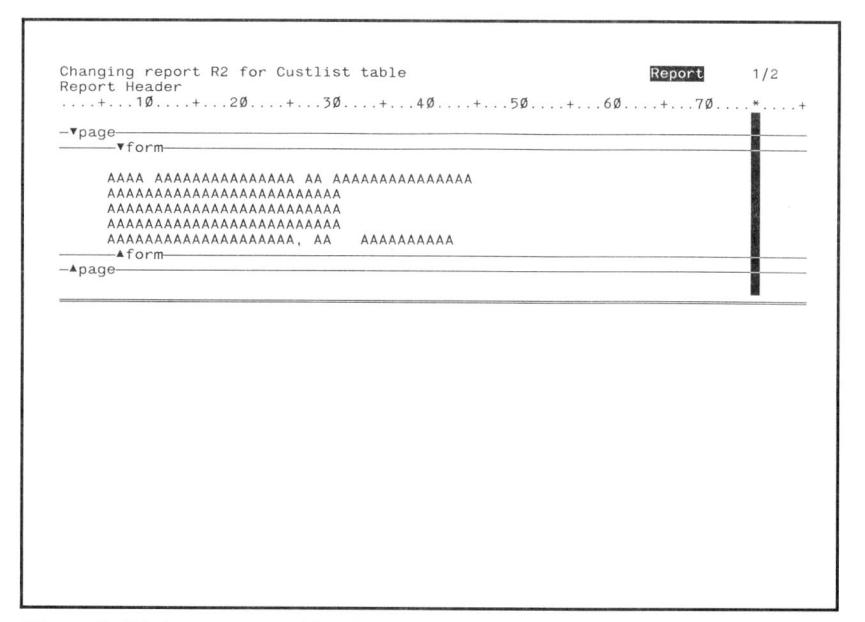

```
Changing report R2 for Custlist table                    Report    1/2
Report Header
....+...1Ø....+...2Ø....+...3Ø....+...4Ø....+...5Ø....+...6Ø....+...7Ø....*....+
—▼page
         —▼form
              AAAA AAAAAAAAAAAAAA AA AAAAAAAAAAAAAA
              AAAAAAAAAAAAAAAAAAAAAAAA
              AAAAAAAAAAAAAAAAAAAAAAAA
              AAAAAAAAAAAAAAAAAAAAAAAA
              AAAAAAAAAAAAAAAAAAAA, AA    AAAAAAAAA
         —▲form
—▲page
```

Figure 8.15: A report specification set up for 1-inch-tall labels

PageLayout, and Length options. Type Ctrl-Backspace to erase the current page length, type in the letter **C** as the new page length, and press Enter.

To ensure that each label prints with an identical height, you'll need to use a fixed line-squeeze setting. To do so, press F10 to call up the Report menu, select Setting, RemoveBlanks, LineSqueeze, Yes, and then Fixed to ensure that any blank lines that are squeezed out of a label are printed at the bottom of the label.

MULTIPLE LABEL COLUMNS

If you want to print more than one label across the page (as when printing two-across or three-across mailing labels), you need to use Paradox's label-format printing mode, with a left margin of zero and a page width equal to the width of each label. For example, suppose you want to print the names and addresses from the CustList table on two-across labels, each of which is four inches wide.

First, to switch to label-printing mode, press Menu (F10) and select the Setting option, then the Labels option, and then Yes. This setting tells Paradox to print as many labels as will fit across a full-width page after you set the width of each label. Next, you need to set the margins to reflect the width of each label (40 characters in this example). First, to set the left margin to zero, press Menu (F10) and select the Setting and Margin options. Press Backspace to erase the current margin setting, type in 0 (zero), and press Enter.

Next, change the page width to 40 characters (assuming your printer prints 10 characters to the inch, and labels are four inches across). To do so, press Menu (F10), and select Setting, then Page-Layout, and Width. Press Ctrl-Backspace to erase the old setting, type in 40, and press Enter. Then, save the new format by pressing DO-IT! (F2).

FINE-TUNING THE LABELS

To print a test run of labels, call up the Report Menu and select Output and either the Printer or Screen option. (If you are using a laser printer, you might need to print labels twice in order to see them. Optionally, you can use the "form feed" script presented in Chapter 19 to eject a page from a laser printer directly from the keyboard.)

If your labels look OK, press DO-IT (F2) to save the label format specification. If the format still needs work, you can continue making adjustments until you get the format you want. Note that if your labels are taller than one inch, you'll need to insert more blank lines within the form band, above the name template. (To do so, move the cursor to the blank line, make sure the Insert mode is on, and press Enter. To delete blank lines, make sure the cursor is in the leftmost column and type Ctrl-Y.)

If the left margin is incorrect on your label, you can use the Margin option under Setting on the Report menu to adjust the left margin setting.

If you are printing multi-column labels, and the printed labels are not properly aligned across the page, you will need to adjust the PageWidth option (on the Settings submenu) to print wider or narrower labels. In some cases, you may need to reduce the size of some field templates (using the Field and Reformat options on the menu) to make the page width sufficiently narrow.

If you want to print three-across labels, you may need to use compressed print, as discussed a little later in this chapter.

For example, if you wanted to print three-across labels, with each label three inches wide, you would need to select Report and Change from the Paradox Main menu, and modify the label format for the CustList table. Then you would need to remove the Mr/Mrs and M.I. field templates and rearrange all the field templates to fit within a 30-character-wide column. Next, you would adjust the page width to 30 (using the Setting, PageLayout and Width menu options) and then save the new format.

PRINTING THE MAILING LABELS

Once you are satisfied with your mailing-label format, save it either by pressing DO-IT! or by calling up the report menu and selecting the DO-IT! option. At any time in the future, you can print mailing labels simply by calling up the Paradox Main menu and selecting the Report and Output options. Specify Custlist as the table to print from, and select the options 2 (for the mailing-labels report format) and Printer from the submenus.

Of course, if you wish to print labels in zip code order, use the usual Modify and Sort options from the Main menu to sort by zip code, then use the Report and Output options to print the mailing labels.

FORM LETTERS

Our Mailing Labels report format is a good first step in getting a form letter started, so once again we'll make a copy of an existing report to help generate a new one. To copy the Mailing Labels report format, select the Tools option from the Main menu. Then select the Copy and Report options from the submenus. Specify the Custlist table. Select 2 (Mailing Labels) as the report to copy. Select 3 as the report to copy to. You'll briefly see this message as Paradox makes the copy:

Copying R2 report for Custlist to R3

When the menu reappears, you can begin creating your form letter. Select Report from the Main menu and Change from the submenu. Once again, specify the Custlist table when requested, and select report 3. When Paradox displays the report description, type Ctrl-Backspace to erase *Mailing Labels,* and enter

Form Letter

as the description. You'll then see the report specification appear with the mailing labels format.

Most letters start with a date at the top of the page. To put in the date, press ↓ three times so the cursor moves inside the form band. Type the current date the way you want it to appear on the letter. Then, put Insert mode on and press the Enter key once or twice. This will insert a blank line or two between the date and the address heading, as in Figure 8.16.

Use the arrow keys to move the cursor to below the city, state, and zip code, and press the Enter key to add some blank lines. (Remember, the Enter key only adds blank lines if the Insert mode is on.) Press ↑, then Ctrl-←, and type in the word **Dear.** Use the → key to put a space after the word *Dear,* then place either the First Name or Mr/Mrs and Last Name fields (depending on which style you prefer) after the word *Dear.* In this example, I've chosen First Name by calling up the Report menu, selecting the usual Field, Place, and Regular options, and then the First Name field choice. Press Enter twice, as usual, to accept the suggested placement and size. You can also type a colon after the template, as shown in Figure 8.17.

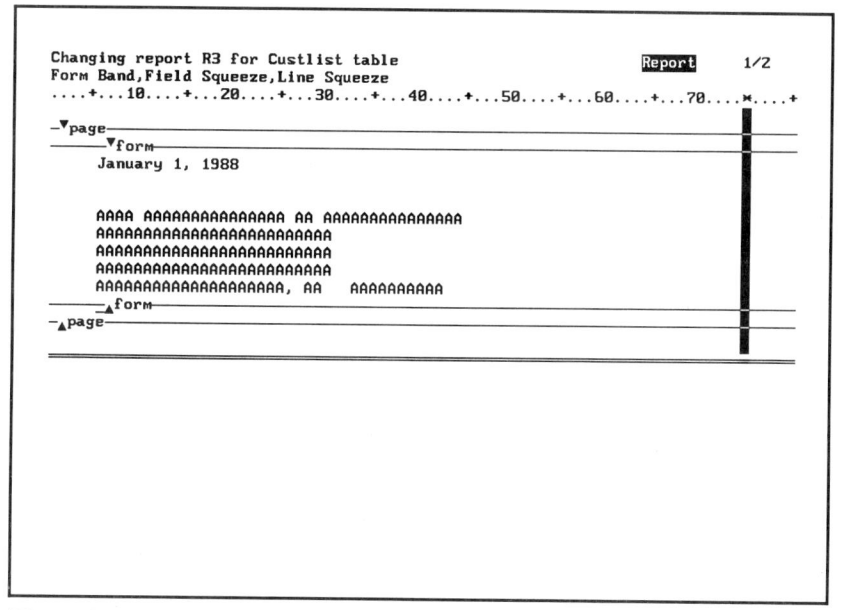

Figure 8.16: The date added to the top of the form letter

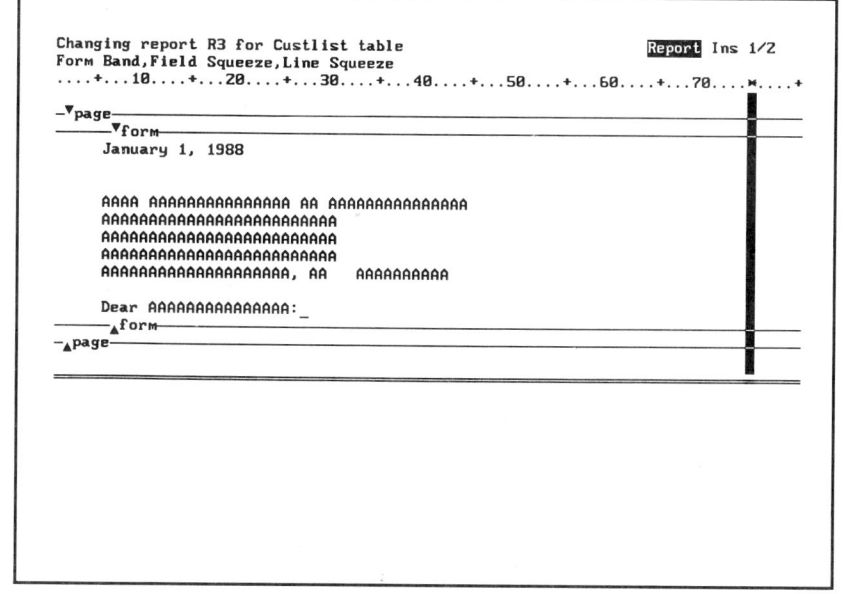

Figure 8.17: A form letter with salutation entered

Press the Enter key a few times to make room, then just type in your letter. Be sure to press Enter at the end of each line, before your text extends beyond the right margin.

You can place fields into the body of your letter at any time using the usual Report, Field, Place, and Regular menu options. In Figure 8.18, I've placed the First Name field into the first paragraph of the letter.

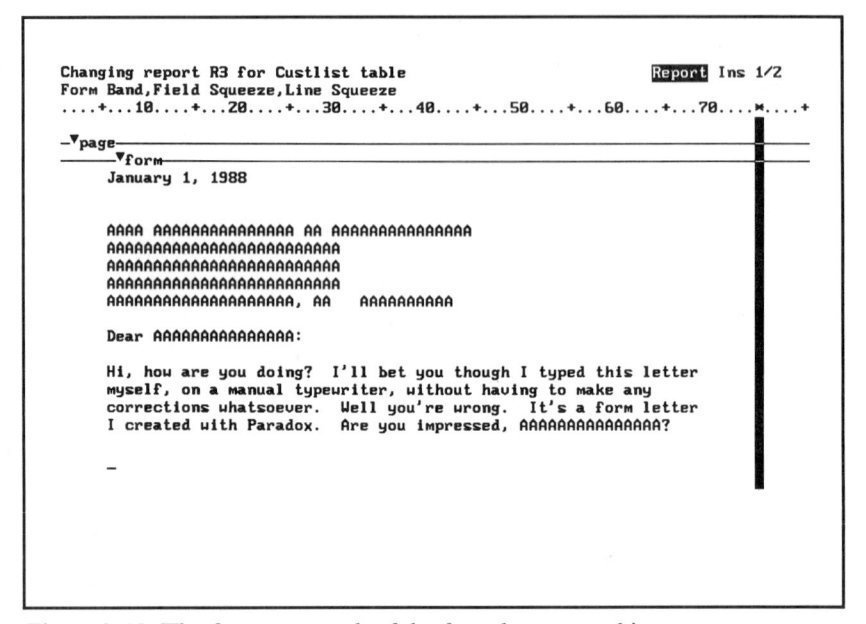

```
Changing report R3 for Custlist table                    Report  Ins 1/2
Form Band,Field Squeeze,Line Squeeze
....+...10....+...20....+...30....+...40....+...50....+...60....+...70....M....+
 ─▼page────────────────────────────────────────────────────────────────
   ─▼form────────────────────────────────────────────────────────────
      January 1, 1988


      AAAA AAAAAAAAAAAAAA AA AAAAAAAAAAAAAA
      AAAAAAAAAAAAAAAAAAAAAAAAAA
      AAAAAAAAAAAAAAAAAAAAAAAAAA
      AAAAAAAAAAAAAAAAAAAAAAAAAA
      AAAAAAAAAAAAAAAAAAAA, AA    AAAAAAAAA

      Dear AAAAAAAAAAAAAA:

      Hi, how are you doing?  I'll bet you though I typed this letter
      myself, on a manual typewriter, without having to make any
      corrections whatsoever.  Well you're wrong.  It's a form letter
      I created with Paradox.  Are you impressed, AAAAAAAAAAAAAA?


      ─
```

Figure 8.18: The first paragraph of the form letter typed in

When typing your letter, be sure to stay within the form band and the right margin. You can use the usual Backspace and arrow keys to make changes and corrections.

PAGE BREAKS

To ensure that each letter is printed on a separate page, you need to tell Paradox where the page break belongs. You do so by simply typing the word PAGEBREAK right into the letter, making sure that it starts in the leftmost column and is the only word on the line. Figure 8.19 shows the complete sample form letter, with the page break properly placed at the bottom.

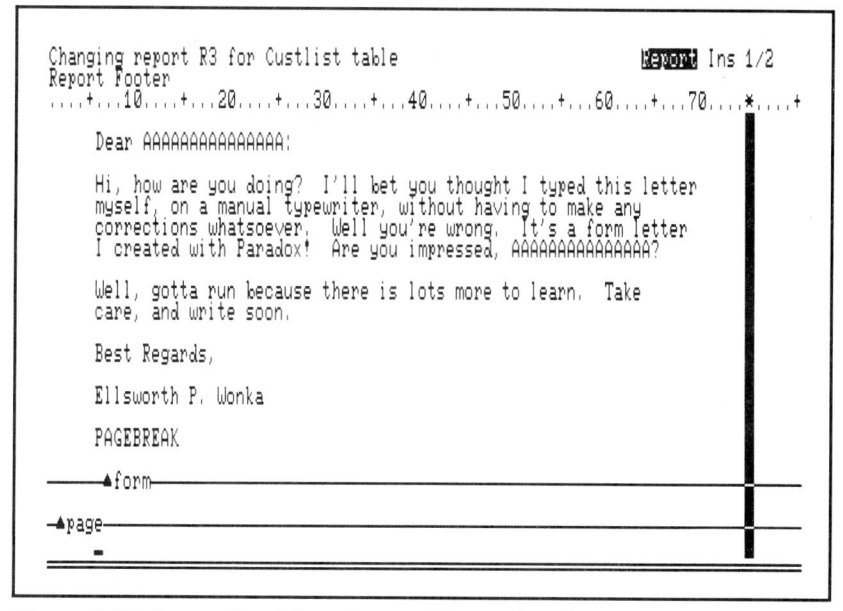

```
Changing report R3 for Custlist table              Report Ins 1/2
Report Footer
....+...10....+...20....+...30....+...40....+...50....+...60....+...70....*....+
     Dear AAAAAAAAAAAAAAA:

     Hi, how are you doing?  I'll bet you thought I typed this letter
     myself, on a manual typewriter, without having to make any
     corrections whatsoever.  Well you're wrong.  It's a form letter
     I created with Paradox!  Are you impressed, AAAAAAAAAAAAAAA?

     Well, gotta run because there is lots more to learn.  Take
     care, and write soon.

     Best Regards,

     Ellsworth P. Wonka

     PAGEBREAK
─────▲form────────────────────────────────────────────────────────────
─▲page────────────────────────────────────────────────────────────────
     ▪
```

Figure 8.19: A completed form letter with page break

SINGLE-SHEET PRINTING

If you are to be printing your letter on single sheets rather than continuous-feed paper, you'll want the printer to pause between each printed page to give you a chance to load a new page. To do so, select the Setting option from the Report menu. Select Wait from the Setting menu, and Paradox will display the following prompt:

    No   Yes
    Do not pause after each page.

Select the Yes option for single-sheet printing.

FORMATTING THE LETTER

For the finishing touches on the format of the form letter, you'll want to make the following menu selections while the mailing label format still appears on the screen. To ensure blank lines and fields are removed, press F10 to call up the Report menu, and select the options Setting, RemoveBlanks, LineSqueeze, Yes, and Fixed. To squeeze out blank fields, call up the Report menu and select Setting, RemoveBlanks, FieldSqueeze, Yes.

To set margins for $8\frac{1}{2}$-by-11-inch paper, call up the Report menu and select Setting, PageLayout, and Length; then type Ctrl-Backspace to erase the current setting, type in **66**, and press Enter. (Given that most printers print six lines to the inch, 66 lines will print on an 11-inch page.)

You may need to experiment with the best margins for your printer. To set a left margin of 5, call up the Report menu, select Setting and Margin, press Ctrl-Backspace to erase the current setting, type in **5**, and press Enter. To set a right margin of 75, call up the menu, select Setting, select PageLayout and Width, and enter a new value of **75**. Press Enter.

To cancel the Labels setting that was originally copied over from the mailing-label format, press F10 and select Setting, Labels, and No.

A TRIAL RUN WITH YOUR FORM LETTER

To test your form letter, just call up the menu and select the Output option as usual. If you select the Printer option, you can use the Break command (Ctrl-ScrollLock) to stop printing.

Remember to press DO-IT! to save the form letter. To print form letters from the Main menu, first remember to sort the table, if necessary, using the Modify and Sort options from the Main and Modify menus. (If mailing labels are printed for the letters, in zip code order, you'll want to print the letters in the same order so that you can match them up easily.) Then select the Report and Output options from the Main and Report menus, and select report 3.

For new form letters, you can erase the body of the letter we've just created (using the Report and Change options) and type in your new letter. If you wish to save the existing form letter, use the Copy option under the Tools menu, as we've done in the past, and make a copy of the letter. Then use the Report and Change options to modify the new form letter.

PRINTING GROUPS OF PAGES

Occasionally, you may need to stop printing a report in the middle (by pressing Ctrl-Break), because the printer runs out of ribbon, or for some other reason. To resume printing where you left off, call up the Paradox Main menu and select Report. From the submenu, select the RangeOutput option and then the table name, report number, and destination as usual. The screen will display the option

> Beginning page number: 1
> Enter first page number to be printed.

To select another starting page, press Backspace, type in the new starting page number, and press Enter. The screen will then display the prompt

> Ending page number:
> Enter last page number to be printed, or press ← for
> last page of report.

Here, you can enter any page number at which to stop printing. Optionally, just press Enter to print all remaining pages in the report.

Note that if you've set the page length option to C (continuous), as when printing mailing labels, Paradox will assume that your entries refer to *records*, rather than pages. For example, if you are printing mailing labels and enter 22 as the starting page, and 500 as the ending page, Paradox will print labels starting at the 22nd record and ending at the 500th record.

USING QUERY FORMS WITH REPORTS

So far we've developed some useful reports for the Custlist table, and have seen techniques for presorting and printing a directory, mailing labels, and form letters. In each case, we printed data for every record in the Custlist table. But suppose we want to send letters to just California residents, or people whose start dates were a year ago, or some other group of individuals. Well, we've already seen how query forms can pull out records that match a certain criterion, so all we have to do now is somehow link these selected records with a report from the Custlist table.

Recall that the query form always stores the results of its searches in a table named Answer. This being the case, we need to perform a query on the Custlist table, then copy the report formats to the Answer table to display data from that table. Let's give it a try, by printing form letters and mailing labels for New York residents only.

Start with only the Main menu showing on the screen (use Clear Image (F8) and Menu (F10) if necessary). Select the Ask option, and specify Custlist as the table to query.

When the query form appears, press Checkmark (F6) while the cursor is still in the leftmost column to put check marks in all the fields on the query form.

Using the → key, move the cursor to the State field and type in NY. Press the DO-IT! (F2) key to perform the query. The two New York residents will appear in the Answer table on the screen, as in Figure 8.20.

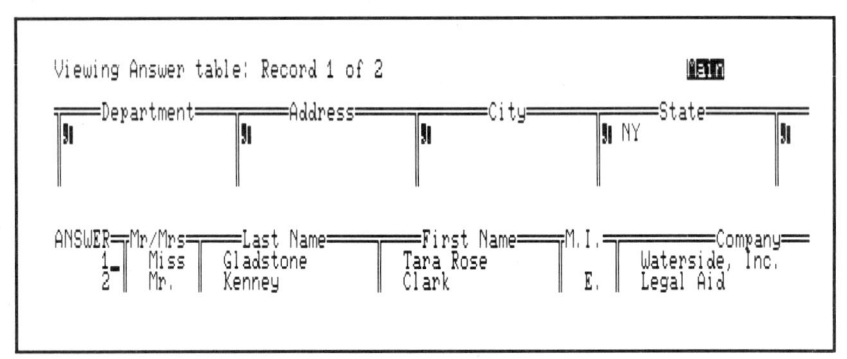

Figure 8.20: New York residents on the Answer table

Now you can sort the Answer table, if you wish, using the Modify and Sort options, being sure to specify Answer as the name of the table to sort, and Same when asked whether to sort to the same table or a new one.

Now you need to copy the report formats from the Custlist table to the Answer table. Here's how:

1. Call up the Main menu (press F10).
2. Select the Tools option from the Main menu.
3. Select the Copy option from the submenu.
4. Select the JustFamily option.
5. Specify Custlist as the table to copy from (the *source* table).
6. Specify Answer as the table to copy to (the *target* table).

When you use JustFamily to copy from one table to another, all report formats and other related items (such as custom forms) are copied from one table's "family" of reports to another. The tables themselves, however, are not altered. Therefore, in this example, we've copied the various report formats from the Custlist table to the Answer table, and used them to print data from the Answer table.

If you've previously performed a copy similar to the one we're performing now, Paradox will double-check before it erases the contents of the previous copy. The screen will display these options:

Cancel   Replace
Do not continue with the family copy

To proceed, select the Replace option. If you've made an error, select Cancel. (When copying JustFamily to the Answer table, you can always safely select the Replace option.)

When the copy is finished, you can print the reports as you normally would, except that you specify the Answer rather than Custlist table when Paradox asks for a table name. In this example, select the Report option from the Main menu and the Output option from the submenu. Specify Answer when prompted for a table name. To print mailing labels, select report 2 and the Printer option. To print form letters, select report 3 and the Printer option.

When you are done printing, use Clear Image (F8) to clear the Answer table and the query form. Of course, you can query for any records you wish, using the techniques we discussed in Chapter 8.

The procedure for copying the reports to the Answer table will always be the same, regardless of the query you perform.

OTHER REPORT OPTIONS

Though the options we've discussed in this chapter are adequate for our needs at this time, the report generator has a few other easy, though useful, capabilities you should know about.

DATES AND TIMES

In our Directory of Customers, the date was automatically printed in the report heading. You can actually place both the current date and the current time any place in your report. Furthermore, you can specify formats for these special fields.

To place the date into a report, put the cursor at the place where you want the date to appear, then call up the Report menu. Select the Field and Place options from the submenus, which bring up the following submenu:

Regular   Summary   Calculated   Date   Time   Page   #Record

Select the Date option, and Paradox will display a menu of eleven format options. Examples of the various date formats are listed below:

DATE FORMAT	EXAMPLE
1) mm/dd/yy	3/31/90
2) Month dd, yyyy	March 31, 1990
3) mm/dd	3/31
4) mm/yy	3/90
5) dd-Mon-yy	3-Mar-90
6) Mon yy	Mar 90
7) dd-Mon-yyyy	3-Mar-1990
8) mm/dd/yyyy	3/31/1990

9) dd.mm.yy   31.03.90
10) dd/mm/yy   31/03/90
11) yy-mm-dd   90-03-31

Use the arrow keys to highlight the date format you want, then press Enter. Paradox will ask you to position the cursor at the place you want the date to appear. Use the arrow keys to position the cursor, if necessary, then press Enter to place the field in the report format.

To place the current time on a report, select the Time option from the submenu. Paradox displays these two formatting options:

Enter the time format to use:
1) hh:mm pm   2) hh:mm:ss (military)

The first option displays the time based on a 12-hour clock, such as 2:55 pm. The second option displays the time based on a 24-hour clock, such as 14:55:00. Select your option and place the field.

If you change your mind about a Date or Time format, call up the Report menu and select the Field and Reformat options. Move the cursor to the field you wish to reformat and press Enter. Depending on the type of the field you specify, Paradox will display a menu of formatting options identical to the menu used when initially placing the field. Select the new format and press Enter.

PAGE NUMBERS

When you first create a report, Paradox automatically displays the page number in the heading. You can, however, display the page number anywhere you wish. First, you might want to remove the suggested placement for the page number. To do this, place the cursor in the page number template on the report specification (shown as 999 on the screen) and select the Field and Erase options from the Report menu. Also, erase the word Page from the heading.

In this example, we'll move the page number to the bottom of each page and center it. Remember, whatever is inside the form band is printed repeatedly on a page. Whatever is outside the form band but inside the page band is printed once on each page. So to display the page number centered on the bottom of each page, you need to place the cursor above the bottom page-band marker, but below the bottom form-band marker. Center the cursor, then call up the menu and select the Field and Place options. Then select the Page option from the submenu, and use the arrow keys to place the page number. (The page number is initially displayed as 999. You can use the ← and → keys to change the size of the page-number template.) Figure 8.21 shows the page number in the Directory report relocated to the bottom of the page.

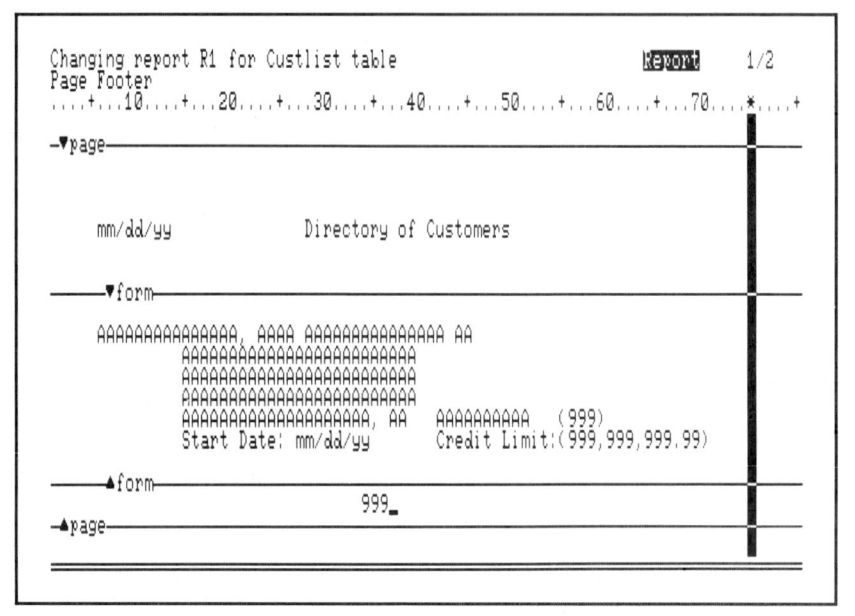

```
Changing report R1 for Custlist table                    Report    1/2
Page Footer
....+...10....+...20....+...30....+...40....+...50....+...60....+...70....*....+
─▼page─────────────────────────────────────────────

       mm/dd/yy           Directory of Customers

    ─▼form─────────────────────────────────────────
         AAAAAAAAAAAAAA, AAAA AAAAAAAAAAAAAA AA
                AAAAAAAAAAAAAAAAAAAAAAAA
                AAAAAAAAAAAAAAAAAAAAAAAA
                AAAAAAAAAAAAAAAAAAAAAAAA
                AAAAAAAAAAAAAAAAAAA, AA   AAAAAAAAA  (999)
                Start Date: mm/dd/yy   Credit Limit:(999,999,999.99)
    ─▲form─────────────────────────────────────────
                              999_
─▲page─────────────────────────────────────────────
```

Figure 8.21: The page number relocated in the Directory report

FORMATTED NUMBERS

You can change the way numbers are displayed in the report as well. Simply move the cursor to some numeric field (such as Credit Limit in the Directory report), call up the menu, and select the Field and Reformat options. Press Enter when the cursor is inside the numeric field, and Paradox will display a list of options, as below:

Digits   Sign-Convention   Commas   International

The Digits option lets you specify the maximum number of whole or decimal digits to display. Just as when you first place a numeric field in a report column, this option will let you use the ← and → keys to increase or decrease the number of digits and decimal places shown in the report column.

The Sign-Convention option displays this submenu:

    NegativeOnly ParenNegative AlwaysSign

The NegativeOnly option places a minus sign in front of negative numbers and no sign in front of positive numbers. (This is the default display for N (numeric) fields.) The ParenNegative option displays negative numbers in parentheses and positive numbers with no sign. (Currency data are always displayed in this format.) The AlwaysSign option displays plus signs in front of positive numbers and minus signs in front of negative numbers.

Selecting the Commas option displays this submenu:

    NoCommas Commas

The NoCommas option does not punctuate the thousands place in numbers (the default setting for N (numeric) fields). The Commas option does punctuate thousands with commas (the default setting for currency data).

The International option displays the submenu shown below:

    U.S.Convention InternationalConvention

If you select U.S.Convention, Paradox uses a period for the decimal separator, and a comma as a digit separator to display numbers (12,345.67). If you select InternationalConvention, Paradox will display numbers with a comma as a decimal separator and a period as the digit separator (12.345,67).

CONDENSED AND EXPANDED PRINT

Most dot matrix and laser printers allow you to use a variety of print sizes, particularly condensed and expanded print. Some printers also allow you to use a variety of fonts. These are activated by sending the printer a special code or *setup string*.

Paradox includes an option that allows you to send these special codes at the beginning of a report. For example, you can send a code for condensed print that will allow you to print up to 132 characters (80 characters is the usual setting) across an 8½-by-11-inch sheet of paper.

Paradox provides setup strings for several IBM-compatible printers, including (at the time of writing) the following:

- IBM PC Graphics Printer and compatibles
- Epson MX and FX series
- Okidata 82, 83, 92, 93, and 192
- HP LaserJet

You can also define codes for other printers.

To send a setup string to the printer, you need to call up the Report menu and select the Setting and Setup options from the submenus. Paradox will display these options:

Predefined   Custom

Selecting the Predefined option displays a menu of ready-to-go printer options, as listed below:

MENU OPTION	EFFECT
StandardPrinter*	Standard print
Small-IBMgraphics	Condensed print on IBM Graphics printer
Reg-IBMgraphics	Regular print on IBM Graphics printer
Small-Epson-MX/FX	Condensed print on Epson MX or FX printer
Small-Oki-92/93	Condensed print on Okidata 92 or 93 printer
Small-Oki-82/83	Condensed print on Okidata 82 or 83 printer

Small-Oki-192	Condensed print on Okidata 192 printer
HPLaserJet	Normal print on HP LaserJet printer
HP-Landscape-Normal	Normal print size in LaserJet Landscape mode
HP-Portrait-66lines	HP LaserJet Portrait mode
Intl-IBMcompatible	Normal size international print on IBM compatible
Intl-IBMcondensed	Condensed print on international IBM

StandardPrinter*, the default option, does not send any special codes to the printer. The other options will send codes, as predefined by the Paradox Custom Configuration program (CCP), discussed in Chapter 16 of the *Paradox User's Guide*. To experiment with the current settings, use the ← and ↓ to highlight an option that matches your current printer, and press Return to select that option.

To test the effects of your selection quickly on a printed report, just press the Instant Report (Alt-F7) key. If you wish to save the printer setup you've selected for future report output, press DO-IT! (F2).

If your printer does not fall into the predefined category, you can select the Custom option to create your own setup string. Paradox will display this prompt:

Printer port:
LPT1   LPT2   LPT3   COM1   COM2   AUX

Most likely, your printer is hooked up to the LPT1 port, so you can just press Enter to select that default value. (If you know for a fact that your printer is connected to some other port, highlight the appropriate port name on the menu and press Enter to select it.)

The next prompt to appear on the screen lets you enter a custom printer setup string:

Setup string:
Enter the setup string to be sent to the printer before printing the report.

The trick here is knowing what code to send. Every printer uses different setup strings, and the only place to find this information is in your printer manual. Furthermore, the code may need some translation. Your custom string can be up to 175 characters long, though most codes are only one or two characters in length.

Many printers use *escape sequences* for setup strings—that is, a press on the Esc key followed by another character. In your printer manual, the escape sequence might be displayed as ESC-A, Esc =, or something similar. The code for the Esc key is 027. So if your printer required the escape sequence ESC 6 to switch to, say, expanded print mode, you would enter

\0276

as your custom setup string. Note that the setup string always begins with a backslash (\).

Some printers use a number, usually in the range of 0 to 31, to put special printer attributes into effect. For example, the Okidata 83A uses code 31 to enter expanded print mode. To put this into effect, you would enter the code

\031

as your custom setup string. (Note that the setup code must contain three digits—hence the leading zero.)

Appendix C of the *PAL User's Guide,* which comes with your Paradox package, shows an ASCII chart that may help you translate a code. ASCII stands for *American Standard Code for Information Interchange* and includes 256 characters used by most microcomputers.

Keep in mind that once a setup string is sent to the printer, it stays in effect until either the printer is turned off or another code is sent. Therefore, if you print mailing labels in condensed print and then immediately print form letters, your form letters may also come out in condensed print. To avoid this situation, just select the Setting, Setup, Predefined, and StandardPrinter* options from the Report menu to cancel the previous printer setup before printing the next report. (This, of course, assumes that you have not used the Paradox Custom Configuration Program to change the StandardPrinter* code.)

TEMPORARY PRINTER REDIRECTION

If you have several printers hooked up to your computer, or a printer that can switch to different fonts or typefaces easily, you can alter the selected port and setup string without modifying the report format. To do so, press F10 to call up the Paradox Main menu, select Report, and then select SetPrinter.

Under the SetPrinter option, you will be given two choices:

    Regular   Override

Selecting Regular specifies the default printer port and print-setup string defined in the report format (under the Report menu Setting option). Selecting Override lets you temporarily bypass the printer port and setup string defined in the report format, and lets you redefine those on the spot.

When you first select Override, you'll be given the options

    PrinterPort   Setup   EndOfPage

To change the printer port (for example, to use the printer connected to your COM1 port), select PrinterPort. You'll be given the options

    Printer port:
    LPT1   LPT2   LPT3   COM1   COM2   AUX

As usual, highlight the port of your choice, and press Enter to select it.

Under the Override menu, you can also select the Setup option, which presents the prompt

    Setup String:
    Enter a setup string to be sent to the printer before printing the report.

As discussed previously, you must enter the setup string as an ASCII number preceded by a backslash. For example, to send ASCII codes 27 (Esc key), 54, and 15 to the printer, enter the setup string as \027\054\015.

MORE CONTROL OVER PAGE LENGTHS

When you print a report, and Paradox ejects one page to start printing the next, it sends a "form feed" character to the printer, which tells the printer to move as many lines as required to move to the top of the next page. The printer calculates how many lines to move by its own page-length setting (not the Paradox page length setting).

If you are attempting to print on pages that are less than 11 inches long, but Paradox "insists" on treating pages as though they were 11 inches long, try changing the end-of-page character from Form Feed to Line Feeds. To do so, starting at the Paradox Main menu, select Report, then SetPrinter, then Override, then EndOfPage. From the submenu that appears, select LineFeed. When you return to the Main menu, select Report and Output, as usual, to print the report.

ADDITIONAL REPORT CAPABILITIES

The basic report-formatting techniques discussed in this chapter will be enough to get you started in developing neatly formatted printed reports. Chapter 14 picks up where this chapter leaves off, and discusses more advanced features of the Paradox report generator, including tabular reports, totals and subtotals, calculated fields, and printing reports from multiple tables. However, before dealing with those topics, we'll look at techniques for developing custom forms for displaying, entering, and editing data on the screen.

SUMMARY

- To create a report format, select the Report and Design options from the Main and Report menus.

- To place a field on a report format, call up the Report menu (F10) and select the Field and Place options from the submenus.

- To squeeze out extraneous lines and blank spaces from a report, select Setting from the Report menu and RemoveBlanks from the submenu. Then select the LineSqueeze and/or FieldSqueeze options.

- To print a trial copy of a report format, select the Output option from the Report menu.
- To save a report format, press the DO-IT! (F2) key.
- To abandon a report format, call up the Report menu and select the Cancel option.
- To presort data before printing a report, use the usual Modify and Sort options from the Main and Modify menus, and sort a table to the same table (not a new table).
- To change page length, page width, or left margin settings, use options under the Report menu Setting option.
- To print continuous data without page breaks, set the Page-Length option to C (for continuous).
- To force a page break into a report, type the word PAGE-BREAK, starting in the leftmost column, where you want the new page to begin.
- To pause between pages for a paper change, set the Wait option to Yes under the Setting option on the Report menu.
- To print a selected group of pages or records in a report, use the Range Output and change the beginning and ending page (record) numbers.
- To use query with reports, query your table in the usual fashion. While the Answer table is showing the results of the query, use the Tools, Copy, and JustFamily options to copy reports from the original table to the Answer table.
- To add dates, times, record numbers, and page numbers to reports, select the appropriate options under the Field and Place options from the Report submenu.
- To use special printer attributes like condensed print or special fonts, select the Setting and Setup options from the Report menu, and either select a predefined code or enter a custom code. See your printer manual for custom codes.

CUSTOM FORMS

CHAPTER 9

WHENEVER YOU SWITCH FROM TABLE VIEW TO FORM View by pressing the Form Toggle (F7) key, Paradox allows you to enter or edit data a single record at a time. Unless you develop your own custom forms, Paradox will display a standard form that it automatically generates for your table, similar to the one shown in Figure 9.1.

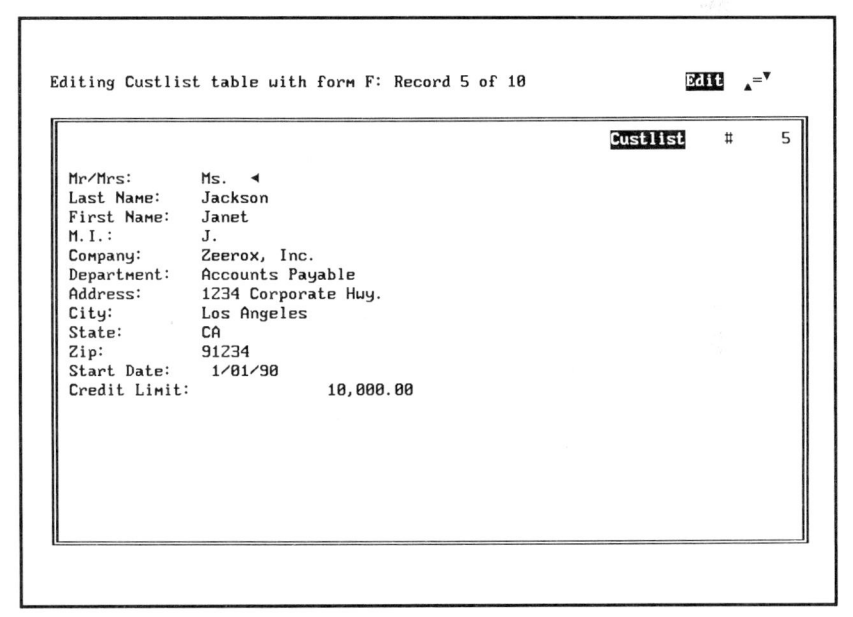

```
Editing Custlist table with form F: Record 5 of 10          Edit

                                                     Custlist   #    5

   Mr/Mrs:        Ms.  ◄
   Last Name:     Jackson
   First Name:    Janet
   M.I.:          J.
   Company:       Zeerox, Inc.
   Department:    Accounts Payable
   Address:       1234 Corporate Hwy.
   City:          Los Angeles
   State:         CA
   Zip:           91234
   Start Date:    1/01/90
   Credit Limit:              10,000.00
```

Figure 9.1: A standard form generated by Paradox

You can easily design and develop your own forms for a table, using commands under the Forms option of the Main menu. Like the Report option, the Forms option allows you to draw a basic format for a form on the screen, as well as make changes to improve the appearance of your form. Some of the keys and menu options work differently with Forms, however. In this chapter, we'll develop a custom form for the Custlist table, shown in Figure 9.2.

Notice that the custom form has certain attributes that make it preferable to the standard form. Boxes and highlights improve the appearance of the form. Some field prompts, such as Starting Date and Zip Code, are spelled out, rather than abbreviated as in the field names. The box at the bottom of the screen displays useful reminders about managing the cursor.

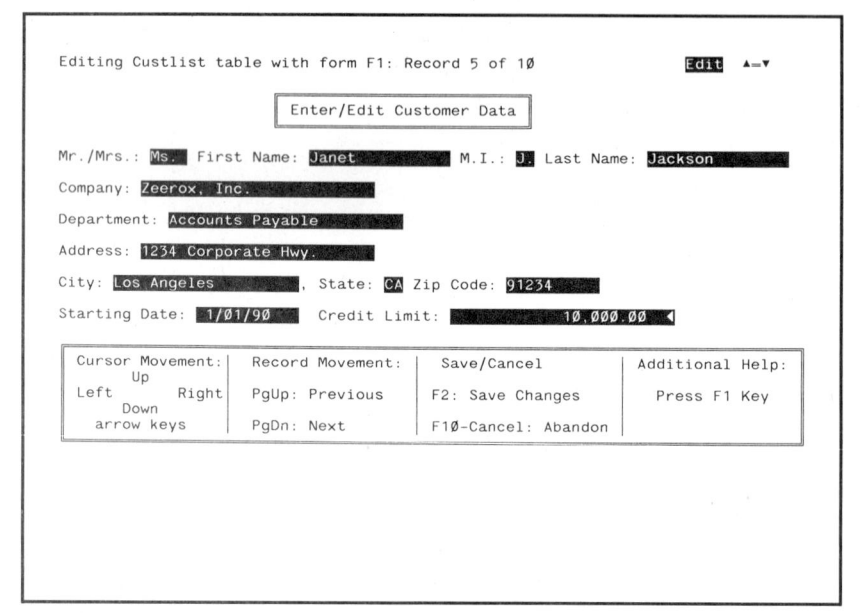

```
Editing Custlist table with form F1: Record 5 of 10                    Edit  ▲═▼
                        ┌─────────────────────────┐
                        │ Enter/Edit Customer Data│
                        └─────────────────────────┘
Mr./Mrs.: Ms.  First Name: Janet          M.I.: J. Last Name: Jackson
Company: Zeerox, Inc.
Department: Accounts Payable
Address: 1234 Corporate Hwy.
City: Los Angeles         , State: CA Zip Code: 91234
Starting Date: 1/01/90    Credit Limit:          10,000.00

┌─────────────────┬──────────────────┬──────────────────┬──────────────────┐
│ Cursor Movement:│ Record Movement: │ Save/Cancel      │ Additional Help: │
│       Up        │                  │                  │                  │
│ Left     Right  │ PgUp: Previous   │ F2: Save Changes │ Press F1 Key     │
│      Down       │                  │                  │                  │
│   arrow keys    │ PgDn: Next       │ F10-Cancel: Abandon│                │
└─────────────────┴──────────────────┴──────────────────┴──────────────────┘
```

Figure 9.2: The custom form for the Custlist table

CREATING A CUSTOM FORM

To create a custom form, select the Forms option from the Main menu. Paradox will display the following submenu:

If you are using Paradox on a network, see "Forms on a Network" in Appendix B.

    Design   Change

Select the Design option to create a new form. Paradox will ask for the name of the table for which the form is being designed. In this example enter Custlist as the table name. Then Paradox displays a menu of form options, as below:

F   1   2   3   4   5   6   7   8   9   10   11   12   13   14

F is the standard form that Paradox creates automatically for the table. You can change this form or select one of the other options, 1–14, for your new form name. In this example, select option 1.

Next, Paradox asks for a description of the form, as below:

Form description:
Enter description of the new form.

Enter any description, up to 40 characters long. As with reports, the description will be displayed later when you select a form to use. For this example, enter the form name

Customer Entry

Then press Enter.

Once you've entered the description, Paradox gives you a blank screen on which to design your form. At the top-left corner of the screen, the prompt

Designing new F1 form for Custlist

reminds you that you are designing form number 1 (F1) for the Cust-List table. Beneath that, the prompt

< 1, 1 >

tells you that the cursor is currently on row 1, column 1, of the form. On the right edge of the screen, the prompt

1/1

tells you that you are on the first page of a one-page form (Page 1 of 1). Let's now discuss techniques for managing the cursor on the form.

MANAGING THE FORM CURSOR

As usual, the ↑, ↓, ←, and → keys move the cursor freely about the screen. In addition, the Ins key toggles the Insert mode on and off. To move text to the right, you can put the Insert mode on and press the Space bar. The Del and Backspace keys erase any text that you've already entered onto the form.

Table 9.1 summarizes the keys to design and edit a form. The Forms menu offers additional techniques for placing, moving, deleting, and copying fields and text on the screen, as later examples will demonstrate.

Table 9.1: Keys for designing and editing forms

Key	Effect
F10	Displays the Report menu
↑	Moves cursor up a line
↓	Moves cursor down a line
→	Moves cursor right a column
←	Moves cursor left a column
Backspace	Moves cursor left, and delete one character
Home	Moves cursor to top of screen
End	Moves to bottom of screen
Ins	Turns Insert mode on/off
Del	Deletes character at cursor
Ctrl-Home	Moves cursor to start of line
Ctrl-End	Moves cursor to end of line

PLACING TEXT ON THE FORM

To place text anywhere on the custom form, just position the cursor and type the text. For example, to center a title at the top of this form, press the ↓ key to move the cursor down one row. Then hold down the → key until the cursor gets to row 2, column 26 (so the cursor position indicator shows < 2,26>). Next, simply type in the title:

Enter/Edit Customer Data

If you make a mistake, you can use the Backspace key, or any if the other keys listed in Table 9.1, to make corrections.

Next, you can type in the prompt for the Mr/Mrs field. Note that the prompt can be any word or words you wish; it need not be the same as the field name. In this example, however, we'll use Mr/Mrs: as the prompt for the field, so first press ↓ three times, then press Ctrl-Home to move the cursor to < 5, 1>. Then type:

Mr/Mrs:

When you've finished typing, press the Space bar or → key once to move the cursor to < 5, 9>. Next you'll place the Mr/Mrs field from the CustList database table on the form.

PLACING FIELDS ON THE SCREEN

The form we are creating will be used to enter or edit data on the Custlist table, so we need to specify positions on the form for entering and changing field data. This is very easy to do; we'll quickly review the basic steps before we actually try it.

To place a field, call up the Form menu (F10) and select the Field option. This brings up the following submenu:

Place   Erase   Reformat   CalcEdit   WordWrap

To place fields from an existing table, select the Place and Regular options.

When you select the Regular option, Paradox will display a menu of existing field names. When you select the field name, Paradox asks where you want to place the field, as below:

Use ↑ ↓ → ← to move to where you want the field to begin . . .
then press ↵ to place it . . .

You use the arrow keys to position the cursor where you want the field to begin, then press Enter. Next, Paradox will ask you to adjust the width of the field:

> Now use → and ← to adjust the width of the field . . .
> press ↵ when finished.

Usually, you'll want the full field size, so you'll just press Enter to use the suggested size. Let's give it a try.

To place the Mr/Mrs field on the form, call up the Forms menu (F10) and select the Field, Place, and Regular options. Select Mr/Mrs as the field to place by pressing Enter. Then press Enter to place the field. Press Enter again to define the size. You'll notice that the field position is displayed as underlines, equal to the size of the field, as in Figure 9.3.

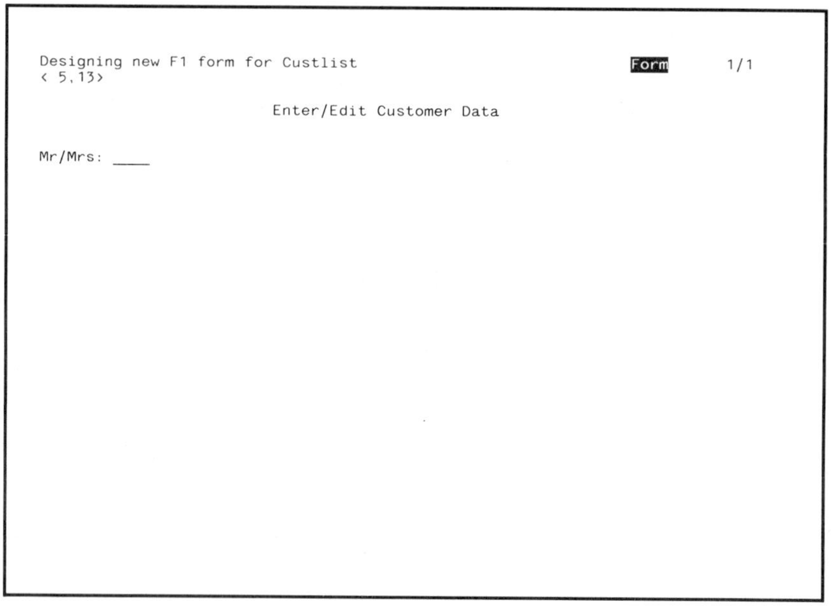

```
Designing new F1 form for Custlist                    Form      1/1
< 5,13>
                    Enter/Edit Customer Data

Mr/Mrs:  ____




```

Figure 9.3: The field prompt and field placed on the screen

Now, to enter a prompt and field for First Name, press → twice. Type

> First Name:

Press → to make a space. Now call up the menu and select Field, Place, and Regular. Press → to highlight the First Name option and press Enter. Press Enter twice in response to the position and size prompts. Now two prompts and two field locations appear on the screen, as below:

    Mr./Mrs.: ____ First Name: _____

Try entering the rest of the field prompts and appropriate field values, so your screen looks like Figure 9.4.

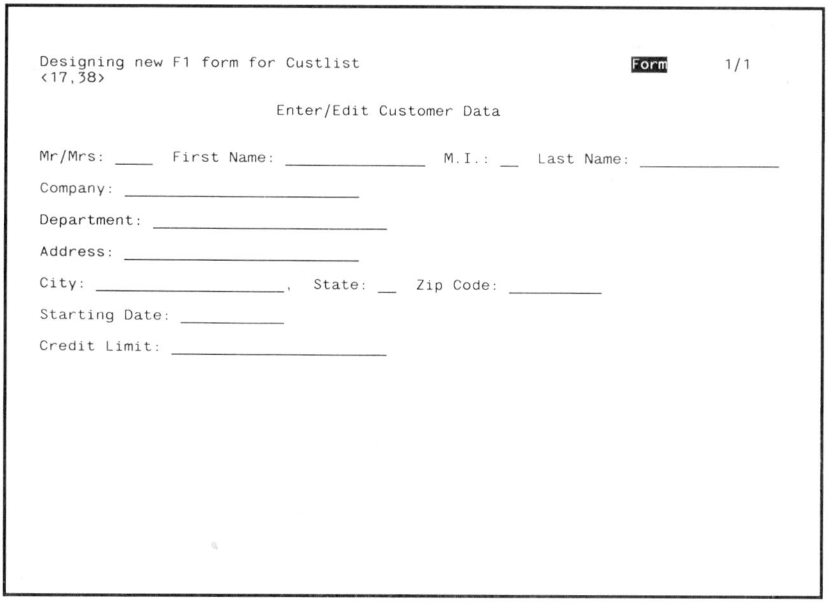

```
Designing new F1 form for Custlist                    Form      1/1
<17,38>
                      Enter/Edit Customer Data

Mr/Mrs: ____   First Name: _____   M.I.: __  Last Name: _____
Company: _____
Department: _____
Address: _____
City: _____, State: __  Zip Code: _____
Starting Date: _____
Credit Limit: _____
```

Figure 9.4: Field prompts and fields on the custom form

To design the form exactly as shown in Figure 9.4, use the cursor coordinates listed below. Remember, to place prompts, simply move the cursor to the coordinates shown below, and type in the prompt exactly as shown. To place fields on the screen, move the cursor to the cursor coordinates shown below, press F10, and select the Field, Place, and Regular options, followed by the appropriate field name.

PROMPT/FIELD	STARTING CURSOR POSITION
M.I.: prompt	<5,44>
M.I. field	<5,50>
Last Name: prompt	<5,54>
Last Name field	<5,65>
Company: prompt	<7,1>
Company field	<7,10>
Department: prompt	<9,1>
Department field	<9,13>
Address: prompt	<11,1>
Address field	<11,10>
City: prompt	<13,1>
City field	<13,7>
, prompt	<13,27>
State: prompt	<13,30>
State field	<13,37>
Zip Code: prompt	<13,41>
Zip field	<13,51>
Starting Date: prompt	<15,1>
Start Date field	<15,16>
Credit Limit: prompt	<17,1>
Credit Limit field	<17,15>

To correct mistakes in prompts, use the usual Backspace and arrow keys. To remove a field that was placed accidentally, move the cursor to the underlines that represent the field on the screen. (Even though you can only see the underlines, you can identify the field by viewing the upper-right corner of the screen when the cursor is within the underlines.) Then, call up the Forms menu (F10), and select the

Field and Erase options. Press Enter to erase the field that the cursor is presently on.

After you have entered all of the prompts and fields, and your screen looks like Figure 9.4, you've finished the basic work of placing the prompts and fields. To enhance the form, you can also add borders, as discussed next.

BORDERS

Borders are another way to enhance a custom form. To draw borders, call up the menu (F10) and select the Border option. The options

    Place   Erase

appear. Select Place to begin drawing a border. A submenu of options will appear, as below:

    Single-line   Double-line   Other

You can draw borders with either a single thin line, double thin lines, or any other character you specify with the Other option. For this example, select the Double-line option. Paradox will display these instructions:

    Use ↑ ↓ → ← to move to a corner of the box or border . . .
    then press ↵ to select it . . .

Use the arrow keys to move the cursor just slightly above and to the left of the title (centered at the top of the screen). Press Enter when you get the cursor to that position. Paradox then displays these instructions:

    Now use ↑ ↓ → ← to indicate the diagonal corner . . .
    press ↵ to finish.

Now use the ↓ and → keys to start drawing a box around the title. As you move the cursor, you'll see the box expand on the screen. Move the cursor to a point where the title is enclosed by the box, and then press Enter. You'll see a box of double lines around the screen title, as in Figure 9.5.

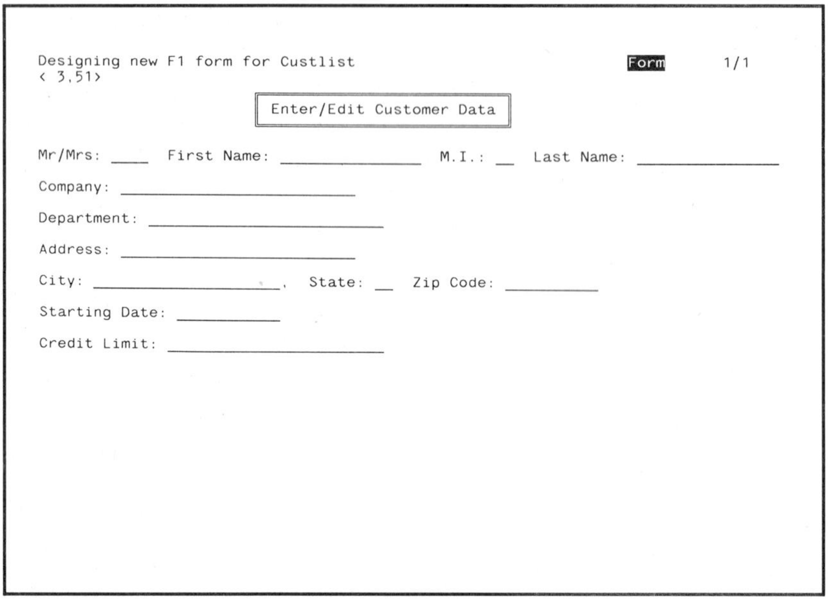

```
Designing new F1 form for Custlist                    Form      1/1
< 3,51>
                     ┌─────────────────────────┐
                     │ Enter/Edit Customer Data │
                     └─────────────────────────┘
Mr/Mrs: ____   First Name: _____   M.I.: __  Last Name: _____
Company: _____
Department: _____
Address: _____
City: _____, State: __  Zip Code: _____
Starting Date: _____
Credit Limit: _____
```

Figure 9.5: A custom form with title and box

MOVING ITEMS ON THE FORM

You may find that you want to make a change to a screen after initially entering data. For example, suppose you want to move the Credit Limit field up next to the Starting Date field. Use the Move option from the Forms menu. Let's give it a try.

Call up the menu and select the Area and Move options. Paradox displays this prompt:

> Use ↑ ↓ → ← to move cursor to a corner of the area to be moved . . .
> then press ↵ to select it . . .

Use the arrow keys to move the cursor to the starting C in Credit Limit. Press Enter to mark the corner. Paradox then displays the following instructions:

> Now use ↑ ↓ → ← to move to the diagonal corner . . .
> press ↵ to define the area . . .

Use the → key to highlight the area to be moved, as in Figure 9.6. (You can, of course, highlight an area of any size to move.) Press Enter when both the prompt and the field area are highlighted.

Paradox then prompts you to drag the highlighted area to its new location on the screen. As you press the ↑ and → keys, the highlight will move on the screen. Keep pressing the arrow keys until the highlight is a few spaces to the right of the Starting Date field, as in Figure 9.7. Then press Enter to complete the move. The highlight will disappear, and the Credit Limit prompt and field will jump to the new location.

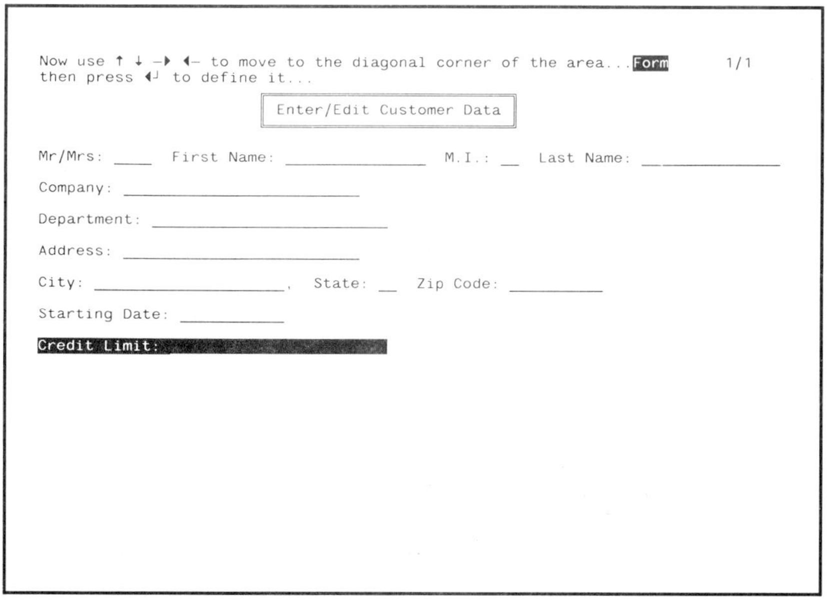

```
Now use ↑ ↓ → ←  to move to the diagonal corner of the area... Form      1/1
then press ↵ to define it...
                        ┌─────────────────────────┐
                        │ Enter/Edit Customer Data │
                        └─────────────────────────┘
Mr/Mrs: ____   First Name: _____   M.I.: __   Last Name: _____
Company: _____
Department: _____
Address: _____
City: _____,  State: __  Zip Code: _____
Starting Date: _____
Credit Limit: _____
```

Figure 9.6: Highlighting the area to move

ADDING HELP TO A FORM

If you wish to make your form easier for a novice to use, you can develop your own "help box," like the one at the bottom of the screen shown in Figure 9.2. To develop one like that shown in the figure, call up the Paradox Main menu, and select the Forms and Change options. Specify CustList as the table, 1 as the form, and press Enter to keep the

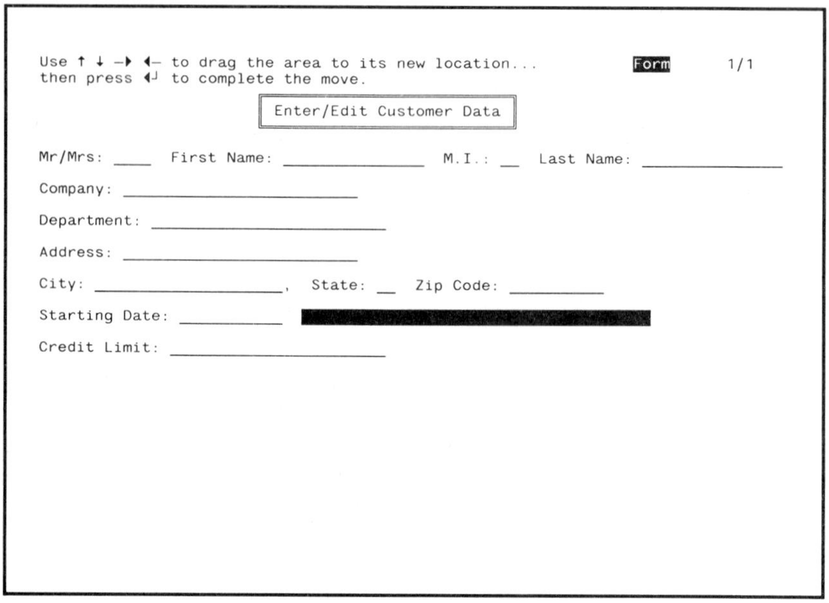

```
         Use ↑ ↓ → ←  to drag the area to its new location...        Form      1/1
         then press ↵ to complete the move.
                              ┌─────────────────────────┐
                              │  Enter/Edit Customer Data │
                              └─────────────────────────┘
         Mr/Mrs: ____   First Name: _____   M.I.: __  Last Name: _____
         Company: _____
         Department: _____
         Address: _____
         City: _____, State: __  Zip Code: _____
         Starting Date: _____   ████████████████████████
         Credit Limit: _____
```

Figure 9.7: The highlighted area moved to a new location

existing description. Then follow these steps to draw the box:

1. Move the cursor to <17, 1>.

2. Call up the Forms menu (F10), and select the Border, Place, and Double-line options.

3. Press Enter to specify the current cursor position as the first corner of the box.

4. Press ↓ six times and → enough times to extend the border to the right edge of the screen.

5. Press Enter to complete the border.

Within the box, type in the text as shown in Figure 9.8. The individual vertical lines can be entered as single-line borders. For example, to fill in the first vertical line, move the cursor to <18,19> (or thereabouts, depending on how you've typed in the text), and call up the menu. Select Border, Place, and Single-line, and press Enter to mark the top of the line. Press ↓ four times to extend the line down four lines,

```
┌─────────────────────────────────────────────────────────────────────┐
│  Changing F1 form for Custlist                        Form    1/1   │
│  <20,76>                                                            │
│                    ┌─────────────────────────┐                      │
│                    │ Enter/Edit Customer Data│                      │
│                    └─────────────────────────┘                      │
│   Mr/Mrs: ____   First Name: _____  M.I.: __  Last Name: _____ │
│   Company: _____                                  │
│   Department: _____                               │
│   Address: _____                                  │
│   City: _____, State: __ Zip Code: _____      │
│   Starting Date: _____  Credit Limit: _____      │
│   ┌─────────────────┬──────────────────┬────────────────────┬──────────────────┐ │
│   │ Cursor Movement:│ Record Movement: │ Save/Cancel:       │ Additional Help: │ │
│   │       Up        │                  │                    │                  │ │
│   │  Left   Right   │ PgUp: Previous   │ F2: Save Changes   │ Press F1 Key     │ │
│   │      Down       │                  │                    │                  │ │
│   │   arrow keys    │ PgDn: Next       │ F10-Cancel: Abandon│                  │ │
│   └─────────────────┴──────────────────┴────────────────────┴──────────────────┘ │
│                                                                     │
│                                                                     │
│                                                                     │
└─────────────────────────────────────────────────────────────────────┘
```

Figure 9.8: Some help text added to a custom form

then press Enter. The single line will appear within the box. Use this same technique to draw other vertical lines inside the box.

COLORING A FORM

If you have a color monitor, you can change the color of any border or area of the screen. You can also control video attributes such as blinking, intensity, and reverse video. The general technique is quite easy. First, you call up the menu and select the Style option. Paradox displays the submenu:

Color Monochrome Fieldnames ShowHighlight

To color an area or border, select Color. To change the video attributes of an area or border, select Monochrome. Next, you'll be prompted to mark the two diagonal corners of the area or border to color by moving the cursor with the arrow keys and pressing Enter.

Next, if you selected Color, you'll be presented with a palette of possible color combinations. Within the palette, you can press ↑ and ↓

to change the foreground color, and → and ← to change the background color. When the color combination is just right, press ↵.

If you selected Monochrome rather than Color, you'll see instructions telling you to press ← and → to experiment with different video attributes. These video attributes are:

Normal	No special video attributes are assigned
Intense	Colors are brightened
Reverse	Foreground and background colors are reversed
Intense-Reverse	Foreground and background colors are reversed and brightened
Blink	Foreground blinks against the background
Non-Blink	Foreground does not blink

To try these features on the current form, we'll first convert a field on the current form to reverse video format. Here are the steps:

1. Move the cursor to the first underline representing the Mr/Mrs field (at position <5,9>).
2. Press Menu (F10), and select Style.
3. Select Monochrome.
4. Select Area.
5. Press ↵ to mark the current cursor position as the beginning of the area.
6. Press → three times to highlight the rest of the Mr/Mrs field, then press ↵.
7. Press the → key until the word Reverse appears in the upper-right corner of the screen.
8. Press ↵.

You'll notice that the field is now displayed in reverse video format. You might want to go ahead and convert all the fields to reverse video, using the same basic techniques discussed above. When you are done, the fields will appear as in Figure 9.9. Later, when you use the form, the reverse video will make it easier to discriminate between the prompts and the data from the database table.

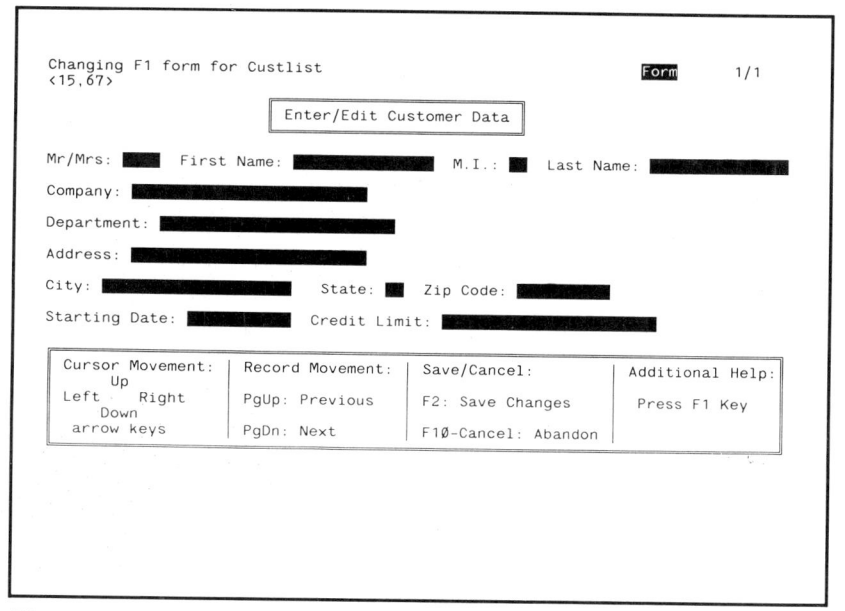

```
Changing F1 form for Custlist                           Form      1/1
<15,67>
                      ┌─────────────────────────┐
                      │ Enter/Edit Customer Data│
                      └─────────────────────────┘
 Mr/Mrs: ███   First Name: ████████████   M.I.: █   Last Name: ████████████
 Company: ███████████████████████
 Department: ████████████████████████
 Address: ██████████████████████████
 City: ████████████████    State: █   Zip Code: ██████████
 Starting Date: ██████████   Credit Limit: ████████████████

 ┌─────────────────┬──────────────────┬───────────────────┬──────────────────┐
 │ Cursor Movement:│ Record Movement: │ Save/Cancel:      │ Additional Help: │
 │        Up       │                  │                   │                  │
 │  Left    Right  │ PgUp: Previous   │ F2: Save Changes  │ Press F1 Key     │
 │       Down      │                  │                   │                  │
 │    arrow keys   │ PgDn: Next       │ F10-Cancel: Abandon│                 │
 └─────────────────┴──────────────────┴───────────────────┴──────────────────┘
```

Figure 9.9: All fields converted to reverse video

If you have a color monitor, you may want to experiment on your own with changing the colors of box borders, or areas on the form. Remember, to do so just press Menu (F10), select the Style and Color options, and follow instructions as they appear at the top of the screen.

SAVING A FORM

When you've finished entering your form, save it by pressing the DO-IT! (F2) key. You'll be returned to the Main menu.

USING A FORM

Generally, you'll want to use a form while entering or editing data. For example, select the View option from the Main menu to view the Custlist table. Press the Edit key (F9) to switch to Edit mode. Then, to use the new form, call up the menu (F10) and select the Image option. From the submenu, select the PickForm option. You'll be given a menu of existing form options, as below:

F 1

To use the new form, select option 1 (or whatever number you have assigned to it). You'll see the custom screen, as in Figure 9.2. Once selected, you can still use the Form Toggle key (F7) to switch back and forth from Form View to Table View.

All keys work the same way on a custom form as they do on the standard form. PgUp and PgDn scroll up and down through records. The arrow keys move the cursor up, down, left, and right, and Backspace and Ctrl-Backspace erase data. Pressing Field View (Alt-F5) allows for more refined editing. As usual, you must press DO-IT! when done editing (if you wish to save your edits), and Clear Image (F8) to clear the screen.

CHANGING A FORM

To modify an existing form, call up the Main menu and select the Forms option. Select Change from the submenu and specify the name of the table with which the form is associated. Paradox will display a menu of existing forms, as below:

F 1

Select the appropriate number for your custom form. You'll have an opportunity to change the description of the form; then the form will appear on the screen, ready for editing. You can use the same keys and menu options that you used to create the form to make changes. The remainder of this chapter discusses other useful techniques for modifying forms.

REFORMATTING FIELDS ON THE FORM

To change the width of a field on the form, call up the Forms menu and select the Field and Reformat options. The screen will prompt you to use the arrow keys to move the cursor to the field you wish to reformat, then press Enter to select that field. You can then use the ← and → keys to increase or decrease the width of the field. As instructed on the screen, press Enter when you are done changing the size of the field.

ERASING PARTS OF THE FORM

To erase the general text placed on a form, use the usual Backspace and Del keys on your keyboard. To remove larger portions of the screen, use one of the techniques listed below. (Because there is no need to remove anything from the current sample form, you may not want to try any of these techniques at the moment.)

ERASING A FIELD

To remove a field from the screen, first move the cursor to the appropriate field hyphens. (Look to the upper-right corner of the screen for the name of the field that the cursor is currently in.) Then, call up the menu and select the Field and Erase options. The screen will ask you to move the cursor to the field you want to erase. If the cursor is already in the field you wish to erase, you can simply press Enter. (Optionally, you can use the arrow keys to highlight a different field to erase, or press Esc to cancel the command and not erase any fields.)

ERASING A BORDER

To erase a border from the screen, call up the Forms menu and select the Border and Erase options. As instructed on the screen, move the cursor to a corner of the box to be erased, and press Enter. Then, as instructed, use the arrow keys again to move the cursor to the opposite (diagonal) corner of the box, and press Enter once again to erase the box.

ERASING AN AREA

To erase a larger area of the screen, call up the menu and select the Area option. From the submenu, select the Erase option. The screen will display the prompt

> Use ↑ ↓ → ← to move to a corner of the area to be removed...
> then press ↵ to select it...

Use the arrow keys to move the cursor as instructed, then press Enter. The screen will ask that you

> Now use ↑ ↓ → ← to move to the diagonal corner of the area to be removed...then press ↵ to erase the area.

As instructed, move the cursor to a diagonal corner. Note that the area you define cannot contain only a portion of a field; if there is a field (or fields) within the area to be erased, *all* of the hyphens that represent that field must be enclosed within the area to be erased. After highlighting the area to erase, press Enter (or Esc to cancel the erasure).

SUMMARY

- To create a custom form, select the Forms option from the Main menu and the Design option from the submenu.
- To use video enhancements on a form, call up the Forms menu and select the Style option.
- To place fields on a form, call up the Forms menu and select the Field and Place options.
- To place borders around text on a form, select the Border and Place options from the Forms menu.
- To move items on the form, select the Area and Move options from the Forms menu.

- To erase parts of a form, select the Area and Erase options from the Forms menu.
- To save a form, press the DO-IT! (F2) key after designing the form.
- To abandon an edited form, select the Cancel option from the Forms menu.
- To use a form for entering or editing data, select the Pick-Form option under the Main menu Image option, and choose a form by number. Use the Form Toggle (F7) key to switch from Table View to Form View.
- To modify an existing form, select Forms from the Main menu and the Change option from the submenu.
- To copy forms, use the Copy and Form options under the Tools option from the Main menu.

GRAPHICS

CHAPTER 10

PARADOX 3 LETS YOU DISPLAY DATA FROM YOUR tables on a variety of common business graphs, such as bar charts, pie charts, line graphs, and so forth. In this chapter, you'll see how easy it is to plot data from tables on graphs and to refine graphs to your own specifications and taste.

This chapter will also describe cross tabulations, or crosstabs, which allow you to quickly summarize data in a table. The resulting summarized table will contain meaningful data that is easy to graph.

A QUICK TOUR OF GRAPHS

Just to show you how quickly you can create a graph, we'll begin by creating a financial summary table named FinSum. Remember, to create a new table, just select Create from the Paradox Main menu. When prompted for a table name, enter FinSum, and then structure the table as shown in Figure 10.1.

After creating the table structure and saving with the F2 key, enter the sample data shown in Figure 10.2 using the usual Modify and Data Entry options from the Paradox Main menu.

VIEWING AN INSTANT GRAPH

To view a quick graph of the data in the FinSum table, first make sure the table is displayed on the workspace. If it is not, press F10 and select View from the Paradox Main menu. Then type in the table name, FinSum, and press Enter or just press Enter and select FinSum from the menu of table names.

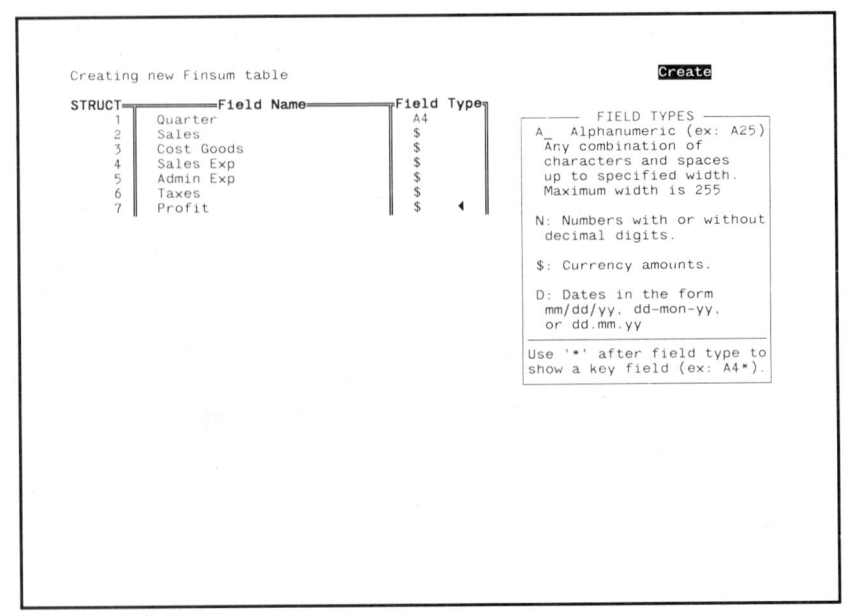

```
Creating new Finsum table                              Create
STRUCT      Field Name           Field Type
  1    Quarter                   A4            ── FIELD TYPES ──
  2    Sales                     $             A_  Alphanumeric (ex: A25)
  3    Cost Goods                $                 Any combination of
  4    Sales Exp                 $                 characters and spaces
  5    Admin Exp                 $                 up to specified width.
  6    Taxes                     $                 Maximum width is 255
  7    Profit                    $    ◄
                                               N: Numbers with or without
                                                  decimal digits.

                                               $: Currency amounts.

                                               D: Dates in the form
                                                  mm/dd/yy, dd-mon-yy,
                                                  or dd.mm.yy

                                               Use '*' after field type to
                                               show a key field (ex: A4*).
```

Figure 10.1: The structure of the FinSum table

```
Quarter   Sales    Cost Goods  Sales Exp  Admin Exp  Taxes   Profit

1-88      140000     96600       7000      15500     8400    12000
2-88      150000     96500       7500      16000     9000    21000
3-88      190000    128700       9500      17500    11400    22900
4-88      210000    147500      12600      18000    12600    19300
1-89      240000    160000      16800      19500    19200    24500
2-89      250000    170000      15000      20000    20000    25000
3-89      270000    187900      16200      21000    21600    23300
4-89      300000    214000      18000      21500    24000    22500
1-90      320000    220000      22400      22500    25600    29500
```

Figure 10.2: Sample data for the FinSum table

If you are using Paradox on a network, see "Graphs on a Network" in Appendix B.

To see a graph of the FinSum table, use the → or Tab key to move the cursor to the Cost Goods field. Then press the Graph key, Ctrl-F7. After a brief pause, the stacked bar graph will appear as in Figure 10.3. Notice that the graph displays data from the Cost Goods field, and all fields to the right.

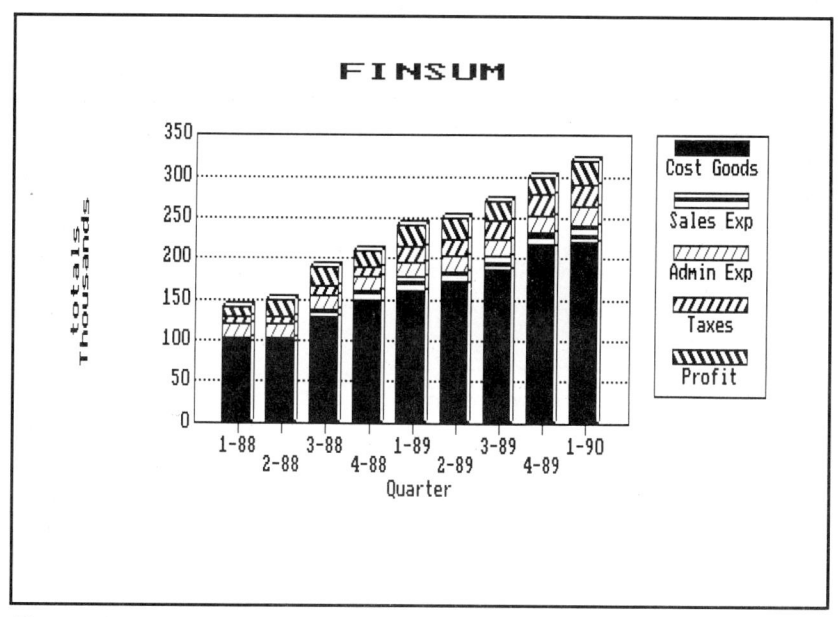

Figure 10.3: An instant graph

HOW PARADOX DESIGNS AN INSTANT GRAPH

The instant graph uses information from the table to determine how to display the graph. First, the way Paradox translates data from the active table into graph elements is determined by the field order in the active table and the location of the cursor when the graph is created. Only numeric values (i.e., those of the N, S, or $ data type) are displayed. On all graphs except pie charts Paradox uses the field that the cursor is positioned in as the *first series* of values to plot data, and all numeric fields to the right of that field as additional series.

Recall that the FinSum table contains fields named Sales, Cost Goods, Sales Exp, Admin Exp, Taxes, and Profits. Prior to displaying the graph shown in Figure 10.3, you positioned the cursor in the Cost Goods field. Notice that the legend to the right of the graph shows that it includes the Cost Goods, Sales Exp, Admin Exp, Taxes, and Profits fields. The Sales field is not included because it is to the left of the cursor on the table view.

As you'll see in the examples that follow, you can use the Rotate (Ctrl-R) key to rotate fields in the table view to determine what fields

> If you do not place the cursor in a numeric field prior to pressing Ctrl-F7 to display a graph, Paradox will only display the message *Active field not numeric*.

are included in and excluded from the graph, as well as the order in which the included fields are displayed in the legend. In addition, you can plot graphs using data from the Answer table that appears after you perform a query. This is an extremely handy feature that allows you to isolate specific records to plot in a graph (e.g., data for 1989 only).

The repeating titles that appear at the bottom of the graph (1–88, 2–88, 3–88, and so forth in Figure 10.3) come directly from values in the leftmost column of the table view. The main title at the top of the graph is the same as the table name. You can change any of the titles on the graph, as well as the type of graph, graph colors, and so forth. But before we go into detail on how to refine some of these features, let's take a moment to view some of the graph types that Paradox offers.

First, you'll need to get back to the workspace. To remove a graph from the screen and get back to the workspace, simply press any key on your keyboard.

EXPLORING GRAPH TYPES

The purpose of graphs is to display information in a form that is easy to understand. This requires more than a bit of creativity on your part and a lot of capability from the graphic tools you use. Paradox allows you to create, modify, display, and print a choice of ten different types of graphs.

Stacked bar	Area graph
Standard bar	Line graph
Rotated bar	Pie chart
3-D bar	Marker graph
X-Y graph	Combined lines/markers

GENERAL TECHNIQUE FOR DISPLAYING SAMPLE GRAPHS

In this section we will illustrate each of these different graph types using the FinSum table. If you would like to create any of the sample graphs yourself, first make sure that the FinSum table is displayed on the workspace. Then follow the general steps below to display the sample graph (specific information for each step is provided for each graph example):

1. Press F10 and select the Image, Graph, and Modify options.

2. When the Customize Graph Type form appears (as in Figure 10.4), select the appropriate graph type for the example by typing in its first letter (e.g., *B* for Bar graph or *3* for 3-D Bar graph).

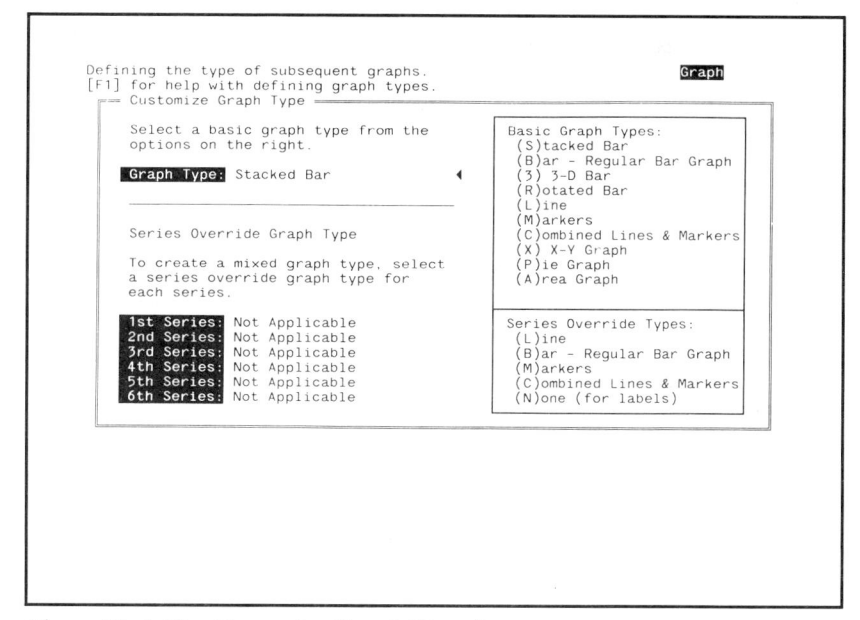

```
Defining the type of subsequent graphs.                    Graph
[F1] for help with defining graph types.
┌── Customize Graph Type ──────────────────────────────────────────┐
│                                                                  │
│   Select a basic graph type from the    Basic Graph Types:       │
│   options on the right.                 (S)tacked Bar            │
│                                         (B)ar - Regular Bar Graph│
│   Graph Type: Stacked Bar          ◄    (3) 3-D Bar              │
│                                         (R)otated Bar            │
│                                         (L)ine                   │
│                                         (M)arkers                │
│   Series Override Graph Type            (C)ombined Lines & Markers│
│                                         (X) X-Y Graph            │
│   To create a mixed graph type, select  (P)ie Graph              │
│   a series override graph type for      (A)rea Graph             │
│   each series.                                                   │
│                                                                  │
│   1st Series: Not Applicable            Series Override Types:   │
│   2nd Series: Not Applicable            (L)ine                   │
│   3rd Series: Not Applicable            (B)ar - Regular Bar Graph│
│   4th Series: Not Applicable            (M)arkers                │
│   5th Series: Not Applicable            (C)ombined Lines & Markers│
│   6th Series: Not Applicable            (N)one (for labels)      │
│                                                                  │
└──────────────────────────────────────────────────────────────────┘
```

Figure 10.4: The Customize Graph Type form

3. Press DO-IT! to save the new graph type definition.

4. Rotate fields, if necessary, using the Rotate (Ctrl-R) key, as indicated in the example.

5. Move the cursor to the field indicated in the example using the Tab key.

6. Press Graph (Ctrl-F7) to view the graph.

By following these steps, and looking closely at the data displayed in the graph, you'll get a better feel for how the order of fields and the cursor's position in the table view determine which fields are plotted on the graph.

STACKED BAR

A stacked bar graph shows the value of each series relative to the total through the "stacking" of series elements. Paradox automatically displays a stacked bar graph if you do not specify a different graph type. You've already seen an example of a stacked bar graph (in Figure 10.3). In this example, we are able to see the relative impact of expense items on total sales, for each quarter.

STANDARD BAR

A standard (vertical) bar graph uses a single bar to represent each data element. This can be useful for comparing values over a period of time. The example in Figure 10.5 was produced by defining the graph type as Bar (B). Then, the Sales field was rotated to the rightmost column of the table, and the cursor moved into the Sales field. The graph shows values from the Sales field only, because there were no numeric fields to the right of the Sales field.

ROTATED BAR

In a rotated bar graph, the X and Y axes are reversed, and the bars are laid out horizontally. Rotated bar graphs are useful for representing performance over time. In our example, Profit per Quarter is illustrated. With the graph type changed to R, the profit field was rotated to the far right location and the cursor was placed on it to get Figure 10.6. (Actually, the graph is slightly customized because Paradox reverses the X and Y axis titles. You'll see how to customize titles a little later in the chapter.)

3-D BAR

A 3-D bar graph is visually appealing and easy to read when there are just a few values plotted. In Figure 10.7, the 3-D graph displays

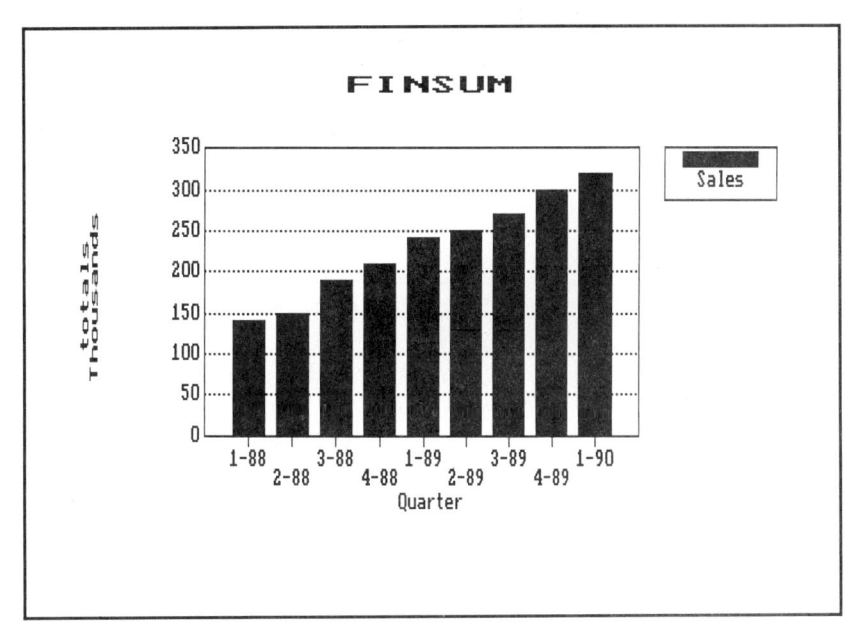

Figure 10.5: A standard bar graph

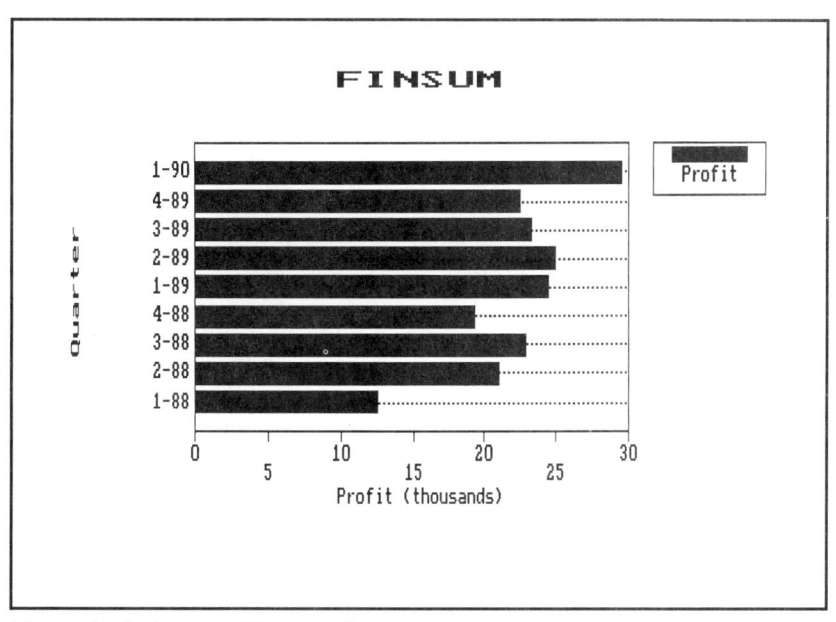

Figure 10.6: A rotated bar graph

only the profit field for quarterly data in 1989. To create this graph, we first set the graph type to 3-D (3).

After returning to the workspace, we isolated 1989 data by selecting Ask from the Main menu, and specifying FinSum as the table to query. In the Quarter field of the query form, we placed the search condition **..89** to isolate records that have 89 as the last two characters of the Quarter field. Then we placed check marks (using the F6 key) in the Quarter and Profit fields of the query form. Pressing DO-IT! (F2) performs the query, creating an Answer table with only 1989 data in it.

Then, we used the Tab key to move the cursor to the Profit field in the Answer table (to display its data on the graph), and pressed Graph (Ctrl-F7) to view the graph. After pressing any key to return to the workspace, you can press Clear Image (F8) to remove the Answer table, then press Up Image (F3) and Clear Image (F8) to remove the query form.

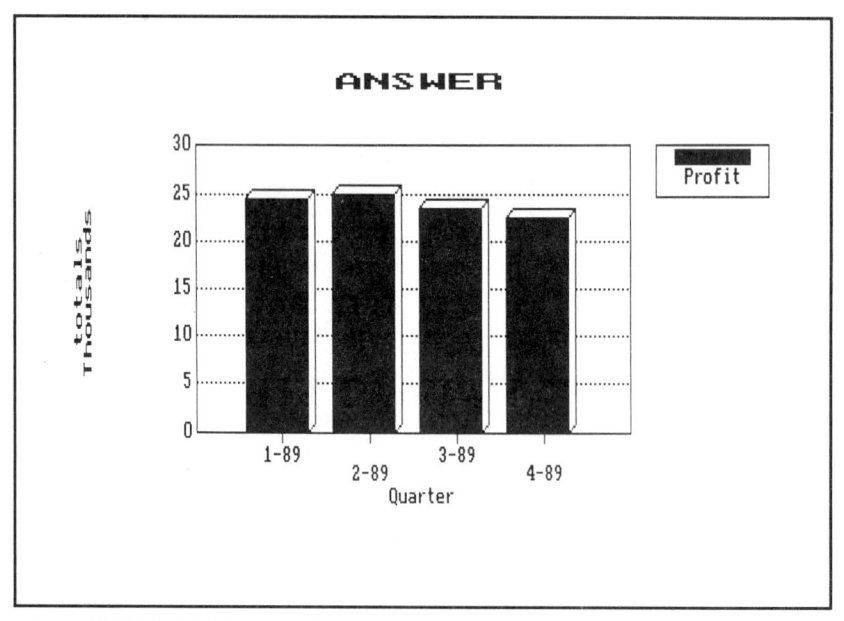

Figure 10.7: A 3-D bar graph

X-Y GRAPH

An X-Y graph uses the values assigned to the X and Y axes, to plot points and a line connecting them. This is useful in showing the relationship between two or more variables.

In Figure 10.8, the graph type was set to X-Y Graph. The Sales field was rotated to the leftmost column of the table field, and the Profit column was rotated to the rightmost column. Because the Sales field is now the leftmost column in the table view, Paradox will use its values as the values to plot along the X-axis.

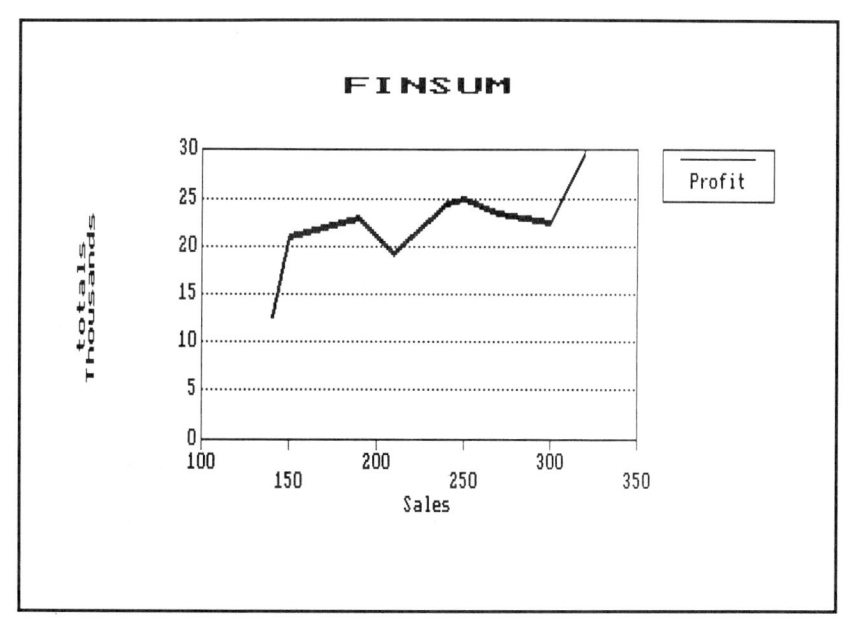

Figure 10.8: An X-Y graph

With the cursor in the Profit field, pressing Ctrl-F7 will produce the X-Y graph shown in Figure 10.8, which shows the relationship between sales and profit for each quarter.

AREA GRAPH

An area graph is actually a different rendering of a stacked bar graph with the smoothness of a line graph. The area graph is often used to show changes in values over a course of time.

In Figure 10.9, the graph type was set to Area (A). Then the fields were placed back into the original order, which is easily accomplished by pressing Clear Image (F8) to remove the current table view from the screen, and then selecting View and the table name (FinSum). The cursor was then placed in the Cost Goods field before the Graph key was pressed.

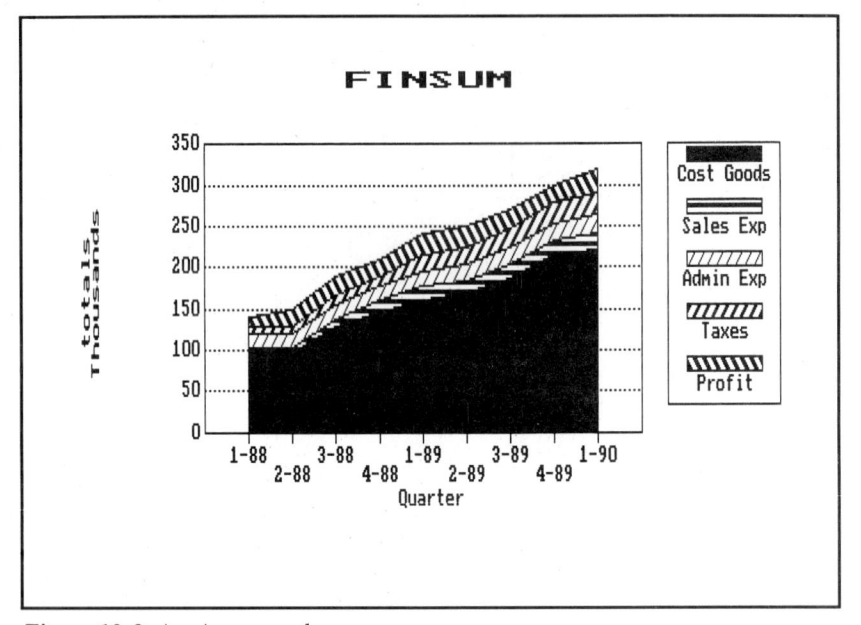

Figure 10.9: An Area graph

LINE GRAPH

A line graph is often used to show the changes in a value (or values) over a course of time. The X-axis on a line graph is usually a progression of time. An X-Y graph can plot any series of values on the X-axis. To produce the graph in Figure 10.10, we selected Line (L) as the graph type, and then rotated the Sales and Cost Goods fields to the rightmost columns. We then placed the cursor in the Sales field before pressing the Graph (Ctrl-F7) key.

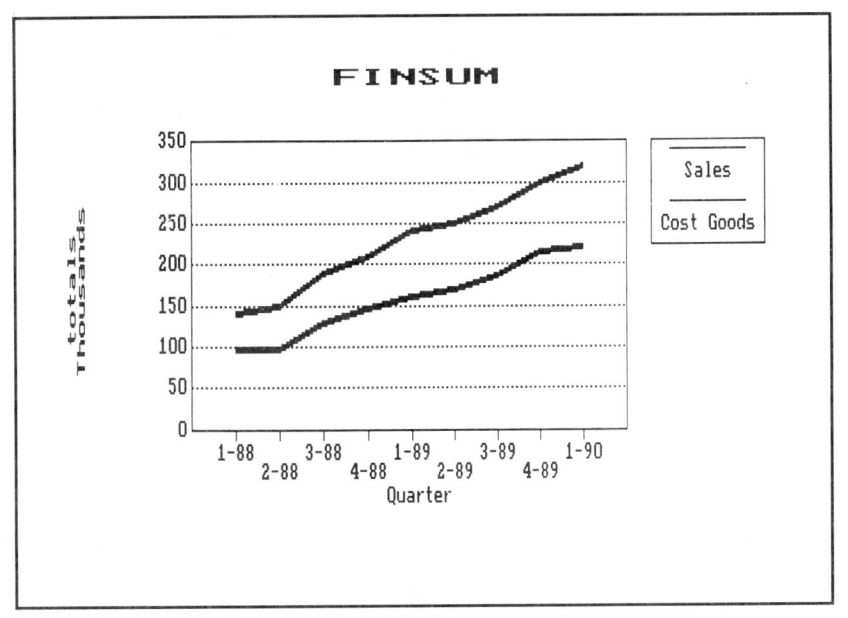

Figure 10.10: A line graph

MARKERS GRAPH

A markers graph represents values in the same way as a line graph, except that the values are marked with symbols rather than with a line. This type of graph emphasizes individual values rather than a sequence of values.

You can produce the graph shown in Figure 10.11 using the settings and cursor position from the line graph example above and changing the graph type to Markers (M).

COMBINED LINES AND MARKERS

A Combined Lines and Markers graph displays both lines and markers, as its name implies, showing progressions of changes but emphasizing discrete points. The graph shown in Figure 10.12 was produced with the same settings as the above graph, and the graph type changed to Combined Lines and Markers (C).

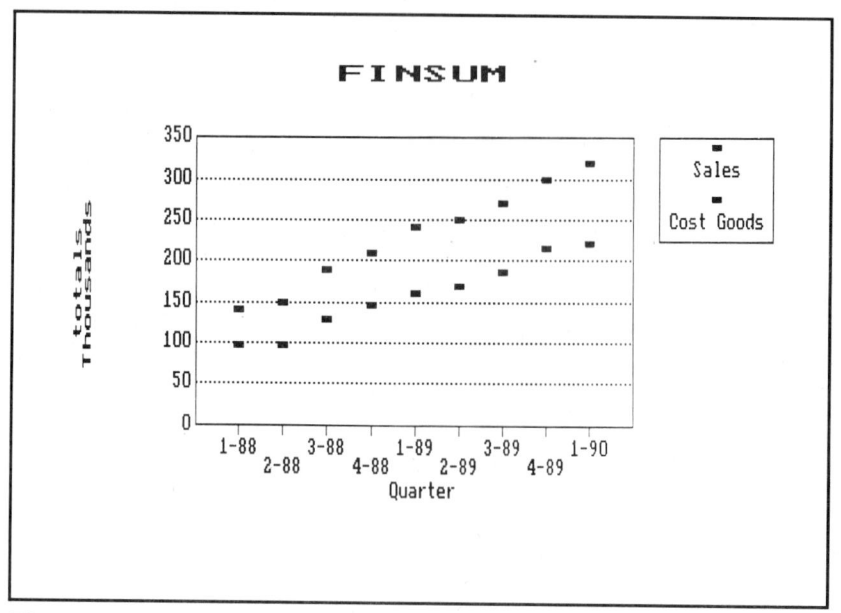

Figure 10.11: A Markers graph

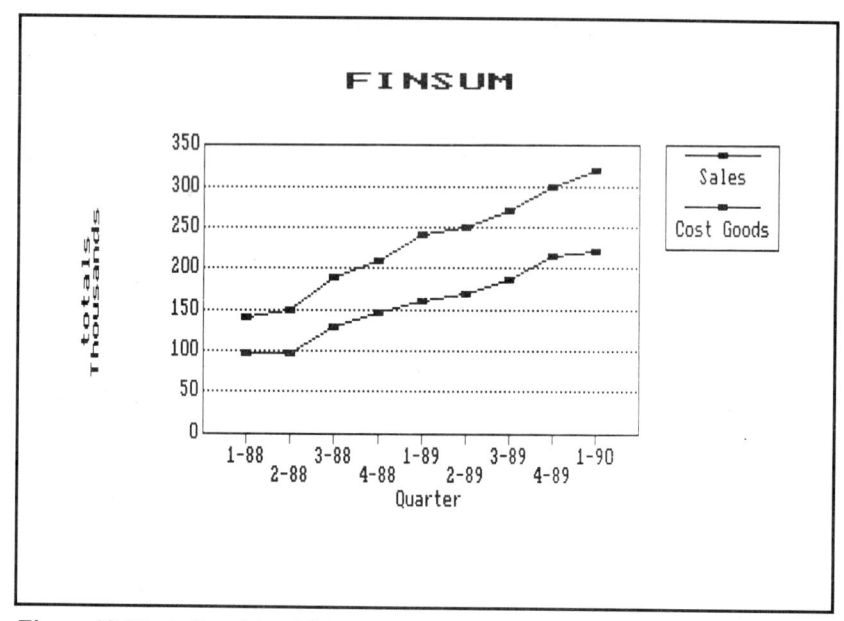

Figure 10.12: A Combined Lines and Markers graph

PIE CHART

The pie chart is an effective image to use when you want to display a proportional breakdown of values within a single whole. The pie chart is one dimensional; that is, it plots one series of values (a single field from the table). Each pie slice represents one record in the table.

The sample pie chart shown in Figure 10.13 was created by first setting the graph type to Pie (P). Then we used a query (as discussed in the example of the 3-D bar graph) to isolate records from 1989, placing check marks in the Quarter and Profit fields. Then, in the resulting Answer table, we placed the cursor in the Profit field prior to pressing the Graph (Ctrl-F7) key. (Note: we also customized the graph a bit, using techniques discussed later in the chapter.)

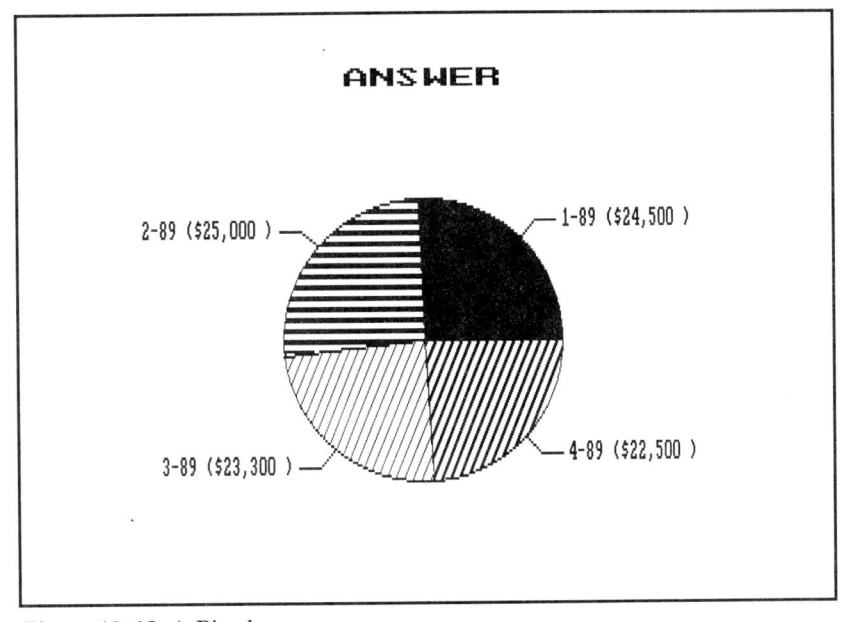

Figure 10.13: A Pie chart

COMBINED GRAPHS

Mixing graph types (normally, the various line, markers, and bar types) can be an effective way of displaying distinctions among the series or types of data being plotted.

The 1st series plotted in a graph is always the field that the cursor is on. The remaining series follow a left-to-right progression of fields to the right of the cursor.

You combine graph types at the Customize Graph Type form utilizing the Series Override Types options. We created the sample graph in Figure 10.14 by first setting the overall graph type to Bar (B) using the usual Image, Graph, and Modify options. Before leaving the Customize Graph Type form, however, we then pressed ↓ to move the cursor to the lower options on the screen. We changed the 1st Series graph type to Combined Lines and Markers by typing the letter C, and then pressed F2 to save the new graph definition.

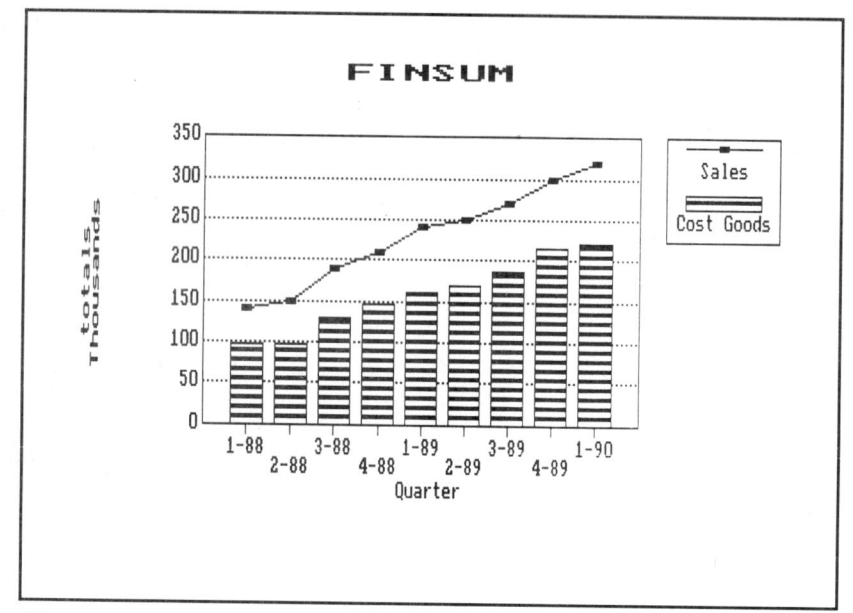

Figure 10.14: A Combined graph

Upon returning to the workspace, we rotated the Sales and Cost Goods fields to the rightmost columns of the table, to graph their values only. Placing the cursor in the Sales field and pressing Graph (Ctrl-F7) then displayed the graph.

CUSTOMIZING GRAPHS

The example "instant" graphs above demonstrate how easy it is to display any type of graph with just a few keystrokes. However, when creating your own graphs, you will probably want to dress them up a bit, perhaps adding your own titles, changing colors, or making other changes.

Let's take a look at how easy it is to customize a graph and save those custom settings for future graphs. We'll change the graph titles to present more meaningful information. To get started, first press Clear All (Alt-F8) to clear any tables from the screen. Then select View from the Main menu, and specify the FinSum table, so that it comes into view on the workspace in its original (unrotated) form. Then, use the Tab key to move the cursor to the Cost Goods field.

SELECTING THE GRAPH TYPE

Next, we'll create a basic stacked bar graph (like the first graph you viewed in this chapter). Press F10 and select the Image, Graph, and Modify options to get to the Customize Graph Type form. Type **S** to select Stacked Bar.

Instead of returning to the workspace you can press Graph (Ctrl-F7) now for a quick view of the graph. After viewing the graph, press any key to return to the Customize Graph Type form.

CUSTOMIZING THE TITLES

Any time the Customize Graph Type form is displayed, you can press F10 to see the Graph menu, which allows you to customize and print graphs. When you press F10, you'll see the following options on the Graph menu:

    Type Overall Series Pies ViewGraph Help DO-IT! Cancel

As usual, if you scroll with the ← and → keys, the first line beneath the options explains each option further. To customize the titles, select Overall, which in turn displays these options:

    Titles Colors Axes Grids PrinterLayout Device Wait

Select Titles, the first option. A form for customizing the graph titles appears, as in Figure 10.15. You can make changes at the left

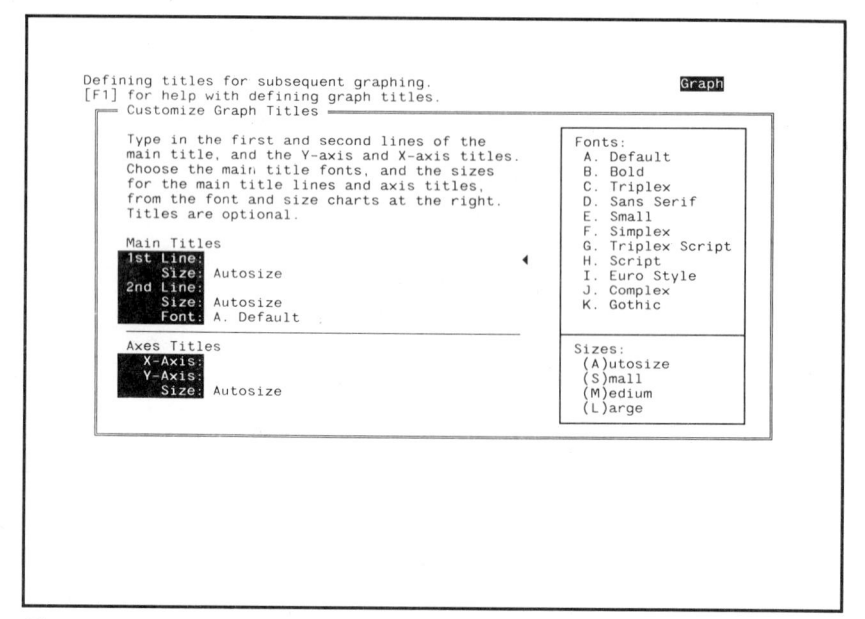

```
Defining titles for subsequent graphing.                    Graph
[F1] for help with defining graph titles.
┌─ Customize Graph Titles ─────────────────────────────────────────┐
│ Type in the first and second lines of the     Fonts:             │
│ main title, and the Y-axis and X-axis titles.    A. Default      │
│ Choose the main title fonts, and the sizes       B. Bold         │
│ for the main title lines and axis titles,        C. Triplex      │
│ from the font and size charts at the right.      D. Sans Serif   │
│ Titles are optional.                             E. Small        │
│                                                  F. Simplex      │
│   Main Titles                                    G. Triplex Script│
│   1st Line:                              ◄       H. Script       │
│       Size: Autosize                             I. Euro Style   │
│   2nd Line:                                      J. Complex      │
│       Size: Autosize                             K. Gothic       │
│       Font: A. Default                                           │
│                                                                  │
│   Axes Titles                                   Sizes:           │
│     X-Axis:                                      (A)utosize      │
│     Y-Axis:                                      (S)mall         │
│       Size: Autosize                             (M)edium        │
│                                                  (L)arge         │
└──────────────────────────────────────────────────────────────────┘
```

Figure 10.15: Form for customizing graph titles

side of the screen. The right side of the screen shows options for fonts (type styles) and sizes.

Go ahead and modify the titles, using the information below. Note that to select a font or size, you merely need to move the cursor to the appropriate Size or Font line at the left of the form, and then press the first letter of the option you want, as listed in the Sizes and Fonts boxes on the right of the form. For example, to make the second line of the title Medium size, move the cursor to the Size option beneath *2nd Line*, and type **M**. To change the font of the title lines, move the cursor to the Font option and type the letter **I**.

    1st Line: **ABC Corporation**
     Size: **Autosize**
    2nd Line: **Quarterly Sales**
     Size: **Medium**
     Font: **I. Euro Style**

X-Axis: **Quarter-Year**

Y-Axis: **Total Sales**

Size: **Autosize**

Note that the Autosize option for graph titles will automatically select a size for the title based upon the number of characters in the title and the size of the space available.

QUICK VIEW OF CHANGES

After modifying the titles you can quickly see the customized graph by pressing the usual Graph (Ctrl-F7) key. Figure 10.16 shows the graph with the new titles added. The new titles appear at the top, bottom, and left side of the graph.

After viewing the graph, simply press any key to return to the Customize Graph Titles form. If you want to try different titles, sizes, or fonts, just make whatever changes you wish to the form and then press Graph (Ctrl-F7) again to view the changes. You can flip back

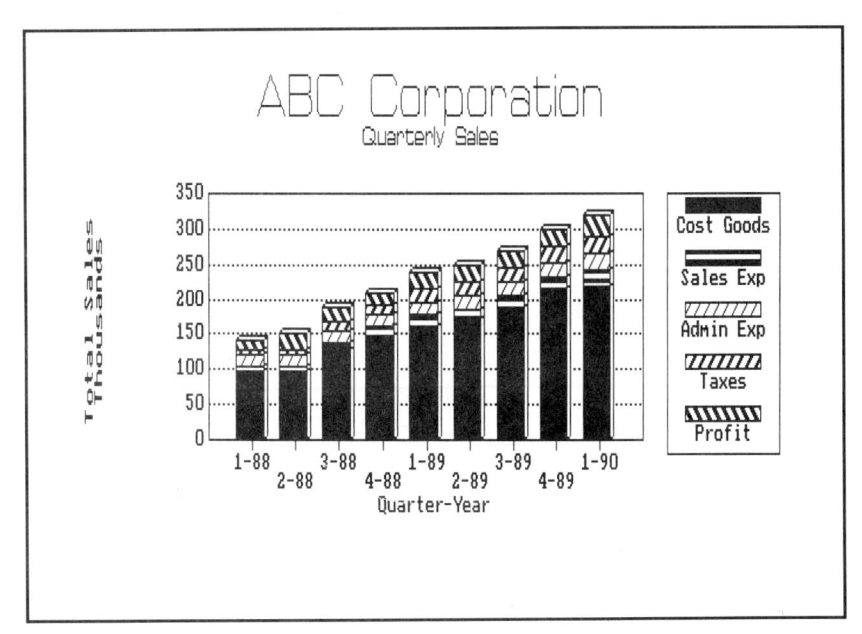

Figure 10.16: Sample graph with new titles added

and forth between the Customize Graph Titles form and the graph as many times as you wish, making whatever changes you desire, until the titles appear exactly as you want them to. Examples of various fonts that you can use for titles are presented in Figure 10.17.

SAVING CUSTOM GRAPH TITLES

When you are satisfied with the titles that you have created for your graph, you can save them for use with future copies of the graph by following the basic steps below:

1. Press F2 to save your work and return to the workspace.
2. Press F10 and select the Image and Graph options.
3. Select Save.
4. As prompted on the screen, type in a file name for the graph (up to eight letters maximum, no spaces or punctuation) and press Enter.

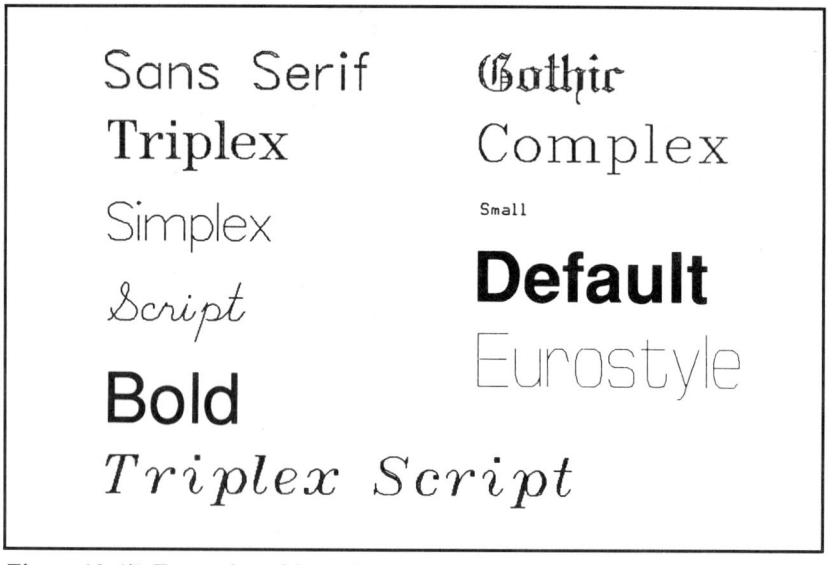

Figure 10.17: Examples of fonts for graph titles

To save the current graph titles in a graph file named MyGraph now, go ahead and press F2 to save the new titles. Press F10, select Image, Graph, and Save, and then type in **MyGraph** and press ⏎.

USING CUSTOM GRAPHS IN THE FUTURE

Because you have saved your custom graph settings in a file, you will be able to use them again at any time in the future. (You can also modify them in the future, or use them as the starting point for developing other graphs.)

To use these saved graph settings, you would start by going through the usual steps for displaying a graph. That is, you would need to use the Main menu View option to bring a table to the workspace (if one were not already displayed). Then, you would rotate the fields (if necessary) and position the cursor in a numeric field for displaying a graph.

At this point, rather than simply pressing the Graph key to view an instant graph, you would need to load the custom graph settings that you saved earlier. The general steps for doing so are listed below:

1. Press F10 and select the Image, Graph, and Load options.

2. When prompted for a graph name, you can press Enter to see the names of existing graph settings.

3. Highlight the name of the graph that contains the custom settings you want, and then press Enter.

4. Now you can press the usual Graph (Ctrl-F7) key to see your graph with the custom settings that you saved earlier.

In this example, you would follow the steps above, specifying MyGraph as the graph file name in step 3.

Note that when you display the graph by pressing Ctrl-F7, the custom settings (e.g., the titles in this example) are used in the new graph. However, the *data* plotted on the graph will reflect the current data stored in the table. This is a great feature, because it allows you to save a custom graph format and use it repeatedly in the future to display current data. You can even experiment with data in the table to try out various what-if scenarios, and then just press the Graph (Ctrl-F7) key to see how your changes look on the graph.

MODIFYING A CUSTOM GRAPH

If you want to make further changes or additions to a custom graph, you can use the same basic techniques that you used to create the graph. That is, after loading the custom graph settings, select the Image, Graph, and Modify options from the Paradox Main menu. Press F10 to access options for further modifying your graph, and make whatever additional changes you wish. (Remember, you can press Ctrl-F7 at any time while modifying a graph to take a quick look at the effects of your changes.)

To save your new changes to the graph, press F2 to return to the workspace, and remember to press F10 and select Image, Graph, and Save to save these new modifications. When Paradox asks for the name of the graph, use the same name that you used to save the graph the first time (MyGraph in this example).

If you forget to save the new modifications, they will be lost when you exit Paradox.

USING ONE CUSTOM GRAPH TO CREATE ANOTHER

In the above examples, you created a stacked bar graph with custom titles. Suppose, now, that you also want to create a line graph that uses these same titles. Rather than creating an entirely new graph and retyping the custom titles, you could use MyGraph as a starting point for the new graph.

To do so, first make sure that the appropriate table for the graph is displayed on the workspace and that the cursor is positioned appropriately for the graph. Then use the Image, Graph, and Load options, as you normally would, to load the graph settings that you want to use as the starting point (MyGraph in this example). Press Ctrl-F7 to view the current graph (just to make sure you've selected the appropriate one), and then press any key to return to the workspace.

Next, press F10 and select Image, Graph, and Modify. Here, you can change the graph type, or press F10 to make other kinds of changes. For example, to create a line graph, simply type the letter **L**. As usual, press Ctrl-F7 when you want to quickly see the effects of your changes. When you are satisfied with the new graph, press DO-IT! (F2).

To save the new graph without losing the original graph, follow the usual steps for saving a graph, but give the new graph a new name. In this example, you would press F10, and select Image, Graph, and Save. Enter a new name, such as MyGraph2, and press Enter.

REFINING GRAPHS

Before we go into the details of refining graphs, let's take a moment to discuss the terms used to describe the various elements that the graph is made of. Depending on the type of graph or chart, Paradox will utilize any or all of the following elements:

Axes: The horizontal (X) and vertical (Y) lines that establish the range of values plotted on the graph. Normally, the X-axis categorizes the data and the Y-axis measures the values. This is true for all Paradox graphs except Pie charts.

Tick marks: These are marks along the axis that divide it into segments. They allow easier reading and indicate the scale of the graph.

Labels: Information placed near the tick marks to identify values on the axes.

Series: A single field from the table that is plotted on the graph.

Legend: The visual key that identifies the different series within the graph.

Scale: The range of values assigned in the graph. This includes the increments used to divide the axis into tick marks.

Slice: Used only on pie charts, a slice represents one graphed value.

REFINING OVERALL SETTINGS

In the examples above, you changed the titles on a graph and saved those new titles. You also saw how to load previously saved custom graph settings to use them again. You can use all those same basic techniques to further customize a graph and save its new settings to be used in the future. In this section, we'll discuss the other features that you can customize. Feel free to experiment with these features on your own using the FinSum table that you created earlier.

THE GRAPH SETTINGS OVERALL SUBMENU

To change features of the entire graph, you need to specify overall settings. To access the submenu with the overall choices, start from the workspace, press F10, and select the usual Image, Graph, and Modify options. When the Customize Graph Type form appears, press F10 to access the Graph menu, and then select Overall. You'll see a submenu with the options below:

    Titles Colors Axes Grids PrinterLayout Device Wait

You've already seen how to use the Titles option from this menu to customize graph titles. In this section we'll discuss the Colors, Axes, and Grids options. (We'll discuss the other options in the section on printing graphs later in this chapter.)

MODIFYING GRAPH COLORS

Selecting Colors from the Overall submenu displays the options shown below:

    Screen Printer Copy

> Only EGA and VGA monitors are capable of displaying Paradox graphs in color.

You can select Screen to change only the colors of the screen display of the graph, or Printer to specify colors for printed copies of the graph. Regardless of whether you select Screen or Printer, Paradox displays the Customize Graph Colors form shown in Figure 10.18. (The figure shows how the form looks on a monochrome monitor. On a color monitor, of course, you'll see the colors in the box at the right.)

The leftmost column in the Customize Graph Colors form lists various parts of the graph that can be colored (such as Background, Frame, First Title Line, and others). To change the graph background color,

GRAPHICS 223

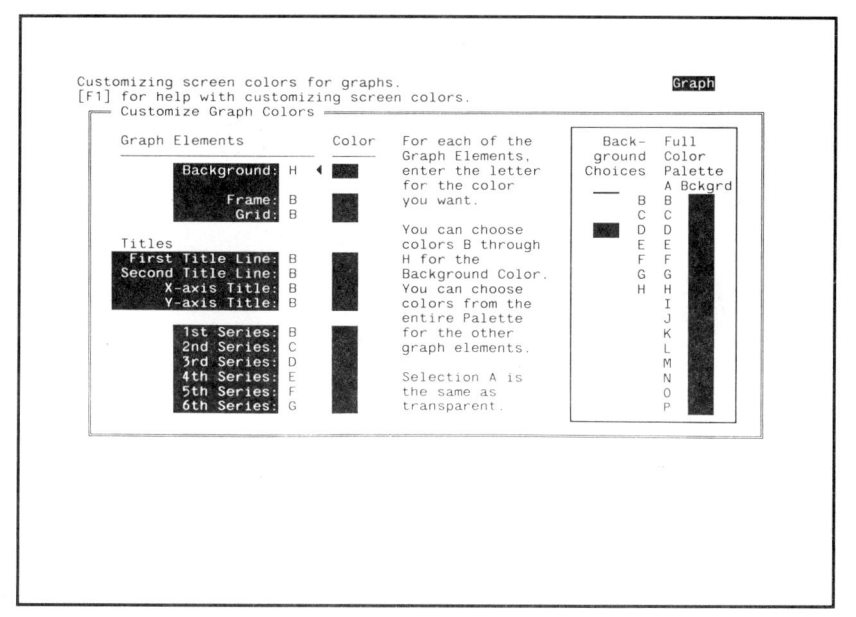

```
┌────────────────────────────────────────────────────────────────────────┐
│  Customizing screen colors for graphs.                          Graph  │
│  [F1] for help with customizing screen colors.                         │
│ ┌─ Customize Graph Colors ─────────────────────────────────────────┐   │
│                                                                        │
│   Graph Elements         Color    For each of the      Back-   Full    │
│   ─────────────                   Graph Elements,      ground  Color   │
│          Background:  H  ◀ ▓▓▓    enter the letter     Choices Palette │
│               Frame:  B    ▓▓▓    for the color        ─────   A Bckgrd│
│                Grid:  B    ▓▓▓    you want.              B     B       │
│                                                          C     C       │
│                                   You can choose         D     D       │
│   Titles                          colors B through       E     E       │
│    First Title Line:  B           H for the              F     F       │
│   Second Title Line:  B           Background Color.      G     G       │
│        X-axis Title:  B           You can choose         H     H       │
│        Y-axis Title:  B           colors from the              I       │
│                                   entire Palette               J       │
│          1st Series:  B           for the other                K       │
│          2nd Series:  C           graph elements.              L       │
│          3rd Series:  D                                        M       │
│          4th Series:  E           Selection A is               N       │
│          5th Series:  F           the same as                  O       │
│          6th Series:  G           transparent.                 P       │
│                                                                        │
└────────────────────────────────────────────────────────────────────────┘
```

Figure 10.18: The Customize Graph Colors form

type in the appropriate color code (a letter in the range of B through H), as indicated by the Background Color Choices near the right side of the screen.

To color an area other than the background, use the ↓ and ↑ keys to move the cursor to any other option on the left side of the form (such as First Title Line). You can select any color from the Full Color Palette options (A through P at the right side of the screen) simply by typing in the letter indicated (for example, M for bright red).

If you are changing screen (as opposed to printer) colors, you can press Ctrl-F7 to see how the graph looks with the new colors. Then press any key to return to the Customize Graph Colors form. You can experiment with various color combinations until you find a color scheme that you like.

When you are satisfied with your color scheme, press DO-IT! (F2) to save it and return to the workspace. Remember, if you want to keep the current color scheme for future displays of the current graph, you need to select the Image, Graph and Save options from the Paradox Main menu, as discussed previously in this chapter.

As an alternative to pressing F2 after changing options on a graphics form, you can press F10 to access the Graph menu. Settings in the current form will not be lost.

MATCHING SCREEN COLORS TO PRINTER COLORS

As an alternative to coloring screen and printer graphs separately, you can select the Copy option from the Overall Colors submenu. Doing so presents the options:

```
ScreenToPrinter   PrinterToScreen
Copy the screen colors to the printer colors
```

Select ScreenToPrinter to copy screen colors to the printed graph, or PrinterToScreen to copy the printed graph's colors to the screen graph.

MODIFYING GRAPH AXES

All graphs, except for Pie charts, have two axes: The X-axis is the horizontal axis at the bottom of the graph, the Y-axis is the vertical axis at the left of the graph. You can customize either axis in a variety of ways.

First, assuming that you are starting from the workspace, you would select Image, Graph, and Modify; then press F10 to get to the Graph menu. Select Overall and Axes from the Graph menu. This brings up the Customize Graph Axes form, shown in Figure 10.19.

The Customize Graph Axes form allows you to choose scaling, tick mark formatting, and tick mark display options, as discussed in the sections that follow.

SCALING

Scaling can best be described as controlling the range of values being displayed. By default, Paradox normally figures out how to scale the graph axes based upon the data being plotted. For example, if the smallest value to be plotted on the graph is 1,000 and the largest value to be plotted is 5,000, Paradox automatically sets up the Y-axis so it extends from 0 to 6,000.

As an alternative to using the automatic scaling method, you can change the scaling technique to Manual (by typing **M**, as indicated under the Set Axis Scaling heading near the right side of the screen).

> Changing the X-Axis scaling feature from (A)utomatic to (M)anual will affect only the X-Y Graph type. Changing the Y-Axis affects all graphs except pie charts.

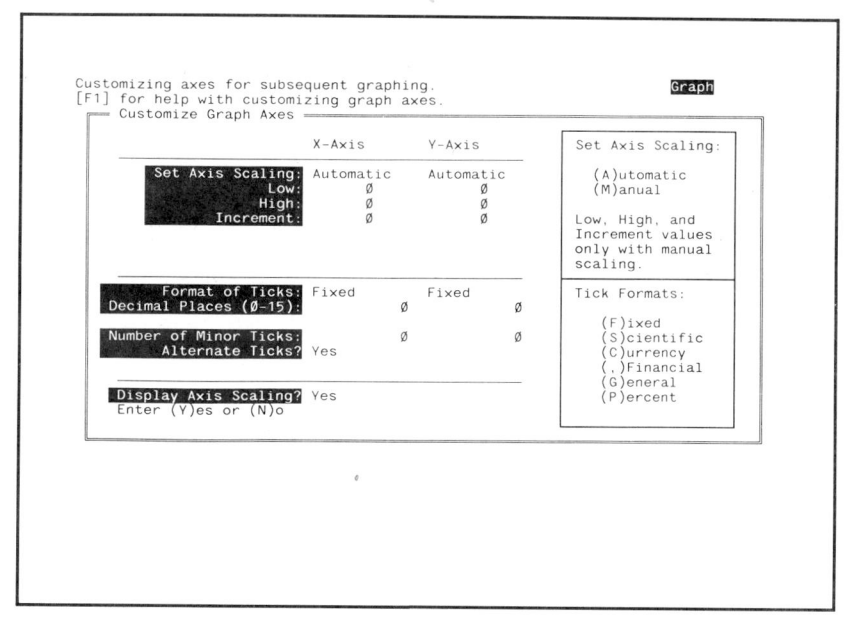

```
Customizing axes for subsequent graphing.              Graph
[F1] for help with customizing graph axes.
┌─ Customize Graph Axes ─────────────────────────────────────────┐
│                     X-Axis        Y-Axis      │ Set Axis Scaling:│
│  Set Axis Scaling: Automatic     Automatic    │                  │
│              Low:      0             0        │  (A)utomatic     │
│             High:      0             0        │  (M)anual        │
│        Increment:      0             0        │                  │
│                                               │  Low, High, and  │
│                                               │  Increment values│
│                                               │  only with manual│
│                                               │  scaling.        │
│   Format of Ticks: Fixed         Fixed        │ Tick Formats:    │
│ Decimal Places (0-15):  0             0       │                  │
│                                               │  (F)ixed         │
│ Number of Minor Ticks:  0             0       │  (S)cientific    │
│      Alternate Ticks? Yes                     │  (C)urrency      │
│                                               │  (,)Financial    │
│                                               │  (G)eneral       │
│  Display Axis Scaling? Yes                    │  (P)ercent       │
│    Enter (Y)es or (N)o                        │                  │
└───────────────────────────────────────────────────────────────┘
```

Figure 10.19: The Customize Graph Axes form

If you change the scaling technique to Manual, you can assign minimum and maximum values that refine the graph display or accentuate a trend or value.

When you set the scaling using the manual mode, make sure the range you select includes all the values to be graphed, or the resulting graph may show inaccurate results. For example, if you set the High end of the Y-Axis to 2,000, and there are values larger than 2,000, these values will only reach the top of the graph. A value of 5,000 would appear as 2,000 in this case.

You can also customize the Increment value of tick marks along the Y-axis of a graph. For example, if you plot values in the range of 0 to 5,000, Paradox will automatically place tick marks at 1,000, 2,000, 3,000, and so on along the Y-axis. However, if you change the tick mark increment value for the Y-axis to 2,000, Paradox will place tick marks at 2,000, 4,000, and 6,000 along that axis.

Customizing the X-axis only makes sense on an X-Y graph, because all other graph types automatically receive their X-axis titles from the leftmost field in the table. That is, there is one tick mark along the X-axis for each record in the table. But an X-Y graph can plot data from any numeric field in the table along the X-axis, and therefore you can customize the low and high values displayed on the X-axis, as well as the increment value of the tick marks.

TICK FORMATS

You can also control the appearance of numbers displayed on the the X and Y axes. Options for tick numbers are displayed at the right side of the Customize Graph Axes form, and summarized below:

(F)ixed	Displays numbers with a fixed number of decimal places.
(S)cientific	Displays numbers in scientific notation.
(C)urrency	Displays numbers in fixed notation with dollar signs.
(,)Financial	Inserts commas, and displays negative numbers within parentheses.
(G)eneral	Displays numbers as they appear in the table to be graphed.
(P)ercent	Displays numbers multiplied by 100 and followed by a % sign (e.g., 0.2 is displayed as 20%).

You can also set the number of decimal places to display with any type of number. Note that if your graph is plotting very large numbers, there may not be enough room to display any decimal places after the whole numbers.

MANAGING AXIS LABELS

When you display a graph using (A)utomatic scaling, every tick mark along the X and Y axis is labeled. The Number of Minor Ticks option allows you to remove labels from some of the tick marks, which can help to "unclutter" a graph that may be too cluttered in (A)utomatic mode. A "minor tick" is a tick mark without a label.

To change the number of tick labels displayed, change the Number of Minor Ticks setting to a number other than zero. For example, if you set Number of Minor Ticks to 1, then only every other tick label is displayed. If you change Number of Minor Ticks to 2, then only every third tick label is displayed (i.e., two successive ticks are left blank), and so forth.

The Alternate Ticks option, which is available only for the X-Axis, lets you determine whether or not long X-axis titles will be staggered onto two separate lines. Changing this setting to No displays X-Axis titles on a single line. Note, however, that if the titles are wider than column space permits, they will run together and be illegible.

The Display Axis Scaling option determines whether the scaling indicator at the left of the graph is displayed. In Figure 10.3, where this option is set to Yes, the word Thousands appears vertically to indicate that the Y-axis values are multiples of 1,000. Changing the Display Axis Scaling option to No would remove "Thousands" from the graph.

SAMPLE CUSTOM AXES

Figure 10.20 shows an example of a Customize Graph Axes form that was used to modify the axes of the graph shown in Figure 10.3.

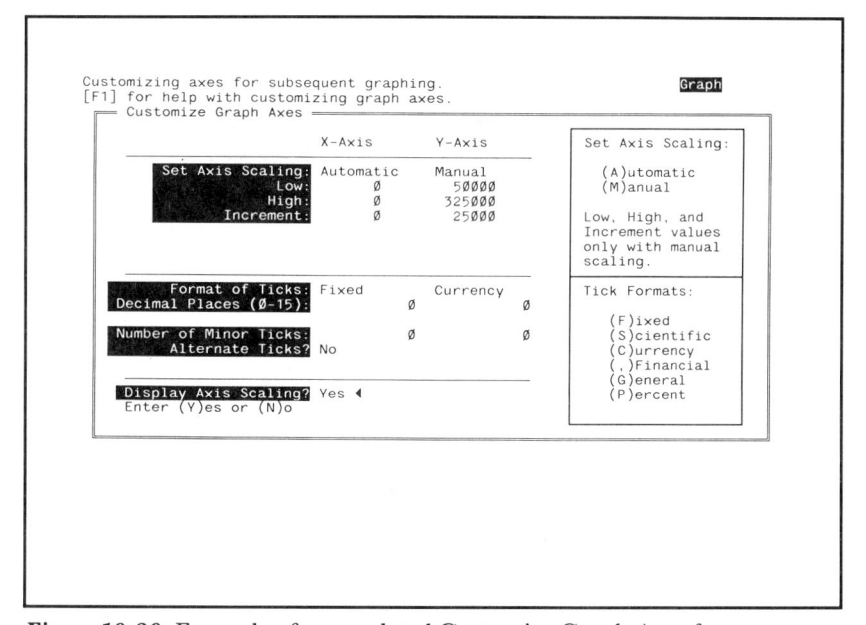

Figure 10.20: Example of a completed Customize Graph Axes form

Note that the Y-Axis setting has been changed to Manual. The Low, High, and Increment settings have been customized, and the format of ticks has been changed to Currency. The X-Axis Alternate Ticks setting has been changed to No.

Figure 10.21 shows the sample stacked-bar graph with these new customization features. Comparing this figure to the one in Figure 10.3, you can see that the values on the Y-axis range from 50 to 325 (thousand), in increments of 25 (thousand). The dollar sign that precedes each X-axis label is displayed because Currency was selected for the Format of Ticks option in the Y-Axis column.

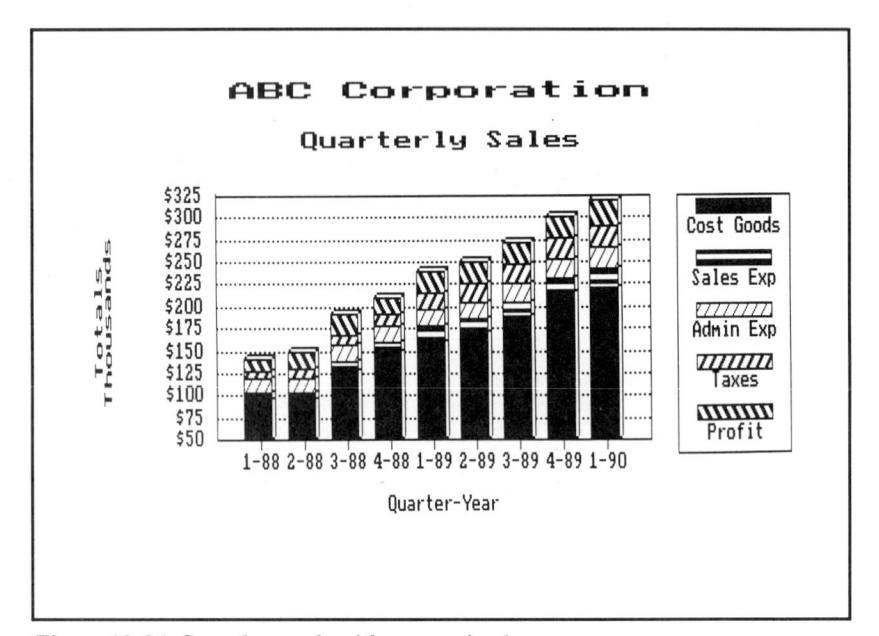

Figure 10.21: Sample graph with customized axes

The X-axis labels are not staggered onto separate rows, because the Alternate Ticks setting was changed to No on the Customize Graph Axes form.

Assuming that you do not want to save these new axis settings for future graphs, you can cancel the current settings now by pressing F10 and selecting Cancel.

MODIFYING GRAPH GRIDS

Paradox automatically displays a graph with a pattern of horizontal grid lines at the tick marks. You can control the grid pattern and colors by selecting the Grids option from the Graph Overall submenu. Doing so displays the Customize Grids and Frames form, as shown in Figure 10.22.

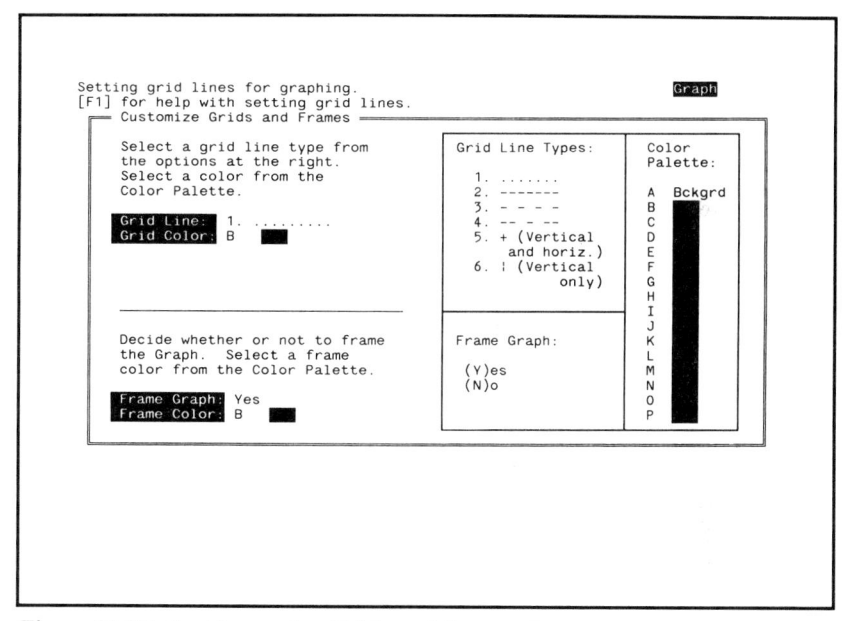

Figure 10.22: the Customize Grids and Frames form

Grid Lines

By default, Paradox uses a series of dots to represent grid lines. Other options for displaying grids are presented in the box labeled Grid Line Types on the Customize Grids and Frames form.

To select a new grid line style, simply type the number (from 1 to 6) to the right of the Grid Line: prompt.

Grid Color

To change the color of the grid lines, use any of the options in the box labeled Color Palette at the right side of the screen (i.e., a letter in the range of A to P). Type the appropriate letter into the box labeled Grid Color on the form.

If you want to remove grid lines, select a color that is the same as the background color, or A (Bckgrd).

Graph Frames

Normally, Paradox display a thin frame around the entire graph (near the edges of your screen). The Frame Graph and Frame Color options let you determine whether to keep this frame (Yes) or remove it (No). You can also select a color for the frame from the Color Palette displayed on the form.

As usual, you can press Ctrl-F7 while experimenting with Grid options to see the effects of any changes. To save the current grid settings for the current session, press DO-IT! (F2). As discussed earlier in this chapter, if you want to use the new grid settings with the current graph in future Paradox sessions, you must return to the workspace and select the Image, Graph, and Save options from the Paradox Main menu.

CUSTOMIZING GRAPH SERIES

In addition to customizing the overall features of a graph, you can customize individual series. To do so, starting from the workspace, select the usual Image, Graph, and Modify options from the Paradox Main menu. Press F10 to bring up the Graph menu, and then select Series. This will bring up the submenu shown below:

Labels MarkersAndFills Colors

MODIFYING LEGENDS AND LABELS

The LegendsAndLabels option allows you to specify how each series and element is labeled on the graph. Select this option to display the Customize Series Legends and Labels form.

Customizing the Graph Legend

Legends identify each series with its style of display. Whenever you create a graph, Paradox automatically creates a legend and uses field names from the table to identify each series plotted on the graph.

To create your own legend labels, make sure that the Use a Legend? box is set to Yes and type in a legend for each series (field) on the graph. (Note that you must be certain to type the legends in the proper order, corresponding to the left-to-right order of fields in the table view—use Ctrl-F7 to switch to the actual graph and back to help you get the order right.)

Interior Labels

Interior labels can be used to display numeric values directly within a graph. These are useful for displaying graphs that must show not only the relationships between values but the actual values as well. By default, Paradox does not display interior labels (it leaves these options set to None).

You can specify which series you wish to label and where to place each label in relation to the plotted point by typing the appropriate letter as listed beneath Label Placement on the form, and as follows:

(C)enter	Places label in middle of point.
(A)bove	Places label above point.
(B)elow	Places label below point.
(R)ight	Places label to the right of the point.
(L)eft	Places label to the left of the point.
(N)one	Omits or resets labels.

Note, however, that interior labels can clutter up a graph, so you should probably limit your use of these options to graphs that display only a few series. For example, Figure 10.23 shows a relatively simple bar graph with interior labels displayed above each bar (using data from a table you've never created). Also, because the graph only plots one series (field), we removed the legend by changing the Use a Legend? option from Yes to No.

If you attempt to display interior labels on graphs that are plotting very large numbers, Paradox will display rows of asterisks rather than the labels.

MODIFYING MARKERS AND FILL PATTERNS

The various forms of bar graphs and area graphs that display more than one series of values use *fill patterns* such as stripes to make it easier

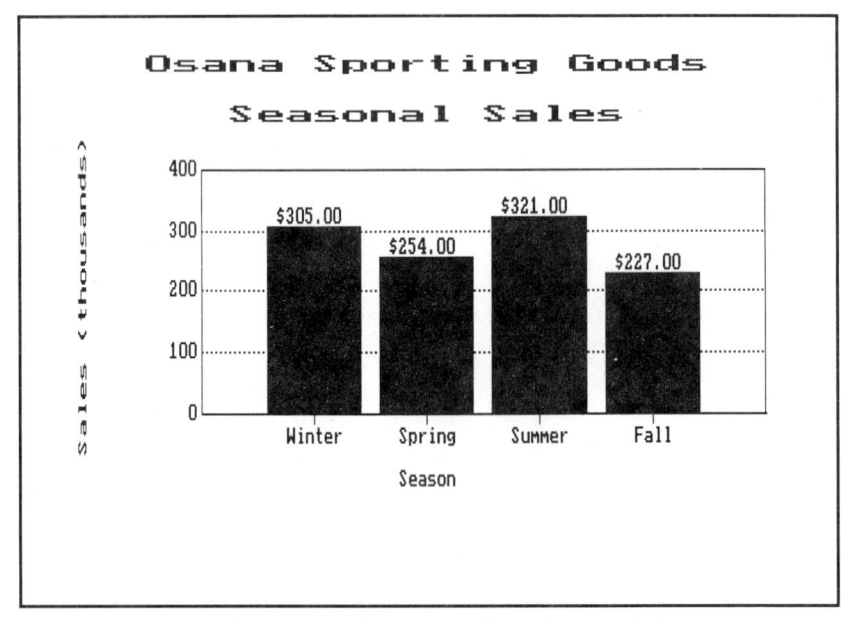

Figure 10.23: Sample graph with interior labels above each bar

for you to distinguish the different series. Marker graphs and Combined Line and Marker graphs use markers to display points that are plotted on the graph.

You can customize the fill patterns or markers for a graph using options from the Customize Fills and Markers form. To get to this form from the workspace, first select the usual Image, Graph, and Modify options from the Paradox Main menu. Then press F10 to get to the Graph menu, and then select Series and MarkersAndFills. Figure 10.24 shows the Customize Fills and Markers form that will appear on your screen.

You can select from 12 fill patterns for each series plotted in the graph by typing in the appropriate letter listed in the Fill Patterns box. For Marker and Combined Lines and Marker graphs, you can select from up to 13 different marker symbols, as indicated by the options A through M in the Marker Symbols box of the form.

As with other techniques discussed in this chapter, you can press Ctrl-F7 to see the effects of a change immediately. To save the changes for the current Paradox session, press DO-IT! (F2) to return to the workspace. If you want to save new settings in a graph for

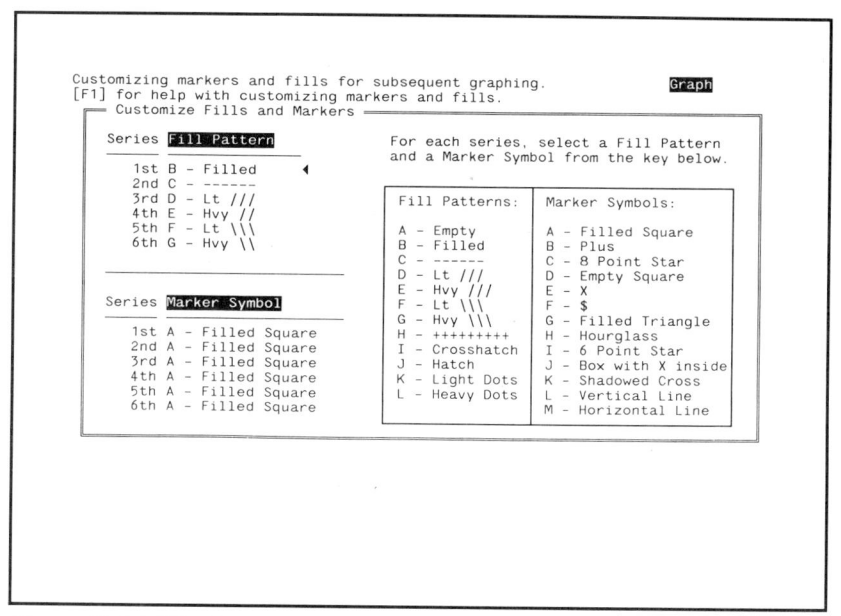

```
Customizing markers and fills for subsequent graphing.        Graph
[F1] for help with customizing markers and fills.
┌─ Customize Fills and Markers ─────────────────────────────────────┐
│                                                                    │
│   Series  Fill Pattern        For each series, select a Fill Pattern│
│      1st  B - Filled     ◄    and a Marker Symbol from the key below.│
│      2nd  C - ------                                               │
│      3rd  D - Lt ///         ┌─ Fill Patterns: ─┬─ Marker Symbols: ─┐│
│      4th  E - Hvy //         │                  │                   ││
│      5th  F - Lt \\\         │  A - Empty       │  A - Filled Square││
│      6th  G - Hvy \\         │  B - Filled      │  B - Plus         ││
│                              │  C - ------      │  C - 8 Point Star ││
│                              │  D - Lt ///      │  D - Empty Square ││
│   ─────────────────────      │  E - Hvy ///     │  E - X            ││
│   Series  Marker Symbol      │  F - Lt \\\      │  F - $            ││
│                              │  G - Hvy \\\     │  G - Filled Triangle│
│      1st  A - Filled Square  │  H - ++++++++    │  H - Hourglass    ││
│      2nd  A - Filled Square  │  I - Crosshatch  │  I - 6 Point Star ││
│      3rd  A - Filled Square  │  J - Hatch       │  J - Box with X inside│
│      4th  A - Filled Square  │  K - Light Dots  │  K - Shadowed Cross││
│      5th  A - Filled Square  │  L - Heavy Dots  │  L - Vertical Line││
│      6th  A - Filled Square  │                  │  M - Horizontal Line│
│                              └──────────────────┴───────────────────┘│
│                                                                    │
└────────────────────────────────────────────────────────────────────┘
```

Figure 10.24: The Customize Fills and Markers form

future Paradox sessions, select the Image, Graph, and Save options from the Main menu.

SPECIAL TECHNIQUES FOR PIE CHARTS

Many of the enhancements that can be added to other types of graphs do not apply to pie charts because they have no axes and can only display a single series (data from a single field). However, Paradox does allow you to customize those features that are unique to pie charts.

If you would like to try out some of these customization features yourself, you'll first need to select a single field from the FinSum table to plot. Profit is a particularly good candidate. So, with the FinSum table displayed in the workspace, press the Ctrl-End key once (or the Tab key repeatedly) until the cursor moves into the Profit field.

To view the pie chart, Press F10, select Image, Graph, and Modify. At the Customize Graph Type form, type the letter **P** (for Pie).

To get a quick view of the default graph, press Ctrl-F7. Figure 10.25 shows how this pie chart will appear on your screen.

Paradox is currently showing asterisks rather than numeric values on the default chart, because the numbers are too large to display (we'll rectify that problem in a moment).

If your screen does not show the custom titles created earlier in this chapter, and you would like to use them, first press any key to remove the graph from the screen, and then press F2 to get back to the workspace.

Then, press F10; select Image, Graph, and Load; and select MyGraph. Then change the graph type to Pie by pressing F10, selecting Image, Graph, and Modify, and typing **P**. Press F2 to save the current settings, and press Ctrl-F7 to see the pie chart with the custom titles.

Now, let's look at a few techniques for customizing pie charts. The starting point and first steps are the same for all graph operations—from the workspace press F10 and select the Image, Graph and Modify options. Then, press F10 to access the Graph menu and select Pies from that menu. This will bring up the Customize Pie Graph form as shown in Figure 10.26.

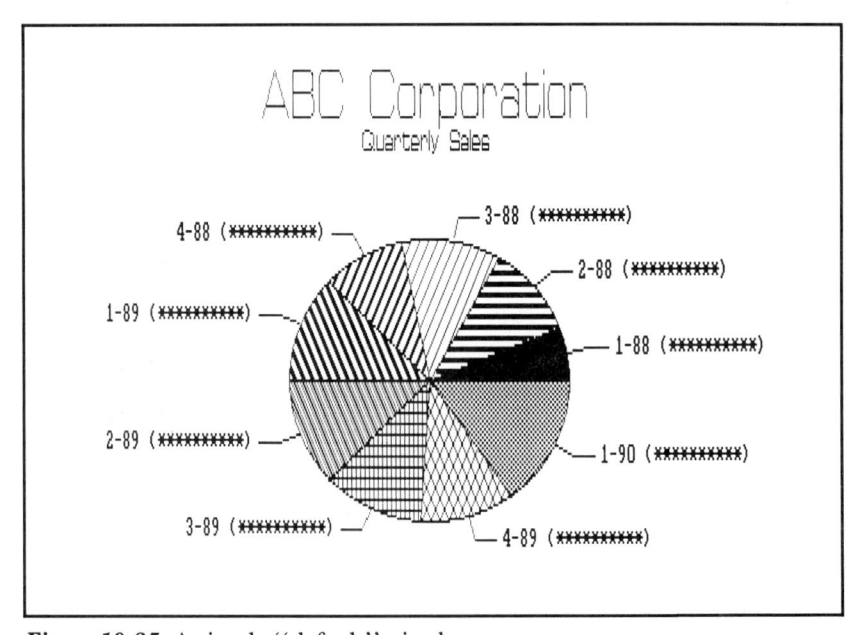

Figure 10.25: A simple "default" pie chart

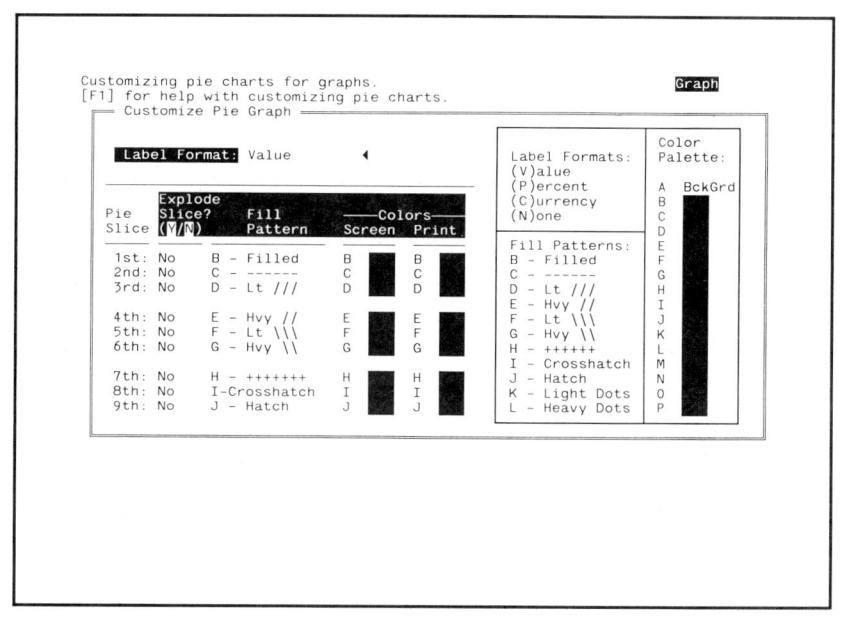

Figure 10.26: The Customize Pie Graph Form

There are four ways to control the appearance of your pie charts, as discussed in the sections that follow.

MODIFYING THE LABEL FORMAT

The slice labels on your graph can be formatted to your choice from a selection of four options:

(V)alue   Each slice will be labeled with the actual table value, if it fits. (This is the default.)

(P)ercent Each slice will be labeled with the percentage of the whole it represents.

(C)urrency Slice labels will be preceded by a dollar sign.

(N)one   No slice labels will be displayed.

Try out various Label Format options (pressing Ctrl-F7 to view the effects of your selections).

CUSTOMIZING PIE SLICES

You can individually explode, fill, or color each slice in a pie chart using options from the bottom half of the Customize Pie Graph form. Fill Patterns and Colors are displayed on the right half of the screen. To explode, or pull out, a slice, change the Explode Slice? option for that series (slice) from No to Yes. As usual, you can quickly see the effects of your change by pressing Ctrl-F7 at any time. Figure 10.27 shows our sample pie chart with the ninth slice exploded and labels displayed in Currency format.

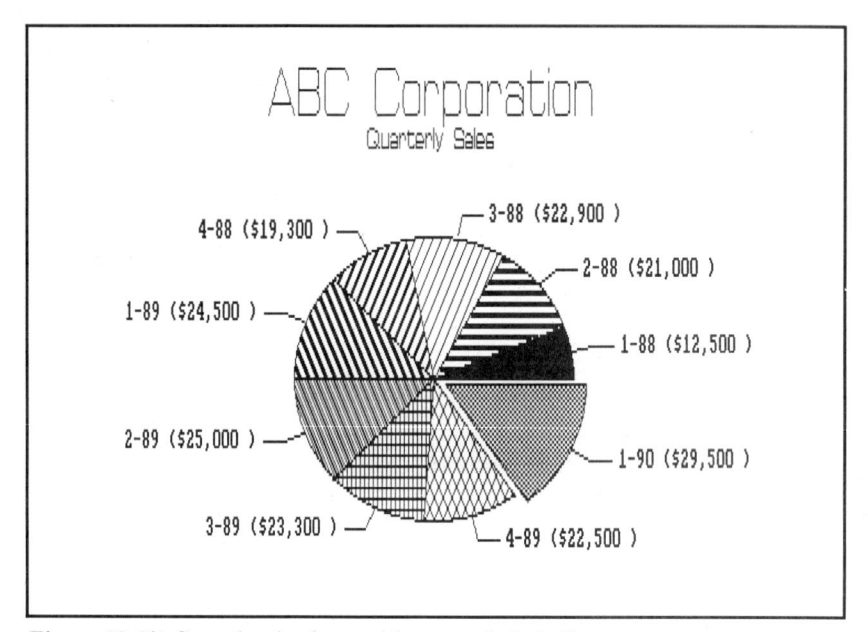

Figure 10.27: Sample pie chart with an exploded slice

As usual, remember to press F2 to save your pie chart settings for the current Paradox session and return to the worksheet. To save your settings permanently in a graph file for future use, select the usual Image, Graph, and Save options from the Paradox Main menu as discussed earlier in this chapter.

PRINTING GRAPHS

Most dot-matrix printers (and all laser printers) can print graphs. Obviously, plotters can produce graphs as well. Before you try printing graphs, however, it's a good idea to make sure Paradox is *configured* to do the job. The next section describes how to do so.

PREPARING THE PRINTER FOR GRAPHS

> You must be logged onto Paradox's directory (usually named \PARADOX3), to run the Custom Configuration program.

Even though you need only go through the graph-printing configuration procedure once (and may have already done so at some time in the past), you may want to take a moment and check your settings. To do so, you need to run the Paradox Custom Configuration program by following these steps:

1. From the Paradox workspace press F10 and select Scripts and Play.
2. Press Enter, highlight Custom, and press Enter again.
3. When asked whether you are using a Black and White monitor right now, answer Yes or No.
4. Select Graphs from the menu that appears.
5. Select Printers from the submenu.
6. If you have only one printer, select 1stPrinter. If you have additional printers, choose the one you want to use to print graphs.
7. Select TypeOfPrinter.
8. Use the ↑, ↓, PgUp, and PgDn keys to scroll through printer manufacturers' names until the cursor is on the manufacturer for your printer, and press Enter.
9. From the list of models that appears next, select your own printer model by positioning the cursor and pressing Enter.
10. If prompted for a mode, highlight the printer mode you wish to use and press Enter.

If you have more than one printer connected to your computer, you will next need to select the Settings and Device options and indicate which port your graphics printer is connected to (if you have only one printer, you need not bother with this step).

When you've finished with the configuration program, select the Return option from each submenu until the Main menu appears, and then press DO-IT! (F2). Select HardDisk or Network (whichever is appropriate for your computer system) from the next submenu. You'll be returned to the DOS prompt at this point, and will have to start Paradox from there using the usual startup procedure.

PRINTING A GRAPH

To print a graph, always begin by viewing the graph on the screen (with the usual Ctrl-F7 key) to make sure that it's ready for printing. Press any key after viewing the graph to return to the workspace. Then, from the workspace, press F10 and select Image, Graph, and ViewGraph. You'll be presented with three options:

    Screen Printer File

These options are summarized below:

Screen	Displays the graph on the screen (just like Ctrl-F7).
Printer	Sends the graph output to the printer or plotter.
File	Sends an image of the current graph to file on disk, for printing later.

To print the graph, select the Printer option. On most printers, there will be a pause of a minute or so as Paradox prepares the graph for printing. You will not have access to Paradox during this pause. However, when the graph is finally printed, you'll be returned to the Paradox workspace.

CUSTOMIZING THE PRINTED GRAPH LAYOUT

By default, Paradox will print graphs so that they fit well on the page. However, you may want to alter the size, or perhaps some other features of your printed graph. To do so, starting from the workspace, press F10 and select the usual Image, Graph, and Modify options. Then, press F10 to access the Graph menu, then select the Overall and PrinterLayout options. The Customize Graph Layout for Printing form will appear on the screen, as in Figure 10.28.

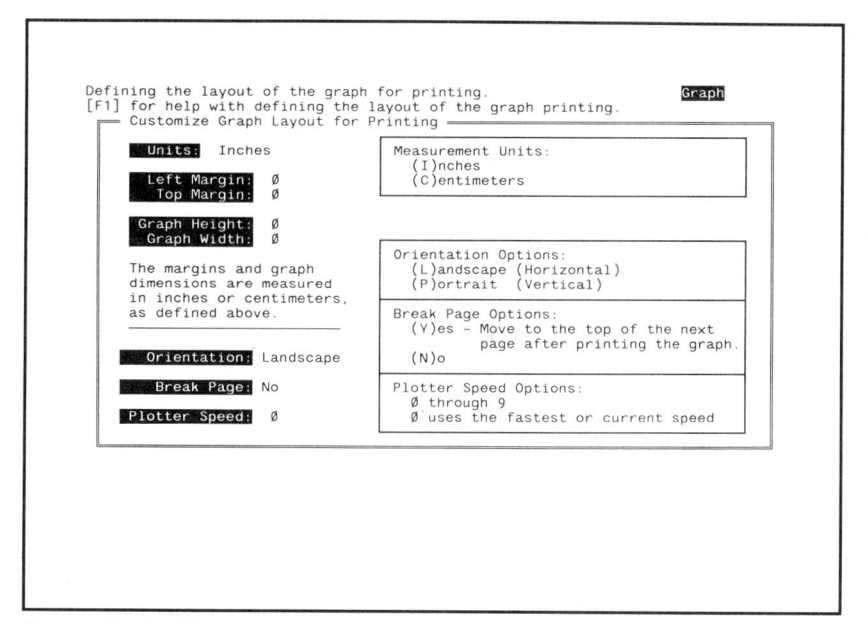

```
Defining the layout of the graph for printing.              Graph
 [F1] for help with defining the layout of the graph printing.
  ┌ Customize Graph Layout for Printing ─────────────────────────┐
  │   Units:  Inches          ┌ Measurement Units: ────────────┐ │
  │                           │     (I)nches                   │ │
  │  Left Margin:  0          │     (C)entimeters              │ │
  │   Top Margin:  0          └────────────────────────────────┘ │
  │ Graph Height:  0                                             │
  │  Graph Width:  0                                             │
  │                           ┌ Orientation Options: ──────────┐ │
  │  The margins and graph    │     (L)andscape (Horizontal)   │ │
  │  dimensions are measured  │     (P)ortrait  (Vertical)     │ │
  │  in inches or centimeters,└────────────────────────────────┘ │
  │  as defined above.        ┌ Break Page Options: ───────────┐ │
  │                           │     (Y)es - Move to the top of the next │
  │                           │             page after printing the graph. │
  │                           │     (N)o                       │ │
  │   Orientation: Landscape  └────────────────────────────────┘ │
  │    Break Page: No         ┌ Plotter Speed Options: ────────┐ │
  │ Plotter Speed: 0          │   0 through 9                  │ │
  │                           │   0 uses the fastest or current speed │
  └──────────────────────────────────────────────────────────────┘
```

Figure 10.28: The Customize Graph Layout for Printing form

The options available on the Customize Graph Layout for Printing form are summarized in Table 10.1.

The Customize Graph Layout for Printing form is like all other forms you've used to customize graphs, so you should have no problem using it. Just note that Paradox will interpret measurements for the margins and the graph height and width as either inches or centimeters, depending upon which option you specify in the Units box near the top of the form.

As usual, press DO-IT! (F2) to save the settings for the current Paradox session and return to the workspace. If you want to save these settings for all future printings of this graph, press F10 after you get to the workspace, and select Image, Graph, and Save, as discussed earlier in this chapter.

SELECTING A TEMPORARY PRINTER

If you have several printers connected to your computer, and want to select one prior to printing a graph, start from the workspace, press F10, and select the Image, Graph, Modify options. Then press F10

Table 10.1: Layout options for printed graphs.

Option	Effect
Units	
(I)nches	Measurements are expressed in inches.
(C)entimeters	Measurements are expressed in centimeters.
Left Margin	Determines the amount of blank space printed to the left of the graph.
Top Margin	Determines the amount of blank space printed above the graph.
Graph Height	Determines the height of the graph.
Graph Width	Determines the width of the graph.
Orientation	
(L)andscape	Prints graph horizontally.
(P)ortrait	Prints graph vertically.
Break Page	
(Y)es	Each graph is printed on a separate page.
(N)o	Multiple graphs can be printed on one page.
Plotter Speed	
(0) through (9)	Controls the speed of the plotter (and therefore, in some cases, the quality of the print). The fastest speed is 0, the slowest speed is 9.

and select Overall, Device, and Printer. Select the printer you want to use for printing, and then press F2 to return to the workspace. Then use the usual technique for printing (press F10 and select Image, Graph, ViewGraph, and Printer).

SAVING GRAPHS FOR PRINTING LATER

As an alternative to printing graphs immediately, you can save them in special files that you can print later, outside of Paradox. You can choose from among three file formats. Starting from the workspace, press F10 and select Image, Graph, Modify. Then press F10 to access the graph menu, and select the Overall, Device, and File options. You'll see three choices, as shown below:

CurrentPrinter   EPS   PIC

Selecting CurrentPrinter defines the file as a printer output file with a .GRF extension. The file will be formatted for the current active printer. You can use the DOS COPY command to print such a file outside of Paradox.

Choosing EPS defines the format of the file as Encapsulated PostScript (using an .EPS extension). There are several word processing programs, including Borland's Sprint, that allow you to embed graphs stored in the EPS format directly into written documents (such as reports and newsletters).

The PIC option will format the graph file for use with Lotus 1-2-3. Files saved in this format are given the extension .PIC. You can use Lotus 1-2-3, Symphony, and many other spreadsheet programs to print the graphs that are stored in this format.

After selecting the type of file, press F10 again, select ViewGraph, and then select File. You'll see the prompt

> File Name:
> Enter the name to be given to the file.

Enter a valid file name (up to eight characters, no spaces or punctuation), and press Enter. There will be a minute or more pause as Paradox saves the file, and then you'll be returned to Paradox.

LIMITING THE DURATION OF A GRAPH

As you've seen previously, Paradox displays a graph on the screen until you press any key to return to the workplace. As an alternative to displaying the graph indefinitely, you can specify how long the graph is to appear on the screen. To set or change the duration (starting from the workspace), select the usual Image, Graph, and Modify options from the Main menu. Then press F10 to get to the Graph menu, and select Overall and Wait.

You will then see the options shown below:

Keystroke   Duration

The Keystroke option allows a graph to remain displayed on the screen until a key (any key) is pressed. This is the usual approach that you are familiar with. If you select Duration, you will see the prompt

Number of seconds to wait:0

Type in a number of seconds to wait and then press Enter. (The default setting, 0, sets the duration to "infinite"; the graph is still displayed until the viewer presses a key.) Press F2 to return to the workspace.

> Displaying graphs for a fixed duration of time can be useful for creating scripts that display multiple graphs. You'll learn about scripts in later chapters of this book.

CROSS TABULATIONS

In Chapter 13 you'll learn techniques for performing calculations on numeric data with Paradox. However, there is one type of calculation, called a *cross tabulation* (or *crosstab*) that is particularly useful when plotting graphs and is available through the graph menus.

CrossTab is most useful in reducing and arranging data from a large table into a smaller table of data that is easier to graph (and generally produces more meaningful graphs as well). Getting CrossTab to produce the results that you want can be a little bit tricky at first, because you must be very careful about how you arrange the field columns and place the cursor in the table view on the screen. However, as you'll see, it's not really difficult, once you learn to adhere to a few rules of thumb.

CREATING A SAMPLE TABLE

In this example, we will use a SalesReg table that stores information about individual salespersons' sales of products by part number. To create the sample table, press F10 to call up the Main menu, select Create, and enter the table name **SalesReg** when prompted. Fill in the table structure as shown in Figure 10.29.

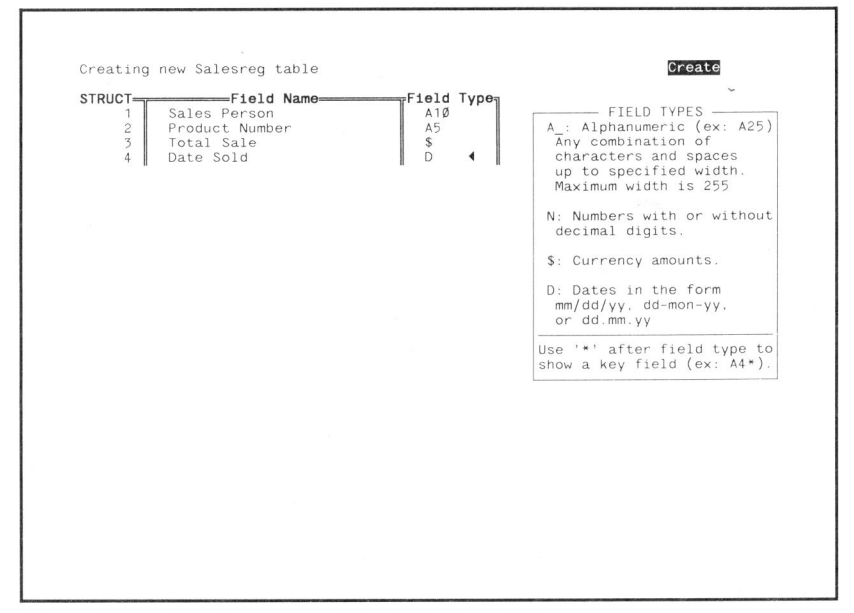

```
Creating new Salesreg table                              Create
STRUCT    Field Name        Field Type
   1    Sales Person         A10              FIELD TYPES
   2    Product Number       A5         A_: Alphanumeric (ex: A25)
   3    Total Sale           $            Any combination of
   4    Date Sold            D            characters and spaces
                                          up to specified width.
                                          Maximum width is 255

                                        N: Numbers with or without
                                          decimal digits.

                                        $: Currency amounts.

                                        D: Dates in the form
                                          mm/dd/yy, dd-mon-yy,
                                          or dd.mm.yy

                                        Use '*' after field type to
                                        show a key field (ex: A4*).
```

Figure 10.29: The structure of the SalesReg table

After you've entered the table structure for the SalesReg table, press the DO-IT! (F2) key to save it. Then fill in some sample data, as shown in Figure 10.30. When finished entering the sample data into the SalesReg table, save your work by pressing DO-IT! Then use Clear Image (F8) to clear the screen.

USING CROSSTAB

If you look at the sample data in Figure 10.30, you'll see that it contains individual sales transactions. Generating a graph directly from this table would lead to a very cluttered and complicated graph,

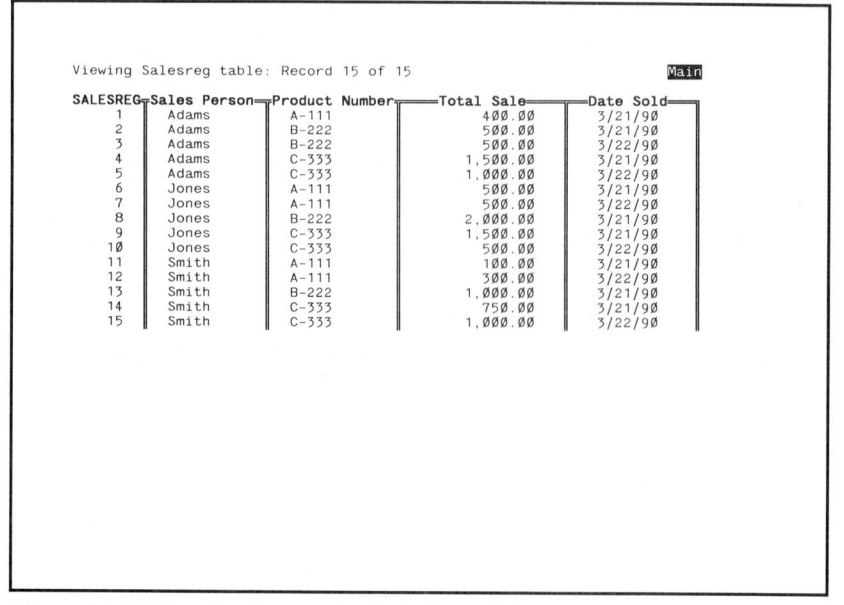

```
Viewing Salesreg table: Record 15 of 15                    Main
SALESREG  Sales Person   Product Number   Total Sale    Date Sold
    1     Adams          A-111               400.00     3/21/90
    2     Adams          B-222               500.00     3/21/90
    3     Adams          B-222               500.00     3/22/90
    4     Adams          C-333             1,500.00     3/21/90
    5     Adams          C-333             1,000.00     3/22/90
    6     Jones          A-111               500.00     3/21/90
    7     Jones          A-111               500.00     3/22/90
    8     Jones          B-222             2,000.00     3/21/90
    9     Jones          C-333             1,500.00     3/21/90
   10     Jones          C-333               500.00     3/22/90
   11     Smith          A-111               100.00     3/21/90
   12     Smith          A-111               300.00     3/22/90
   13     Smith          B-222             1,000.00     3/21/90
   14     Smith          C-333               750.00     3/21/90
   15     Smith          C-333             1,000.00     3/22/90
```

Figure 10.30: Sample data on the SalesReg table

because there are so many records, and no meaningful, summarized (totaled) results.

A better way to graph data in the SalesReg table would be to first summarize the records into a smaller table of total sales. More specifically, you might want to cross tabulate the table to determine each salesperson's totals sales for each product. Notice that we've mentioned three fields in this description of the cross tabulation; we want each *salesperson*'s *total sales* for each *product (number)*.

When a summary involves three fields such as this, CrossTab is the tool to use to get instant results. That's because a crosstab always requires exactly three fields of data to work with to generate a result. These fields are:

- **Row values:** One field in the starting table must contain values that will be summarized into unique rows in the crosstab table.

- **Column values**: A second field in the original table will be summarized into unique columns of information in the crosstab table.

- **Summary values**: A third field, which must be numeric, will be use to display the results of some calculation at the intersection of each row and column in the crosstab table.

Using the SalesReg table as an example, if we make Sales Person the field for row values, Product number the field for column values, and Total Sales the field for summary values, the resulting table will contain the total sales for each salesperson and each product; in other words, each salesperson's total sales for each product.

Notice that we've used the term *total* sales in the above description. Most likely, you will use CrossTab to generate totals. However, CrossTab can actually perform any one of several operations on the field used as the summary value, as described below:

- **Sum**: Summary values are totals for each row and column pair. In the SalesReg example, this would be the total sales for each person and each product.

- **Min**: Summary values for each row and column pair are the smallest of all individual values. In the SalesReg example, this would be the smallest individual sale for each Sales Person, for each Part.

- **Max**: Summary values for each row and column pair are the largest of all individual values. In the SalesReg example, this would be the largest individual sale for each Sales Person, for each Part.

- **Count**: Summary values for each row and column pair indicate how many records refer to that row and column pair. In the SalesReg example, this would be the the total number of records in the SalesReg table for each sales person, for each part.

GENERATING A CROSSTAB

Enough about crosstab "theory," let's go ahead and generate one. First, the table that you want to use for the crosstab must be on the workspace. If the SalesReg table is not on your screen right now, press F10 and select View from the Main menu. When prompted for the table name, press Enter and select SalesReg from the list of table names.

Next, press F10 to get to the Main menu once again, and select the Image, Graph, and CrossTab options. The following options will be displayed:

> 1) Sum 2) Min 3) Max 4) Count
> Generate a crosstab based on the sum of the values in the table.

We mentioned earlier how CrossTab can perform these various operations. For this example, select Sum. Next, the following instructions are displayed on the screen:

> Use → and ← to move to the column containing crosstab row labels ...
> then press ↵ to select it ...

The field that you select for row labels will determine what information will be listed down the left side of the crosstab table. (This field also specifies the sort order of rows in the generated crosstab table.) For our example, we want to use the Sales Person field for the row labels, so move the cursor to the Sales Person field and press Enter.

Next, the following instructions are displayed:

> Use → and ← to move to column containing crosstab column labels...
> then press ↵ to select it...

The field you select for the column labels will be listed across the top of the crosstab table. In our example, we want to use Product Number as column titles, so move the cursor to the Product Number field and press Enter.

Next, the screen displays these instructions:

> Use → and ← to move to column containing crosstab values...
> then press ↵ to generate the crosstab.

Paradox is asking which field to perform calculations on. In this example, simply move the cursor to the Total Sale field and press Enter. You'll see the message *Creating CROSSTAB* appear briefly on the screen, and then you'll see the generated crosstab table, as in Figure 10.31.

Notice that the generated table is automatically named CROSSTAB by Paradox. As you can see, the crosstab table displays exactly the data we requested. Each row refers to an individual sales person, and each column refers to an individual product. At the intersection of each row and column is the total of all sales for the row and column pair.

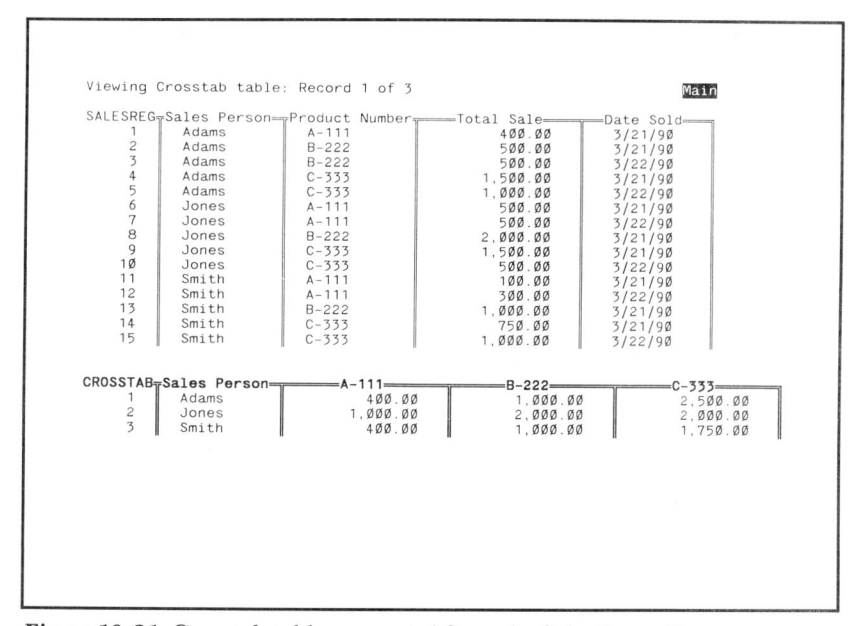

```
Viewing Crosstab table: Record 1 of 3                              Main
SALESREG┬Sales Person═╤Product Number╤═════Total Sale═══╤═══Date Sold═╕
   1    │ Adams       │ A-111        │         400.00  │    3/21/90  │
   2    │ Adams       │ B-222        │         500.00  │    3/21/90  │
   3    │ Adams       │ B-222        │         500.00  │    3/22/90  │
   4    │ Adams       │ C-333        │       1,500.00  │    3/21/90  │
   5    │ Adams       │ C-333        │       1,000.00  │    3/22/90  │
   6    │ Jones       │ A-111        │         500.00  │    3/21/90  │
   7    │ Jones       │ A-111        │         500.00  │    3/22/90  │
   8    │ Jones       │ B-222        │       2,000.00  │    3/21/90  │
   9    │ Jones       │ C-333        │       1,500.00  │    3/21/90  │
  10    │ Jones       │ C-333        │         500.00  │    3/22/90  │
  11    │ Smith       │ A-111        │         100.00  │    3/21/90  │
  12    │ Smith       │ A-111        │         300.00  │    3/22/90  │
  13    │ Smith       │ B-222        │       1,000.00  │    3/21/90  │
  14    │ Smith       │ C-333        │         750.00  │    3/21/90  │
  15    │ Smith       │ C-333        │       1,000.00  │    3/22/90  │

CROSSTAB┬Sales Person═╤═══A-111═══╤═══B-222═══╤═══C-333═══╕
   1    │ Adams       │   400.00  │ 1,000.00  │ 2,500.00  │
   2    │ Jones       │ 1,000.00  │ 2,000.00  │ 2,000.00  │
   3    │ Smith       │   400.00  │ 1,000.00  │ 1,750.00  │
```

Figure 10.31: Crosstab table generated from the SalesReg table

GRAPHING A CROSSTAB TABLE

> If your graph uses custom features that you defined earler, and you prefer that it look like the example in the figure, remove all custom settings by selecting Image, Graph, Reset, and Ok from the Main menu, and then press Ctrl-F7 again to view the graph.

To see an instant graphic result of a crosstab table, just press the Graph (Ctrl-F7) key. As you can see in Figure 10.32, the resulting graph shows the total sales for each sales person, for each part. The stacked bar graph is particularly lucid in this case because it shows both the overall total sales for each salesperson, and sales of individual products for each sales person (as indicated in the graph legend).

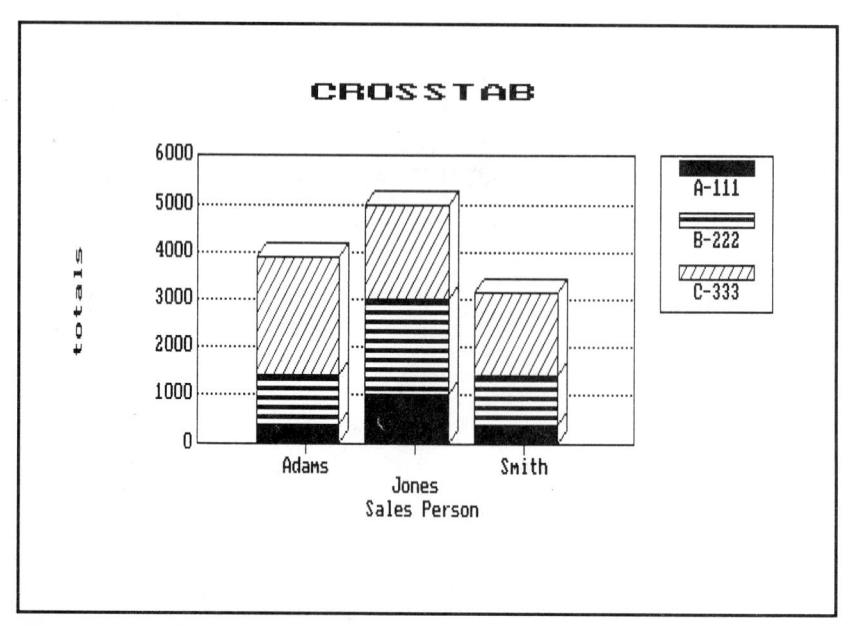

Figure 10.32: Graph generated from a crosstab table

As usual, when you are finished viewing the graph, simply press any key to return to the workspace.

ARRANGING FIELDS FOR CROSSTABS

The fields in the SalesReg were already arranged to make the crosstab easy. However, when creating crosstabs on your own, you may need to use the Rotate (Ctrl-R) key to rearrange fields in the table view *before* you start the cross tabulation process. Keep in mind these important points about the order of fields in the table view when generating your own crosstabs:

- If the field used for row labels has any fields to the left of it, those fields are combined to create the row labels.
- The field used for column labels must be to the right of the field(s) used for row values.

The first rule is a little tricky to understand, but perhaps an example will help clarify the matter. Let's try a crosstab using the Product Number column as the row labels field. Assuming your CROSSTAB table is still on the screen, press Clear Image (F8) to erase it. Next, press F10 and select Image, Graph, CrossTab, and Sum.

Move the cursor to the Product Number field and press Enter to mark that field for row labels. Next, move the cursor to the Date Sold field and press Enter to mark it as the column labels field. Finally, move the cursor to the Total Sale field and press Enter to mark Total Sale as the crosstab values field and to generate the crosstab table.

Figure 10.33 shows the resulting CROSSTAB table. Notice that each row no longer represents an individual salesperson. Instead, each row in the crosstab table now represents an individual Sales Person and Product Number pair. That's because when you marked Product Number as the field to use for row values, the Sales Person field was to the left of it, so Paradox assumed that you wanted to combine Sales Person and Product Number when generating unique values for the rows in the crosstab table.

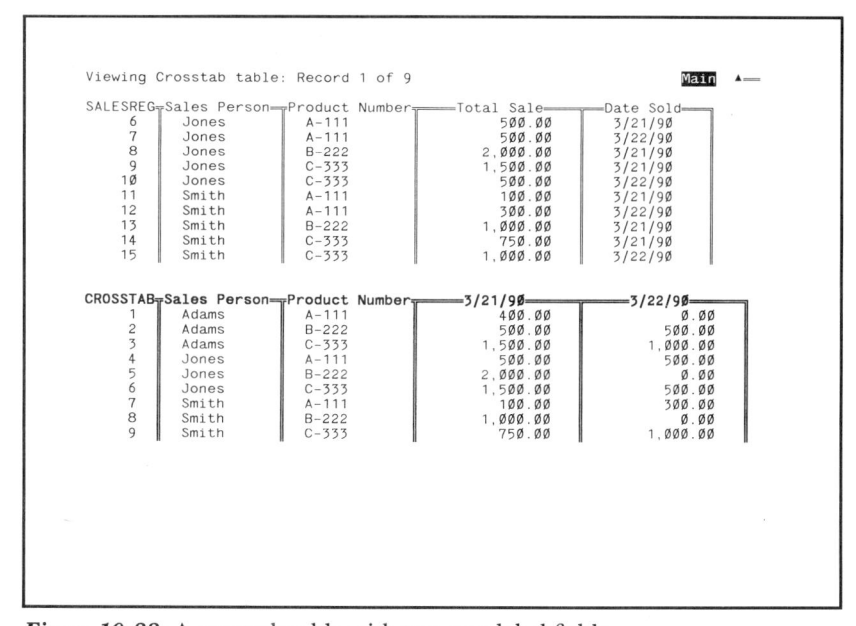

```
Viewing Crosstab table: Record 1 of 9                          Main
    SALESREG  Sales Person  Product Number   Total Sale    Date Sold
         6    Jones         A-111              500.00      3/21/90
         7    Jones         A-111              500.00      3/22/90
         8    Jones         B-222            2,000.00      3/21/90
         9    Jones         C-333            1,500.00      3/21/90
        10    Jones         C-333              500.00      3/22/90
        11    Smith         A-111              100.00      3/21/90
        12    Smith         A-111              300.00      3/22/90
        13    Smith         B-222            1,000.00      3/21/90
        14    Smith         C-333              750.00      3/21/90
        15    Smith         C-333            1,000.00      3/22/90

    CROSSTAB  Sales Person  Product Number   3/21/90       3/22/90
         1    Adams         A-111              400.00          0.00
         2    Adams         B-222              500.00        500.00
         3    Adams         C-333            1,500.00      1,000.00
         4    Jones         A-111              500.00        500.00
         5    Jones         B-222            2,000.00          0.00
         6    Jones         C-333            1,500.00        500.00
         7    Smith         A-111              100.00        300.00
         8    Smith         B-222            1,000.00          0.00
         9    Smith         C-333              750.00      1,000.00
```

Figure 10.33: A crosstab table with two row label fields

But suppose that the generated crosstab table is not really displaying the results you were looking for. That is, you wanted to use Product Number as the row labels field, rather than the Product Number and Sales Person field combination. In that case, you would need to press Clear Image (F8) to erase the current CROSSTAB table. Then, move the cursor to the Sales Person field in the SalesReg table view, and press Ctrl-R to rotate that field to the rightmost column.

If you repeat the steps to generate the crosstab table and specify Product Number as the field for row labels, the resulting table will display a single row for each unique part number.

A SHORTCUT METHOD FOR CROSSTABS

If your work requires many cross tabulations, you may want to use the shortcut CrossTab (Alt-X) key option. When you use the CrossTab key Paradox will not prompt you for fields to use for row, column, and summary values. Instead, it will assume that you've already ordered the columns in the table, and positioned the cursor, following the rules below:

- The data in the field that the cursor is in, and all fields to its left will become the row labels.

- The data in the second from the rightmost field becomes the column labels.

- The data in the rightmost field becomes the values. The field must be numeric. The field is then summed for every row and column.

- All other fields in the table are ignored.

You can use the usual Rotate (Ctrl-R) key to arrange the columns in the table view prior to using the CrossTab key. After you've arranged the order of columns, you must also remember to put the cursor in the row-value field prior to pressing CrossTab (Alt-X).

To demonstrate, we'll use the CrossTab key to generate a table of total sales for each salesperson and each part number (as in our first sample crosstab). The first step is to use the Rotate (Ctrl-R) key to arrange the fields in the SalesReg table as shown in Figure 10.34.

```
Viewing Salesreg table: Record 1 of 15                    Main
SALESREG Sales Person   Date Sold    Product Number    Total Sale
    1     Adams          3/21/90       A-111              400.00
    2     Adams          3/21/90       B-222              500.00
    3     Adams          3/22/90       B-222              500.00
    4     Adams          3/21/90       C-333            1,500.00
    5     Adams          3/22/90       C-333            1,000.00
    6     Jones          3/21/90       A-111              500.00
    7     Jones          3/22/90       A-111              500.00
    8     Jones          3/21/90       B-222            2,000.00
    9     Jones          3/21/90       C-333            1,500.00
   10     Jones          3/22/90       C-333              500.00
   11     Smith          3/21/90       A-111              100.00
   12     Smith          3/22/90       A-111              300.00
   13     Smith          3/21/90       B-222            1,000.00
   14     Smith          3/21/90       C-333              750.00
   15     Smith          3/22/90       C-333            1,000.00
```

Figure 10.34: Columns are arranged for an "instant" crosstab

Notice that the columns are now properly arranged for the crosstab. That is, the row values field (Sales Person) is in the leftmost column, the columns values field (Product Number) is the second-to-last column, and the summary field (Total Sale) is the rightmost column.

Prior to pressing CrossTab, however, you must make sure to position the cursor. In this case, you need to move the cursor to the Sales Person field. Then press CrossTab (Alt-X), and Paradox quickly generates the crosstab table, without asking any questions. (The resulting table looks exactly like the one in Figure 10.31 above.)

SUMMARY

- To produce an "Instant" graph, View your table, move the cursor to a numeric field, and press the Graph (Ctrl-F7) key.
- To select a type of graph, select Image, Graph, and Modify from the Main menu.

- To refine a graph, select Image, Graph, and Modify from the Main menu, then press F10 to access the Graph menu.
- To save custom graph settings, select Image, Graph, and Save from the Main menu.
- To load previously saved graph settings, select Image, Graph, and Load from the Main menu.
- To design the layout of a printed graph, select Image, Graph, and Modify from the Main menu. Then press F10 and select Overall and PrinterLayout.
- To print a graph, first view it on the screen, Then select Image, Graph, Viewgraph, and Printer from the Main menu.
- To summarize data in a table for graphing, select CrossTab from the Graph options menu.

SCRIPTS

CHAPTER 11

SOME TASKS IN PARADOX NATURALLY REQUIRE several keystrokes to perform. A simple example is the printing of a customer directory in alphabetical order. You need to call up the Main menu, select the Modify and Sort options, fill out the sort form, then call up the menu again, select the Report option, and so on.

You don't have to repeat all these keystrokes every time you wish to perform the task, however. Instead, you can record the required keystrokes in a Paradox *script,* then play them all back by selecting only a few menu options. In other words, you can make your entire task a single menu item and access it as you would any other Paradox menu item. Let's create a script for printing a customer directory in alphabetical order, and then we'll discuss some general techniques that you can use with scripts.

YOUR FIRST SCRIPT

If you are using Paradox on a network, see "Scripts on a Network" in Appendix B.

Though there are several ways you can begin recording a script, the easiest is to call up the Main menu (F10) and select the Scripts option. This brings up the following submenu:

   Play   BeginRecord   QuerySave   ShowPlay   ReportPlay
   Editor

To begin recording a script, select the BeginRecord option. Paradox will ask for a name for the script, as below:

   Script:
   Enter name for new script.

The name you give to a script can be up to eight characters long and cannot contain spaces or punctuation. In this example, enter the script name as

    Director

and press Enter. (*Note:* If you enter the name of an existing script, Paradox will double-check for permission before replacing the old script with the new one. Select the Cancel option to rename the new script, or the Replace option to replace the old script with the new one.)

From this point on, all of your keystrokes will be recorded and stored in a script named Director. When space permits, the letter R will appear in the upper-right corner of the screen to remind you that you are recording a script.

First, press Clear All (Alt-F8) to clear everything from the screen. (In general, it's a good idea to start every script by pressing Clear All, so that you begin with a blank workspace.) Now, sort the Custlist table into alphabetical order by selecting the Modify and Sort options from the Main menu. When Paradox asks for the name of the table, type in or select Custlist. Select the Same option from the submenu, then sort by last name, first name, and middle initial by filling out the sort form as in Figure 11.1. Press DO-IT! after specifying the sort order, and wait for Paradox to finish sorting.

When the sorted Custlist table appears on the screen, call up the menu (F10) and select the Report and Output options. Once again, type in or select Custlist. Select report 1, then select the Printer option. Paradox will print the Directory of Customers.

When the printing is done, stop recording the script by calling up the menu (F10) and selecting the Scripts and End-Record options. To play back the script, call up the menu (F10) and select the Scripts option. From the submenu, select the ShowPlay option. Paradox will ask for the name of the script to play, as below:

    Script:
    Enter name of script to play, or press ↵ to see a list of scripts.

You can either type in the script name, Director, or press Enter to see a list of script names. As with table names, you can highlight the

```
Sorting Custlist table                              Sort
┌─────────────────────────────────────────────────────────┐
│ Number fields to set up sort order (1, 2, etc.). If you want a field sorted │
│    in descending sequence, follow the number with a "D" (e.g., "2D").       │
│         Ascending is the normal sequence and need not be indicated.         │
└─────────────────────────────────────────────────────────┘
          Mr/Mrs
     1    Last Name
     2    First Name
     3_ ◄ M.I.
          Company
          Department
          Address
          City
          State
          Zip
          Phone
          Start Date
          Credit Limit
```

Figure 11.1: A sort form filled out for alphabetical sort

name of the script and press Enter to select it. When Paradox asks if you want the script played Fast or Slow, select Fast.

You'll now see Paradox play back all your keystrokes, exactly mimicking every step you used to print the sorted directory. Furthermore, the Director script will be saved automatically when you exit Paradox, so you can use it over and over again in the future.

This simple example does not demonstrate the full potential of scripts. But when you begin performing more complex tasks in Paradox, requiring perhaps hundreds of keystrokes, you'll really begin to appreciate the power of being able to record the steps taken in performing a task, and then repeat them at any time in the future by selecting a script name from the Scripts submenu.

VIEWING A RECORDED SCRIPT

You can look at the contents of a recorded script by calling up the Main menu and selecting the Scripts and Editor options. From the submenu, select Edit. Paradox will ask for the name of the script to edit. In this example, type in or highlight the name Director. You'll see the recorded script as in Figure 11.2.

Notice that the script contains all the keystrokes and menu options you selected during recording. You can change or modify the script, using the usual keys for moving the cursor, but don't do so now. We'll discuss techniques for customizing and enhancing scripts later in the book. For now, just call up the menu (F10) and select the Cancel and Yes options.

```
Changing script Director                                    Script
....+....10....+....20....+....30....+....40....+....50....+....60....+....70....+....80
ClearAll {Modify} {Sort} {Custlist} {Same} Down "1" Down
"2" Down "3" Do_It! Menu {Report} {Output} {Custlist} {1}
{Printer} Menu {Scripts} {End-Record}
```

Figure 11.2: A recorded script ready for editing

THE SCRIPTS MENU

Now let's briefly discuss what each option under Scripts provides. You will recall that the Scripts submenu consists of the following options:

**Play   BeginRecord   QuerySave   ShowPlay   RepeatPlay
Editor**

The Play option allows you to play back a previously recorded script, as does the ShowPlay option. The Play option, however, displays only the net results of the entire script (a printed directory in the Director example), without displaying the menus and keystrokes along the way as the script is being played.

The BeginRecord option, as we discussed, allows you to name a script and begin recording keystrokes. If you call up the menu (F10) and select Scripts after selecting BeginRecord, you'll see these options:

Cancel   End-Record   Play   QuerySave   ReportPlay

The End-Record option stops recording your script. The Cancel option discards all recorded keystrokes since the last BeginRecord session and returns you to the workspace. The Play and RepeatPlay options select another script and play it *inside* the script currently being recorded. This advanced technique is discussed in later chapters.

The ShowPlay option plays back a script, showing menus and keystrokes along the way. Before playing back a script, ShowPlay presents these options:

Fast   Slow

The Fast option plays the script rapidly, and the Slow option plays back the script very slowly. The Slow option is usually used when developing more complex scripts that need to be analyzed in slow motion for changes and enhancements.

The RepeatPlay option lets you play a script any number of times. When you select RepeatPlay, you'll be prompted for the name of the script to play, as usual. After you enter the script name, you'll see the prompt and instructions below:

Enter number of times to repeat:
Enter the number of times to play the script or "c" for
continuous play.

Enter any number, or the letter **C**, and press Enter. The script will be repeated as many times as you've specified. If you entered C, for continuous play, the script will be played repeatedly until you press Ctrl-Break. (Hold down the Ctrl key and press the key labeled Break. The key may have Break written on the side and Pause or Scroll lock written on top.)

The QuerySave option saves a query form set up through the Ask option. We'll see examples of the power of this option in later chapters. But for now, suffice it to say that queries involving multiple tables can become quite complicated. QuerySave lets you record a complex query and play it back at any time, just as a recorded script allows you to record and play back keystrokes.

The Editor option presents this submenu:

   Write   Edit

The Write option allows you to write your own PAL (Paradox Application Language) program. Until you become familiar with PAL you won't want to use this option. The Edit option allows you to change or modify existing scripts or PAL programs.

INSTANT SCRIPTS

Another way to record a script is simply to press Instant Script Record (Alt-F3). As with the BeginRecord option, an R will appear in the upper-right corner of the screen (when room permits), and all keystrokes will be recorded. To stop recording an instant script, press Alt-F3 again. To play back an instant script, press Instant Script Play (Alt-F4). Paradox will instantly play back your keystrokes exactly as you recorded them.

Paradox stores the instant script in a file named Instant. To save an instant script, you'll need to change its name, because Paradox can save only one instant script at a time. To do so, call up the Tools option and select Rename. Then select the Script option and change the name of the instant script to some new, unique name.

Whenever you use Instant Script Record, Paradox automatically erases the existing instant script. Therefore, if you do not intentionally save your instant script after recording, it will be lost the next time you press Instant Script Record.

THE PAL MENU

If you are in the middle of an operation when you decide to begin recording a script, you may not be able to get to the Main menu to select the Scripts options. To get around this, you can call up the PAL menu by pressing Alt-F10. The PAL menu also provides the BeginRecord, End-Record, and Play options, which are identical to those options under the Scripts menu.

AUTOEXECUTE SCRIPTS

If you give the name *Init* to a script, it will be played automatically each time Paradox is started. Paradox always stores scripts with the name you assign followed by the extension .SC (for example, Director.SC). When Paradox first starts up, it looks on the program disk for a file named Init.SC. If it finds Init.SC, Paradox plays the script immediately before displaying the Main menu. If no Init.SC script is found, Paradox runs normally. (We'll discuss this in greater detail when we get to the PAL language.)

BEING CREATIVE

As with most Paradox functions, the best way to learn about scripts is simply to experiment with them. You certainly can't do any harm by recording keystrokes and playing them back. A good way to practice, however, might be to create a script called Labels that sorts Custlist data into zip code order, then prints mailing labels.

In later chapters we'll see how we can combine scripts with PAL to create very powerful customized systems. Before we get to that point, however, we need to enhance our present skills by learning to manage multiple tables. We'll get started on this topic in the next chapter.

SUMMARY

- To record a script, call up the Main menu (F10) and select the Scripts and BeginRecord options. Enter a name for the script, using a maximum of eight letters and no spaces or punctuation.

- If the main menu is not available when you want to start or stop recording a script, press Alt-F10 and use the Pal menu inserted.

- To stop recording, call up the Main menu and select the Scripts and End-Record options.

- To play back a script, call the Main menu and select the Scripts option. Then select either the Play or ShowPlay options.

- To view a recorded script, select the Editor and Edit options from the Scripts and Editor menus.

- To record a script instantly, press Instant Script Record (Alt-F3) to begin recording keystrokes. To stop recording, press Alt-F3 again. To play back an instant script, press Instant Script Play (Alt-F4). To save an instant script, you must rename it by selecting the Rename and Script options from the Tools submenu.

PART II

MULTIPLE TABLES IN A DATABASE

DATABASE DESIGN WITH MULTIPLE TABLES

CHAPTER 12

UP TO THIS POINT, ALL OF OUR WORK WITH PARADOX has used single tables to teach and demonstrate the important "nuts and bolts" of managing data stored in a single table. With that important information under our belts, we can begin to look into some of the more sophisticated aspects of Paradox database management.

The techniques used to manage multiple tables are largely the same as the techniques used to manage a single table, so we certainly have not wasted any time in previous chapters. However, several new concepts come into play when managing multiple tables; those concepts are what this chapter is all about.

Many applications, such as those that manage a mailing list or customer list, require only a single table. Larger business applications typically require more complex designs, using several related tables. The task of determining how to divide data into separate, related tables is called *database design*.

THE ONE-TO-ONE DATABASE DESIGN

The *one-to-one* relationship is the simplest and perhaps most common database design. The customer list developed in previous chapters used a one-to-one design. The term *one-to-one* stems from the fact that for each field in the table, there is another related field. In the customer table, for each one customer name, there is one company affiliation, one address, one city, one state, and so forth. As a reminder, Figure 12.1 shows the structure of the Custlist table used in previous chapters.

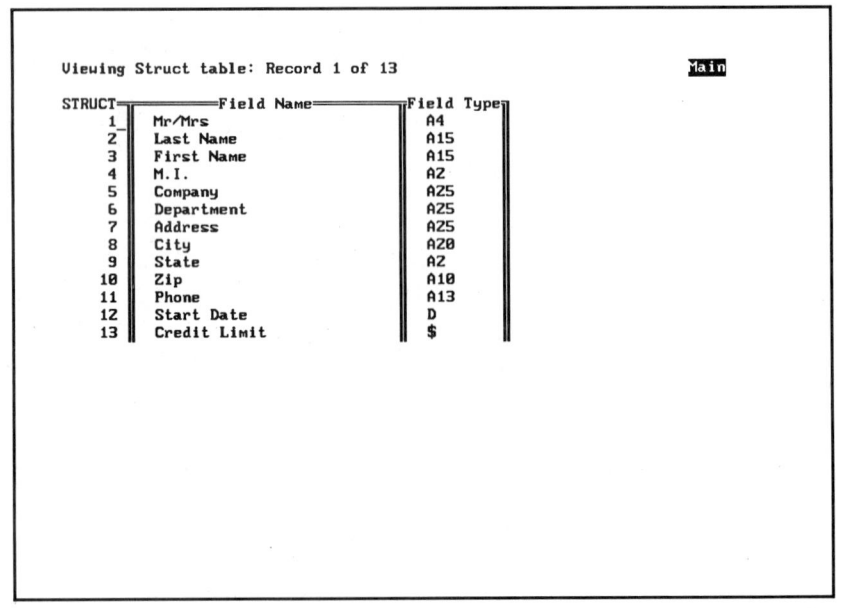

```
Viewing Struct table: Record 1 of 13                    Main
STRUCT       Field Name          Field Type
    1     Mr/Mrs                  A4
    2     Last Name               A15
    3     First Name              A15
    4     M.I.                    A2
    5     Company                 A25
    6     Department              A25
    7     Address                 A25
    8     City                    A20
    9     State                   A2
   10     Zip                     A10
   11     Phone                   A13
   12     Start Date              D
   13     Credit Limit            $
```

Figure 12.1: One-to-one database design illustrated in the structure of the Custlist table

THE ONE-TO-MANY DATABASE DESIGN

The *one-to-many* database design is used in situations where many (usually an unknown number) items of data are associated with another data item. For example, in an accounts-receivable system, each individual customer might charge several items during the course of the month. In other words, there could be many charge transactions placed by one customer.

If you attempt to design the database for an accounts-receivable system using a single table, you'll quickly see the problems inherent in the design. If the table has a single record for each charge transaction, where do you store the customer's name, address, city, state, zip code, and so forth? If you store this information with each charge transaction, there will be a great deal of redundant data.

For example, even though there are only three unique customers (Smith, Miller, and Jones) in the charge transactions listed in Figure

12.2, the table uses a lot of disk space because of all the redundant data in the name and address fields. A data-entry operator will waste a lot of time typing the name and address of each customer repeatedly. Furthermore, if one of the customers moves and changes their address, that address will have to be changed in many different records.

```
Last Name    First Name  Address          City          Charge
Jones        Fred        345 Grape St.    Encinitas     6457.42
Smith        Albert      345 C St.        San Diego        5.10
Smith        Albert      345 C St.        San Diego     1000.00
Adams        Martha      P.O. Box 1107    Alameda         76.50
Smith        Albert      345 C St.        San Diego     4567.89
Adams        Martha      P.O. Box 1107    Alameda         99.00
Adams        Martha      P.O. Box 1107    Alameda        123.45
Adams        Martha      P.O. Box 1107    Alameda       3245.69
Jones        Fred        345 Grape St.    Encinitas      333.33
Smith        Albert      345 C St.        San Diego      596.43
Jones        Fred        345 Grape St.    Encinitas      764.32
```

Figure 12.2: Example of a poor accounts-receivable database design

One solution to the problems with this design is to store one record for each customer, and have several fields for charges. But such a design limits the number of transactions that can be assigned to a particular customer to the number of fields allocated for transactions in the table. It also makes it virtually impossible to answer questions such as, "How many charge transactions this month involved part number A-123?"

USING A COMMON FIELD TO RELATE TABLES

To resolve the inherent problems in trying to store accounts-receivable data in a single table, the data can be stored on two separate tables. Then a single *common field* (or *key field*) can be used to *relate* the two tables.

Figure 12.3 shows the structures of two tables named Customer and Charges. The Customer table contains a single record for each customer in the hypothetical accounts-receivable system. Each customer is assigned a unique customer number in the field named CustNo. The Charges table stores each individual charge transaction

Structure of the Customer table

Field	Field Name	Field Type	Description
1	CustNo	N*	Customer number
2	LName	A15	Last name
3	FName	A10	First name
4	Address	A25	Address
5	City	A20	City
6	State	A2	State
7	Zip	A10	Zip code
8	Phone	A13	Phone number
9	Last_Updat	D	Last updated
10	Start_Bal	$	Starting balance
11	Chg_Curr	$	Current charges
12	Pay_Curr	$	Current payments
13	Bal_30	$	Balance last month
14	Bal_60	$	Balance 2 months ago
15	Bal_90	$	Balance 3 months ago
16	Bal_90Plus	$	Balance over 3 months
17	Terms	A20	Credit terms

Structure of the Charges Table

Field	Field Name	Field Type	Description
1	CustNo	N	Customer number
2	Part_No	A5	Part number
3	Qty	N	Quantity purchased
4	Unit_Price	$	Unit price
5	Date	D	Date of purchase

Figure 12.3: The structures of the Customer and Charges tables

on a single record. The CustNo field in the Charges table identifies which customer in the Customer table the transaction belongs to.

Note that the common field in the two tables, CustNo, has been given the exact same Field Name and Field Type in both table structures. This is essential to the success of relational database design. Notice also that the type of the CustNo field is marked with an asterisk, indicating that it is the key field. Paradox uses this field when sorting the table and when rejecting duplicate entries (a process we'll examine later in this chapter).

Figure 12.4 shows sample listings of the two tables. It is easy to see which charges belong to which customers, as the arrows linking customer number 1001 to his charges indicate.

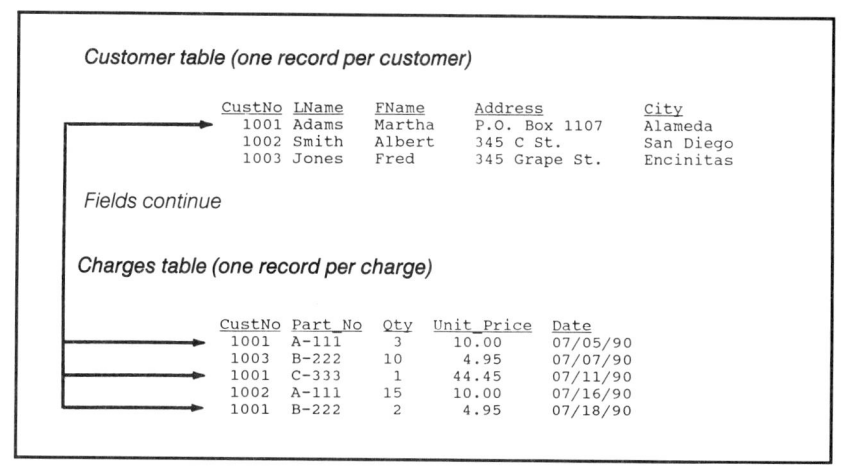

```
Customer table (one record per customer)

          CustNo  LName  FName   Address         City
          1001    Adams  Martha  P.O. Box 1107   Alameda
          1002    Smith  Albert  345 C St.       San Diego
          1003    Jones  Fred    345 Grape St.   Encinitas

Fields continue

Charges table (one record per charge)

          CustNo  Part_No  Qty  Unit_Price  Date
          1001    A-111     3    10.00      07/05/90
          1003    B-222    10     4.95      07/07/90
          1001    C-333     1    44.45      07/11/90
          1002    A-111    15    10.00      07/16/90
          1001    B-222     2     4.95      07/18/90
```

Figure 12.4: Sample data from the Customer and Charges tables

Note that dividing the information into two separate tables minimizes the redundant data. Each customer and his address (and other related information) fills a single record on the Customer table. Each transaction for each customer requires one record on the Charges table. Only the customer number is repeated on both tables, and there is no limit to the number of transactions that can be assigned to each customer.

GUIDELINES FOR CREATING A COMMON FIELD

The common field that relates the two tables is an important one, and there are a couple of guidelines that you should follow when designing your own databases and choosing common fields.

Make Common Fields Unique

If there is a one-to-many relationship involved, the common field on the "one" side of the relationship must be unique to each record.

Otherwise, there will be no way of matching a given record with the appropriate record on the "many" side of the relationship. For example, suppose the last-name field (LName) rather than CustNo was the common field between the Customer and Charges tables discussed above.

Furthermore, suppose there are ten customers with the last name Smith on the Customer table. If one of the charges in the Charges table is charged to Smith, you have no way of knowing which Smith it refers to. You could refine the relationship a bit by trying to link the two tables by both last and first name, but if you have two customers with the same first and last name your problem will not be solved.

The customer number is the best way to set up the common field between the Customer and Charges tables, because you can then ensure that each customer has a unique customer number. That way, when a record on the Charges table refers to customer number 1005, there can be no ambiguity about which customer on the Customer table gets the bill (assuming, of course, that only one customer has been assigned the number 1005).

To make matters easier, a Paradox table can easily be set up to reject any duplicate entries in the common field on the "one" side of the one-to-many relationship. We'll see how this is accomplished a little later in this chapter.

Make Common Fields Arbitrary

A second guideline in creating common fields is to make them meaningless. A four-digit number (from 1001 to 9999) is a good choice, because it has no other meaning in the database.

If you decide to place encoded information into the customer number (for example, by assigning numbers such as SDC5112, where SD stands for San Diego, C5 stands for credit rating of 5, and 112 is the customer number), you might have some difficulty in ensuring that each customer has a unique number. Furthermore, if the encoded information changes (the customer moves away from San Diego or his credit rating changes), you'll have to change his customer number. As soon as you change the customer number on the Customer table, you have to make sure both that the new number is not already in use and that the same change is made to all the CustNo fields in any related tables.

To avoid this problem, put any meaningful information into a field of its own, and make the customer number a plain, arbitrarily (or sequentially) assigned number.

THE MASTER-TABLE/TRANSACTION-TABLE STRUCTURE

One of the most common applications of the one-to-many design is the master-table/transaction-table relationship. In this design, the master table keeps track of current, ongoing balances, while the transaction table records individual transactions that affect those balances. The master table tells us the status of things at the moment, while the transaction tables maintain a history, or audit trail, of the events that produced those current balances.

A retail-store inventory database provides a good example. The master table stores one record for each item that is kept in stock and the quantity currently in stock. Two other tables are used to keep track of individual sales transactions and individual purchases (items received into the stock room or warehouse).

Through a process called *updating*, Paradox can subtract the quantities of items sold from the appropriate in-stock quantity on the master table. The quantities of items received into the stock room can be added to the appropriate in-stock quantities. The net result is that the master table reflects the true quantity of each item in stock, while the tables recording individual sales and purchase transactions still retain their useful information.

The accounts-receivable system can be structured with a master-table/transaction-table relationship as well. The master table records the customer number, name, address, and current balance for each credit customer. Charges and payments can be stored in separate tables. Each charge and payment transaction can then be assigned to a customer, through the customer number, so there is no ambiguity about which customer each charge and payment transaction belongs to.

Through updating, the current charges can be added to each customer's balance, and his payments can be subtracted from his balance. Thus, current information is readily available (current balances), and historical information (the individual charges and payments that produced the balances) is maintained. Updating techniques are discussed in more detail in Chapter 15.

THE MANY-TO-MANY DATABASE DESIGN

The *many-to-many* relationship occurs in situations such as scheduling or exploded inventories. For example, when scheduling students for classes, there will be many students in each of many classes, and many classes each with many students. In an exploded inventory, a manufacturer might produce many products from many components. Likewise, each of many components might be used in many products. Let's discuss each example independently.

A SCHEDULING DATABASE

The class scheduling problem mentioned above is the classic example of the many-to-many relationship. To avoid redundancies in storing data, all of the necessary information is split into several tables. The Courses table contains information about each course or each section of each course. Each course has a unique number assigned to it, which is the common field that links specific students to specific courses. The structure and sample data for the Courses table are shown in Figure 12.5. (This table is simplified, because each course might really be offered in several different sections or time slots.)

The Students table contains one record for each student in the school. To identify students individually, each student is assigned a unique student number. The structure and sample data for the Students table are shown in Figure 12.6.

To link the many students to their appropriate courses, a third table—called a *linking* table—contains one record for each student enrolled in each class. For this example, the linking table is called SCLink and has the structure and sample data shown in Figure 12.7. From the contents of the SCLink table, you can clearly see that student number 10001 is enrolled in courses B-222 and C-333. Student number 10002 is enrolled in courses A-111, B-222, and C-333.

Structure of the Courses table

Field	Field Name	Field Type	Description
1	CourseID	A5*	Course number
2	Course Name	A20	Course name
3	Instructor	A15	Instructor's name
4	Room Number	N	Room number

Other relevant fields can be included

Sample Courses data

```
CourseID  Course Name   Instructor      Room number
A-111     Algebra       Mr. Jones       551
B-222     Botany        Miss Smith      901
C-333     Chemistry     Mrs. Pauling    321
```

Figure 12.5: The structure and sample contents of the Courses table

Structure for the Students table

Field	Field Name	Field Type	Description
1	StudentID	N*	Student number
2	Last Name	A10	Last name
3	First Name	A10	First name
4	Address	A20	Address
5	City	A20	City
6	State	A2	State
7	Zip	A5	Zip code
8	Phone	A13	Phone number

Sample Students data

Fields continue

```
StudentID  Last Name  First Name  Address
10001      Adams      Angela      123 A St.
10002      Baker      Bobbi       345 B st.
10003      Carlson    Carla       345 C St.
```

Figure 12.6: The structure and sample contents of the Students table

As Figure 12.8 shows, the SCLink table provides a sort of "map" as to which students are enrolled in which courses. There are no redundant data on either the Students or Courses tables; each contains a single record for a single student or course. The SCLink table does contain many redundant records, of course, but since there are only two fields on the table, little disk storage space is wasted. Furthermore, the Students and Courses tables are easy to maintain, because each contains only one record per student or per course, respectively.

In some situations, the linking table will contain more than two fields, as the next section demonstrates.

```
Structure for the SCLink table

Field    Field Name    Field Type    Description
  1      StudentID         N         Student number
  2      CourseID          A5        Course number


Sample SCLink data

StudentID    CourseID
10001        B-222
10001        C-333

10002        A-111
10002        B-222
10002        C-333

10003        A-111
10003        C-333
```

Figure 12.7: The structure and sample contents of the SCLink table

```
Students table                        SCLink table
                                      StudentID  CourseID
                                      10001      B-222
                                      10001      C-333       CourseID   Course Name
StudentID  Last Name   First Name     10002      A-111       A-111      Algebra
10001      Adams       Angela         10002      B-222       B-222      Botany
10002      Baker       Bobbi          10002      C-333       C-333      Chemistry
10003      Carlson     Carla          10003      A-111
                                      10003      B-222
                                      10003      C-333
```

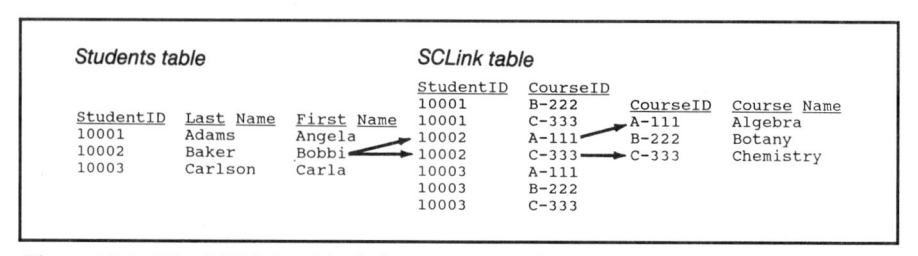

Figure 12.8: The SCLink table links students to the courses

AN EXPLODED INVENTORY DATABASE

Another example of a many-to-many relationship among tables is the *exploded inventory* model. One table, named Product, stores one record for each type of product the company produces. The structure and sample data for the Product table are shown in Figure 12.9. (In Chapter 13, we'll see how the Needed field can be used to calculate the number of components needed to produce a certain number of products.) Of course, you can also include other fields, such as as the quantity in stock, selling price, and so forth, but this table just shows some basic fields to present the structure.

Structure for the Product table

Field	Field Name	Field Type	Description
1	Product Number	A5*	Product number
2	Product Name	A25	Product name
3	Needed	N	Quantity to manufacture

Other relevant fields can be included

Sample data for the Product table

Product Number	Product Name	Needed
A-123	Personal Computer	100
B-123	Minicomputer	50
C-123	Mainframe Computer	20

Figure 12.9: The structure and sample contents for the Product table

A second table, named Componen, contains one record for each type of component that the manufacturer purchases to create its products. Each component has a unique component number, stored in the field named Component Number. The structure and sample data for the Componen table are shown in Figure 12.10. (Again, you might want to include other relevant information, such as purchase price, date of last shipment received, quantity on order, expected date of next shipment, vendor, and so forth.)

```
Structure for the Componen table

Field    Field Name           Field Type    Description
1        Component Number     A7*           Component number
2        Component Name       A21           Component name
3        In_Stock             N             Quantity in stock


Other relevant fields can be included.

Sample data for the Componen table

Component Number    Component Name              In_Stock
TT-1234             80286 microprocessor            500
UU-1234             Color monitor                   500
VV-1234             Monochrome monitor              500
WW-1234             Hard disk                       500
YY-1234             Floppy controller               500
ZZ-1234             Floppy disk drive               500
```

Figure 12.10: The structure and sample contents for the Componen table

There is a many-to-many relationship between the Product and Componen tables, because each product uses many components, and each component is used in many products. A linking table, named Linker in this example, sets up the relation between these two tables, describing which products use which components.

Because some products use more than one of a particular component, the Linker table includes the quantity of each component required to produce each product. This information is stored in the Qty_Used field of the Linker table. The structure and sample contents of the Linker table for this example are shown in Figure 12.11.

Note that product number A-123 uses one component number TT-1234 and two component numbers ZZ-1234. You can see the relationships among the Product, Linker, and Componen tables in Figure 12.12, which uses arrows to show which components make up product number B-123.

Using standard Paradox query forms, you can use these three tables to answer questions such as, "If I plan to manufacture 75 personal computers and 50 business computers, how many of each component will I need?" or "Given that I've manufactured 22 personal

> Field moves are abbreviated in Figure 12.12 to fit them on the page

DATABASE DESIGN WITH MULTIPLE TABLES 277

Structure of the Linker table

Field	Field Name	Field Type	Description
1	Product Number	A5	Product number
2	Component Number	A7	Component number
3	Qty_Used	N	Quantity used

Sample data for the Linker table

```
Product Number  Component Number  Qty Used
A-123           TT-1234           1
A-123           VV-1234           1
A-123           YY-1234           2
A-123           ZZ-1234           2
B-123           TT-1234           1
B-123           UU-1234           1
B-123           YY-1234           2
B-123           ZZ-1234           2
C-123           TT-1234           1
C-123           UU-1234           1
C-123           WW-1234           1
C-123           YY-1234           1
C-123           ZZ-1234           1
```

Figure 12.11: The structure and sample contents of the Linker table

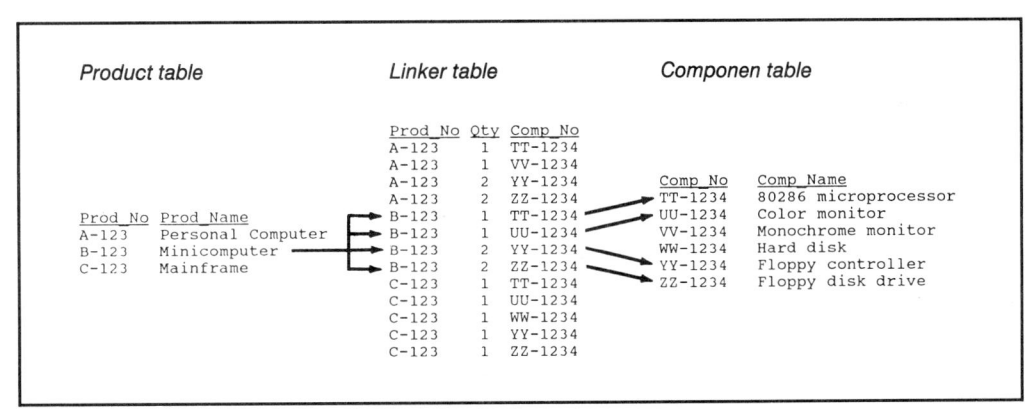

```
Product table           Linker table                    Componen table

                        Prod_No  Qty  Comp_No
                        A-123    1    TT-1234
                        A-123    1    VV-1234
                        A-123    2    YY-1234
                        A-123    2    ZZ-1234           Comp_No   Comp_Name
Prod_No  Prod_Name      B-123    1    TT-1234           TT-1234   80286 microprocessor
A-123    Personal Computer  B-123    1    UU-1234       UU-1234   Color monitor
B-123    Minicomputer   B-123    2    YY-1234           VV-1234   Monochrome monitor
C-123    Mainframe      B-123    2    ZZ-1234           WW-1234   Hard disk
                        C-123    1    TT-1234           YY-1234   Floppy controller
                        C-123    1    UU-1234           ZZ-1234   Floppy disk drive
                        C-123    1    WW-1234
                        C-123    1    YY-1234
                        C-123    1    ZZ-1234
```

Figure 12.12: Relationships among the Product, Linker, and Componen tables

computers and 17 business computers today, how many of each component are left in stock?'' Chapter 13 provides examples of querying many-to-many tables.

NORMALIZING A DATABASE

The techniques for dividing data into separate, related tables have been formalized in database management literature into a theory called *normalization*. The process of normalizing a database involves three rules:

1. Remove all redundant data.
2. Remove all partial dependencies.
3. Remove all transitive dependencies.

Each step in this process produces a database in one of what are called the *normal forms* of database design.

REMOVE REDUNDANT DATA

The first step in normalizing a database is to remove repeating data from the single table and place it in a separate table, using a common field to link the redundant information. When you've removed the redundant data from a single table by placing it into two separate related tables, the database is said to be in the *first normal form* of database design.

The sample accounts-receivable design discussed earlier in this chapter and illustrated in Figures 12.3 and 12.4 demonstrates a database in the first normal form; the redundant customer names and addresses have been removed from the Charges table and placed in a separate Customer table.

REMOVE ALL PARTIAL DEPENDENCIES

Partial dependencies may occur in a database that contains more than one common field. In that situation, any information that is not dependent on all common fields should be removed and placed in a separate table.

For example, the Linker table in the exploded inventory example contains two common fields: Product Number, which acts as the link to the Products table, and Component Number, which forms the link to the Componen table. This table also included the Qty – Used field, which is directly dependent on *both* the product number and component number (because it describes how many of each component each product requires).

Any other information stored on this database would be dependent on only one of the common fields (either Product Number or Component Number). For example, the product name would be directly relevant only to the Prod – No field. To avoid any such partial dependencies, all information that is specific to individual products is stored on the separate Products table, and all information that is specific to individual components is stored in the Componen table. When only the data that are directly relevant to all common fields in a table record remain in the table, the database has reached the *second normal form*.

REMOVE TRANSITIVE DEPENDENCIES

The third step in normalizing a database design is to remove the *transitive dependencies*: those fields that are occasionally (though not always) dependent on some other non-common field in the same record. For example, in the Componen table, where information about components purchased by the manufacturer is listed, you might want to place the name and address of the vendor who supplies the component. However, if this were the only component purchased from that vendor and you later stopped using that component and deleted the record, you would lose the vendor's name and address. Hence, the dependence between the particular component and the vendor was a temporary, or transitive, one.

To avoid this situation, you could store a vendor code in the Componen table and use that to relate each component to a vendor in a separate table of vendors' names and addresses named Vendors. That way, your list of vendors would remain intact, regardless of the components you were using at a particular moment.

To use a bookkeeping example, you wouldn't want the chart of accounts to be dependent on (or derived from) the individual transactions that transpired within a given month, because some accounts might not be used in that particular month.

When all the transitive dependencies have been removed from the records, the database is said to be in the *third normal form*.

THE FULLY NORMALIZED DATABASE

Like most theories, perhaps this discussion tends to make abstract what is actually intuitively obvious. When you take away all the fancy terminology, a *fully normalized* database is one that is easy to manage because the data are grouped into tables of similar information. For example, in an inventory system, the data are simply divided into product information, component information, vendor information, and information that defines which components go into which products. If you think about it for a moment, it makes perfect sense to store information in such a manner.

Furthermore, if you look at most manual systems that are used to store and manage information, you'll often find that the information is already structured in the third normal form. So don't let a lot of theory confuse you. Strive to reduce the redundancies in your tables and make particular bodies of information independent and easy to work with, and you'll find that your databases will naturally fall into the desired third normal form.

A WORKING INVENTORY EXAMPLE

To demonstrate some hands-on techniques for creating and using multiple related tables, we'll work through the steps required to set up an inventory-management system. We'll also use this sample inventory system in examples in later chapters.

MASTER INVENTORY TABLE

We'll name the master inventory table *Mastinv*. To create this table, first clear any data currently on the screen (Alt-F8). Then select the Create option and enter the table name Mastinv. Type in the table structure as shown in Figure 12.13, and press DO-IT! (F2) when you have finished.

REJECTING DUPLICATE ENTRIES

We can see in Figure 12.13 that the type of the Part No field is marked with an asterisk. As mentioned earlier, this informs Paradox

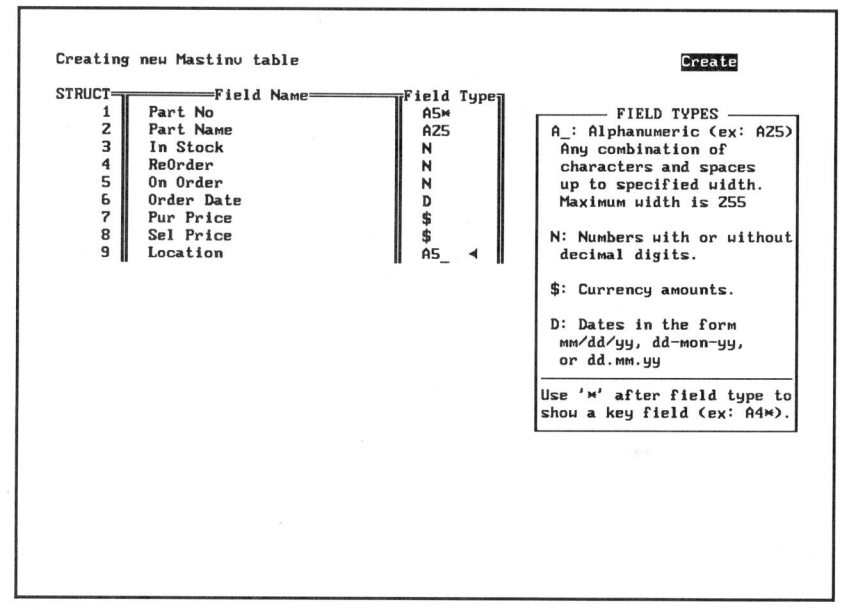

```
Creating new Mastinv table                                    Create
STRUCT       Field Name        Field Type
   1    Part No               A5*         ┌──── FIELD TYPES ────
   2    Part Name             A25         │ A_: Alphanumeric (ex: A25)
   3    In Stock              N           │ Any combination of
   4    ReOrder               N           │ characters and spaces
   5    On Order              N           │ up to specified width.
   6    Order Date            D           │ Maximum width is 255
   7    Pur Price             $           │
   8    Sel Price             $           │ N: Numbers with or without
   9    Location              A5_    ◄    │ decimal digits.
                                          │
                                          │ $: Currency amounts.
                                          │
                                          │ D: Dates in the form
                                          │ mm/dd/yy, dd-mon-yy,
                                          │ or dd.mm.yy
                                          │
                                          │ Use '*' after field type to
                                          │ show a key field (ex: A4*).
```

Figure 12.13: The structure for the Mastinv table

that the field is a key field. Knowing this, Paradox will automatically reject any duplications in the field, and it will always keep the table in sorted order by this field. Let's now take a moment to see how Paradox handles duplicate entries in the Part No field of the Mastinv table.

From the Main menu, select the Modify and DataEntry options and specify the Mastinv table. Type in two records, using the information shown below:

Part No	Part Name	In Stock
A-100	Gershwin Bicycle	10
A-100	Nikono Bicycle	50

When you press the DO-IT! key, Paradox will show a new table named Keyviol, which displays the records with identical part numbers (see Figure 12.14).

To remedy this situation, you must first edit the Keyviol table so that there are no duplicate part numbers. Press Edit (F9) and change the second part number to A-101.

```
Viewing Keyviol table: Record 1 of 2                    Main
MASTINV┬Part No┬════════Part Name═══════╤═In Stock═╤═ReOrder═╤

KEYVIOL┬Part No┬════════Part Name═══════╤═In Stock═╤═ReOrder═╤
     1─│ A-100 │ Gershwin Bicycle       │    10    │         │
     2─│ A-100 │ Nikono Bicycle         │    50    │         │
```

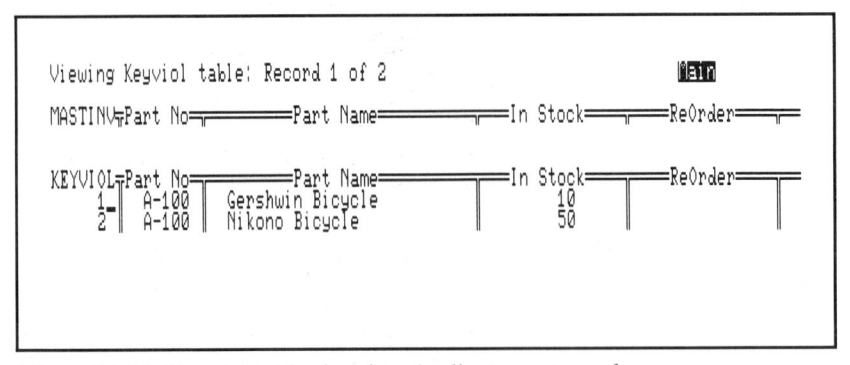

Figure 12.14: Keyviol table showing duplicate part numbers

Next, add these records to the Mastinv table by following these steps:

1. Save the new Keyviol data (press DO-IT!).
2. Call up the Tools option from the Main menu.
3. Select the More and Add options.
4. Enter Keyviol as the name of the table from which to add records (the source table).
5. Enter Mastinv as the name of the table to which the records will be added (the target table).
6. Select New Entries.

Paradox will add the corrected records to the Mastinv file and return to viewing the Mastinv table.

Now, take a moment to complete these two records and to add some more data to the Mastinv file, as shown in Figure 12.15. (Use the Edit (F9) key to begin making changes.) When done, press the DO-IT! key to save the new data and then Clear Image (F8) to clear the screen.

An important point to keep in mind with the Mastinv table is that once initial values for the quantity in stock have been entered, they need not be modified manually. The In Stock, On Order, and Pur Price fields will all be maintained automatically through updating procedures, which we'll discuss in Chapter 15.

```
Part No  Part Name            In Stock  ReOrder  On Order  Order Date  Pur Price  Sel Price  Location
A-100    Gershwin Bicycle        10        5         0      1/31/90     450.00     675.00    J-111
A-101    Nikono Bicycle          50       35         0      1/31/90     375.00     562.50    J-112
A-200    Racing Bicycle           2        3         1      2/01/90     600.00     900.00    M-991
B-100    Safety Helmet (Nikono)  50       10         0      2/15/90      20.00      30.00    L-111
B-111    Safety Helmet (Carrera)  2       10         0      1/31/90      40.00      60.00    J-333
B-112    Safety Helmet (Ozzy)     0       10        25      1/31/90      15.00      22.50    L-225
C-551    Hobie Skateboard        50       75         0      4/15/90      45.00      67.50    S-911
C-559    Flexie Skateboard       25       75        50      4/15/90      15.00      22.50    S-912
```

Figure 12.15: Sample data on the Mastinv table

Notice also that Part No is the first (topmost) field defined in this table. This is intentional, because we can use the first field in a table to validate entries made in the related tables and to look up related information as well. We'll see how to perform these operations in a moment, when we create the related Sales table.

THE SALES TABLE

The Paradox sample tables include a table named Sales, which we will use in the following examples. If you have copied this table to your hard disk, and want to keep it for future use, you might want to change its name so that it does not conflict with the Sales table we'll create in this section. To do so, call up the Main menu (F10), select the Tools and Rename options, and select Sales as the name of the table to rename. When prompted, enter a new name for the table, such as OrigSales, and press Enter.

In our example, the Sales table will store individual sales transactions. Select the Create option from the Main menu, enter the table name Sales, and fill in the table structure as shown in Figure 12.16.

Notice that we did *not* specify Part No as a key field on this table. (That is, we did not put an asterisk next to the part-number field type.) In this table, we do not expect each transaction to have a unique part number. Only the Mastinv file needs to have a unique part number for every record. Since the Sales table might have any number of individual sales transactions for a given product, we do not want Paradox to reject duplicates in this field. When you've entered the table structure for the Sales table, press the DO-IT! key.

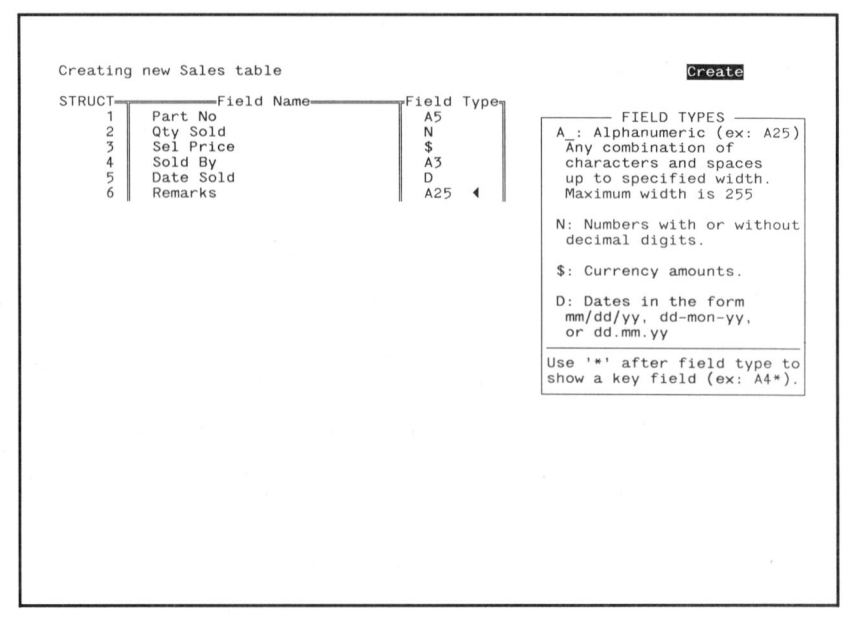

```
Creating new Sales table                              Create
STRUCT     Field Name          Field Type
   1    Part No                  A5         ─── FIELD TYPES ───
   2    Qty Sold                 N          A_: Alphanumeric (ex: A25)
   3    Sel Price                $             Any combination of
   4    Sold By                  A3            characters and spaces
   5    Date Sold                D             up to specified width.
   6    Remarks                  A25 ◀         Maximum width is 255

                                              N: Numbers with or without
                                                 decimal digits.

                                              $: Currency amounts.

                                              D: Dates in the form
                                                 mm/dd/yy, dd-mon-yy,
                                                 or dd.mm.yy

                                              Use '*' after field type to
                                              show a key field (ex: A4*).
```

Figure 12.16: The structure of the Sales table

Notice also that we've used the field name Sel Price in this table, using the same field name and field type as the Sel Price field on the Mastinv table. By doing so, we can use the *automatic fill-in* feature that Paradox offers to copy the appropriate selling price automatically from the Mastinv table onto the Sales table during data entry and editing. We'll now discuss how to set up this automatic fill-in feature.

AUTOMATIC VALIDATION AND FILL-IN

Let's take a moment to think about entering data into the Sales table. Suppose whoever is typing sales transactions into this table accidentally enters an invalid part number (for example, a part number with no corresponding record on the Mastinv table). If that error is allowed into the Sales table, it may be very difficult to find and correct later. This error can be avoided altogether by asking Paradox to validate any entry into the Part No field against part numbers listed in the Mastinv table.

Suppose the person entering the data into the Sales table does not even *know* the correct part number or the correct selling price. How does the person go about getting the necessary information? By using Paradox's HelpAndFill feature, you can provide a quick and easy technique that allows the person entering data to look up part numbers quickly on the Mastinv table, and to automatically fill in the selling price stored on the Mastinv table as the selling price on the Sales table.

Your options for defining look-ups and validations across two related tables are shown in the TableLookup option under ValCheck in the Edit menu. Before actually trying them out, however, let's take a moment to discuss all the options in a general sense. The two main options for defining table look-ups are

JustCurrentField   AllCorrespondingFields

Let's discuss each of these options.

JustCurrentField

The JustCurrentField option checks any data entered into the common field against all existing entries in the look-up table. In this example, a part number entered into the Part No field in the Sales table will be compared against all entries in the Part No field. If you select JustCurrentField, you'll be given the options

PrivateLookup   HelpAndFill

The PrivateLookup option checks the entry in the current table against the first field in the look-up table, but does not provide any view of, or access to, the look-up table. Instead, invalid entries are simply rejected with the error message

Not one of the possible values for this field.

Like PrivateLookup, the HelpAndFill option also checks the entry in the current field against entries in the first field of the look-up table, but in addition allows you to view the look-up table, browse through it to find the information you need, and automatically copy that information to the current table. In the inventory system we've discussed, if you needed to enter a sales transaction for a Nikono Bicycle, but did not know the part number, HelpAndFill would let you locate the part name quickly on the Mastinv table, and press a key to copy the part number from the Mastinv table to the Sales table.

AllCorrespondingFields

The AllCorrespondingFields option under TableLookup works much like the JustCurrentField entry, but copies values in *all* fields with identical field names from the lookup table to the current table. (In this example, Sel Price exists on both Mastinv and Sales, so data can be copied from the Sel Price field in the Mastinv table to the Sel Price field in the Sales table).

When you select AllCorrespondingFields, you'll be given the options

FillNoHelp   HelpAndFill

The FillNoHelp option checks the entry in the current field against all entries in the first field of the look-up table. If the entry is valid, fields that have the same name as fields on the look-up table are automatically filled with the appropriate values from the look-up table. There is no way, however, to view the look-up table on the screen.

The HelpAndFill option checks the entry in the current field against all entries in the first field of the look-up table. If the entry is valid, fields that have the same name as fields on the look-up table are filled automatically with the appropriate values from the look-up table, just as with the FillNoHelp option above. However, you may optionally view the look-up table, select a value to fill in, which in turn also fills in all fields that have field names in common with the look-up table.

Using the Mastinv and Sales tables as an example, suppose you wish to enter a transaction into the Sales table for a Nikono bicycle, but do not know the part number. The HelpAndFill feature would allow you to look up the appropriate part number on the Mastinv table and copy both the part number and the selling price from the Mastinv table into the current record on the Sales table.

REFINING THE SALES TABLE

Now that we are familiar with these advanced database features, how can we use them to beef up the Sales table? As mentioned previously, we intentionally defined Part No as the first (topmost) field in the Mastinv table structure so that we could use the field for data validation and look-ups. Furthermore, we've used the field name Sel Price on both the Mastinv and Sales tables, so we could copy data from Mastinv into Sales during data entry and editing.

To add these features to the Sales table, make sure the Sales table is on the screen. (If not, select View from the Main menu, and specify Sales as the table to work with). Next, enter the Edit mode by pressing F9. Call up the Edit menu (F10), and select the ValCheck and Define options.

When Paradox asks you to select the field to validate, move the cursor to the Part No field and press Enter. You'll see the usual menu of ValCheck options. Select TableLookup. Paradox presents the prompt

> Enter name of table to check values against,
> or press ↵ for a list of tables.

Mastinv contains all the valid part numbers, so specify Mastinv as the look-up table. From the next menu to appear—

> JustCurrentField   AllCorrespondingFields

—select AllCorrespondingFields. (Since both Mastinv and Sales contain the Sel Price field, we might as well copy the selling price from the Mastinv table to the Sales table, which can only be done using the AllCorrespondingFields option.)

The next options to appear are

> FillNoHelp   HelpAndFill

There is no need to "hide" the Mastinv table from whoever is entering data in this example, so select the HelpAndFill option to provide both validation with help and automatic fill-in. When the process is done, press F2 to save the new ValCheck selections.

EXPERIMENTING WITH HELP AND FILL-IN

Now we can enter some sample data into the Sales table and experiment with the help and fill-in features we've added to this table. First, clear the screen clutter by pressing Clear All (Alt-F8). Then select View and specify the Sales table. Next, press Edit (F9) to begin entering data. The blank Sales table appears on the screen. Notice the message at the top of the screen:

> Press [F1] for help with fill-in

This prompt appears because we've assigned the HelpAndFill option to this field.

Testing the Table Look-up Validation

Enter the part number **K-456** into the Part No field, and press Enter. Since there is no corresponding value in the Mastinv table, the screen displays the error message

> Not one of the possible values for this field.

Hence, the basic validation feature of the table look-up works fine—it rejects this invalid part number.

Testing the Table Look-up Help Feature

Now, let's get some help finding a *valid* part number. As instructed on the screen, press F1 to get some help. The Mastinv table appears on the screen, along with the prompt

> Move to the record to be selected
> Press [F2] to select the record; Esc to cancel; [F1] for help

Here is the basic help we've selected through our table look-up. By pressing F1, we've been presented with a list of parts in the Mastinv table, and we can now simply select a part number by positioning the cursor and pressing F2, as instructed on the screen. (Had we selected PrivateLookup rather than HelpAndFill under the TableLookup option, we would not have access to this table on the screen.)

Now, just for the sake of exercise, suppose that the Mastinv table is very large, and we need to find the part number for a helmet. We can use the Zoom key, as with any other table. In this example, press → to move the cursor to the Part Name field, and type Ctrl-Z to start Zoom. When Paradox asks for a value to search for, enter **..Helmet..**

and press Enter. The cursor drops to the first record with the word *Helmet* in the Part Name field. If this were not the correct record, you could use Zoom Next (Alt-Z) to find the next record with Helmet in the Part Name field. Now that we've located the proper record, let's try the automatic fill-in feature.

Testing the Automatic Fill-In

As the prompt at the top of the screen indicates, you can press F2 to select the current record. Note that the current record lists B-100 as the part number, and $30.00 as the selling price. Press F2 to select this record, and the Mastinv table will disappear from the screen. The Sales table appears on the screen with the part number B-100 in the Part no field, and $30.00 in the Sel Price field, as shown in Figure 12.17. (The image is in Form View, rather than Table View, in this example.)

Even though the Sel Price field is filled in automatically, you can still change it if you like when you move the cursor into that field. Use the usual Backspace key or Field View (Alt-F5) to do so.

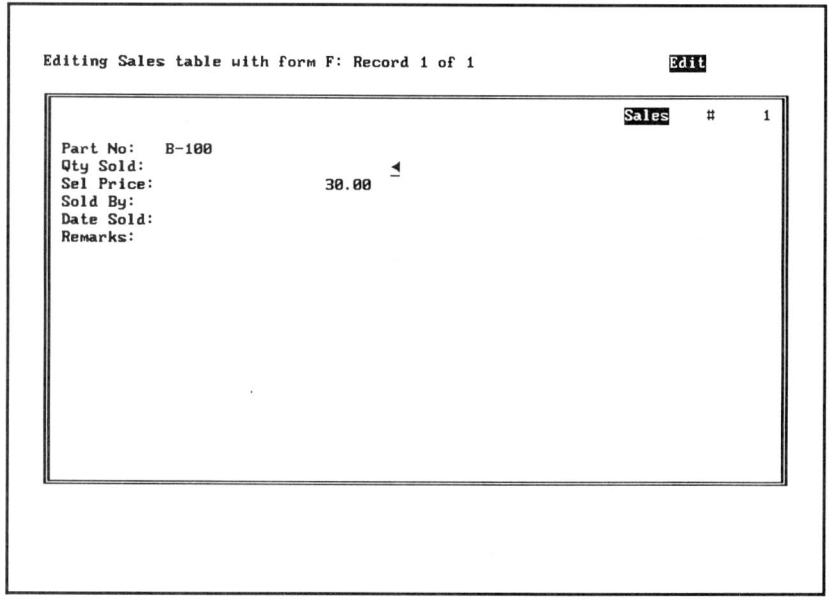

```
Editing Sales table with form F: Record 1 of 1              Edit

                                                     Sales   #    1
 Part No:   B-100
 Qty Sold:                              ◄
 Sel Price:             30.00
 Sold By:
 Date Sold:
 Remarks:
```

Figure 12.17: The Sel Price field automatically filled in from Mastinv table

As mentioned previously, when the Mastinv table is displayed on the screen to offer look-up help, it also displays the prompts

> Move to the record to be selected
> Press [F2] to select the record; Esc to cancel; [F1] for help

As we have seen, pressing F2 copies data from the Mastinv table to the Part No and Sel Price fields on the Sales table. You can also press the F1 key to get additional help (the standard Paradox help screen). Optionally, you can press Esc to remove the Mastinv table image from the screen and return to the Sales table image without copying any data.

Take some time now to enter some more sample data into the Sales table to help with future examples. If you like, you can use Form View (F7) to enter records one at a time, rather than Table View. (The help and fill-in features will work the same in either view.) Figure 12.18 shows some sample data that you can enter.

When done entering the sample data into the Sales table, save your work by pressing DO-IT! (F2). Then use Clear Image (F8) to clear the screen.

```
Editing Sales table: Record 12 of 12                                    Edit
SALES  Part No  Qty Sold  Sel Price  Sold By  Date Sold        Remarks
    1   B-100      1         30.00     JAK     6/01/90
    2   C-551      2         67.50     JAK     6/01/90
    3   A-200      1        900.00     JAK     6/01/90
    4   C-559      5         22.50     BBG     6/05/90
    5   A-100      5        675.00     BBG     6/05/90
    6   B-112      2         22.50     BBG     6/05/90
    7   A-101      1        562.50     JAK     7/01/90
    8   B-111      2         60.00     JAK     7/01/90
    9   C-551      1         67.50     JAK     7/01/90
   10   A-100      3        675.00     BBG     7/15/90
   11   B-112     -2         22.50     BBG     8/01/90    Return and Refund
   12   A-100      1        675.00     JAK     8/01/90
```

Figure 12.18: Sample data on the Sales tables

THE PURCHASE TABLE

Finally, we'll add another table for recording individual purchases (new stock) to the inventory system. Use the Create option from the Main menu to name the table Purchase, and give it the structure shown in Figure 12.19. Notice that once again, the Part No field is *not* marked as a key field. Only the master file needs to reject duplicate part numbers. Press DO-IT! after entering the structure for the Purchase table.

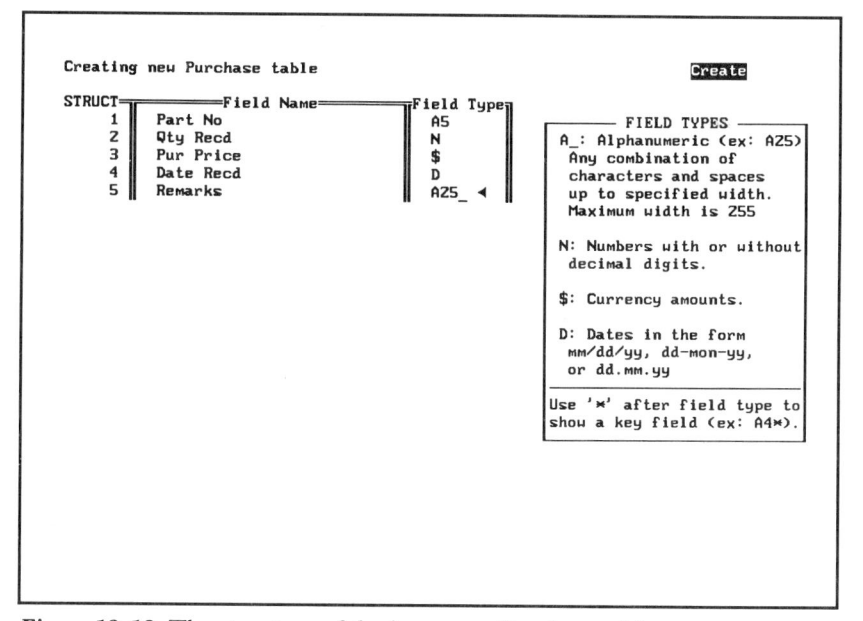

```
Creating new Purchase table                                    Create
STRUCT       Field Name        Field Type
   1      Part No                 A5              FIELD TYPES
   2      Qty Recd                N         A_: Alphanumeric (ex: A25)
   3      Pur Price               $         Any combination of
   4      Date Recd               D         characters and spaces
   5      Remarks                 A25       up to specified width.
                                            Maximum width is 255

                                            N: Numbers with or without
                                               decimal digits.

                                            $: Currency amounts.

                                            D: Dates in the form
                                               mm/dd/yy, dd-mon-yy,
                                               or dd.mm.yy

                                            Use '*' after field type to
                                            show a key field (ex: A4*).
```

Figure 12.19: The structure of the inventory Purchase table

Once again, we'll place a validity check on the Part No field. Call up the Main menu and select the Modify and Edit options, then specify the Purchase table. Call up the menu again and select the ValCheck and Define options. Specify the Part No field when requested. Select the TableLookup option and specify Mastinv as the table against which to validate part numbers. There is no need to use automatic fill-in on multiple fields in this example, so select JustCurrentField and HelpAndFill. Save the validity check by pressing DO-IT! when done.

Use Edit (F9) or the Modify and DataEntry options to add the data shown in Figure 12.20 to the Purchase table. Press DO-IT! when done entering data. Then press Clear (F8) to clear the screen.

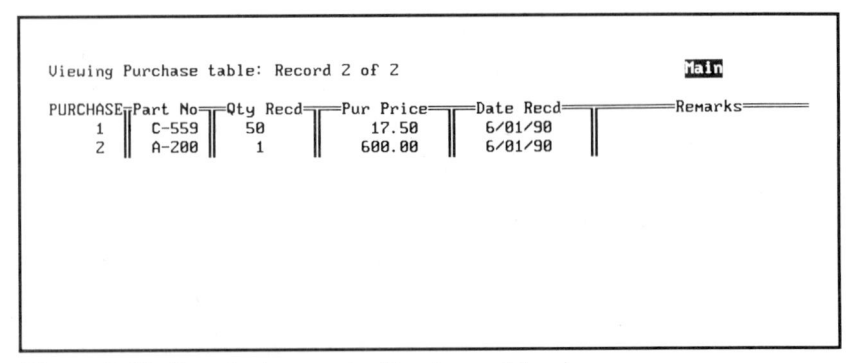

```
Viewing Purchase table: Record 2 of 2                              Main
PURCHASE=Part No=Qty Recd=Pur Price=Date Recd=========Remarks=======
   1    | C-559 |   50  |   17.50  |  6/01/90 |
   2    | A-200 |    1  |  600.00  |  6/01/90 |
```

Figure 12.20: Sample data on the Purchase table

Before we can really put the inventory system to work, we have to learn some specific techniques for managing numbers in a table, performing updates, querying multiple tables, and using advanced report techniques. These are the subjects of the next few chapters.

SUMMARY

- In larger business applications, data are usually stored in several separate tables. Multiple tables can save disk space by avoiding redundant data.

- Multiple tables allow easy access to both current and historical data, as in the example of master and transaction tables used in inventories.

- *Common fields* are used to relate data among multiple tables. Usually, the common field is a key field on one of the tables (for example, a customer-number or part-number field).

- A *key field* is one that contains a unique entry for each record in the table.

- To specify a key field in a table, mark it with an asterisk in the Field Type column when defining the structure.
- To validate entries in one table against values in another table, use the TableLookup option under the ValCheck menu.
- Only the first field in a table can be used as a look-up field.
- Any fields that have identical names in two related tables can be used for automatic fill-in.

ADVANCED QUERIES AND CALCULATIONS

CHAPTER 13

IN THIS CHAPTER WE'LL DISCUSS SOME MORE advanced features of the Ask option, including querying multiple tables and performing calculations. We'll use the inventory tables we developed in the last chapter for our examples.

QUERYING MULTIPLE TABLES

When querying multiple tables, there are two points to keep in mind:

1. You must fill out a query form for each table.
2. You must provide *examples* to link records from the two separate tables.

Other than these two items, the techniques for querying multiple tables are the same as for querying a single table. Let's first work through a somewhat simple example.

Suppose you wish to see the part number, quantity sold, and selling price for each item in the Sales table. To do so, you call up the Main menu and select the Ask option. Specify the Sales table and place check-plus symbols in the appropriate columns, as in the upper part of Figure 13.1. (Remember, placing check-plus symbols by pressing Alt-F6 displays duplicates, whereas placing check marks alone (F6) does not.) When you press DO-IT!, Paradox shows the appropriate data, as in the lower part of Figure 13.1.

Now suppose you also want to see the part names. Because these are not stored on the Sales table, you'll have to get them from the Mastinv table. To do so you'll first need to clear the Answer table (F8), then call up a query screen for the Mastinv table (press Menu (F10), select Ask, and specify the Mastinv table). Place a check mark in the Part Name field. Figure 13.2 shows how the screen looks with

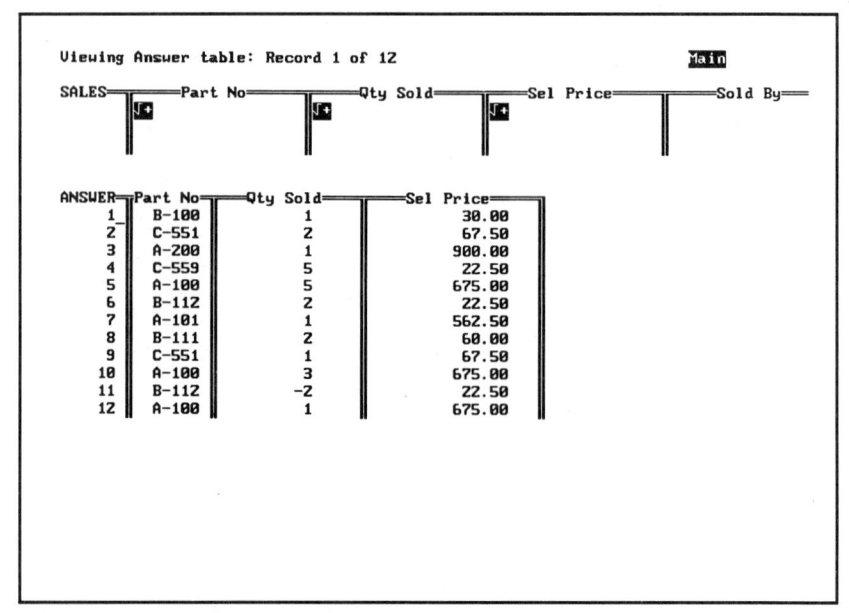

Figure 13.1: A query for the Sales table

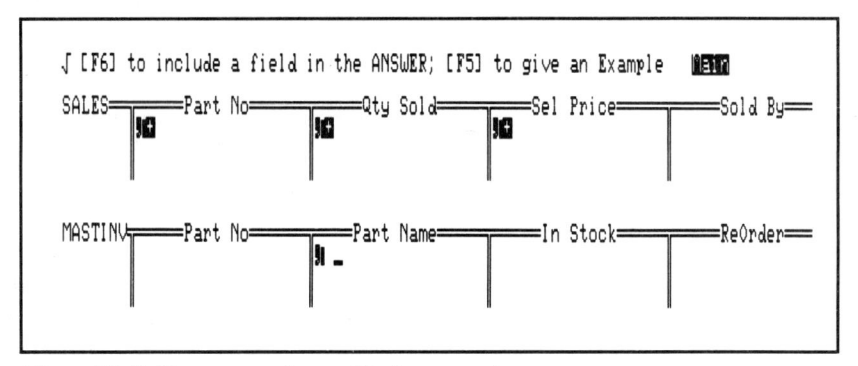

Figure 13.2: Two query forms filled out on the screen

both query forms partially filled in (we're not ready to press DO-IT! yet, however).

ENTERING EXAMPLES

Now we need to find a way to tell Paradox that the two tables are linked by the Part No field. That is, when Paradox displays a sales transaction for part number A-100, we want to be sure it displays the appropriate part name from the Mastinv table. We define such a relationship with an *example*.

To enter an example, first move the cursor to the field on which the relationship is based. In this case, move the cursor to the Part No field of the Mastinv query form. Then press the Example (F5) key. Now you can type in any example that comes to mind. The actual content of the example is unimportant, because the example just acts as a place holder for performing comparisons. This time, type in **ABC** as the example, and press Enter. You'll notice that the example is highlighted, as in Figure 13.3.

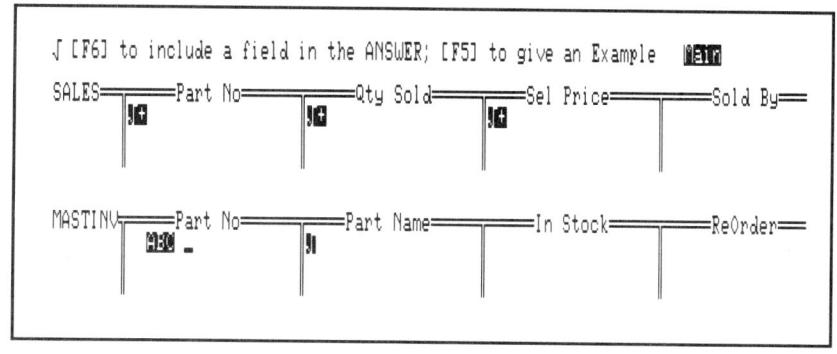

Figure 13.3: An example entered on the Mastinv query form

Now we need to enter the same example into the Part No field on the Sales query form. First, press Up Image (F3) to move the cursor up to the Sales query form. Then, move the cursor to the Part No field, press Example (F5) and type in the same example used in the Mastinv query form (ABC). Press Enter when done. Figure 13.4 shows how the two query forms look now, with examples in the Part No field of each query screen.

The query in Figure 13.4 tells Paradox to link the Mastinv and Sales tables by common Part No fields and to display the Part No, Part Name, Qty Sold, and Sel Price fields of these tables. Pressing DO-IT! performs the query and displays the result in the Answer table, as in Figure 13.5.

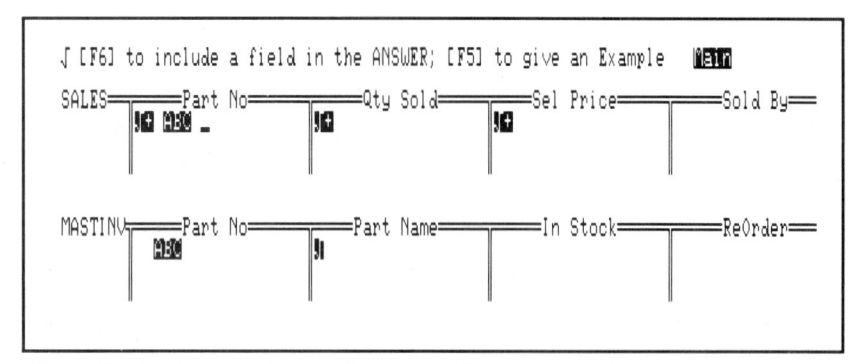

Figure 13.4: Examples in the Sales and Mastinv query forms

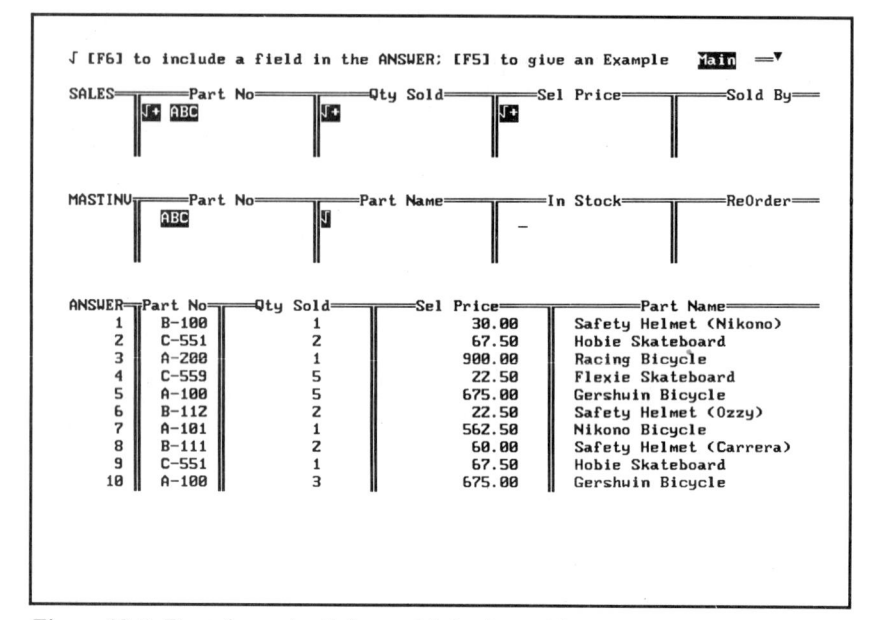

Figure 13.5: Data from the Sales and Mastinv tables

These are the important points to remember about examples:

- They are entered by first pressing the Example (F5) key.
- They must match exactly on the two query forms, telling Paradox to look for matching Part No fields when displaying data.

We could have used anything as the example—a single letter such as X, any number such as 9999, or a name such as Ronald. Again, the example only acts as a means of showing that we're looking for data that match between the two tables. Hence, had we used Ronald as the example on the Mastinv query form, we would have had to use Ronald as the example on the Sales query form as well. Keep in mind that examples may contain only letters and numbers. Punctuation marks and blank spaces cannot be used.

SEARCHES WITH MULTIPLE TABLES

Of course, you can perform all the usual types of searches with multiple tables. For example, to see only sales by salesperson JAK, fill in the Sales query form as you normally would for such a search. Once again, to view part names (available only on the Mastinv table), fill in a query form for the Mastinv table, and place a check mark in the Part Name field. Then place examples into the Part No fields on both the Mastinv and Sales query forms. (*Note:* The Up Image (F3) and Down Image (F4) keys let you move the cursor back and forth between query forms. Clear Image (F8) clears the Answer table or a query form from the screen, and Clear All (Alt-F8) clears everything from the screen.)

Figure 13.6 shows a query for all sales by salesperson JAK, with a check mark in the Part Name field of the Mastinv table and identical examples linking the two tables via the Part No field. The top query displays records from the Sales table that have JAK as the salesperson, and the bottom query adds part names to the display, based on matching part numbers in the two tables.

Let's try another query, phrasing it in English first. We want to tell Paradox to show the part number, date, part name, and purchase price of all items sold between July 1 and July 15. Let's take it one step at a time. First of all, the "all items sold" portion of the request immediately refers to the Sales table. The part name and purchase price data, however, are on the Mastinv table. So the first thing you need to do is call up query forms for the Sales and Mastinv tables. Then, for the "show the part number, date, part name, and purchase price" portion of the request, place check marks as in Figure 13.7. (Note that I've used the Rotate key to rearrange the columns.)

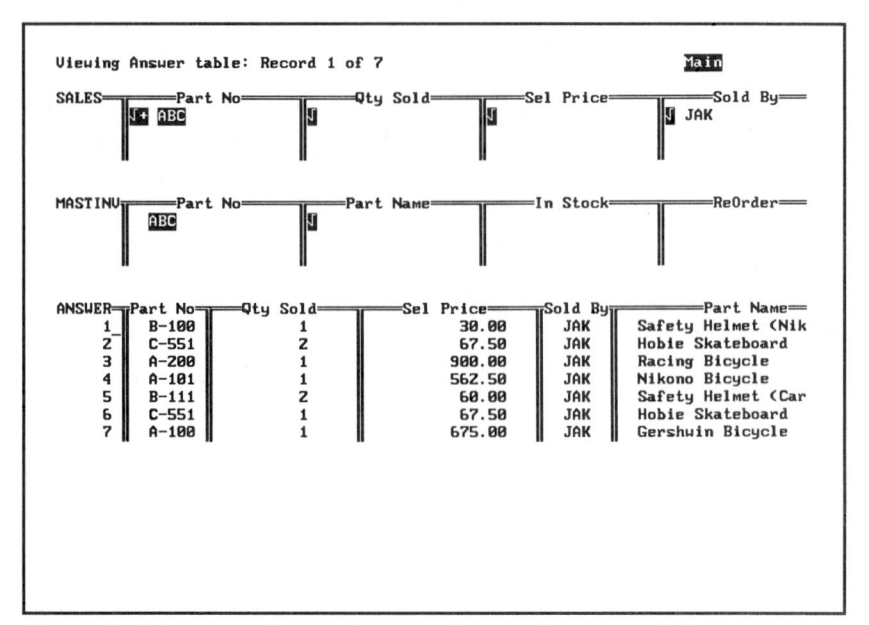

```
Viewing Answer table: Record 1 of 7                              Main
SALES═══╤══Part No══╤══╤══Qty Sold══╤══╤══Sel Price══╤══╤══Sold By══╕
        │ +  ABC    │  │            │  │             │  │ JAK       │


MASTINV═╤══Part No══╤══Part Name══╤══In Stock══╤══ReOrder══╕
        │    ABC    │             │            │           │


ANSWER══╤═Part No═╤═Qty Sold═╤═Sel Price═╤═Sold By═╤═Part Name══════
      1 │  B-100  │    1     │   30.00   │  JAK    │ Safety Helmet (Nik
      2 │  C-551  │    2     │   67.50   │  JAK    │ Hobie Skateboard
      3 │  A-200  │    1     │  900.00   │  JAK    │ Racing Bicycle
      4 │  A-101  │    1     │  562.50   │  JAK    │ Nikono Bicycle
      5 │  B-111  │    2     │   60.00   │  JAK    │ Safety Helmet (Car
      6 │  C-551  │    1     │   67.50   │  JAK    │ Hobie Skateboard
      7 │  A-100  │    1     │  675.00   │  JAK    │ Gershwin Bicycle
```

Figure 13.6: A query of two tables for sales by salesperson JAK

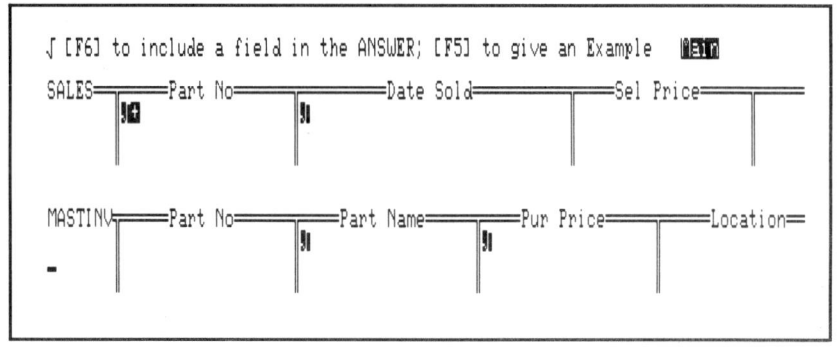

```
√ [F6] to include a field in the ANSWER; [F5] to give an Example    Main
SALES═══╤══Part No══╤══╤══Date Sold══╤══╤══Sel Price══╕
        │ +         │  │             │  │             │


MASTINV═╤══Part No══╤══Part Name══╤══Pur Price══╤══Location══╕
        │           │             │             │            │
   -
```

Figure 13.7: A request to see part number, date, part name, and purchase price

Now, for the "all items sold between July 1 and July 15" portion of the query, we need to fill in the appropriate search formula, as in Figure 13.8.

So far, so good. But now we need an example to link the two tables. Of course, this will be in the Part No field (since this is the only field that links the two tables). Put examples into the Part No field of

ADVANCED QUERIES AND CALCULATIONS 301

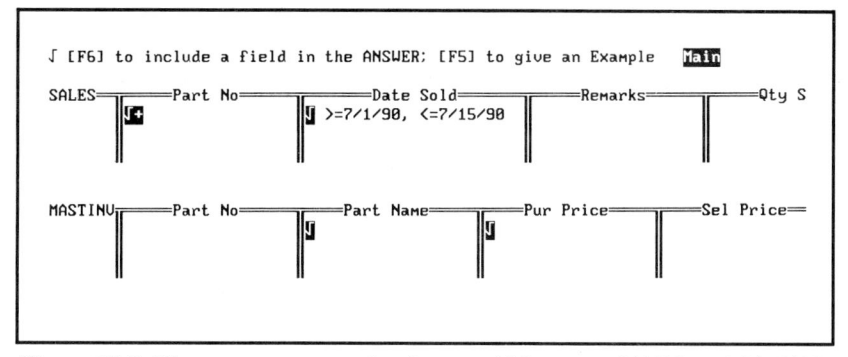

```
√ [F6] to include a field in the ANSWER; [F5] to give an Example    Main
SALES══════Part No══════════Date Sold═════════Remarks════════════Qty S
        √+            √ >=7/1/90, <=7/15/90



MASTINV════Part No══════════Part Name════════Pur Price═════════Sel Price
                       √               √
```

Figure 13.8: The query narrowed to items sold between 7/1/90 and 7/15/90

each query form (don't forget to press F5 first), as shown in the upper portion of Figure 13.9. Press DO-IT!, and you'll see the results shown in the lower portion of the figure.

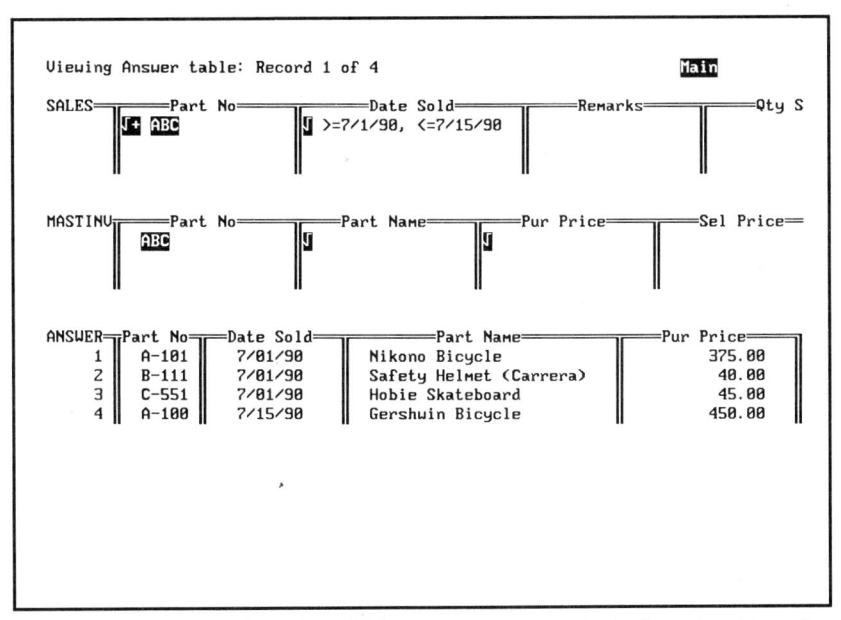

```
Viewing Answer table: Record 1 of 4                              Main
SALES══════Part No══════════Date Sold═════════Remarks════════════Qty S
        √+ ABC         √ >=7/1/90, <=7/15/90



MASTINV════Part No══════════Part Name════════Pur Price═════════Sel Price
           ABC         √               √


ANSWER═Part No══Date Sold═════════Part Name═══════════Pur Price
   1    A-101    7/01/90     Nikono Bicycle             375.00
   2    B-111    7/01/90     Safety Helmet (Carrera)     40.00
   3    C-551    7/01/90     Hobie Skateboard            45.00
   4    A-100    7/15/90     Gershwin Bicycle           450.00
```

Figure 13.9: A query for sales within a range of dates, including data from the Mastinv table

AND *AND* OR *QUERIES WITH MULTIPLE TABLES*

And and Or queries with multiple tables are similar to And and Or queries with a single table. For an And query, place the search conditions on the same line. For instance, to display all sales of part number A-100 by salesman BBG, place the search criteria on the same line of the Sales query form. To pull in the part name from the Mastinv table, simply enter an example in each of the two Part No fields and check the Part Name field on the Mastinv query form, as shown in Figure 13.10.

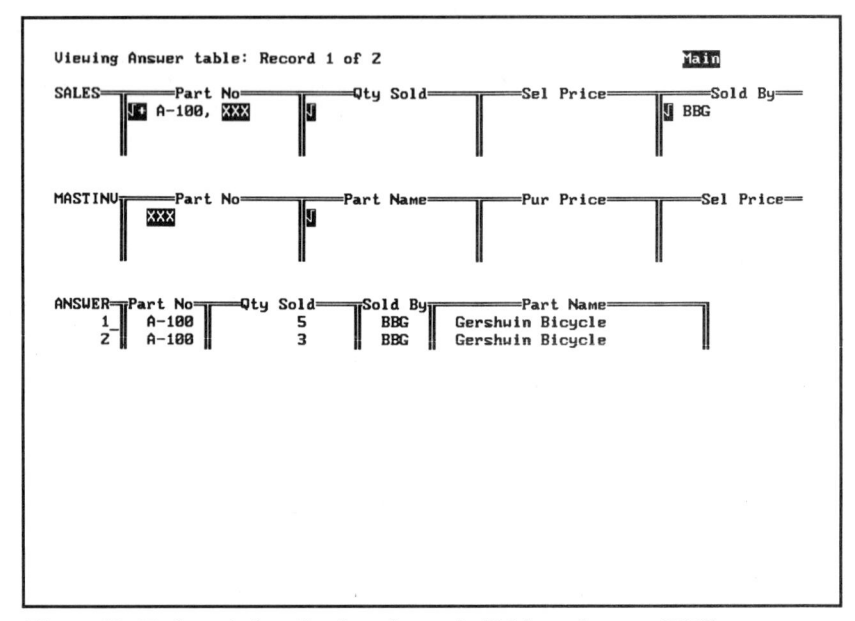

```
Viewing Answer table: Record 1 of 2                         Main
SALES    Part No          Qty Sold      Sel Price       Sold By
         A-100, XXX       y                             y BBG

MASTINV  Part No          Part Name     Pur Price       Sel Price
         XXX              y

ANSWER   Part No   Qty Sold   Sold By   Part Name
    1    A-100         5        BBG     Gershuin Bicycle
    2    A-100         3        BBG     Gershuin Bicycle
```

Figure 13.10: Search for all sales of part A-100 by salesman BBG

Suppose that you want to display records from the Sales table that contain part numbers A-100, A-101, or A-200. Furthermore, you want to display the part name from the MastInv table. In Chapter 7, you saw how to construct an Or query by stacking query criteria onto separate rows. As an alternative to stacking query conditions, you can use the Or operator.

Figure 13.11 shows an example query. The condition *A-100 or A-101, or A-200* specifies records that have either A-100, A-101, or A-200 as the part number. ABC is an example (entered using the usual F5 key) that links the Sales table to the MastInv table via the common Part No field. As you can see near the bottom of the figure, the query displays the requested records.

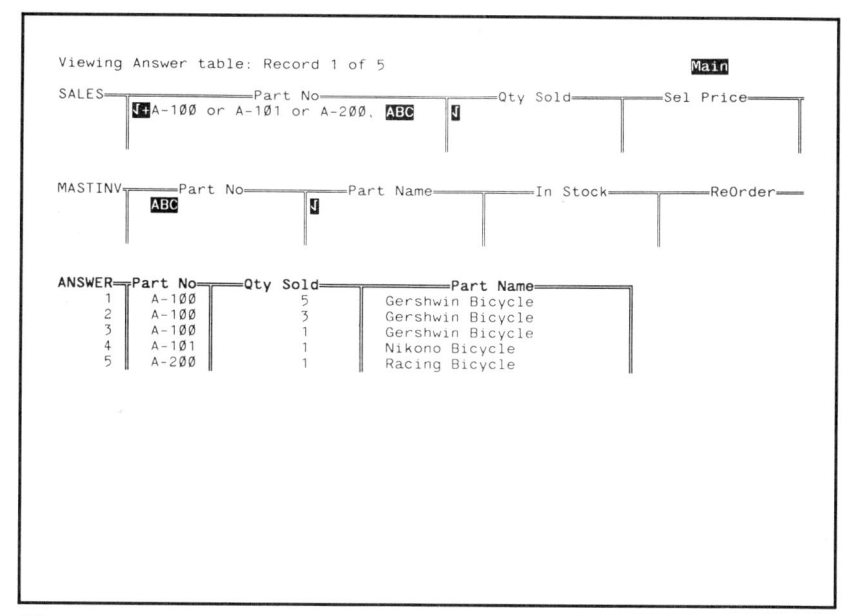

```
Viewing Answer table: Record 1 of 5                              Main
SALES        Part No                    Qty Sold        Sel Price
      ✓+A-100 or A-101 or A-200, ABC     ✓


MASTINV      Part No      Part Name     In Stock        ReOrder
             ABC          ✓


ANSWER  Part No   Qty Sold       Part Name
   1    A-100        5           Gershwin Bicycle
   2    A-100        3           Gershwin Bicycle
   3    A-100        1           Gershwin Bicycle
   4    A-101        1           Nikono Bicycle
   5    A-200        1           Racing Bicycle
```

Figure 13.11: A query for part numbers starting with A-

Note that the query criteria and the example are separated by a comma (both in Figures 13.10 and 13.11). Remember to separate query criteria from examples when developing your own queries. (If you forget, Paradox will display the message *Missing comma* when you press F2, and you will need to press the Backspace key to back up and insert the comma.)

Incidentally, since part numbers A-100, A-101, and A-200 represent all part numbers in the inventory tables beginning with the letter

A, you could have entered this query as shown in Figure 13.12 and received the same results.

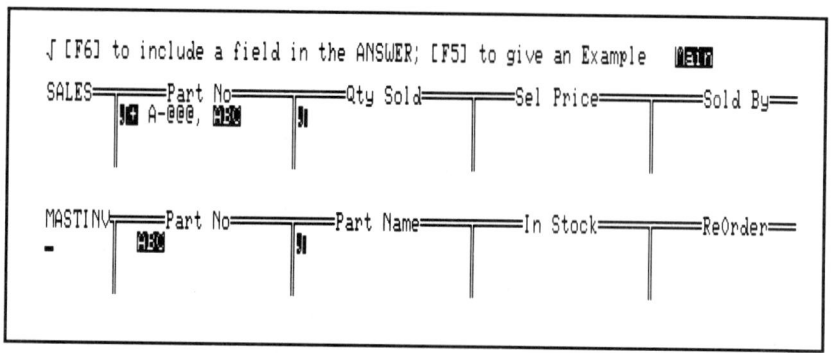

```
√ [F6] to include a field in the ANSWER; [F5] to give an Example    Main
SALES══╤═Part No═══════╤═Qty Sold═══════╤═Sel Price══════╤═Sold By══
       │ A-@@@, ABC    │ ✓              │                │
       │               │                │                │

MASTINV╤═Part No═══════╤═Part Name══════╤═In Stock═══════╤═ReOrder══
       │ ABC           │ ✓              │                │
```

Figure 13.12: A query for part numbers starting with A-

DISPLAYING NON-MATCHING RECORDS

Usually when you create a query that displays data from two tables, Paradox displays only records that have matching values on the two tables. For example, if you were to display data from the Purchase table, with part names from the MastInv table, Paradox would display only the two records from the Purchase table that have part numbers C-559 and A-200.

If you want to display all records from a table, whether or not there are matching records on a related table, you need to use the *inclusion operator* (!). Figure 13.13 shows an example, where records from the Purchase and MastInv table are displayed. Note that, as usual, check marks are used to display selected fields, and an example (ABC) is used to link the files. The inclusion operator (!) in the query for the MastInv table ensures that all records from the MastInv table are displayed.

As you can see from the results of the query, all records from the MastInv table are displayed. The Qty Recd field is blank in all records except for part numbers A-200 and C-559, which are the only part numbers listed in the Purchase table.

> The type of query that the inclusion operator performs is sometimes called an *outer join*.

ADVANCED QUERIES AND CALCULATIONS **305**

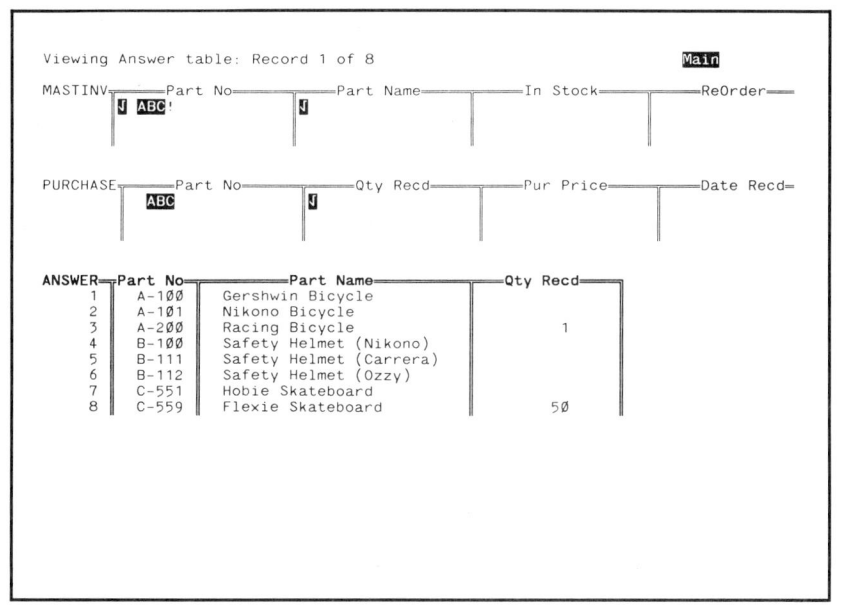

```
Viewing Answer table: Record 1 of 8                          Main
MASTINV┬──Part No──────┬──Part Name──────┬──In Stock──────┬──ReOrder──
       │ √ ABC         │ √               │                │
       │               │                 │                │


PURCHASE┬──Part No─────┬──Qty Recd──────┬──Pur Price─────┬──Date Recd═
        │ ABC          │ √              │                │
        │              │                │                │


ANSWER┬─Part No──────┬──Part Name──────────────┬──Qty Recd──
  1   │  A-100       │  Gershwin Bicycle       │
  2   │  A-101       │  Nikono Bicycle         │
  3   │  A-200       │  Racing Bicycle         │      1
  4   │  B-100       │  Safety Helmet (Nikono) │
  5   │  B-111       │  Safety Helmet (Carrera)│
  6   │  B-112       │  Safety Helmet (Ozzy)   │
  7   │  C-551       │  Hobie Skateboard       │
  8   │  C-559       │  Flexie Skateboard      │     50
```

Figure 13.13: An outer join using the ! operator

USING QUERIES TO CALCULATE RESULTS

To perform calculations, you can use the following arithmetic operators in your query forms:

OPERATOR	*FUNCTION*
+	Addition
–	Subtraction
*	Multiplication
/	Division
( )	Used for grouping

We've seen how to use arithmetic operators in queries before. For instance, if you performed the query shown in Figure 13.14, you'd

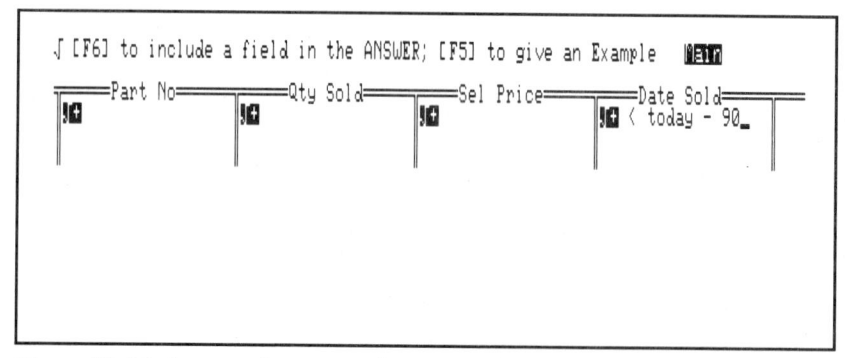

```
√ [F6] to include a field in the ANSWER; [F5] to give an Example   Main
══Part No══════════Qty Sold══════════Sel Price══════════Date Sold══
                                                         < today - 90_
```

Figure 13.14: A query for transactions more than 90 days old

see records with dates less than (earlier than) today's date minus 90 days (that is, transactions that are over 90 days old).

With the addition of the *Calc* option and examples, you can perform more interesting calculations, such as sums, averages, frequency distributions, projections, and more. The Calc option can be used with the sum, average, max, min, and count operators listed in Table 13.1.

Table 13.1: Operators used with the Calc option

Calc Operator	Calculates	With Field Types
sum	Total of values	N, $, S
average	Average of values	N, $, S, D
max	Highest value	A, N, $, S, D
min	Lowest value	A, N, $, S, D
count	Number of values	A, N, $, S, D

In its simplest form, the Calc option will calculate data on all records of a field. For example, the query in Figure 13.15 requests a sum of the Qty Sold field and returns the answer 22.

Had we used the Calc average option rather than Calc sum in the query form, Paradox would have displayed 1.83, the average of all

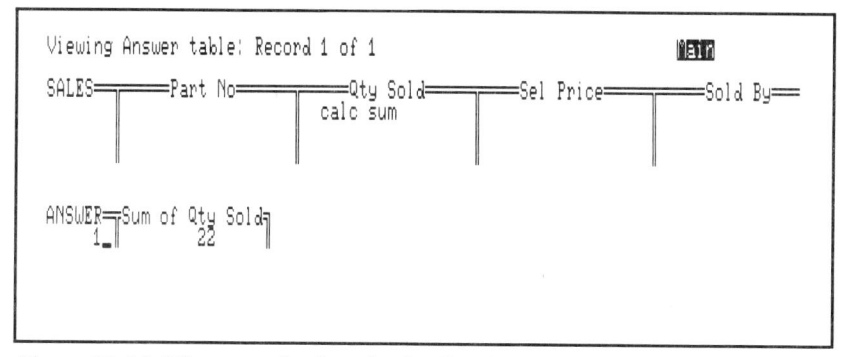

```
Viewing Answer table: Record 1 of 1                    Main
SALES═══╤═Part No═══════╤═Qty Sold═╤═Sel Price═╤═Sold By══
        │               │ calc sum │           │
        │               │          │           │
        │               │          │           │
ANSWER═╤═Sum of Qty Sold╕
   1_│      22         │
```

Figure 13.15: The sum of values in the Qty Sold field

the Qty Sold values. The query Calc max would display 5, the highest value in the Qty Sold field. Calc min would have displayed −2, the smallest value, and Calc count would have displayed 5, indicating that there are 5 different values in the Qty Sold field. (The request Calc Count All would have displayed 12, the total number of records in the table.)

CALCULATIONS ON GROUPS OF RECORDS

Using check marks in fields of interest has a different effect on calculations than on normal queries. A checked field in the query form with a Calc option indicates a group of records on which to perform a calculation. For example, look at the query form in Figure 13.16. The check mark in the Part No field indicates that calculations should be based on groups of like part numbers. Calc sum in the Qty Sold field indicates that the sums should be calculated on this field for each unique part number. The results are shown in the Answer table.

The query in Figure 13.17 requests the sum of the quantity sold for each salesperson. In this instance, the Sold By field is checked for totaling, and the Calc sum operator is placed (as before) in the Qty Sold field.

Checking multiple fields in a Calc query will create even more groups. For example, in Figure 13.18, both the Part No and Sold By fields are checked. Calc sum again appears in the Qty Sold field. The end result is the quantity of each item sold by each salesperson.

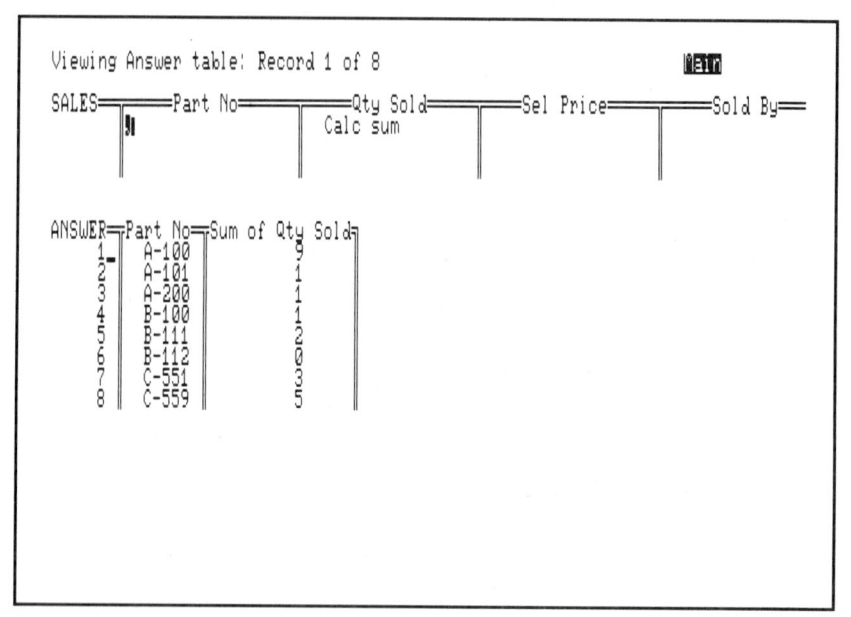

```
Viewing Answer table: Record 1 of 8                    Main
  SALES╤═════Part No═════╤═════Qty Sold═════╤═════Sel Price═════╤═════Sold By══
       │¶                │    Calc sum      │                   │
       │                 │                  │                   │


  ANSWER╤Part No╤Sum of Qty Sold╗
      1 │ A-100 │       9       │
      2 │ A-101 │       1       │
      3 │ A-200 │       1       │
      4 │ B-100 │       1       │
      5 │ B-111 │       2       │
      6 │ B-112 │       0       │
      7 │ C-551 │       3       │
      8 │ C-559 │       5       │
```

Figure 13.16: The sum of the Qty Sold field for each part number

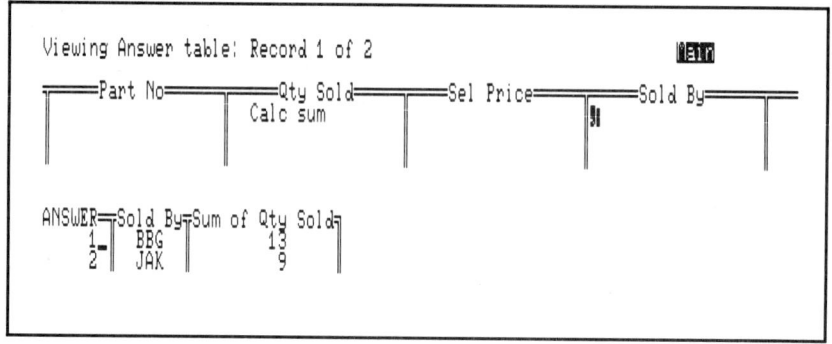

```
Viewing Answer table: Record 1 of 2                    Main
  ═════Part No═════╤═════Qty Sold═════╤═════Sel Price═════╤═════Sold By══
                   │    Calc sum      │                   │¶
                   │                  │                   │


  ANSWER╤Sold By╤Sum of Qty Sold╗
      1 │  BBG  │      13       │
      2 │  JAK  │       9       │
```

Figure 13.17: The sum of quantities for each salesperson

FREQUENCY DISTRIBUTIONS

The *Calc Count All* operator combined with a checked field (or fields) provides a quick and easy frequency distribution. For example, suppose you select Ask and specify Custlist as the table to

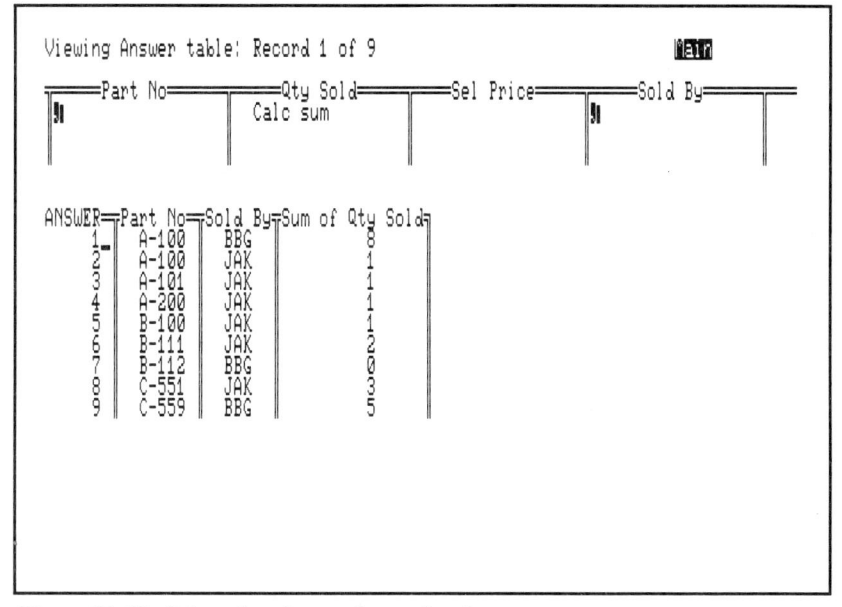

```
Viewing Answer table: Record 1 of 9                    Main
┌─Part No══════════╤═Qty Sold═══════════╤═Sel Price═══════╤═Sold By═══════┐
│ ▌                │     Calc sum       │                ▌│               │
│                  │                    │                 │               │


  ANSWER══Part No══Sold By══Sum of Qty Sold═
     1     A-100    BBG              8
     2     A-100    JAK              1
     3     A-101    JAK              1
     4     A-200    JAK              1
     5     B-100    JAK              1
     6     B-111    JAK              2
     7     B-112    BBG              0
     8     C-551    JAK              3
     9     C-559    BBG              5
```

Figure 13.18: Sales of each part by each salesperson

query. Then you place a check mark in the State field, along with the Calc count all operator, and you'll get a display counting the number of individuals residing in each state, as in Figure 13.19.

CALCULATIONS WITH EXAMPLES

Using examples with calculations allows you to display the results of calculations of two or more fields, add a constant to a field, or project "what-if" situations. For instance, the Sales table has a field for quantity sold and a field for selling price. The actual dollar amount for the transaction, however, is the quantity sold times the selling price.

To calculate the actual dollar value of each transaction, you could set up a query screen for the Sales table as in Figure 13.20. Note that Qty and Price are *examples* of data found in the Qty Sold and Sel Price field. Next to the Price example (followed by a comma) is the instruction to multiply the quantity by the price. When Calc is used in this fashion, it will display the results of the calculation as a separate field, as shown in the Answer table in Figure 13.20.

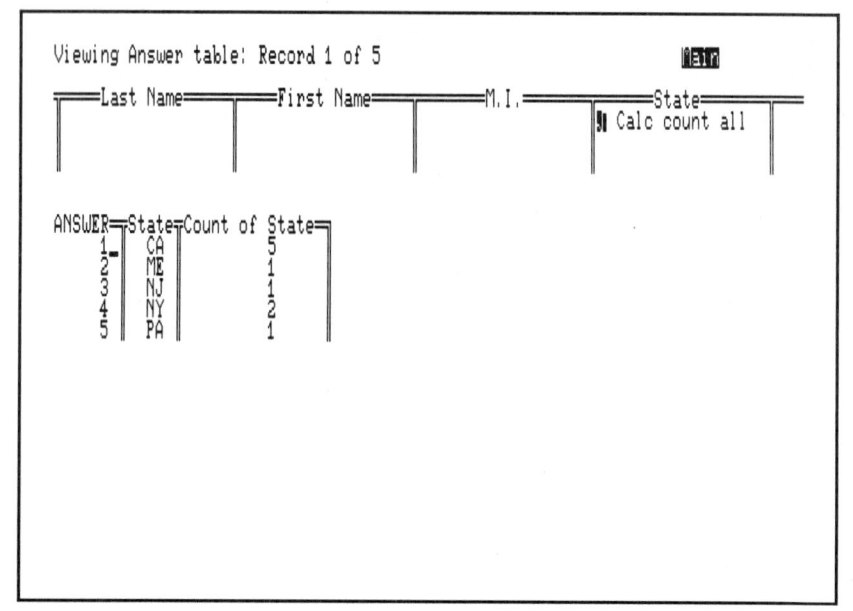

```
Viewing Answer table: Record 1 of 5                    Main
   ═Last Name══════ ═First Name══════ ═M.I.══ ═══State═══
                                              ¶ Calc count all


ANSWER═State═Count of State═
   1      CA        5
   2      ME        1
   3      NJ        1
   4      NY        2
   5      PA        1
```

Figure 13.19: Frequency distribution of states in the Custlist table

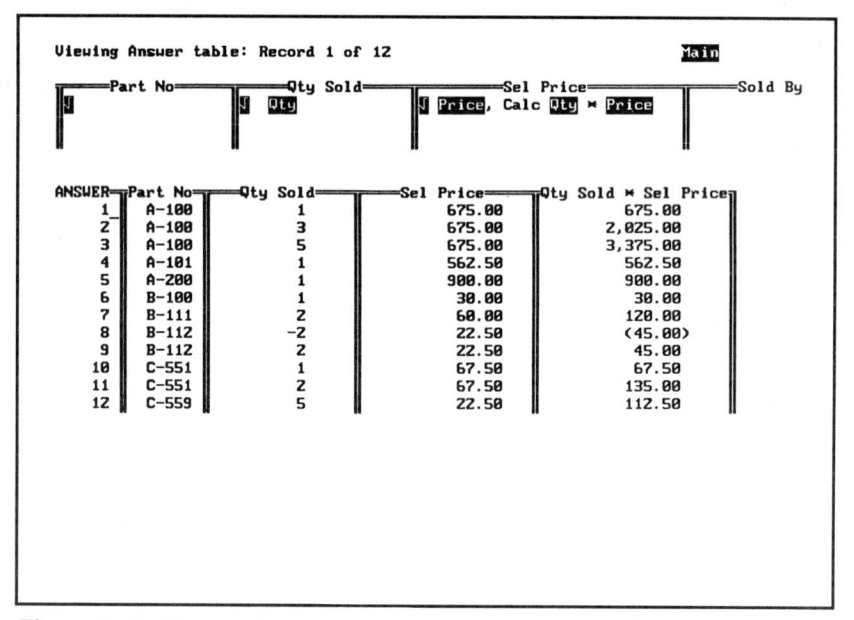

```
Viewing Answer table: Record 1 of 12                    Main
   ═Part No══ ═Qty Sold══ ═══Sel Price═══════ ═Sold By
   ¶          ¶ Qty       ¶ Price, Calc Qty * Price


ANSWER═Part No═ ═Qty Sold═ ═Sel Price═ ═Qty Sold * Sel Price═
   1    A-100       1         675.00         675.00
   2    A-100       3         675.00       2,025.00
   3    A-100       5         675.00       3,375.00
   4    A-101       1         562.50         562.50
   5    A-200       1         900.00         900.00
   6    B-100       1          30.00          30.00
   7    B-111       2          60.00         120.00
   8    B-112      -2          22.50         (45.00)
   9    B-112       2          22.50          45.00
  10    C-551       1          67.50          67.50
  11    C-551       2          67.50         135.00
  12    C-559       5          22.50         112.50
```

Figure 13.20: The total sales price calculated using examples

ADVANCED QUERIES AND CALCULATIONS 311

> If you need a quick reference to query form operators while creating your own queries, just press the F1 key.

Notice in Figure 13.20 that the last column in the Answer table is named *Qty Sold * Sel Price*. Paradox automatically assigns the calculation expression as the table name, unless you specify your own name using the *as* operator. For example, the query in Figure 13.21 displays the results of the expression Qty * Price in a column labeled Subtotal, because of the additional *as Subtotal* used in the query form.

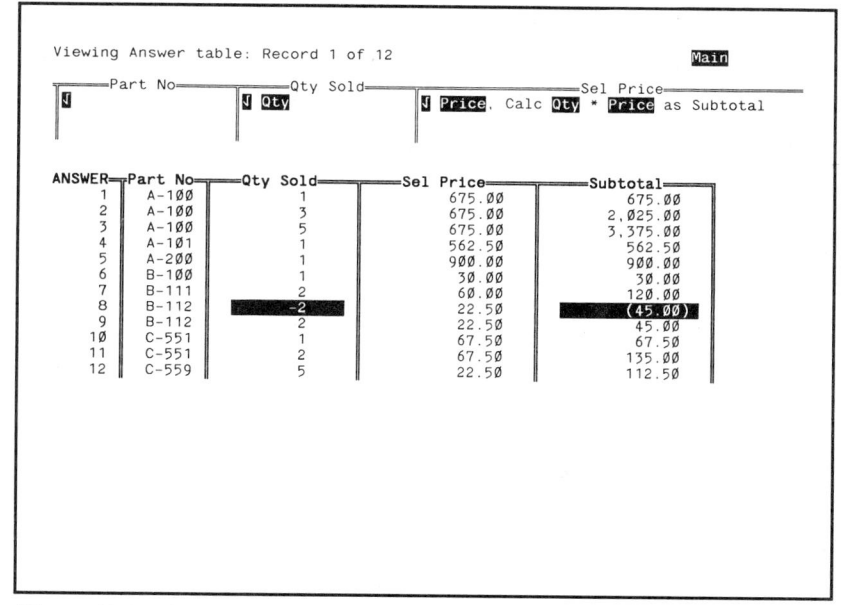

```
Viewing Answer table: Record 1 of 12                           Main
     ┌─Part No─┐ ┌──Qty Sold──┐ ┌──────────Sel Price──────────┐
     │√        │ │√ Qty       │ │√ Price, Calc Qty * Price as Subtotal

ANSWER ┬─Part No─┬─Qty Sold─┬─Sel Price─┬─Subtotal─
     1 │ A-100   │    1     │   675.00  │   675.00
     2 │ A-100   │    3     │   675.00  │ 2,025.00
     3 │ A-100   │    5     │   675.00  │ 3,375.00
     4 │ A-101   │    1     │   562.50  │   562.50
     5 │ A-200   │    1     │   900.00  │   900.00
     6 │ B-100   │    1     │    30.00  │    30.00
     7 │ B-111   │    2     │    60.00  │   120.00
     8 │ B-112   │   -2     │    22.50  │  (45.00)
     9 │ B-112   │    2     │    22.50  │    45.00
    10 │ C-551   │    1     │    67.50  │    67.50
    11 │ C-551   │    2     │    67.50  │   135.00
    12 │ C-559   │    5     │    22.50  │   112.50
```

Figure 13.21: Calculated field is named Subtotal using the *as* operator

You can perform multiple calculations in a single query form by using two or more Calc expressions, separated by commas. Figure 13.22 shows an example where the subtotal is calculated using the expression *Calc Qty * Price as Subtotal*, and a third field displays the total with 6% tax added using the expression *Calc 1.06*(Qty * Price) as Total*. Though not visible on the screen, the Qty Sold field contains the example Qty (as in Figures 13.20 and 13.21).

Note that you can place the Calc instruction in any field of the query form, even one that is not used directly in the calculation. Because the calculated field is always displayed in the results of a query, it need not be checked (using F6).

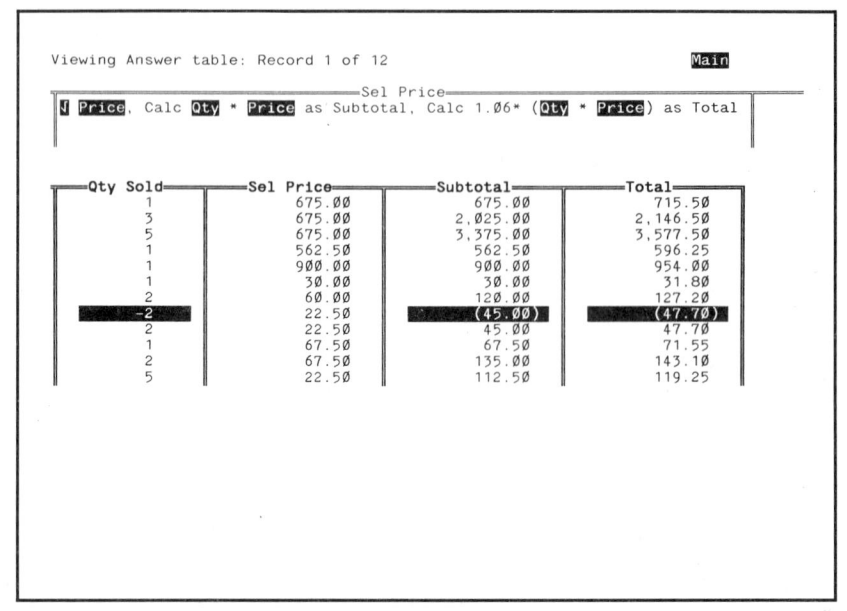

```
Viewing Answer table: Record 1 of 12                    Main
                    ─Sel Price─
│ Price, Calc Qty * Price as Subtotal, Calc 1.06* (Qty * Price) as Total │

┌─Qty Sold─┬─Sel Price─┬──Subtotal──┬───Total───┐
│    1     │  675.00   │   675.00   │   715.50  │
│    3     │  675.00   │ 2,025.00   │ 2,146.50  │
│    5     │  675.00   │ 3,375.00   │ 3,577.50  │
│    1     │  562.50   │   562.50   │   596.25  │
│    1     │  900.00   │   900.00   │   954.00  │
│    1     │   30.00   │    30.00   │    31.80  │
│    2     │   60.00   │   120.00   │   127.20  │
│   -2     │   22.50   │  (45.00)   │  (47.70)  │
│    2     │   22.50   │    45.00   │    47.70  │
│    1     │   67.50   │    67.50   │    71.55  │
│    2     │   67.50   │   135.00   │   143.10  │
│    5     │   22.50   │   112.50   │   119.25  │
```

Figure 13.22: Two calculations in a field

You can also use a field from another table in a calculation. Figure 13.23 shows a sample query where ABC is used as the example to link the Sales and MastInv tables on the common field PartNo (the order of fields in the query form have been rearranged using the Rotate (Ctrl-R) key). Note that Qty is used as the example for the Qty Sold field, and Price is the example used in the Sel Price field of the MastInv table. The expression *Calc Qty * Price as Subtotal* displays the selling price using the Sel Price field from the MastInv table.

PERFORMING QUERIES IN A MANY-TO-MANY DESIGN

Back in Chapter 12, we discussed the *many-to-many* relationship, using the examples of students and courses, joined by a linking table, and an exploded inventory database, where products and components were joined by an example. It is quite easy to perform queries

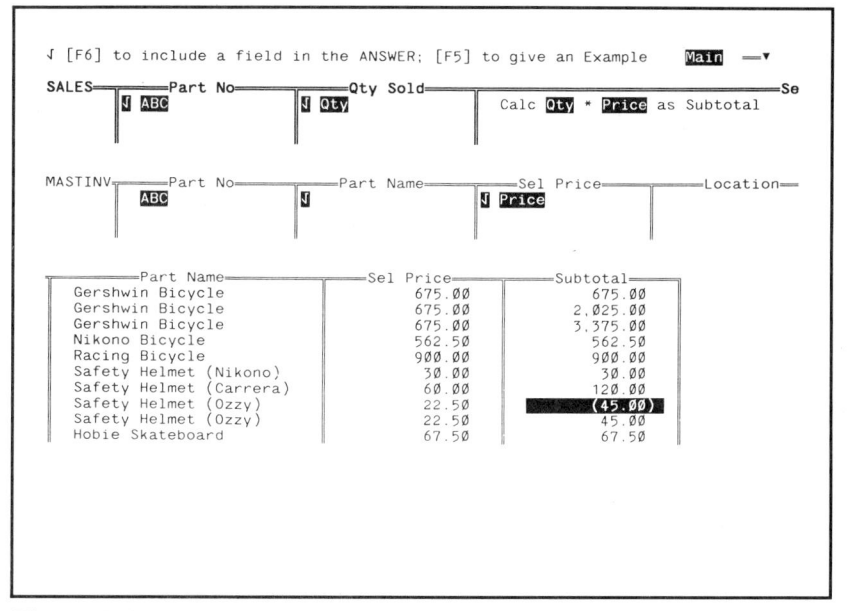

```
√ [F6] to include a field in the ANSWER; [F5] to give an Example   Main  —▼
SALES========Part No=========┬=========Qty Sold=========┬==========================Se
        │ ABC           │ Qty           │  Calc Qty * Price as Subtotal


MASTINV======Part No=========Part Name=========Sel Price=========Location===
        │ ABC    │ √      │ √ Price  │


            ========Part Name========Sel Price========Subtotal====
              Gershwin Bicycle            675.00          675.00
              Gershwin Bicycle            675.00        2,025.00
              Gershwin Bicycle            675.00        3,375.00
              Nikono Bicycle              562.50          562.50
              Racing Bicycle              900.00          900.00
              Safety Helmet (Nikono)       30.00           30.00
              Safety Helmet (Carrera)      60.00          120.00
              Safety Helmet (Ozzy)         22.50         (45.00)
              Safety Helmet (Ozzy)         22.50           45.00
              Hobie Skateboard             67.50           67.50
```

Figure 13.23: A query using two tables to perform a calculation

on tables related in such a manner. To display data from all three tables, use one example to relate the linking table to one of the tables, and another example to relate the linking table to the other table. An example will demonstrate.

Figure 13.24 shows a sample query that will display a list of all students, with the names of the courses that they are enrolled in. Note that the example 9999 links the Students table to the SCLink table, and the example XXXXX links the Courses table to the SCLink table. Check marks in the fields specify which fields to display in the answer table. Figure 13.25 shows the results of the query in the Answer table.

To look at the students and courses data from a different angle, listing courses with the names of the students enrolled in each course, place the Courses query form at the top and the Students query form at the bottom, and use the same technique of examples and check marks to define the relationships and the fields to display. Figure 13.26 shows an example query. Figure 13.27 shows the results of the query, wherein courses are listed in order, with students enrolled in each.

314   MASTERING PARADOX

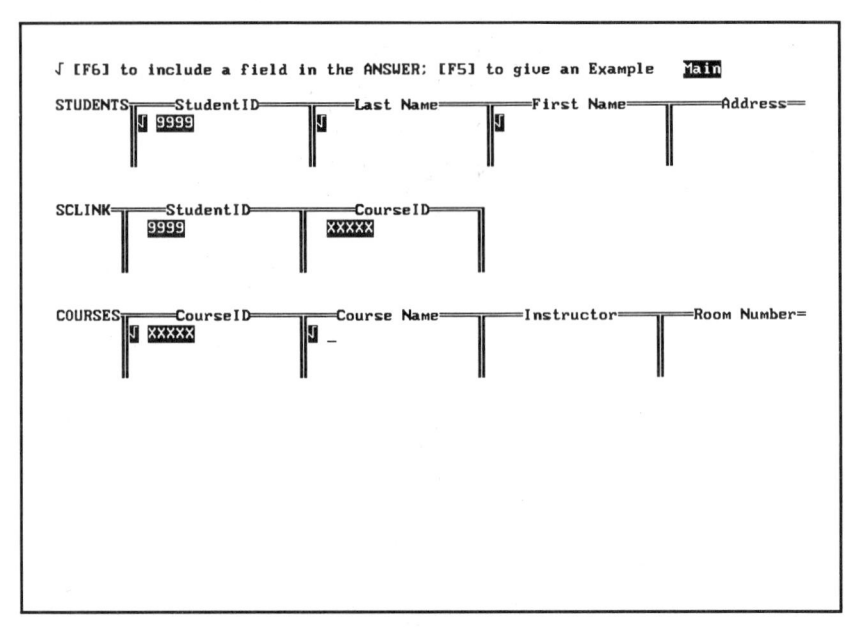

CH. 13

```
√ [F6] to include a field in the ANSWER; [F5] to give an Example    Main
STUDENTS    StudentID         Last Name      First Name       Address
           √ 9999            √              √

SCLINK      StudentID         CourseID
            9999              XXXXX

COURSES     CourseID          Course Name    Instructor       Room Number
           √ XXXXX           √
```

Figure 13.24: Queries to link three related tables

```
Viewing Answer table: Record 1 of 7                              Main
ANSWER      StudentID     Last Name    CourseID     Course Name
  1         10001         Adams         B-222        Botany
  2         10001         Adams         C-333        Chemistry
  3         10002         Black         A-111        Algebra
  4         10002         Black         C-333        Chemistry
  5         10003         Carlson       A-111        Algebra
  6         10003         Carlson       B-222        Botany
  7         10003         Carlson       C-333        Chemistry
```

Figure 13.25: The results of the query shown in Figure 13.24

CALCULATIONS IN A MANY-TO-MANY DESIGN

Chapter 12 presented the basic model for an "exploded inventory" database, where a manufacturer keeps many different components in stock and produces several different products. The

```
√ [F6] to include a field in the ANSWER; [F5] to give an Example      Main
COURSES═╤═CourseID═════════╤═══Course Name═══════╤═Instructor═══════╤═Room Number═
        │√ COURSE          │√                    │                  │
        │                  │                     │                  │

SCLINK══╤═StudentID════════╤═CourseID════════════╕
        │√ STUDENT         │  COURSE             │
        │                  │                     │

STUDENTS╤═StudentID════════╤═Last Name═══════════╤═First Name═══════╤═Address═════
        │√ STUDENT         │√                    │√ _               │
```

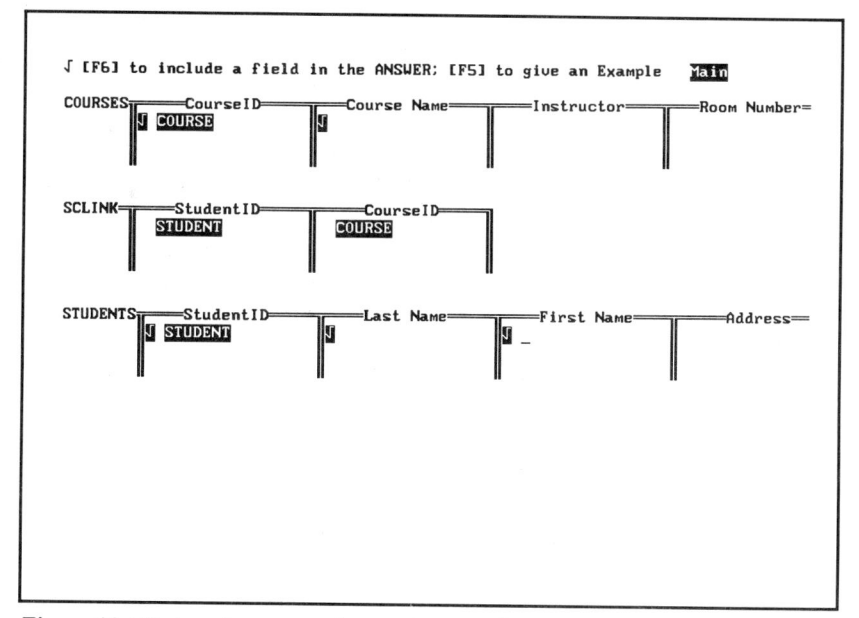

Figure 13.26: Another query for students and courses

```
Viewing Answer table: Record 1 of 7                                    Main
ANSWER╤═CourseID═══╤══════Course Name═══╤═StudentID═══╤═Last Name═══╤═First Na
    1 │  A-111     │  Algebra           │   10002     │  Black      │  Sandra
    2 │  A-111     │  Algebra           │   10003     │  Carlson    │  Carla
    3 │  B-222     │  Botany            │   10001     │  Adams      │  Andy
    4 │  B-222     │  Botany            │   10003     │  Carlson    │  Carla
    5 │  C-333     │  Chemistry         │   10001     │  Adams      │  Andy
    6 │  C-333     │  Chemistry         │   10002     │  Black      │  Sandra
    7 │  C-333     │  Chemistry         │   10003     │  Carlson    │  Carla
```

Figure 13.27: The results of the query shown in Figure 13.26

many-to-many relationship is based on the fact that each product manufactured consists of many components, and each component is used in many different products.

Suppose the user of this database wanted to know how many of each component is necessary to build 50 of product number A-123. The query shown in Figure 13.28 displays the answer. The top query, based on the Linker table, limits calculations to part number A-123. The CCCCCCC example links the component number in the Linker table to the Componen table, and check marks assure that the appropriate fields are displayed. The Y example holds the Qty Used value to aid in the calculation. The formula Calc Y * 50 multiplies the quantity required to produce the product by 50—the quantity to manufacture in this example.

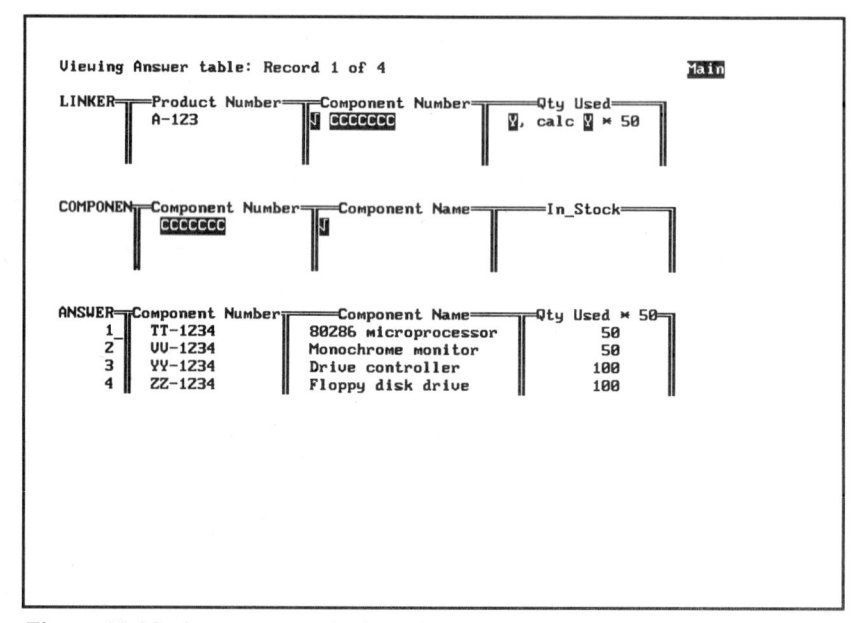

```
Viewing Answer table: Record 1 of 4                            Main
  LINKER──┬─Product Number─┬─Component Number─┬─Qty Used─────┐
          │     A-123      │ ✓ CCCCCCC        │ ✓, calc Y * 50│


  COMPONEN─┬─Component Number─┬─Component Name─┬─In_Stock─┐
           │    CCCCCCC       │     Y          │          │


  ANSWER─┬─Component Number─┬─Component Name────┬─Qty Used * 50─┐
    1    │     TT-1234      │  80286 microprocessor│    50       │
    2    │     VV-1234      │  Monochrome monitor  │    50       │
    3    │     YY-1234      │  Drive controller    │   100       │
    4    │     ZZ-1234      │  Floppy disk drive   │   100       │
```

Figure 13.28: A query to calculate the number of components required to manufacture 50 of product A-123

As the Answer table in Figure 13.28 shows, the manufacturer would need 50 of component numbers TT-1234 and VV-1234 and 100 each of components YY-1234 and ZZ-1234 to manufacture 50 personal computers (product number A-123). To calculate components needed for a different product, change the A-123 condition to the appropriate product name. To change the quantity of products being produced, change the 50 in the calculation to the number of products you wish to produce.

The simple query above is useful for calculating the number of components required to produce a single product. But suppose you wish to make a more "global" calculation to determine the number of each component required to manufacture several of each product? Such a calculation would require several steps.

First, you'd need to fill the Needed field on the Product table with the number of each product you wish to produce. Figure 13.29 shows an example in which the manufacturer wishes to produce 100 personal computers, 50 minicomputers, and 20 mainframe computers.

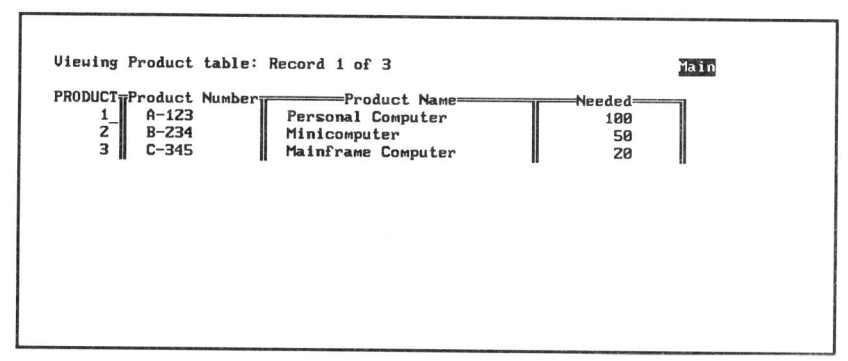

```
Viewing Product table: Record 1 of 3                    Main
PRODUCT┬Product Number┬─────Product Name─────┬──Needed──
     1 │    A-123     │ Personal Computer    │   100
     2 │    B-234     │ Minicomputer         │    50
     3 │    C-345     │ Mainframe Computer   │    20
```

Figure 13.29: The Needed field filled in the Product table

Next, you'll need to create a temporary table that holds all of the fields required to perform the calculation. Figure 13.30 shows just such a query. The top query, based on the Linker table, calculates the number of each component required to produce each product by multiplying the Qty Used field by the number of each item needed. (Y is the query example for the quantity of each component required, and X is the query example for the number of each product being manufactured.) The PPPPP example links the PC Link table to the Product table, and the CCCCCCC example links the Linker table to the Componen table. Check marks ensure that the appropriate fields will be displayed in the Answer table.

Figure 13.31 displays the Answer table that the query in Figure 13.30 produces. While the Answer table contains the appropriate data, it needs to be summarized a bit to be of real use.

To see the data in the Answer table in a better light, you'll want totals based on individual component numbers. To create such a table, copy the Answer table to a new table and use Calc sum to calculate the totals. In this example, you can copy the Answer table to a

```
√ [F6] to include a field in the ANSWER; [F5] to give an Example     Main
LINKER═╤═Product Number═╤═Component Number═╤═Qty Used═══╗
       │    PPPPP        │    CCCCCCC       │ Y, Calc X * Y

PRODUCT╤═Product Number═╤═Product Name═╤═Needed═══╗
       │ √ PPPPP         │ √            │ X

COMPONEN╤═Component Number═╤═Component Name═╤═In_Stock═══╗
        │ √ CCCCCCC        │                │
```

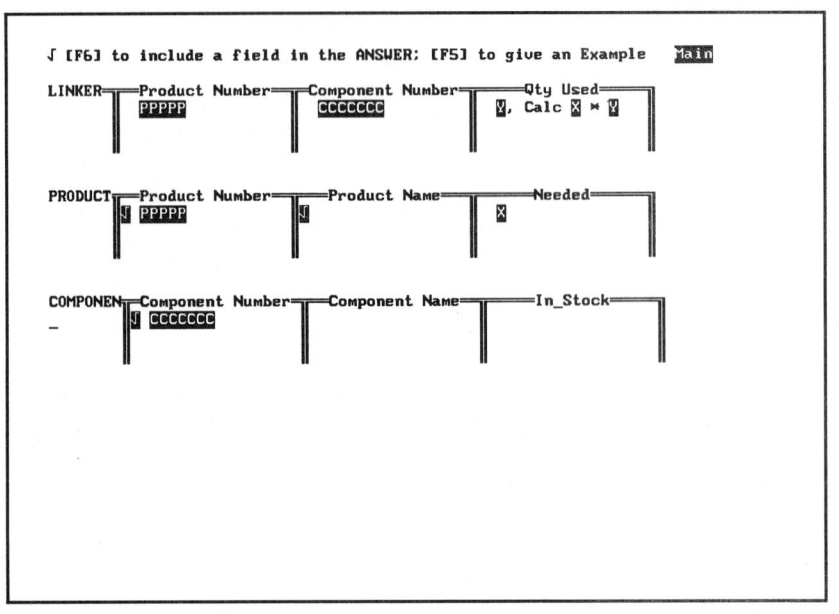

Figure 13.30: A query to calculate the number of components required to manufacture several products

```
Viewing Answer table: Record 1 of 13                                Main
ANSWER╤═Product Number═╤═Product Name═════╤═Component Number═╤═Needed * Qty Used═╗
   1  │    A-123       │ Personal Computer│    TT-1234       │       100
   2  │    A-123       │ Personal Computer│    UU-1234       │       100
   3  │    A-123       │ Personal Computer│    YY-1234       │       200
   4  │    A-123       │ Personal Computer│    ZZ-1234       │       200
   5  │    B-234       │ Minicomputer     │    TT-1234       │        50
   6  │    B-234       │ Minicomputer     │    UU-1234       │        50
   7  │    B-234       │ Minicomputer     │    YY-1234       │       100
   8  │    B-234       │ Minicomputer     │    ZZ-1234       │       100
   9  │    C-345       │ Mainframe Computer│   TT-1234       │        20
  10  │    C-345       │ Mainframe Computer│   UU-1234       │        20
  11  │    C-345       │ Mainframe Computer│   VV-1234       │        20
  12  │    C-345       │ Mainframe Computer│   YY-1234       │        20
  13  │    C-345       │ Mainframe Computer│   ZZ-1234       │        20
```

Figure 13.31: The answer table produced by the query in Figure 13.30

new table named Joined using the Main menu options Tools, Copy, Table. Specify Answer as the table to copy, and Joined as the name of the table to copy to. (If a table named Joined already exists, select Replace to replace its contents with the contents of the Answer table.)

Next, clear the screen to make some room (type Alt-F8), and select Ask from the Main menu. Specify Joined as the table to query, place a check mark in the Component number field (as this is the field we wish to group by), and Calc sum in the Needed * Qty Used field. Press F2, and the Answer table will display the results, as shown in Figure 13.32.

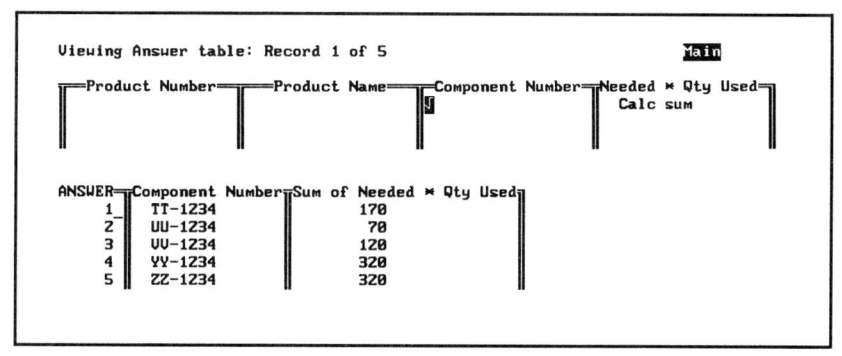

```
Viewing Answer table: Record 1 of 5                    Main
┌─Product Number─┬─Product Name─┬─Component Number─┬─Needed * Qty Used─┐
│                │              │                  │    Calc sum       │
│                │              │                  │                   │
│                │              │                  │                   │
│                │              │                  │                   │
ANSWER─┬─Component Number─┬─Sum of Needed * Qty Used─┐
   1   │   TT-1234        │         170              │
   2   │   UU-1234        │          70              │
   3   │   VV-1234        │         120              │
   4   │   YY-1234        │         320              │
   5   │   ZZ-1234        │         320              │
```

Figure 13.32: The totals of components required to manufacture products listed in Figure 13.29

As the table shows, the manufacturer would need 170 of part number TT-1234 to produce the number of products specified in the Product table (Figure 13.29). You'll need 70 of part number UU-1234, and so forth.

This example shows how you can actually break a query into several steps to perform more complex tasks. Notice the basic steps we used. First, we created an Answer table containing the basic information we need, using one query. Then, we copied the Answer table to a new table, and performed a query on that new table. With a little practice, you should be able to perform similar complex queries of your own.

ASKING ABOUT SETS OF RECORDS

In some situations you may need to ask questions about categories or *sets* of records in a table. To allow you to do so, Paradox offers *set queries*. To demonstrate the power and flexibility of set queries, we'll use two new sample tables. Figure 13.33 shows one of these tables, named PartList, that includes information about individual parts in an inventory. (Note that the table is similar to MastInv created earlier, but includes a new field named Category.)

```
Viewing Partlist table: Record 1 of 8                    Main
PARTLIST┬Part No──────┬──Part Name──────────┬─Category─
   1    │   A-100     │ Gershwin Bicycle    │  BIKE
   2    │   A-101     │ Nikono Bicycle      │  BIKE
   3    │   A-200     │ Racing Bicycle      │  BIKE
   4    │   B-100     │ Safety Helmet (Nikono)│ HELMET
   5    │   B-111     │ Safety Helmet (Carrera)│ HELMET
   6    │   B-112     │ Safety Helmet (Ozzy) │ HELMET
   7    │   C-551     │ Hobie Skateboard    │  SKATE
   8    │   C-559     │ Flexie Skateboard   │  SKATE
```

Figure 13.33: Sample table named PartList

Figure 13.34 shows a second sample table, named CustSale, that includes records of sales transactions, including customers' names.

CREATING SET QUERIES

A set query generally consists of one query form that defines the set, and a query form from a related table that compares records to the set. There are three *set* operators that you can use to compare records to the set:

> **only** Displays records that have only the values in the set.
>
> **no** Displays records that do not match any values in the set.
>
> **every** Displays records that match (at least) every record in a set.
>
> **exactly** Displays records that have exactly the same values as the set; no more and no less (a combination of *only* and *every* above).

```
Viewing Custsale table: Record 1 of 17                    Main
CUSTSALE    Customer Name      Part No       Qty
    1       Andy Adams         A-100          1
    2       Andy Adams         A-101          1
    3       Andy Adams         A-200          1
    4       Andy Adams         B-100          1
    5       Andy Adams         B-111          2
    6       Andy Adams         B-112         10
    7       Andy Adams         C-551          1
    8       Andy Adams         C-559          5
    9       Bob Baker          A-100          3
   10       Charlie Chap       A-100          5
   11       Charlie Chap       B-112          2
   12       Charlie Chap       C-551          2
   13       Debra Doe          C-551          2
   14       Debra Doe          C-559          1
   15       Edie Edwards       A-100          1
   16       Edie Edwards       A-101          1
   17       Edie Edwards       A-200          1
```

Figure 13.34: Sample CustSale table

Figure 13.35 shows an example set query, using the sample PartList and CustSale tables. (The queries were created using the usual Ask option from the main menu.) The top query in the figure defines the set as BIKE category. Note that the word Set must be included under the table name, as in the Figure. BIKE is a query condition that defines the set as records that have BIKE in the category field. ABC in the Part No field is an example (entered with the usual F5 key), that links the PartList table to the CUSTSALE table via the common field, Part No.

The CustSale query form has a check mark in the Customer Name field, because this is the field we want the query to display. The Part No field contains the example ABC, preceded by the *every* operator. Note that, what the query is asking, is for a display of customers who have bought every bike (i.e., all products in the BIKE category).

The answer to the query appears at the bottom of Figure 13.35. Notice that customers Andy Adams and Edie Edwards are displayed. If you refer back to Figure 13.34, you'll see that the answer is indeed correct; only these two customers have purchased every type of BIKE.

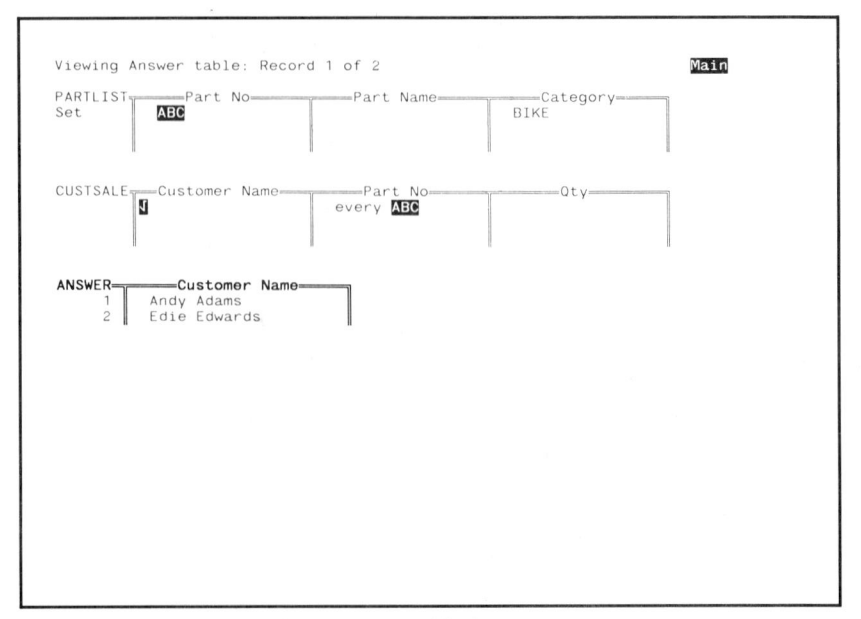

```
Viewing Answer table: Record 1 of 2                          Main
PARTLIST┬──Part No──┬──┬──Part Name──┬──┬──Category──┐
Set     │   ABC     │  │             │  │   BIKE     │
        │           │  │             │  │            │


CUSTSALE┬──Customer Name──┬──┬──Part No──┬──┬──Qty──┐
        │   √             │  │ every ABC │  │       │
        │                 │  │           │  │       │


ANSWER┬──┬──Customer Name──┐
    1 │  │ Andy Adams      │
    2 │  │ Edie Edwards    │
```

Figure 13.35: An example set query with the *every* operator

Suppose you want to see lists of customers who have not purchased any bikes. You would use the *no* operator, as in Figure 13.36. The Answer table displays Debra Doe. Again, referring back to the Figure 13.34, you can see that, indeed, Debra Doe has not purchased any item from the BIKE category.

Now, suppose you want to see a list of customers who have bought *only* bikes, and not other products from any other categories. In this case, you would use the *only* operator, as in Figure 13.37. Its Answer table displays customer names Bob Baker and Edie Edwards. Referring once again back to Figure 13.34, you can see that these two customers have purchased *only* products from the BIKE category, and no products from any other category. (Even though Charlie Chap and Andy Adams have purchased bikes, they are excluded from the display because they have also purchased other products outside of the BIKE category.)

Finally, suppose you want to see customers who have purchased exactly those products that make up the BIKE category; that is, customers who have bought every type of bike, and no other product. In this case, you would use the *exactly* operator, as in Figure 13.38. Once

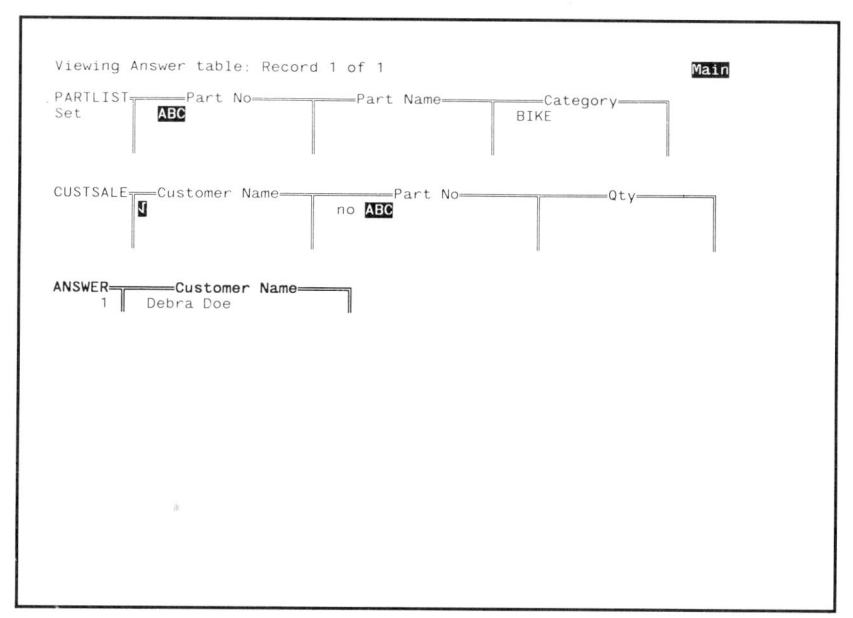

Figure 13.36: A set query using the *no* operator

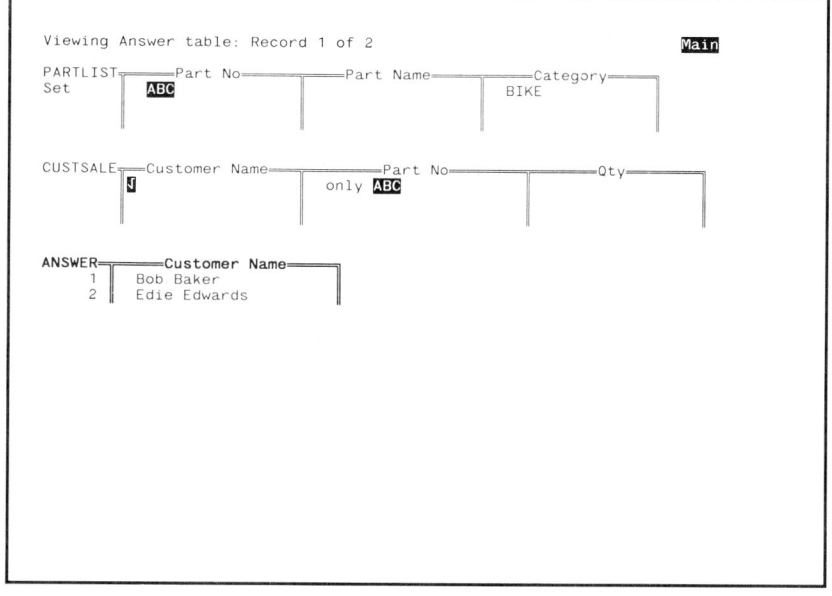

Figure 13.37: A set query using the *only* operator

again, if you refer back to Figure 13.34, you'll see that Edie Edwards has indeed purchased each product in the BIKE category, and nothing more.

COMPARING RECORDS TO SUMMARY VALUES

In the preceding examples you saw how set queries can let you compare records in one table to a set of records in another table. You can also use set queries to compare records in a table to a summary calculation within that table, such as an average or sum. You can use any of the summary operators (average, count, max, min) to perform such an analysis.

Figure 13.39 shows an example using the CustList table. The first line of the query includes Set in the leftmost column, and the example *limit* in the Credit Limit field. Because there are no search criteria in the top line of the query, *set* defines all records in the table.

The second line of the query includes check marks in the Last Name and Credit Limit fields, as these are the fields we want to see in the Answer table. The second line *does* include a search criteria,

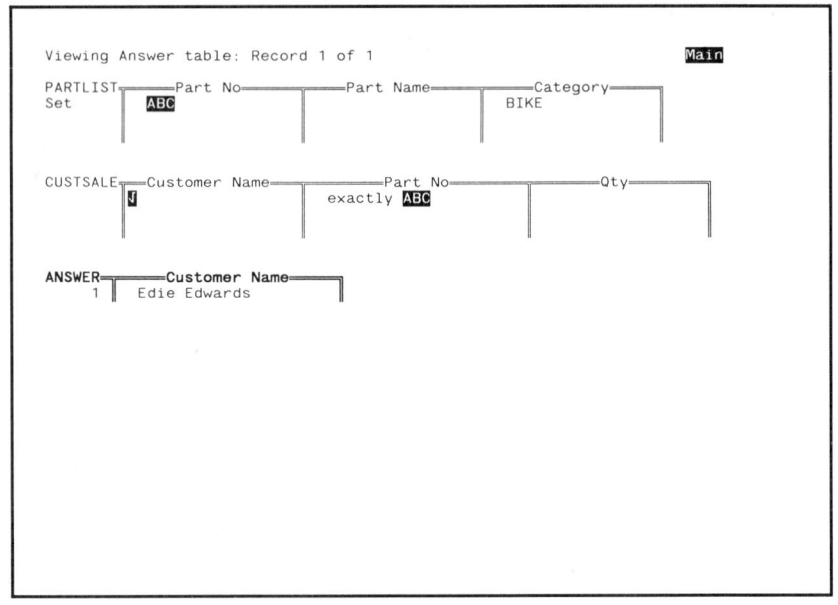

```
Viewing Answer table: Record 1 of 1                         Main
     PARTLIST    Part No        Part Name       Category
     Set         ABC                            BIKE


     CUSTSALE    Customer Name        Part No              Qty
                 √                    exactly ABC


     ANSWER      Customer Name
          1     Edie Edwards
```

Figure 13.38: A set query using the *exactly* operator

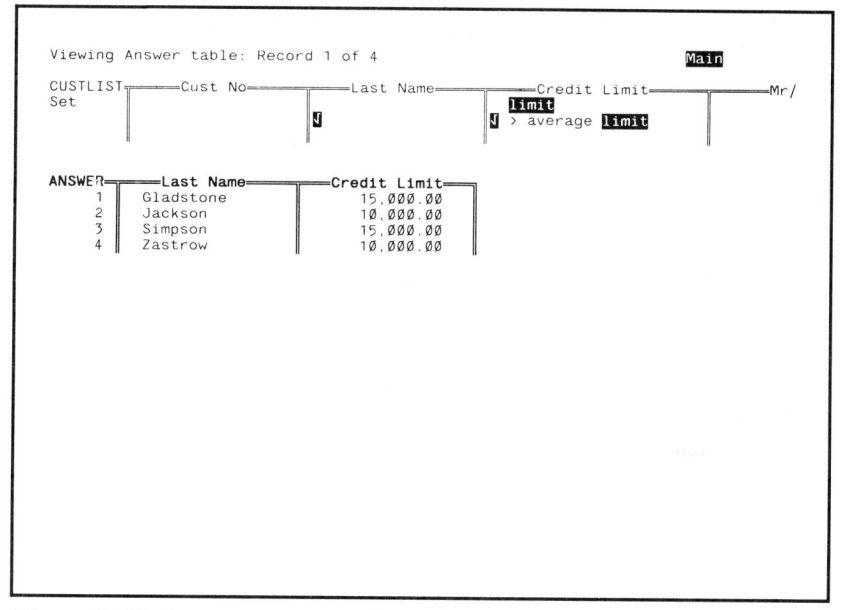

```
Viewing Answer table: Record 1 of 4                    Main
CUSTLIST┬─────Cust No────┬────Last Name────┬────Credit Limit────┬────Mr/
Set     │                │                 │      limit         │
        │                │       √         │   √ > average limit│

ANSWER┬────Last Name─────┬────Credit Limit─┐
   1  │   Gladstone      │    15,000.00    │
   2  │   Jackson        │    10,000.00    │
   3  │   Simpson        │    15,000.00    │
   4  │   Zastrow        │    10,000.00    │
```

Figure 13.39: A set query comparing values to an average

> *average limit*. This condition restricts the records displayed in the Answer table to those that have Credit Limits that are greater than the average Credit Limit.

Note that if, in Figure 13.39, you used > *min limit* in place of > *average limit*, the Answer table would display records that have values that are greater than the smallest credit limit. Using the criterion = *max limit* instead would display those records that have the highest credit limits in them.

THE GROUPBY OPERATOR

Check marks in the first line of set queries serve two purposes; they define which fields to display, and also define which fields to group answers by. In some situations, you might not want to perform both operations (i.e., you may want to group records by a field, but not display that field). In these situations, you can use the *groupby* operator, rather than a check mark, in the query form. To place the groupby operator in a query form, you press Shift-F6.

> This hypothetical example also assumes that the MastInv table includes a column named CATEGORY.

To demonstrate, suppose that the CustSale table back in Figure 13.34 contained a field named Customer Number, but did not contain customer names. Instead, a table named CustList contained customer names and addresses, and also a field named Customer Number to link names and addresses to customer numbers in the CustSale table.

Now suppose you want to set a query to see which cities and states contain customers that have purchased *only* skateboards (and no other products). Your first step would be to select Ask and create a set query for the MastInv table, as at the top of Figure 13.40. Notice that Set and SKATE define the set as records with SKATE as the category. ABC is used to link the MastInv table to the CustSale table.

The second query, based on the CustSale table, uses *only ABC* to find customers who have purchased only skateboards. Note, however, that none of the fields in the second query form are checked, because the data we want to display is stored in yet another table. But Paradox needs to know which field to use for grouping in the second table. To indicate this you would press groupby (Shift-F6) rather than check (F6) in the Customer Number field. (The groupby operator appears as a G, as you can see in the Figure.) Now Paradox will isolate groups of *customers* that have purchased only skateboards.

The last query form contains the example CUSTNO, to relate it to the CUSTNO field in the CustSale table. The City and State fields are checked in this last query form. As you can see in the Answer table, Manhattan Beach, California is the only city with customers that have purchased only skateboards.

HANDLING BLANKS IN QUERY CALCULATIONS

When you begin developing queries with more complex calculations, you may be alarmed to find that Paradox does not treat a blank field as zero. Instead, a calculation such as Calc $X + Y + Z$ will display a blank if any of the fields referenced contains a blank (even if the other two fields contain numbers). No need to panic over this. You can use the Paradox Custom Configuration program to reconfigure Paradox to treat empty fields as zeros when performing calculations. See Chapter 14 of the *Paradox User's Guide* for details.

ADVANCED QUERIES AND CALCULATIONS 327

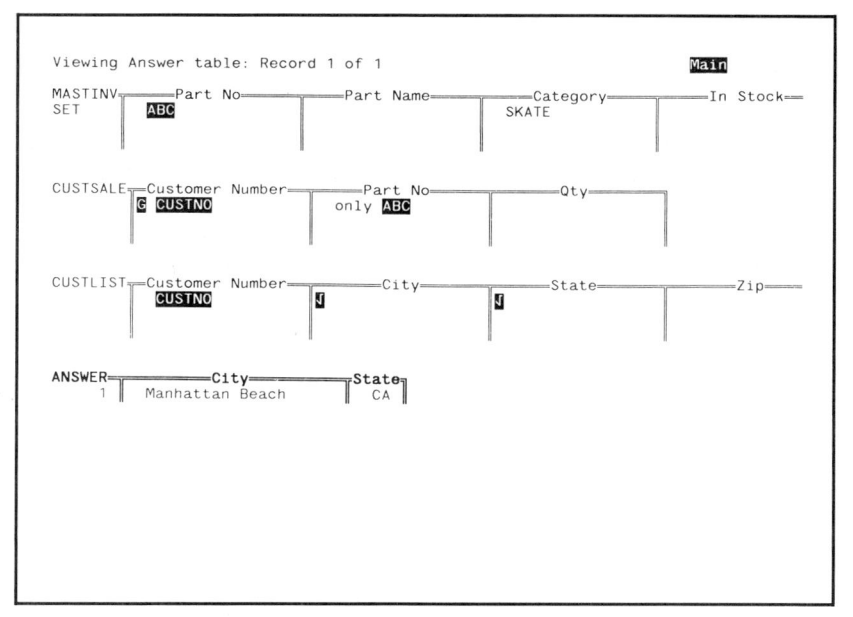

```
Viewing Answer table: Record 1 of 1                         Main
MASTINV┬──Part No──────┬──Part Name──────┬──Category──────┬──In Stock══
SET    │ ABC           │                 │  SKATE         │

CUSTSALE┬═Customer Number═┬══Part No══┬══Qty══┐
        │ G CUSTNO        │ only ABC  │       │

CUSTLIST┬═Customer Number═┬══City══┬══State══┬══Zip══┐
        │ CUSTNO          │ √      │ √       │       │

ANSWER┬═════════City══════┬═State═┐
      1 │ Manhattan Beach │  CA   │
```

Figure 13.40: Sample set query using the groupby operator.

SAVING QUERIES

As we've seen in this chapter, some queries can become quite complex, especially those involving two or more tables. (Even though we've used a maximum of three tables in our examples, Paradox can simultaneously query as many related tables as you wish.) To save yourself the trouble of retyping a query each time you want to use it, you can save a query for future use.

To do so, build the complete query on the screen in the usual manner, and test it (using the F2 key). If the query produces the results you want, press F8 to clear the Answer table, then save the query by calling up the Main menu (F10), and selecting the Scripts and QuerySave options. You'll be given the prompt

    Query script name:
    Enter name to be given to new query script.

Enter a name for the script (eight letters maximum, no spaces or punctuation), and press Enter.

To use the query in the future, you'll probably want to first clear the screen (Alt-F8), then select Scripts and Play from the Main menu. You'll see the prompt

> **Move to the record to be selected**
> **Press [F2] to select the record; Esc to cancel; [F1] for help**

Type in the name of the saved query, or press Enter to see a list of saved queries (and scripts) and select the query name by highlighting and pressing Enter in the usual fashion.

The query will appear on the screen, in exactly the format you saved it. You can then press F2 to perform the query, or use the usual arrow keys to modify the query if you wish.

If the query actually involves several steps, as in the example of the exploded-inventory calculation above, you can store all the keystrokes needed to produce the query rather than the queries themselves. To do so, press Instant Script Record (Alt-F3), press Clear All (Alt-F8), and then type all the keystrokes necessary to perform the entire query. When you are done, press Alt-F3 again to stop recording the keystrokes.

Paradox will save the script under the name Instant. To assign a more descriptive name to the script, call up the Main menu and select the Tools, Rename, and Script options. Enter Instant as the name of the script to rename, and enter a new name for the script (as usual, eight letters maximum length, no spaces or punctuation).

To perform the query steps at a later moment, call up the menu and select Scripts and either Play or ShowPlay. Enter the name of the script and press Return as usual. All of the necessary steps to perform the query will take place on the screen.

QUERY SPEED-UP

Large queries that do not use key fields can sometimes take a long time to complete. The QuerySpeedup option under the Tools menu can help speed up most queries. See the section "Speeding Up Queries" in Chapter 16 for more information on this option.

SUMMARY

- To link multiple tables in a query, you enter *examples* of matching data in the field that links the two tables.

- To enter an example on a query form, first press the Example (F5) key, then type in an example.

- To display fields from two tables, just place check-mark or check-plus symbols in the appropriate fields of the query forms, and use an example to relate the two tables.

- To perform calculations on numeric fields, you can use the Calc command with the average, sum, max, min, or count operators.

- To calculate subtotals of unique items in a field, use a check mark with the Calc sum command.

- To determine frequency distributions, use the Calc count all command.

- To display a new field based on the calculations of two or more existing fields, use examples to define fields in the calculation, and place the fields in a formula.

- When querying multiple tables, Paradox displays only matching records from the tables, unless you use the inclusion operator (!).

- The *As* operator lets you assign a field name to a calculated fields.

- Set queries allow you to ask questions about groups, or categories, of records. Set queries require that you place the word Set beneath the table name in the query form, and use one of the set operators *only*, *no*, *every*, or *exactly*.

ADVANCED REPORT AND FORM TECHNIQUES

CHAPTER 14

THIS CHAPTER DISCUSSES ADVANCED TECHNIQUES that you can use to create custom reports and forms. The more advanced report techniques we'll discuss include tabular reports; totals, subtotals, and grouping; calculated fields; and techniques for printing reports using data from multiple tables. Advanced techniques for forms include forms that access multiple tables, multiple-page forms, and calculated fields.

To begin with, we'll take a look at some of the basic options available for tabular reports. We'll assume that you are already adept at selecting menu items and moving the cursor at this point. Rather than spend time demonstrating all of these techniques with hands-on examples, we'll present the tabular-report capabilities in a more general form, which you should be able to incorporate into your own reports with a little practice.

TABULAR REPORTS

As you may recall from Chapter 8, when you select the Report option from the Main menu, one of the submenus that appears presents the options

   Tabular   Free-form

When you select Free-form, Paradox displays a suggested free-form report format on the screen. Similarly, the Tabular option presents a suggested tabular report format on the screen. Figure 14.1 shows the suggested report format that Paradox would display for a tabular report of the Sales table.

Looking at the sample tabular report format in Figure 14.1, you can see that the field names and column titles are enclosed within the

CH. 14

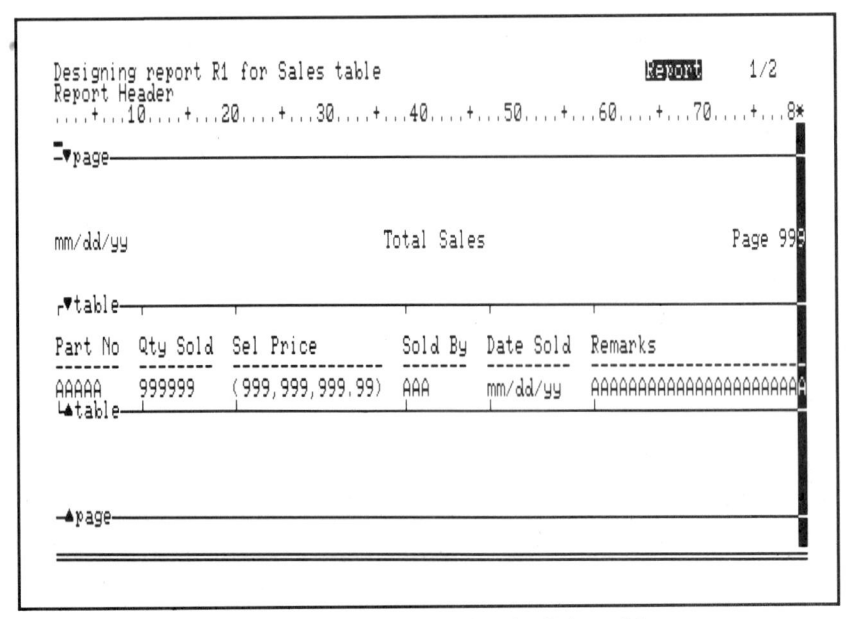

```
Designing report R1 for Sales table                    Report    1/2
Report Header
....+...10....+...20....+...30....+...40....+...50....+...60....+...70....+...8*
─▼page─────────────────────────────────────────────────────────────────


mm/dd/yy                         Total Sales                      Page 999

  ┌▼table──────────────────────────────────────────────────────────
  Part No  Qty Sold  Sel Price         Sold By  Date Sold  Remarks
  -------  --------  ----------------  -------  ---------  ----------------------
  AAAAA    999999    (999,999,999.99)  AAA      mm/dd/yy   AAAAAAAAAAAAAAAAAAAAAA
  └▲table──

─▲page─────────────────────────────────────────────────────────────────
```

Figure 14.1: The suggested report format for the Sales table

table band. (The word *table* appears on the line marking the table band, next to the upward and downward pointing triangles.) Generally speaking, the fields within the table band are printed once for each record in the table. The column titles and underlines are printed at the top of each page.

THE TABULAR REPORT MENU

When designing a tabular report, you can press Menu (F10) at any time to call up the Report menu. Doing so will present the options

    Field TableBand Group Output Setting Help DO-IT!
    Cancel

These options can be summarized as follows:

    Field   Places, deletes, or formats a field on the report
    TableBand   Copies, resizes, deletes, or inserts a field

Group	Specifies groups, either for general format or for subtotals
Output	Prints the report
Setting	Formats the printed page, prints single sheets, and specifies printer-setup strings.
Help	Provides help while formatting the report
DO-IT!	Saves the current report format
Cancel	Abandons the current report format

The Help, DO-IT!, and Cancel options above should all be obvious to you by now. The other options need some additional explanation.

MANAGING REPORT COLUMNS

One of the first steps in formatting a tabular report will probably be to get the report columns formatted to your liking. Options for managing the individual columns are available in the TableBand menu. The following sections briefly discuss these basic options. Each is very easy to use, and when you use them, you'll be given simple instructions on the screen to help you out.

INSERTING COLUMNS

To insert a new column into the report, call up the menu, select TableBand, and then select Insert. The screen will ask that you

> USE ↑ ↓ → ← to show where the new column should be placed... then press ← to insert it.

Move the cursor to the report column to the right of the position where you want the new report column to appear. When you press Enter, Paradox will attempt to insert a new, empty, report column to the left of the cursor position. If there is not enough room in the report format for the new column, an error message will tell you so. You can make more room by deleting another report column (using the TableBand and Erase options from the menu), resizing a different column (using the TableBand and Resize menu options), or increasing the width of the printed report (using the Setting and PageLayout options).

Once inserted, the new report column will be 15 characters wide. You can define a field for the column using the Field and Place menu options. You can also resize the column using the TableBand and Resize menu options.

ERASING COLUMNS

To remove a column from the report format, select Tableband from the report menu, and Erase from the submenu. When you do so, Paradox will instruct you to move the cursor to the column to erase and then press Enter. (To change your mind, and not erase any columns, press Esc.)

When you press Enter, the column, its heading, and the underline under the heading will disappear. All columns to the right will shift to the left to fill in the gap left by the erased column.

RESIZING COLUMNS

To expand or contract the width of a report column, select the Resize option from the TableBand menu. As instructed, move the cursor to the column you want to resize. If you plan to shrink the column width, be sure to place the cursor on the same line as the field template (for example, the AAA or 999 or mm/dd/yy portion of the table band), either to the left or right of the template. That way, you won't erase anything as you narrow the column width. If you plan to expand the column width, you can place the cursor in the field template, within the underline, or in the column heading.

After positioning the cursor, press Enter. The screen displays the instructions

    Now use ← to contract the column, → to expand it...
    press ↵ when finished.

Use the arrow keys to widen or narrow the column, then press Enter when done.

Note that you can expand the width of a column only as far as the margins in the report allow. If you do not have enough room to widen the column to your liking, make more room by either deleting another report column (using the TableBand and Erase options from the menu), resizing a different column (using the TableBand and Resize menu options), or by increasing the width of the printed report (using the Setting and PageLayout options).

If you make a numeric field too narrow to display the values in that field, the numbers will appear as asterisks in the printed report. If that happens, use the Report and Change options to bring the report format back onto the screen. Then select the TableBand and Resize options once again, and widen the field as necessary. Press F2 to save the new report format.

MOVING COLUMNS

There are two ways to move columns on the report format. If you simply want to rotate the fields, use the Rotate (Ctrl-R) key. This key works in the same fashion on the table band as it does on table images on the screen.

A second technique for moving a column is to select the Move option on the TableBand menu. When you select Move, the screen displays the instructions

> Use ↑ ↓ → ← to indicate the column to be moved...
> then press ↵ to select it.

Move the cursor into the report column that you wish to move, then press Enter. Next, the screen asks that you

> Now use → and ← to show the new location for the column...
> press ↵ to move it.

Move the cursor to the new location for the column, and press Enter. The column will move to the new location, and all other columns will shift accordingly to make room.

COPYING COLUMNS

If you want a column to appear in more than one place on the report, use the TableBand and Copy options from the Report menu to copy the column. When you select TableBand and Copy from the menu, the screen will ask that you

> Use ↑ ↓ → ← to indicate the column to be copied...
> then press ↵ to select it.

Move the cursor to within the report column to be copied, then press Enter. The screen then asks that you

> Now use → and ← to show the location for the copy...
> press ↵ to place it.

Move the cursor to the right of the position that you want to place the copy, and press Enter. The copy will appear to the left of the cursor position, and all other fields will shift to make room for the copy. As mentioned in the discussion of moving columns above, you can resize or erase another field, if necessary, to make room for the new column. Optionally, you can change the report width to make room for the copy.

MANAGING FIELDS

In tabular reports, you have at your disposal many options for placing and formatting report columns. All of these options appear under the Field option on the Report menu. When you select Field, the following submenu appears on the screen:

> Place   Erase   Reformat   Justify   CalcEdit   WordWrap
> Lookup

These options can be summarized as follows:

OPTION	*FUNCTION*
Place	Adds a new field to the report format
Erase	Removes a field from the report format
Reformat	Formats the field display

Justify   Aligns the data within the report column

WordWrap   Wraps long alphanumeric fields within a report column

Lookup   Displays related information from a separate table

These options are discussed in more detail in the sections that follow.

GENERAL TECHNIQUES FOR PLACING AND FORMATTING FIELDS

When you select Place from the Field menu, the following submenu is displayed on the screen:

```
Regular  Summary  Calculated  Date  Time  Page
#Record
```

These options can be summarized as follows:

OPTION	*FUNCTION*
Regular	Places a field from the table on the report
Summary	Places a subtotal, total, average, count, lowest value, or highest value calculation on the report
Calculated	Calculates and displays the results of arithmetic operations on two or more fields
Date	Places the current date on the report
Time	Places the current time on the report
Page	Places the current page number on the report
#Record	Places the record number on the report

Each of these options uses the same general techniques for placing and formatting the field. Once you determine what you want to place on the report, the screen will display the instructions

Use ↑ ↓ → ← to indicate where the field should begin...
then press ⏎ to place it.

Use the arrow keys to move the cursor to the exact location where you want the field to appear. (If the field is to appear as a report column, you would need to use the TableBand and Insert options first to create a new, empty column for the field.)

You can place a field anywhere on the report format. How and when it is displayed on the printed report will be determined by its position within the various report bands, as discussed later. For now, suffice it to say that you may move the cursor to any position on the report format, and press Enter to place the field. When you press Enter, the field template will appear to the right of the cursor (assuming there is enough room for the field).

If there is not enough room to place the field where you want it, Paradox will present a warning message. You can either move the cursor to a new position to place the field or press Esc to cancel the field placement.

If you cancel the operation, you may be able to move things around on the report format to make more room. For example, you can use the Insert option under the TableBand menu to insert a new field, and the Resize option to widen that field. You can use the Erase or Resize option under the TableBand menu to resize or erase an existing field. You can also erase or move any literals (such as headings) that might be in the way, to make more room for the field.

Once you do get the field placed on the report, the screen will ask you to format the field. The way you format the field will depend on the data type of that field, as discussed below.

Formatting Alphanumeric Fields

If you've just placed an alphanumeric field on the report, the field template (or *mask*, as it is also called) will appear as a row of A's, which match the width of the field. The screen will display the prompt

> Now use → and ← to indicate how many characters to show...
> press ⏎ when finished.

To make the field narrower, press the ← key as many times as necessary. To widen the field, use the → key. (Note, however, that you cannot widen the field beyond its width in the table.) Press Enter after selecting the appropriate width for the field.

Formatting Date Fields

If you are attempting to place a Date field on the report format, the screen will display a menu of date formats before placing the field. These formats, along with sample dates, are listed below:

DATE FORMAT	EXAMPLE
1) mm/dd/yy	12/1/90
2) Month dd, yy	December 1, 1990
3) mm/dd	12/01
4) mm/yy	12/90
5) dd-Mon-yy	1-Dec-90
6) Mon yy	Dec 90
7) dd-Mon-yyyy	1-Dec-1990
8) mm/dd/yyyy	12/01/1990
9) dd.mm.yy	12.01.90
10) dd/mm/yy	12/01/90
11) yy-mm-dd	90-12-01

Select a date format from the menu, and press Enter. The field mask will then appear on the report format.

Formatting Numeric Fields

If the field you've placed on the report is numeric or currency, the field mask will appear on the screen as a series of nines separated by commas (for example, 999,999,999,999). The screen will display the instructions

> Now use → and ← to adjust the number of whole digits to show... press ↵ to set the number of digits.

Use the ← key to narrow the number display or → to widen it. Press Enter when done, and the screen will display the instructions

> Use the → and ← keys to adjust the number of decimal places... then press ↵ to set the number of decimals.

Pressing → increases the number of digits displayed to the right of the decimal point, while pressing ← decreases the number of digits in the decimal portion. Press Enter after setting the number of decimal places you would like.

The maximum width of a numeric field is 12 whole digits, or 20 digits if decimal places are used. Once the field is placed and sized, you can use the Reformat option under the Field menu to reformat the number according to a variety of international standards.

PLACING REGULAR FIELDS

A *regular field* is any field that is stored in the table for which you are developing the report. When you select the Regular option from the Place menu, the screen displays a menu of field names on the current table. As usual, to select a field, just move the highlight to that field and press Enter. Once you've selected the field, place it on the report and format it using the general techniques discussed above.

Remember, you can place a regular field anywhere on the report. Referring back to Figure 14.1, the fields in the table band—Part No, Qty Sold, Sel Price, and so on—are all regular fields from the table named Sales. (These are the "suggested" fields that Paradox placed on the report automatically.)

PLACING CALCULATED FIELDS

A *calculated field* is one that is based on calculations of two or more other fields in the table. The calculations may involve any single data type, such as numeric (and currency) fields, date fields, and alphanumeric fields. Each type of calculation uses slightly different rules, as discussed below.

Calculated Numeric Fields

Numeric calculations are probably the most common ones used in reports. For example, the Sales table includes a field named Sel Price (the unit price), and a field named Qty Sold (the quantity sold). It does not include a field to store the *extended price*, which is the unit price times the quantity sold. However, you could still *display* the extended price by adding a calculated field to the report format.

To enter a calculated field, you must place the field names in square brackets ([ ]) and use any of the arithmetic operators below to create the appropriate calculation:

+   Addition

−   Subtraction

*   Multiplication

/   Division

( )   Grouping

Numeric fields may also use the *summary operators* listed below in their expressions:

Sum	Sum of the field
Average	Average of the field
Count	Count of the field
High	Highest value in the field
Low	Lowest value in the field

These summary operators allow you to perform summary calculations within a report column. When using summary operators, you must place the expression within parentheses after the operator, using the general syntax

Sum(*field name or expression***)**

For example, the expression

Sum([Sel Price] * [Qty Sold])

demonstrates the correct syntax for displaying the sum of the products of the Sel Price and Qty Sold fields.

Summary calculations are usually used in conjunction with *groups,* a topic we will discuss later in this chapter. A sample invoice-printing report format, shown towards the end of this chapter, demonstrates this use of summary operators.

You may also use constants in calculated fields. These are simply numbers that do not vary in value. For example, a calculation of 6 percent sales tax might be a constant, because the 6 percent is used for all calculations.

Let's look at some examples of calculated numeric fields. Suppose you wish to place a report column to show the extended price on a report for the Sales table. To do so, you would select the Calculated option from the menu, and enter the expression

[Sel Price] * [Qty Sold]

Note that the field names are placed within brackets, and the * symbol is used to signify multiplication.

If you wished to add 6 percent sales tax to the calculation, you could multiply the expression by the constant 1.06, as shown:

([Sel Price] * [Qty Sold]) * 1.06

Note that the constant is not enclosed in brackets. Furthermore, to ensure that the *Sel Price* * *Qty Sold* calculation is performed first, that part of the expression is enclosed in parentheses.

Parentheses are used in calculated fields the same way they are used in general math; they ensure that a particular operation takes place first, regardless of the normal order of precedence. For example, in general terms, the formula

10 + 5 * 2

equals 20, because the rules of operator precedence dictate that multiplication and division take place before addition and subtraction. However, the calculation

(10 + 5) * 2

equals 30 (15 times 2), because the parentheses force the addition to take place before the multiplication.

When using parentheses in expressions, make sure that the expression includes an equal number of open and closed parentheses, or the calculation will not work. For example, the sample expression

(([Qty]*[Price]) – ([Price]*[Discount])) * 1.06

is valid, because there are exactly three open and three closed parentheses. The expression below is incorrect, because there is one too many closing parentheses:

((([Qty]*[Price]) – ([Price]*[Discount])) * 1.06)

If you enter an expression with unbalanced parentheses (or some other syntax problem) Paradox will reject the entry and display the message

Syntax error in expression.

You can use the Backspace key or Field View (Alt-F5) to make corrections and try again.

The entire expression that you use in a calculated field can contain any number of fields, operators, and constants, so long as the overall length of the expression does not exceed 175 characters.

Figure 14.2 shows a sample printed report using data from the table named Sales. Note the various calculated fields used to display some of the columns.

Calculated Date Fields

Date fields may also be calculated using the arithmetic operators + (plus) and – (minus). Date fields also support the use of the summary operators discussed in the previous section. A simple example of a calculated date field would be

[Date Sold] + 30

which would display the date 30 days after the date sold. The expression

[Date Sold] – 30

would display the date 30 days prior to the date sold.

Figure 14.3 shows a sample report, using a field named Date Shipped, which is a regular field in the table, and a calculated field displayed as Payment Due, which is not stored in the table. Instead, the Payment Due field is calculated using the expression *[Date Shipped] + 30*.

Calculated Alphanumeric Fields

The only arithmetic operator allowed with alphanumeric fields is the + sign. Using this operator, alphanumeric fields can be joined to

```
10/28/90        Sample Report with Calculated Fields        Page 1

Part No   Qty Sold   Sel Price    Subtotal      Tax    Total Price
-------   --------   ---------    --------      ---    -----------
B-100        1          30.00        30.00     1.80         31.80
C-551        2          67.50       135.00     8.10        143.10
A-200        1         900.00       900.00    54.00        954.00
C-559        5          22.50       112.50     6.75        119.25
A-100        5         675.00     3,375.00   202.50      3,577.50
B-112        2          22.50        45.00     2.70         47.70
A-101        1         562.50       562.50    33.75        596.25
B-111        2          60.00       120.00     7.20        127.20
C-551        1          67.50        67.50     4.05         71.55
A-100        3         675.00     2,025.00   121.50      2,146.50
B-112       -2          22.50       (45.00)   (2.70)       (47.70)
A-100        1         675.00       675.00    40.50        715.50
```

Calculated fields

[Qty Sold] * [Sel Price]

([Qty Sold] * [Sel Price]) * .06

([Qty Sold] * [Sel Price]) * 1.06

Figure 14.2: A sample report with calculated numeric fields

```
Customer                                    Date
Number     Customer Name    Product Name    Shipped    Payment Due
--------   -------------    ------------    -------    -----------
1001       Joe Smith        Wool socks      10/28/90   11/27/90
1002       Wanda Miller     Wool muffler    10/30/90   11/29/90
1009       Jackson Ho       Oil lamp        10/30/90   11/29/90
1088       Basil Irwin      Wool socks      11/01/90   12/01/90
1088       Basil Irwin      Wool muffler    11/01/90   12/01/90
```

Calculated field

[Date Shipped] + 30

Figure 14.3: A sample report with a calculated date field

one another, to constants (enclosed in quotation marks), or to special printer codes.

In the sample calculated field below, the constants "Dear " and ":" are both enclosed in quotation marks. Both constants are joined to the contents of the First Name field using the + operator:

"Dear " + [First Name] + ":"

When printing a record with *Wanda* in the First Name field, this expression would display

Dear Wanda:

In the calculated field below, there is a single blank space between the two quotation marks. This blank space is used to join the First Name and Last Name fields, once again using the + operator:

[First Name] + " " + [Last Name]

The expression above would display a record with *Wanda* in the First Name Field and *Smith* in the Last Name field as

Wanda Smith

If you know the codes your printer uses for special features such as boldface, underlining, expanded, and compressed print, you can use these codes in calculated alphanumeric fields to take advantage of these printer features. (All printers use different codes, so you'll need to look them up in your printer manual.)

Chapter 8 discussed general techniques for converting "written" codes to numeric codes for use in Paradox. For example, the Esc key is always code 27, which in Paradox is expressed as \027. (These codes are always preceded by a backslash.)

Suppose that your printer uses a particular set of special codes for the following printer attributes:

Begin expanded print	Esc-A
End expanded print	Esc-B

Begin compressed print   15

End compressed print   29

If you placed your report title on the report format using the calculated field

"\027A" + "Monthly Sales Summary" + "\027B"

the title would appear on the report in expanded print.

You may also place a calculated field with a printer code in it on the report with no other text. For example, using the sample codes above, if you were to place a calculated field containing "\015" (including the quotation marks) just above the report table, and the code "\029" (again including the quotation marks) just beneath the report table band, the body of the report (the column titles, underlines, and data) would be displayed in compressed print. Figure 14.4 shows the position of the title and the compressed print codes on a sample report format (these of course appear as AAA masks on the report specification screen).

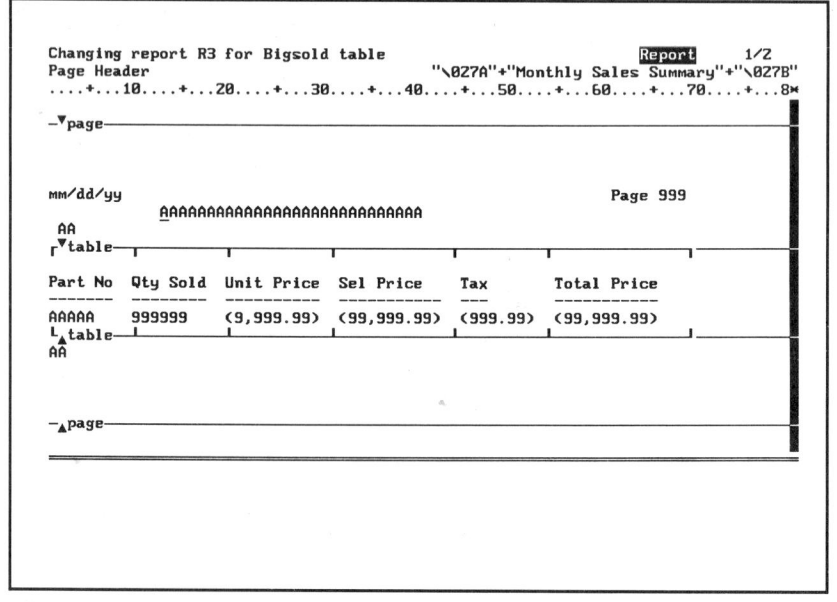

Figure 14.4: Special printer codes added to a report format

Note in Figure 14.4 that the title is intentionally off center, to the left. This is because the title will be printed larger than appears on the screen, so some adjustment must be made to make the title appear centered on the printed report. You may have to use a little trial-and-error to get expanded print properly centered on your own printer.

You can see the AA field masks for the codes for starting and ending compressed print, just above and below the table band in the leftmost column.

Using PAL Functions in Calculated Fields

You can also use *PAL functions* from the Paradox Application Language to perform calculations on data displayed in a report. We can provide some examples of PAL functions in this introductory book, but for more complete coverage you'll need to refer to Chapter 21 of the *PAL User's Guide* that came with your Paradox package.

The PAL FORMAT function lets you refine the display format of your data. For example, suppose you want the numbers in the Total Price column of Figure 14.2 (p.344) to be displayed with leading dollar signs. In that case, you would use the calculated field

FORMAT("W12.2,E$C",([Qty Sold]*[Sel Price])*1.06)

rather than just *([Qty Sold] * [Sel Price]) * 1.06* to display the contents of that field.

As another example, suppose you have a table that contains the previous year's oil sales of all oil-exporting countries, and you want to print a report that calculates and displays the percentage of the world's oil that each country sold. Let's assume that the table is named OilExprt, that the field that stores the sales amount for each country is named Exported, and that this field is Numeric or Currency.

When designing the report format, you would add the calculated field

[Exported] / CSUM("OilExprt","Exported") * 100

This formula divides the export amount (*Exported*) for the current record by the sum of the exported amounts in the entire table (*CSUM("OilExprt", "Exported")*), multiplies it by 100, and displays the result as a two-digit percentage (e.g. 20 for 20%).

If you wanted more control over the output, you could use this formula instead

```
FORMAT("W6.2",[Exported] /
CSUM("OilExprt","Exported") * 100) + "%"
```

which would display the result in the format 20.00%. (The formula is broken onto two lines only to fit within the margins of this book; when typing it in as a calculated field expression you would type it as one long line.)

Editing Calculated Fields

If you discover an error in a calculated field after placing it on the report format, you can edit it by calling up the report menu and selecting the Field and CalcEdit options. This method is particularly useful for correcting long expressions, because it saves you from having to retype the entire calculation.

When you select CalcEdit, Paradox presents the familiar instructions:

> Press ↑ ↓ → ← to move to the field you want to edit...
> then press ↵ to correct it.

As instructed, move the cursor to the field you wish to edit and press Enter. The expression will be displayed at the top of the screen, with the cursor at the right end.

You can then enter the Field View mode (by typing Alt-F5) to help edit the expression. Once in Field View mode, you can use the Field View keys to make corrections. When done, press Enter to leave Field View, then press Enter again to place the edited expression back into the report.

Calculating Blanks as Zeros

By default, Paradox does not treat a blank value in a numeric field as a zero value. Instead, it ignores the record altogether, which might lead to misleading averages or lowest-value calculations in some reports. To have Paradox treat blanks as zeros, you need to reconfigure Paradox to use the Paradox Custom Configuration program, discussed in Chapter 14 of the *Paradox User's Guide*, that came with your Paradox package.

PLACING SUMMARY FIELDS

Summary fields are used to display totals and subtotals in reports. They can also be used to display an average, count, highest value, or lowest value. (We'll see some examples of summary fields in a later section of this chapter.) When you select Summary from the Place menu, you'll see the following options:

Regular   Calculated

If the field you want to summarize is a regular field from the current table, select Regular. You'll see a list of field names from that table. Select the field name you want to summarize.

If the field you wish to summarize is a calculated field, you will be asked to enter the calculation, rather than the name of the field to summarize. For example, if you wish to total (or summarize) the selling price times the quantity sold, you could enter the calculation

[Sel price] * [Qty Sold]

After you've selected the regular field, or defined the calculated field expression, you'll be given the options

Sum   Average   Count   High   Low

These options can be summarized as follows:

OPTION	*FUNCTION*
Sum	Displays the sum of the field
Average	Displays the average of the field
Count	Displays the number of fields
High	Displays the highest value in the field
Low	Displays the lowest value in the field

Select the type of calculation you want from the options listed. The next menu displayed is

PerGroup   Overall

The PerGroup option is used for subtotals. The Overall option is used for overall totals or running (cumulative) totals. Select the option you want, then place and format the field in the usual manner, as instructed on the screen. Figure 14.5 shows a sample report with summary fields used as subtotals and totals, and a highest date value.

PLACING THE DATE FIELD

The Date option under the Field and Place menus displays the current date on the report. (Note that Paradox automatically places the current date in the report heading as well.) When you select this option,

```
10/28/90                    Total Sales                 Page   1

Part No  Qty Sold  Sel Price  Sold By  Date Sold  Total Sale
-------  --------  ---------  -------  ---------  ----------

A-100       1        675.00    JAK      8/01/90      675.00
A-100       3        675.00    BBG      7/15/90    2,025.00
A-100       5        675.00    BBG      6/05/90    3,375.00
                                                   ---------
                                        Subtotal: 6,075.00
                        Total number of transactions:      3
                                     Date of last sale: 8/01/90


A-101       1        562.50    JAK      7/01/90      562.50
A-101       2        562.50    JAK      7/02/90    1,125.00
A-101       1        562.50    BBG      7/01/90      562.50
A-101       3        562.50    JAK      7/01/90    1,687.50
                                                   ---------
                                        Subtotal: 3,937.50
                        Total number of transactions:      4
                                     Date of last sale: 7/02/90
                                                   =============
                                     Grand Total:   10,012.50
```

Summary Fields
Per-group sum of Calculated field
  [Qty Sold] * [Sel Price]

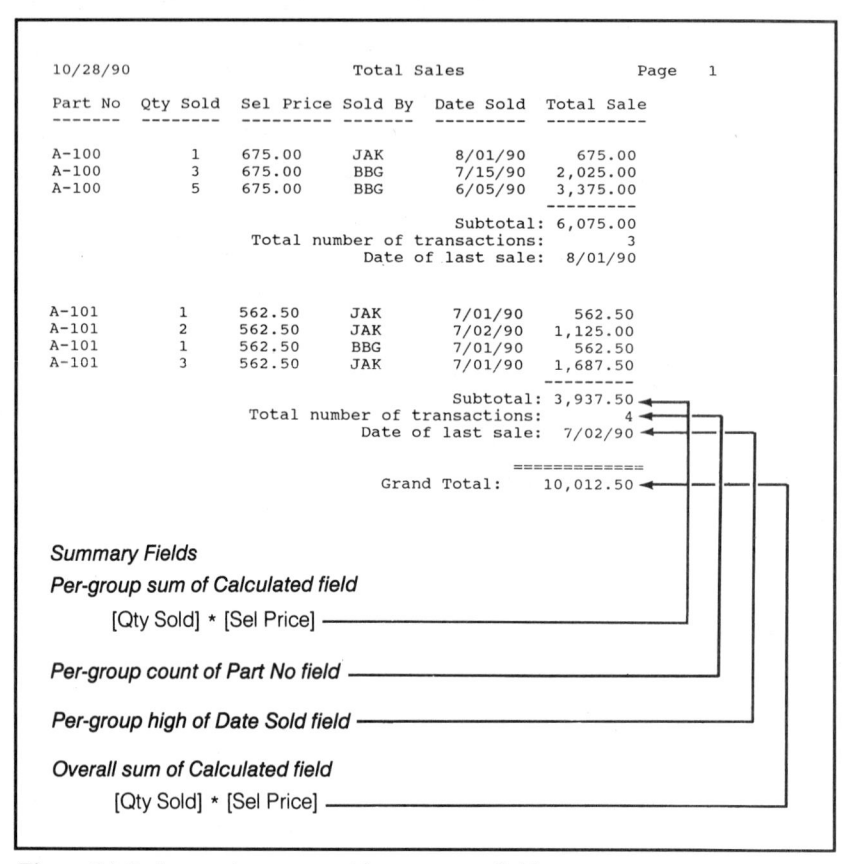

Per-group count of Part No field

Per-group high of Date Sold field

Overall sum of Calculated field
  [Qty Sold] * [Sel Price]

Figure 14.5: A sample report with summary fields

you'll be prompted to place and format the date in the usual manner.

The current date displayed is the one stored in your system. You can set that date directly from the DOS prompt, by entering the DATE command and pressing Enter. To change the system date from within Paradox, type Ctrl-O, enter the DATE command at the DOS prompt, and press Enter. Fill in the new date in the format shown on the screen. Then give the EXIT command and press Enter to return to Paradox.

PLACING THE TIME FIELD

The Time option under the Place menu lets you put the current time in the printed report. When you select this option, you'll be given two options for displaying the time:

> **Enter the time format to use:**
> **1) hh:mm pm   2) hh:mm:ss (military)**

The first option prints the time in the 12-hour clock format (with AM or PM). The second option displays the time in the 24-hour clock format used in the military.

Like the Date field mentioned above, the Time field uses the current system time. You can adjust the system time by entering the TIME command at the DOS prompt, and pressing Enter. (As with the Date field, you can escape to DOS temporarily using Ctrl-O to do this from within Paradox.) Be sure to enter the time in the format suggested on your screen.

PLACING THE PAGE FIELD

The Page field displays the page number on each page of the report. Paradox automatically places this field at the top of the report. However, if you prefer to place the page number elsewhere, you can use this option to place the page number wherever you wish (though you should place it in the Page band, and outside the other bands, to prevent the page number from being displayed in several places on the printed page).

PLACING THE #RECORD FIELD

The #Record field numbers records that are displayed in the report. When you select this option, Paradox displays the submenu

   Overall   Per-Group

If you select Overall, records will be numbered consecutively from the top of the report to the bottom. If you select Per-Group, records will be numbered individually within groups (for example, subtotal groups). Once you select an option, you'll be prompted to place and format the #Record field in the usual manner.

If you place the #Record field in the report table band, each record will be assigned a number. If you place the #Record field in the page footer, it will count the number of records on each page. Placing the #Record field in the report footer displays the total count of all record numbers printed in the report.

Up to now, we've only briefly discussed *grouping* and the various tabular *report bands,* so some of this discussion about the #Record field may be a bit confusing at the moment. We'll deal with these important topics in a moment. But first, we need to discuss a couple of other options on the Field menu.

COLUMN ALIGNMENT

By default, Paradox automatically right-justifies Numeric and Currency values in report columns, and left-justifies Alphanumeric and Date fields. To change these default settings, call up the Report menu and select the Field and Justify options. You'll be given the standard instructions to

   Use ↑ ↓ → ← to move into the field you want to justify...
   then press ↵ to select it.

After moving the cursor to the report column of interest, and pressing Enter, you'll be given the options

   Left   Center   Right   Default

These can be summarized as follows:

OPTION	FUNCTION
Left	Aligns values with the left edge of the column
Center	Centers values within the column
Right	Aligns values with the right edge of the column
Default	Returns to the alignment Paradox uses by default

Select the option you wish to use for the current field. You will see the effects of your selection when you print the report. Figure 14.6 shows examples of left-justified, centered, and right-justified columns.

```
Left                    Center                   Right              Default

Adams                    Adams                    Adams              Adams
Bartholomew              Bartholomew              Bartholomew        Bartholomew
Cat                      Cat                      Cat                Cat

9,876.54                 9,876.54                 9,876.54           9,876.54
1.23                     1.23                     1.23               1.23
-11.00                   -11.00                   -11.00             -11.00

March 31, 1953           March 31, 1953           March 31, 1953     March 31, 1953
November 15, 1950        November 15, 1950        November 15, 1950  November 15, 1950
September 30, 1987       September 30, 1987       September 30, 1987 September 30, 1987
```

Figure 14.6: Examples of report-column justification

WORD-WRAP

Another feature of Paradox reports is word-wrapping, where long alphanumeric fields are broken into several lines, as necessary, on the printed report. For neatness, long text is broken between words, rather than between characters. Hence, this feature lets you display the full contents of a long alphanumeric field within in a narrow column, thereby allowing more room for other columns.

Figure 14.7 shows the "suggested" report format displayed by Paradox when developing a report for the Mastinv table. As you can see, the Pur Price field extends beyond the right margin. To make room for the Pur Price field within the margins, you could narrow, and word-wrap, the longer Part Name field.

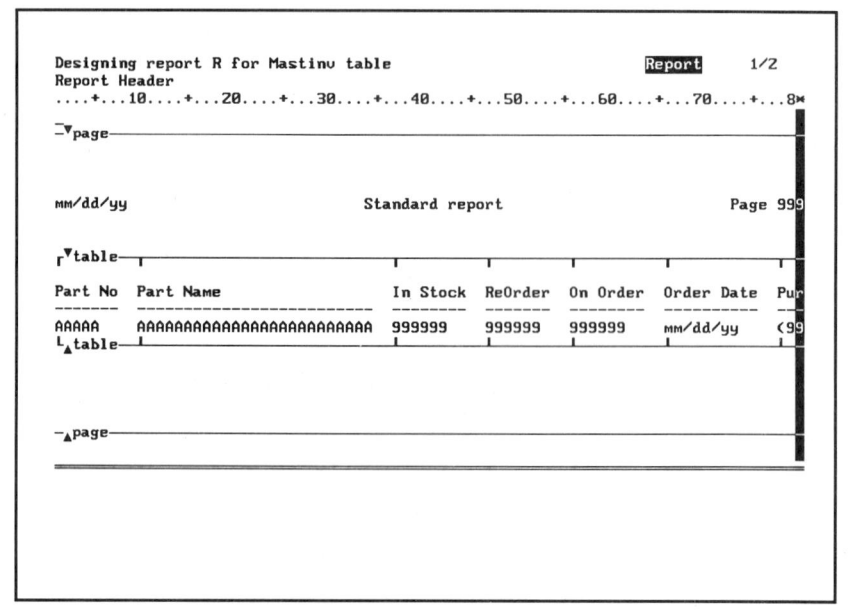

```
Designing report R for Mastinv table                    Report   1/2
Report Header
....+...10....+...20....+...30....+...40....+...50....+...60....+...70....+...8▶
 ▼page
 
 
 mm/dd/yy                          Standard report                  Page 999
  ▼table
  
 Part No  Part Name                In Stock   ReOrder   On Order   Order Date   Pu
 -------  ------------------------ --------   -------   --------   ----------   ---
 AAAAA    AAAAAAAAAAAAAAAAAAAAAAAA  999999     999999    999999    mm/dd/yy     <99
  ▲table
 
 
 ▲page
```

Figure 14.7: Paradox's suggested report format for the Mastinv table

To word-wrap the field, first reduce the size of the field to the width you desire. You can use the Field and Reformat menu options to do so. Then use the TableBand Resize options from the menu to narrow the entire column. Next, call up the menu and select Field and WordWrap. The screen asks that you move the cursor to the field to word-wrap, then press Enter to select that field (using the usual instructions at the top of the screen).

Next, the screen presents the prompt

> **Number of lines: 1**
> Enter the number of lines to wrap onto,
> or press ↵ to leave unchanged.

The maximum number of lines for displaying a single field is 255. Paradox will use only as many lines as necessary to display the entire contents of the field, up to the limit you set here. For this example, you can set a fairly small number, such as 3.

For the word-wrapped field, there will be an unpredictable number of lines printed on the row. (In this example, some Part Names may require only one line, some may require more lines.) If you wish to make sure that there is always a blank line between records displayed on the report, you can add the BLANKLINE keyword at the bottom of the table band. Figure 14.8 shows the narrowed Part Name field, with the BLANKLINE keyword added in the appropriate place.

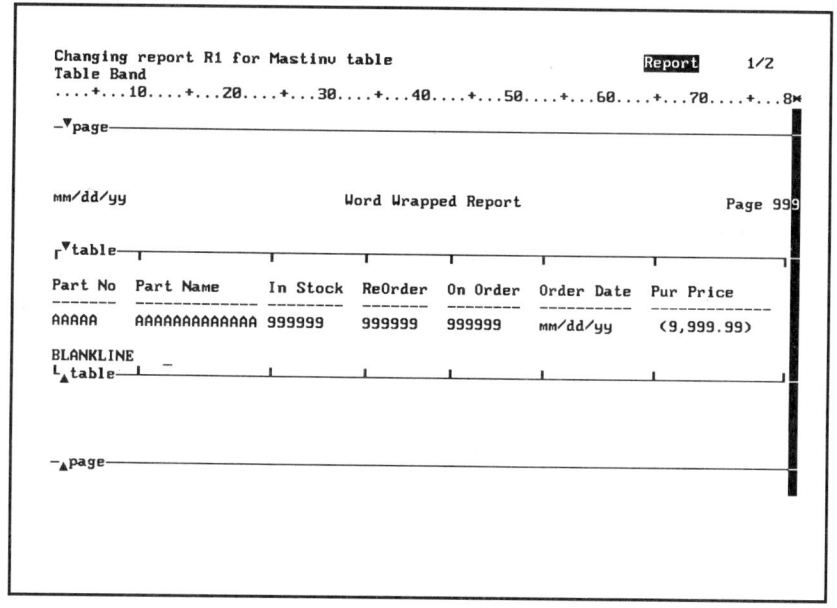

```
Changing report R1 for Mastinv table                    Report    1/2
Table Band
....+...10....+...20....+...30....+...40....+...50....+...60....+...70....+...8»
 —▼page
 
 
 mm/dd/yy                        Word Wrapped Report              Page 999
  ▼table
  
 Part No   Part Name         In Stock   ReOrder   On Order   Order Date   Pur Price
 -------   ---------------   --------   -------   --------   ----------   ---------
 AAAAA     AAAAAAAAAAAAAA    999999     999999    999999     mm/dd/yy     (9,999.99)
 BLANKLINE
  ▲table
  
  
 —▲page
```

Figure 14.8: A report format with a word-wrapped Part Name field and BLANKLINE keyword

Figure 14.9 shows a sample of the printed report. Notice that the part names are broken into two or more lines, where necessary, to fit within the column. The names are broken between words (rather than between characters). Paradox will attempt to wrap every word in the field. However, if any single word is wider than the column, then Paradox will break the word between letters. Also, as you can see in the report, the BLANKLINE keyword has put a blank line between each printed record in the body of the report.

```
10/28/90                Sample Word Wrapped Report

Part No  Part Name      In Stock  ReOrder  Order Date  Pur Price
-------  -------------  --------  -------  ----------  ---------
A-100    Bicycle              10        5     1/31/90     450.00

B-112    Safety                0       10     1/31/90      15.00
         Helmet (Ozzy)

C-551    Hobie                50       75     4/15/90      45.00
         Skateboard

C-559    Flexie               25       75     4/15/90      15.00
         Skateboard
```

Figure 14.9: The sample report with a word-wrapped Part Name field

GROUPING

Grouping allows you to display subtotals and other calculations within like groups of data (for example, total sales for all part number A-100 sales, all part number B-200 sales, and so forth). But beyond subtotals, grouping also allows you to organize data for a display that is easier to read. For example, a customer list could be grouped by state or zip code and a financial report could be grouped by day, week, or month.

You can also nest groups within groups, to as many as 16 levels, to display subtotals and sub-subtotals (and sub-sub-subtotals, and so on). On a large customer list, you could group records by state and, within each state, group records by county. Within each county, you could group records by city. As you'll see in this section, there is almost no limit to the ways in which Paradox will allow you to define groups for your reports.

A NOTE ON REPORT BANDS

Before discussing grouping and *group bands* in detail, perhaps a brief discussion of tabular report bands, in general, will help reduce any confusion later in this section. When Paradox first displays its suggested report format on the screen, the report has two bands: the page band and the table band. A report can actually have up to four types of bands, as illustrated in Figure 14.10. The various types of bands can be summarized as follows:

- **Report band**: Everything in the report band is printed once each time the report is printed. Hence, the report band would be used to display a cover page for a lengthy report of several pages, or a grand total at the end of the report.
- **Page band**: Information within the page band is printed once on each page of the report. Paradox automatically fills in the current date, report description, and page number in the page band, which you can use or delete.
- **Group band**: The optional group band is nested between the page band and the table band. This band determines how records from the table will be grouped on the printed page. A single report can contain up to 16 group bands, which means that you can have up to 16 levels of grouping. Any headers or footers placed within the group band will be displayed at the top and bottom of each group. If a report contains subtotals, you would typically place the subtotal as a footer in the group band, so that the subtotal is displayed at the bottom of each printed group.
- **Table band**: The table band is the innermost band and represents the main body of the report. The table band contains headings for fields from the table being displayed, as well as data from the table itself. The table band prints as many records from the table as will fit on the printed page.

PLACING GROUP BANDS IN THE REPORT

We'll discuss specific menu selections for defining group bands in a moment. But first, we need to discuss general techniques for inserting group bands. Remember that group bands must be inserted between the page and table bands, simply because a given page might contain several groups, and a given group might contain several records.

If your report contains several levels of groupings, the groups should be defined with the most important grouping level as the outermost band, and the least important group as the innermost band.

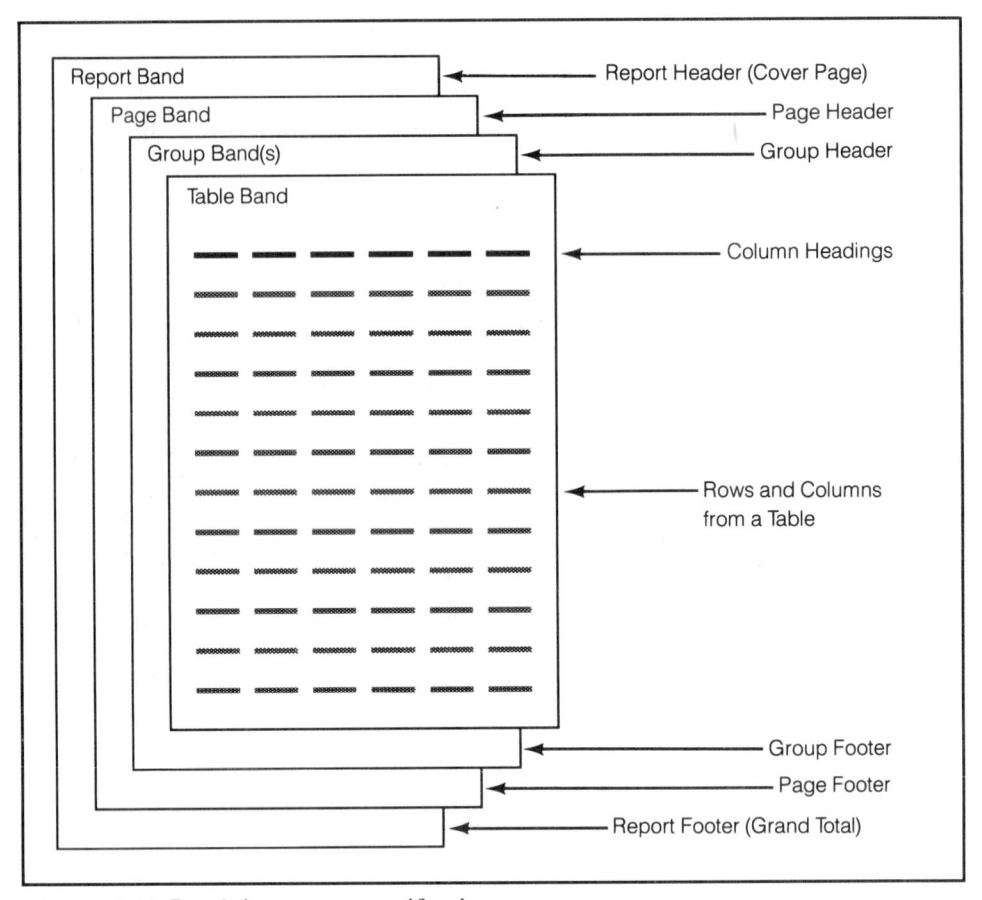

Figure 14.10: Bands in a report specification

In other words, the outermost group band specifies the broadest range of records, while the innermost group band specifies the narrowest range of records.

For example, if you were to group records in a report by State, County, and City, clearly State is the broadest range, and hence would be the outermost group band. County would be the next group band, because there are more counties than states, yet fewer counties than cities. City would be the innermost group band, because there are more cities than either states or counties.

Figure 14.11 shows a sample report specification with three levels of grouping for State, County, and City. Group bands appear with

ADVANCED REPORT AND FORM TECHNIQUES   359

triangles, followed by the word *group,*, and the name of the field that the group is based on. Also, the group identification is indented to show its level within the group bands, as shown below (the table band is not shown so that you can see the group bands more clearly):

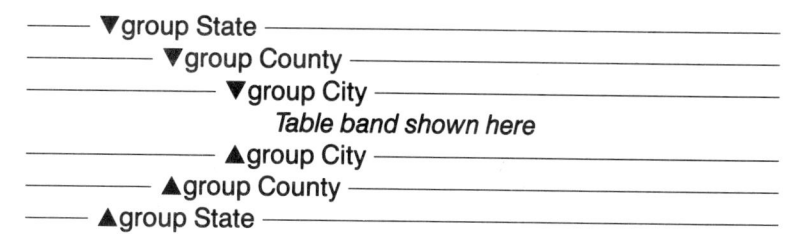

```
────── ▼group State ──────────────────────────────
           ────── ▼group County ─────────────────────
                    ────── ▼group City ────────────────
                           Table band shown here
                    ────── ▲group City ────────────────
           ────── ▲group County ─────────────────────
────── ▲group State ──────────────────────────────
```

Figure 14.12 shows a page printed from the report specification shown in Figure 14.11. Even though this is only a single page from the report, you can see how the report is grouped by states, and by counties within the same state, and by cities within the same county. Additional pages would be in the same format.

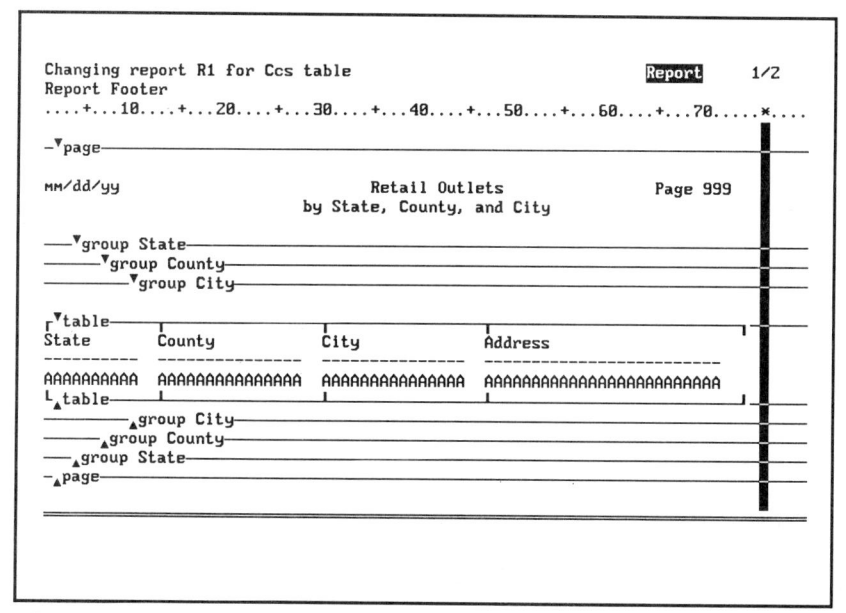

```
Changing report R1 for Ccs table                    Report   1/2
Report Footer
....+....10....+....20....+....30....+....40....+....50....+....60....+....70.....*....
─▼page──────────────────────────────────────────────

MM/dd/yy                       Retail Outlets                Page 999
                            by State, County, and City

  ──▼group State──────────────────────────────────
    ──▼group County────────────────────────────────
      ──▼group City──────────────────────────────────
 ┌▼table─────┬─────────────────┬─────────────────┬──────────────────────────┐
 │State      │County           │City             │Address                   │
 │───────    │─────────────    │─────────────    │──────────────────────    │
 │AAAAAAAAA  │AAAAAAAAAAAAAA   │AAAAAAAAAAAAAA   │AAAAAAAAAAAAAAAAAAAAAAAA  │
 └▲table─────┴─────────────────┴─────────────────┴──────────────────────────┘
      ──▲group City──────────────────────────────────
    ──▲group County────────────────────────────────
  ──▲group State──────────────────────────────────
─▲page──────────────────────────────────────────────
```

Figure 14.11: A Report specification with three grouping levels

```
10/29/90                    Retail Outlets                Page 4
                       By State, County, and City

State         County            City              Address
-----------   ---------------   ---------------   --------------------
California    Los Angeles       Culver City       123 A St.
California    Los Angeles       Culver City       2345 Beach St.
California    Los Angeles       Culver City       345 Callaway

California    Los Angeles       Duarte            2776 Adams Ave.
California    Los Angeles       Duarte            982 Vickers Way

California    Los Angeles       Whittier          1 Fashion Plaza
California    Los Angeles       Whittier          77 Alton Pkwy

California    San Diego         Del Mar           88 15th. St.

California    San Diego         Encinitas         1086 Crest Dr.
California    San Diego         Encinitas         11 Santa Fe Dr.
California    San Diego         Encinitas         2001 Wotan St.

California    San Diego         La Jolla          191 Silverado
California    San Diego         La Jolla          21 Prospect Ave.
California    San Diego         La Jolla          71 Wall St.

Colorado      Acton             Boulder           11801 Rocky Hwy
Colorado      Acton             Boulder           27 Route 11
```

Figure 14.12: The printed report grouped by State, County, and City

Note also that Paradox has sorted each group: the states are in alphabetical order (California comes before Colorado); within the states, the counties are in alphabetical order (Los Angeles comes before San Diego); and within the counties, cities are alphabetized (Del Mar comes before Encinitas). Paradox automatically sorts the data within the groups, in either ascending or descending order.

The sample report in Figure 14.12 only shows a basic grouping. As we'll see, there are many ways to format the grouped report.

Whenever you insert a group into a report specification, Paradox will ask that you

    USE ↑ ↓ → ← to show where you want the group inserted...
    then press ↵ to place it.

If you are entering the first group band, move the cursor to any column position between the page band and the table band, and press Enter. If you are inserting an additional group band, be sure to move the cursor above, below, or between existing group bands, depending on the new band's logical position. (Using the example above, the County group band would be inserted between the existing State and City bands.) Press Enter when the cursor is properly positioned for the group.

THE GROUP MENU

When you select Group from the tabular Report menu, you'll see the following submenu:

> Insert   Delete   Headings   SortDirection   Regroup

These options can be summarized as follows:

OPTION	FUNCTION
Insert	Adds a new grouping to the report
Delete	Deletes an existing group
Headings	Determines when group headings are printed
SortDirection	Specifies how data are sorted within groups
Regroup	Changes an existing grouping definition

INSERTING GROUPS

The Insert option under the Group menu lets you define a group for the report. When you select this option, you'll see the following submenu:

> Field   Range   NumberRecords

These options are discussed individually in the sections below.

Grouping by Field

If you select the Field option from the Group Insert submenu, Paradox will display a list of all field names. Select the field you wish to group by in the usual manner (by highlighting and pressing Enter).

Paradox will then ask you to move the cursor to the place you want the group to be inserted. If this is the first grouping level, just move the cursor to anywhere between the page band and table band, then press Enter. If this is not the first defined group, be sure to place the cursor at the right grouping level, relative to other grouping levels, then press Enter.

Figures 14.11 and 14.12 display a report specification with three levels of grouping, each of these levels being a field from the table (State, County, and City). Figure 14.11 shows the proper nesting of the three fields, with State as the outermost, County in the middle, and City innermost.

Grouping By Range

The second option on the Group Insert submenu is Range. This option lets you define a range of values for a group that will depend on the data type of the group. Selecting this item first displays a menu of field names. Select the field to group by in the usual manner. Depending on the data type of that field, you'll be given one of three options, as outlined in the following sections.

Numeric Range If the field you select under the Range option is Numeric or Currency, Paradox will display the prompt

> Size of range:
> Example: 10 produces 0-9, 10-19, etc.

The range you select determines how records are grouped. For example, if the field being grouped on was the price of a house, and you entered 25,000, the first displayed group would list houses costing in the range of 0 to $25,000.00. The second group would list houses costing in the range of $25,001 to $50,000. The third printed group would list houses costing in the range of $50,001 to $75,000, and so forth up to the most expensive house.

If, on the other hand, you had selected a field representing the number of bedrooms in a house, and specified 1 as the range, the report would group all houses with zero bedrooms (if any), then all houses with one bedroom, then all houses with two bedrooms, and so forth up to whatever the largest number of bedrooms available was.

After you select the range, you'll be prompted to place the cursor and insert the group. Again, move the cursor to anywhere between the page and table bands, or to the appropriate place in relation to other defined groups, and press Enter.

Date Range   If the field you select under the Range option is the Date data type, you'll see the prompt

>   Day   Week   Month   Year

Selecting the Day option groups together records that have exactly the same date. For example, Jan. 1, 1990 would form one group, Jan. 2, 1990 would form the second group, and so forth for all the records in the table.

Selecting Week groups together records that fall within the same week (from Sunday to Saturday). Note that these records might cross two months, if the first of the month falls between a Sunday and the following Saturday. For example, records with dates in the range December 23, 1990 to December 29, 1990 would fall in one group, records with dates in the range December 30, 1990 to January 5, 1991 would form the next group, and so forth.

If you select the Month option, records that fall within the same month will be grouped together. For example, one group would contain all records with January dates, the next group would consist of records with all February dates, and so forth.

If you select Year, records that have dates with identical years will be grouped together. For example, all records with 1990 dates would be grouped together, followed by the 1991 records, and so forth.

After you have selected a date range, you'll be prompted to position the cursor at the group insertion point, and press Enter.

Alphanumeric Range   If the field you select to group by under the Range option is the Alphanumeric data type, you'll see the prompt

>   Number of initial characters for range:
>   Use 1 to group by first letter, 2 to group by first two letters, etc.

If you enter a 1 in response to this prompt, all records that begin with the letter A will be grouped together, all records that begin with the letter B will be grouped together, all records that begin with the letter C will be grouped together, and so forth. If you selected 2, all records that begin with the letters AA would be grouped together, then all records beginning with the letters AB would be grouped together, followed by all records beginning with the letters AC, and so forth up to ZZ.

If the number you enter here equals the length of the field being grouped on, all records with identical values would be grouped together. For example, if you were to select Last Name, with a length of 15 characters, as the grouping field, and entered 15 as the number of initial characters, then all records with the last name Adams would be grouped together, followed by all records with the last name Bowser (or whatever last name was next in alphabetical order), and so forth.

After you specify the number of initial letters to group by, you'll be prompted to insert the group, as discussed previously.

Grouping by Number of Records

The NumberRecords option under the Range menu lets you define grouping sizes that are constant in size, and do not depend on values in any fields. When you select this option, you'll see the prompt

Number of records:
Enter number of records to group on:

If you were to enter a number such as 5, any group would have a maximum of five records in it. Blank lines (discussed in a moment) would separate each group of five records. (However, if the number of records in the report was not evenly divisible by five, the last group would have fewer records.)

Note that the NumberRecords option does not actually sort or organize records in any way. Instead, it merely creates "white space" on the report, which has the psychological effect of making the report more pleasing to the eye. For example, Figures 14.13 and 14.14 show two copies of the same report. The only difference between the two is that the report in Figure 14.14 displays records in groups of five, using the NumberRecords option.

In this example, there are 18 records in the table. As you can see, the last group on the report in Figure 14.14 has only three records, because there are no more records in the table to fill out the group.

ADVANCED REPORT AND FORM TECHNIQUES 365

```
Mr/Mrs   Last Name         First Name        M.I.  Company
------   ---------------   ---------------   ----  ------------------------

Miss     Abzug             Ann               Z.
Mr.      Adams             Andy              A.
Ms.      Davis             Randi
Miss     Gladstone         Tara Rose               Waterside, Inc.
Ms.      Jackson           Janet             J.    Zeerox, Inc.
Mr.      Kenney            Clark             E.    Legal Aid
Mr.      Macallister       Mark              S.    BBC Publishing
Dr.      Rosiello          Richard           L.    Raydontic Labs
Mrs.     Simpson           Susan             M.    SMS Publishing
Dr.      Zastrow           Ruth                    Scripts Clinic
Mr.      Wilson            Jackson           J.    Rancho Enterprises
Mrs.     Salvatore         Annette           Q.
Ms.      Stark             Robin             D.    Starkland Systems
Dr.      Wallace           Doug                    Wallace Productions
Mr.      Newell            Jeff              J.    Irvine Construction
Mr.      Pickett           Scott             K.    Adept Software
Miss     Petricca          Mary Ann                Biotech International
Mr.      Mendez            David                   Jet Plumbing, Inc.
```

Figure 14.13: A report with no groups

```
Mr/Mrs   Last Name         First Name        M.I.  Company
------   ---------------   ---------------   ----  ------------------------

Miss     Abzug             Ann               Z.
Mr.      Adams             Andy              A.
Ms.      Davis             Randi
Miss     Gladstone         Tara Rose               Waterside, Inc.
Ms.      Jackson           Janet             J.    Zeerox, Inc.

Mr.      Kenney            Clark             E.    Legal Aid
Mr.      Macallister       Mark              S.    BBC Publishing
Dr.      Rosiello          Richard           L.    Raydontic Labs
Mrs.     Simpson           Susan             M.    SMS Publishing
Dr.      Zastrow           Ruth                    Scripts Clinic

Mr.      Wilson            Jackson           J.    Rancho Enterprises
Mrs.     Salvatore         Annette           Q.
Ms.      Stark             Robin             D.    Starkland Systems
Dr.      Wallace           Doug                    Wallace Productions
Mr.      Newell            Jeff              J.    Irvine Construction

Mr.      Pickett           Scott             K.    Adept Software
Miss     Petricca          Mary Ann                Biotech International
Mr.      Mendez            David                   Jet Plumbing, Inc.
```

Figure 14.14: A report with groups of five records

Even though the reports displayed are not in any particular order, we could have used the Modify Sort options under the Main menu to presort these records into alphabetical order by name, prior to printing either report.

GROUP HEADERS, FOOTERS, AND BLANK LINES

You can place a header at the top and a footer at the bottom of each group on a printed report, to identify the group or display subtotals. The header or footer may consist of any number of lines you wish. A group header must appear inside its appropriate group band on the report specification, above the table band. The group footer must appear within the appropriate group band beneath the table band. Both the header and the footer can include fields from the table, which may be placed using the usual Field, Place, and Regular options from the Report menu.

Figure 14.15 shows a sample report with two levels of grouping and subtotals. Records are grouped and subtotaled by part number. Each part-number group has a header (for example, *Part number: A-100*) and a footer (for example, *Total sales for part number A-100:*).

Within each part-number group, records are grouped and subtotaled by salesperson. Each salesperson group also has a header (for example, *Salesperson: BBG*) and a footer (for example, *Total sales for salesperson BBG:*). Note also the use of blank lines to separate the various groups.

Figure 14.16 shows the report specification that was used to print the report shown in Figure 14.15. Let's take a look at it piece by piece, as it demonstrates many of the techniques we've discussed in this chapter.

Before looking at the group bands, take a look inside the table band. The Qty column contains the field Qty Sold, which appears as the mask *999*. The Unit Price column contains the Sel Price field, which is displayed as the mask *99,999.99*. The Total Price column is a calculated field, based on the expression *[Qty Sold] * [Sel Price]*. The fields are arranged and sized using the Field and TableBand options from the Report menu.

Now, locate the top of the group band for the Part No field. Within this group band, near the top, is a blank line and the group header

   Part number: AAAAA

The blank line is inserted in the usual manner, by positioning the cursor, making sure the insert mode is on, and pressing Enter.

```
                          Sales Summary
                   By Part Number and Sales Person
10/29/90                                                        Page 1

Part No   Sold By   Date Sold   Qty   Unit Price   Total Price
-------   -------   ---------   ---   ----------   -----------

Part number:  A-100

    Salesperson: BBG
A-100     BBG        7/15/90     3      675.00       2,025.00
A-100     BBG        6/05/90     5      675.00       3,375.00
A-100     BBG        6/05/90     5      675.00       3,375.00
A-100     BBG        8/01/90    10      675.00       6,750.00
                                                   ------------
              Total sales for salesperson BBG:      15,525.00
    Salesperson: JAK
A-100     JAK        6/01/90     1      675.00         675.00
A-100     JAK        7/01/90     1      675.00         675.00
A-100     JAK        8/01/90     1      675.00         675.00
A-100     JAK        8/03/90     2      675.00       1,350.00
A-100     JAK        8/02/90     3      675.00       2,025.00
                                                   ------------
              Total sales for salesperson JAK:       5,400.00
                                                   ==============
              Total sales for part number A-100:    20,925.00

Part number:  A-200

    Salesperson: BBG
A-200     BBG        6/05/90     2      900.00       1,800.00
A-200     BBG        6/21/90     2      900.00       1,800.00
A-200     BBG        6/01/90     3      900.00       2,700.00
A-200     BBG        6/15/90     5      900.00       4,500.00
                                                   ------------
              Total sales for salesperson BBG:      10,800.00
    Salesperson: JAK
A-200     JAK        7/01/90     1      900.00         900.00
A-200     JAK        6/01/90     2      900.00       1,800.00
A-200     JAK        7/01/90     2      900.00       1,800.00
A-200     JAK        6/01/90    17      900.00      15,300.00
                                                   ------------
              Total sales for salesperson JAK:      19,800.00
                                                   ==============
              Total sales for part number A-200:    30,600.00

                        Grand Total of Sales:       51,525.00
```

Figure 14.15: A sample report with two levels of subtotals

(Remember, to remove lines, including blank lines, move the cursor to the leftmost column of the line to be deleted and type Ctrl-Y.) The text for the header is simply typed in. *AAAAA* is the mask for the Part No field, placed by positioning the cursor and selecting the Field, Place, and Regular options from the Report menu, and Part No from the menu of field names.

The footer for the Part No group appears between the Sold By and Part No group bands beneath the table band. The footer appears on

```
Changing report R5 for Bigsold table                      Report    1/2
Page Footer
....+...10....+...20....+...30....+...40....+...50....+...60....+...70....+...8▶
 ──▼group Part No─────────────────────────────────────────────────────────────
 Part number: AAAAA
  ──▼group Sold By────────────────────────────────────────────────────────────
    Salesperson: AAA
 ┌▼table─┬────────┬──────────┬───┬────────────┬────────────┐
 Part No  Sold By  Date Sold  Qty  Unit Price   Total Price
 ───────  ───────  ─────────  ───  ──────────   ───────────
 AAAAA    AAA      mm/dd/yy   999  (99,999.99)  (999,999.99)
 └▲table─┴────────┴──────────┴───┴────────────┴────────────┘
                                  ─────────────
                   Total sales for salesperson AAA: (999,999.99)
  ──▲group Sold By────────────────────────────────────────────────────────────
                                  =============
                   Total sales for part number AAAAA: (999,999.99)
 ──▲group Part No─────────────────────────────────────────────────────────────

 ─▲page───────────────────────────────────────────────────────────────── ─ ──
```

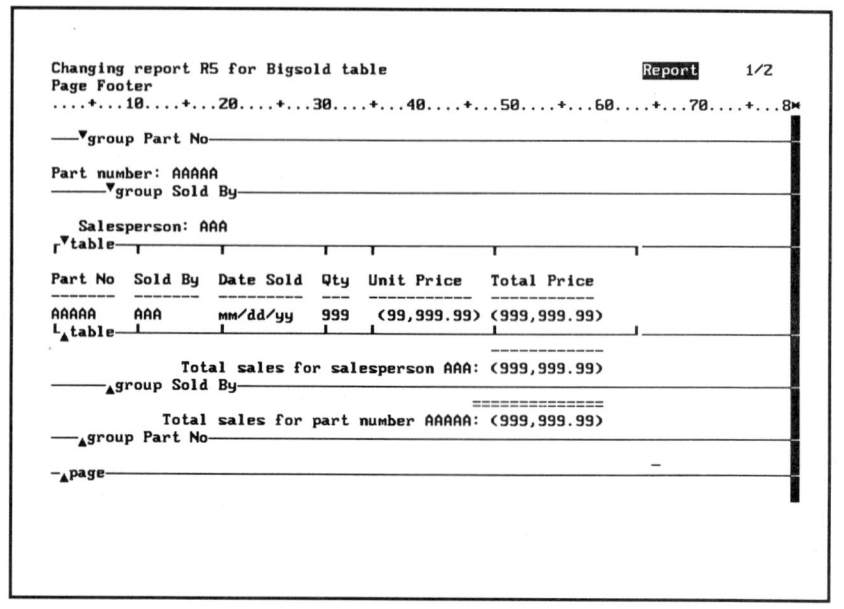

Figure 14.16: A report specification with group headers and footers

the report specification as follows:

Total sales for part number AAAAA: (999,999.99)

The text is typed in, and *AAAAA* is once again the mask for the Part No field, placed using the Field, Place, and Regular options from the Report menu. The *(999,999.99)* mask shows the subtotal for the group on the printed report. It is placed by calling up the Report menu and selecting the Field, Place, Summary, and Calculated menu options. The expression for the field is once again *[Qty Sold] * [Sel Price]*, and the Sum and Per Group options have been selected to specify totals for the current group of records. Note also the equal-signs bar in the report footer, which is typed in from the keyboard.

Now locate the group band for the Sold By field. Above the table band, the group has a blank line and the header

Salesperson: AAA

Salesperson is typed in, and *AAA* is the mask for the Sold By field, placed using the usual Field, Place, and Regular options from the Report menu.

The footer for the Sold By group appears within the Sold By group band, beneath the table band. It appears as

Total sales for salesperson AAA: (999,999.99)

AAA is the mask for the Sold By field, again placed using the Field, Place, and Regular menu options. The *(999,999.99)* mask is placed using the Field, Place, Summary, Calculated, and Sum menu options and the expression *[Qty Sold] * [Sel Price]*. The PerGroup option is selected, rather than the Overall option, because this is a subtotal. This footer also includes a series of hyphens, which you can also see on the printed report in Figure 14.15.

Finally, notice the grand total at the bottom of the printed page in Figure 14.15. On the report specification, this appears beneath the page band, so that it is printed only once at the end of the report, rather than at the bottom of each page. (Though the screen does not show a marker for the report band, this grand total is actually in the report band.)

The *(999,999.99)* mask next to the *Grand Total of Sales:* title is another Summary field, placed using the usual Field, Place, Summary, and Calculated options. The expression for the calculation is once again *[Qty Sold] * [Sel Price]*. However, unlike the subtotal fields, this field is an Overall (rather than PerGroup) sum, because it displays the total of all records, not just individual groups of records.

REMOVING GROUPING VALUES FROM THE TABLE BAND

In some reports, you might prefer to display the grouping field in the group header only. For example, in the small group below, the part number A-100 appears only once at the top of the group. The part number does not appear within the records that fall into this group:

```
Part number: A-100
       BBG     7/15/90           3       675.00      2,025.00
       BBG     6/05/90           5       675.00      3,375.00
```

BBG	6/05/90	5	675.00	3,375.00
BBG	8/01/90	10	675.00	6,750.00

To achieve this result, simply remove the grouping field from the Table band (using the TableBand Erase submenu). To leave an indentation beneath the group heading, as above, you can use the Field Erase options to remove the field without removing the entire column. Then use the Del (or Delete) key to remove the column heading and underline. Finally, use TableBand and Resize to adjust the blank column to the width you want for the indentation.

DELETING GROUPS

To delete a group band from a report specification, select the Delete option from the Group menu. Paradox will ask that you identify the group band by positioning the cursor. Before deleting the group, Paradox will ask for confirmation:

    Cancel Ok

Select Cancel to change your mind and keep the group band intact. Select Ok to delete the group band.

GROUP HEADINGS

Group headings are placed in the upper portion of a group band and, like footings, are printed once for each group. In addition, they are repeated on the next page if the group is split into two or more pages.

If you prefer that group headings not be repeated on a second page, select the Headings option from the Group menu. After you identify the group heading, Paradox will present these options:

    Page Group

The Group option prevents group headings from being displayed on a second page. The Page option retains the default setting (group headings at the top of each group, and on any "spillover" pages).

SORTING GROUPS

By default, Paradox will display groups sorted in ascending order. To display a group in descending order, select SortDirection from the Group submenu. Paradox will ask that you identify which group to sort by positioning the cursor. Then you'll be given these options:

Ascending   Descending

Ascending, the default setting, displays groups in the normal order (smallest to largest). Selecting Descending will display the group in descending (largest to smallest) order.

CHANGING GROUPS

You can always redefine groups in a report specification by selecting the Regroup option from the Group menu. When you choose Regroup, Paradox will ask that you identify the group to redefine by positioning the cursor. Then you'll be given the following options:

Field   Range   NumberRecords

From this point on, changing a group band definition is exactly the same as initially inserting a group.

TABULAR REPORT SETTINGS

You may recall that calling up the menu while designing a tabular report brings up these options:

Field   TableBand   Group   Output   Setting   Help   DO-IT!   Cancel

The Setting option allows you to define general report-format settings, as displayed on this submenu:

Format   GroupRepeats   PageLayout   Margin   Setup   Wait

These options can be summarized as follows:

OPTION	FUNCTION
Format	Defines how group and table headers should be displayed, whether as a table of groups or as a group of tables
GroupRepeats	Determines whether to repeat the constant field value within a group
PageLayout	Sets page dimensions (same as for a free-form report)
Margin	Specifies a left margin (same as for a free-form report)
Setup	Specifies a setup string (same as for a free-form report)
Wait	Pauses for paper change between pages (same as for a free-form report)

The Format option provides this submenu:

TableOfGroups   GroupsOfTables

Selecting the TableOfGroups option (the default setting) produces a table that displays individual column headings only at the top of each page, as in Figure 14.17. The GroupsOfTables option produces a group of tables that repeats column headings each time the grouping changes, as in Figure 14.18.

The GroupRepeats option lets you decide whether to repeat the constant value (for instance, the part number) used to define the group in each record. Your options are

Retain   Suppress

```
10/11/90              Total Sales                    Page 1

Part No  Sold By  Date Sold  Qty Sold  Unit Price   Total Sale
-------  -------  ---------  --------  ----------   ----------

A-100    BBG      1/01/90       5        650.00       3,250.00
A-100    BBG      1/11/90       3        700.00       2,100.00
A-100    BBG      2/01/90       7        650.00       4,550.00
A-100    BBG      2/02/90       7        700.00       4,900.00
A-100    BBG      3/04/90       9        650.00       5,850.00
A-100    BBG      3/05/90       5        700.00       3,500.00
                              Sales Person Subtotal: 24,150.00
A-100    JAK      1/01/90       1        700.00         700.00
A-100    JAK      1/11/90       3        700.00       2,100.00
A-100    JAK      1/31/90       5        700.00       3,500.00
A-100    JAK      2/06/90       1        450.00         450.00
A-100    JAK      3/03/90       3        450.00       1,350.00
                              Sales Person Subtotal:  8,100.00
                              Part Number Subtotal:  32,250.00

B-112    BBG      1/01/90      10         25.00         250.00
B-112    BBG      1/18/90       0         25.00           0.00
B-112    BBG      2/02/90       2         25.00          50.00
B-112    BBG      2/02/90       2         25.00          50.00
B-112    BBG      3/18/90       4         25.00         100.00
B-112    BBG      3/25/90       6         25.00         150.00
                              Sales Person Subtotal:    600.00
B-112    JAK      1/21/90       2         70.00         140.00
B-112    JAK      2/02/90       3         55.00         165.00
B-112    JAK      2/02/90       5         55.00         275.00
B-112    JAK      3/01/90       4         70.00         280.00
B-112    JAK      3/15/90       6         70.00         420.00
B-112    JAK      3/25/90       1         55.00          55.00
                              Sales Person Subtotal:  1,335.00
                              Part Number Subtotal:   1,935.00
```

Figure 14.17: Table of groups: column headings at top of page only

Retain is the default option, whereby the value is repeated in every record of the group, as follows:

PART NO	SOLD BY	DATE SOLD	QTY SOLD	SEL PRICE	TOTAL SALE
A-100	BBG	7/02/90	3	700.00	2,100.00
A-100	BBG	7/02/90	5	650.00	3,250.00
A-100	BBG	7/03/90	7	700.00	4,900.00
A-100	BBG	7/03/90	9	650.00	5,850.00

```
10/11/90              Total Sales                  Page 1

Part No   Sold By   Date Sold   Qty Sold   Unit Price      Total Sale
-------   -------   ---------   --------   ----------      ----------

A-100     BBG       1/01/90     5          650.00          3,250.00
A-100     BBG       1/11/90     3          700.00          2,100.00
A-100     BBG       2/01/90     7          650.00          4,550.00
A-100     BBG       2/02/90     7          700.00          4,900.00
A-100     BBG       3/04/90     9          650.00          5,850.00
A-100     BBG       3/05/90     5          700.00          3,500.00
                                Sales Person Subtotal:    24,150.00

Part No   Sold By   Date Sold   Qty Sold   Unit Price      Total Sale
-------   -------   ---------   --------   ----------      ----------

A-100     JAK       1/01/90     1          700.00            700.00
A-100     JAK       1/11/90     3          700.00          2,100.00
A-100     JAK       1/31/90     5          700.00          3,500.00
A-100     JAK       2/06/90     1          450.00            450.00
A-100     JAK       3/03/90     3          450.00          1,350.00
                                Sales Person Subtotal:     8,100.00
                                Part Number Subtotal:     32,250.00

Part No   Sold By   Date Sold   Qty Sold   Unit Price      Total Sale
-------   -------   ---------   --------   ----------      ----------

B-112     BBG       1/01/90     10         25.00             250.00
B-112     BBG       1/18/90     0          25.00               0.00
B-112     BBG       2/02/90     2          25.00              50.00
B-112     BBG       2/02/90     2          25.00              50.00
B-112     BBG       3/18/90     4          25.00             100.00
B-112     BBG       3/25/90     6          25.00             150.00
                                Sales Person Subtotal:       600.00

Part No   Sold By   Date Sold   Qty Sold   Unit Price      Total Sale
-------   -------   ---------   --------   ----------      ----------

B-112     JAK       1/21/90     2          70.00             140.00
B-112     JAK       2/02/90     3          55.00             165.00
B-112     JAK       2/02/90     5          55.00             275.00
B-112     JAK       3/01/90     4          70.00             280.00
B-112     JAK       3/15/90     6          70.00             420.00
B-112     JAK       3/25/90     1          55.00              55.00
                                Sales Person Subtotal:     1,335.00
                                Part Number Subtotal:     1,935.00
```

Figure 14.18: Groups of tables: column headings repeated in each group

Selecting the Suppress option will suppress the grouping field after it is displayed in the first row of the group, as follows:

Part No	**Sold By**	**Date Sold**	**Qty Sold**	**Sel Price**	**Total Sale**
A-100	BBG	7/02/90	3	700.00	2,100.00
	BBG	7/02/90	5	650.00	3,250.00

BBG	7/03/90	7	700.00	4,900.00
BBG	7/03/90	9	650.00	5,850.00

SUMMARY REPORTS

A commonly used report format in all kinds of business settings is the summary report. This type of report shows only totals rather than individual transactions. Figure 14.19 is an example of a summary report based on the Sales table, showing the total sales for each item.

```
9/01/90    Summary Report    Page 1

                          Date of Most
Part No  Total Sales      Recent Sale
-------  -----------      -----------
A-100       6,050.00        8/01/90
A-101         450.00        7/01/90
A-200         800.00        6/01/90
B-100          55.00        6/01/90
B-111         100.00        7/01/90
B-112           0.00        8/01/90
C-551         195.00        7/01/90
C-559         155.00        6/05/90

Total:      7,805.00
```

Figure 14.19: A summary report based on the Sales Table

To print such a report, you need to remove all fields from within the table band of the report specification, leaving only headings for the fields you want. Then you need to create a group band based on part number. Within the group band (but outside the table band), you can place Part No as a regular field. The Total is a per-group summary field with the formula *[Qty Sold] * [Sel Price]*. The Date of Most Recent Sale is a per-group summary field using the High option, rather than the Sum option, from the Summary submenu.

The grand total at the bottom of the report (outside the page band) is an overall summary field with the formula *[Qty Sold] * [Sel Price]*. Figure 14.20 shows the report specification for the Summary report. Note that the field masks for the report columns are outside of, and beneath, the table band.

```
Changing report R2 for Sales table                    Report  Ins 1/2
Table Header
....+...10....+...20....+...30....+...40....+...50....+...60....+...70....+...8*
      ─▼page────────────────────────────────────────────────────────────
          mm/dd/yy   Summary Report    Page 999
      ──▼group Part No─────────────────────────────────────────────────
          ─▼table─┐
                  │              Date of Most
          Part No Total Sales    Recent Sale
          ─────── ───────────    ───────────
          ─▲table─┴─────────────
          AAAAA   (999,999.99)   mm/dd/yy
      ──▲group Part No─────────────────────────────────────────────────
      ─▲page────────────────────────────────────────────────────────────
          Total:  (999,999.99)
```

Figure 14.20: The report specification for the summary report

PRINTING REPORTS FROM MULTIPLE TABLES

In Chapter 12 we discussed the value of storing data on separate related tables, to minimize redundancy and allow maximum access to all of the data. However, there are times when you'll want to list related information from separate tables simultaneously on a report. For example, you might want to list part names from the MastInv table with sales data from the Sales table.

Paradox lets you incorporate data from other tables in a report, provided that the common field that relates a foreign table to the current table is *keyed*. For example, the Sales and MastInv tables that we created in Chapter 12 both included a common field named Part No to relate part numbers in the Sales table to information about individual products in the MastInv table. Because each part on the MastInv table *must* have a unique part number, the Part No field was keyed by marking it with an asterisk, as Figure 14.21 shows.

> To view or alter the structure of a table, select Modify, Restructure, and the table name from the Paradox Main menu (as discussed in Chapter 16).

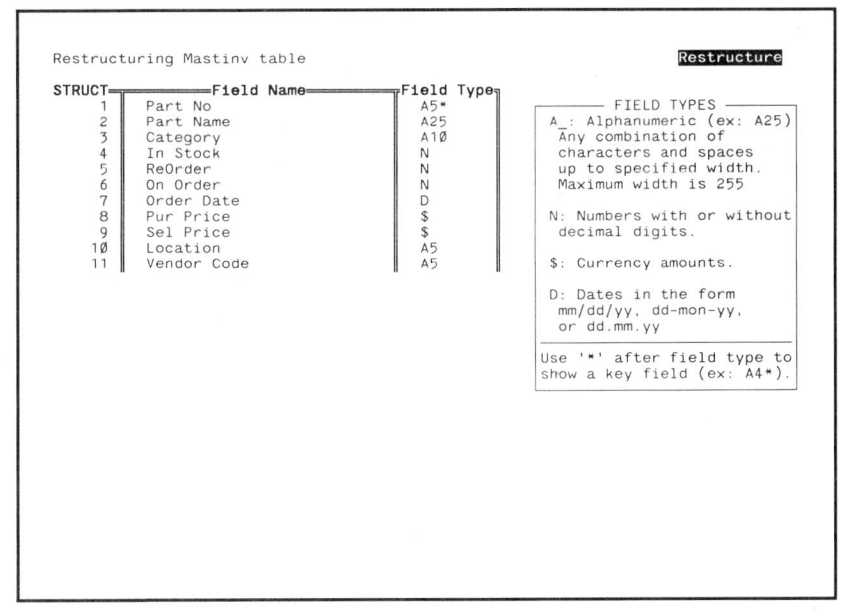

```
Restructuring Mastinv table                               Restructure
STRUCT       Field Name            Field Type
   1      Part No                  A5*          ─── FIELD TYPES ───
   2      Part Name                A25          A_: Alphanumeric (ex: A25)
   3      Category                 A10          Any combination of
   4      In Stock                 N            characters and spaces
   5      ReOrder                  N            up to specified width.
   6      On Order                 N            Maximum width is 255
   7      Order Date               D
   8      Pur Price                $            N: Numbers with or without
   9      Sel Price                $            decimal digits.
  10      Location                 A5
  11      Vendor Code              A5           $: Currency amounts.

                                                D: Dates in the form
                                                mm/dd/yy, dd-mon-yy,
                                                or dd.mm.yy

                                                Use '*' after field type to
                                                show a key field (ex: A4*).
```

Figure 14.21: MastInv table with keyed Part No field

To include the Part Name field in a report that displays information from the Sales table, select Report, Design, Sales, and a report number from the Paradox Main menu. When prompted, enter any report description that you wish. You can then select Either Tabular, or Freeform (in this example, we'll assume that you've selected Tabular).

When the "suggested" format for the Sales table report appears, use the basic editing techniques described earlier in this chapter to add, delete, or reformat fields. In Figure 14.22, the Remarks field has been deleted, and the Sel Price field has been narrowed to make more space available.

Add a new column to the table band by moving the cursor to the Qty Sold column and selecting TableBand and Insert from the Main menu. Then, to widen the new column (as necessary), select TableBand and Resize from the menus. Follow the instructions on the screen to size the new column.

Next, to include data from the MastInv table, you need to "tell" Paradox how the Sales and MastInv table are related to one another. To do so, you need to select Field, Lookup, and Link from the menus.

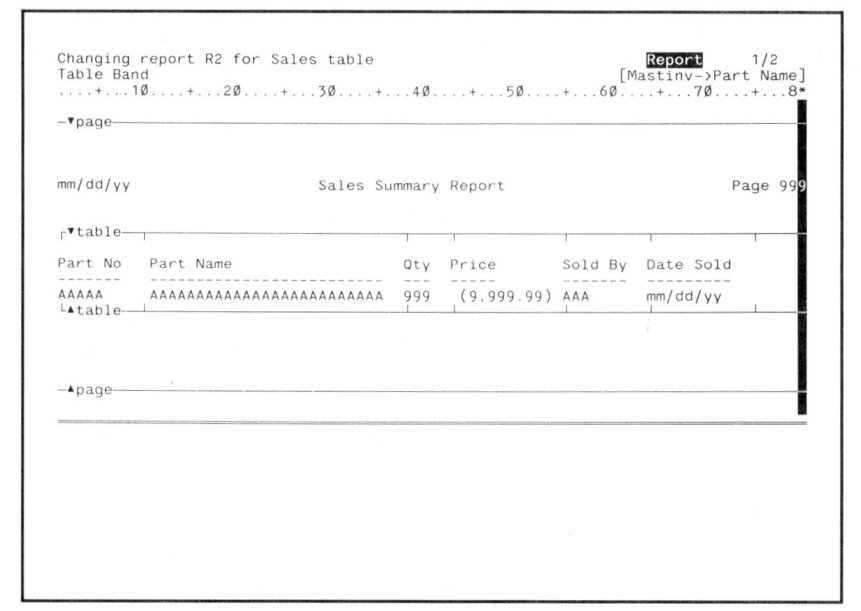

```
Changing report R2 for Sales table                        Report    1/2
Table Band                                              [Mastinv->Part Name]
....+...10....+...20....+...30....+...40....+...50....+...60....+...70....+...8*
─▼page─────────────────────────────────────────────────────────────────────


mm/dd/yy                        Sales Summary Report                  Page 999

 ┌▼table─┬───────────────────────────┬────┬────────┬────────┬─────────┐
 Part No  Part Name                   Qty  Price    Sold By  Date Sold
 ───────  ──────────────────────────  ───  ───────  ───────  ─────────
 AAAAA    AAAAAAAAAAAAAAAAAAAAAAAAAA  999  (9,999.99) AAA    mm/dd/yy
 └▲table─┴───────────────────────────┴────┴────────┴────────┴─────────┘


─▲page─────────────────────────────────────────────────────────────────────
```

Figure 14.22: Sales report format with Part Name from the MastInv table

Paradox will prompt you for the name of the table containing the related data. In this example, you would enter (or select) MastInv.

Next, Paradox displays the prompt *Select SALES field to match Part No in MASTINV*, and displays the names of all fields in the Sales table. In this example, Part No is the common field that relates records in the Sales table to records in the MastInv table, so you would select Part No. At this point, all you've done is "told" Paradox that the Sales and Mastinv Table are related to each other via the common Part No field.

Now you can place any field from the MastInv table on the report format. For example, to place the Part Name field in the new column, press Menu (F10) and select Field, Place, and Regular as you normally would to place a field on the format. However, when you do, you will notice that the menu of field names now includes an option shown as [Mastinv·>]. When you select [Mastinv->], the menu will display field names from the MastInv Table. Select any field name you wish (Part Name in this particular example).

Paradox will now take you through the usual steps for placing and sizing a field on the report format. You may want to type in a column title, and underlines so that the new column matches the others in the report (as in the example of the Part Name field in Figure 14.22).

You can add as many fields from the MastInv table as you wish. When you are done designing the report format, press F2 to save it. When you use the Main menu Report and Output options to print the completed report, it will show the appropriate part name for each sales transaction, as Figure 14.23 shows.

```
9/24/90                  Sales Summary Report                    Page   1

Part No    Part Name                  Qty    Price     Sold By   Date Sold
-------    -------------------------  ---    -----     -------   ---------
B-100      Safety Helmet (Nikono)      1      30.00     JAK      6/01/90
C-551      Hobie Skateboard            2      67.50     JAK      6/01/90
A-220      Racing Bicycle              1     900.00     JAK      6/01/90
C-559      Flexie Skateboard           5      22.50     BBG      6/05/90
A-100      Gershwin Bicycle            5     675.00     BBG      6/05/90
B-112      Safety Helmet (Ozzy)        2      22.50     BBG      6/05/90
A-101      Nikono Bicycle              1     562.50     JAK      7/01/90
B-111      Safety Helmet (Carrera)     2      60.00     JAK      7/01/90
C-551      Hobie Skateboard            1      67.50     JAK      7/01/90
A-100      Gershwin Bicycle            3     675.00     BBG      7/15/90
B-112      Safety Helmet (Ozzy)       -2      22.50     BBG      8/01/90
A-100      Gershwin Bicycle            1     675.00     JAK      8/01/90
```

Figure 14.23: Sales table report showing Part Names

USING SUMMARY OPERATORS IN REPORTS

As mentioned earlier in this chapter, you can use *summary operators* in calculated fields, in place of Summary fields, to calculate totals, subtotals, and other group values. The summary operators are Sum(), Average(), Count(), High(), and Low(), each of which has the same function as the equivalent option from the Summary menu. In addition, the keyword *group* can be used inside a summary expression to specify calculations for a single group on the report (just as PerGroup is used with Summary fields).

In this section we'll demonstrate a report that prints invoices using summary calculations. The structure of the table that this report prints its data from is shown in Figure 14.24. (This table might actually be created from an Answer table that combines information from a customer list and a table of orders or charges.)

Samples of the invoices are shown in Figure 14.25. Though the figure shows two invoices on a single page, the report can easily print individual invoices on separate pages, as we'll demonstrate.

```
Viewing Struct table: Record 1 of 12                          Main
  STRUCT          Field Name           Field Type
     1      Customer number              A5
     2      Last Name                    A15
     3      First Name                   A15
     4      Address                      A30
     5      City                         A20
     6      State                        A2
     7      Zip Code                     A10
     8      Part Number                  A5
     9      Part Name                    A20
    10      Qty                          S
    11      Unit Price                   $
    12      Date Sold                    D
```

Figure 14.24: The structure of a table used to print invoices

```
Customer number: 1001                    Invoice date:   2-Nov-90
   Andy Adams
   123 Grape St.
   Santa Monica, CA  91234


Date Sold   Part No.  Part Name              Qty   Unit Price   Item Total
---------   --------  --------------------   ---   ----------   ----------
 4/01/90    A-111     Avacado tree             5        75.00       375.00
 4/01/90    B-333     Rubber tree              1       120.00       120.00
 4/01/90    K-011     Wildflower seeds         1         5.00         5.00
 4/01/90    E-901     Decorative ferns         5         7.50        37.50
                                                                ----------
                                              Order total:          537.50
                                              Sales Tax:             32.25
                                                                ----------
                                          Total amount due:         569.75
Thank you!


- - - - - - - - - - - - - - - - - - - - - - - - - - - - - - - - - - - - -

Customer number: 8881                    Invoice date:   2-Nov-90
   Sandra Smith
   2071 Melba St.
   Venice, CA  92345
Date Sold   Part No.  Part Name              Qty   Unit Price   Item Total
---------   --------  --------------------   ---   ----------   ----------
 4/02/90    A-111     Avacado tree             1        75.00        75.00
 4/02/90    B-333     Fountain                 1       250.00       250.00
 4/02/90    K-011     Decorative ferns        10         7.50        75.00
                                                                ----------
                                              Order total:          400.00
                                              Sales Tax:             24.00
                                                                ----------
                                          Total amount due:         424.00
Thank you!


- - - - - - - - - - - - - - - - - - - - - - - - - - - - - - - - - - - - -
```

Figure 14.25: Sample invoices

Figure 14.26 shows the report specification used to print the invoices. Notice that the customer information (name, address, and so forth) is displayed as a header in the Customer number group band, so that these are displayed only once on each invoice. The individual transactions are displayed in the table band. The order total, sales tax, and invoice total are displayed as the Customer number group band footer.

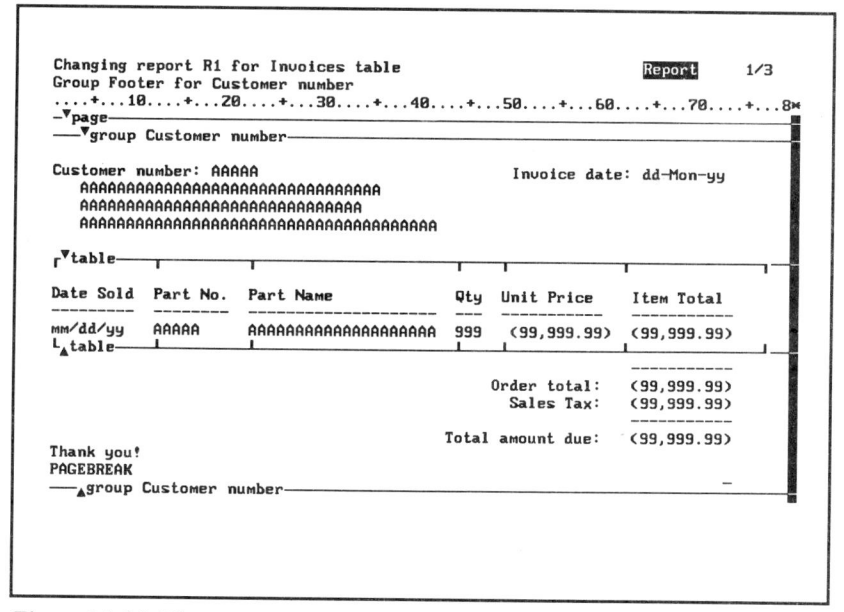

```
Changing report R1 for Invoices table                    Report   1/3
Group Footer for Customer number
....+...10....+...20....+...30....+...40....+...50....+...60....+...70....+...8»
 -▼page
  ─▼group Customer number─────────────────────────────────────────

 Customer number: AAAAA                         Invoice date: dd-Mon-yy
         AAAAAAAAAAAAAAAAAAAAAAAAAAAAAA
         AAAAAAAAAAAAAAAAAAAAAAAAAA
         AAAAAAAAAAAAAAAAAAAAAAAAAAAAAAAAAA
   ┌▼table─┬─────────┬────────────────────┬──────┬──────────┬────────────┐
   │Date Sold Part No.  Part Name             Qty  Unit Price  Item Total │
   │────────  ────────  ──────────            ───  ──────────  ────────── │
   │MM/dd/yy  AAAAA     AAAAAAAAAAAAAAAAAA    999  (99,999.99) (99,999.99)│
   └▲table─┴─────────┴────────────────────┴──────┴──────────┴────────────┘
                                                  ──────────
                                      Order total:  (99,999.99)
                                        Sales Tax:  (99,999.99)
                                                  ──────────
                                   Total amount due: (99,999.99)
 Thank you!
 PAGEBREAK
  ─▲group Customer number─────────────────────────────────────────
```

Figure 14.26: The report specification for printing invoices

In the table band, the item total is a calculated field based on the expression

[Qty] * [Unit Price]

In the group footer the order total is a calculated field based on the expression

Sum([Qty]*[Unit Price],group)

Note that the expression calculates the sum of the total sale (which is calculated as *Qty* * *Unit Price*). The *group* keyword, preceded by a comma, assures that the calculation is for the current group (invoice) only. (Note also that the *group* expression is placed inside the parentheses for the Sum operator, as required.)

The sales tax in the footer is also a calculated field, based on the expression

    Sum([Qty]*[Unit Price],group)*.06

The invoice total is another calculated field, based on the expression

    Sum([Qty]*[Unit Price],group)*1.06

For your general information (though this does not pertain to summary operators per se), the customer name is displayed in the group header as a calculated field using the expression

    [First Name]+" "+[Last Name]

The city, state, and zip code are also a single calculated field, based on the expression

    [City]+", "+[State]+" "+[Zip Code]

The invoice date in the group header is placed using the usual Field, Place, and Date options from the Report menu.

To print each invoice on a separate page, the PAGEBREAK keyword appears at the bottom of the Customer number group band. Finally, to display column titles on each invoice, the GroupsOfTables option under the Setting Format menu options has been selected.

MULTIPLE-PAGE FORMS

On a table with many fields, it may not be possible to enter and edit data with a single custom form. In that case, you'll need to divide the form into several pages. Employment forms, tax forms, and others often require several pages of screens. A single Paradox form can consist of up to 15 "pages" of screens.

To add pages to a form, call up the menu (press F10) while editing the form, and select the Page option. You will be given these two new options:

Insert   Delete

To add a page, select the Insert option. Paradox will then display these options:

After   Before

To add a page following the form currently being edited, select the After option. To insert a page before the current form, select the Before option. A new screen for creating the new page will appear. Near the top of the screen, a symbol, such as 2/2, will tell you how many pages are on the form and which page you are viewing. For example, 1/2 indicates that you are viewing the first page of a two-page form.

While creating or editing a form with multiple pages, you can use the PgUp and PgDn keys to scroll up and down through the pages. You can also use PgUp and PgDn in conjunction with the Move command to move portions of a screen from one page to another.

When you use the multiple-page form to enter or edit data on a table, the PgUp and PgDn keys will move you from page to page, as well as through records. For example, if you are editing record number 1 (a two-page record), pressing PgDn will display the second page of record number 1. Pressing PgDn again will display the first page of record number 2.

To delete a page from a form, move to the page you want to delete and call up the menu. Select the Page option, then the Delete option. Be careful with this option. Once you delete a page, it cannot be retrieved. You would have to reinsert a new page, as well as reenter all the text and fields. (Of course, if you are editing an already existing form, you can Cancel all changes, in which case the deletion would not be saved and the page would remain intact.)

DISPLAY-ONLY FIELDS

When you use multiple-page forms, it's a good idea to carry over some identifying piece of information from one page to the next so you can always see, at a glance, which record you're working with.

Figure 14.27 shows the structure of a hypothetical table named Taxform. Suppose this table, which stores all the information to fill out a 1040 tax form, has 200 fields. You can easily set up a multiple-page form using the Page and Insert options, but let's look at a technique for carrying information over from one page to the next.

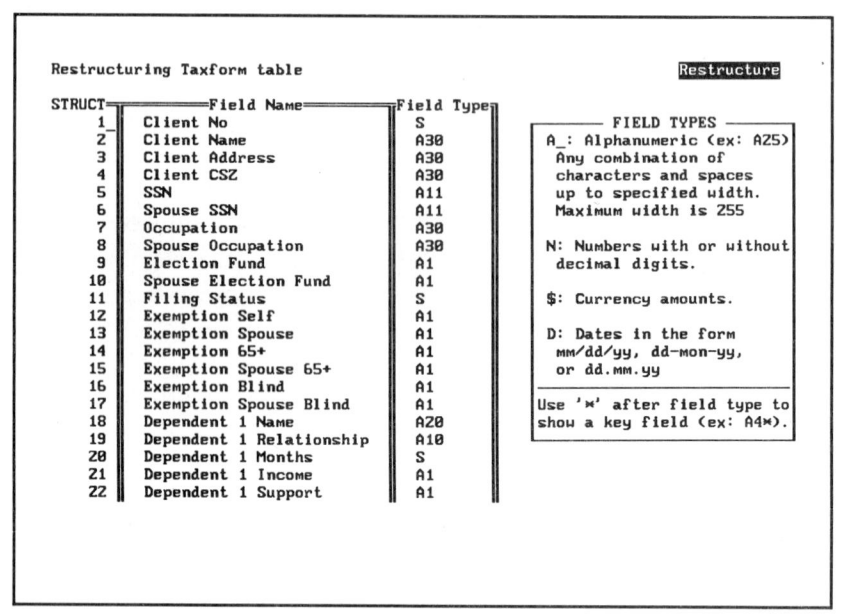

```
Restructuring Taxform table                                    Restructure
STRUCT     Field Name            Field Type
    1   Client No                    S              ── FIELD TYPES ──
    2   Client Name                  A30          A_: Alphanumeric (ex: A25)
    3   Client Address               A30          Any combination of
    4   Client CSZ                   A30          characters and spaces
    5   SSN                          A11          up to specified width.
    6   Spouse SSN                   A11          Maximum width is 255
    7   Occupation                   A30
    8   Spouse Occupation            A30          N: Numbers with or without
    9   Election Fund                A1              decimal digits.
   10   Spouse Election Fund         A1
   11   Filing Status                S            $: Currency amounts.
   12   Exemption Self               A1
   13   Exemption Spouse             A1           D: Dates in the form
   14   Exemption 65+                A1              mm/dd/yy, dd-mon-yy,
   15   Exemption Spouse 65+         A1              or dd.mm.yy
   16   Exemption Blind              A1
   17   Exemption Spouse Blind       A1           Use '*' after field type to
   18   Dependent 1 Name             A20          show a key field (ex: A4*).
   19   Dependent 1 Relationship     A10
   20   Dependent 1 Months           S
   21   Dependent 1 Income           A1
   22   Dependent 1 Support          A1
```

Figure 14.27: The structure of a hypothetical Taxform table

Figure 14.28 shows the first page of the custom form. All fields on this form were placed using the Put and Regular options. Therefore, you'll have complete access to all these data later when entering or editing information through the form.

Figure 14.29 shows the third page (of five, as indicated by *3/5* in the upper-right corner) of this form. The data inside the borders are carry-overs from the first page and cannot be changed. They are only to identify the individual for whom the tax form was entered. These were placed using the Field, Place, and DisplayOnly options from the menu. (The field on the left is Client No; the field on the right is Client Name.)

ADVANCED REPORT AND FORM TECHNIQUES 385

```
Changing F1 form for Taxform                        Form    1/5
<19, 1>
 Client Number  _____              Social Security Number
 Client Name    _____ _____
 Address        _____ Spouse's SSN
                _____ _____
                                     Occupation
                                     _____
                                     Spouse Occupation
                                     _____
       $1.00 to presidential election fund?   _ (Y/N)
       If joint return, $1.00 from spouse?   _ (Y/N)
 FILING STATUS  _____    1. Single
                          2. Married filing joint return
                          3. Married filing separate return
                          4. Head of Household
                          5. Qualifying widow(er)
```

Figure 14.28: The first page of the custom form for tax table

```
Changing F1 form for Taxform                        Form    3/5
< 2, 13>                                   DisplayOnly, Client No
   Client : _____           _____
Moving Expense.............................. _____
Employee Business Expenses................... _____
IRA Deduction................................ _____
       IRA Payments.......................... _____
Payments to a Keogh.......................... _____
Penalty on early withdrawal of savings....... _____
Alimony Paid................................. _____
Deduction for a married couple when both work.. _____
Disability Income............................ _____
```

Figure 14.29: The third page of the custom form for the Taxform table

Figure 14.30 shows how this page of the form looks after entering some data into the completed form. The client name and number appear on the form for identification purposes but cannot be changed.

Since Paradox allows a regular field to be placed on a form only once, you cannot place the same regular field on different pages of a form. However, the DisplayOnly option allows you to place a field for display only on as many pages of the form as you wish. You can also use the Put and #Record options under the Forms menu to place a record number on any page of a form.

CALCULATED FIELDS

We've seen how to perform calculations on data in tables using the Ask and Report options, but you can also perform immediate calculations on a custom form. For example, recall the structure of the Sales table, shown in Figure 14.31. Even though there is no field for storing the results of the calculation *[Qty Sold] * [Sel Price]*, we can display these results on a form using a calculated field.

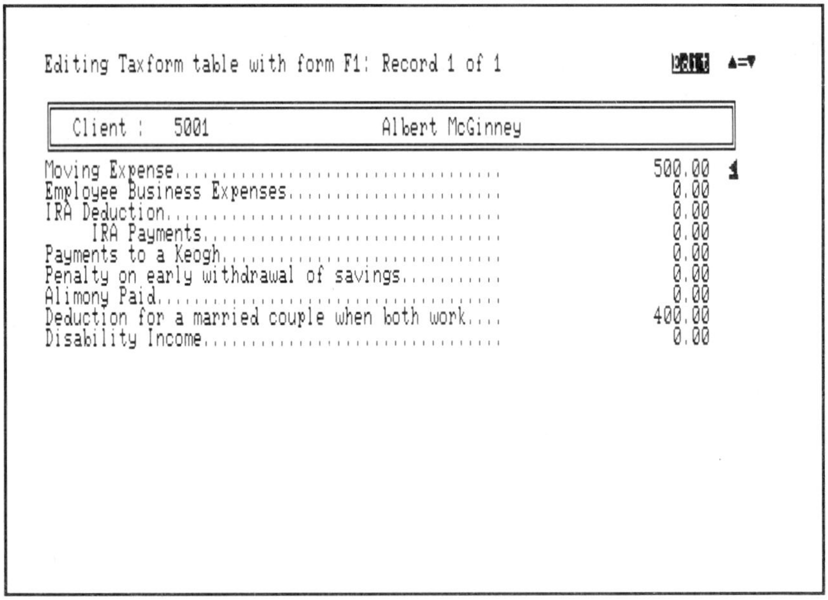

Figure 14.30: The third page of the Taxform data-entry form

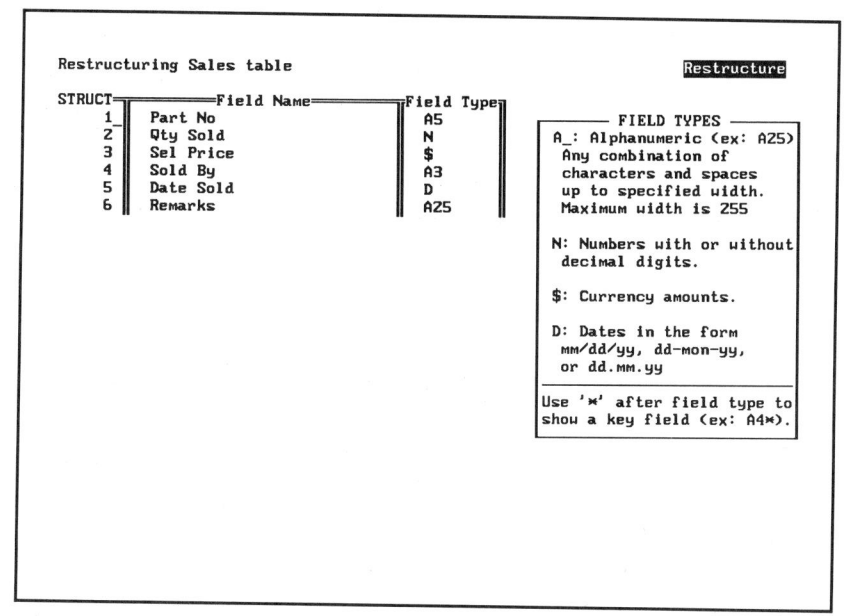

```
Restructuring Sales table                                    Restructure
STRUCT       Field Name          Field Type
  1     Part No                    A5              FIELD TYPES
  2     Qty Sold                   N          A_: Alphanumeric (ex: A25)
  3     Sel Price                  $          Any combination of
  4     Sold By                    A3         characters and spaces
  5     Date Sold                  D          up to specified width.
  6     Remarks                    A25        Maximum width is 255

                                              N: Numbers with or without
                                                 decimal digits.

                                              $: Currency amounts.

                                              D: Dates in the form
                                                 mm/dd/yy, dd-mon-yy,
                                                 or dd.mm.yy

                                              Use '*' after field type to
                                              show a key field (ex: A4*).
```

Figure 14.31: The structure of the Sales table

Take a look at the form in Figure 14.32. All the fields except one were placed on this form using the usual Field, Place, and Regular options from the Forms menu. The field next to the *Total:* prompt was placed by selecting the Field, Place, and Calculated options from the menus. The expression entered into the field is *[Qty Sold] * [Sel Price]*.

When you use this form to enter or edit data, Paradox will not let you move the cursor to this calculated field. However, when you enter or change data in the Qty Sold and/or Sel Price fields, Paradox will immediately calculate and display the results of the calculation, as shown in Figure 14.33.

COMBINING MULTIPLE FORMS FOR MULTIPLE TABLES

For the remainder of this chapter, we'll discuss how to create forms for entering, viewing, and editing data from multiple related tables. These forms, called *multitable forms* allow you to view data from several related tables simultaneously, thereby making it easier to work with several tables at once.

```
Changing F1 form for Sales                              Form      1/1
<18, 1>
┌─────────────────────────────────────────────────────────────────┐
│ Enter a Sales Transaction                                       │
└─────────────────────────────────────────────────────────────────┘

Date: _____              Sold By: ___
Part Number: _____
Quantity:    _____
Unit Price:  _____
Total:       _____

    ┌─────────────────────────────────────────────────────────────┐
    │   Remarks:  _____                 │
    └─────────────────────────────────────────────────────────────┘
```

Figure 14.32: The form for the Sales table

```
Editing Sales table with form F1: Record 1 of 12          Edit   —▼
┌─────────────────────────────────────────────────────────────────┐
│ Enter a Sales Transaction                                       │
└─────────────────────────────────────────────────────────────────┘

Date:   6/01/90              Sold By: JAK
Part Number: C-551
Quantity:    3
Unit Price:  67.50
Total:       202.50

    ┌─────────────────────────────────────────────────────────────┐
    │   Remarks:                         ◄                        │
    └─────────────────────────────────────────────────────────────┘
```

Figure 14.33: A calculated total on a data-entry form

ADVANCED REPORT AND FORM TECHNIQUES 389

We will also discuss techniques for developing *multirecord forms*, which allow you to display multiple records from a single table. By combining multitable, and multirecord forms onto a single screen, you can develop truly powerful forms that provide the best access to information stored in tables.

Figure 14.34 shows a multitable, multirecord form. Though it *appears* as though all the information on the form is stored in a single table, there are actually three tables involved. The information in the upper left corner (not in a box) is from one table; the customer name and address are from a second table. The individual orders in the box centered near the bottom of the screen come from yet a third table. (Actually, as you'll see, some of the data in the bottom box comes from yet a fourth table.)

The basic procedure for developing a multitable form, like the one shown in Figure 14.34, is summarized below:

1. Create the *subform(s)* that will later be included in a larger *master* form, making them small enough so that they will fit.

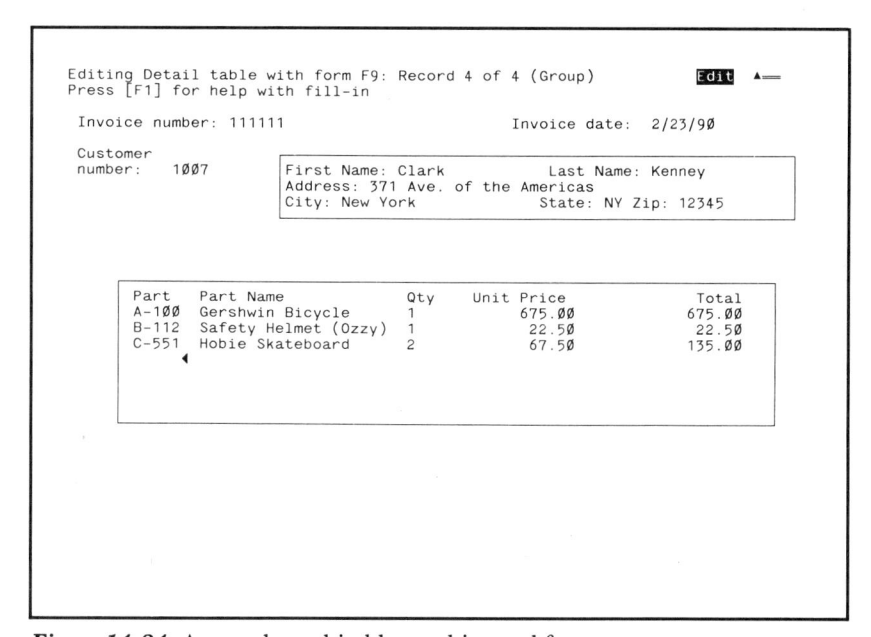

```
Editing Detail table with form F9: Record 4 of 4 (Group)      Edit
Press [F1] for help with fill-in

 Invoice number: 111111                    Invoice date:  2/23/90
 Customer
 number:     1007       First Name: Clark          Last Name: Kenney
                        Address: 371 Ave. of the Americas
                        City: New York            State: NY Zip: 12345


              Part   Part Name            Qty   Unit Price         Total
              A-100  Gershwin Bicycle      1       675.00         675.00
              B-112  Safety Helmet (Ozzy)  1        22.50          22.50
              C-551  Hobie Skateboard      2        67.50         135.00
```

Figure 14.34: A sample multitable, multirecord form

2. Create the master form, and use menu options to read the subform onto the screen and position it according to your tastes.

But, before you can develop the appropriate forms, you need to create the tables with the information that the forms will provide access to, as discussed in the next section.

TABLES USED IN THE SAMPLE FORM

To demonstrate the power of multitable, multirecord forms, we'll use a new set of tables best suited to illustrate some techniques for creating these forms. If you would like to follow along and try developing the sample form, you will need to create these tables (using the usual Create option from the Paradox Main menu).

First, you'll need to create a table named Invoices that has the rather simple structure shown in Figure 14.35. Notice that the Invoices table contains only information about invoices as a whole; only an invoice number, customer number, invoice date, and invoice total.

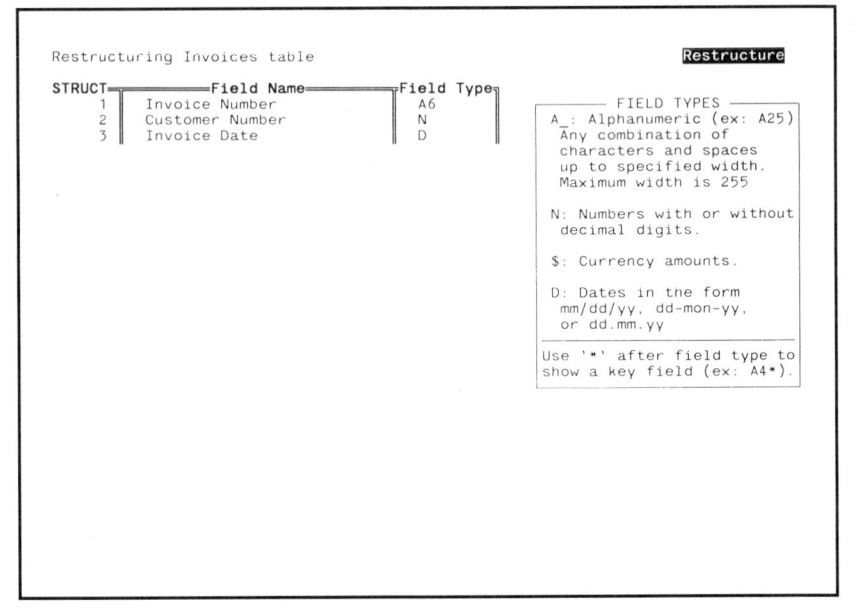

```
Restructuring Invoices table                                    Restructure
STRUCT      Field Name              Field Type
   1     Invoice Number                 A6           ──── FIELD TYPES ────
   2     Customer Number                N           A_: Alphanumeric (ex: A25)
   3     Invoice Date                   D            Any combination of
                                                     characters and spaces
                                                     up to specified width.
                                                     Maximum width is 255

                                                    N: Numbers with or without
                                                     decimal digits.

                                                    $: Currency amounts.

                                                    D: Dates in the form
                                                     mm/dd/yy, dd-mon-yy,
                                                     or dd.mm.yy

                                                    Use '*' after field type to
                                                    show a key field (ex: A4*).
```

Figure 14.35: Structure of the Invoices table

The invoice *detail*, that is, the individual customer orders or purchases that are included on a single invoice, is stored in a second table named Detail. Again, use the Create option from the Paradox Main menu to create this table with the structure shown in Figure 14.36.

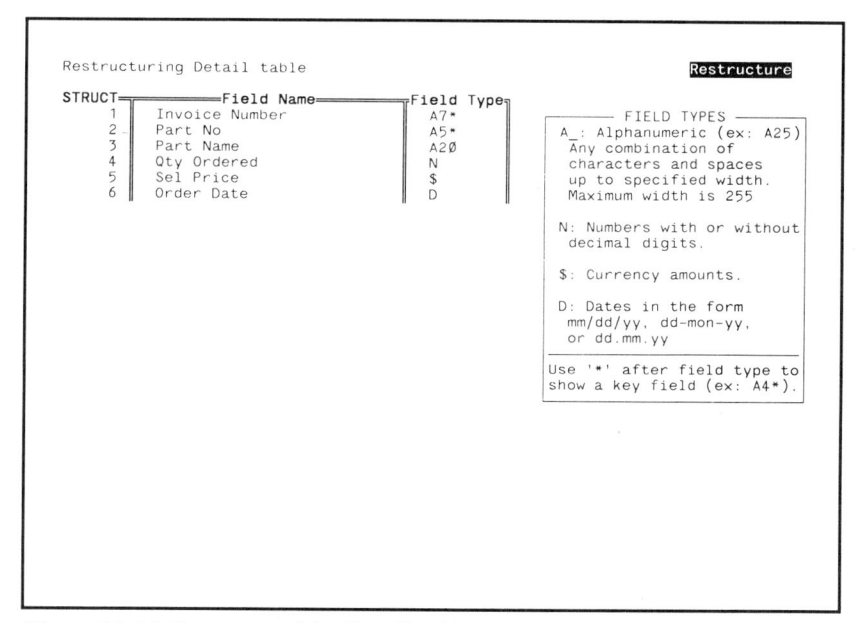

```
Restructuring Detail table                                    Restructure
STRUCT      Field Name           Field Type
   1     Invoice Number             A7*              ——— FIELD TYPES ———
   2     Part No                    A5*          A_: Alphanumeric (ex: A25)
   3     Part Name                  A20          Any combination of
   4     Qty Ordered                N            characters and spaces
   5     Sel Price                  $            up to specified width.
   6     Order Date                 D            Maximum width is 255

                                                 N: Numbers with or without
                                                 decimal digits.

                                                 $: Currency amounts.

                                                 D: Dates in the form
                                                 mm/dd/yy, dd-mon-yy,
                                                 or dd.mm.yy

                                                 Use '*' after field type to
                                                 show a key field (ex: A4*).
```

Figure 14.36: Structure of the Detail table

Notice in Figure 14.36 that Invoice Number and Part No fields are both keyed (marked with an asterisk). When developing multitable forms, you must make certain that the field relating a *subordinate* (or *child*) table to the master-form table is indexed. But, recall also that once you mark a field as a key, each record in that field must contain a unique value. This creates a bit of a dilemma for us.

First of all, we want groups of records in the Detail table to refer to a single invoice. But if we make Invoice Number, alone, a keyed field in the Detail table, we will only be allowed to enter one "detail" record for each invoice. To get around this problem, we've keyed the Detail table on two fields, Invoice Number and Part No.

By making two fields into keyed fields, we change the "uniqueness" restriction so that each record must have a unique "pair" of values. By making both Invoice Number and Part No keyed fields, we can enter several records with the same invoice number but different part numbers, such as the records below:

INVOICE NUMBER	PART NO
111111	A-100
111111	B-222
111111	C-551

A third table will store information about individual customers. You can use the CustList table we used in previous chapters to quickly build a new table named CustData for this example. From the Paradox Main menu, select Tools, Copy, Table, and enter CustList as the name of the table to copy. When prompted, enter CustData as the name of the new table.

Next, you need to modify the new CustData table to include a field containing customer numbers that relates each record to a customer in the Invoices table. To do so, select Modify and Restructure from the main menu, and enter CustData as the table to modify. When the table structure appears on the screen, press the Ins (or Insert) key on your keyboard to add a new field. Give this field the name Customer Number, and the N data type, as shown in Figure 14.37.

Press F2 after changing the table structure, and you will see the new CustData table on the screen. To add customer numbers, press Edit (F9), and then assign each customer a unique number, as in Figure 14.38.(Don't be concerned if your particular copy of the CustData table shows different customer data; just assign each customer a unique number starting with number 1001.)

Now, as mentioned earlier, this table must be keyed on the field that relates it to the Invoices table if you want to develop a multitable form. So you will need to press F2 after adding the customer numbers to save those changes. Then press F10 and select the Modify and Restructure options. Enter CustData as the table to restructure, and mark the Customer Number field as a key by placing an asterisk to the right of the N, as in Figure 14.39. Press F2 after adding the asterisk.

ADVANCED REPORT AND FORM TECHNIQUES

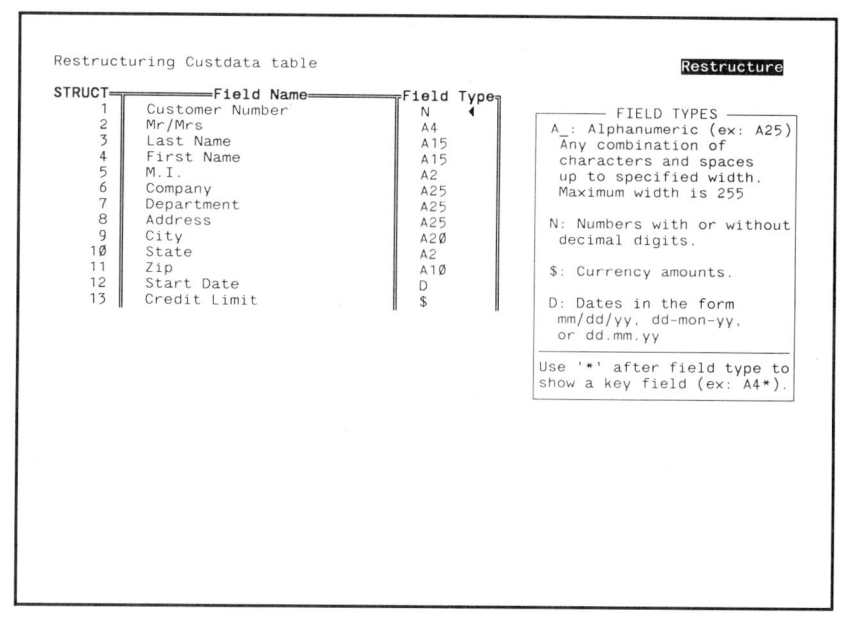

```
Restructuring Custdata table                                    Restructure
STRUCT         Field Name         Field Type
   1      Customer Number              N      ◄        ─── FIELD TYPES ───
   2      Mr/Mrs                       A4              A_: Alphanumeric (ex: A25)
   3      Last Name                    A15                 Any combination of
   4      First Name                   A15                 characters and spaces
   5      M.I.                         A2                  up to specified width.
   6      Company                      A25                 Maximum width is 255
   7      Department                   A25
   8      Address                      A25             N: Numbers with or without
   9      City                         A20                decimal digits.
  10      State                        A2
  11      Zip                          A10             $: Currency amounts.
  12      Start Date                   D
  13      Credit Limit                 $               D: Dates in the form
                                                          mm/dd/yy, dd-mon-yy,
                                                          or dd.mm.yy

                                                       Use '*' after field type to
                                                       show a key field (ex: A4*).
```

Figure 14.37: The CustData table structure

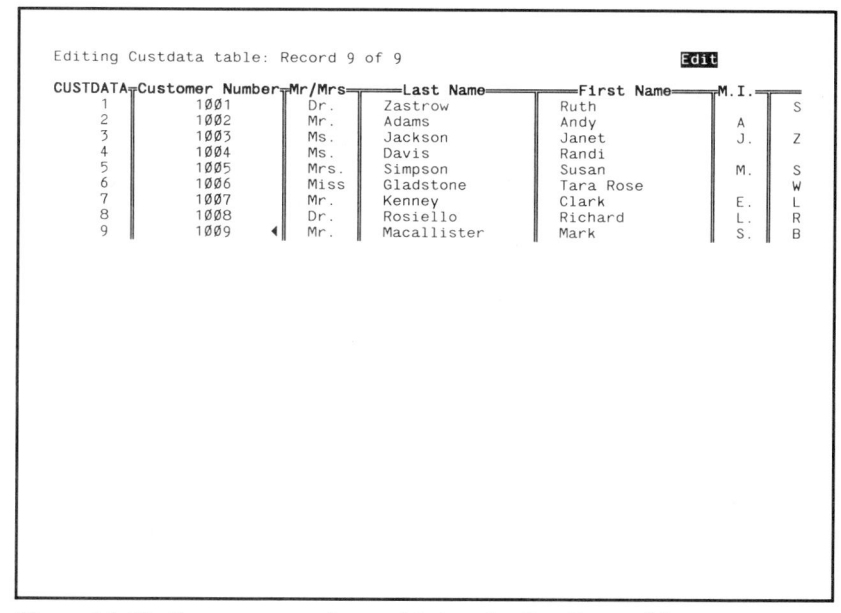

```
Editing Custdata table: Record 9 of 9                              Edit
CUSTDATA Customer Number  Mr/Mrs     Last Name      First Name      M.I.
   1         1001          Dr.       Zastrow         Ruth                   S
   2         1002          Mr.       Adams           Andy            A.
   3         1003          Ms.       Jackson         Janet           J.     Z
   4         1004          Ms.       Davis           Randi
   5         1005          Mrs.      Simpson         Susan           M.     S
   6         1006          Miss      Gladstone       Tara Rose              W
   7         1007          Mr.       Kenney          Clark           E.     L
   8         1008          Dr.       Rosiello        Richard         L.     R
   9         1009       ◄  Mr.       Macallister     Mark            S.     B
```

Figure 14.38: Customer numbers added to the CustData table

```
Restructuring Custdata table                              Restructure
STRUCT    Field Name         Field Type
   1   Customer Number         N*              ── FIELD TYPES ──
   2   Mr/Mrs                  A4         A_: Alphanumeric (ex: A25)
   3   Last Name               A15            Any combination of
   4   First Name              A15            characters and spaces
   5   M.I.                    A2             up to specified width.
   6   Company                 A25            Maximum width is 255
   7   Department              A25
   8   Address                 A25         N: Numbers with or without
   9   City                    A20            decimal digits.
  10   State                   A2
  11   Zip                     A10         $: Currency amounts.
  12   Start Date              D
  13   Credit Limit            $           D: Dates in the form
                                              mm/dd/yy, dd-mon-yy,
                                              or dd.mm.yy

                                           Use '*' after field type to
                                           show a key field (ex: A4*).
```

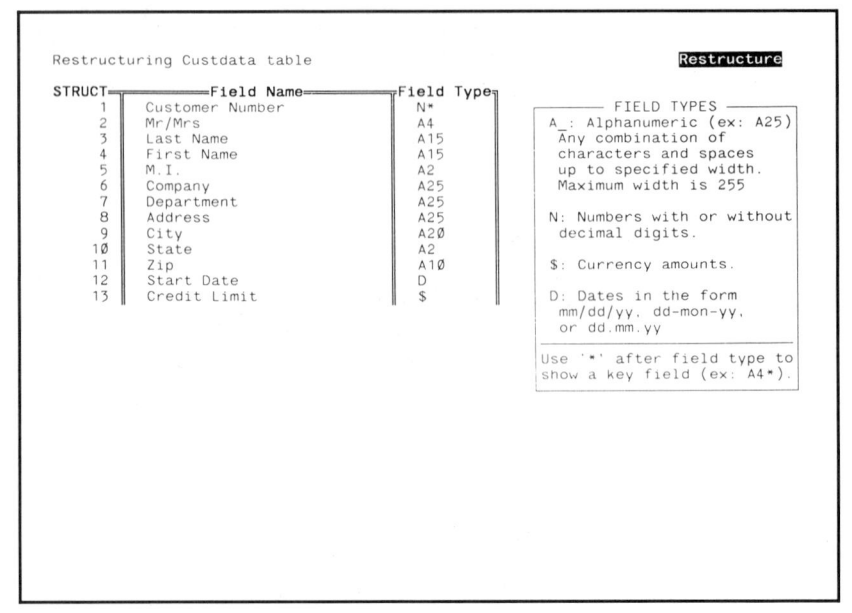

Figure 14.39: CustData table Customer Number field is keyed

So now you have the Invoices table, which contains a single record for each invoice. You also have a table named Detail that contains a single record for each order on the invoice. Detail is keyed on the Invoice Number field so that it can be related to the Invoices table. (It is also keyed on the PartNo field so that multiple records can be entered for each invoice number.) You also have a table named CustData, which is keyed on the Customer Number field, so that it too can be related to the Invoices table.

But, actually, a fourth table, one that stores information about each product that customers might order, will come in very handy here. You can use the MastInv table, created in earlier chapters, as this fourth table.

To check the structure of the MastInv table, select Modify and Restructure from the Main menu, and enter MastInv as the table to restructure. If the Part No field on your MastInv table is not keyed, add an asterisk to the Field Type column of that field as shown in Figure 14.40. (If you added the Category field described in Chapter 13, don't worry about it; this example will work fine with or without that field.) Then press F2 to save the new structure.

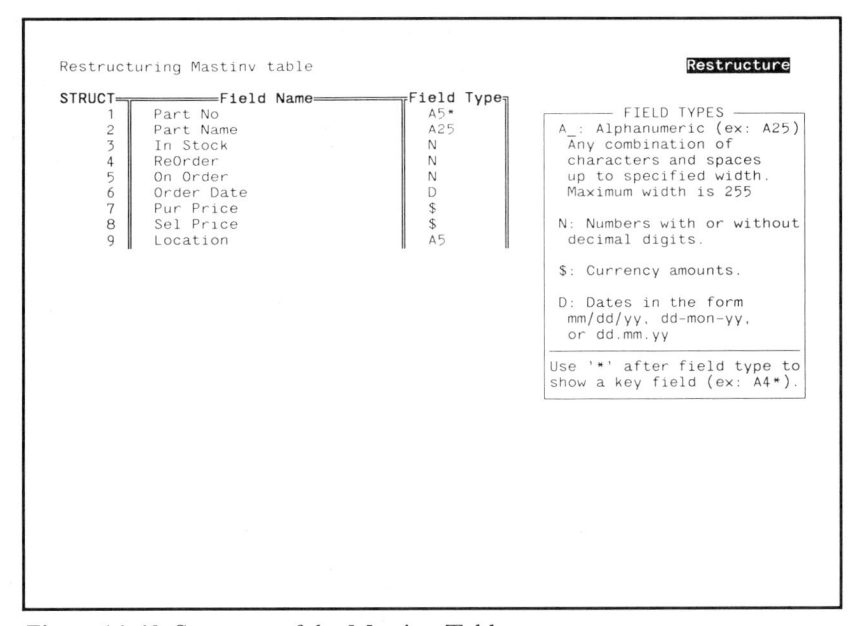

```
Restructuring Mastinv table                              Restructure
STRUCT     Field Name          Field Type
   1    Part No                 A5*          ──── FIELD TYPES ────
   2    Part Name               A25         A_: Alphanumeric (ex: A25)
   3    In Stock                N             Any combination of
   4    ReOrder                 N             characters and spaces
   5    On Order                N             up to specified width.
   6    Order Date              D             Maximum width is 255
   7    Pur Price               $
   8    Sel Price               $           N: Numbers with or without
   9    Location                A5            decimal digits.

                                             $: Currency amounts.

                                             D: Dates in the form
                                                mm/dd/yy, dd-mon-yy,
                                                or dd.mm.yy

                                             Use '*' after field type to
                                             show a key field (ex: A4*).
```

Figure 14.40: Structure of the Mastinv Table

Figure 14.41 shows some sample data on the MastInv table. Don't be concerned if the sample data in your MastInv table does not exactly match the sample data shown in Figure 14.41. Just be sure that each record in your MastInv table has a unique value in the Part No field.

```
Viewing Mastinv table: Record 1 of 8                           Main
MASTINV  Part No          Part Name           In Stock    ReOrder
   1     A-100     Gershwin Bicycle              10          5
   2     A-101     Nikono Bicycle                50         35
   3     A-200     Racing Bicycle                 2          3
   4     B-100     Safety Helmet (Nikono)        50         10
   5     B-111     Safety Helmet (Carrera)        2         10
   6     B-112     Safety Helmet (Ozzy)           0         10
   7     C-551     Hobie Skateboard              50         75
   8     C-559     Flexie Skateboard             25         75
```

Figure 14.41: Sample data in the MastInv table.

The basic process for developing multitable forms goes like this:

DESIGNING A SUBFORM

Now that you've developed all of the appropriate tables for the fancy form, you can begin developing subforms. To design the small embedded form for displaying customer information, first press Clear All (Alt-F8) to clear your screen of any clutter. Then select Forms and Design from the Main menu, and specify CustData as the table for which you want to create a form. Select any unused form number, such as 9, and enter any description when prompted (such as *Partial CustData form*).

Next, develop a small form in the upper left corner of the forms design screen, containing the fields that you want the final master form to display. Remember, to place text on a form, just position the cursor to where you want the text to begin, and start typing. To display field data from a table on a form, press F10 and then select Field, Place, and Regular and a field name from the menus that appear, and follow instructions that appear on the screen.

Figure 14.42 shows the sample subform used for the CustData table. When creating this form, start typing the word First (in First Name) at row 2, column 2, as indicated by the <2,2> near the upper-left corner of the screen. After typing in the text shown and placing the fields, you can draw the box around the form using the usual Border, Place, and Single-line options from the menu.

▰ The underscores shown in Figure 14.42 are "placeholders" for fields placed using the Field and Place options from the menu, as discussed in Chapter 9.

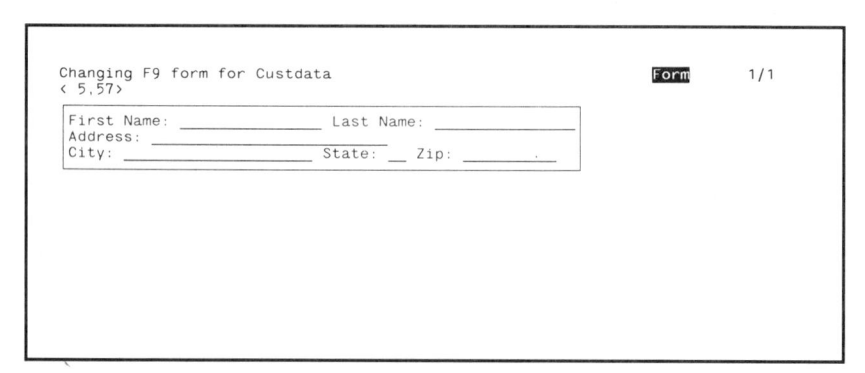

```
Changing F9 form for Custdata                    Form      1/1
< 5,57>
┌─────────────────────────────────────────────────────────────┐
│ First Name: _____    Last Name: _____ │
│ Address: _____                                   │
│ City: _____          State: __  Zip: _____    │
└─────────────────────────────────────────────────────────────┘
```

Figure 14.42: Sample subform for the CustData table

Notice that the Customer Number field is *not* included on the Cust-Data subform. That's because the Customer Number from the Invoices table will be used on the Master form, so we need not (and, actually, cannot) place the Customer Number field in this sub-form. After you have created the form shown in Figure 14.42, press F2 to save it. You'll be returned to the Paradox main menu.

DEVELOPING A MULTIRECORD SUBFORM

The next step will be to create the subform that displays individual line items (the larger box shown in Figure 14.34). This particular form has a unique feature; it displays several records from a single table. As you'll see in this section, it is fairly easy to create such a multirecord form.

To begin, select Forms and Design from the Paradox Main menu. When prompted for a table name, specify Detail. Then select 9 as the number for the report (though you could use any number). When prompted for a description, type in **Partial Detail Form** and press Enter.

Figure 14.43 shows how the sample form should look when you first create it on the screen. The word **Part** begins at row 2 column 3 (<2,3> on the indicator near the upper left corner of the screen). The field beneath the Unit Price column title is actually the Sel Price field. When you place the Part No, Part Name, and Qty fields on this form, Paradox will initially suggest very wide columns. You can use the ← key, when prompted, to narrow these fields to the widths shown in the figure.

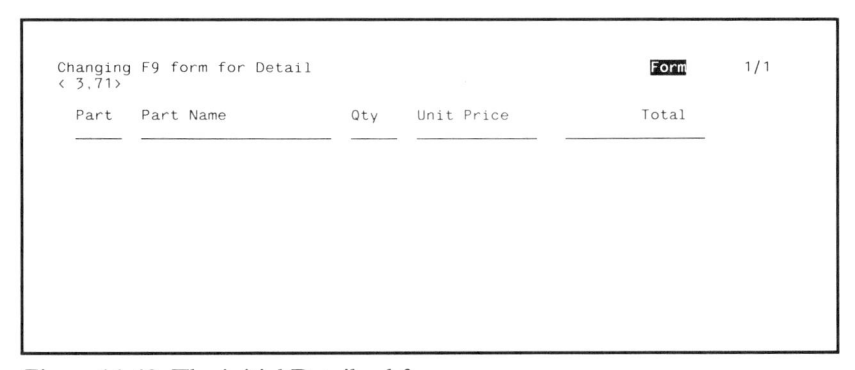

```
Changing F9 form for Detail                              Form      1/1
< 3,71>
  Part    Part Name            Qty     Unit Price         Total
  ____    _____            ___     _____         _____
```

Figure 14.43: The initial Detail subform

The field under the Total column is actually a calculated field that you can place on the form (at about row 3, column 55) by selecting the Field, Place, and Calculated options from the menu. When prompted for an expression, type **[Qty Ordered] * [Sel Price]** and then press Enter.

The next steps involve extending the fields on the form downward, to display multiple records from the table. To do so, begin by positioning the cursor to the the first underscore character of the Part No field (about row 3, column 3). When the cursor is properly placed, you should see the field name Part No near the upper right corner of the screen.

Next, press F10 to call up the menu, and select Multi. Paradox presents the options:

Tables   Records

Select Records (later, you'll see how to use the Tables option) and then select Define to specify a multirecord region (or area) on the form. The screen prompts you to move the cursor to a corner of the region to define. The cursor is already properly placed, so just press ←⏎.

Next, the screen prompts you to move to a diagonal corner. Press (or hold down) the → key until all the fields are highlighted (right up to the very last underscore in the Total field) and then press Enter.

Next, the screen prompts you to use ↓ or ↑ to add or delete repeating rows. Press ↓ six times to extend the region downward. Your screen should look like Figure 14.44. Press Enter to finish defining the multirecord region.

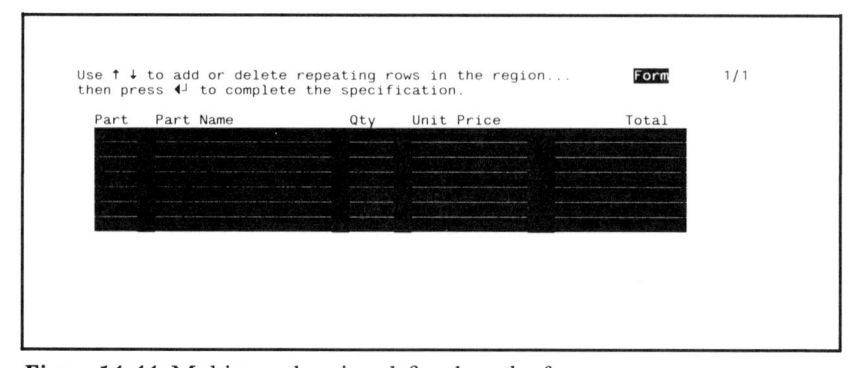

Figure 14.44: Multirecord region defined on the form

Finally, you can draw a box around the multirecord region by moving the cursor to row 1, column 1, and selecting Border, Place, and Single-line. Press Enter to mark the upper left corner of the box, then use the → and ↓ keys to extend the box to the lower right corner of the region, as shown in Figure 14.45. (Press Enter to finish drawing the box.)

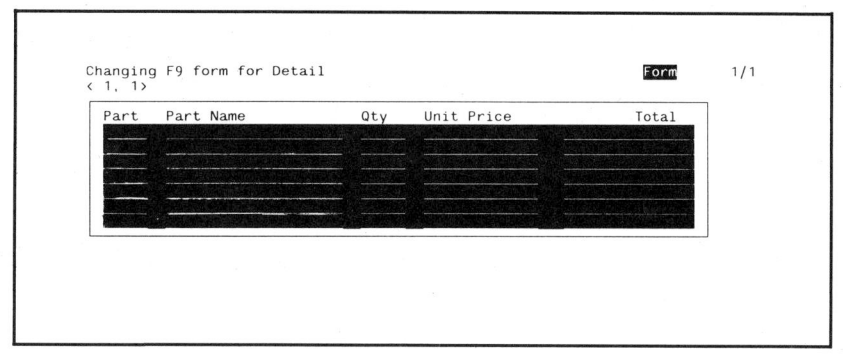

Figure 14.45: Multirecord region with a box drawn around it

When you have completed the form, press F2 to save it.

DEVELOPING THE MASTER FORM

The final step in combining the multiple forms is to create the master form and place the subforms onto it. You start by using the usual techniques. That is, select Forms and Design from the Main menu. When prompted for a table name, enter Invoices (in this example), and select any unused form number (we'll use 1 in this example).

When prompted for a form description, you can type in any description, such as *Master order-entry form* and then press Enter. When the design screen appears, a good starting point is to "read in" the subforms, so you can see how much room you have left over for fields from the Invoices database.

To read in the subform for the CustData table, press F10 to call up the menu, then select Multi. Again, the submenu displays:

Tables Records

You want to place a form from another table, so select the Tables option, and then select Place from the submenu that appears. The next submenu offers the options:

Linked   Unlinked

These options let you define whether or not the "foreign table" (CustData) is linked (or related) to the current table (Invoices). In this example, the table is indeed linked (via the common Customer Number field), so select Linked.

Next, the screen prompts you for the name of the foreign table. Press Enter and select CustData. Then, when prompted for the form to embed from the CustData table, select number 9.

Paradox then displays the prompt *Select INVOICES field to match Customer Number in CUSTDATA*. In this case, you want to select Customer Number, as this is the field that links (relates) the Invoices table to the CustData table.

Immediately, a highlighted box appears near the lower right corner of the screen. This box shows you the size of the sub-form. You can use the ↑, ↓, ←, and → keys to move this box to any position on the screen. In this example, press ↑ about 15 times, and then ← twice, to move the box up and to the left, as shown in Figure 14.46. Press Enter after positioning the box.

Next, you can place the subform for the Detail table on the Master form. Follow the same basic steps that you followed to place the CustData form. That is, press F10 and select Multi. Again, select Tables.

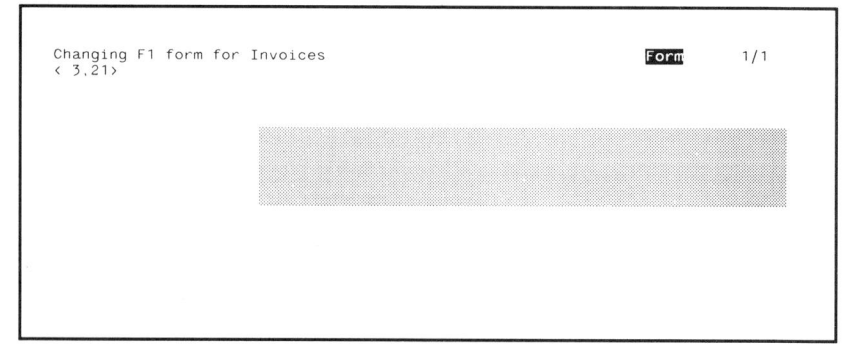

```
Changing F1 form for Invoices                          Form      1/1
< 3,21>
```

Figure 14.46: The CustData subform positioned on the master form

(You do *not* select Records here. That option allows you to create a multirecord region on a new form. You select Tables at this point because the multirecord subform has already been created, and now you want to *use* that subform.)

Select Place and then select Linked. When prompted for a table name, press Enter and select Detail. Select form number 9 when prompted. Paradox asks that you select the field that links the Invoices table to the Detail table. In this example, select Invoice Number.

Again, a highlighted image demonstrating the size of the subform appears on the screen. Press ↑ twice, and ← about four times to move the box up and center on the screen. Press Enter after positioning the box.

Finally, you need to place fields from the Invoices table onto this master form. First, move the cursor to row 2 column 2 and type **Invoice number:**. Press → once, then press F10 to call up the menu. Select Field, Place, and Regular from the menu, and then select the field name Invoice Number. Press Enter in response to the prompts that follow.

Move the cursor to row 2 column 48, type **Invoice date:**, and then press →. Press F10 to call up the menu, and select Field, Place, and Regular. Select the field name Invoice Date and, again, press Enter in response to all prompts that follow.

Next, move the cursor to row 4 column 2, and type **Customer**. Then move the curser down to row 5 column 2 and type **number:**. Press → once, then press F10 to access the menus. Select the Field, Place, and Regular options, and select Customer Number. Press Enter, then press ← a few times to reduce the size of the underscores so that they no longer intersect with the box representing the Cust-Data table. (Figure 14.47 shows an acceptable size for this field.) Press Enter after sizing the field.

The completed form appears in Figure 14.47. You can save it by pressing the F2 key, which will bring you back to the Paradox main menu.

A FEW FINISHING TOUCHES

You've actually completed the master form at this point, but you can add a few finishing touches to make the form easier to use. These

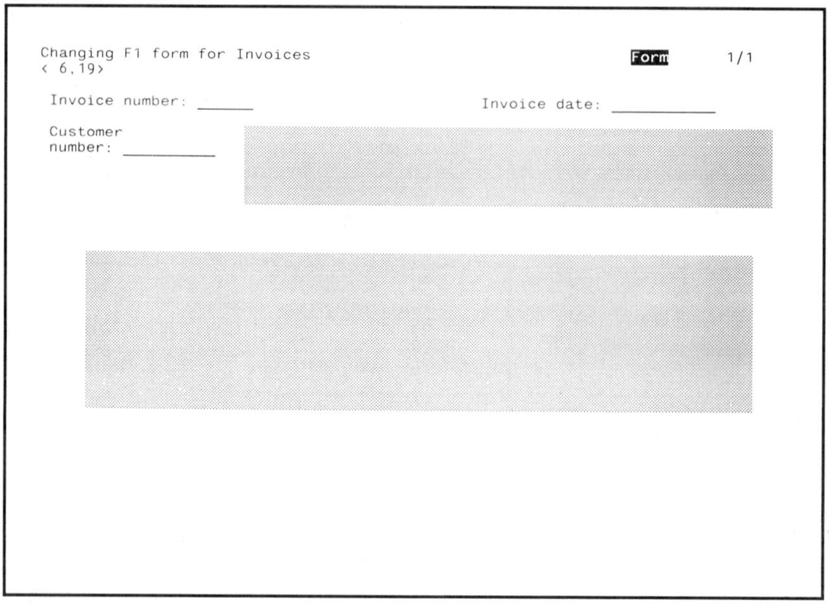

```
Changing F1 form for Invoices                           Form    1/1
< 6,19>
  Invoice number: _____              Invoice date: _____
    Customer
    number: _____
```

Figure 14.47: The master form with two embedded forms.

finishing touches focus on the help-and-fill options that we originally discussed in Chapter 12, and they will allow you to look up information on the various tables as needed (so you do not have to memorize part numbers and customer numbers).

First, you need to bring the master form onto the screen. To do so, select Modify and Edit from the Paradox main menu. When prompted for a table name, press Enter and select Invoices. Then, press F10 again, and select the Image, PickForm, and 1 options.

To add a help-and-fill option to the Customer Number field, press the Tab key twice so the cursor lands in that field. Then press F10 and select the ValCheck and Define options. Press Enter when prompted to move to a field, select TableLookup, and press Enter when prompted for a table name. Select CustData as the lookup table. Select AllCorrespondingFields and then select HelpAndFill.

To add a help-and-fill feature to the Part No field in the lower box, first press the DownImage (F4) key twice to move the cursor to the Part No field (beneath the Part column heading). Press F10, select ValCheck and Define, and then press Enter. Select TableLookup and, when prompted for a table name, press Enter and select MastInv. Select AllCorrespondingFields, and then select HelpAndFill.

To save these new features, press F10 once again, select Image and KeepSet. Then press F2 to save the entire order-entry form.

USING THE MULTITABLE FORM

To try out the new multitable form, use it to enter a sample order. Press Clear All (Alt-F8) to start with a clear workspace. Then select the Modify and Edit options from the Main menu. Specify Invoices as the table to edit, and then switch to the custom form by pressing F10 and selecting the options Image, PickForm, and 1.

Type in an invoice number, such as 111111 and press Enter. To enter the current date as the invoice date, press the space bar three times and then press Enter.

Rather than entering a customer number arbitrarily, press F1 to get some help-and-fill help. A table of existing customers will appear. Press ↓ a few time to move the cursor to one of the choices (such as customer 1006), and then press F2 to select that customer.

When the order-entry form appears, you will notice that the customer's name and address did *not* automatically appear on the screen. This is normal. You must *re-sync* the tables to get this information to actually appear when entering new data. To do so, you can use either of two techniques:

- Press the "Re-Sync-Links" key (Ctrl-L).
- Press DownImage (F4) to move to the next "image" (box).

The customer name and address (which as you recall, is actually stored on the CustData table) appears on the form. Very handy! Now, let's try the help-and-fill in the "Detail" box. Press DownImage (F4) once or twice until the cursor lands beneath the Part column title. Press F1 to get some help in selecting a part number.

Again, you can move the cursor to any part number, using the ↓ and ↑ keys, and then press F2 to select whichever part number the cursor is on at the moment (such as A-100). Press Enter twice to move the cursor to the Qty field, and type a quantity. When you press Enter, the total sale calculation appears in the right-most column.

You can then either type in a new unit price (rather than using the "suggested" unit price from the MastInv table), or press Enter to add another order for this invoice. You may want to experiment with this form now on your own, pressing F1 whenever the cursor is in the Part column to get help in selecting a part number, and pressing F2 to select a part number from the MastInv table that appears. (Note that if you leave the Qty column blank on one of these lines, the calculated total remains blank.)

USING THE CURSOR ON A MULTITABLE FORM

You've already gained a little experience with the keys used to navigate a multitable form. In general, each subform that appears on the screen in a multitable form acts like any single "regular" form on the screen. That is, you can use the Tab, or arrow keys to move from field to field. However, these keys do not allow you to move from one subform to the next.

To move to the next subform on the screen, you must press the DownImage (F4) key. To move "up" to the previous subform, you must press the UpImage key (F3).

On a multitable form being used to edit existing data, the PgDn and PgUp keys work only when the cursor is in one of the fields for the "master" form. In this situation, the PgDn key moves down one record and the PgUp key moves up one record. When the cursor is in any of the subforms, the PgUp and PgDn keys either make data seem to disappear or just sound a beep. (If you do inadvertently press PgDn while the cursor is in a subform, and data disappears, press PgUp as many times as necessary to bring the missing data back onto the screen.)

As usual, when you are done entering or editing data via a multitable form, press F2 to save your changes, or press F10 and select Cancel to cancel them all.

HOW PARADOX MANAGES MULTITABLE FORMS

> When a multitable form forbids you from changing or deleting information, you can still access any single table represented on the multitable form, using the usual table view or form view, to make changes.

As you gain experience using multitable forms, you may find that Paradox occasionally refuses to let you delete or change certain information once it has been entered. That's because Paradox uses a built-in scheme, called *referential integrity*, to protect the relationships among data in the related tables. Paradox applies four basic rules to editing on multitable forms:

- You cannot delete a record in the master table while linked records in the detail tables depend on it. For example, if a customer on the CustData table has outstanding orders in the Invoices table, you cannot delete that customer until you've deleted his outstanding orders.

- If you change a linking field in the master record, Paradox automatically changes the values in the detail tables. For example, if you change a customer's ID number on the CustData table, all outstanding orders for that customer on a separate Orders table are automatically changed to that new number.

> Paradox 3.5 lets you link up to nine detail tables to a master table, while Paradox 3.0 allows only five when creating multitable forms.

- Once you begin editing a table using a multitable form, you cannot switch to table view using the usual Form Toggle (F7) key. You must press F2, or press F10 and select Cancel, to end the current multitable editing session.

- On a network, a multitable form places a full lock on all the tables accessed on the form. Other users on the network will be able to access the locked data *only* if they use the same multitable form.

SUMMARY

Complete mastery of the Paradox report generator will require some practice as well as a knowledge of the tools that are available to you. In this section, we've had a chance to develop a report with calculated fields, summary fields, subtotals, and totals. We've also been able to discuss many general options available from the Report menu. But the key to mastering the report generator is simply practice.

Creating reports is very much an iterative process. You design a little, make a quick printout (using Instant Report or the Output option from the Report menu), then design a little more and see the results. Keep doing so until your report looks exactly as you want it to, and save the report specification with the DO-IT! key.

Particular topics of importance that we've discussed in this chapter are summarized below:

- To insert, delete, copy, move, or modify fields in a tabular report, select the TableBand option from the Report menu.

- To place fields in a tabular report format, call up the Report menu and select Field.

- To display the results of calculations on fields in a record, enter a calculated field using the Field, Place, and Calculated options from the Report menu.

- To group records in a report, select the Group option from the Report menu.

- To display subtotals in a report, place a summary field at the bottom of a group band.

- To display grand totals in a report, place a summary field in the report band at the bottom of the report specification.

- To include multiple groups (or subtotals of subtotals), use nested group bands.

- To insert blank lines in a report specification, press Enter while Insert mode is on.

- To delete blank lines in a report specification, move the cursor to the leftmost column of the blank line and type Ctrl-Y.

- To specify sort orders for groups in a report, select the Sort-Direction option from the Group submenu.

- To print summary reports, remove all field templates from the table band and place them in the group band beneath.

- To display data from multiple tables in a report, make sure the common field is keyed, and then select the Field, Lookup, and Link options from the menu.
- You can create forms that display data from multiple tables, as well as forms that display multiple records from one table, using the Multi option on the forms design screen menu.

AUTOMATIC UPDATING

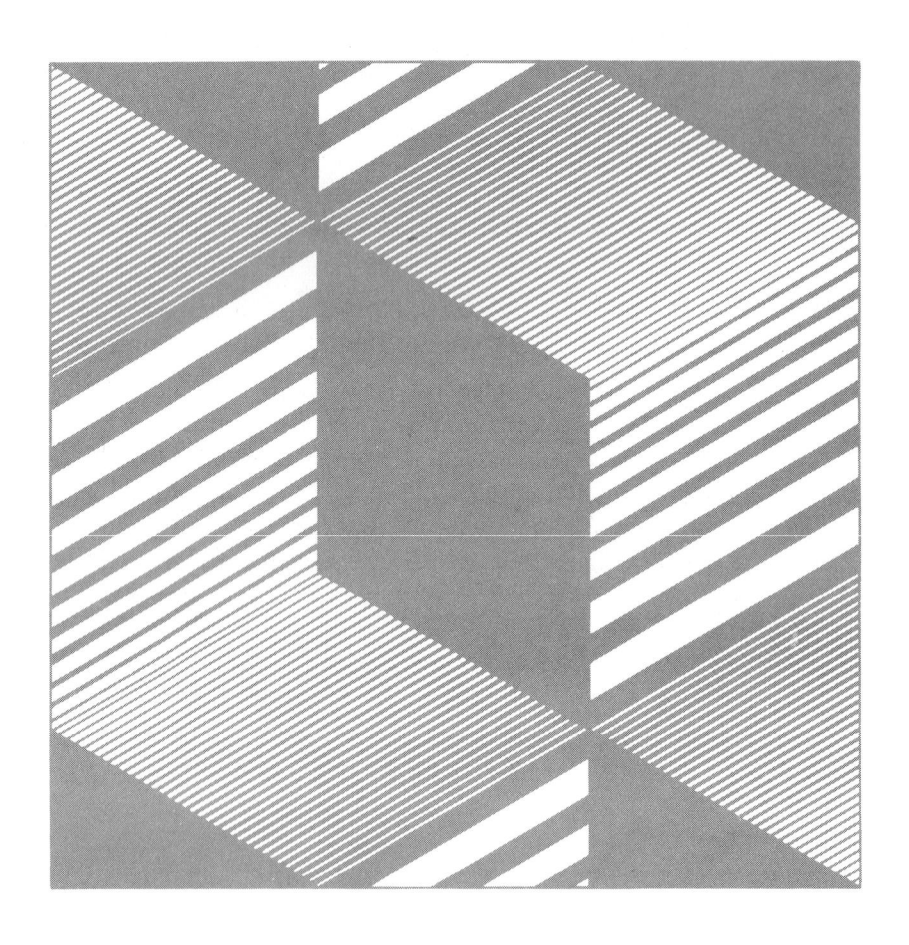

CHAPTER 15

UPDATING IS A PROCESS WHEREBY THE CONTENTS of one table are modified based on the contents of another. In this chapter, we'll show a technique for updating the Mastinv table based on the contents of the Sales and Purchase tables that we developed in Chapter 12. That is, the quantities of items sold will be subtracted from the in-stock quantities, and the purchases (items received) will be added to the in-stock quantities. Furthermore, items from the Purchase table will be subtracted from the on-order quantities (which assumes that these items were actually received), and the current purchase price in the Mastinv table will be changed to reflect the current purchase price in the Purchase table.

Before we begin, we need to discuss one problem that always accompanies an updating procedure. That is, how to differentiate between records that have already been updated (or *posted to* the Mastinv table) and those that have not. If we sell five racing bicycles and record this on the Sales table, then update the Mastinv table, the in-stock quantity of the racing bicycles will properly be decreased by five. However, we have to be sure not to update this same transaction again in the future, or the in-stock quantity on the Mastinv table will erroneously be decreased by five once again.

One way to handle this situation is to move all records that have already been updated from the Sales and Purchase tables onto separate *history tables*. This technique offers several advantages:

1. The current Sales and Purchase tables can be kept relatively small for quicker processing and easier access to current data.

2. On a floppy disk system, large history tables can periodically be transferred to other disks, thereby avoiding the problem of running out of disk space.

3. History tables encourage the use of *adjustment transactions* to make corrections, which leave a permanent audit trail of all events that have influenced the Mastinv table.

Let's set up some history tables for our inventory system.

HISTORY TABLES

A history table generally has the same structure as the associated transaction table. In this example, we'll create a history table named Salhist with the same structure as the Sales table. Select the Tools, Copy, and Table options from the Main and submenus. Specify Sales as the table to copy from and Salhist as the table to copy to.

Once the copy is complete, make sure the Salhist table is empty. To do so, select the Tools, More, and Empty options and specify Salhist as the table to empty. Select Ok when Paradox asks you to verify your request.

To create a history table for the Purchase table, named Purhist, select the Tools, Copy, and Table options, and specify Purchase as the table to copy from and Purhist as the table to copy to. Again, to ensure that you're starting with an empty table, select the Tools, More, and Empty options and specify Purhist as the table to empty. Select Ok when Paradox asks you to verify.

Now our entire inventory database consists of five tables, as shown in Figure 15.1. At the moment, the Sales and Purchase tables have some data on them, and both history tables are empty. After performing an update, the Sales and Purchase tables will be empty, and the Salhist and Purhist tables will contain the updated records.

As new sales and purchases occur, these will be added to the Sales and Purchase tables. However, as soon as an automated update takes place, the new records in Sales and Purchase will be added to the Salhist and Purhist tables. Hence, both history tables will tend to grow indefinitely, while Sales and Purchases grow only between updates.

AUTOMATING AN UPDATE PROCEDURE

Updating involves quite a few steps, so your best bet is to record all the required keystrokes in a script. If you're planning on following along

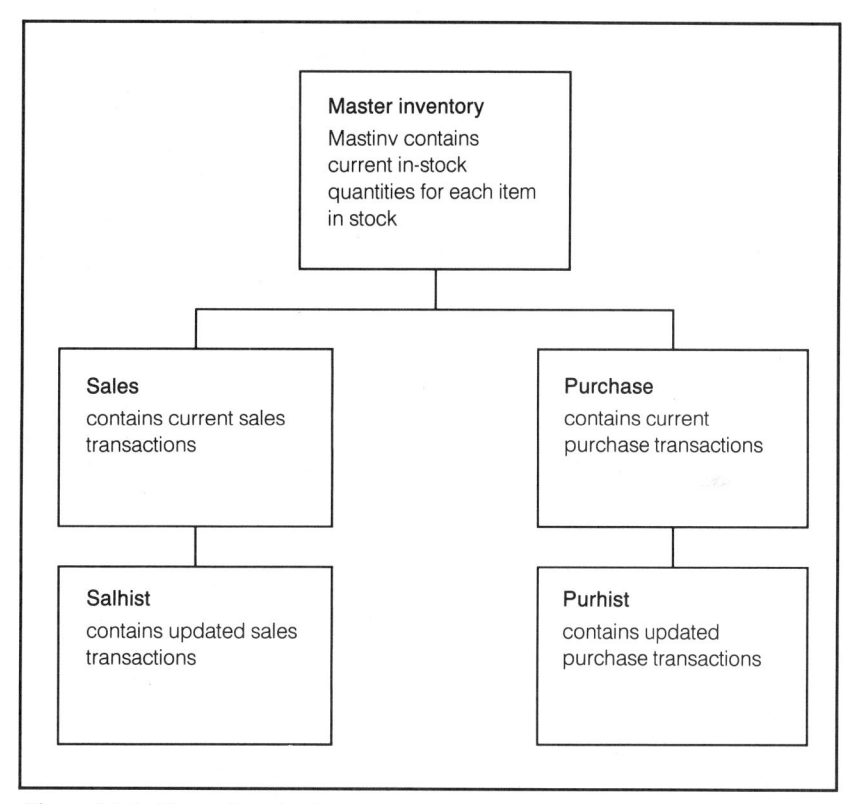

```
                    ┌──────────────────────┐
                    │ Master inventory     │
                    │ Mastinv contains     │
                    │ current in-stock     │
                    │ quantities for each item │
                    │ in stock             │
                    └──────────┬───────────┘
                  ┌────────────┴────────────┐
        ┌─────────┴────────┐      ┌─────────┴──────────┐
        │ Sales            │      │ Purchase           │
        │ contains current sales  │ contains current   │
        │ transactions     │      │ purchase transactions│
        └─────────┬────────┘      └─────────┬──────────┘
        ┌─────────┴────────┐      ┌─────────┴──────────┐
        │ Salhist          │      │ Purhist            │
        │ contains updated sales  │ contains updated   │
        │ transactions     │      │ purchase transactions│
        └──────────────────┘      └────────────────────┘
```

Figure 15.1: Five tables in the inventory system

on-line at this point, make sure you have a few minutes to complete all the necessary steps. Once you've saved all the keystrokes, you need only play the script to perform a complete update in the future.

RECORDING THE SCRIPT

To start recording the script, call up the Main menu and select the Scripts and BeginRecord options. Then enter the name Invupdat for the script. To be sure the script always starts with a clear screen, press Clear All (Alt-F8). Now we can begin the update.

SUMMARIZING THE SALES TRANSACTIONS

The first step in performing the update is to total and summarize all the sales transactions. To do so, select Ask from the Main menu and specify the Sales table. Place a check mark in the Part No column and the instruction

    Calc sum

in the Qty Sold column, as shown in Figure 15.2. Press F2. The summarized table will appear on the screen as in the bottom of Figure 15.2.

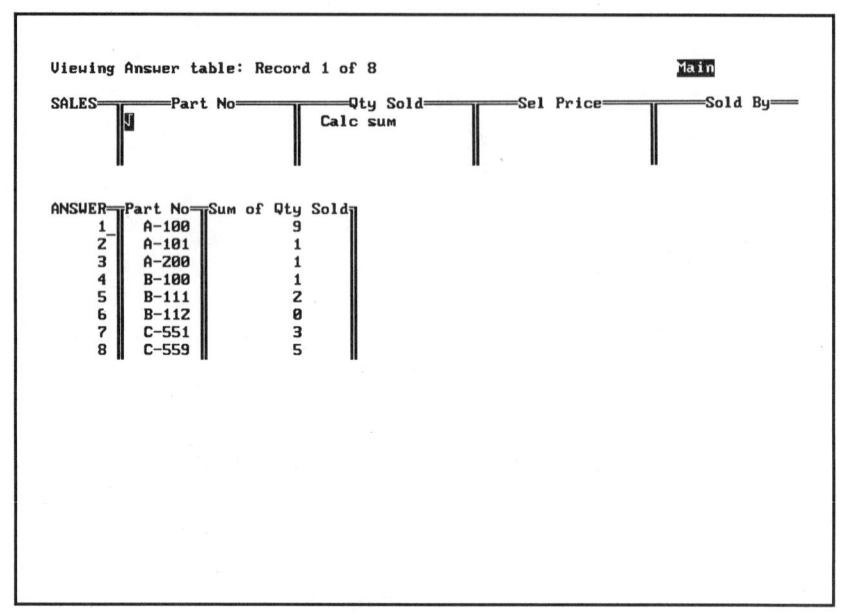

```
Viewing Answer table: Record 1 of 8                              Main
SALES=======Part No=========Qty Sold=========Sel Price=========Sold By===
       √                    Calc sum



ANSWER==Part No==Sum of Qty Sold=
     1   A-100          9
     2   A-101          1
     3   A-200          1
     4   B-100          1
     5   B-111          2
     6   B-112          0
     7   C-551          3
     8   C-559          5
```

Figure 15.2: Summary (totals) of sales transactions

SUBTRACTING SALES FROM MASTER QUANTITIES

The next step is to subtract the sums in this Sum of Qty Sold field from the Mastinv table. Follow these steps to do so:

1. Press Up Image (F3).

2. Press Clear Image (F8).

3. Call up a query form for the Answer table (call up the menu (F10), select Ask, and specify the Answer table).

4. Enter an example in the Part No field (move the cursor to the Part No field, press F5, type **XXX**, and press Enter).

5. Enter an example in the Sum of Qty Sold field (press F5 and type Sqty).

The query form should now look like the top of Figure 15.3.

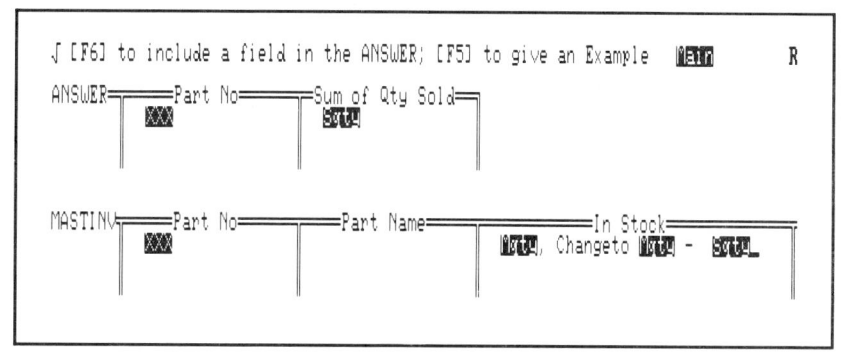

```
√ [F6] to include a field in the ANSWER; [F5] to give an Example    Main    R
ANSWER╤═══Part No═══╤═══Sum of Qty Sold═══╗
       │   XXX      │   Sqty              │


MASTINV╤═══Part No═══╤═══Part Name═══╤═══In Stock═══════════════╗
       │   XXX       │               │  Mqty, Changeto Mqty - Sqty
```

Figure 15.3: A query to update Mastinv from the Sales table

Next, fill in a query form for the Mastinv table that will subtract the sums of quantities sold from the in-stock quantities. Here are the steps:

1. Bring up a query form for Mastinv (call up the menu, select Ask, and specify the Mastinv table).

2. Enter an Example for the Part No field (move the cursor to the Part No field, press F5, type **XXX**, and press Enter).

3. Enter an example and formula in the In Stock field. (Move the cursor to the In Stock field, press F5, and type **Mqty**. Then type in a comma and a space, followed by the command

    Changeto Mqty – Sqty

    Remember to press the Example (F5) key before entering Mqty and Sqty.)

The query form for the Mastinv table should look like the lower one in Figure 15.3. Perform the query by pressing DO-IT!. You'll see the Changed table, which displays copies of changed records with their original values. But before you check that actual changes have taken place on the Mastinv table, we have some more work to do.

MOVING RECORDS TO THE HISTORY TABLE

Next, we need to move the updated records from the Sales table to the Salhist table, then empty all records from the Sales table. Here are the steps:

1. Clear the screen (press Alt-F8).
2. Append records from the Sales table to the bottom of the Salhist table (select the Tools, More, and Add options, and specify Sales as the source table to copy from and Salhist as the target table to copy to).
3. Empty the Sales table (call up the menu, select Tools, More, and Empty, specify the Sales table, and select Ok).

That takes care of the Sales table. Now let's do the same for the Purchase table. This update is a little more complex, because we need to add quantities from Purchase to quantities in Mastinv, then subtract these same values from the Mastinv OnOrder field, updating the purchase price at the same time. The first task is to summarize the purchase transactions.

SUMMARIZING THE PURCHASE TRANSACTIONS

In order to summarize the purchase transactions, you must follow these steps:

1. Clear the screen (press Alt-F8).
2. Call up a query form (select Ask and specify Purchase).
3. Calculate the sum of the quantity ordered and the highest purchase price for each individual part number (place a check mark in the Part No field, the instruction Calc sum in the Qty Recd field, and the instruction Calc max in the Pur Price field, as shown in the top of Figure 15.4).

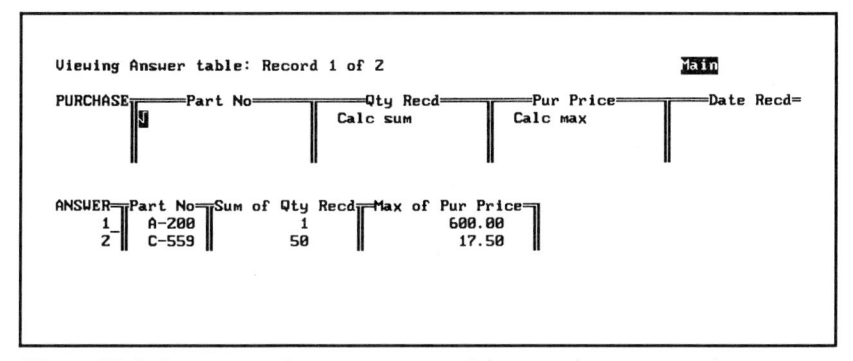

```
Viewing Answer table: Record 1 of 2                              Main
PURCHASE┬──Part No──┬──────┬──Qty Recd─┬──────┬──Pur Price─┬──────┬──Date Recd─
        │ y         │      │ Calc sum  │      │ Calc max   │      │
        │           │      │           │      │            │      │


ANSWER┬─Part No─┬─Sum of Qty Recd─┬─Max of Pur Price─┐
    1 │ A-200   │        1        │      600.00      │
    2 │ C-559   │       50        │       17.50      │
```

Figure 15.4: A query and answer summarizing purchase transactions

4. Press DO-IT! to perform the query.

Note that we've used Calc max to calculate the purchase price with which to update the Mastinv table purchase price. Ideally, we would want the most recent purchase price, but there is no command to calculate the most recent price. Calc max will calculate the most recent *date* when used in a Date field, but Pur Price is a Currency field. So, since we can't calculate the most recent purchase price, we've used the next best value—the highest purchase price. (Since prices seem to always go up, this is a reasonable alternative.)

ADDING PURCHASES TO MASTER QUANTITIES

After the Answer table has appeared, fill in query forms to update the Mastinv table from the Answer table. These are the steps:

1. Move up to the query form (press F3).

2. Delete the query form (press F8).

3. Call up a query form for the Answer table (call up the menu, select Ask, and specify Answer as the table to query).

4. Type in examples. (Put the cursor in the Part No field, press F5, and type **XXX**. Move the cursor to the Sum of Qty Recd field, press F5, and type **Pqty**. Move the cursor to the Max of Pur Price field, press F5, and type **Pprice**.)

Your query form should look like the top of Figure 15.5.

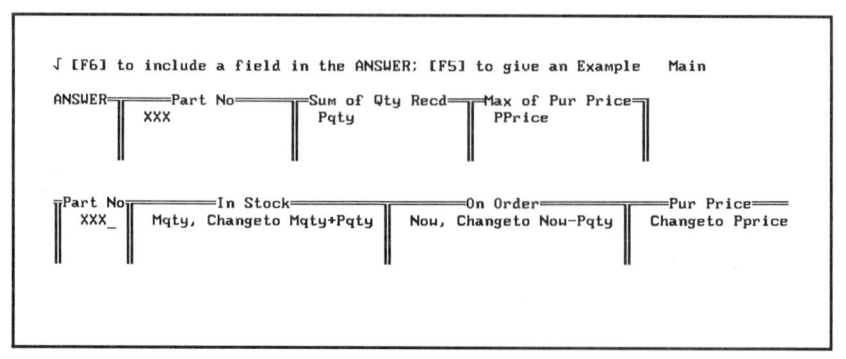

```
√ [F6] to include a field in the ANSWER; [F5] to give an Example    Main
ANSWER╤═══════Part No═══════╤═══Sum of Qty Recd═╤═Max of Pur Price═╗
      │        XXX          │        Pqty       │       PPrice     ║


  ╥Part No╤════════════════╤═══In Stock═══════╤═══════On Order═══════╤══Pur Price══╗
  ║  XXX_ │   Mqty, Changeto Mqty+Pqty        │  Now, Changeto Now-Pqty │ Changeto Pprice ║
```

Figure 15.5: A query to update Mastinv from the Purchase table

Next, enter examples and formulas into a query form for the Mastinv table that will add purchases to the in-stock quantities, subtract them from the on-order quantities, and replace the value in the Pur Price field with the maximum of the latest purchase price. To do this, follow these steps:

1. Call up a query form for Mastinv (press Menu, select Ask, and specify Mastinv).

2. Place an example in the Part No field (move the cursor to the Part No field, press F5, and type **XXX**).

3. Place examples and a formula in the In Stock field. (Move the cursor to the In Stock field, press F5, and type **Mqty**. Then type a comma and the instruction **Changeto**, press F5 again, type **Mqty** and a + sign, press F5 again, and type **Pqty**.)

4. Place examples and a formula in the On Order field. (Move the cursor to the On Order field, press F5, type **Now**, a comma, and the **Changeto** instruction; press F5, type **Now**, then enter a minus sign (hyphen), press F5, and type **Pqty**.)

5. Place an example and formula in the Pur Price field. (Move the cursor to the Pur Price field, type in the command **Changeto**, press F5, and type **Pprice**.)

The examples and formulas in the Mastinv query should appear as they do in Figure 15.5. Note, however, that I've rearranged the columns to better fit them on the screen. Be sure to get the right formula in the right field. (Also note that the previous Answer table may still be showing on your screen.)

When both query forms are complete, perform the update by pressing F2.

MOVING PURCHASE TRANSACTIONS TO THE PURHIST TABLE

The last step in the update is to move all purchases from the Purchase table to the Purhist table, and then empty the Purchase table. This is done by following these steps:

1. Clear the screen (press Alt-F8).
2. Copy records to Purhist (select the Tools, More, and Add options, and specify Purchase as the source table with records to copy and Purhist as the target table to which the records will be copied).
3. Empty the Purchase table (call up the menu, select the Tools, More, and Empty options, specify Purchase as the table to empty, and select Ok).
4. Clear the screen (press Alt-F8).

COMPLETING THE SCRIPT

You can stop recording the Invupdat script now by selecting the Script and End-Record options from the menus.

VERIFYING THE UPDATE

If you are using Paradox on a network, see "Update Queries on a Network" in Appendix B.

To verify that the update worked properly, view the Mastinv table. As Figure 15.6 shows, some values in the In Stock, On Order, and Pur Price columns have changed. For example, part number C-559 now shows 70 units in stock, because five were sold and 50 were received. There are no Flexie Skateboards on order because of the 50 that were received. The purchase price is now $17.50, as was indicated on the Purchase table.

```
Part No  Part Name                In Stock  ReOrder  On Order  Order Date  Pur Price  Location
-------  ----------------------   --------  -------  --------  ----------  ---------  --------
A-100    Gershwin Bicycle                1        5         0     1/31/90     450.00  J-111
A-101    Nikono Bicycle                 49       35         0     1/31/90     375.00  J-112
A-200    Racing Bicycle                  2        3         0     2/01/90     600.00  M-991
B-100    Safety Helmet (Nikono)         49       10         0     2/15/90      20.00  L-111
B-111    Safety Helmet (Carrera)         0       10         0     2/15/90      40.00  J-333
B-112    Safety Helmet (Ozzy)            0       10        25     1/31/90      15.00  L-225
C-551    Hobie Skateboard               47       75         0     4/15/90      45.00  S-911
C-559    Flexie Skateboard              70       25         0     4/15/90      17.50  S-912
```

Figure 15.6: The Mastinv table after an automated update

Also, if you view either the Sales or Purchase tables, you'll see that both are empty. Viewing the Salhist and Purhist tables will show where the data went.

To test the whole procedure again, add a couple of records to both the Sales and Purchase tables. Now call up the menu, select Scripts and either Play or ShowPlay, and specify the Invupdat script. Then just sit back and relax for a couple of minutes while the script performs the new update and takes care of all the transactions.

DEVELOPING A SCHEDULE

Systems that use automated updating should be run on some kind of a schedule. In inventory systems, updates are often performed every day. (Bookkeeping systems, on the other hand, are often posted only once a month.) You should develop a routine for updating, such as the one below:

1. Add new transactions to the Sales and Purchase tables during business hours.

2. Print current Sales and Purchase reports at the end of each day.

3. Make any necessary corrections *before* the update is performed.

4. Perform the update after verifying sales and purchases.

5. Print the current master inventory data after the update.

Notice that the schedule specifies that current sales and purchases be printed before the update, since these records will be moved off the current Sales and Purchase tables during the update. Any corrections should be made before the update (though this is not essential). The master inventory table is then updated and contains only up-to-the-minute data.

CORRECTING UPDATED TRANSACTIONS

Occasionally, you may discover that a sales or purchase transaction which has already been updated was incorrect. This might be caused by a typographical error, or perhaps by an individual returning an item and receiving a refund.

One way to rectify this situation would be to edit the Salhist or Purhist table directly, then edit the Mastinv table directly. However, doing so leaves no audit trail to explain the change.

The preferred method for making such a correction would be to make an *adjustment transaction*. For example, you may have noticed that the Sales database (see Figure 12.18) contained a record with the following data:

Part_No	Qty_Sold	Sel_Price	Sold_By	Remarks
B-112	-2	22.50	BBG	Return and Refund

Notice that the number sold is a negative number (-2), and the Remarks field (which, as you see, can be a very useful field to have) explains the situation. During updating, this negative value will be subtracted from the In Stock quantity (thereby increasing the quantity). This method provides an accurate In Stock quantity as well as a record of the change in the Salhist table for future auditing.

A MASTER INVENTORY REPORT

You may want to develop some formatted reports for your master inventory table, though a simple Instant Report (Alt-F7) will tell you a lot. Perhaps the most important data you'll need, however, is a list of items that must be reordered. To get this information, simply view records with reorder points that are greater than the sum of the In Stock and On Order fields. Figure 15.7 shows a query that will pull these records out of the Mastinv table for you.

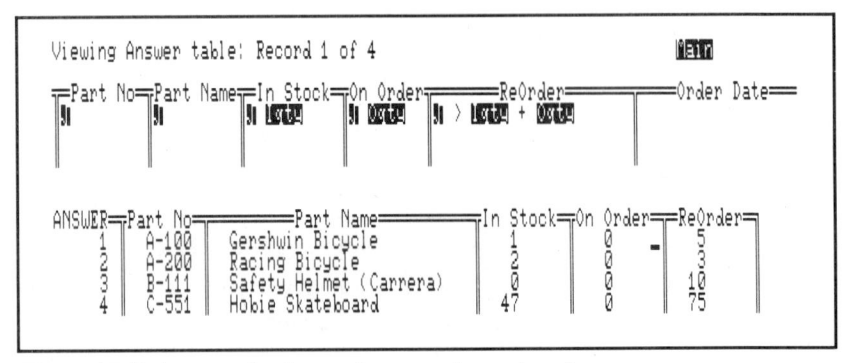

```
Viewing Answer table: Record 1 of 4                          Main
┌Part No┬Part Name┬In Stock┬On Order┬════ReOrder════┬═Order Date═
│       │         │ Check  │ Check  │ > Check + Check│
│       │         │        │        │                │

ANSWER┬Part No──┬─────Part Name─────┬In Stock┬On Order┬ReOrder┐
    1 │ A-100   │ Gershwin Bicycle  │   1    │   0    │   5
    2 │ A-200   │ Racing Bicycle    │   2    │   0    │   3
    3 │ B-111   │ Safety Helmet (Carrera) │ 0 │   0    │  10
    4 │ C-551   │ Hobie Skateboard  │  47    │   0    │  75
```

Figure 15.7: A query for items that must be ordered

Of course, you can develop formatted reports for your Mastinv table and use the JustFamily copying procedure we discussed earlier to print data based on queries from the table.

SUMMARY

- Automatic updating allows you to change the values in one table based on the values in another.
- To avoid errors during updating procedures, you can copy updated records to separate history tables as soon as the update is complete.
- To perform an update, first summarize and total data in the transaction table, then set up query forms for the Answer and master tables with appropriate examples and formulas.
- To copy updated transactions to a history table, use the Tools, More, and Add options.

- To empty updated transactions from a transaction table, use the Tools, More, and Empty options.

- To correct transactions that have already been updated, enter *adjustment transactions* into the current transaction tables.

MANAGING FILES

CHAPTER 16

AS YOU DEVELOP MORE PARADOX *OBJECTS* (TABLES, forms, reports, and scripts), you'll need to learn techniques for managing them. The Tools option from the Main menu provides options for renaming, copying, deleting, and viewing objects. The Tools menu also provides options for importing and exporting data between Paradox and other database or spreadsheet programs, as well as for protecting data. We've used several options from the Tools menu already in previous chapters. In this chapter, we'll round out our knowledge of the Tools capability and discuss general techniques for managing objects.

When you select Tools from the Main menu, the submenu displays the following options:

    Rename QuerySpeed ExportImport Copy Delete Info
    Net More

We'll discuss each of these options below (except for Net, which is the option for networking. If you are using Paradox on a network, be sure to read your *Network Administrator's Guide*, as many of these options perform differently on a network).

RENAMING OBJECTS

■ If you are using Paradox on a network, see "Tools on a Network" in Appendix B.

To rename a table or other object, select the Rename option from the Tools menu. The submenu will provide these options:

    Table Form Report Script Graph

Once you select one of these options, Paradox will help you identify the object you want to rename, then ask for the new name. If the new name you enter is the same as an existing name, Paradox will ask for confirmation before deleting the original object and replacing it with the object being renamed.

The Rename option can be especially useful with the Answer table. If you perform a complex query whose results you wish to save for future use, simply rename the Answer table. The renamed Answer table will be as readily available as any other Paradox table.

COPYING OBJECTS

To make copies of objects, select Copy from the Tools menu. The submenu will display the following options:

Table   Form   Report   Script   JustFamily   Graph

Copying is useful for making backups of important data or for creating a new form or report that is similar to an existing form or report. When you decide to copy a table, Paradox will ask for the name of the table to copy and a name for the copy. The copy will include all the objects associated with the original table, including forms and reports.

The Form and Report options copy forms and reports. These are used primarily when you want to design a new form or report that is similar to an existing form or report. Paradox will display two options when you copy a report or form: SameTable and DifferentTable. Select SameTable if you want to copy the form or report to a new number in the same table, or DifferentTable to copy the form or report to a different table. Paradox will prompt you for the name of the table that contains the form or report, the number of the form or report to copy, and a number for the copied form or report.

The Scripts and Graph options let you make copies of scripts and graphs.

The JustFamily option copies all the objects associated with a table (for instance, forms and reports) without copying the table itself.

DELETING OBJECTS

The Delete option from the Tools menu provides these options:

Table   Form   Report   Script   QuerySpeedup   KeepSet
ValCheck   Graph

As you can see, the Delete option allows you to delete anything, including image settings and validity checks assigned to a table.

Do be careful, however, when deleting objects. Once deleted, they cannot be recovered. Before deleting an object, Paradox will double-check and allow you to change your mind, using the usual display:

Cancel   Ok

Select Ok to delete or Cancel to cancel your request.

COPYING RECORDS FROM ONE TABLE TO ANOTHER

In Chapter 15 we saw a technique for moving copies of records from one table to another using the Tools, More, and Add options. These options can also be used to combine information from several tables into a single table. There are a few minor catches to watch out for when using the Tools, More, and Add options:

- The two tables must have compatible structures. This means that you cannot add records from a table containing Last Name, First Name, and Address fields to a table containing Amount, Qty, and Date fields. If you wish to combine tables with incompatible structures, you should use multiple-query forms, then rename the Answer table, thereby creating a new table with a new structure.

- If two compatible tables are combined but the receiving table has a key field, records that violate the rule of uniqueness in the key field will be displayed in the Keyviol table. As discussed earlier, you can edit or delete records in the Keyviol table, then use Tools, More, and Add once again to add records from the Keyviol table to the receiving table. You must do so immediately though, because the Keyviol table is erased when you exit Paradox. (Optionally, just copy the Keyviol table using Tools Copy, and edit the copied Answer table when it's convenient to do so.)

REMOVING RECORDS FROM A TABLE

You can remove individual records from a table by simply pressing the Del key while in the Edit mode, or by using the Delete option in a query form. But you can also remove records from a table that match records in another table by using the Tools, More, and Subtract options. Let's look at an example.

Suppose you have an accounts-receivable system in which you bill clients at the end of the month for purchases made during the previous month. You store these charges on a table named Charges, as shown in Figure 16.1.

```
Viewing Charges table: Record 1 of 7                              Main
   CHARGES  Cust No   Part No      Qty      Unit Price    Purchase Date
      1      1001     A-111         2         100.00       10/01/90
      2      1009     B-222         4          20.00       10/09/90
      3      1002     A-111         5         100.00       10/15/90
      4      1003     A-111         6          25.00       10/30/90
      5      1005     J-555         1         550.00       11/07/90
      6      1004     K-444         2         447.00       11/11/90
      7      1001     S-911         1      42,000.00       11/12/90
```

Figure 16.1: Charges on the Charges table

At the end of November, you want to isolate charges for the month of October. You could set up a query like the one in Figure 16.2 to pull out all records with purchase dates in October.

Next, using the Tools, Rename, and Table options, you rename the Answer table as Billed. Now the Billed table contains only transactions for the month of October, as shown in Figure 16.3. Now you could use Tools, Copy, and JustFamily to copy a report specification

```
Viewing Answer table: Record 1 of 4                          Main
CHARGES╤═Cust No═╤═Part No═╤═Qty═╤═Unit Price═╤═Purchase Date═╗
       ║ √+      ║ √+      ║ √+  ║ √+         ║ √+ 10/00/00   ║


ANSWER╤═Cust No═╤═Part No═╤═Qty═╤═Unit Price═╤═Purchase Date═╗
    1 ║ 1001    ║ A-111   ║  2  ║  100.00    ║  10/01/90     ║
    2 ║ 1009    ║ B-222   ║  4  ║   20.00    ║  10/09/90     ║
    3 ║ 1002    ║ A-111   ║  5  ║  100.00    ║  10/15/90     ║
    4 ║ 1003    ║ A-111   ║  6  ║   25.00    ║  10/30/90     ║
```

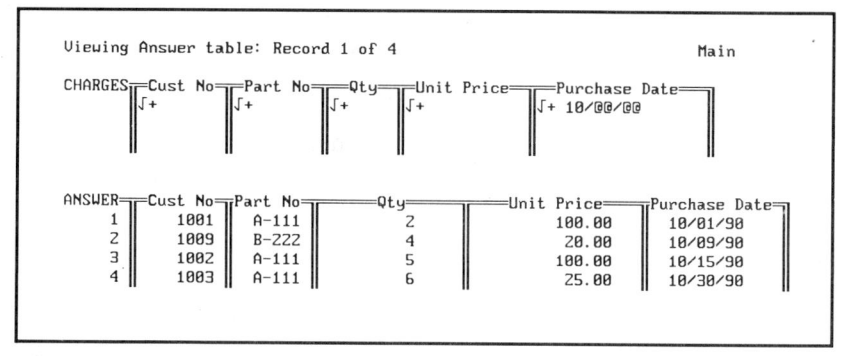

Figure 16.2: A query for charges in the month of October

```
Viewing Billed table: Record 1 of 4                          Main
BILLED╤═Cust No═╤═Part No═╤═Qty═╤═Unit Price═╤═Purchase Date═╗
    1 ║ 1001    ║ A-111   ║  2  ║  100.00    ║  10/01/90     ║
    2 ║ 1009    ║ B-222   ║  4  ║   20.00    ║  10/09/90     ║
    3 ║ 1002    ║ A-111   ║  5  ║  100.00    ║  10/15/90     ║
    4 ║ 1003    ║ A-111   ║  6  ║   25.00    ║  10/30/90     ║
```

Figure 16.3: Charges for the month of October on the Billed table

for printing invoices from any other table to the Billed table in order to print invoices.

Once the October transactions have been billed, they should be removed from the Charges table using the Tools, More, and Subtract options. Paradox will prompt you for the table names. Specify Billed as the table containing the transactions to be subtracted and Charges as the table from which to subtract these records. When done, the Charges table will no longer contain charges for the month of October, as shown in Figure 16.4.

EMPTYING A TABLE

In the last chapter, we saw how the Tools, More, and Empty options allow you to empty all transactions from a table. This is

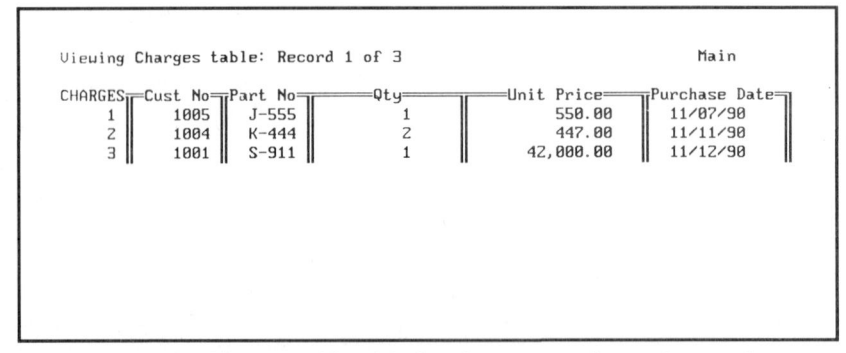

```
Viewing Charges table: Record 1 of 3                              Main
  CHARGES┬─Cust No─┬─Part No─┬────Qty────┬───Unit Price═┬─Purchase Date┐
    1    │  1005   │  J-555  │     1     │      550.00  │   11/07/90
    2    │  1004   │  K-444  │     2     │      447.00  │   11/11/90
    3    │  1001   │  S-911  │     1     │   42,000.00  │   11/12/90
```

Figure 16.4: The Charges table with October transactions subtracted

particularly useful in systems with automated updating, where updated transactions are copied to a history file (using Tools, More, and Add), then deleted from the current transactions table.

Selecting the Tools, More, and Empty options always asks for the name of the table to empty records from. Before actually erasing all the records, Paradox presents these options:

Cancel   Ok

To proceed, select Ok. If you change your mind, select Cancel. Use caution when making this decision. Once records are erased from a table, they cannot be retrieved.

PROTECTING DATA

There are two ways to protect a table or other object in Paradox. The *password* technique ensures that unauthorized users, who don't know the password you assign, can neither read nor change information in a table. The *write-protect* technique allows anybody to read data in a table, but prevents accidental changes to the data in a table.

Both protection schemes are available from the Tools, More, and Protect options. When selected, Paradox displays the following options:

Password   ClearPasswords   Write-protect

PASSWORD PROTECTION

If you select the Password option from the Protect submenu, Paradox will first display this menu:

Table   Script

(As discussed in Chapter 19, scripts can be encrypted so that they cannot be read or changed by users.) Once you select an option, Paradox will ask for the name of the table or script to protect. Then you'll see these instructions:

Password:
Enter new owner password, or press ← to remove all passwords.

Before you type in your password, note these important points:

- Case counts. That is, the password *Hello* is *not* the same as *hello*. Therefore, pay attention to case as you enter your password.

- The password does not appear on the screen as you type it. This is a safety precaution to prevent others from watching what you enter on the screen. If you type away madly waiting for something to appear on the screen, you will actually be entering your password as you do so.

- Once you enter your password, there is no way to view the table or script, or to remove the password if you do not know the password. Therefore, you should write down your password and store it in a safe place where you can find it easily.

- For obvious reasons, if your data is sensitive enough to deserve password protection, you should avoid obvious passwords like you first name, initials, or nickname. (Pet names are also common, and obvious, passwords.)

- If you decide to bail out now after reading the above, you can just press the Esc key to do so.

Once you decide on a password, type it in and press Enter. The screen will verify that you've typed it correctly by displaying the prompt

Password:
Enter password a second time to confirm.

Type in the same password again. (If you don't get it right, the screen will inform you of this. You can try again, or press Esc until the Main menu reappears to start all over.)

If you correctly enter your password a second time, you'll see a large form for entering *auxiliary passwords*. Unless you are working on a network, auxiliary passwords will probably not be necessary. To bypass the auxiliary passwords, press F2. You'll see the message

Encrypting...

at the bottom right corner of the screen, and then be returned to the Main menu.

In the future, when you attempt to view or work with the password-protected table, you'll see the message below before Paradox gives you any access to the table:

Password:
Enter password for this table to view it.

If you attempt to edit a protected script, using the Scripts Editor and Edit options from the menu, you'll be given the instructions

Password:
Enter script password before you can edit it.

You must type in the correct password to proceed. Again, the password will *not* appear on the screen as you type it, so type carefully. Press Enter after typing in the password.

If you do not enter the correct password, Paradox will display the error message

Invalid password

and allow you to try again. If you cannot enter the correct password, your only alternative is to press Esc and return to the higher-level menu.

REACTIVATING PASSWORDS

Once you access a password-protected table or script by entering the appropriate password, Paradox allows you to access that table or script as often as you wish during the current session (that is, until you exit Paradox) without reentering the password.

This is convenient, as it can become tedious to reenter the password each time you need a table or script. But there is a drawback: If you walk away from your computer during the current session, anybody who sits down at your computer can also access all your password-protected tables and scripts without reentering the passwords. (This is even more of a problem on a network.)

To work around this problem, you can select the Tools, More, Protect, and ClearPasswords options from the menus. Doing so clears all the passwords that you've entered in the current session, so that the passwords will need to be reentered to access the tables or scripts again. (This option also clears the screen, as Alt-F8 does.)

When you select ClearPasswords, you'll be given the options

   Cancel   Ok

Selecting Ok will clear the previous password entries. Selecting Cancel cancels the commands, and retains free access to the scripts and tables during the current session.

WRITE PROTECTION

The Write-protect option on the Protect submenu acts as a temporary stopgap measure to prevent accidental changes to a table. A write-protected table can be viewed at any time, but cannot be changed in any way until the write-protection is removed. Unlike password-protection, write-protection can easily be removed by anyone without the use of a password.

If you attempt to change a write-protected table, Paradox will display a message such as

   This table is write-protected and cannot be modified

You cannot modify the table until the write-protection is removed.

When you select Write-protect from the Protect submenu, Paradox will ask for the name of the table to protect. Enter the table name in the usual manner. The screen will then display the options:

   Set   Clear

Select Set to enforce write-protection on the table. Select Clear to disable the previous write-protection.

SETTING A DIRECTORY

If you are a hard disk user who stores files on many different directories, you may occasionally wish to change the default directory for accessing files (objects). Normally, Paradox assumes that all objects are stored on the current directory (C:\PARADOX3 on most hard disk systems). You can change this by selecting the Tools, More, and Directory options. Paradox will then ask for the new working directory, as below:

**Directory: C:\PARADOX3\
Enter new working directory specification (e.g. a:\data or b:)**

Type in the drive specification (for instance, C:) and the directory name.

When you change directories, Paradox will delete all current temporary tables (for example, Answer and Keyviol). This avoids splitting a single application (such as accounts-receivable tables) onto separate directories.

Before changing directories, Paradox will ask for verification using the usual options:

   Cancel   Ok

GENERAL FILE INFORMATION

The Info option from the Tools menu provides a powerful and convenient way for viewing and printing your Paradox objects.

When you select the Info option, the following submenu is displayed:

Structure   Inventory   Family   Who   Lock

VIEWING TABLE STRUCTURES

If you select the Structure option from the Info submenu, Paradox will ask for the name of the table for which you wish to view the structure. As usual, you can type in a table name or press Enter to see a menu of existing tables, and then select a table by highlighting and pressing Enter. Paradox will then display the table structure as in Figure 16.5.

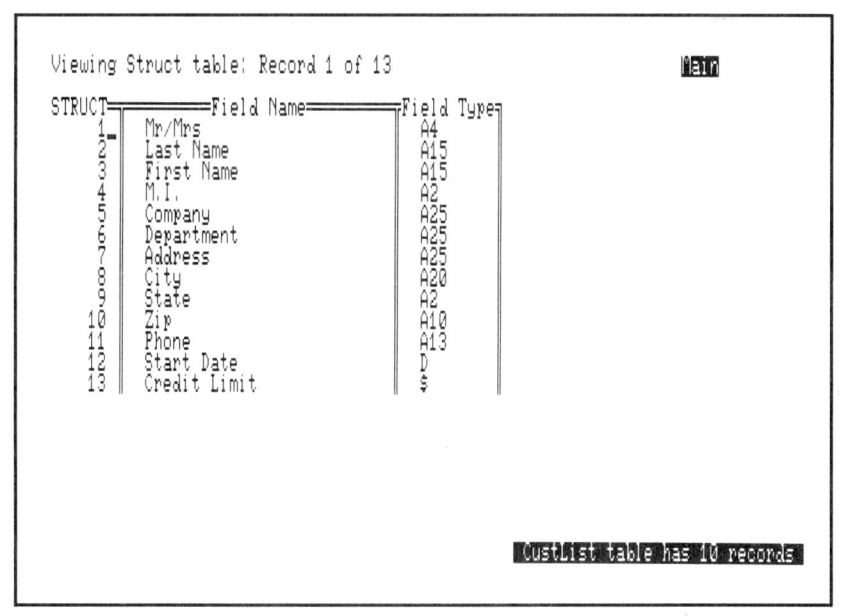

```
Viewing Struct table: Record 1 of 13                              Main
STRUCT     Field Name       Field Type
   1       Mr/Mrs           A4
   2       Last Name        A15
   3       First Name       A15
   4       M.I.             A2
   5       Company          A25
   6       Department       A25
   7       Address          A25
   8       City             A20
   9       State            A2
  10       Zip              A10
  11       Phone            A13
  12       Start Date       D
  13       Credit Limit     $

                                        CustList table has 10 records
```

Figure 16.5: A sample display from the Tools Info Structure option series

Although you can edit this structure using the usual arrow, Ins, and Del keys, you should not do so unless you plan on renaming the table after making your modifications. Info is really designed only to allow you to view a structure. Use the Modify and Restructure options to modify the structure of a table.

VIEWING THE FILE INVENTORY

Selecting the Inventory option from the Info submenu presents the following options:

Tables   Scripts   Files

These options present directories of existing objects. As the option names imply, selecting Tables displays the names of existing tables, Scripts displays the names of scripts, and Files displays the names of any files. Each option shows the name and the date of the last modification displayed in a special table named List, as shown in Figure 16.6.

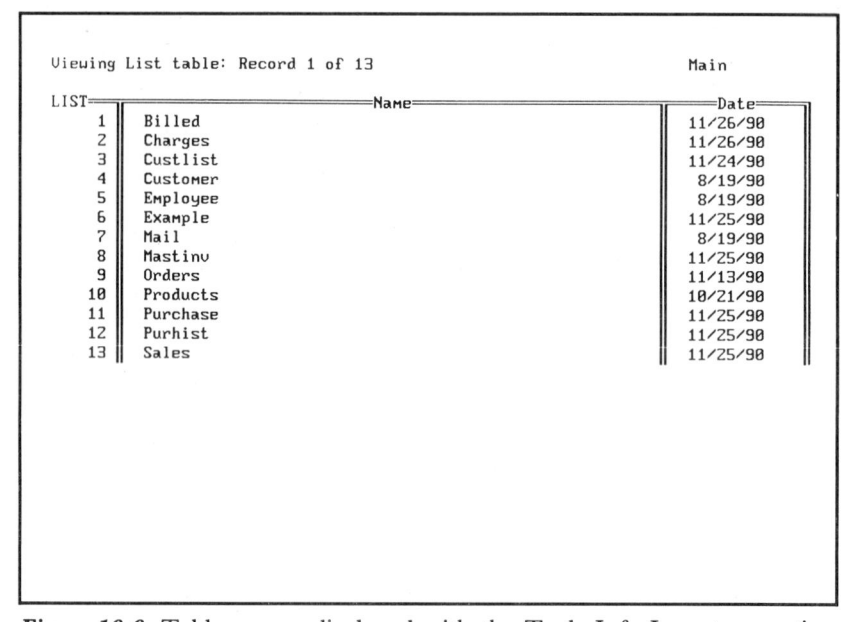

```
Viewing List table: Record 1 of 13                                Main
LIST                         Name                              Date
    1    Billed                                              11/26/90
    2    Charges                                             11/26/90
    3    Custlist                                            11/24/90
    4    Customer                                             8/19/90
    5    Employee                                             8/19/90
    6    Example                                             11/25/90
    7    Mail                                                 8/19/90
    8    Mastinv                                             11/25/90
    9    Orders                                              11/13/90
   10    Products                                            10/21/90
   11    Purchase                                            11/25/90
   12    Purhist                                             11/25/90
   13    Sales                                               11/25/90
```

Figure 16.6: Table names displayed with the Tools Info Inventory option series

When you first select either the Tables or Scripts option, Paradox will display this prompt:

Directory:
Enter directory for list of tables, or press ⏎ for working directory

Just pressing the Enter key will display tables or scripts on the currently logged drive. You can enter another drive or directory name instead, using the usual syntax (for instance, A: or C:\accounts).

Selecting the Files option from the Inventory submenu lets you view any group of files. When selected, Paradox will show this prompt:

Pattern:
Enter DOS directory pattern (e.g. *.TXT, or ⏎ for working directory)

You can use a question mark as a "wild-card" for a single character, or an asterisk for a group of characters. For example, *.* displays all files, while *.WRK displays only those files with the extension .WRK (Symphony worksheets, for example). The pattern *.DB? displays files with any first name and the letters DB as the first two characters of a three-character extension (that is, .DB, .DBF, .DBA, and so on).

You can specify a drive and directory as well. For example, the pattern C:\dbase*.DBF will display the names of all dBASE database files on a directory named dbase on drive C.

To print a copy of the screen, press Instant Report (Alt-F7). To clear the display, press Clear Image (F8).

VIEWING FAMILIES

The Family option from the Info submenu displays a table name and its associated objects (or *family*). When you select this option, Paradox will ask that you enter the table name, and then it will display the family as shown in Figure 16.7. Notice that the Custlist table includes validity checks in a VAL file (that is, a file named Custlist.VAL), two forms (named Custlist.F and Custlist.F1), and four reports (Custlist.R, .R1, .R2, .R3). (Your screen might show other family members.)

RESTRUCTURING A TABLE

Once you've created a table, added some data to it, and used it for a while, you may find that you want to change something about its

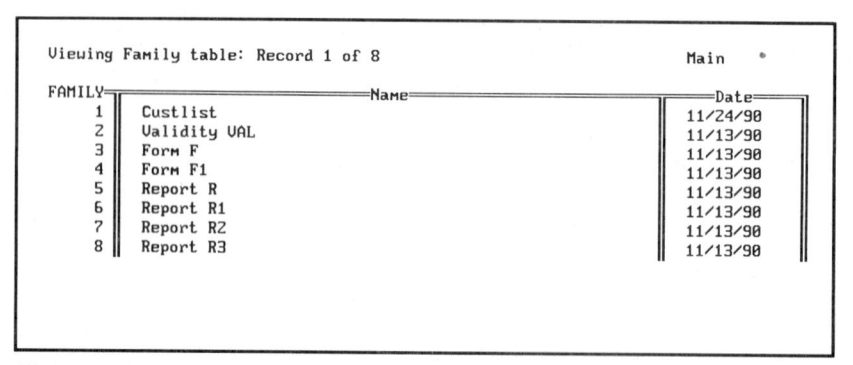

```
Viewing Family table: Record 1 of 8                    Main
FAMILY              Name                         Date
   1   Custlist                                  11/24/90
   2   Validity VAL                              11/13/90
   3   Form F                                    11/13/90
   4   Form F1                                   11/13/90
   5   Report R                                  11/13/90
   6   Report R1                                 11/13/90
   7   Report R2                                 11/13/90
   8   Report R3                                 11/13/90
```

Figure 16.7: The family of objects for the Custlist table

basic structure. For example, you might want to add a field for storing the phone number to the Custlist table. Or you may need to lengthen a field such as Company or Address.

ADDING A NEW FIELD

To modify the structure of a table, first select the Modify option from the Main menu, which brings up this familiar submenu:

   Sort   Edit   CoEdit   DataEntry   MultiEntry   Restructure

Then select the Restructure option. Paradox will ask for the name of the table to restructure. The current table structure appears on the screen, ready for editing.

You can use the arrow keys, as usual, to move the cursor around and make changes. The Ins and Del keys allow you to insert and delete fields.

SAVING THE NEW STRUCTURE

When you're satisfied with your new table structure, just press the DO-IT! (F2) key to save it. Paradox will display some messages as it updates the standard form and report formats, then return to the Main menu.

CHANGING YOUR MIND

If you make a mistake while restructuring a table and want to go back to the original structure, do *not* press the DO-IT! key. Instead, call up the menu (F10) and select the Cancel option. Paradox will ask for confirmation before canceling your current change.

DELETING A FIELD

To delete a field while the table structure is displayed, simply move the cursor to that field and press the Del key. Because doing so automatically erases all the data stored in the deleted field, Paradox will ask for confirmation before deleting the field, after you press DO-IT! (F2). You'll see the options

    Delete   Oops!

Select the Delete option to delete the field and all data stored in it. Optionally, select Oops! to cancel the deletion. At that point, you need to reinsert the deleted field, or call up the menu and select Cancel to recover the original table structure.

RENAMING A FIELD

To change the name of a field, simply move the cursor to the appropriate field name in the structure and type in the new name.

REARRANGING FIELDS

You can rearrange the order of fields in a table structure (though you can achieve a similar effect by just modifying the image on the screen in View or Edit mode). To move a field to a new position, place the cursor in the new position for the field and press the Ins key to insert a blank line. Type in the field name exactly as it is spelled in the original position. When you press the Enter key, Paradox will move the field from its original position to its new position.

CHANGING THE LENGTH OF A FIELD

Lengthening an alphanumeric field (for instance, from A20 to A25) will generally not cause any problems, though you might have to change the format of a custom form or report later to accommodate the new width (as discussed later in this chapter).

Shortening an alphanumeric field (for example, from A25 to A20) may cause some data loss if there are existing data longer than the new width. When you shorten an alphanumeric field and press DO-IT! Paradox will warn you if there is a potential data loss, then give you these three options for handling the potential loss:

Trimming   No-Trimming   Oops!

Selecting the Trimming option will simply truncate all data that are too long, so that they fit into the new width. Selecting the No-Trimming option will place all data that do not fit into a temporary table named Problems. You can then change the data in the Problems table and add them to the original table using the Tools option (discussed in this chapter). The Oops! option allows you to bow out gracefully and either re-enter the field width, or call up the menu and select Cancel to retain the original table structure.

CHANGING THE TYPE OF A FIELD

You can change field types (alphanumeric, numeric, currency, date), though the results may be similar to shortening an alphanumeric field (as discussed above). If there is a potential data loss, Paradox will warn you and give you the Trimming, No-Trimming, and Oops! options discussed above.

Generally, you won't want to change the type of data in a field. But in case you've made an error at the outset, it's easy enough to do. If you remember to put numeric values in either numeric or currency fields, dates in date fields, and everything else in alphanumeric fields, you probably will never have to change a field type.

Note: Paradox also offers the S field type for *short numbers*. A short field can contain whole numbers (no decimal places) in the range of −32,767 to 32,767. Until you are an experienced Paradox user, you should avoid using this field type. It has the advantage of conserving memory, but the small range of acceptable numbers makes it very restrictive. For example, the number 1.1 is not acceptable because it has a decimal place, and the zip code 40001 is too large.

SPEEDING UP QUERIES

The QuerySpeed option from the Tools menu allows you to enhance the speed of often-used queries. For example, if you regularly perform an automated update, you can use QuerySpeed to reduce the time required to perform the update.

To use this feature, fill out query forms as you normally would. (You can use the Scripts and QuerySave options to save the query.) While the query form is displayed, select the Tools and QuerySpeed options from the menu. In most cases, future queries using the same fields will run more quickly.

There are situations where QuerySpeed will not speed up or will even slow down a query. For example, if a query is based on a key field, Paradox will display this message:

No speedup possible

That's because the key field is already used to maximize the speed of the query.

The QuerySpeed option works by creating secondary index files (or key fields) that are updated whenever a query is performed. These secondary index files have two costs associated with them:

- They consume disk space.
- They require some time to update.

The significance of the first cost depends on how much disk space you have on your computer. If you're using a hard disk, this cost will be negligible for a single speed-up. However, each speed-up will require more index files, and the disk space will mount up if you attempt to use this option with every query form.

The second cost, time, is a different matter. If a table is very small, it may very well take more time to update the index and perform the query than it did to perform the query in the first place. Hence, QuerySpeed could actually slow things down. However, for an average-to-large-size table, QuerySpeed will probably enhance the speed noticeably.

INTERFACING WITH OTHER SOFTWARE SYSTEMS

The ExportImport option under the Tools menu allows you to transfer data to and from other software systems. When you select this option, your choices are

    Export   Import

Selecting either option displays the following submenu:

    Quattro Pro   1-2-3   Symphony   dBase   Pfs   Reflex
    Visicalc   Ascii

Let's first discuss each of these options in general terms, then look at some creative ways to import and export data. One important point to keep in mind is that Paradox always converts data through copies of files. In all cases, your original data are left unchanged, and converted data are copied to a new file with a name you provide. (Paradox will prompt you for the name before converting.)

QUATTRO PRO

Quattro Pro can interact directly with Paradox tables, so it may not even be necessary to import/export your Paradox tables.

Selecting Quattro Pro lets you import data from a Quattro spreadsheet into a Paradox table, or export data in a Paradox table to a Quattro spreadsheet. When importing spreadsheet data, keep in mind that Paradox tables store information in even columns (fields) and rows (records), whereas spreadsheets let you arrange text, numbers, and formulas in any manner you wish.

If your spreadsheet uses headings, underlines, or other characters to improve the spreadsheet's appearance, do not attempt to import these into a Paradox table. Instead, use Quattro's File, Xtract, and

Values option to extract even columns and rows of data (and one row of column titles, if possible) into a separate table (perhaps named Temp). Then, use Paradox to import data from the Temp table.

1-2-3 AND SYMPHONY

If you select 1-2-3 from the Export or Import submenu, you'll be given the options

    1) 1-2-3 Release 1A   2) 1-2-3 Release 2

Select the appropriate option for your version of 1-2-3. (The version number appears on the copyright screen when you first run 1-2-3.)

If you select the Symphony option from the Export or Import submenu, you'll see the options

    1) Symphony Release 1.0   2) Symphony Release 1.1

Select the appropriate option for your version of Symphony. (Again, the version number is displayed on the copyright screen when you first run Symphony.)

When importing or exporting on a hard disk with several directories, be sure to include the directory name as required. For example, to import a 1-2-3 spreadsheet named Sales from the directory named Lotus on drive C, enter the name of the file to import as *C:\Lotus\Sales*.

When you export data to Symphony or 1-2-3, the table fields and records will be stored in individual columns and rows. The file will have the name you assigned, plus the appropriate extension for your version of 1-2-3 or Symphony; .WKS for Release 1A of 1-2-3, .WK1 for Release 2 of 1-2-3, .WRK for Symphony Release 1.0, and .WR1 for Symphony Release 1.1. Once you export the Paradox file, you can use the usual File Retrieve options in Symphony or 1-2-3 to read the exported file into the spreadsheet. (Examples later in the chapter demonstrate techniques for exporting and graphing Paradox data using Lotus products.)

When importing 1-2-3 or Symphony data, Paradox will look for files on the specified directory, with the appropriate extension. For example, if you opt to import a 1-2-3 spreadsheet from Release 2 of

1-2-3, and specify C:\Lotus\Sales as the file to import, Paradox will search the Lotus directory in drive C for a file named Sales.WK1.

Paradox cannot reliably import the data that are randomly placed about a spreadsheet. Instead, it needs to import even columns and rows, where the top row contains the field names for the database table. If your spreadsheet contains labels or formulas outside of an even row-and-column orientation, you should first use the File Xtract option in 1-2-3 or Symphony to extract only the field names and values beneath them. (On a Symphony spreadsheet, this would be the database [_DB] range.) Then from Paradox, import the extracted file only.

Paradox will assign data types to the imported data based on the following table:

LOTUS COLUMN	PARADOX FIELD
Label	Alphanumeric (A)
Number	Numeric (N)
Number formatted as Currency, or with fixed two decimals	Currency ($)
Date (formatted as Date)	Date (D)

Any column storing the results of calculations will be imported as values. Paradox will not import the formulas themselves.

DBASE II, III, AND IV

dBASE III and IV use identical file structures, so select dBASE III to import or export dBASE IV data.

Transferring data to and from dBASE is a simple, straightforward process, since both systems store data in records and fields. To export data to dBASE, select the dBase option from the menu, then either dBASE II or dBASE III from the submenu. Paradox will copy data to the file name you provide, adding the usual dBASE .DBF extension (for instance, Partodb3.DBF).

Importing dBASE data is just as easy as exporting. When importing data, however, dBASE logical fields will be converted to alphanumeric fields with a length of one character, and memo fields will be trimmed to a maximum of 255 characters and stored as alphanumeric data.

FRAMEWORK

Though there is no command to interface with Framework, you can bypass this simply by using the dBase or Ascii option. Just export a Paradox table as a dBASE III database, then use the Framework @dbasefilter function to read the converted file.

When you're working with Framework and you want to send data to Paradox, bring the data you want to transfer to the desktop and select the Write DOS Text File option from the Disk menu. Framework will create a delimited file with the extension .TXT (such as Fwtopar.TXT).

In Paradox, create an empty table that resembles the Framework file structure and use the Ascii and Delimited options to import the file.

REFLEX

Importing and exporting Reflex data with Paradox is a simple, straightforward process, because both store data in a similar format. When exporting, Paradox will allow you to choose Version 1.0 or Version 1.1 of Reflex. When importing, Paradox handles these minor version differences automatically.

PFS

The Pfs option stores data in Pfs (or IBM Filing Assistant) format with the file name extension .PFS.

When importing data from Pfs or IBM Filing Assistant, first make sure that the file you are importing has the file name extension .PFS. (If it does not, use the DOS Rename command to change the file name.)

Since Pfs does not use data types, Paradox will make reasonable assumptions about data types during the conversion. Attachment pages will be trimmed to a maximum length of 255 characters and stored as alphanumeric data.

VISICALC

The Visicalc option lets you import and export data stored in Data Interchange Format (DIF). The exported file will be assigned the file name extension .DIF.

VisiCalc and many other spreadsheet programs allow you to store data in DIF format. Any file that you convert to DIF format can be imported into Paradox by selecting the Import and Visicalc options from the ExportImport submenus. Keep in mind that Paradox stores data in fields and records, and therefore the data being imported should have a consistent row-and-column format. Paradox cannot import a spreadsheet that contains data stored randomly throughout the rows and columns. Also, extraneous characters like boxes and asterisks, used to enhance the appearance of the spreadsheet on the screen, will not be converted easily. Remove these before exporting to Paradox.

ASCII

When you select the Export and Ascii options from the Export-Import menu, you'll be given the options below:

    Delimited   Text

If you select Import, and then Ascii, you'll be given the choice

    Delimited   AppendDelimited   Text

A delimited file is one in which fields are separated by commas and each record is terminated by a carriage return/linefeed combination. Typically, character data are enclosed in quotation marks. When you use the DOS TYPE command to view a delimited file, it will typically look something like the example in Figure 16.8. The carriage return/linefeed at the end of each record causes each new record to begin on a new line in the screen, as in the figure.

When you export a delimited file, Paradox creates a file with the name you provide and the extension .TXT (unless you provide a different file name extension). The ASCII file shown in Figure 16.8 is a Paradox table exported in delimited format. This is a common format that many software systems can import. Hence, you can export data from Paradox to just about any software system by exporting to a delimited ASCII file, then using the other software package to import the delimited file. (Examples using word processors are presented in the next section.)

```
C:\paradox > type transfer.dat
"Miss","Abzug","Ann","Z.","","","301 Crest Dr.","Encinitas","CA","92024","(123)5
55-1111","3/01/1990",7500.00
"Mr.","Adams","Andy","A.","","","234 Ocean View Dr.","San Diego","CA","92038","(
213)555-9999","1/15/1990",2500.00
"Ms.","Davis","Randi","","","","371 Oceanic Way","Manhattan Beach","CA","90001",
"(555)555-1111","3/01/1990",7500.00
"Miss","Gladstone","Tara Rose","","Waterside, Inc.","Acquisitions","P.O. Box 121
","New York","NY","12345","(415)555-1111","2/28/1990",15000.00
"Ms.","Jackson","Janet","J.","Zeerox, Inc.","Accounts Payable","1234 Corporate H
wy.","Los Angeles","CA","91234","(616)555-0011","1/01/1990",10000.00
"Mr.","Kenney","Clark","E.","Legal Aid","","371 Ave. of the Americas","New York"
,"NY","12345","(333)222-1111","1/31/1990",5000.00
"Mr.","Macallister","Mark","S.","BBC Publishing","Foreign Sales","121 Revelation
 Dr.","Bangor","ME","00001","(333)888-0109","3/15/1990",7500.00
"Dr.","Rosiello","Richard","L.","Raydontic Labs","Accounts Payable","P.O. Box 77
112","Newark","NJ","00123","(222)555-9898","3/15/1990",7500.00
"Mrs.","Simpson","Susan","M.","SMS Publishing","Software Division","P.O. Box 280
2","Philadelphia","PA","23456","(333)555-0101","1/01/1990",15000.00
"Dr.","Zastrou","Ruth","","Scripts Clinic","Internal Medicine","4331 La Jolla Sc
enic Dr.","La Jolla","CA","92037","(818)555-3258","1/01/1990",10000.00

C:\paradox >
```

Figure 16.8: The Custlist table exported to ASCII delimited format

Paradox can also import delimited ASCII files (also called *text files* and *sequential data files* in some software systems). When importing delimited ASCII files, Paradox assumes that individual fields are separated by commas. (You can, however, use the Paradox Custom Configuration program to specify a different delimiter.) The imported data will be stored on a new table with the field names Field 1, Field 2, Field 3, and so forth. Data types in the imported table are determined on a "best guess" basis. (Of course, you can use the Modify and Restructure options from the Paradox Main menu to change the field names and data types in the imported table if you wish.)

AppendDelimit lets you import ASCII data into an existing Paradox table. If the table you are importing records into is keyed, you'll be given the options below:

NewEntries   UpDate

If you select NewEntries, Paradox attempts to append the imported records to the bottom of an existing table. If you select Update, Paradox attempts to replace records in an existing table with imported records that have identical key fields.

Because the ASCII file has no field names, Paradox simply attempts to append records based upon the order of the fields. That is, the first field in the ASCII file is imported into the first field in the Paradox table, the second field in the ASCII file is imported into the second field of the Paradox table, and so on.

Any data that cannot be imported, because of non-matching fields or conflicting data types are stored in a table named Problems. This table shows the record number of the record that could not be imported, the first 80 characters of that record, and the reason that the importation failed. You can use this information, if necessary, to modify the ASCII file (using any text editor with a "nondocument" mode), and try again later.

The Text option lets you import and export text files consisting of single lines of information. When importing Text files, the new table will have a single field named Text, containing a single line from the imported file. When exporting Text files, the Paradox table may contain only a single alphanumeric field. Each record in the Paradox table becomes a line in the exported text file.

INTERFACING WITH WORD PROCESSORS

The Ascii option from the ExportImport menu is particularly useful for interfacing with word processors. In the following exercises, we'll use WordStar as the example word processor, although most word processors have similar capabilities.

EXPORTING A REPORT

You can export Paradox reports to word processors either for further editing or for inclusion in other documents. To send a copy of a report to a word processor, first make an ASCII text file copy of the report. Call up the Paradox Report menu and select the Output option. Enter a table name when requested (such as Custlist), and specify a report (for example, 1 for the directory). From the submenu, select the File option and enter a file name (such as Transfer). When complete, there will be a copy of your report on disk with the file name you assigned plus the extension .RPT (in this example, Transfer.RPT).

Exit Paradox and call up your word processor. Then, simply edit the Transfer.RPT file as you would any other.

If you wish to embed the transferred report in an existing document, first begin editing the existing document. Move the cursor to the place where you want to embed the Paradox report and simply read in the file. For example, in WordStar, type ^KR and the name of the file to read in (that is, Transfer.RPT), then press Enter.

MAILMERGE FILES FOR FORM LETTERS

Word processors with mailmerge capabilities for writing form letters mostly use the ASCII delimited format for storing data. In this section, we'll see how to export Paradox data to a WordStar MailMerge file. First, from the Paradox Main menu, choose the Tools option, then select the ExportImport, Export, Ascii, and Delimited options. Enter the name of the table to export (such as Custlist), and a name for the exported file (such as Transfer.DAT). When the export is complete, exit Paradox.

From the DOS A> or C> prompt, you can use the TYPE command to verify that the export took place. On a hard disk system, enter the command

    TYPE Transfer.DAT

On a floppy disk system, enter the command

    TYPE B:Transfer.DAT

(assuming, of course, that you named the exported file Transfer.DAT). You'll see the data from the table stored on a delimited file, with commas as the delimiters. (Incidentally, this is also the format used to store BASIC sequential data files.) Figure 16.8 shows the Custlist table exported to ASCII delimited format.

Next, call up your word processor and enter the appropriate commands to set up a form letter. Figure 16.9 shows a sample form letter set up in WordStar. The .OP command eliminates page numbers, the .DF (Data File) command specifies the name of the file with names and addresses (Transfer.DAT in this example). The .RV (Read Variable) command defines the structure of the file. Notice that the .RV command lists all fields, even though we do not use all of the fields in the letter. Keep in mind that the .RV command assigns names to *all* fields in the data file, not just the ones you want to use. The number of fields in the .RV command must match exactly the number of fields in the data file. The .PA command at the bottom of the letter starts each letter on a new page.

```
              C:FORMLET.TXT  PAGE 1 LINE 14 COL 52        INSERT ON
L----!----!----!----!----!----!----!----!----!----!----!--------R
.OP                                                               <
.DF Transfer.DAT                                                  M
.RV Title, Lname, FName, MI, Co, Dept, Add, City, State, Zip, Date, Amount  M
                                                                  <
&Title/o& &Fname& &MI/o& &LName&                                  <
&Co/o&                                                            <
&Dept/o&                                                          <
&Add&                                                             <
&City&, &State&  &Zip&                                            <
                                                                  <
Dear &Fname&:                                                     <

    How do you like getting these form letters from me?  I'll
bet you thought I hand typed this letter, but not so.  By
combining Paradox and Wordstar, I was able to use Paradox with
Wordstar's nifty formatting capabilities, like justified right
margin, ^Sunderline^S, ^Bboldface^B, ^Xstrikeout^X, and so on._   <
                                                                  <
Best Regards                                                      <
                                                                  <
Albert Winney                                                     <
.PA
```

Figure 16.9: A WordStar form letter

Within the form letter, variable names defined in the .RV command are placed by surrounding the name with ampersands (for instance, &LName&). The /o used in some variable names means "omit if no data." This keeps blank fields from appearing as blank lines or spaces.

WORDPERFECT FORM-LETTER FILES

WordPerfect uses a very unusual format for storing data to be merged into form letters. Each field is terminated with a ^R (Ctrl-R) and a carriage return, and each record is terminated with a ^E (Ctrl-E) and a carriage return. You can't export Paradox files to this exact format, but you can use WordPerfect's search-and-replace capabilities to convert the ASCII file field delimiters to ^R characters and insert the ^E at the end of each record. Below, we'll work through the steps to convert an exported Paradox ASCII file to a WordPerfect data file for printing form letters.

First of all, you should probably use some character other than a comma as the delimiter (field separator) in the converted ASCII file, because this character might actually exist inside one of the fields, as in the company name *ABC Records, Inc*. We wouldn't want WordPerfect to convert this comma to a ^R character, because it is not a field delimiter. To avoid any confusion about the field delimiters, we'll have Paradox use an unusual character (@ in this example) as a field separator in the exported text file.

To change the field delimiter, run Paradox in the usual fashion, and select the menu options Scripts and Play. Enter Custom as the script to play.

When the Configuration menu appears at the top of the screen, select the options Ascii and Separator. Press Backspace to erase the default delimiter (a comma) and type in the @ character. Press Return, then select the options Return and DO-IT!. Select either HardDisk or Network from the next menu, depending on the type of computer you have. You've just reconfigured Paradox to place an @ sign, instead of a comma, between fields in exported ASCII text files. (After completing this exercise, you might want to repeat the process and put a comma back in as the separator.)

Now, run Paradox in the usual manner. Select Tools, ExportImport, Export, Ascii, and Delimited from the menus. Specify the name of the table to export (we'll use the CustList table in this example). Enter a drive, directory, and name for the copied file. On a hard disk, this might be C:\WP\Data.TXT, assuming WordPerfect is stored on a directory named WP on drive C. On a two-floppy system, place a disk in drive B, and name the file B:Data.TXT.

Next, exit Paradox using the usual Exit and Yes menu options. To verify the exportation, use the TYPE command to view the contents of the Data.TXT file. On a hard disk, log onto the WordPerfect disk (enter the command CD\WP and press Enter). Then enter the command TYPE DATA.TXT and press Enter. On a floppy disk system, enter the command TYPE B:DATA.TXT. The file should look something like the example in Figure 16.8.

Now, run WordPerfect in the usual manner, specifying Data.TXT as the file to edit. (That is, at the DOS prompt, type in the command WP DATA.TXT and press Enter.) You should see the delimited ASCII file on your screen.

Now, you need to place a ^E and carriage return at the end of each record. To do so, follow these steps:

1. Type Alt-F2.
2. Enter N in response to the *Confirm?* prompt.
3. Press Enter in response to the *Srch:* prompt (this appears as [HRt]).
4. Press F2.
5. Type Ctrl-E and press Enter in response to the *Replace with:* prompt (it appears on the screen as ^E[HRt]).
6. Press F2.

WordPerfect will put a ^E at the end of each record; you'll be able to see the effect on your screen.

Next, you need to replace all the @ delimiters with a Ctrl-R and carriage return. To do so, follow these steps:

1. Press Home-Home-↑ to move to the top of the file.
2. Type Alt-F2.
3. Enter N in response to the *Confirm?* prompt.
4. Type @ in response to the *Srch:* prompt.
5. Press F2.
6. Type Ctrl-R and press Enter in response to the *Replace with:* prompt (it appears on the screen as ^R[HRt]).
7. Press F2.

Finally, you need to get rid of the quotation marks. Here are the steps to do so:

1. Press Home-Home-↑ to move to the top of the file.
2. Type Alt-F2.
3. Enter N in response to the *Confirm?* prompt.
4. Type " in response to the *Srch:* prompt.
5. Press F2.
6. Type F2 in response to the *Replace with:* prompt.

All of the quotation marks are removed from the file. If you now type Home-Home-↑ to move the cursor to the top of the screen, the first Paradox record should look something like the following (of course, the actual data might be different):

```
Miss^R
Abzug^R
Ann^R
Z.^R
^R
301 Crest Dr.^R
Encinitas^R
CA^R
92024^R
(555)555-1212^R
3/01/1990^R
7500.00^E
```

Notice that each field starts on a new line (The Company and Department fields are blank in this record.) Each field ends with a Ctrl-R, and each record ends with a ^E, just as WordPerfect requires. Save the data file by pressing F7, selecting Yes, pressing Enter, and selecting Yes again.

Next you can use WordPerfect to create your form letter. We can't go into detail on how to do that here, but basically you need to use the Alt-F9 menu to place fields in the document. The field numbers on the CustList table are listed below:

FIELD	CODE
Mr/Mrs	F1
LName	F2
FName	F3
M.I.	F4
Company	F5
Department	F6
Address	F7
City	F8
State	F9
Zip code	F10
Phone	F11
Start Date	F12
Credit Limit	F13

You'll want to use the Alt-F9 and F options to lay out the recipient's address at the top of the form letter (but below the letter date) so that it looks something like this:

```
^F1^ ^F3^ ^F4^ ^F2^
^F5?^
^F6?^
^F7^
^F8^, ^F9^ ^F10^
```

Note the use of a single space between each field position. The question marks prevent any empty Company or Department fields from being printed as blank lines, like Paradox's LineSqueeze option. The comma in the last line is the comma placed between the City and State fields.

Type in the body of the letter. (You can also use Alt-F9, F to place fields in the body of the letter.) Save the completed form letter in the usual manner (the F7 key), using a file name such as FormLet.TXT.

To merge the form letter with the data file, run WordPerfect, type Ctrl-F9, and select 1 (Merge). Specify FormLet.TXT (in this example) as the Primary file, and Data.TXT (in this example) as the Secondary file. The letters will be created on the screen, and you can scroll through them and make any necessary changes using the usual WordPerfect techniques. You might want to save the completed form letters under a new file name, or perhaps print them immediately (using Shift-F7 1).

RUNNING EXTERNAL PROGRAMS

You can temporarily suspend Paradox and exit back to the DOS A> or C> prompt without having to save or clear any open tables. This is very useful for using DOS commands such as FORMAT or COPY during a session in Paradox. You can even change floppy disks while the DOS prompt is showing, as long as you put the original disks back in their drives before returning to Paradox.

To suspend the current Paradox session, first try to work your way back to the Main menu. For example, if you happen to be editing a table, form, or report specification, save these. While it is not absolutely necessary, it is safer to do so. (Should anything go wrong while Paradox is suspended, any data being edited might be lost.) You need not clear any tables from the screen, however.

Next, select the Tools, More, and ToDOS options from the menu, or type Ctrl-O. Paradox will display a warning message and the DOS prompt. While Paradox is suspended, and the DOS prompt is showing, you'll need to keep in mind a few rules to protect the suspended Paradox:

- Don't load any RAM resident programs, such as desktop tools, keyboard enhancers, or memory-resident spelling checkers. Similarly, don't use the DOS PRINT or MODE commands.

- Do not ERASE, RENAME, or modify any Paradox objects that were in use when you suspended the current Paradox session.

- If you use the DOS CHDIR or CD command to change directories, be sure to go back to the original directory before returning to Paradox.

- If you change floppy disks, be sure to put the original disks back in their drives before returning to Paradox.
- Always return to Paradox and exit properly before turning off the computer.

To return to your Paradox session from the DOS A> or C> prompt, just type the command EXIT at the DOS prompt, then press Enter. Your Paradox session will reappear on the screen as though you'd never left (assuming you've followed the rules above). If at anytime you forget whether or not Paradox is suspended, enter the EXIT command at the DOS prompt (after replacing the appropriate disks if necessary). If Paradox is not in suspension, the DOS prompt will simply reappear.

Note that while Paradox is suspended, you may not be able to run all of your programs, because the suspended Paradox still occupies 420K of memory. If you need more memory, you can exit to DOS using the DOS Big key (Alt-O). DOS Big leaves only 100K of Paradox in memory while Paradox is suspended, leaving more room for other programs. The only disadvantage to using DOS Big is that it takes longer to get back into Paradox from the DOS prompt when you enter the EXIT command. Note also that DOS Big works only on hard disk systems, and not on computers with floppy disk drives only.

SUMMARY

- To rename a Paradox object, use the Tools and Rename options.
- To copy Paradox objects, use the Tools and Copy options.
- To delete Paradox objects, use the Tools and Delete options.
- To copy records from one table to another, use the Tools, More, and Add options.
- To remove records from one table that match records in another table, use the Tools, More, and Subtract options.

- To empty a table of all records (thereby closing the table), use the Tools, More, and Empty options.
- To protect data with passwords or write-protection, use the Tools, More, and Protect options.
- To define a new working directory, use the Tools, More, and Directory options.
- To view general information about files, use the Tools and Info options.
- To change the structure of a table, select the Modify and Restructure options from the Main menu.
- To add a new field to a table, use the Ins key to make space and enter the new field name and field type.
- To delete a field from a table, move the cursor to the field and press the Del key.
- To move a field to a new location, use the Ins key to make room for a new field, then type in the field name exactly as it appears in its original position.
- To save a modified table structure, press the DO-IT! (F2) key.
- To cancel modifications to a table structure, call up the menu and select the Cancel option.
- To update forms or reports after modifying a table structure, use the Change option from the Forms or Reports Main-menu option.
- To speed up often used queries, use the Tools and Query-Speedup options.
- To import and export data, use the Tools and ExportImport options.
- You can read a delimited ASCII text file into an existing table using the AppendDelimited option.
- You can temporarily suspend Paradox and return to the DOS prompt using the Tools, More, and ToDOS menu options, the Ctrl-O key, or the DOS Big (Alt-O) key.

PART III

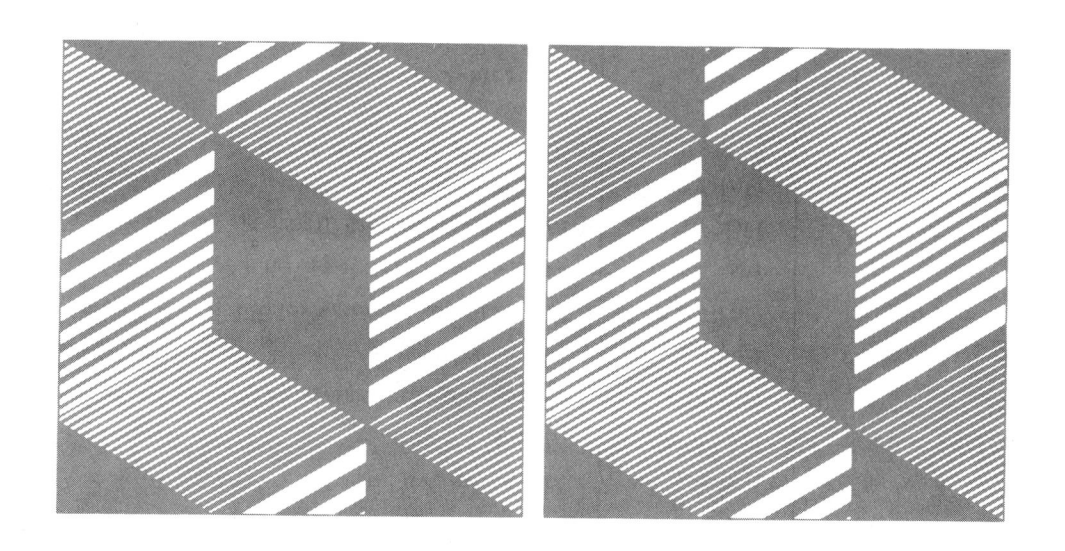

THE PARADOX APPLICATION LANGUAGE

INTRODUCTION TO PAL PROGRAMMING

CHAPTER 17

MOST DATABASE-MANAGEMENT SYSTEMS REQUIRE A considerable amount of programming to gain full control in accessing data. Paradox, on the other hand, provides substantial power in managing data without any programming whatsoever. Nonetheless, there will always be "power users" who want to extend the built-in capabilities of Paradox to create custom systems for special applications.

For the power users Paradox offers PAL, the Paradox Application Language. We've already seen how to record a series of keystrokes and store them in a script using the Script and BeginRecord options. With PAL, you can extend the power of scripts beyond recorded keystrokes to entire programs.

In this chapter, we'll cover the basics of designing and developing PAL programs, and discuss in detail some of the more commonly used commands. In the next chapter, we'll look at some PAL programs designed to manage a mailing system. We'll use the more common commands in examples so you can see how they work. For more technical information on all the PAL commands and functions, refer to the *PAL User's Guide*, which comes with Paradox.

CREATING A PAL PROGRAM

To create a PAL program, you can use the PAL editor or any word processor that has a nondocument mode. (If you use an external word processor, be sure to use the extension .SC in your file name.) To access the PAL editor, call up the Paradox Main menu and select the Scripts, Editor, and Write options. Paradox will ask for a file name. Enter a name (eight letters maximum with no spaces or punctuation) and press Enter. In this example, enter the name **Test1**.

The PAL editor provides a blank screen to work with. The keys for creating and editing command files are the same as those used for creating forms and reports, as listed in Table 17.1.

Table 17.1: Keys used for creating and editing command files

KEY	FUNCTION
←	Moves left one character
Ctrl-←	Moves left one screen
→	Moves right one character
Ctrl-→	Moves right one screen
↑	Moves up a line
↓	Moves down a line
Home	Moves to first line
Ctrl-Home	Moves to first character on line
End	Moves to last line
Ctrl-End	Moves to last character of line
Ins	Toggles Insert mode on/off
Del	Erases character at cursor
Ctrl-Y	Deletes all to right of cursor, or entire line if cursor is in leftmost column
Enter	Moves down a line, or creates a new blank line if Insert mode is on
Ctrl-V	Turns vertical ruler on or off

We can test a simple program here. Type the lines below, *exactly* as shown:

```
? "Test Test Test"
SLEEP 10000
```

Use the various editing keys to make corrections if necessary.

SAVING A PAL PROGRAM

When you've entered your program, call up the Editor menu by pressing Menu (F10). You'll be given these options:

Read   Go   Print   Help   DO-IT!   Cancel

The Go option will save your program as well as play it right away. The DO-IT! option will save the program and return to the Paradox menu. The Cancel option allows you to abandon the current program (and the current changes), and Help provides a help screen.

The Read option allows you to combine scripts, which is very useful to more advanced programmers. For example, you might find that you can write a large portion of a program by recording keystrokes or saving a query form. With the Read option, you can incorporate a recorded script or query form directly into the current PAL program.

For now, select the DO-IT! option to save your program and return to the Paradox menu. Paradox automatically adds the extension .SC to the file name you provide. Hence, if you name your program Test1, it will be stored on disk as Test1.SC.

RUNNING A PAL PROGRAM

A PAL program is no different than any other script. To run the program, call up the Main menu and select the Scripts and Play options. When requested, enter the name of the script, or press Enter to view a menu of existing scripts and select one by highlighting it. In this example, enter or highlight the name Test1. You'll see the screen clear, then the message

Test Test Test

appear on the screen for about 10 seconds. Then the Paradox Main menu reappears. Let's discuss why.

The ? command means "display." Therefore, the command

? "Test Test Test"

displays the words in quotes on the screen. The SLEEP command causes Paradox to pause. The 10000 tells Paradox to pause for 10,000 milliseconds, or 10 seconds. Therefore, the "Test Test Test" message stays on the screen for about 10 seconds before the program ends and returns to the Paradox Main menu.

Notice that the menu disappeared while the program was running, then reappeared when the program was done. This has to do with the *PAL canvas*, which we'll discuss next.

THE PAL CANVAS

When you become involved with programming in PAL, you have to become familiar with the concept of the PAL canvas. Basically, whenever a PAL program is running, it takes over the screen and "hides" any events that might be occurring on the Paradox workspace (for example, menus, tables, and so on). This keeps Paradox invisible and in the background. As we'll see later, the WAIT and ECHO commands allow you to bring Paradox out of the background into the foreground temporarily, even while a program is running.

CANCELING A PAL SCRIPT

Once you begin running a PAL script, it keeps running until it is fully played out, or until Paradox encounters an error. When you develop more complex scripts, particularly those that use *looping*, you may make a mistake that makes the script behave unpredictably and go into a performance of some routine without ever stopping. To get out of such a dilemma, press the Break key (the Ctrl-ScrollLock combination on IBM PC keyboards, and Ctrl-Pause on the IBM AT keyboard) to cancel the script. You'll be given the option to Cancel or Debug. Select Cancel to terminate the script and return to the Paradox workspace. Select Debug to use the PAL debugger, discussed in Chapter 19.

DEBUGGING

When you write your own programs in PAL, you're likely to make errors quite often. Programming errors are called "bugs" in computer jargon (because an error was once caused by a moth flying into the earliest computer). Getting rid of errors is therefore called *debugging*.

When Paradox encounters a bug in a program, it will stop running the program and present you with these options:

Cancel   Debug

Selecting Cancel simply stops the program and returns you to the Paradox Main menu. Selecting the Debug option displays the line where the error occurred, and a brief description of the problem. (In some cases, the line below the offending line will appear, but the error message will help you figure out the problem.) The instructions

Type Ctrl-Q to Quit

will also appear. After viewing and understanding the error, you can type Ctrl-Q to quit and return to the Paradox menu. Then use the editor to correct the line and try again. (*Note:* For more advanced debugging techniques with complex programs, see Chapter 19 in this book, and Chapter 11 of the *PAL User's Guide.*)

EDITING A PAL PROGRAM

To fix or change a PAL program, select the Scripts, Editor, and Edit options, and enter the name of the program to edit. The script will appear on the screen. At this point, all editing keys work as they usually do. After editing the program, call up the menu and select Go to run the program, or DO-IT! to save the program and run it later using the Scripts and Play options.

With the basics of creating, running, debugging, and editing PAL programs under our belts, let's take a look at the basic commands used in creating and running PAL programs.

INTERACTING WITH THE USER

Most programs use commands for presenting information to and getting information from the user. PAL includes many commands for such interactions, a few of which are listed below:

COMMAND	FUNCTION
CLEAR	Erases the PAL canvas
ACCEPT	Gets information from the user
?	Prints information on a new line
??	Prints information on the same line
@	Positions the cursor
STYLE	Defines colors, blinking, and other effects on the PAL canvas
GETCHAR( )	Gets a character of information from the user

Let's try out some of these commands to see how they work. From the Paradox menu, select the Scripts, Editor, and Write options, and enter the file name Testuser. Then enter the program shown in Figure 17.1. After typing in each line, press the Enter key to move to the beginning of the next line. To put blank lines into the script, press the Enter key while the cursor is still on a blank line. Notice that some lines start with a semicolon (;). Be sure you don't leave these semicolons out, or the program won't run correctly. (We'll discuss the function of these semicolons and the text that follows them later in the chapter.)

Let's discuss what each *routine* in this sample program does. The first routine simply states the name of the program (Testuser.SC) and its function:

```
;-------------------------------------------------------------- Testuser.SC
;------------------------------------------------ Test user-interface commands.
CLEAR                       ;Clear the screen
STYLE ATTRIBUTE 30          ;Yellow letters on blue
@ 1,10                      ;Cursor to row 1, column 10
?? "This is yellow on blue"
```

The CLEAR command makes sure that the PAL canvas is clear before running the rest of the program. The STYLE ATTRIBUTE 30

```
;--------------------------------------- Testuser.SC
;----------------------- Test user-interface commands.
CLEAR                           ;Clear the screen
STYLE ATTRIBUTE 30              ;Yellow letters on blue
@ 1,10                          ;Cursor to row 1, column 10
?? "This is yellow on blue"

STYLE REVERSE                   ;Reverse video
@ 3,10
?? "This is reverse video"

STYLE REVERSE, BLINK            ;Reverse and blinking
@ 5,10
?? "This is blinking"

STYLE ATTRIBUTE 40              ;Get user name
@ 7,10
?? "Enter your name, then press <-' : "
ACCEPT "A25" TO MyName

@ 9,10
?? "Enter a number from 1 to 5 then press <-' : "
ACCEPT "N" PICTURE "#" MIN 1 MAX 5 TO X

STYLE ATTRIBUTE 95
@ 20,10
?? "Your Name is ",MyName," and you entered ",X

STYLE ATTRIBUTE 175
@ 24,10
?? "Press any key to return to Paradox menu..."
Y = GETCHAR()
```

Figure 17.1: The Testuser.SC PAL program

command sets the display style for a color monitor to yellow letters on a blue background. (I'll show you all the color combinations a little later in this chapter.) The command @ 1,10 places the cursor at the first row of the tenth column on the screen. The command *?? "This is yellow on blue"* displays the sentence enclosed in quotation marks on the screen, beginning at the cursor position.

The next routine displays the sentence ''This is reverse video'' in reverse video on the third row, tenth column of the screen:

```
STYLE REVERSE    ;Reverse video
@ 3,10
?? "This is reverse video"
```

Notice that the word ATTRIBUTE is not used when selecting a display enhancement rather than a color combination. Display enhancements include REVERSE, BLINK, and INTENSE.

The next routine displays the sentence "This is blinking" on the fifth row, tenth column, of the screen:

```
STYLE REVERSE, BLINK    ;Reverse and blinking
@ 5,10
?? "This is blinking"
```

Two STYLE parameters are defined: REVERSE and BLINK. The two enhancements are separated by a comma, and once again the ATTRIBUTE command is not used.

Now the routine gets a little trickier, as shown below:

```
STYLE ATTRIBUTE 40    ;Get user name
@ 7,10
?? "Enter your name, then press <-' : "
ACCEPT "A25" TO MyName
```

The colors are changed using STYLE ATTRIBUTE, and on the seventh row, tenth column, the sentence "Enter your name, then press <-' :" is displayed. (The Enter key is represented by a less-than sign followed by a hyphen and apostrophe.) The ACCEPT command then waits for alphanumeric data with a maximum length of 25 characters ("A25") to be typed in. Whatever the user types is stored in a *variable* named MyName.

The variable name MyName is completely arbitrary. I could have used the variable name X, HaHaHa, or Bowser. Any variable name would do. The important point about variables is that they can store data which can be used later in the program, as we'll see in a moment. However, unlike data stored in tables, variables are transient and cease to exist when the program stops running. For now, keep in mind that whatever the user (or yourself) types in response to the "Enter your name" request is stored in the variable named MyName.

The next routine positions the cursor on the screen at row 9, column 10:

```
@ 9,10
?? "Enter a number from 1 to 5 then press <-' : "
ACCEPT "N" PICTURE "#" MIN 1 MAX 5 TO X
```

The ?? command then displays the request to enter a number between 1 and 5, followed by a press on the Enter key. The ACCEPT command waits for a number ("N") that is one digit long (PICTURE "#") and has a minimum value of 1 and a maximum value of 5. Whatever the user types is stored in a variable named X. (If a number out of the range is typed in, Paradox will reject it and ask for a new number. The program will continue running only after a number within the defined range has been entered.)

Next the program uses the data stored in the variables to display a simple message at row 20, column 10, using yet another color combination. This routine is shown below:

```
STYLE ATTRIBUTE 95
@ 20,10
?? "Your Name is ",MyName," and you entered ",X
```

Notice how the variable data is combined with *literal* data. That is, Paradox displays "Your Name is", followed by the contents of the MyName variable, followed by the words " and you entered ", and the contents of variable X. Hence, had you entered "Albert" as your name, and "2" as the number, this line would display

Your Name is Albert and you entered 2

Notice that the literal data is enclosed in quotation marks, while variable names are not. Commas are used to separate the literals from the variables. This syntax is very common and often used in PAL programs.

The last routine in the program displays the message "Press any key to return to Paradox menu..." at the bottom of the screen (row 24):

```
STYLE ATTRIBUTE 175
@ 24,10
?? "Press any key to return to Paradox menu..."
Y = GETCHAR( )
```

The GETCHAR( ) function, rather than the ACCEPT command, is used in this example. That's because ACCEPT allows data of any length to be entered, followed by a press on the Enter key. The GETCHAR( ) function "expects" only a single keystroke and stores the results of that keystroke in a variable. (Actually, GETCHAR( ) stores the ASCII code of the keystroke in the variable, but we need not concern ourselves with such details yet.)

Figure 17.2 shows the results of running the Testuser program, though your screen may look slightly different depending on the type of monitor you have. Pressing any key will end the program and return you to the Paradox Main menu.

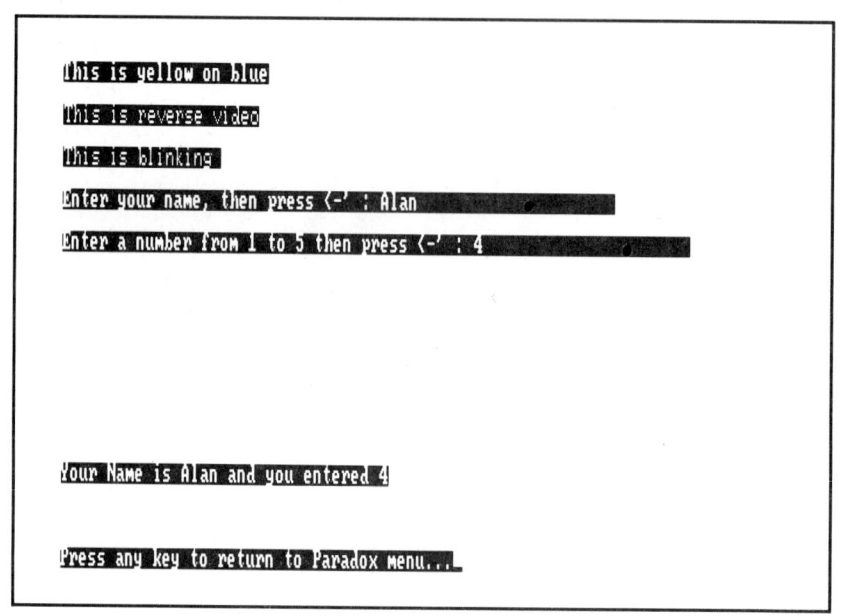

```
This is yellow on blue
This is reverse video
This is blinking
Enter your name, then press <-' : Alan
Enter a number from 1 to 5 then press <-' : 4




Your Name is Alan and you entered 4

Press any key to return to Paradox menu...
```

Figure 17.2: Results of the Testuser.SC program

LOOPING

One of the most common techniques used in programming is *looping*. Looping allows a program to perform a task repeatedly without repeating many lines. For example, we briefly discussed the STYLE ATTRIBUTE command, which allows you set up color combinations on the screen. Suppose you wish to know what all the possible color combinations are? Well, since there are 255 of them, you could spend a great deal of time and effort trying each one out individually. A better way would be to write a program with a loop that repeats itself 255 times, incrementing the attribute number, and displaying each one on the screen.

Loops are set up in PAL programs using the WHILE and ENDWHILE commands. There *must* be an ENDWHILE command associated with each WHILE command in a program. This is the general syntax for the WHILE and ENDWHILE loop:

WHILE <some condition exists>
   <do this command>
   <and this command>
   <and whatever other commands you want to do>
ENDWHILE

Often, a variable is used with a loop to terminate the loop after a certain number of repetitions. If you have a color monitor, try entering and running the program named Colors in Figure 17.3 to test this out. As in the last example, select Scripts, Editor, and Write to enter the PAL editor. Type in the script name **Colors** when prompted, and press Enter. Then type in the script *exactly* as it is shown in Figure 17.3. After typing in the script, call up the PAL menu (press F10), and select Go to save and play the script.

```
;--------------------------------------- Colors.SC.
;-- Shows colors used with STYLE ATTRIBUTE command.
;---------------------------- Loop from 0 to 255.
Counter = 0
WHILE Counter <= 255
      STYLE ATTRIBUTE Counter
      ?? FORMAT("W5",Counter)
      Counter = Counter + 1
ENDWHILE
@ 24,1
?? "Press any key when done viewing colors..."
X = GETCHAR()
```

Figure 17.3: The Colors.SC program

As you'll see, the script displays all the possible color combinations in each of the attribute numbers. In the future, you can use these numbers with the STYLE ATTRIBUTE command to set up a color combination. For example, to display yellow letters on a blue background, use the following command in your program:

STYLE ATTRIBUTE 30

Now let's discuss how the Colors program produces its display. The first three lines in the program are simply programmer comments (they don't affect the program in any way):

; --- Colors.SC.
;------------- Shows colors used with STYLE ATTRIBUTE command.
; -- Loop from 0 to 255.

The next line creates a variable named Counter and assigns the number zero to it:

Counter = 0

Next, a loop is set up that will repeat itself as long as the number stored in the Counter variable is less than or equal to 255:

WHILE Counter < = 255

Within the loop, the program sets the STYLE ATTRIBUTE to whatever number is currently stored in the Counter variable:

STYLE ATTRIBUTE Counter

The next line displays the number currently stored in the Counter variable on the screen. To standardize the format of the displayed number, the PAL FORMAT command is used. It specifies that the Counter variable must be displayed with a width of five characters ("W5"):

?? FORMAT("W5",Counter)

Since we don't want the next pass through the loop to repeat the same STYLE ATTRIBUTE, the next line in the program increments the number stored in the Counter variable by 1. This is accomplished by indicating that the variable equals itself plus 1, as shown below:

    Counter = Counter + 1

The ENDWHILE command marks the bottom of the loop. All commands between the WHILE and ENDWHILE loop will be repeated until the stated condition, Counter < = 255, is no longer true.

To keep the color display from suddenly disappearing from the screen when the looping is done, the GETCHAR( ) function waits for the user to press any key, as shown below:

    @ 24,1
    ?? "Press any key when done viewing colors..."
    X = GETCHAR( )

When the user presses any key after viewing colors, the PAL canvas with all the colors displayed disappears from the screen, and the Paradox Main menu reappears.

AVOIDING THE INFAMOUS INFINITE LOOP

The command *Counter = Counter + 1* in the Colors.SC script is a very important one, not only because it makes sure that the next STYLE ATTRIBUTE is displayed, but also because it guarantees that the loop will end at some point. WHILE...ENDWHILE loops must *always* include some command to assure that the loop does not attempt to run forever (called an *infinite loop*).

For example, if you look at the small routine below, you'll see that the WHILE condition says, "Repeat this loop as long as the value of counter is less than 1001":

    Counter = 1
    WHILE Counter < 1001
      ? "Hello"
    ENDWHILE

However, the value of the Counter variable never changes; it is *always* equal to 1. Hence, this script would attempt to print the word *Hello* on the screen forever. The only way to terminate this loop would be to press the Break key on the keyboard when you grew tired of seeing Hellos written on the screen.

To avoid an infinite loop, be sure there is some way for the WHILE condition to end eventually. In the above example, you would merely need to increment the Counter variable with each pass through the loop so that Counter eventually reaches a number greater than 1000, as shown here:

```
Counter = 1
WHILE Counter < 1001
    ? "Hello"
    Counter = Counter + 1
ENDWHILE
```

There are other ways to ensure that loops will not run forever, as future examples in this book will demonstrate.

MAKING DECISIONS

There are basically two techniques used in PAL to make decisions while a program is running. One is the fairly simple IF...THEN...ELSE...ENDIF command clause, used for making decisions when there are only one or two possible outcomes. The other is the SWITCH...CASE...OTHERWISE...ENDSWITCH clause, used for making a decision when several mutually exclusive alternatives exist. We'll discuss and test each type independently.

IF...THEN...ELSE...ENDIF

The PAL IF...THEN...ELSE...ENDIF commands mean pretty much the same thing they do in English. The basic syntax for this structure is as follows:

```
IF <this condition exists> THEN
    <do this command>
    <and this command>
    <and whatever other commands are listed here>
```

```
ELSE
    <do this command instead>
    <and this one too>
    <and any others listed here>
ENDIF
```

The ELSE command is entirely optional. That is, an IF decision might also have this syntax:

```
IF <this condition exists> THEN
    <do this command>
    <and any others listed here>
ENDIF
```

In this case, the ELSE situation is assumed to be, "Don't do anything." The required ENDIF command marks the end of the decision clause; commands beneath ENDIF are not dependent on anything that happened within the IF...ENDIF clause. Let's look at an example by typing in the command file shown in Figure 17.4.

```
;-------------------------------- Iftest.SC
;---- Test IF...THEN...ELSE...ENDIF commands.
CLEAR
@ 10,1
;------------------------ Get a number from the user.
?? "Enter a whole number "
ACCEPT "N" TO X
;------------------- Display one message or the other.
IF MOD(X,5) = 0 THEN
   @ 15,1
   ?? X, " is evenly divisible by 5"
ELSE
   @ 15,1
   ?? X, " is NOT evenly divisible by 5"
ENDIF
SLEEP 5000
```

Figure 17.4: A program to test the IF...ENDIF clause

The program is a relatively simple one. First it asks the user to enter a whole number. The user's answer is stored in a variable named X:

```
;-------------------------------------------------------------------- Iftest.SC
;------------------------------ Test IF...THEN...ELSE...ENDIF commands.
CLEAR
```

```
@ 10,1
; ---------------------------------------------------- Get a number from the user.
?? "Enter a whole number "
ACCEPT "N" TO X
```

Next, an IF command tests to see if the number entered is evenly divisible by 5. It does so by testing the *modulus* of the number when divided by 5. The PAL MOD function divides the two numbers and tests the result. If the modulus (remainder) is zero, the number is evenly divisible by 5. Otherwise, the number is not evenly divisible by 5. Hence, if the number is indeed evenly divisible by 5, the program displays the number (X) followed by the message "is evenly divisible by 5", as shown below:

```
; ------------------------------------------- Display one message or the other.
IF MOD(X,5) = 0 THEN
   @ 15,1
   ?? X, " is evenly divisible by 5"
```

However, if the number is not evenly divisible by 5 (ELSE), the program displays the number and the message "is NOT evenly divisible by 5", as shown below:

```
ELSE
   @ 15,1
   ?? X, " is NOT evenly divisible by 5"
ENDIF
```

The ENDIF command marks the end of the IF clause, so the last command pauses the program for about five seconds before returning control to the Paradox Main menu, regardless of what occurred within the IF...ENDIF commands:

```
SLEEP 5000
```

SWITCH...CASE...OTHERWISE...ENDSWITCH

In some situations, decisions may involve more alternatives than a simple IF...ELSE...ENDIF clause can handle. In such situations, a SWITCH...CASE...OTHERWISE...ENDSWITCH clause can be called into play. This is the basic syntax for this clause:

```
SWITCH
   CASE <this occurs> :
      <do these commands>
   CASE <this occurs> :
      <do these commands>
   CASE <this occurs> :
      <do these commands>
   OTHERWISE <if none of the above> :
      <do these commands>
ENDSWITCH
```

There can be any number of CASE commands within the SWITCH-...ENDSWITCH commands. The OTHERWISE command is entirely optional. Hence, the following syntax is acceptable:

```
SWITCH
   CASE <this occurs> :
      <do these commands>
   CASE <this occurs> :
      <do these commands>
   CASE <this occurs> :
      <do these commands>
ENDSWITCH
```

The difference is that in the first syntax, if none of the CASE options occurs, the OTHERWISE option performs its commands. In the latter syntax, if none of the CASE options occurs, nothing at all happens. (That is, nothing between the SWITCH and ENDSWITCH commands happens.)

It is important to keep in mind that options within a SWITCH-...ENDSWITCH clause are mutually exclusive. That is, as soon as a CASE option performs its commands, all other CASEs and the OTHERWISE are ignored. Figure 17.5 shows a sample program named Testcase that demonstrates the SWITCH...ENDSWITCH clause.

This program begins by clearing the screen, setting a color combination, and asking the user to enter a number between 1 and 4. The

```
;-------------------------------- Testcase.SC
;--- Test SWITCH, CASE, OTHERWISE, and ENDSWITCH.
CLEAR
STYLE ATTRIBUTE 40
@ 12,10
?? "Enter a number from 1 to 4, then press <-' : "
ACCEPT "N" PICTURE "#" TO X

;-------------------- Respond to entry.
@ 15,10
STYLE REVERSE, BLINK
SWITCH
     CASE X = 1 :
          ?? "You entered a one"
     CASE X = 2 :
          ?? "You entered a two"
     CASE X = 3 :
          ?? "You entered a three"
     CASE X = 4 :
          ?? "You entered a four"
     OTHERWISE  :
          BEEP BEEP BEEP
          ?? "I said from 1 to 4!"
ENDSWITCH
SLEEP 4000
STYLE
```

Figure 17.5: The Testcase.sc program

user's answer is stored in a variable named X, as shown below:

```
; ----------------------------------------------------------- Testcase.SC
; ----------- Test SWITCH, CASE, OTHERWISE, and ENDSWITCH.
CLEAR
STYLE ATTRIBUTE 40
@ 12,10
?? "Enter a number from 1 to 4, then press <–' : "
ACCEPT "N" PICTURE "#" TO X
```

Next, the program positions the cursor at row 15, column 10 on the screen, and sets the style to reverse video and blinking:

```
; ---------------------------------------------------------------- Respond to entry.
@ 15,10
STYLE REVERSE, BLINK
```

Next, a SWITCH...ENDSWITCH clause decides what to do based on the user's entry. If the user entered a 1, the program displays the message "You entered a one". If the user entered a 2, the program displays "You entered a two", and so on. If the user did not enter a number between 1 and 4, the OTHERWISE option takes over, sounds three beeps (via the PAL BEEP command), and displays the message "I said from 1 to 4!"

```
SWITCH
   CASE X = 1 :
      ?? "You entered a one"
   CASE X = 2 :
      ?? "You entered a two"
   CASE X = 3 :
      ?? "You entered a three"
   CASE X = 4 :
      ?? "You entered a four"
   OTHERWISE :
      BEEP BEEP BEEP
      ?? "I said from 1 to 4!"
ENDSWITCH
```

The SLEEP command then pauses for about four seconds, the STYLE command (with no attributes) sets the STYLE back to the default settings, and control is returned to the Paradox Main menu.

```
SLEEP 4000
STYLE
```

Note that each CASE statement, as well as the optional OTHERWISE statement, is followed by a colon. Also, even though there is only a single command associated with each CASE statement in this example, a CASE statement may have any number of commands associated with it. The same holds true for the OTHERWISE command.

The SWITCH...ENDSWITCH clause is often used with custom menus in PAL. We'll see how next.

CUSTOM MENUS

You can create your own menus, which are similar to the menus Paradox shows at the top of the screen, using the SHOWMENU...TO <variable> commands. Your menus can include help messages, which appear below the menu as each option is highlighted. This is the basic syntax for the SHOWMENU command:

```
SHOWMENU
    <option 1> : <help message 1>,
    <option 2> : <help message 2>,
    <option n> : <help message n>
TO <choice>
```

where options are displayed at the top of the screen, help messages (descriptions of the menu items) are displayed beneath highlighted menu options, and <choice> is any variable name to store the selected option. Note that commas separate the options. To try this out, enter and play the PAL program named Testmenu, shown in Figure 17.6.

```
;---------------------------------- TestMenu.SC
;-------------- Test commands for displaying menus.
CLEAR
SHOWMENU
    "Beep"    : "Make a few beeps",
    "Flash"   : "Display a flashing message",
    "Colors"  : "Play the Colors script",
    "Nothing" : "Don't do anything"
TO Choice

;--------------- Respond to menu choice.
SWITCH
    CASE Choice = "Beep" :
        BEEP BEEP BEEP BEEP
    CASE Choice = "Flash" :
        @ 12,20
        STYLE BLINK
        ?? "Here is your flashing message..."
        SLEEP 5000
    CASE Choice = "Colors" :
        CLEAR
        PLAY "Colors"
ENDSWITCH
```

Figure 17.6: The Testmenu program

This sample program demonstrates both the SHOWMENU command and a technique for responding to a menu selection with a SWITCH...ENDSWITCH clause. When you play this program, you'll see this menu at the top of the screen:

Beep Flash Colors Nothing
Make a few beeps

If you move the highlight to other menu options, their help messages will be displayed beneath the menu. You can select a menu option by typing the first letter of the option or by moving the highlight to the option and pressing Enter (as with any other Paradox menu).

The menu appears on the screen because of the SHOW-MENU...TO <variable> clause in the Testmenu program, shown below:

```
;-------------------------------- Display a menu, store selection in Choice.
SHOWMENU
   "Beep"    : "Make a few beeps",
   "Flash"   : "Display a flashing message",
   "Colors"  : "Play the Colors script",
   "Nothing" : "Don't do anything"
TO Choice
```

Whichever option is selected from the menu when the program is run is stored in the variable Choice. Once again, this variable name is entirely arbitrary. I've used the name Choice only because it is descriptive.

Note the syntax of the SHOWMENU...TO <variable> clause. Within the clause, menu options to be displayed are enclosed in quotation marks. (To ensure that the "first-letter" method of choosing menu items works properly, you should make each option start with a unique letter.)

Next to each menu option, after a colon, is the help message to be associated with the option. This, too, is enclosed in quotation marks. Each menu option and help message, except the last, is followed by a comma.

Beneath the SHOWMENU...TO clause is a SWITCH-...ENDSWITCH clause that responds to the selected menu item. Within the SWITCH...ENDSWITCH clause, the first CASE sounds four beeps if the user selects Beep from the menu:

```
;--------------------------------------------------- Respond to menu choice.
SWITCH
   CASE Choice = "Beep" :
      BEEP BEEP BEEP BEEP
```

The second CASE displays a flashing message if the Flash option is selected:

```
CASE Choice = "Flash" :
  @ 12,20
  STYLE BLINK
  ?? "Here is your flashing message..."
  SLEEP 5000
```

The third CASE runs the Colors.SC program if the Colors option is selected:

```
CASE Choice = "Colors" :
  CLEAR
  PLAY "Colors"
ENDSWITCH
```

(This choice works only if the Colors program, discussed earlier in this chapter, has already been created and is stored on the same disk as the Testmenu program.) Notice the syntax of the command. The PLAY command in a PAL program is identical to selecting the Scripts and Play options from the Paradox Main menu. The script or program name is enclosed in quotation marks.

If the Nothing option is selected, nothing happens, because there is no CASE or OTHERWISE option to cover this alternative. In any case, control is returned to the Paradox Main menu after a selection is made and the appropriate commands, if any, are performed.

SCRIPT CONVENTIONS

In previous examples in this chapter and in Chapter 11 we've seen many different types of scripts, in several different forms. Chapter 6 discussed *instant scripts*, which are recorded as you select commands and then stored in a script named Instant.SC. This chapter includes more complex scripts, which you create with the PAL editor. In the next chapter, we'll see yet another type of script called the *keyboard macro*.

All of these different types of scripts have certain elements in common, and any type of script may use any of these elements. The conventions that all scripts use are discussed in this section.

MENU SELECTIONS

If a script is designed to select items from one of the Paradox menus, the appropriate menu selection must be enclosed in curly braces and spelled exactly as it is spelled on the menu. For example, if the script is to select the Modify and Sort options from the Paradox Main menu, then the instructions to do so would be written into the script as

{Modify} {Sort}

A script can select any menu item, as long as the item is available on the current menu. For example, the selection {Sort} alone will generate an error if the {Modify} menu has not already been called up. If you are not sure of the series of menu selections you need, try selecting the items from the keyboard without any scripts involved, and jot down notes as you select menu items. Optionally, record the menu selections as you make them, and then copy the recorded keystrokes from the Instant.SC script to a new script name.

LITERAL KEYSTROKES

Literal keystrokes refer to any keystrokes that would otherwise be typed in at the keyboard. Literal keystrokes must be enclosed in double quotation marks within the script. When Paradox sees text enclosed in quotation marks within a script, it types those exact letters, just as though they were being typed in from the keyboard by a person. For example, if you want your script to type the name *Palm Springs*, then that section of the script must be written as

"Palm Springs"

Suppose you want your script to select the Modify and Restructure options from the menu, then type in the name CustList as the table to restructure. The series of elements would need to be

{Modify} {Restructure} "CustList"

Here, the menu selections are enclosed in curly braces, and the literal name CustList is enclosed in quotation marks.

SPECIAL KEYS

In addition to the basic letters and numbers that appear on your keyboard, a script can also press the special keys such as Enter, ↑, ↓, and so forth. These special key names are *not* enclosed in quotation marks, but are instead typed in by name. The names for these keys are listed in Table 17.2.

Table 17.2: Key names used in scripts

KEY NAME	PAL NAME
Spacebar	Space
↓	Down
←	Left
→	Right
↑	Up
Alt-F10	PalMenu
Alt-F3	InstantRecord
Alt-F4	InstantPlay
Alt-F5	FieldView
Alt-F6	CheckPlus
Alt-F7	InstantReport
Alt-F8	ClearAll
Alt-F9	CoeditKey
Alt-K	KeyLookup
Alt-L	LockKey
Alt-O	DOSBig
Alt-R	Refresh
Alt-X	CrossTab
Alt-Z	ZoomNext
Backspace	Backspace
Ctrl-←	CtrlLeft
Ctrl-→	CtrlRight

Table 17.2: Key names used in scripts (continued)

KEY NAME	PAL NAME
Ctrl-Backspace	CtrlBackspace
Ctrl-Break	CtrlBreak
Ctrl-D	Ditto
Ctrl-End	CtrlEnd
Ctrl-F	FieldView
Ctrl-Home	CtrlHome
Ctrl-PgDn	CtrlPgDn
Ctrl-R	Rotate
Ctrl-V	VertRuler
Ctrl-Y	DeleteLine
Ctrl-F6	CheckDescending
Ctrl-F7	GraphKey
Ctrl-O	DOS
Ctrl-Z	Zoom
Shift-F6	GroupBy
Del (or Delete)	Del
End	End
Enter	Enter
Esc	Esc
F1	Help
F2	DO_IT!
F3	UpImage
F4	DownImage
F5	Example
F6	Check
F7	FormKey
F8	ClearImage
F10	Menu

Table 17.2: Key names used in scripts (continued)

Key Name	PAL Name
Home	Home
Ins (or Insert)	Ins
PgDn	PgDn
PgUp	PgUp
Shift-Tab	ReverseTab
Tab	Tab

Note that DO_IT! is spelled with an underscore, not a hyphen.

Suppose you want your script to call up the Paradox Main menu, select the the Tools, Info, Inventory, and Files options, type in *.TXT as the pattern of file names to view, and then press Enter. The script would look like this:

Menu {Tools} {Info} {Inventory} {Files} "*.TXT" Enter

where *Menu* presses the Menu (F10) key, {*Tools*} {*Info*} {*Inventory*} {*Files*} select items from the menu, "*.TXT" is typed in literally when Paradox displays the prompt for entering a file name pattern, and *Enter* presses the Enter key.

COMMANDS AND FUNCTIONS

Any PAL script may also contain any one of the many PAL commands and functions. We've seen some examples of commands, such as STYLE, CLEAR, and WHILE...ENDWHILE in this chapter, and some functions as well, such as UPPER( ), GETCHAR( ), and MOD( ). There are many more PAL commands and functions, and these are discussed in the *PAL User's Guide*.

Commands and functions have very specific rules of syntax and other requirements that must be adhered to strictly. Those many requirements are far too numerous to list here, and your best source for the specifics about a PAL command or function is the *PAL User's Guide* that comes with your Paradox package.

Commands and functions are usually entered in all uppercase, (though this is more for stylistic, rather than technical, reasons). All of the sample scripts in this chapter demonstrate the use of PAL commands in scripts.

FIELD NAMES

Field Names from the currently open table can be used in scripts by placing square brackets around the name of the field. Note, however, that the field name must refer to a field that is on the currently active table. In the sample routine below, the first line uses the VIEW command to make the CustList table active. The second command displays the data in the Last Name field, for the current record, on the screen:

```
VIEW "CustList" Enter
? [Last Name]
```

VARIABLES

In this chapter we've seen the use of *variables* in PAL scripts as well. As discussed, a variable is a temporary "holding place" for information used in a script. Unlike information stored in tables, information stored in variables is temporary—it ceases to exist when the script stops running.

There are a few basic rules about variables that you need to adhere to for successful use in macros, as listed below:

- Variable names may be up to 132 characters in length.
- The first character must be a letter, A-Z or a-z.
- Subsequent characters in the variable name may be letters, numbers, or the punctuation marks ., $, !, or _.
- Blank spaces are *not* allowed in variable names.
- Variable names cannot be the same as a Paradox keyword— a PAL command, a PAL function, a menu selection, or a key name.

Examples of valid and invalid variable names are listed in Table 17.3.

Table 17.3: Examples of valid and invalid variable names

Variable Name	Type	Explanation
YourName	Valid	
My_Name	Valid	
X15	Valid	
Any_Day_Now	Valid	
Fig13.33	Valid	
Income$	Valid	
Hardy Har	Invalid	Contains a blank space
1stEntry	Invalid	Does not begin with a letter
$Income	Invalid	Does not begin with a letter
"Hello"	Invalid	Does not begin with a letter
Style	Invalid	Same as a command
MenuChoice	Invalid	Same as a function name
Ditto	Invalid	Same as a key name

The trickiest variable names to avoid are those that duplicate commands, function names, and key names. Table 17.2 lists all the key names. If you do inadvertently use a reserved word as a variable name, PAL will display an error message such as

Syntax error: Expecting a variable name

You'll need to edit the script and use a different variable name.

For your own convenience, you might also want to avoid using table names as variable names. For example, if your script operates on a table named Mastinv, you can avoid potential confusion by not using Mastinv as a variable name in that script.

Variables are assigned values in several ways within scripts. One is to use the equal sign (=), as you would in general mathematics. For example, the command below creates a variable named LoopCounter, and stores the number 1 in it:

```
LoopCounter = 1
```

The command below stores the name Albert in a variable named PersonName:

```
PersonName = "Albert"
```

The value in a variable may be changed using the equal sign operator as well. For example, the command below adds 1 to the current value of the LoopCounter variable:

```
LoopCounter = LoopCounter + 1
```

The command below adds the word *Dear* and a blank space to the front of whatever is stored in the variable named PersonName:

```
Salute = "Dear  " + PersonName
```

In the above example, if the variable named PersonName contains Albert, then this command stores *Dear Albert* in a variable named Salute.

Many commands, such as SHOWMENU and ACCEPT, also automatically assign values to variables, as earlier examples demonstrated. For example, the command below:

```
ACCEPT A25 TO PersonName
```

waits for the user to type in an alphanumeric value with a maximum length of 25 characters, and stores that entry in a variable named PersonName.

Other commands and functions operate on data already stored in variables. For example, the small script below displays the prompt *Enter you name:* on the screen, then waits for the user to type in his name and press Enter. The ? command displays the user's name on the screen in all uppercase letters (because of the UPPER function):

```
? "Enter your name: "
ACCEPT "A20" TO PersonName
? UPPER(PersonName)
```

In the next chapter, we'll see all of these elements used within a practical application of PAL scripts.

STRUCTURED PROGRAMMING

Now, before we try to do anything too practical with our new knowledge of basic PAL programming techniques, we should discuss why the sample programs in this chapter look the way they do. You'll notice that most programs include comments (sentences in plain English preceded by a semicolon) and indentations. Such techniques are part of the *structured* approach to programming, and are designed to help you write programs that are easy to debug and modify.

There are two basic and fairly simple rules for structured programming that you can use to make your PAL programming a bit easier:

1. Use comments to identify the program and major routines in plain English.

2. Indent commands that fall within "clauses."

Figure 17.7 shows a program, identical to the Testmenu program that we just developed, which does not follow these two basic rules of structured programming.

The unstructured program will run as well as the structured one, but it is difficult to decipher the purpose of the program and the function of each major section of the program. Figure 17.6 shows the same program with comments and indentations.

Notice that the comments stand out very clearly and, therefore, make the program easy to decipher. Even though Paradox requires only that a comment be preceded by a semicolon, the use of hyphens brings the comments to the foreground, making it easy to scan through the comments quickly to review the purpose of the major routines in the program.

```
CLEAR
SHOWMENU "Beep":"Make a few beeps","Flash":
"Display a flashing message","Colors":
"Play the Colors script","Nothing":
"Don't do anything" TO
Choice
SWITCH
CASE Choice = "Beep":BEEP BEEP BEEP BEEP
CASE Choice = "Flash":@ 12,20
STYLE BLINK
?? "Here is your flashing message..."
SLEEP 5000
CASE Choice = "Colors":CLEAR
PLAY "Colors"
ENDSWITCH
```

Figure 17.7: An unstructured PAL program

Indentations are used in all commands that form clauses to make the clauses stand out more clearly. In the unstructured program, all the commands look like a single string of indecipherable code. In the structured program, it is clear that there are two major clauses in the program: one for displaying the menu (SHOWMENU...TO <variable>) and another for making decisions (SWITCH...ENDSWITCH).

In the sample programs in the next chapter, we'll adhere to the basic rules of structured programming to try to make the programs as readable as possible. First, take a moment to review the various programming techniques we discussed in this chapter.

SUMMARY

- To create or edit a PAL program, use the Scripts and Editor options from the Paradox Main menu.

- To run a PAL program, use the Scripts and Play options from the Paradox Main menu, or the Go option from the Editor menu.

- To display information on the screen from within a program, use the STYLE, ?, ??, and @ commands.

- To get information from the user while a program is running, use the ACCEPT command or GETCHAR( ) function.

- To set up a loop in a program, use the WHILE-...ENDWHILE commands.

- To make simple if...then decisions in a program, use the IF...THEN...ELSE...ENDIF commands.
- To make decisions where several mutually exclusive alternatives exist, use the SWITCH...CASE...OTHERWISE...ENDSWITCH commands.
- To generate menus from within a program, use the SHOWMENU...TO <variable> commands.
- A script is composed of any combination of the basic script elements: menu selections, literal keystrokes, special key names, PAL commands and functions, field names, and variables.

A SAMPLE PAL APPLICATION

CHAPTER 18

The Paradox Personal Programmer, discussed in Chapter 20, lets you develop applications with little or no programming.

ONE OF THE MAIN REASONS THAT PEOPLE DEVELOP custom applications with a programming language is to simplify the use of the end product. As an example of this, in this chapter we'll develop some PAL programs that automate a mailing-list management system, using the Custlist table. When the user plays the script named Mail, the screen displays a menu containing these options:

    Add Sort Print Change Exit

The user can select items from this custom menu to perform a variety of tasks. He need not know anything about Paradox itself, because all options are fully automated.

Each of the menu options has a PAL script associated with it. Each of the scripts is accessed from the Mail script, which presents the menu. We can envision the relationship among the various scripts (programs) as shown in Figure 18.1.

We'll discuss each program in the sample application independently. If you are planning to follow along on-line, be sure to store these programs on the same disk as your Custlist table, which we created in the first few chapters of this book.

THE MAIN MENU

The main menu program for the sample application is named Mail.SC. You can create it with the PAL editor. Type it in as shown in Figure 18.2.

Let's discuss how the Mail.SC program works. The program begins with some opening comments and the CLEARALL command, as shown below. CLEARALL clears any existing tables from

```
                    ┌─────────────────────┐
                    │ Mail.SC             │
                    │ Presents menu       │
                    │ Add                 │
                    │ Sort                │
                    │ Print               │
                    │ Change              │
                    │ Exit                │
                    └─────────────────────┘
```

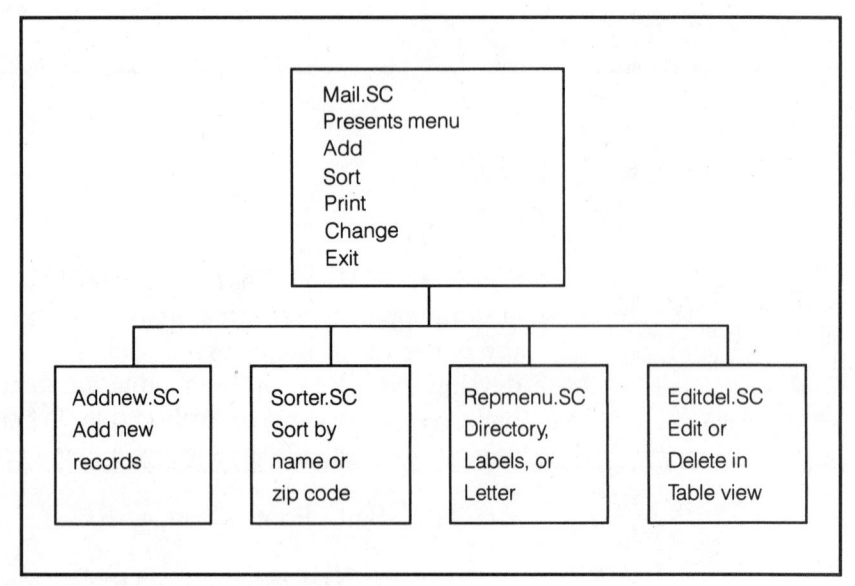

Figure 18.1: Relationships of programs in the mailing system

the Paradox workspace, so the program begins with a "clean slate":

```
;-------------------------------------------------------------------- Mail.SC
; ------------------------------------------ Script to integrate mailing system.
CLEARALL
```

The next routine in the program sets a style attribute and prints the title "Mailing List Management System" and some opening instructions. Any information between the TEXT...ENDTEXT commands in a program is displayed on the screen exactly as typed into the program:

```
; -------------------------------------------------------- Display opening screen.
STYLE ATTRIBUTE 30
CLEAR
@ 8,25
?? "Mailing List Management System"
STYLE
@ 10,1
TEXT
    Select options from the menu above, either by highlighting and
```

```
;------------------------------------- Mail.SC
;----------- Script to integrate mailing system.
CLEARALL
;----------------- Display opening screen.
STYLE ATTRIBUTE 30
CLEAR
@ 8,25
?? "Mailing List Management System"
STYLE
@ 10,1
TEXT
          Select options from the menu above, either by highlighting
          and pressing Enter, or by typing in the first letter of
          the option.  Moving the highlight with the cursor arrow
          keys displays a brief description of each option.

ENDTEXT
;------------- Set up loop to repeat menu.
Choice = " "
WHILE Choice <> "Exit"
     ;---------------- Show Paradox-style menu.
     SHOWMENU
        "Add"   : "Add new records",
        "Sort"  : "Sort data into alphabetical or zip code order",
        "Print" : "Print directory, labels, or letters",
        "Change" : "Change or delete data",
        "Exit"  : "Return to Paradox"
     TO Choice
     ;---------- Branch to new script based on choice.
     SWITCH
        CASE Choice = "Add" :
            PLAY "Addnew"
        CASE Choice = "Sort" :
            PLAY "Sorter"
        CASE Choice = "Print" :
            PLAY "Repmenu"
        CASE Choice = "Change" :
            PLAY "Editdel"
     ENDSWITCH
ENDWHILE
;------------- Exit selected.
CLEAR
STYLE REVERSE
@ 12,24
?? "Returning to Paradox Main menu..."
SLEEP 1000
```

Figure 18.2: The Mail.SC program

pressing Enter, or by typing in the first letter of the option. Moving the highlight with the cursor arrow keys displays a brief description of each option.
ENDTEXT

Next, a WHILE...ENDWHILE loop is set up that will repeatedly redisplay the menu on the screen, as long as the user does not opt to exit from the mailing system. Note that the variable Choice is used to control the loop, which repeats as long as this variable does not contain the word *Exit:*

```
;------------------------------------------------ Set up loop to repeat menu.
Choice = " "
WHILE Choice < > "Exit"
```

Within the WHILE loop, the SHOWMENU command displays the menu and help messages. The user's selection is stored in the variable named Choice:

```
;------------------------------------------------ Show Paradox-style menu.
SHOWMENU
   "Add" : "Add new records",
   "Sort" : "Sort data into alphabetical or zip code order",
   "Print" : "Print directory, labels, or letters",
   "Change" : "Change or delete data",
   "Exit" : "Return to Paradox"
TO Choice
```

Next, a SWITCH...ENDSWITCH clause passes control to another program, based on the user's menu selection. (This part of the program will work properly only after you've created the other programs discussed in this chapter.)

```
;---------------------------------- Branch to new script based on choice.
SWITCH
   CASE Choice = "Add" :
      PLAY "AddNew"
   CASE Choice = "Sort" :
      PLAY "Sorter"
   CASE Choice = "Print" :
      PLAY "RepMenu"
   CASE Choice = "Change" :
      PLAY "EditDel"
ENDSWITCH
ENDWHILE
```

When an outside script is accessed by this program, it will perform its tasks and then return control to the Mail.SC program. At this point, all other CASE options are ignored, and control falls to the

ENDWHILE command. If the user did not select Exit, the loop will repeat and the menu will reappear at the top of the screen.

When the user does select Exit, none of the CASE statements will be selected, and the WHILE...ENDWHILE loop will end. At this point, control will fall to the last routine in the program, which displays a closing message, pauses briefly, and then returns to the Paradox Main menu:

```
; -------------------------------------------------------------------- Exit selected.
CLEAR
STYLE REVERSE
@ 12,24
?? "Returning to Paradox main menu..."
SLEEP 1000
```

When first played, the Mail.SC program displays the opening messages and menu shown in Figure 18.3. After a menu option is selected and a task is performed, the menu will reappear on the screen and the user can either make another selection or choose Exit to leave the mailing system and return to the Paradox Main menu.

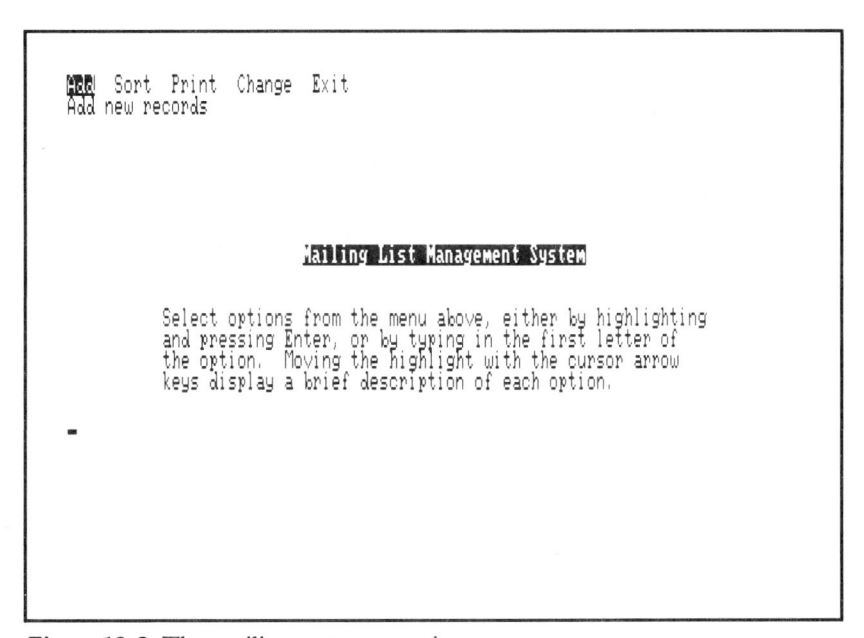

```
Add  Sort  Print  Change  Exit
Add new records




                    Mailing List Management System

            Select options from the menu above, either by highlighting
            and pressing Enter, or by typing in the first letter of
            the option.  Moving the highlight with the cursor arrow
            keys display a brief description of each option.


■
```

Figure 18.3: The mailing system opening screen

ADDING NEW RECORDS

When the user selects Add from the main menu, Paradox displays the custom form (which we developed earlier), ready to accept new data, as shown in Figure 18.4. The Addnew.SC program, shown in Figure 18.5, allows the user to enter new data through this custom form.

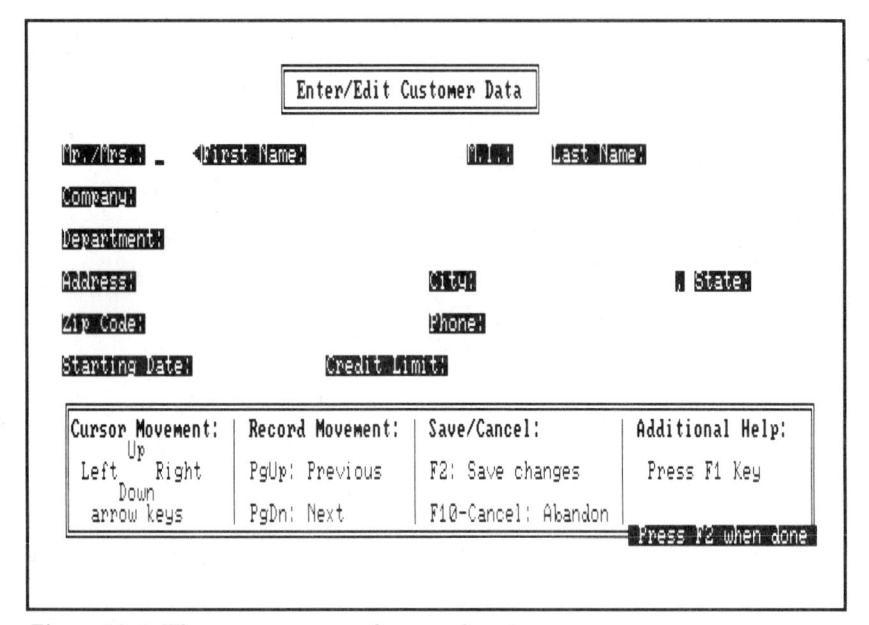

Figure 18.4: The custom screen for entering data

```
;------------------------------------ Addnew.SC.
;--- Script to add new records to Custlist table.

;--- Make menu selections.
CLEARALL {Modify} {DataEntry} {Custlist}
MENU {Image} {PickForm} {1}
;--- Allow new records until F2 is pressed.
WAIT TABLE
      MESSAGE "Press F2 when done"
UNTIL "F2"
;--- Save new records, then clear everything.
DO_IT!
CLEARALL
CLEAR
```

Figure 18.5: The Addnew.SC program

This program begins with the usual opening comments, the CLEARALL command to clear the workspace, and then keystrokes similar to those in a recorded script, as shown below:

```
CLEARALL {Modify} {DataEntry} {Custlist}
MENU {Image} {PickForm} {1}
```

The keystrokes *{Modify} {DataEntry} {Custlist}* select the Modify and DataEntry options from the menu and specify Custlist as the table to add records to. Notice that the keystrokes are placed inside curly braces, as discussed in Chapter 17.

The second set of keystrokes, *MENU {Image} {PickForm} {1}*, calls up the menu and selects the Image and PickForm options and form number 1. MENU is a command that calls up the menu, so it is not enclosed in braces.

The next routine keeps the custom form for entering records on the screen until the user presses DO-IT! (F2). The WAIT command is used in situations where a Paradox table or form is displayed on the screen, and you want to hold that table or form until a certain key is pressed. This keeps the PAL canvas in the background and the Paradox workspace in the foreground until some event occurs. Notice the syntax of the command, shown below:

```
; -- Allow new records until F2 is pressed.
WAIT TABLE
    MESSAGE "Press F2 when done"
UNTIL "F2"
```

The WAIT TABLE portion tells Paradox to wait before returning to the PAL canvas, and allows changes to the entire table. The MESSAGE portion displays the message "Press F2 when done" in the lower-right corner of the screen, so the user knows how to get back to the PAL program. The UNTIL portion defines which key terminates the WAIT.

Other options for the WAIT command are WAIT RECORD, which allows a single record to be modified or added, and WAIT FIELD, which allows changes to only a single field.

Once the user is done entering records and presses F2, the last lines in the program are played:

```
; -- Save new records, then clear everything.
DO_IT!
CLEARALL
CLEAR
```

The DO_IT! command (which uses an underline rather than a hyphen when used as a PAL command) saves the newly added records. (When the user presses DO-IT! (F2) in the performance of this program, the only action that takes place is that the WAIT pause ends. The program itself then performs a DO_IT! to actually save the new records.) The CLEARALL command clears the form from the workspace, and the CLEAR command clears the PAL canvas. At this point, the program is done and returns control to the calling program, Mail.SC, which in turn redisplays the mailing-system menu.

SORTING DATA

When the user selects Sort from the menu, the screen displays this submenu:

```
Alphabetical   ZipCode   None
```

The user can select a sorting option, and PAL will automatically perform the sort. If the user selects None, control is simply returned to the mailing-system menu. This portion of the mailing system is handled by the Sorter.SC program, shown in Figure 18.6.

The Sorter program begins with the usual opening programmer comments, followed by a routine that displays a menu of sort options, as shown below:

```
;----------------------------------------------------------------- Sorter.SC.
;----------------------------------------------- Script to display options and sort.
CLEARALL
CLEAR
SHOWMENU
   "Alphabetical" : "Alphabetical order by name",
```

```
;---------------------------------------- Sorter.SC.
;----------------- Script to display options and sort.
CLEARALL
CLEAR
SHOWMENU
  "Alphabetical" : "Alphabetical order by name",
  "ZipCode" : "Zip code order for bulk mailing",
  "None" : "Don't sort, return to menu"
TO SChoice

;--- Create message about waiting.
IF SChoice <> "None" THEN
    Msg = "Sorting the data, please wait"
    STYLE REVERSE, BLINK
    @ 12,25
    ?? Msg
ENDIF

;---------- Sort accordingly.
SWITCH
    CASE SChoice = "Alphabetical" :
        SORT "Custlist" ON "Last Name", "First Name"
    CASE SChoice = "Zip Code" :
        SORT "Custlist" ON "Zip", "Last Name"
ENDSWITCH
CLEAR
```

Figure 18.6: The Sorter.SC program

```
    "ZipCode" : "Zip code order for bulk mailing",
    "None" : "Don't sort, return to menu"
TO SChoice
```

The user's selection is stored in a variable named SChoice. If the user does not select the None option, the program displays a blinking message: "Sorting the data, please wait". The IF clause shown below displays the message (assuming the user did not select None):

```
;------------------------------------------ Create message about waiting.
IF SChoice <> "None" THEN
    Msg = "Sorting the data, please wait"
    STYLE REVERSE, BLINK
    @ 12,25
    ?? Msg
ENDIF
```

The final routine sorts the database according to the user's request. Note the use and syntax of the PAL SORT command, which bypasses the need to fill out the sort form:

```
;  ------------------------------------------------------------------ Sort accordingly.
SWITCH
   CASE SChoice = "Alphabetical" :
      SORT "Custlist" ON "Last Name", "First Name"
   CASE SChoice = "Zip Code" :
      SORT "Custlist" ON "Zip", "Last Name"
ENDSWITCH
CLEAR
```

The general syntax for the SORT command is as follows:

SORT "<table name>" ON "<field 1>",
"<field 2>",... "<field n>"

This form of the command will sort the table to itself (just as selecting the Same option from the Sort submenu). An optional TO clause can be used to store sorted data on a separate table, using this syntax:

SORT "<table name>" ON "<field 1>",..."<field n>" TO
"<table name>"

In this example, sorted records will be stored on the second table name in the command. You can also specify descending orders with the SORT command by placing the letter D after the field name but before the comma. For example, the command

SORT "Custlist" ON "Zip" D, "Last Name", TO "Zipdesc"

sorts the Custlist table in descending zip code order, with last names in alphabetical order within common zip codes. The sorted records are placed in a table named Zipdesc.

PRINTING REPORTS

If the user selects Print from the mailing-system main menu, the following submenu appears:

Directory   Labels   FormLetter   None

The user can pick any option and the program will automatically print the report. After selecting the type of report to print, the following submenu appears, offering the user a simplified querying capability:

AllRecords   City   State   ZipCode

Selecting AllRecords displays data for every record in the table. Selecting City presents the prompt

Limit print run to what city?

The user can type in the name of any city, and press Enter. The printed report will then contain only those records that contain the requested city.

The State option displays the prompt

Limit print run to what State?

In response to this prompt, the user may type in the two-letter abbreviation of any state, and the report will include records for only that state.

Selecting ZipCode allows the user to specify a range of zip codes to print the directory, mailing labels, or form letter from. This option first presents the prompt

Enter lowest zip code to include:

The user can type in any zip code value and press Enter. The screen then displays the prompt

Enter highest zip code to include:

The user types in the highest zip code value, and presses Enter. For example, if the user types in 90000 as the lowest zip code, and 99999 as the highest zip code, the report will include only records with zip codes in the range 90000 to 99999.

Of course, the user might request a query value for which there are no records. For example, if the user asks to print records for Kalamazoo residents, but there are no Kalamazoo records, the script displays the message

No records matched the requested query!

and passes control back to the main menu.

However, assuming the user enters a search value for which there are matching records, the program proceeds normally, beginning with the next prompt:

Are records already sorted into desired order? (Y/N)

If the records have not already been sorted, then the user can enter N, for No. In this case, the screen displays the message

Sorting records...

and sorts the records. (For a directory report, the records are sorted into alphabetical order by name. For mailing labels for a form letter, records are sorted into zip code order.)

If for some reason the printer is not ready to display the report when the sorting is complete, the screen displays the prompt

Prepare printer then press any key!

The user can turn on the printer (or set it on-line), and press any key to proceed. The requested report is printed, in the appropriate sorted order, and limited to the city, state, or zip code range requested (unless, of course, the AllRecords option was selected to print all the records). The PAL script to perform all of these tasks and present the menus and prompts, RepMenu.SC, is shown in Figure 18.7. We'll examine the various routines that the program uses in the following discussion.

The program begins with the usual identifying comments and then displays the menu of report options using the usual SHOW-MENU command. The user's selection is stored in a variable named RChoice, as shown below:

```
; -------------------------------------------------------------- Repmenu.SC
; ------------------------------------ Display report options and print report.
CLEAR
SHOWMENU
"Directory"  : "Directory of Customers",
"Labels"    : "Mailing Labels",
"FormLetter" : "Print Form Letter",
"None"      : "Return to Menu"
TO RChoice
```

A SAMPLE PAL APPLICATION   505

```
;---------------------------------------- RepMenu.SC
;------------ Display report options and print report.
CLEAR
SHOWMENU
    "Directory" : "Directory of Customers",
    "Labels" : "Mailing Labels",
    "Form Letter" : "Print Form Letter",
    "None": "Return to Menu"
TO RChoice

;---------------- If no report selected, return to menu.
IF RChoice = "None" THEN
    CLEAR
    RETURN
ENDIF

;--------- Display simple menu of query options.
CLEAR
SHOWMENU
    "AllRecords" : "Print data for all records",
    "City"       : "Limit mailing to a particular city",
    "State"      : "Limit mailing to a particular state",
    "ZipCode"    : "Limit mailing to a particular zip code range"
TO QChoice

;--- Bring up the query form, and
;--- fill in all fields with CheckPlus.
MENU {Ask}{CustList}CHECKPLUS

;--- Ask for query information,
;--- and fill in query form.
STYLE ATTRIBUTE 30
SWITCH
    CASE QChoice = "City":
        @ 12,5
        ?? "Limit print run to what city? "
        ACCEPT "A25" TO LookUp
        [City] = LookUp
    CASE QChoice = "State":
        @ 12,5
        ?? "Limit print run to what State? "
        ACCEPT "A5" TO LookUp
        [State] = LookUp
    CASE QChoice = "ZipCode":
        @ 12,5
        ?? "Enter lowest zip code to include: "
        ACCEPT "A10" TO LookUp1
        @ 14,5
        ?? "Enter highest zip code to include: "
        ACCEPT "A10" TO LookUp2
        [Zip] = ">="+LookUp1+",<="+LookUp2
ENDSWITCH

@ 24,1 CLEAR EOL
?? "Querying..."
;----- Perform the query, and copy report
;----- formats to the Answer table.
DO_IT!

;--- If Answer table ends up empty,
;--- cancel the operation.
IF (NRECORDS("Answer")=0) THEN
    BEEP BEEP
    @ 24,1 CLEAR EOL
    ?? "No records matched the requested query!"
    SLEEP 5000
    CLEARALL
    CLEAR
    RETURN
ENDIF
```

Figure 18.7: The RepMenu.SC program

```
;--- If Answer table OK, copy report formats to it.
{Tools}{Copy}{JustFamily}{CustList}{Answer}
{Replace}

;-------- Check on sort order, allow only Y or N answer.
Answer = " "
WHILE Answer <> "Y" AND Answer <> "N"
    @ 12,1 CLEAR EOS
    @ 12,10
    STYLE ATTRIBUTE 30
    ?? "Are records already sorted into desired order? (Y/N) "
    Answer = UPPER(CHR(GETCHAR()))
    ?? Answer
ENDWHILE

;-------- Sort if No selected.
IF Answer = "N" THEN
    STYLE REVERSE, BLINK
    @ 24,1 CLEAR EOL
    STYLE BLINK
    ?? "Sorting records..."
    IF RChoice = "Directory" THEN
        SORT "Answer" ON "Last Name", "First Name"
    ELSE
        SORT "Answer" ON "Zip", "Last Name"
    ENDIF ;(rchoice)
    CLEAR
ENDIF ;(answer)


;-------------------------- Make sure printer is ready.
WHILE PRINTERSTATUS() = False
    BEEP
    @ 12,1 CLEAR EOS
    @ 12,10
    STYLE REVERSE,BLINK
    ?? "Prepare printer then press any key!"
    Nothing = GETCHAR()
ENDWHILE

;-------------------------- Print requested report.
STYLE
CLEAR
? "Printing requested report..."
SWITCH
    CASE RChoice = "Directory" :
        REPORT "Answer" "1"

    CASE RChoice = "Labels" :
        REPORT "Answer" "2"

    CASE RChoice = "Form Letter" :
        REPORT "Answer" "3"

ENDSWITCH
;--- Eject one more page (optional).
PRINT "\F"

CLEARALL
CLEAR
```

Figure 18.7: The RepMenu.SC program (continued)

If the user decides not to print any reports (by selecting None), the program simply clears the screen and returns control to the calling program (Mail.SC). Note the use of the RETURN command to exit the program and return to the calling program:

```
;---------------------------------------- If no report selected, return to menu.
IF RChoice = "None" THEN
   CLEAR
   RETURN
ENDIF
```

Next, the program displays its simplified "mini-query" menu to the user. Once again, it uses the SHOWMENU command, as shown below. Note that the user's menu selection is stored in a variable named QChoice:

```
;-------------------------------------- Display simple menu of query options.
CLEAR
SHOWMENU
   "AllRecords" : "Print data for all records",
   "City"       : "Limit mailing to a particular city",
   "State"      : "Limit mailing to a particular state",
   "ZipCode"    : "Limit mailing to a particular zip code range"
TO QChoice
```

After the user makes his selection, the program calls up the query form for the CustList table, and places checkmarks in all the fields. (Since the PAL canvas is still in control of the screen, the user does not see this take place.) Because the cursor is automatically in the leftmost column of the query form when it is brought to the screen, the single CHECKPLUS keystroke places check-plus marks in every field:

```
;-------------------------------------------------- Bring up the query form, and
;-------------------------------------------------- fill in all fields with CheckPlus.
MENU {Ask}{CustList}CHECKPLUS
```

Now the program asks the user for the value to search for. If the user opts to limit records to a particular city, the routine below asks for the name of the city, stores the user's entry in a variable named LookUp, and then places that value into the City field on the query form. Once again, the field name [City] is enclosed in brackets, while the variable name LookUp is not:

```
;-------------------------------------------------------- Ask for query information,
;-------------------------------------------------------- and fill in query form.
STYLE ATTRIBUTE 30
SWITCH
   CASE QChoice = "City":
      @ 12,5
      ?? "Limit print run to what city? "
      ACCEPT "A25" TO LookUp
      [City] = LookUp
```

If the user opts to limit the report to a particular state, a routine similar to the one above asks for the name of the state, and places that name in the State field on the query form:

```
CASE QChoice = "State":
   @ 12,5
   ?? "Limit print run to what State? "
   ACCEPT "A5" TO LookUp
   [State] = LookUp
```

If the user opts to limit records to a range of zip codes, the program asks for the highest and lowest zip code values:

```
CASE QChoice = "ZipCode":
   @ 12,5
   ?? "Enter lowest zip code to include: "
   ACCEPT "A10" TO LookUp1
   @ 14,5
   ?? "Enter highest zip code to include: "
   ACCEPT "A10" TO LookUp2
   [Zip] = ">=" + LookUp1 + ",<=" + LookUp2
ENDSWITCH
```

The low value is stored in a variable named LookUp1, and the high value is stored in a variable named LookUp2. The appropriate expression is then placed into the Zip field of the query form. Note that this is done with the line

```
[Zip] = ">=" + LookUp1 + ",<=" + LookUp2
```

where *[Zip]* is the field name on the currently active query form, "> = " and ", < = " are literal text, and *LookUp1* and *LookUp2* are variables. Hence, if the user entered 10000 as the low value, and 19999 as the high value, the Zip field on the query form would receive the proper expression *> = 10000, < = 19999.*

Notice that there is no CASE clause for the AllRecords menu option. If the user selects this option, we want the query form to contain only the check-plus marks, because we want the query to display all the records in the table.

Next, the program clears the bottom line of the screen, presents the message "Querying...", and performs the query by pressing the DO-IT! key, as shown below:

```
@ 24,1 CLEAR EOL
?? "Querying..."
; ---------------------------------------- Perform the query, and copy report
;------------------------------------------------- formats to the Answer table.
DO_IT!
```

As a safety precaution, the program checks to make sure that some records made it to the Answer table. It uses the NRECORDS function to count how many records are in the Answer table. If this value is zero, the routine below beeps twice, displays an error message for about 5 seconds, clears the PAL canvas and the Answer table, and passes control back to the main menu, Mail.SC, using the RETURN command:

```
;-------------------------------------------- If Answer table ends up empty,
;-------------------------------------------------------- cancel the operation.
IF (NRECORDS("Answer") = 0) THEN
    BEEP BEEP
    @ 24,1 CLEAR EOL
    ?? "No records matched the requested query!"
    SLEEP 5000
    CLEARALL
    CLEAR
    RETURN
ENDIF
```

Assuming that the Answer table does not end up empty, the PAL keystrokes below copy all the report formats from the CustList table to the Answer table, using the usual Tools, Copy, and JustFamily menu options:

```
;------------------------------ If Answer table OK, copy report formats to it.
{Tools} {Copy} {JustFamily} {CustList} {Answer}
{Replace}
```

It is necessary to copy the report formats into the Answer table so that they can be used to print only those records that are in the Answer table.

Now the program asks about the sort order. It uses a technique that forces the user to enter either Y or N as a response. It uses a variable named Answer (which has nothing to do with the Answer table) to store the user's answer.

The WHILE loop repeats as long as the variable named Answer does not equal Y and does not equal N. Within the loop, the @ 12,1 CLEAR EOS command clears the screen from row 12 down (EOS stands for End Of Screen). The GETCHAR( ) function reads the next keystroke, storing it as an ASCII number. The CHR function converts this number to the appropriate letter (the one that was actually typed), and the UPPER function converts that letter to uppercase (so that a *y* or *n* entry is converted to *Y* or *N*). The ?? Answer command displays this converted answer on the screen:

```
; -------------------------- Check on sort order, allow only Y or N answer.
Answer = " "
WHILE Answer <> "Y" AND Answer <> "N"
    @ 12,1 CLEAR EOS
    @ 12,10
    STYLE ATTRIBUTE 30
    ?? "Are records already sorted into desired order? (Y/N) "
    Answer = UPPER(CHR(GETCHAR( )))
    ?? Answer
ENDWHILE
```

If the user recently sorted the table using the Sort option from the Mail.SC main menu, he can answer Y to the "Are records already sorted into the desired order?" prompt, and bypass the wait required to sort the records at this point. If the user answers N in response to the prompt, the routine below presents a blinking message, "Sorting records...", on the screen. Then it sorts the Answer table into the appropriate order for the report being printed: into alphabetical order by last and first name for directory reports, or into zip code order for the other report options:

```
;  -------------------------------------------------------------- Sort if No selected.
IF Answer = "N" THEN
    STYLE REVERSE, BLINK
    @ 24,1 CLEAR EOL
    STYLE BLINK
    ?? "Sorting records..."
    IF RChoice = "Directory" THEN
        SORT "Answer" ON "Last Name", "First Name"
    ELSE
        SORT "Answer" ON "Zip", "Last Name"
    ENDIF ;(rchoice)
    CLEAR
ENDIF ;(answer)
```

Note the use of nested IF clauses in the routine above. The first IF clause bypasses all the commands within the routine if the user's answer was not N. However, if the user's answer was N, all of the commands within that routine are executed. As required, each IF clause has its own ENDIF associated with it. To keep track of which ENDIF goes with which IF, the comments *;(rchoice)* and *;(answer)* are placed next to the ENDIFs. Since these are only comments (because of the leading semicolon), they do not have any effect on the routine. Paradox automatically assumes that an ENDIF relates to the IF at its same level of nesting. The comments next to the ENDIFs are simply for our own clarification.

Next, the program contains a routine to ensure that the printer is ready to accept the report. The PAL PRINTERSTATUS( ) function evaluates to false if the printer is not ready, or true if the printer is ready. A WHILE loop holds the program in suspension until the printer is ready (that is, it repeats itself as long as the printer is not ready). Within this WHILE loop, the program beeps and displays a blinking message. The CLEAR EOL command clears the screen from the cursor position to the end of the line. The GETCHAR( ) function waits for any key to be pressed. The results of the keypress are stored in a variable named Nothing (since this variable only exists to make the GETCHAR( ) funtion work properly):

```
;-------------------------------------------------------- Make sure printer is ready.
WHILE PRINTERSTATUS( ) = False
    BEEP
    STYLE REVERSE, BLINK
    @ 12,10 CLEAR EOL
    ?? "Prepare printer then press any key!"
    Nothing = GETCHAR( )
ENDWHILE
CLEAR
```

Finally, the program is ready to print the reports. In the routine below, the CLEAR and ? commands clear the screen and display a message on the screen. Then a SWITCH...ENDSWITCH clause prints the appropriate report, based on the user's earlier request (stored in the RChoice variable).

The routine uses the PAL REPORT command, which follows the general syntax

REPORT "<table name>","<report identifier>"

where <*table name*> is the name of the table containing the data to print, and <*report identifier*> is the number of the report assigned when the report was initially designed. As you may recall from Chapter 8, we assigned the number 1 to the directory report, the number 2 to the mailing labels, and 3 to the form letter. Furthermore, this program already used the Tools, Copy, and JustFamily options to copy these report formats to the Answer table. Therefore, the command below prints mailing labels for the Answer table:

REPORT "Answer","2"

The routine to print the appropriate report is shown below:

```
;-------------------------------------------------------- Print requested report.
STYLE
CLEAR
? "Printing requested report..."
```

```
    SWITCH
      CASE RChoice = "Directory" :
        REPORT "Answer" "1"
      CASE RChoice = "Labels" :
        REPORT "Answer" "2"
      CASE RChoice = "Form Letter" :
        REPORT "Answer" "3"
    ENDSWITCH
```

The small routine below causes the printer to eject an extra page after the report is printed. Many printers will not need this extra page, though some laser printers might require it. If your printer automatically ejects an extra page at the end of the printed reports, you can just leave this entire routine out:

```
;-------------------------------------------------- This small routine is optional.
PRINT "\F"
```

On some printers, you may need to eject only the last page when printing mailing labels. (That's because mailing labels use a "continuous" page length, and leave the printer waiting for an "eject" after the last "page" is printed.) If that is the case, leave out the small routine above, and place the PRINT "\F" statement in the CASE clause for printing labels, as shown below:

```
CASE RChoice = "Labels" :
  REPORT "Answer" "2"
  PRINT "\F"
```

The last two commands in the RepMenu.SC simply clear the workspace and the PAL canvas:

```
CLEARALL
CLEAR
```

Then, the program ends and passes control back to the calling program: Mail.SC in this example.

EDITING THE MAILING LIST

When the user selects the Change option from the mailing-system main menu, the program first presorts the table into alphabetical order, making it easier to find a particular person by name, and then displays this prompt:

    Enter last name to look up
    Or just press Enter to exit: _

The user can enter a last name, and the Custlist table will appear on the screen, ready for editing, with the cursor at the first record with the requested last name. Since the table is sorted, any other individuals with the same last name will be beneath the cursor, as shown in Figure 18.8.

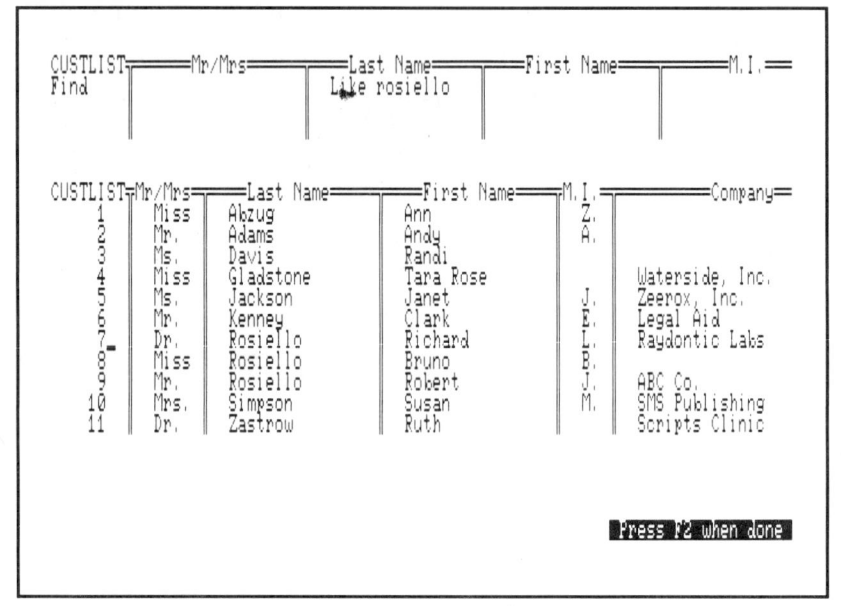

```
CUSTLIST======Mr/Mrs==========Last Name=======First Name=======M.I.==
Find                          Like rosiello



CUSTLIST=Mr/Mrs========Last Name=======First Name====M.I.========Company=
   1    Miss    Abzug           Ann            Z.
   2    Mr.     Adams           Andy           A.
   3    Ms.     Davis           Randi
   4    Miss    Gladstone       Tara Rose            Waterside, Inc.
   5    Ms.     Jackson         Janet          J.    Zeerox, Inc.
   6    Mr.     Kenney          Clark          E.    Legal Aid
   7    Dr.     Rosiello        Richard        L.    Raydontic Labs
   8    Miss    Rosiello        Bruno          B.
   9    Mr.     Rosiello        Robert         J.    ABC Co.
  10    Mrs.    Simpson         Susan          M.    SMS Publishing
  11    Dr.     Zastrow         Ruth                 Scripts Clinic




                                                          [Press F2 when done]
```

Figure 18.8: The screen after the request to edit Rosiello's data

If there is no name that matches the requested name, the program displays this message:

    There is nobody named <Smith>

The user can edit and delete as many records as he wishes using this program. Pressing Enter rather than entering a name to look up returns control to the mailing-system menu. This portion of the mailing system is handled by the EditDel.SC program, shown in Figure 18.9.

Let's look at how the EditDel program works. The program begins with opening comments and then sorts that table into

```
;---------------------------------------- EditDel.SC
;----------------------- Edit/Delete data in a table.
;---------------------Presort into alphabetical order.
STYLE REVERSE,BLINK
CLEAR
@ 12,10
?? "Presorting to simplify editing..."
SORT "Custlist" ON "Last Name" "First Name" "M.I."
BEEP
;--------------------- Set up loop for editing.
CLEAR
StillAtIt = TRUE
WHILE StillAtIt
      CLEARALL
      CLEAR
      STYLE ATTRIBUTE 30
      @ 12,10
      ?? "Enter last name to look up "
      @ 14,10
      ?? "Or just press Enter to exit: "
      ACCEPT "A20" TO LookUp

      ;---------- If no entry, exit.
      IF ISBLANK(LookUp) THEN
          @ 24,1 CLEAR EOL
          ?? "Returning to menu..."
          QUITLOOP
      ENDIF

      @ 24,1
      ?? "Setting pointer to " + Lookup
      ;----- Perform a "find" query.
      MENU {Ask} {Custlist}
      [Last Name] = "Like " + LookUp
      [#] = "Find"
      DO_IT!

      ;----- If no match, warn user.
      IF (NRECORDS("Answer") = 0) THEN
          BEEP
          @ 24,1 CLEAR EOL
          ?? "There is nobody named "+LookUp
          SLEEP 5000
          LOOP
      ENDIF

      ;-- Allow full editing from cursor position.
      EDITKEY
      WAIT TABLE
          MESSAGE "Press F2 when done"
          UNTIL "F2"
      ;-- Save Changes.
      DO_IT!
ENDWHILE
CLEAR
RETURN
```

Figure 18.9: The EditDel.SC program

alphabetical order, as shown below:

```
;---------------------------------------------------------------------------- EditDel.SC
;---------------------------------------------------------- Edit/Delete data in a table.
;------------------------------------------------ Presort into alphabetical order.
STYLE REVERSE,BLINK
CLEAR
@ 12,10
?? "Presorting to simplify editing..."
SORT "CustList" ON "Last Name" "First Name" "M.I."
BEEP
```

Next, a loop is set up so the user can repeatedly enter names to look up and edit. This loop is controlled by a variable named StillAtIt. Within the loop, the program asks the user to enter a name to look up (or press Enter), and stores the user's entry in a variable named LookUp, as shown below:

```
;------------------------------------------------------------- Set up loop for editing.
CLEAR
StillAtIt = TRUE
WHILE StillAtIt
   CLEARALL
   CLEAR
   STYLE ATTRIBUTE 30
   @ 12,10
   ?? "Enter last name to look up "
   @ 14,10
   ?? "Or just press Enter to exit: "
   ACCEPT "A20" TO LookUp
```

If the user simply presses Enter, rather than entering a name, the program drops out of the loop immediately. Note the use of the PAL ISBLANK function to test whether the LookUp variable is a blank. The PAL QUITLOOP command terminates the WHILE loop in this case, passing control to the first command beneath the ENDWHILE command:

```
;------------------------------------------------------------------- If no entry, exit.
IF ISBLANK(LookUp) THEN
   @ 24,1 CLEAR EOL
```

```
    ?? "Returning to menu..."
    QUITLOOP
ENDIF
```

If the user enters a name, the program displays a message indicating that it is looking up the requested individual, as shown below:

```
@ 24,1
?? "Looking for " + LookUp
```

Next, the program calls up the Paradox menu, selects Ask, and specifies CustList as the table to query, as shown below:

```
; ---------------------------------------------------------- Perform a "find" query.
MENU {Ask} {CustList}
```

Next, the word "Like" and the requested last name are placed into the Last Name field on the query form, and the command "Find" is placed into the leftmost column. Note the use of square brackets to indicate fields on the query form. The [#] symbol stands for the leftmost column, where commands like Find and Delete are entered. The DO_IT! command then performs the "Find" query (which displays actual table data ready for editing, rather than an Answer table):

```
[Last Name] = "Like " + LookUp
[#] = "Find"
DO_IT!
```

Now it gets a little tricky. Although a find query displays the original table rather than the Answer table, it does create an Answer table that is simply not shown on the screen. Therefore, we can determine whether the program found an individual with the requested last name by counting the number of records in the (invisible) Answer table. If there are no records in the Answer table (NRECORDS = 0)—that is, no record matches the requested last name—the program informs the user of this fact in the routine below:

```
; ---------------------------------------------------------- If no match, warn user.
IF (NRECORDS("Answer") = 0) THEN
```

```
    BEEP
    @ 24,1 CLEAR EOL
    ?? "There is nobody named " + LookUp
    SLEEP 5000
    LOOP
ENDIF
```

(The LOOP command skips all remaining commands between the current position and the ENDWHILE command, but does not in itself terminate the loop.)

If there is a match (or several matches) for the requested last name, the program switches the user to Edit mode (by issuing the EDITKEY command), then waits for the user to finish editing. When the user has finished editing (signified by pressing F2), the program saves his changes and repeats the loop asking for the next person to edit:

```
    ;-- Allow full editing from cursor position.
    EDITKEY
    WAIT TABLE
       MESSAGE "Press F2 when done"
       UNTIL "F2"
    ;-- Save changes.
    DO_IT!
ENDWHILE
CLEAR
RETURN
```

This marks the end of the program and the end of the mailing-list system.

After you have typed in all of the programs (scripts) shown in this chapter using the PAL editor (or an outside word processor), you can use the mailing system. (Of course, you'll also need the CustList table we created in Chapter 2, and the report formats we created in Chapter 8.)

To use the mailing system anytime, select the Scripts and Play options from the Paradox Main menu. Specify Mail as the name of the script to play. The Mail menu will replace the Paradox Main menu until you select Exit. At that point, you'll be returned to the Paradox Main menu, and all your work with the Mail system will be safely stored on disk.

SPEEDING UP MAIL

For all its user-friendliness, and constant resorting, the Mail system has one drawback: it can get to be rather slow when there are many records in the CustList table. To speed things up, you can create *secondary indexes* of fields that are commonly used for searching. (They are called secondary indexes because Paradox automatically creates a primary index for the key field in the table, if it has one.) In this application, the Last Name field is searched quite regularly to locate a record to edit. Also, the Zip field might be searched often if you often specify ranges of zip codes for mailings.

The QuerySpeed menu option we discussed earlier creates secondary indexes, but does not necessarily create the best possible indexes for a given application. For example, if you use QuerySpeed to create an index for a query on the State field, but don't really search the State field often, the secondary index is somewhat wasteful, because there is some extra time involved in keeping all secondary indexes up to date. Instead of using the QuerySpeed option, you can use the PAL INDEX command to create indexes for specific, and often used, fields.

The basic syntax of the INDEX command is

    INDEX [MAINTAINED] "<table name>" ON "<field name>"

where the optional *[MAINTAINED]* portion is used only with tables that already have a primary index (based on a key field). *<table name>* is the name of the table the index file is for, and *<field name>* is the name of the field that is indexed.

To create indexes of the Last Name and Zip fields for the CustList table, enter the PAL script editor using the usual Scripts, Editor, and Write menu options. Enter a name, such as MIndex, for the script when prompted, and type in the two commands below:

    INDEX "CustList" ON "Last Name"
    INDEX "CustList" ON "Zip"

Press F2 when done, then select Scripts, Play, and MIndex from the Main menu to run the script.

Though you won't see any immediate effects, Paradox will create four files, named CustList.X02, CustList.Y02, CustList.X0A, and CustList.Y0A. Paradox will automatically maintain and use these files as necessary in the future. You need not do anything else after running the MIndex script once. (However, if a blackout or some other small disaster causes Paradox to terminate abruptly, the indexes may become corrupted, and your searches may then behave strangely. If that occurs, just play the MIndex script again to rebuild the index files.)

I hope this sample system has given you a basic idea of how PAL programs work, and has presented enough general techniques to get you started on your own programs, if you are so inclined. Again, let me state that it is not necessary to program Paradox; most work can be handled easily working through the normal Paradox menus. But if you enjoy programming or have a strong desire to develop a customized application, PAL will allow you to do so.

There is also another way to create customized applications in Paradox, and that is to use the Paradox Personal Programmer, which comes with your Paradox package. The Personal Programmer lets you build custom applications through menu selections, much like the menu selections on the Paradox Main menu. You tell the Personal Programmer what you want your custom application to do, and it writes the PAL scripts for you. We'll discuss the Paradox Personal Programmer in Chapter 20.

SUMMARY

In this chapter, we've discussed some general programming techniques that you can use to create custom applications using PAL. Some of the commands that are especially useful to programmers are summarized below:

- The TEXT...ENDTEXT commands allow a program to display many lines of text without repeated ? or ?? commands.
- The WAIT command halts a PAL program while the user interacts with a form or table display.

- The SORT command sorts a table without going through the usual menu procedures.
- The REPORT command prints a report without going through the usual menu selection process.

HANDY TIPS AND SCRIPTS

CHAPTER 19

THIS CHAPTER DISCUSSES GENERAL TECHNIQUES for managing scripts, and also presents some handy scripts that you can use in your own custom applications. One particularly useful script converts numbers (such as *123.45*) to words (such as *one hundred twenty three and 45/100*) for applications that write checks. Another handy script prints multicolumn mailing labels in any format you desire. Both of these scripts also involve some advanced PAL programming concepts and techniques.

TIPS ON SCRIPTS

We shall begin our discussion by looking at several handy techniques you can use with your scripts.

RUNNING SCRIPTS FROM DOS

To run an existing script without first going through the Paradox opening screen, simply enter the name of the script next to the Paradox3 command from the DOS prompt. For example, on a hard disk, the command

    C> PARADOX3 Mail

runs Paradox and the Mail.SC script immediately (assuming that the script is on the current directory and Paradox is accessible from that directory).

AUTOMATIC SCRIPTS

Another way to make a script run immediately is to assign it the name Init.SC. When Paradox first runs, it looks for a script named

Init.SC and processes all commands in the script immediately, before providing access to the Main menu. If a script contains the EXIT command, it will return to the DOS prompt when done.

PROTECTING SCRIPTS

Using the Tools, More, Protect, Password, and Script options, you can assign passwords to scripts. Once the password is assigned, the script cannot be viewed or edited by anyone who does not know the password. Furthermore, the script will be encrypted, so that neither the DOS TYPE command nor an external word processor can view its contents. Passwords are discussed in greater detail in Chapter 16.

PRINTING SCRIPTS

To print a PAL script, press Menu (F10) while the script is displayed in the PAL editor. Then simply select Print from the menu to print your script.

USING EXTERNAL WORD PROCESSORS TO EDIT SCRIPTS

An unprotected script is a simple ASCII file that can be created and edited with any text editor or word processor. When you use an external word processor to create or edit a script, be sure to follow these guidelines:

- Store the script on a directory or disk that is available to Paradox.
- Always specify the extension .SC with the script file name. The PAL editor does this automatically, but an external word processor will not.
- Create or save the script as an ASCII file (also called a DOS text file).

The last point is an important one, because most word processors add formatting codes, which Paradox cannot read, if you do not explicitly store the file as an ASCII file. In WordStar, you create ASCII files by specifying N (Nondocument), rather than D (Document) mode before you enter the name of the file to edit or create. With WordPerfect, you need to press Ctrl-F5 and select 1 (DOS Text File Format Save) when saving the completed script. Other word processors will use other techniques for storing ASCII files (or DOS text files).

You can configure Paradox to invoke the word processor of your choosing automatically when you select Script Editor from the Main menu. For instructions on how to do so, see the discussion of the PAL editor configuration in Chapter 16 of the *Paradox User's Guide*.

RUNNING EXTERNAL PROGRAMS FROM SCRIPTS

To run an external DOS program from within a PAL script, use the PAL RUN command. Doing so has the same effect as selecting Tools, More, and ToDos from the menus, or typing Ctrl-O. (You can also mimic the DOS Big key, Alt-O, by using the command RUN BIG instead.)

With RUN or RUN BIG, you can run any DOS command (such as DIR, COPY, MKDIR), any DOS batch file (with the extension .BAT), or any program that is normally run from the DOS prompt (such as Lotus 1-2-3, dBASE, or a word processor). Within the script, put the name of the command or program in quotation marks. For example, the following command runs the DOS COPY program, and copies all scripts (.SC files) from the current drive to drive A:

```
RUN "COPY *.SC A:"
```

The command below runs Lotus 1-2-3, assuming that 1-2-3 is accessible from the current disk and directory (either because it is stored on the same directory as Paradox or because of the DOS PATH setting). Note the use of RUN BIG in this case, to make more memory available to 1-2-3:

```
RUN BIG "123"
```

Do not use the RUN or RUN BIG commands to run programs that stay resident in memory (like the DOS MODE and PRINT commands). These programs will likely prevent you from returning to the suspended Paradox program.

If you want your script to exit to the DOS prompt without running a program, you can use the commands below in the script instead of the RUN command:

{Tools} {More} {ToDos}

With this option, you'll need to enter the EXIT command at the DOS prompt to get back into Paradox. The script will resume playing where it left off.

You can use the SLEEP command with RUN to set up a delay before Paradox is reinstated. This is useful if you want the user to read something on the screen before Paradox erases it. The maximum delay is 30 seconds (entered in the SLEEP command as 30,000 milliseconds). As an example, the command below exits to DOS from within a script, displays a directory of Paradox database (.DB) files, then pauses for 20 seconds before returning to Paradox:

RUN SLEEP 20000 "DIR *.DB"

See the discussion of running external programs in Chapter 16 for more important information on suspending Paradox.

KEYBOARD MACROS

A *keyboard* macro is a sort of miniature script that is assigned to a particular key or pair of keys (such as Alt-1). You assign a script to a particular keystroke using the PAL SETKEY command, using the general syntax

SETKEY <key code> <commands>

The <*key code*> is a special code that represents the key to be pressed. You can assign a macro to any key you want—even the letter A, for instance. However, you really wouldn't want to do that, because you need the letter A for general typing. Instead, you'll probably want to assign macros to keys that are not already used in Paradox, such as Alt-F or Ctrl-F10. The codes for these unassigned keys are listed in Table 19.1. (*Note*: Though listed, the Alt-Z key is actually used as Zoom Next in Paradox, and Alt-R and Alt-L are used in networked environments for locking records and refreshing the screen. If you use these options in Paradox, you'll want to avoid assigning custom macros to these keys.)

Table 19.1: Common key codes for keyboard macros.

KEYS	CODE	KEYS	CODE	KEYS	CODE
Alt-A	−30	Alt-1	−120	Shift-F1	F11
Alt-B	−48	Alt-2	−121	Shift-F2	F12
Alt-C	−46	Alt-3	−122	Shift-F3	F13
Alt-D	−32	Alt-4	−123	Shift-F4	F14
Alt-E	−18	Alt-5	−124	Shift-F5	F15
Alt-F	−33	Alt-6	−125	Shift-F6	F16
Alt-G	−34	Alt-7	−126	Shift-F7	F17
Alt-H	−35	Alt-8	−127	Shift-F8	F18
Alt-I	−23	Alt-9	−128	Shift-F9	F19
Alt-J	−36	Alt-0	−129	Shift-F10	F20
Alt-K	−37				
Alt-L	−38	Alt-F1	F31	Ctrl-F1	F21
Alt-M	−50	Alt-F2	F32	Ctrl-F2	F22
Alt-N	−49	Alt-F10	F30	Ctrl-F3	F23
Alt-O	−24			Ctrl-F4	F24
Alt-P	−25			Ctrl-F5	F25
Alt-Q	−16			Ctrl-F6	F26
Alt-R	−19			Ctrl-F7	F27
Alt-S	−31			Ctrl-F8	F28
Alt-T	−20			Ctrl-F9	F29
Alt-U	−22			Ctrl-F10	F30

Table 19.1: Common key codes for keyboard macros (continued).

KEYS	CODE	KEYS	CODE	KEYS	CODE
Alt-V	−47				
Alt-W	−17				
Alt-X	−45				
Alt-Y	−21				
Alt-Z	−44				

The <*commands*> portion of the keyboard macro is the text, keystrokes, or commands that you want the key to perform. Some examples will best demonstrate the use of SETKEY.

A KEYBOARD MACRO TO TYPE A NAME

Suppose you have a table containing names and addresses, and most of the addresses have Los Angeles as the city name. You can create a keyboard macro that automatically types Los Angeles for you when you type a particular key. Suppose you decide to use Alt-C as the key for the macro (the letter C reminds you that this macro is for typing in the City). The PAL command to set up the macro would be

```
SETKEY −46 "Los Angeles"
```

In this case, the command portion (Los Angeles) is enclosed in quotation marks because the macro types literal text (as opposed to performing PAL commands). The −46 is the code for the Alt-C keystrokes, derived from Table 19.1.

A MACRO TO EJECT A PAGE

If you have a laser printer, chances are you know how it often leaves a printed page inside the machine until you eject the page. You can set up a keyboard macro that will eject a page from the printer right from the keyboard. In the example below, the appropriate command, PRINT "\F", is assigned to the Alt-E (for eject) keystroke:

SETKEY −18 PRINT "\F"

In this example, −18 is the code for the Alt-E keystroke, and PRINT "\F" is the command to eject a page from the printer. PRINT is not enclosed in quotation marks, because it is a PAL command.

A MACRO TO DISPLAY SCRIPT INVENTORY

This sample macro demonstrates how to select Paradox menu items from within a keyboard macro. To display all script names on the screen, you select the menu items Tools, Info, Inventory, and Scripts. To store these in a script assigned to the Alt-S (for scripts) keystrokes, you would use the command

SETKEY −31 MENU{Tools}{!Info}{Inventory}{Scripts}Enter

Note that in this example, menu selections are enclosed in curly braces. Pressing the Enter key is signified by the key name Enter, which is not enclosed in curly braces because it is the name of a key rather than a menu item.

ACTIVATING THE SETKEY COMMANDS

To activate the keyboard macros, you need to place the SETKEY commands in a PAL script and play that script using the usual Scripts and Play menu options. For example, to place the three sample keyboard macros in a script named KeyMacs.SC, you would select Scripts, Editor, and Write from the Paradox Main menu, and type in the SETKEY commands as shown in Figure 19.1. Note that several comments are included to clarify what each SETKEY command does. After you've created the script shown in the figure, save it using the usual DO-IT! key.

Before the keyboard macros will actually work, you need to play the script. In this example, just select Scripts and Play from the Paradox Main menu, and specify KeyMacs as the script to play. Nothing

```
;-- Assign keyboard macros.
;--- Alt-C types Los Angeles.
SETKEY -46 "Los Angeles"
;--- Alt-E ejects a page.
SETKEY -18 PRINT "\F"
;--- Alt-S displays script inventory.
SETKEY -31 MENU{Tools}{Info}{Inventory}{Scripts}Enter
```

Figure 19.1: Keyboard macros assigned in a script

will appear on your screen, as this script does not display anything. However, the keyboard macros will be available to you for the rest of the current Paradox session.

Once assigned, typing Alt-E will eject a page from the printer, while typing Alt-S will display a list of all scripts on the current disk and directory. If you call up a table in the Edit mode, and place the cursor in a new blank record, then type Alt-C, the name *Los Angeles* will be typed automatically into the field.

Of course, you can store all of your SETKEY commands in a script named Init.SC. As discussed above, Paradox *always* runs the script named Init.SC at startup. Therefore, your keyboard macros will be available as soon as Paradox is up and running on your computer.

KEYBOARD MACRO LIMITATIONS

A SETKEY command cannot be longer than a single line. Using the PAL editor, that means your limit is about 130 characters. If a script is longer than that, you'll need to treat it as a script played with the usual Scripts and Play menu options, rather than as a keyboard macro.

Of course, there is a way around this problem. Suppose you have a macro named BigGuy.SC that is many lines long, but you would like to invoke it by pressing Alt-B. Simply have your Alt-B command activate the BigGuy.SC script using the PAL PLAY command as shown:

SETKEY −48 PLAY "BigGuy"

Note that the PLAY command is not enclosed in quotation marks, but the script name (BigGuy in this example) is.

CANCELING KEYBOARD MACROS

If at any time you want to cancel a macro assignment to a keystroke, run a script containing the SETKEY command with the appropriate keystroke code but no command. For example, the script below cancels the effects of the Alt-C, Alt-E, and Alt-S keys whenever the script is run:

```
;---- Cancel previous keyboard macro assignments.
SETKEY -46
SETKEY -18
SETKEY -31
```

DEBUGGING PAL SCRIPTS

Whenever Paradox encounters something in a PAL script that it cannot "digest," it stops executing the script and displays the options

Cancel   Debug

If you select Cancel, you'll simply be returned to the Paradox workspace. Optionally, you can select Debug to enter the PAL Debugger and get some help in correcting the problem.

When you select Debug, the screen displays the *current command* (the one that caused the error), a brief description of the error (called an *error message*), the name of the script with the error in it, the line number of the current command, and the option

Type Control-Q to Quit

to exit the debugger.

There are two other ways to enter the PAL debugger. One is to interrupt the script as it is playing by pressing the Break key. Doing so will display the Cancel and Debug options. Select Debug at that point. A second way to start the debugger is to place the command DEBUG right in your script at exactly the point where you want debugging to begin. Then save and play the script.

While the debugger is active, you can press PALMenu (Alt-F10) to call up the Debugger menu. This menu displays the options

Value Step Next Go MiniScript Where? Quit Pop Editor

Each of these options is discussed below.

THE VALUE OPTION

The Value option on the Debugger menu let's you enter an expression to test its current value. This option is particularly useful when an expression caused the error. For example, suppose you receive the error message while a script is attempting to execute the line

? SQRT(X)

(which means, "Print the square root of the value stored in the variable named X"). If you call up the debugger, select Value, and enter X as the value to check, the bottom right corner of the screen will display the value stored in the variable named X. If, for example, this number is then displayed as -123, you will know the problem: you cannot take the square root of a negative number, and X contains a negative number.

You may also enter a complete expression, or even a PAL function, as the value to check. For example, if the error occurred in a long expression such as

(Cost − (Discount * Cost)) * 1.06

you could enter just the expression *Discount * Cost* to see what this portion of the faulty expression evaluates to.

The PAL functions listed in Table 19.2 can also provide useful information about the current environment in which the error occurred. (See the *PAL User's Guide* that comes with your Paradox package, for more information on these functions.)

As an example of using PAL functions as values, suppose a script fails because it cannot find a value in a table named Charges. To see if the Charges table exists, select Value and enter the expression

ISTABLE("Charges")

Table 19.2: Functions that can help in debugging.

Function	Display
ARRAYSIZE(*arrayname*)	Dimensions of named array
ATFIRST( )	Is current record the first record?
ATLAST( )	Is current record the last record?
CHECKMARKSTATUS( )	Is field in query form checked?
DIRECTORY( )	Name of current directory
DIREXISTS(*directory name*)	Does named directory exist?
DRIVESPACE()	Amount of space available on disk
FIELD()	Name of current field
FIELDSTR()	Contents of current field
FIELDTYPE()	Type of current field
IMAGETYPE()	Type of current image
ISASSIGNED(*variable*)	Has variable been assigned a value?
ISENCRYPTED(*table name*)	Is table password-protected?
ISEMPTY(*table name*)	Is the named table empty?
ISFIELDVIEW()	Is the current field in Field View?
ISFILE(*file name*)	Does the named file exist?
ISFORMVIEW()	Is the current table in form view?
ISINSERTMODE()	Is the insert mode on?
ISTABLE(*table name*)	Does the table exist?
ISVALID()	Are the field contents valid?
MEMLEFT()	How much RAM memory is left?
NIMAGES()	Number of images on the workspace
NKEYFIELDS(*table name*)	Number of key fields in the table
NRECORDS(*table name*)	Number of records in the table

Table 19.2: Functions that can help in debugging.

FUNCTION	DISPLAY
PRINTERSTATUS()	*Is printer ready to accept data?*
RECNO()	Current table record number
SYSMODE()	Current operating mode
TABLE()	Table currently in use
VERSION()	Version of Paradox in use

If the table exists, the lower right corner of the screen will display *True*. Otherwise, it will display *False*.

Perhaps the table exists (the screen displays *True*), but the script is still not working properly. Perhaps the table is empty. Entering the value

ISEMPTY("Charges")

will display *True* if the table is empty, *False* if it is not.

Suppose in the above example, the screen displays *False* in response to the ISTABLE( ) function. In that case, perhaps the script is currently logged onto the wrong directory. You could test this by typing in the function

DIRECTORY( )

as the value to check; the screen will display the current directory.

Note that if the expression you enter as the value to test causes an error in itself, then you'll be placed in the debug mode to debug *that* error. To "pop" back up to the original error, call up the PAL menu (Alt-F10), and select Pop.

THE STEP OPTION

If you entered the Debugger through the Break key or the DEBUG command in a script, you can select Step from the Debugger menu, or just type Ctrl-S, to play the script one step at a time.

Stepping through a script a single line at a time lets you follow the logic of the script in a slower one-command-at-a-time manner. When the stepping process comes to an erroneous line, it will display the error as it normally would. At that point, you may have enough information from the previous steps to figure out what caused the error.

THE NEXT OPTION

This option is used in conjunction with Step to skip over the line that caused the error in the script and proceed with the next line. This lets you check the script for other errors, if possible, before dealing with the current error. You can activate Next either from the Debugger menu or by typing Ctrl-N.

THE GO OPTION

Selecting Go from the Debugger menu, or typing Ctrl-G, resumes executing the script from the current command. This is particularly handy if you've corrected the error with the Editor option from the Debugger menu and want to proceed with the script without starting it from the first line.

THE MINISCRIPT OPTION

The MiniScript option lets you create and execute a small script on the spot, which may help you to proceed with your debugging. For example, if the error in your script was caused by a nonexistent variable (such as the calculation $X = Y + Z$, where the Z variable is not defined), you can enter a miniscript such as $Z = 0$ to assign a value to the variable Z temporarily. Then select Go from the debugger menu to proceed with the script. (Later, you'll have to come back and edit the script so that Z does actually have a value.)

Like Value on the debugger menu, it is possible to enter a miniscript that contains an error of its own. When that occurs, the debugger will again detect *that* new error and allow you to fix it. As discussed before, you need to select Pop from the Debugger menu to pop back up to the level that caused the original problem in the script.

THE WHERE? OPTION

Selecting Where? from the debugger, or typing Ctrl-W, displays the nesting level at which the error occurred. For example, suppose the script named Mail.SC plays a script named RepMenu.SC, and RepMenu.SC in turn plays a script named Labels.SC. If an error occurs in Labels.SC, you want to know what series of scripts led to the error. Where? will show you, as in Figure 19.2. As you can see, Mail.SC called RepMenu.SC, which in turn called Labels.SC, which is where the error occurred.

THE POP OPTION

As discussed under Value and MiniScript above, the Pop option (which can also be activated by typing Ctrl-P) leaves the current level

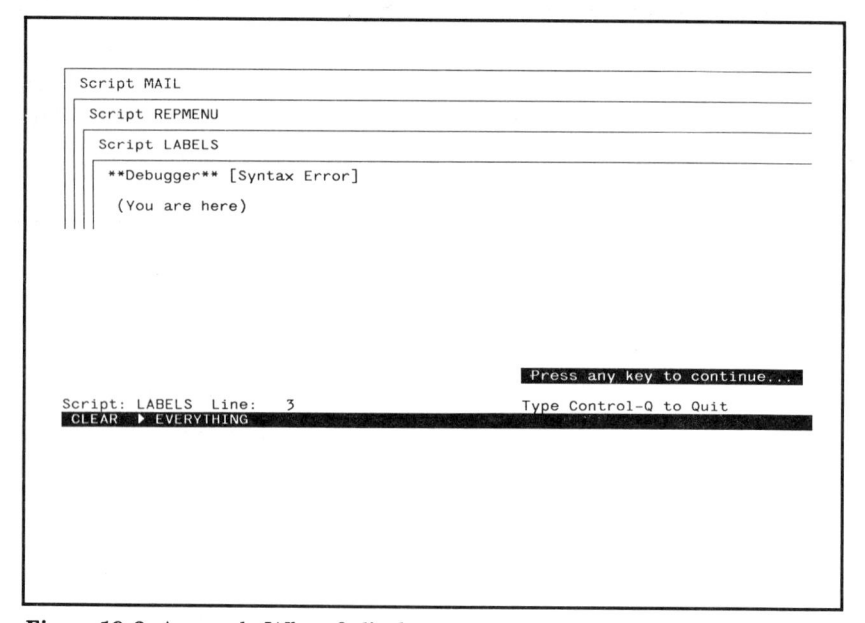

```
Script MAIL
 Script REPMENU
  Script LABELS
   **Debugger** [Syntax Error]
   (You are here)




                                            Press any key to continue...
Script: LABELS  Line:   3               Type Control-Q to Quit
 CLEAR  ▶ EVERYTHING
```

Figure 19.2: A sample Where? display

of debugging and pops back up to the next highest level (and thus to the previous error).

THE EDITOR OPTION

Selecting the Editor option, or typing Ctrl-E, brings you straight from the debugger into the PAL editor, with the cursor at the line that caused the error. You can correct the error at that point using the usual PAL Editor editing keys. When done, call up the menu (F10) and select Go to save and replay the corrected script.

THE QUIT OPTION

Selecting Quit from the Debugger menu, or typing Ctrl-Q, ends the debugger and cancels the entire script play. You'll be returned to the Paradox workspace with no scripts running.

USING RECORD NUMBERS IN TABLES

You may have noticed by now that the record numbers in Paradox tables are not constant. For example, when you sort a table to itself (by using the Same rather than the New option), each record in the table receives a new number. Similarly, when you query a table, the Answer table assigns new record numbers to records, which will not match the record numbers in the original table.

You can add your own constant record number to a table simply by adding a field to store record numbers in. To simplify the maintenance of this field, I'll show you a script that will automatically assign a record number to each new record in a table.

Let's use the Custlist table to demonstrate a technique for managing constant record numbers. Figure 19.3 shows the original Custlist table with a new field, named RecNo, added via the Modify and Restructure options. Notice that I've used the short number (S) data type. (If your table is likely to have more than 32,000 records in it, be sure to use the N data type instead.)

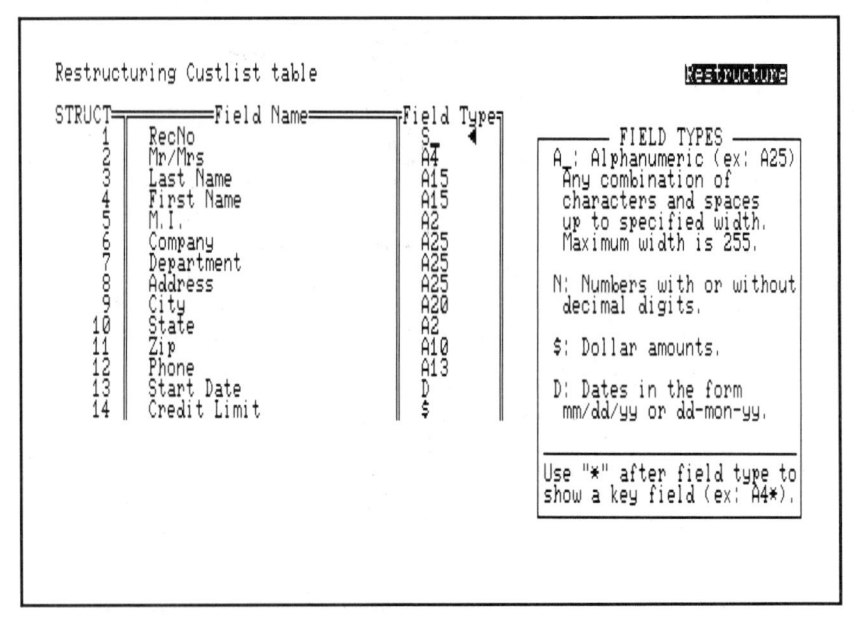

```
Restructuring Custlist table                              Restructure
STRUCT======Field Name=========Field Type
    1    RecNo                  S              ┌──── FIELD TYPES ────┐
    2    Mr/Mrs                 A4             │ A : Alphanumeric (ex: A25)
    3    Last Name              A15            │   Any combination of
    4    First Name             A15            │   characters and spaces
    5    M.I.                   A2             │   up to specified width.
    6    Company                A25            │   Maximum width is 255.
    7    Department             A25            │
    8    Address                A25            │ N: Numbers with or without
    9    City                   A20            │   decimal digits.
   10    State                  A2             │
   11    Zip                    A10            │ $: Dollar amounts.
   12    Phone                  A13            │
   13    Start Date             D              │ D: Dates in the form
   14    Credit Limit           $              │   mm/dd/yy or dd-mon-yy.
                                               │
                                               │ Use "*" after field type to
                                               │ show a key field (ex: A4*).
```

Figure 19.3: The Custlist table with a new field added

Figure 19.4 shows the Custlist table after adding the new field and saving the structure. Notice that the RecNo field is still blank in every record.

Figure 19.5 shows a PAL script named Fillrec.SC that will automatically scan the Custlist table for records that have a blank in the RecNo field and enter the record number into the RecNo field.

To use a similar script for a different table, just change the table name *Custlist* in the following command to whatever table name you wish to use:

   EDIT "Custlist"

If you use a field name other than RecNo, change the name *RecNo* in the following commands to the appropriate field name:

   MOVETO [RecNo]
   SCAN FOR ISBLANK([RecNo])

The TYPEIN command types the record number (RecNo) into the field, and MESSAGE displays the record number on the screen so you can see the script's progress.

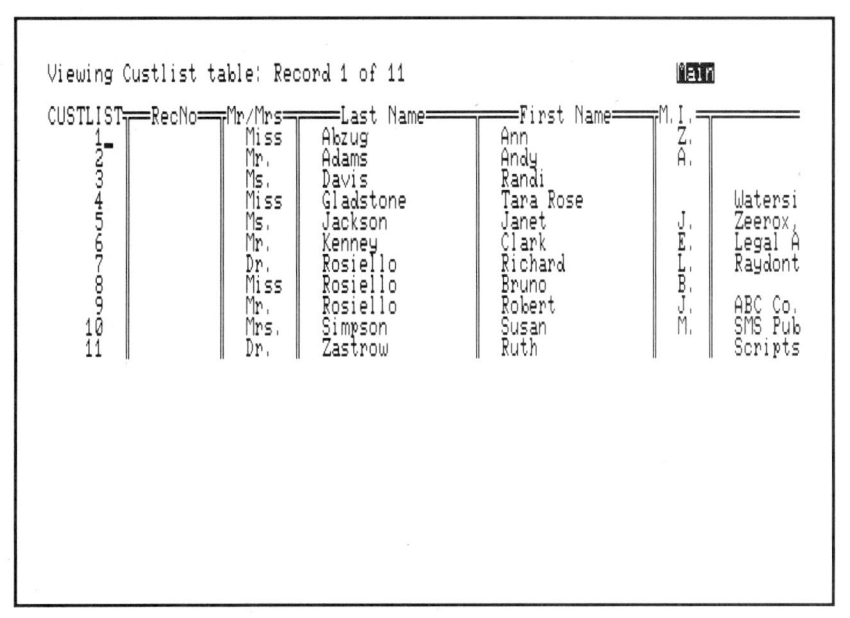

```
Viewing Custlist table: Record 1 of 11                    Main
CUSTLIST═══RecNo═══Mr/Mrs═══════Last Name══════First Name══════M.I.═══
        1       Miss       Abzug          Ann              Z.
        2       Mr.        Adams          Andy             A.
        3       Ms.        Davis          Randi
        4       Miss       Gladstone      Tara Rose                 Watersi
        5       Ms.        Jackson        Janet            J.       Zeerox
        6       Mr.        Kenney         Clark            E.       Legal A
        7       Dr.        Rosiello       Richard          L.       Raydont
        8       Miss       Rosiello       Bruno            B.
        9       Mr.        Rosiello       Robert           J.       ABC Co.
       10       Mrs.       Simpson        Susan            M.       SMS Pub
       11       Dr.        Zastrow        Ruth                      Scripts
```

Figure 19.4: The Custlist table with a blank RecNo field

```
;------------------------------------------- Fillrec.SC
;--- Automatically fills in RecNo field on Names table.
CLEARALL
EDIT "Custlist"              ; edit custlist table
MOVETO [RecNo]               ; move to RecNo field
SCAN FOR ISBLANK([RecNo])    ; find blank record
    TYPEIN RECNO()           ; enter record number
    MESSAGE RECNO()          ; show progress
ENDSCAN                      ; repeat for next blank
? "All Done!"
BEEP
DO_IT!                       ; save changes
```

Figure 19.5: The Fillrec script

After you play the Fillrec script (using the Scripts and Play options), the Custlist table will have record numbers in the RecNo field, as shown in Figure 19.6.

After you sort the table to itself, the RecNo field will still contain the original record numbers, as shown in Figure 19.7. To get the records back in their original order, simply sort the table again, based on the RecNo field.

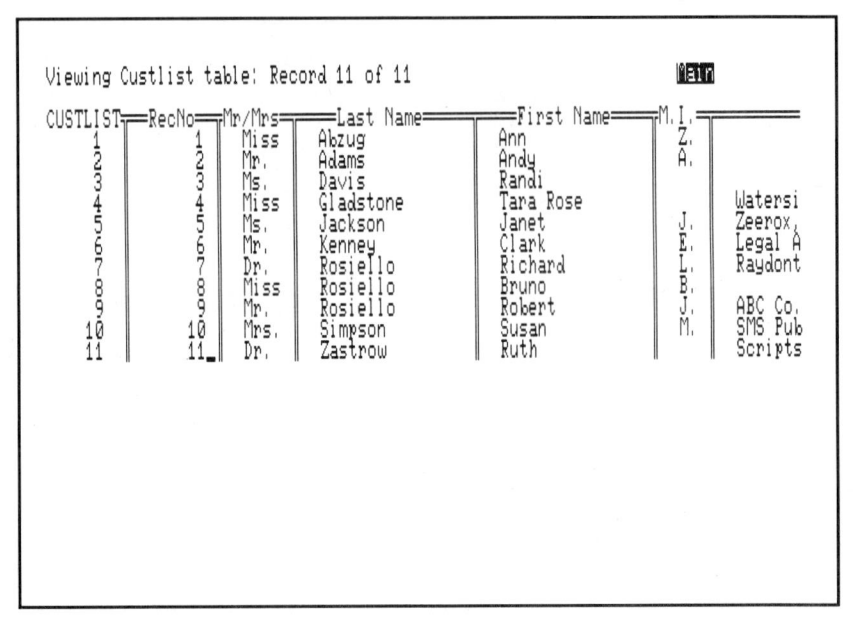

```
Viewing Custlist table: Record 11 of 11                Main
CUSTLIST══RecNo══Mr/Mrs══════Last Name══════First Name══M.I.══
     1         1    Miss     Abzug           Ann          Z.
     2         2    Mr.      Adams           Andy         A.
     3         3    Ms.      Davis           Randi
     4         4    Miss     Gladstone       Tara Rose          Watersi
     5         5    Ms.      Jackson         Janet        J.    Zeerox
     6         6    Mr.      Kenney          Clark        E.    Legal A
     7         7    Dr.      Rosiello        Richard      L.    Raydont
     8         8    Miss     Rosiello        Bruno        B.
     9         9    Mr.      Rosiello        Robert       J.    ABC Co.
    10        10    Mrs.     Simpson         Susan        M.    SMS Pub
    11        11    Dr.      Zastrow         Ruth               Scripts
```

Figure 19.6: Record numbers in the RecNo field

```
Viewing Custlist table: Record 1 of 11                 Main
CUSTLIST══RecNo══Mr/Mrs══════Last Name══════First Name══Zip══
     1         7    Dr.      Rosiello        Richard      00123
     2         9    Mr.      Rosiello        Robert       11111
     3         4    Miss     Gladstone       Tara Rose    12345
     4         6    Mr.      Kenney          Clark        12345
     5        10    Mrs.     Simpson         Susan        23456
     6         3    Ms.      Davis           Randi        90001
     7         5    Ms.      Jackson         Janet        91234
     8         1    Miss     Abzug           Ann          92024
     9        11    Dr.      Zastrow         Ruth         92037
    10         2    Mr.      Adams           Andy         92038
    11         8    Miss     Rosiello        Bruno        99999
```

Figure 19.7: The Custlist table sorted by zip code

If you query the table, the Answer table will still show the original record numbers, as shown in Figure 19.8. After the query, you can use the Image, GoTo, and Record options to jump to the appropriate record in the original table and make changes if you wish.

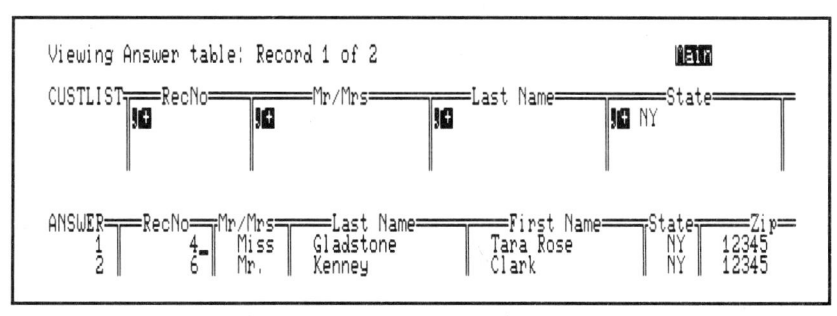

```
Viewing Answer table: Record 1 of 2                           Main
CUSTLIST==RecNo======Mr/Mrs=======Last Name=====State=====
         |          |            |              | NY
         |          |            |              |

ANSWER==RecNo==Mr/Mrs=====Last Name========First Name======State====Zip==
    1      4    Miss      Gladstone        Tara Rose        NY      12345
    2      6    Mr.       Kenney           Clark            NY      12345
```

Figure 19.8: The Answer table with original record numbers

TRANSLATING NUMBERS INTO WORDS

If you were to write a script to manage accounts payable using Paradox and you wanted to print checks from a table, you'd need the ability to translate dollar amounts, expressed as figures, into words. This is one of the few capabilities that Paradox does not already have. However, you can write a PAL script to perform the translation for you.

The first thing you'll need is an *array* that contains all the unique English words for numbers. You can create this by entering and playing the Numwords.SC script shown in Figure 19.9.

The Numwords script creates an array of 90 subscripted variables named Word. (Subscripted variables all have the same name, but different subscripts.) The subscript, in this example, matches the word stored in the variable. Hence, Word[17] is "SEVENTEEN", and Word[90] is "NINETY".

Once you play the Numwords script, other PAL procedures will have full access to these subscripted variables. Next, you'll need a *procedure* to translate a number to words. Figure 19.10 shows such a procedure, named Translat.SC. You can type it in using the usual Scripts editor.

What makes a procedure different from a regular script is that when you play a procedure, it is loaded into RAM memory but not

```
;-------------------------------- Numwords.SC
;-- Create an array of unique words for numbers.
ARRAY Word[90]
Word[1]  = "ONE"
Word[2]  = "TWO"
Word[3]  = "THREE"
Word[4]  = "FOUR"
Word[5]  = "FIVE"
Word[6]  = "SIX"
Word[7]  = "SEVEN"
Word[8]  = "EIGHT"
Word[9]  = "NINE"
Word[10] = "TEN"
Word[11] = "ELEVEN"
Word[12] = "TWELVE"
Word[13] = "THIRTEEN"
Word[14] = "FOURTEEN"
Word[15] = "FIFTEEN"
Word[16] = "SIXTEEN"
Word[17] = "SEVENTEEN"
Word[18] = "EIGHTEEN"
Word[19] = "NINETEEN"
Word[20] = "TWENTY"
Word[30] = "THIRTY"
Word[40] = "FORTY"
Word[50] = "FIFTY"
Word[60] = "SIXTY"
Word[70] = "SEVENTY"
Word[80] = "EIGHTY"
Word[90] = "NINETY"
```

Figure 19.9: The Numwords.SC script

immediately executed. To access the procedure after loading it into memory, treat the procedure name as any PAL function. For example, after creating the Numwords and Translat scripts, you can create a third script, as below, to test the procedure:

```
;-------------------------------------------------------------- Trantest.SC
;---------------------------------------------- Test the translation procedure.
PLAY "NumWords";---------------------------------- Load English words.
PLAY "Translat"; ---------------------------- Load translation procedure.
AnyNumber = 1
WHILE AnyNumber > 0
    @ 9,2
    ?? "Enter a number from 1 to 999999.99"
    @ 11,2
    ?? "(or 0 to exit) : "
    ACCEPT "$" TO AnyNumber
    @ 15,1 CLEAR EOS
    ? TRANSLAT(AnyNumber)
    SLEEP 3000
ENDWHILE
CLEAR
```

```
;---------------------------------------- Translat.SC
;------- PAL procedure to convert a $ number to words.
PROC TransLat(Amount)

;-------------------------- Set up initial variables.
Counter = 1
Start = 1
Hold = STRVAL(Amount)
String = SPACES(9-LEN(Hold))+Hold
English = " "

;---------------- Loop through thousands and hundreds.
WHILE Counter <= 2

   ;------ Split out hundreds, tens, and ones.
   Chunk = SUBSTR(String,Start,3)
   Hun = NUMVAL(SUBSTR(Chunk,1,1))
   Ten = NUMVAL(SUBSTR(Chunk,2,2))
   One = NUMVAL(SUBSTR(Chunk,3,1))

   ;-------------- Fix possible error in Ten variable.
   IF Ten = "Error" THEN
      Ten = One
   ENDIF

   ;------------------------- Handle hundreds portion.
   IF NUMVAL(Chunk) > 99 THEN
      English = English + Word[Hun] + " HUNDRED "
   ENDIF

   ;-------------------------- Handle second 2 digits.
   IF Ten > 0 THEN
      SWITCH

         ;-------------- Translate even tens and teens.
         CASE MOD(Ten,10)=0 OR (Ten>9 AND Ten<20) :
            English = English + Word[Ten]

         ;-- Translate numbers evenly divisible by 10.
         CASE Ten > 9  AND MOD(Ten,10) <> 0 :
            Ten=NUMVAL(SUBSTR(STRVAL(Ten),1,1))*10
            English=English+Word[Ten]+" "+Word[One]

         ; -------------Translate number less than 10.
         CASE Ten < 10 :
            English = English + Word[One]

      ENDSWITCH

   ENDIF ;(Ten > 0)

   ;-------------------- Add "Thousand" if necessary.
   IF Amount > 999.99 AND Counter = 1 THEN
      English = English +" THOUSAND "
   ENDIF

   ;--------------- Prepare for pass through hundreds.
   Start = 4
   Counter = Counter + 1

ENDWHILE ;(counter <= 2)

;------------------------------- Tack on the pennies.
IF INT(Amount) > 0 THEN
   English = English + " AND "
ENDIF

English = English + SUBSTR(String,8,2)+"/100"

;---------- End procedure, return English translation.
RETURN English
ENDPROC
```

Figure 19.10: The Translat.SC procedure

In the Trantest script, the command

    PLAY "Numwords"

loads the array of words into memory, and

    PLAY "Translat"

loads the translation procedure. The command

    ACCEPT "$" TO AnyNumber

allows the user to enter any number. (The Translat procedure works only with the $ data type, with numbers in the range of 0.01 to 999,999.99.) To translate a number to words, the Trantest script simply uses the command

    ? TRANSLAT(AnyNumber)

Notice how the syntax is identical to any other PAL function. Once a script is defined and loaded as a procedure, it can be treated as though it were a built-in Paradox capability.

Let's take a look at the Translat procedure now. Notice that the first command (beneath the comments) is PROC. It is this command, in conjunction with ENDPROC, that causes this script to be treated as a procedure. The procedure name is defined (Translat), and a single parameter named Amount is passed, as shown below:

```
; -------------------------------------------------------------------- Translat.SC
; ------------------------ PAL procedure to convert a $ number to words.

PROC Translat(Amount)
```

Within the main body of the procedure, numerous commands manipulate the passed number and build an English translation using variables from the Words array. At the bottom of the procedure are these commands:

```
; -------------------------------- End procedure, return English translation.
RETURN English
ENDPROC
```

The *RETURN English* command returns control to the calling program, along with the translated number stored in the variable named English. The *ENDPROC* command marks the end of the procedure.

A practical application of the translation procedure would be, of course, to print checks from data stored in a table. Figure 19.11 shows a sample table named Checks, which stores data to write checks from. Notice that the field named Written is blank in all records.

Figure 19.12 shows a sample script named Checkprn.SC that can print a check for each record in the Checks table. The routine also marks each check as having been written by placing the letter Y in the Written field. Hence, this script never prints the same check twice, because the SCAN command accesses only records that have a blank Written field.

```
CheckNo   Check Date   To Whom                    Amount    Written
-------   ----------   -------                    ------    -------
   1001    12/02/90    American Financial           20.00
   1002    12/02/90    Federated Partners           13.11
   1003    12/15/90    Sandy Eggo Utilities          6.01
   1004    12/15/90    Frankly Unctuous            100.00
   1005    12/16/90    Borscht Microprocessors     123.45
   1006    12/16/90    MicroPotatoChips          1,234.56
   1007    12/20/90    Salisbury Finance        12,345.67
   1008    12/21/90    Woosk Matilda           123,456.78
   1009    12/02/90    HereWeGo Enterprises        888.08
   1010    12/02/90    StillAtIt Co.               808.08
   1011    12/02/90    UpForGrabs, Ltd.          8,080.80
```

Figure 19.11: A table with data for writing checks

Within the SCAN . . . ENDSCAN loop, the script prints the check number, followed by 40 blank spaces, followed by the check date. Then the script prints a blank line and the name of the recipient, followed by 10 blank spaces and the dollar amount. The script then prints another blank line and the translated dollar amount. Undoubtedly, the lines that control spacing within the SCAN . . . ENDSCAN loop will have to be modified for different check formats.

PREPARSED PROCEDURE LIBRARIES

For the more advanced database programmer, Paradox offers *preparsed procedure libraries.* Like the Translat procedure we created earlier

```
;-------------------------------- Checkprn.SC
;-------------------- Sample program to print checks.
CLEARALL
CLEAR
;-------------------- Create index of English words.
PLAY "Numwords"
;----------------------- Load translation procedure.
PLAY "Translat"

;--------------- Call in "Checks" table in Edit mode.
EDIT "Checks"

;--------------- Send ? and ?? outputs to printer.
PRINTER ON

; --- Loop through records with blank "printed" field.
SCAN FOR ISBLANK([Written])
     Dollars = FORMAT("W12.2,E$C*",[Amount])
     ? [Checkno],SPACES(40),[Check Date]
     ?
     ? [To Whom], SPACES(10), Dollars
     ?
     ? TRANSLAT([Amount])
     ?
     ;----------------- Mark check as written.
     MOVETO [Written]
     TYPEIN "Y"
ENDSCAN ;--------------- (for checks not printed yet)

;-------------------------- End of Checkprn.SC script.
DO_IT!          ;---- Save edits to the Checks table.
CLEARALL
CLEAR
```

Figure 19.12: The Checkprn.SC script

in this chapter, a preparsed procedure is loaded into memory, and can be played at any time from within a script. There are, however, certain advantages to preparsed procedures. They are already translated from PAL into a language more readily understood by the computer (preparsed), and therefore are executed much more quickly than regular procedures. Also, you can store up to 50 different procedures in a single library, which helps organize many procedures into a single file.

The commands used for preparsed procedure libraries are CREATELIB, WRITELIB, READLIB, and INFOLIB. Let's try one out to get a feel for them.

PROCEDURE TO CREATE A LIBRARY

We'll begin by developing a couple of procedures to translate dates from the Paradox MM/DD/YY or Mon-DD-YY format to the English format of Month Date, Year (for example, January 1, 1990). Two procedures will be required, one to assign all the month names to variables in an array, and another to perform the translation. Since we want to store both procedures in a single library, we'll put them in a single file named Makelib.SC. So, use the Scripts, Editor, and Write options to first create the script shown in Figure 19.13.

```
;------------------------------ Makelib.SC
;--- Create a preparsed library of date
;--- translation aids named Dateproc.LIB

CREATELIB "Dateproc"

;------------ Make an Array of month names.
PROC Dateword()
     ARRAY CMonth[12]
     CMonth[1]  = "January"
     CMonth[2]  = "February"
     CMonth[3]  = "March"
     CMonth[4]  = "April"
     CMonth[5]  = "May"
     CMonth[6]  = "June"
     CMonth[7]  = "July"
     CMonth[8]  = "August"
     CMonth[9]  = "September"
     CMonth[10] = "October"
     CMonth[11] = "November"
     CMonth[12] = "December"
     RETURN
ENDPROC

;----- Engdate procedure to convert
;----- MMDDYY dates to English.
PROC Engdate(mmddyy)
     Engdate = CMonth[MONTH(mmddyy)] + " "+
               STRVAL(DAY(mmddyy))+", "+
               STRVAL(YEAR(mmddyy))
RETURN Engdate
ENDPROC

WRITELIB "Dateproc" Dateword
WRITELIB "Dateproc" Engdate
```

Figure 19.13: The Makelib.SC script

Let's discuss the Makelib.SC script. The CREATELIB command beneath the opening comments tells Paradox that it is to create a preparsed procedure library named Dateproc.LIB (Paradox automatically assigns the extension .LIB to the file name you specify):

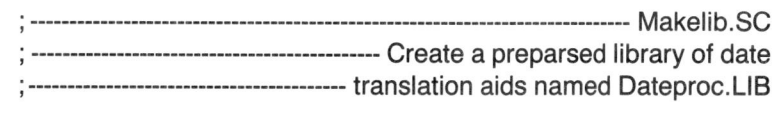

```
;-------------------------------------------------------------- Makelib.SC
;-------------------------------------- Create a preparsed library of date
;-------------------------------------- translation aids named Dateproc.LIB

CREATELIB "Dateproc"
```

Next, a procedure named Dateword is listed. Like all procedures, it begins with the PROC command and ends with the ENDPROC command. Since no parameters are passed to this procedure, empty parentheses follow the procedure name. Within the procedure, an array named CMonth consisting of 12 variables is defined. Each array element is assigned the name of a month, (in proper order, of course). Hence, after the Dateword procedure is executed, the variable CMonth(6) will equal "June", CMonth(10) will equal "October", and so on:

```
;------------------------------------------------ Make an Array of month names.
PROC Dateword( )
    ARRAY CMonth[12]
    CMonth[1] = "January"
    CMonth[2] = "February"
    CMonth[3] = "March"
    CMonth[4] = "April"
    CMonth[5] = "May"
    CMonth[6] = "June"
    CMonth[7] = "July"
    CMonth[8] = "August"
    CMonth[9] = "September"
    CMonth[10] = "October"
    CMonth[11] = "November"
    CMonth[12] = "December"
    RETURN
ENDPROC
```

The next procedure, named Engdate, actually translates the Paradox Date data into an English date. Since one parameter is passed to this procedure (a date in MM/DD/YY format), a single parameter is specified after the procedure name, Engdate.

Within the Engdate procedure, a variable named Engdate is assigned the English month name corresponding to the date number, followed by a blank space, followed by the day converted to a character string, followed by a comma and a space, followed by the year converted to a character string. The procedure uses the PAL MONTH, DAY, and YEAR functions to isolate these portions of the date. Since CMonth is a character string, all the pieces of the Engdate variable need to be character strings. Therefore, the PAL STRVAL function, which converts numeric values to character strings, is used in the procedure. The procedure ends by returning the variable Engdate:

```
;-------------------------------------------------- Engdate procedure to convert
;-------------------------------------------------- MMDDYY dates to English.
PROC Engdate(mmddyy)
   Engdate = CMonth[MONTH(mmddyy)] + " " +
      STRVAL(DAY(mmddyy)) + ", " +
      STRVAL(YEAR(mmddyy))
RETURN Engdate
ENDPROC
```

The last two lines of the Makelib.SC script store the Dateword and Engdate procedures in the Dateproc.LIB procedure file:

```
WRITELIB "Dateproc" Dateword
WRITELIB "Dateproc" Engdate
```

After creating and saving the Makelib.SC script, you can play it using the usual Scripts and Play options from the menu. Nothing will happen on the screen, however the new Dateproc.LIB procedure file will be created and stored on disk.

USING THE PROCEDURE LIBRARY

To use the procedure library, you need to create a script that uses the READLIB command to load the procedures into memory. Figure 19.14 shows an example. You can create this script using the usual Scripts, Editor, and Write options from the menu, assigning the name Testlib.

The Testlib.SC script works in the following fashion. First, the READLIB command loads the Dateword and Engdate procedures from the Dateproc.LIB library into memory. The Dateword( ) command accesses the Dateword procedure, which in turn creates the array of words for dates:

```
;----------------------------------------------------------- Open procedure library.
READLIB "Dateproc" Dateword, Engdate
```

```
;---------------------------------- Execute the Dateword procedure
;------------------------------------------------------------ to load array.
Dateword( )
```

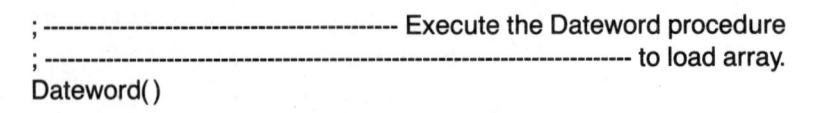

Next, the script asks that you enter a date in MM/DD/YY format. It stores your entry in a variable named AnyDate:

```
;---------------------------------------------------- Ask for a MM/DD/YY date.
@ 12,5
?? "Enter a valid date in MM/DD/YY format : "
ACCEPT "D" TO AnyDate
```

Next the script displays the English translation of the date you entered at row 15, column 5 on the screen:

```
;------------------------------------------------------------------------ Print results.
@ 15,5
?? Engdate(AnyDate)
```

Finally, the script pauses for a few seconds before returning to the Paradox Main menu:

SLEEP 3000

```
;---------------------------------- Testlib.SC
;------ Script to test the Dateproc procedures.

;---------------- Open procedure library.
READLIB "Dateproc" Dateword, Engdate

;---------------- Execute the Dateword procedure
;----------------  to load array.
Dateword( )

;---------------- Ask for a MM/DD/YY date.
@ 12,5
?? "Enter a valid date in MM/DD/YY format : "
ACCEPT "D" TO Anydate

;---------------- Print results.
@ 15,5
?? Engdate(AnyDate)

SLEEP 3000
```

Figure 19.14: The Testlib.SC script

To test the Testlib.SC script, use the usual Scripts and Play options after creating and saving the script. Fill in a date when requested, such as 12/10/90. The script will display the English translation, December 10, 1990.

MODIFYING PROCEDURE LIBRARIES

Since procedure libraries are stored in a special preprocessed format, you cannot edit them directly. Instead, you need to edit the script used to create the library (Makelib.SC in this example), then play that script again to recreate the .LIB procedure library. You can add, delete, or change procedures in the Makelib.SC script as often as you wish. Just be sure to play that procedure after any changes so that the .LIB script is updated accordingly.

CHECK-PRINTING REVISITED

Let's take a look at a way to combine some existing scripts and procedures into a single procedure library to speed up the process of printing checks. We'll use a few fancy techniques with the PAL editor to create the procedure library. We'll name the procedure library Proclib1.LIB (for procedure library 1), and create it with a script named Proclib1.SC.

First, use Scripts, Edit, and Write from the menu to create a script named Proclib1. When the script editor appears, press Menu and select Read. Enter the name Makelib to read the Makelib script onto the screen. Change the line that reads

    CREATELIB "Dateproc"

to

    CREATELIB "Proclib1"

so that the script will create a library named Proclib1.SC. You may also want to change the opening comments, as I've done in Figure 19.15.

```
;-------------------------------- ProcLib1.SC
;--- Create a pre-parsed library of check
;--- writing procedures named DateProc.LIB

CREATELIB "ProcLib1"

;------------ Make an Array of month names.
PROC DateWord()
     ARRAY CMonth[12]
     CMonth[1] = "January"
     CMonth[2] = "February"
     CMonth[3] = "March"
     CMonth[4] = "April"
     CMonth[5] = "May"
     CMonth[6] = "June"
     CMonth[7] = "July"
     CMonth[8] = "August"
     CMonth[9] = "September"
     CMonth[10] = "October"
     CMonth[11] = "November"
     CMonth[12] = "December"
     RETURN
ENDPROC

;----- EngDate procedure to convert
;----- MMDDYY dates to English.
PROC EngDate(mmddyy)
     EngDate = CMonth[MONTH(mmddyy)] + " "+
               STRVAL(DAY(mmddyy))+", "+
               STRVAL(YEAR(mmddyy))
RETURN EngDate
ENDPROC

PROC NumWords()
     ;-- Create an array of unique words for numbers.
     ARRAY Word[90]
     Word[1] = "ONE"
     Word[2] = "TWO"
     Word[3] = "THREE"
     Word[4] = "FOUR"
     Word[5] = "FIVE"
     Word[6] = "SIX"
     Word[7] = "SEVEN"
     Word[8] = "EIGHT"
     Word[9] = "NINE"
     Word[10] = "TEN"
     Word[11] = "ELEVEN"
     Word[12] = "TWELVE"
     Word[13] = "THIRTEEN"
     Word[14] = "FOURTEEN"
     Word[15] = "FIFTEEN"
     Word[16] = "SIXTEEN"
     Word[17] = "SEVENTEEN"
     Word[18] = "EIGHTEEN"
     Word[19] = "NINETEEN"
     Word[20] = "TWENTY"
     Word[30] = "THIRTY"
     Word[40] = "FORTY"
     Word[50] = "FIFTY"
     Word[60] = "SIXTY"
     Word[70] = "SEVENTY"
     Word[80] = "EIGHTY"
     Word[90] = "NINETY"
     RETURN
ENDPROC
```

Figure 19.15: The Proclib1.SC script

```
PROC TransLat(Amount)
;-- Procedure to convert a $ number to words.
;-------------------------- Set up initial variables.
Counter = 1
Start = 1
Hold = STRVAL(Amount)
String = SPACES(9-LEN(Hold))+Hold
English = " "

;---------------- Loop through thousands and hundreds.
WHILE Counter <= 2

    ;------ Split out hundreds, tens, and ones.
    Chunk = SUBSTR(String,Start,3)
    Hun = NUMVAL(SUBSTR(Chunk,1,1))
    Ten = NUMVAL(SUBSTR(Chunk,2,2))
    One = NUMVAL(SUBSTR(Chunk,3,1))

    ;------------ Fix potential error in Ten variable.
    IF Ten = "Error" THEN
        Ten = One
    ENDIF

    ;------------------------- Handle hundreds portion.
    IF NUMVAL(Chunk) > 99 THEN
        English = English + Word[Hun] + " HUNDRED "
    ENDIF

    ;-------------------------- Handle second 2 digits.
    IF Ten > 0 THEN
        SWITCH

            ;------------ Translate even tens and teens.
            CASE MOD(Ten,10)=0 OR (Ten>9 AND Ten<20) :
                English = English + Word[Ten]

                ;-- Translate numbers evenly divisible by 10.
                CASE Ten > 9  AND MOD(Ten,10) <> 0 :
                    Ten=NUMVAL(SUBSTR(STRVAL(Ten),1,1))*10
                    English=English+Word[Ten]+" "+Word[One]

                ; -------------Translate number less than 10.
                CASE Ten < 10 :
                    English = English + Word[One]

        ENDSWITCH

    ENDIF ;(Ten > 0)

    ;--------------------- Add "Thousand" if necessary.
    IF Amount > 999.99 AND Counter = 1 THEN
        English = English +" THOUSAND "
    ENDIF

    ;--------------- Prepare for pass through hundreds.
    Start = 4
    Counter = Counter + 1

ENDWHILE ;(counter <= 2)

;------------------------------ Tack on the pennies.
IF INT(Amount) > 0 THEN
    English = English + " AND "
ENDIF

English = English + SUBSTR(String,8,2)+"/100"
```

Figure 19.15: The Proclib1.SC script (continued)

```
;---------- End procedure, return English translation.
RETURN English
ENDPROC

WRITELIB "ProcLib1" DateWord
WRITELIB "ProcLib1" EngDate
WRITELIB "ProcLib1" NumWords
WRITELIB "ProcLib1" Translat
```

Figure 19.15: The Proclib1.SC script (continued)

Next, press the End key to move the cursor to the bottom of the script. Move the cursor so that it is above the two WRITELIB commands, press Insert, and then press Return a few times to add a few blank lines. Then, press Menu and select Read. Enter Numwords as the name of the procedure to read in, and press Enter. You'll see the Numwords.SC script appear on the screen. To change this into a procedure, place the command

PROC NumWords( )

above the ARRAY command, and the commands

RETURN
ENDPROC

at the bottom of Numwords, as shown in Figure 19.15. You may also want to add indentations just to pretty things up, as I've done in Figure 19.15. (Move the cursor to the beginning of each line, make sure Insert mode is on, and press the Space bar 5 times. Tedious, I know!)

Next, read the Translat.SC procedure into this procedure file. To do so, first make sure the cursor is below the Numwords procedure, but above the two WRITELIB commands. Then, call up the menu, select Read, and enter Translat as the name of the file to read. The Translat procedure was originally created with the PROC and ENDPROC commands, so you don't need to add anything to it.

Finally, move the cursor to the bottom of the procedure file. Replace the two lines that read

WRITELIB "Dateproc" Dateword
WRITELIB "Dateproc" Engdate

with the four lines below:

    WRITELIB "Proclib1" Dateword
    WRITELIB "Proclib1" Engdate
    WRITELIB "Proclib1" Numwords
    WRITELIB "Proclib1" Translat

This will make sure that all four procedures are stored in the new Proclib1 procedure library. Press DO-IT! to save the new script. Figure 19.15 shows the Proclib1.SC script in its entirety.

To create the new Proclib1.LIB procedure library, select the Scripts and Play options as usual, and play Proclib1. Not much will happen on the screen, but when the Main menu returns, the Proclib1.LIB library will have been created.

Now, we need a script that can access these procedures to print checks. Our original Checkprn.SC script (Figure 19.12) is close, but not quite adequate. So, we'll use Checkprn.SC to create a new script named Chekprn2.SC.

To do so, select Scripts, Editor, and Write from the menu. Enter **Chekprn2** as the name of the new script. Then, press Menu, select Read, and specify Checkprn as the file to read in.

Next, you'll need to remove the two PLAY commands shown below (using Ctry-Y):

    ; -- Create index of English words.
    PLAY "Numwords"
    ; -- Load translation procedure.
    PLAY "Translat"

and put in these lines instead:

    ; -- Load procedure library.
    READLIB "Proclib1" Dateword, Engdate, Numwords, Translat
    ; -- Load date and number arrays.
    Dateword( )
    Numwords( )

The READLIB command will read in the preparsed procedures, and the Dateword( ) and Numwords( ) commands will set up the number and month arrays we've discussed earlier in the chapter.

To use the new date-translation procedure on printed checks, change the line that reads

? [Checkno],SPACES(40),[Check Date]

to

? [Checkno],SPACES(40),Engdate([Check Date])

which uses the Engdate procedure to translate the [Check Date] field from the Checks table. Figure 19.16 shows the entire Chekprn2.SC script.

Before you can test it all, you'll need to call up the Checks table (described earlier in this chapter) using the Modify and Edit options from the menu. Then, use → to scroll over to the field named Written

```
; -------------------------------------- Chekprn2.SC
; -------------------- Sample program to print checks.
CLEARALL
CLEAR

;--------------- Load procedure library.
READLIB "Proclib1" Dateword, Engdate, Numwords, Translat

;--------------- Load date and number arrays.
Dateword()
Numwords()

; -------------- Call in "Checks" in table in Edit mode.
EDIT "Checks"

; -------------- Send ? and ?? output to printer.
PRINTER ON

; -- Loop through records with blank "printed" field.
SCAN FOR ISBLANK([Written])
     Dollars = FORMAT("W12.2,E$C*",[Amount])
     ? [Checkno],SPACES(40),EngDate([Check Date])
     ?
     ? [To Whom], SPACES(10), Dollars
     ? " "
     ? TRANSLAT([Amount])
     ? " "
     ;---------------- Mark check as written.
     MOVETO [Written]
     TYPEIN "Y"
ENDSCAN ;--------------- (for checks not printed yet)

;------------------------ End of Checkprn.SC script.
DO_IT!           ;---- Save edits to the Checks table.
CLEARALL
CLEAR
PRINTER OFF
```

Figure 19.16: The Chekprn2.SC script

and remove the *Y* from any records that might have it. (Recall that the check printing procedure puts a Y in the Written field, so that it does not accidentally print the same check twice. Of course, if you have real check data in the Checks table, you'd do better to wait until you've added some more checks before printing.)

To test the new script and procedures, save the Checks table with DO-IT!, call up the menu, select Scripts and Play, and specify Chekprn2 as the script to play. Unless you have a particularly slow printer, you should notice increased speed over the previous script used to print checks.

LOOKING INTO PROCEDURES

You can look at the names and sizes of procedures in a procedure library using the INFOLIB command. To see a list of procedures in the Proclib1.LIB procedure file, select Scripts, Editor, and Write from the menu, enter a name for the script, such as PeekLib, and enter this single line:

INFOLIB "Proclib1"

Call up the menu and select Go. You'll see a temporary table named List containing the names and sizes of the procedures in the Proclib1.LIB file, as shown in Figure 19.17.

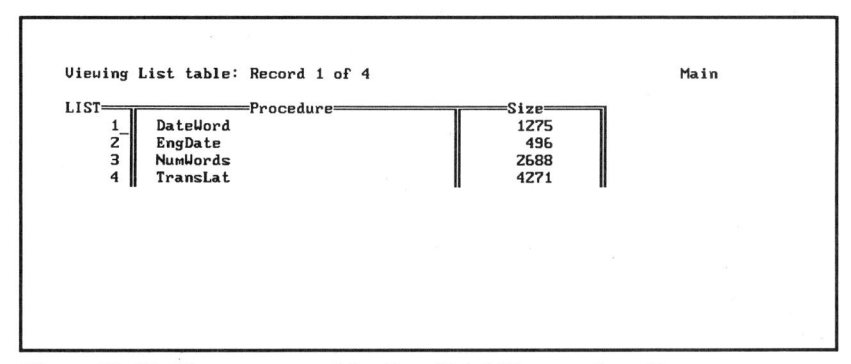

```
Viewing List table: Record 1 of 4                              Main
LIST          Procedure            Size
    1    DateWord              1275
    2    EngDate                496
    3    NumWords              2688
    4    TransLat              4271
```

Figure 19.17: The contents of the Proclib1.LIB procedure file

SUMMARY

In this chapter, we've discussed more basic techniques for managing scripts, and looked at some sample scripts using advanced PAL techniques. Space here does not permit us to go into as much detail as the 500-plus page *PAL User's Guide* that comes with your Paradox package, but hopefully the information presented here has given you a good overview of the potential of PAL scripts and enough basic techniques to get you started on developing scripts of your own.

Some specific points to keep in mind that were discussed in this chapter are listed below:

- You can include a script name next to the PARADOX3 command at the DOS prompt to have Paradox run the script immediately at startup.

- You can have a script run automatically every time Paradox is first run by assigning the name Init.SC to the script.

- The Tools, More, Protect, Password, and Script options let you assign passwords to scripts to prevent others from viewing or changing the script's contents.

- To print a copy of a script, call up the menu while editing the script and select Print.

- You can use any text editor or word processor to create or modify a script, as long as you remember to include the extension .SC in the file name, and save the script as an ASCII (DOS Text) file.

- The RUN and RUN BIG commands let you run external programs from within a PAL script.

- Keyboard macros are miniature scripts that are assigned to a particular keystroke through the SETKEY command.

- The PAL debugger provides menu options that can help you locate and correct errors in a script.

THE PARADOX PERSONAL PROGRAMMER

CHAPTER 20

AS DISCUSSED PREVIOUSLY, AN *APPLICATION* IS A SET of Paradox tables, report formats, forms, PAL programs, and perhaps other objects that work together to perform a particular job, such as managing an inventory, an account, or a payroll. The application typically has a menu system of its own that temporarily replaces the more general Paradox menus with menus that are specific to the job at hand.

The real beauty of an application is that it allows you to develop complete systems that others can use easily; even people with no Paradox experience whatsoever. In fact, others who may be interested in using your application don't even need to have Paradox at all! Instead, they can use a smaller *Paradox Runtime* package, which costs less than Paradox, and requires less disk space. This is particularly beneficial if you decide to market your application on a large scale.

One way to develop applications, as we saw in Chapter 18, is to write a lot of PAL scripts. This technique can be quite tedious, and also requires a good deal of knowledge about PAL and general programming techniques. A second way to develop applications is with the Paradox Personal Programmer, which came with your Paradox package.

The Personal Programmer lets you develop applications by presenting menus and asking you to *describe* the application you wish to develop. You define what tables, reports, and forms are required, and design a system of menus that link the various pieces of the application into an integrated system. After you've described your application through your menu selections, the Personal Programmer automatically writes all the necessary PAL scripts to convert your description into a real working application.

REQUIREMENTS AND LIMITATIONS

The Personal Programmer is a very large program; to use it you will need quite a bit of computer hardware and a little Paradox experience.

HARDWARE REQUIREMENTS

As a minimum, your computer system must have the following features:

- At least 640K RAM
- A hard disk with at least 2 megabytes (2,000K) of available space
- All other basic requirements for running Paradox, and the Paradox program already installed on the computer

Though you can't use the Personal Programmer on a computer without a hard disk, your users may be able to use the application you develop with the Personal Programmer on a computer with only two floppy disk drives. Whether or not other users can use the developed application on smaller computers will, of course, be determined by how much disk space the final application requires.

EXPERIENCE REQUIREMENTS

As an application developer, you need to know the basics of using Paradox. You don't need to know anything about PAL, the Paradox Application Language (discussed in Chapters 17 through 19 of this book), but it certainly doesn't hurt to have some familiarity with PAL. In some cases, very complex or sophisticated applications may require some PAL programming.

In this chapter, we'll see how ability to record a PAL script (discussed in Chapter 11) can help overcome some of the limitations of the Personal Programmer.

If you already are an experienced PAL programmer, you'll find the Personal Programmer a great productivity tool in helping you build applications. The PAL programs that the Personal Programmer develops adhere to the basic principals of *structured programming*, making it easy to modify the applications that the Personal Programmer develops, if you are so inclined.

There are a few limitations that the Personal Programmer imposes, although these are by no means strict. Briefly, Paradox sets the following limits for a single application:

- A maximum of 15 tables
- A maximum of 15 selections per custom menu
- A maximum of 10 levels of menus

If you are using Paradox on a network, you need to change to a local drive before running the Personal Programmer; it cannot be run from a network drive. In fact, if memory is tight you may have to unload network drivers to regain enough memory to run the Personal Programmer. Also, you cannot use the Personal Programmer to build multiuser applications, or SQL Link applications.

PLANNING AN APPLICATION

In this section, we'll discuss general techniques for planning an application, using an inventory-management system as an example. Rather than plan an application that the Personal Programmer is able to create easily, we'll purposely design an application that goes a bit beyond the capabilities of the Personal Programmer. After all, in any "real-world" situation, you'll probably want to design your own applications without limitations. When the Personal Programmer falls short of meeting the needs of our example application, I'll show you how to bypass the Personal Programmer's limitations to develop the application you want.

AN INVENTORY MANAGEMENT SYSTEM

When you want to build your own application, it's a good idea to start with a large goal, such as the development of an inventory-management system, and break it down into smaller, easier goals. To do this, you must create a diagram of the various tables used in the application and a *menu tree* of the tasks required to manage those data.

THE INVENTORY SYSTEM TABLES

The database structure we'll use for the inventory example will be identical to the structure discussed in Chapter 15, and shown in Figure 15.1. To recap, the master inventory table will hold a single record for each item that the business keeps in stock. Each of these items must be assigned a unique part number (or product number). This table will also store information about the current status of each item, including the quantity in stock, the reorder point, the quantity on order, the date the last order was placed, and so forth.

The Sales table will store current sales transactions. The SalHist table stores sales transactions that have already been posted (their quantities have already been subtracted from the in-stock quantities in the Mastinv table). The Purchase table will store items received from the manufacturers (or distributors). The Purhist table will store posted transactions (items that have been received and their quantities already added to the Mastinv table in-stock quantities).

Figure 20.1 shows the the five tables used in the inventory system we'll develop in this chapter. There are a couple of one-to-many relationships in this database structure. For each item in the Mastinv table, there will likely be many sales transactions and many purchase transactions.

THE APPLICATION MENU TREE

After deciding how to store the data for the application, you'll want to develop a *menu structure* that simplifies the task of managing the data. A general rule of thumb when developing applications with multiple tables is to provide an individual menu for managing each table. That is, each table should have a menu selection that allows the user to add new data, edit and delete data, look up information, and print reports. Any general tasks, such as updating, can also be assigned a menu selection. All of the various tasks and submenus can then be linked together through a higher level main menu.

```
                    ┌─────────────────────┐
                    │  Master inventory   │
                    │  Mastinv contains   │
                    │  current in-stock   │
                    │  quantities for each item │
                    │  in stock           │
                    └─────────────────────┘
```

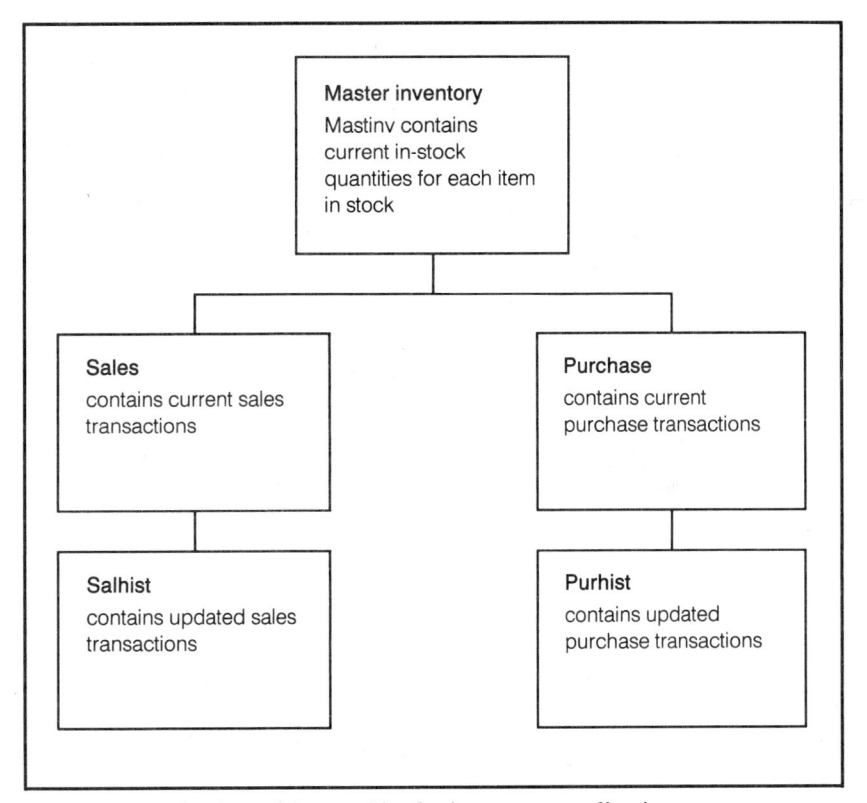

Figure 20.1: The five tables used in the inventory application

Planning the menu structure (or *menu tree* as it is often called) before using the Personal Programmer will greatly simplify the development of your application. A preplanned menu structure breaks the larger task of developing the application into smaller, more manageable chunks. It also provides a road map to guide you through the Personal Programmer, and makes it easier to take a break from time to time and resume your work at a later point.

The menu structure for the sample inventory-management system we'll develop in this chapter is shown in Figure 20.2. Notice that several of the main menu options branch to submenus for managing information on the Mastinv, Sales, and Purchase tables. The master inventory submenu branches down even further to a second submenu, to allow the user of the application to select a particular report to print.

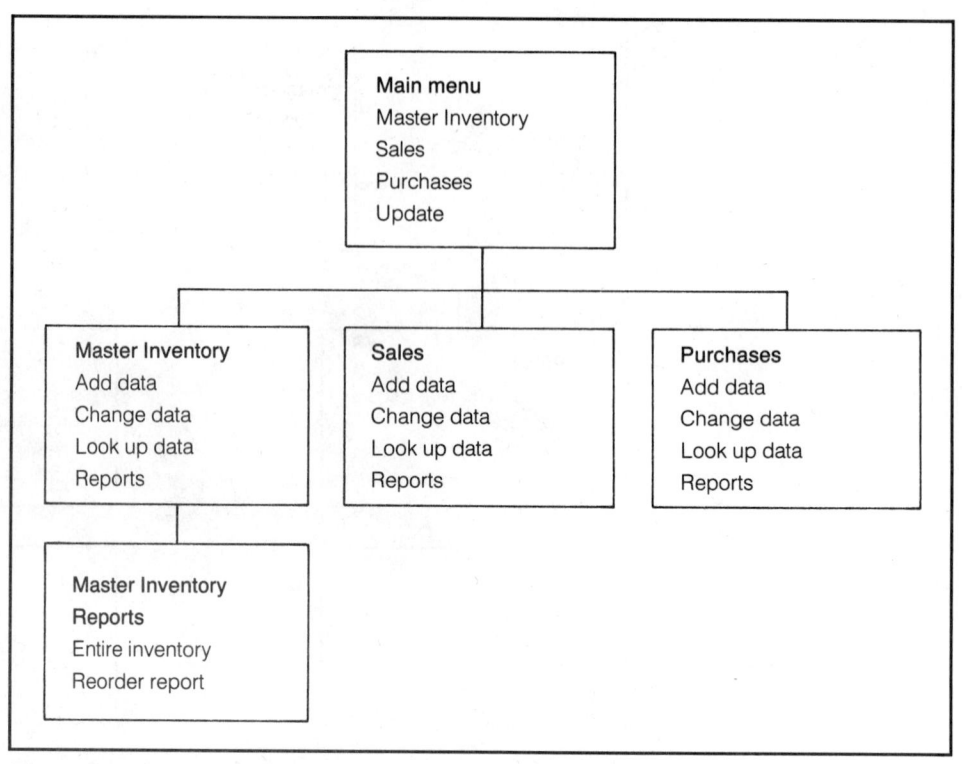

```
┌─────────────────────────────────────────────────────────────────┐
│                      ┌──────────────────┐                       │
│                      │ Main menu        │                       │
│                      │ Master Inventory │                       │
│                      │ Sales            │                       │
│                      │ Purchases        │                       │
│                      │ Update           │                       │
│                      └──────────────────┘                       │
│    ┌──────────────────┬──────────────────┬──────────────────┐   │
│    │ Master Inventory │ Sales            │ Purchases        │   │
│    │ Add data         │ Add data         │ Add data         │   │
│    │ Change data      │ Change data      │ Change data      │   │
│    │ Look up data     │ Look up data     │ Look up data     │   │
│    │ Reports          │ Reports          │ Reports          │   │
│    └──────────────────┘                                         │
│    ┌──────────────────┐                                         │
│    │ Master Inventory │                                         │
│    │ Reports          │                                         │
│    │ Entire inventory │                                         │
│    │ Reorder report   │                                         │
│    └──────────────────┘                                         │
└─────────────────────────────────────────────────────────────────┘
```

Figure 20.2: The menu structure for the inventory application

As we develop the sample application, you might want to refer back to this figure from time to time to keep track of where we are in the development process.

Now, be forewarned that in this chapter, I will intentionally take you into some "dead-ends" where the Personal Programmer falls short. If you are just trying to follow instructions to get the job done, you might be irritated by these intentional dead-ends. But be patient. Learning how to react to, and overcome, the limitations of the Personal Programmer is an important part of mastering this valuable tool. Hopefully, the intentional dead-ends that I overcome in this chapter will help you to do the same when developing custom applications of your own.

CREATING A DIRECTORY FOR THE APPLICATION

Each application that you develop should be stored on its own directory on your hard disk, to avoid conflicting file names and general confusion. To create a new directory for your application, start from your root directory (the one that is logged when you first start your computer), and use the DOS MKDIR or MD command to enter the name of the new directory. The directory name can be up to eight characters long, with no spaces or punctuation.

We'll store the sample application in this chapter on a directory named InvMgr. To create the directory, enter the series of commands below at the DOS prompt (pressing Enter after each command):

```
CD\
MD\INVMGR
CD\INVMGR
```

These commands ensure that you start from the root directory (*CD*), create a new directory named INVMGR (*MD\\INVMGR*), and log onto that new directory (*CD\\INVMGR*).

When developing or modifying your application, you'll want to be sure to always log onto the appropriate directory first.

COPYING OBJECTS

If you plan to use existing tables, report formats, forms, or scripts for your application, you may want to copy these onto the new directory before starting the Personal Programmer. To do so, be sure you are logged onto the new directory, and use the DOS COPY command with the appropriate file name and extension. The file-name extensions that Paradox uses for various objects are listed in Table 20.1.

As an example, a table named CustList would be stored on disk as Custlist.DB. Its validity checks, if any, would be stored in the file Custlist.VAL. Its image settings, if any, would be stored in Custlist.SET. Report and form file-name extensions use the number you selected when designing the report. For example, report number 1 for the Custlist table is Custlist.R1. Form number 3 for the Custlist table is Custlist.F3.

Table 20.1: Paradox file-name extensions

OBJECT	EXTENSION
Table	.DB
Form	.F<number>
Report format	.R<number>
Script	.SC
Validity check	.VAL
Image setting	.SET

To use the DOS COPY command to copy objects to the application directory, enter the COPY command, followed by the name of the directory that the object is stored on, and the name of the object to copy. For example, to copy the Custlist table to the current directory, you would enter the command

```
COPY C:\PDOX35\Custlist.DB
```

at the DOS prompt.

For the current example application, you need not copy any Paradox objects. We'll begin with a blank directory.

STARTING THE PERSONAL PROGRAMMER

If you cannot access the Personal Programmer on your computer, it may not be installed yet. See the Appendix for installation instructions.

To start the Personal Programmer, you need to perform three basic steps:

- Log onto the directory that the application is to be created on.
- Enter the DOS PATH command so that both the Personal Programmer and Paradox are accessible from the current directory.
- Enter the command PPROG.

For the current example, in which we are developing the application on a directory named InvMgr, you would follow these steps (assuming the DOS command prompt is currently on your screen):

1. Type **CD \INVMGR** and press ← to log onto the InvMgr directory (if you have not already done so).
2. If you did not already change your Autoexec.BAT file to include the PARADOX35 and PARADOX35\PPROG directories during the installation process (discussed in the Appendix), type **PATH C:\PDOX35;C:\PDOX35\-PPROG** and press ←.
3. Type **PPROG** and press ← to start the Personal Programmer.

You'll see an introductory graphic screen similar to the one you see when first starting Paradox, and then the Personal Programmer Main menu and initial instructions, as shown in Figure 20.3.

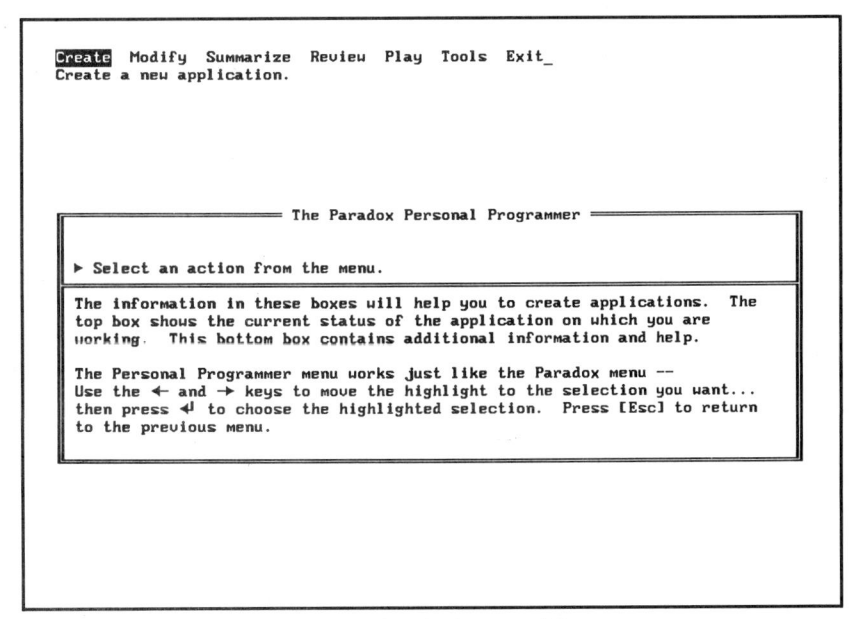

```
Create  Modify  Summarize  Review  Play  Tools  Exit_
Create a new application.




                  ═══ The Paradox Personal Programmer ═══
  ► Select an action from the menu.

  The information in these boxes will help you to create applications.  The
  top box shows the current status of the application on which you are
  working.  This bottom box contains additional information and help.

  The Personal Programmer menu works just like the Paradox menu --
  Use the ← and → keys to move the highlight to the selection you want...
  then press ↵ to choose the highlighted selection.  Press [Esc] to return
  to the previous menu.
```

Figure 20.3: The opening screen for the Personal Programmer

The options on the Main menu are summarized below:

OPTION	EFFECT
Create	Creates a new application
Modify	Changes an existing application
Summarize	Prints a summary of the application
Review	Views the menu structure of the application
Play	Runs the application or a PAL script
Tools	Copies, deletes, or renames the application, changes settings or the current directory
Exit	Leaves the Personal Programmer and returns to DOS

You select items from the Personal Programmer menu in exactly the same way you select them from the Paradox menus. To leave a submenu and return to a higher-level menu, press the Esc key; select DO-IT! or Cancel if the options are presented. We'll see examples of these various options as we develop the sample inventory manager.

CREATING THE APPLICATION

It will take quite a bit of time to develop the entire inventory application, so we'll break it down into pieces so that you can take a break from time to time, and resume where you left off. (See Modifying An Application later in this chapter for information.)

To create an application, select Create from the Personal Programmer Main menu. The screen displays the prompt

Application name:
Enter a name for the new application:

The application name can be from one to five characters long, with no spaces or punctuation. For this example, type in the application name **Inv** and press Enter.

SELECTING TABLES FOR THE APPLICATION

The next step in creating an application is to create the tables or specify which existing tables to use for the application. The menu at the top of the screen displays the options

ExistingTable   NewTable   RemoveTable   DO-IT!   Cancel

These options can be summarized as follows:

ExistingTable	Selects an existing table for use in the application
NewTable	Creates a new table for use in the application
RemoveTable	Removes a table from the application
DO-IT!	Finishes selection of tables for the application
Cancel	Cancels table selections and returns to the Main menu

> Don't worry if the borrowed table structure has a blank field at the end of it; just press F2 to save the structure.

For the inventory example, we'll assume that the tables do not already exist. Therefore, select the NewTable option, type in the table name **Mastinv** when prompted, and press Enter. Figure 20.4 shows the structure of the Mastinv table. You can type it in exactly as shown in the figure. (Optionally, if you already created the Mastinv table back in Chapter 12, call up the Menu (F10), select Borrow, and type **\PDOX-35\Mastinv** as the structure to borrow.) When you have the structure entered correctly, as in Figure 20.4, press the DO-IT key (F2) to save it.

Next, create the structure of the Sales table. Select NewTable, and enter **Sales** as the table name. Type in the structure exactly as shown in Figure 20.5. (If you previously created the Sales table back in Chapter 12, you can borrow its structure by pressing Menu (F10) and selecting Borrow. Specify **\PDOX35\Sales** as the structure to borrow. Note that you must also change the name of the Sel Price field to Unit Price, so the structure matches that in Figure 20.5.) Press F2 to save the completed Sales table structure.

Next, create the structure for the Purchase table. Select NewTable from the menu, and enter the table name **Purchase**. Structure the table

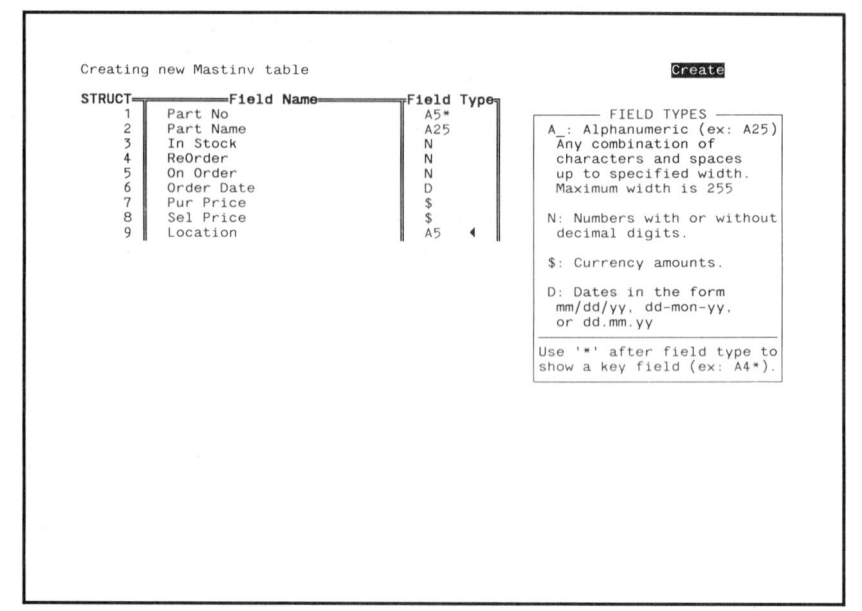

```
Creating new Mastinv table                              Create
STRUCT    Field Name            Field Type
   1    Part No                  A5*           ── FIELD TYPES ──
   2    Part Name                A25           A_: Alphanumeric (ex: A25)
   3    In Stock                 N             Any combination of
   4    ReOrder                  N             characters and spaces
   5    On Order                 N             up to specified width.
   6    Order Date               D             Maximum width is 255
   7    Pur Price                $
   8    Sel Price                $             N: Numbers with or without
   9    Location                 A5   ◄           decimal digits.

                                               $: Currency amounts.

                                               D: Dates in the form
                                                  mm/dd/yy, dd-mon-yy,
                                                  or dd.mm.yy

                                               Use '*' after field type to
                                               show a key field (ex: A4*).
```

Figure 20.4: The structure of the Mastinv table

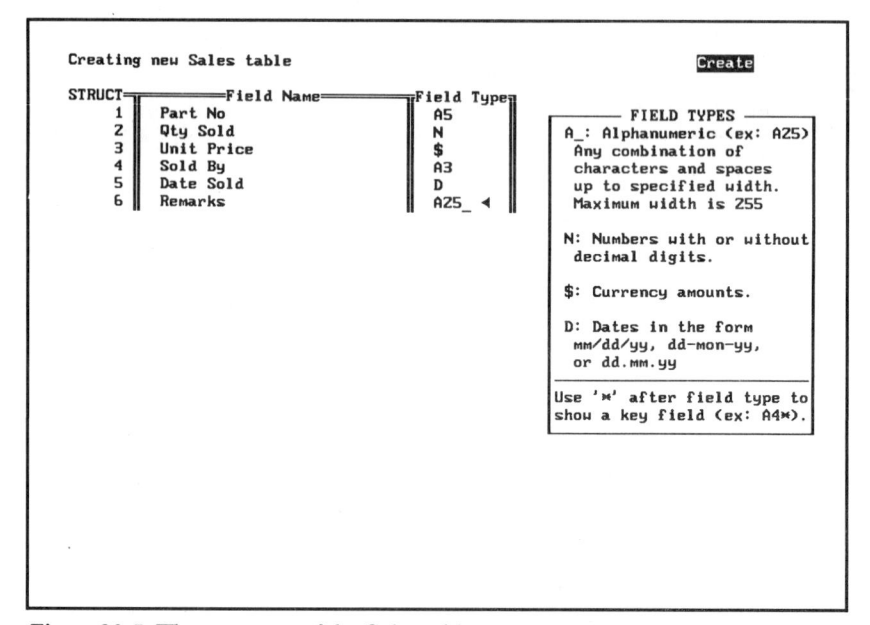

```
Creating new Sales table                                Create
STRUCT    Field Name            Field Type
   1    Part No                  A5            ── FIELD TYPES ──
   2    Qty Sold                 N             A_: Alphanumeric (ex: A25)
   3    Unit Price               $             Any combination of
   4    Sold By                  A3            characters and spaces
   5    Date Sold                D             up to specified width.
   6    Remarks                  A25  ◄        Maximum width is 255

                                               N: Numbers with or without
                                                  decimal digits.

                                               $: Currency amounts.

                                               D: Dates in the form
                                                  mm/dd/yy, dd-mon-yy,
                                                  or dd.mm.yy

                                               Use '*' after field type to
                                               show a key field (ex: A4*).
```

Figure 20.5: The structure of the Sales table

exactly as shown in Figure 20.6. (Once again, if you already created this table back in Chapter 12, press F10, select Borrow, and specify **\PDOX35\Purchase** as the structure to borrow.) Press F2 when the table structure matches that shown in Figure 20.6.

Next, create the history files. Select NewTable, and enter the table name **Salhist**. Since its structure is identical to the Sales table structure, press Menu (F10), select Borrow, and enter **Sales** as the name of the structure to borrow. Press F2 when the structure of the Salhist table matches the structure of the Sales table shown in Figure 20.5.

To create the Purhist table, select NewTable, and enter the table name **Purhist**. Since its structure is identical to the Purchase table structure, press Menu (F10), select Borrow, and enter **Purchase** as the name of the structure to borrow. Press F2 when the structure of the Purhist table matches the structure of the Purchase table shown in Figure 20.6.

The screen displays the names of the tables selected for the application, as shown below:

Selected tables:
Mastinv Sales Purchase Salhist Purhist

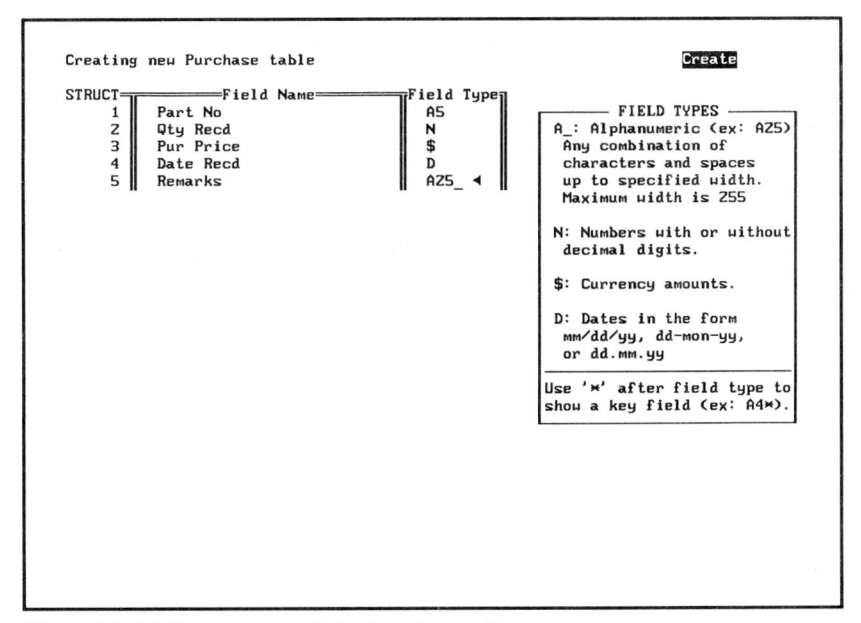

```
Creating new Purchase table                                     Create
STRUCT        Field Name          Field Type
  1    Part No                    A5            ── FIELD TYPES ──
  2    Qty Recd                   N            A_: Alphanumeric (ex: A25)
  3    Pur Price                  $             Any combination of
  4    Date Recd                  D             characters and spaces
  5    Remarks                    A25  ◄        up to specified width.
                                                Maximum width is 255

                                                N: Numbers with or without
                                                   decimal digits.

                                                $: Currency amounts.

                                                D: Dates in the form
                                                   mm/dd/yy, dd-mon-yy,
                                                   or dd.mm.yy

                                                Use '*' after field type to
                                                show a key field (ex: A4*).
```

Figure 20.6: The structure of the Purchase table

These are the five tables we'll use in this application, so select DO-IT! from the top menu to finish selecting tables. The Personal Programmer will now ask you to type in a description of each table.

Type in **Master inventory file** as the description of the Mastinv table, and press Enter. Type in **Current sales transactions** as the description of the Sales table, and press Enter. Enter **Current purchases (items received)** as the description of the Purchase table. Enter **Posted sales transactions** as the description of the Salhist table, and **Posted purchases (items received)** as the description of the Purhist table. After entering all the table descriptions, you'll see the message

> Preparing to create the main menu

at the bottom of the screen.

DEFINING THE MAIN MENU

Your next task is to define the main menu for the application. You define each menu item, up to a maximum of 20 characters, as it is to appear on the screen, and a descriptive message, up to 60 characters, for each item. You'll notice on the screen that the word *Main* appears in the upper-right corner of the box, and the reminder

> Designing MAIN menu

appears within the help box on the screen, as shown in Figure 20.7 (yours won't show the inventory system main menu yet). Later, when you develop submenus, these same messages will help you keep track of which submenu you are working on.

When entering menu items, remember that these menus will work just like the Paradox menus. The user of your application can select options either by highlighting and pressing Return, or by typing in the first letter of the option. Therefore, you might want to ensure that each option begins with a unique letter.

As you enter menu items and descriptions, you can use the following keys to make changes and corrections if necessary:

KEY	EFFECT
→, ←	Moves the highlight between menu items

```
Master Inventory  Sales  Purchases  Update                    Main
Update the master inventory from Sales and Purchases


================= The Paradox Personal Programmer =================
Creating new Inv application.
Designing MAIN menu.
► Enter the names of menu selections and their descriptions.

Menu selection names can be up to 20 characters long, descriptions up to 60.

← and → move you around the menu you are designing. [Ins] inserts a new
selection, [Del] deletes the highlighted selection. [F9] allows you to edit
the highlighted selection name or its description; when you are finished
editing, press [Enter].

When you are finished designing the current menu level, press [F2] or
press [F10] and select DO-IT! from the menu.
```

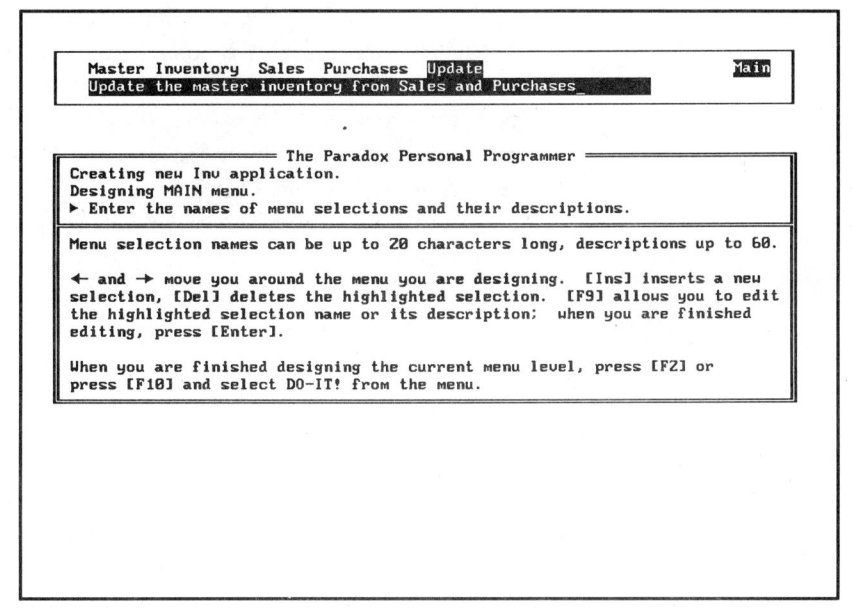

Figure 20.7: The main menu for the inventory system defined

Ins	Inserts a new item to the left of the current one
Del	Deletes the highlighted menu item
F9	Edits the highlighted selection below:

The F9 key makes use of the following keys to edit the highlighted item:

KEY	EFFECT
Backspace	Moves cursor back and erases
Ctrl-Backspace	Erases entire entry
Enter	Finishes item edit and moves to description
Esc	Cancels the edit
DO-IT!	Finishes editing session

For the inventory application, enter the menu selections shown in the main menu of Figure 20.2. That is, for the first item, type in the item **Master Inventory,** press Enter, then type the description **Manage the master inventory file** and press Enter again. For the second main menu item, type in **Sales**, press Enter, type in the description **Manage current sales transactions** and press Enter again. For the third menu item, type in **Purchases** and the description **Manage current purchases (items received)**. As the fourth selection, type in the name **Update**, and enter the description **Update the master inventory from Sales and Purchases**.

When you've finished creating the main menu, your screen will look like Figure 20.7. To save the main menu, press F2. The Personal Programmer will add the menu option Leave to your menu.

ASSIGNING ACTIONS TO MENU ITEMS

The next phase in the application development process is to begin assigning actions to menu items. In other words, now is the time to tell the Personal Programmer what to do when the user selects the currently highlighted menu item. The menu below appears on the screen:

SpecifyAction   DO-IT!   Cancel

These options can be summarized as follows:

OPTION	EFFECT
SpecifyAction	Assigns actions to menu items
DO-IT!	Saves work so far and returns to Main menu
Cancel	Abandons work so far and returns to Main menu

Select the SpecifyAction option to assign actions to the Master menu item (which is blinking on the screen).

After you select SpecifyAction, the Action menu below appears on the screen:

Menu   View   Report   DataEntry   Edit   Script   Help
NotDefined   Cancel

These options can be summarized as follows:

OPTION	EFFECT
Menu	Displays a submenu to the user
View	Lets the user view data
Report	Lets the user print a report
DataEntry	Lets the user enter new data
Edit	Lets the user change or delete data
Script	Plays a script for the user
Help	Shows a help screen to the user
NotDefined	Skips the current item
Cancel	Sends the user back to the previous menu

The Action menu is where you'll do most of your work in the Personal Programmer. You need to assign an action to every menu item in your system. If for some reason you are not ready to assign an action to an item, you can select NotDefined and come back to that item later. You can also press Esc to work backwards and exit the Personal Programmer.

THE MASTER INVENTORY SUBMENU

In the current inventory application, the Master Inventory menu selection branches to a submenu of choices for managing the master inventory file. To assign this action to the item, select Menu from the Action menu.

As you begin to design the submenu of the master-inventory table, the upper-right corner of the screen reminds you that you are now designing a submenu for the Master Inventory selection from the inventory-system main menu. You create a submenu using the same technique as for a main menu: type in the menu items and a brief description of each item. Referring back to Figure 20.2, recall that we want this menu to display the options Add data, Change data, Look up data, and Reports.

Type in **Add data** as the first menu item, and **Add new products to the master inventory** as the description. As the second submenu item, enter **Change data** as the menu item, and **Edit/delete master inventory items** as the description. For the third submenu item, enter **Look up data** as the item, and **Look up information in the master inventory** as the description. Finally, enter **Reports** as the fourth menu item, and **Print master inventory reports** as the description. Press ← four times to scroll back to the first selection. Your screen should look like Figure 20.8.

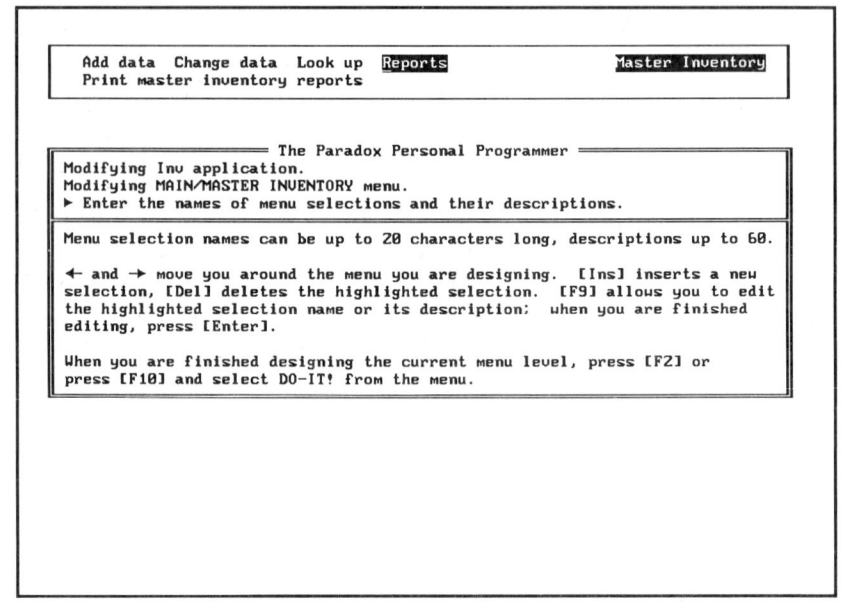

```
┌──────────────────────────────────────────────────────────────────────────┐
│    Add data  Change data  Look up  Reports                Master Inventory│
│    Print master inventory reports                                         │
└──────────────────────────────────────────────────────────────────────────┘
┌──────────────── The Paradox Personal Programmer ────────────────┐
│ Modifying Inv application.                                       │
│ Modifying MAIN/MASTER INVENTORY menu.                            │
│ ► Enter the names of menu selections and their descriptions.     │
├──────────────────────────────────────────────────────────────────┤
│ Menu selection names can be up to 20 characters long, descriptions up to 60.│
│                                                                  │
│ ← and → move you around the menu you are designing. [Ins] inserts a new│
│ selection, [Del] deletes the highlighted selection. [F9] allows you to edit│
│ the highlighted selection name or its description; when you are finished│
│ editing, press [Enter].                                          │
│                                                                  │
│ When you are finished designing the current menu level, press [F2] or│
│ press [F10] and select DO-IT! from the menu.                     │
└──────────────────────────────────────────────────────────────────┘
```

Figure 20.8: The Master Inventory submenu defined

Press F2 when you've finished defining the submenu. Your next step is to assign an action to each item on this submenu.

Master Inventory Data Entry

When users select *Add data* from the submenu, we want them to be able to add new records to the master inventory file. So, select Specify-Action from the top menu, then DataEntry from the Action menu. The screen will ask which table or tables you want the user to add data to, using the following menu:

> SelectTable AllTables DO-IT! Cancel

The SelectTable option lets you select a table (or several tables) to add data to. The AllTables option selects all tables for entering data. Obviously, we only want to add data to a single table here, so select SelectTable. When prompted, specify Mastinv as the name of the table to use, and then select DO-IT! to indicate that you are finished selecting tables for this menu item.

The next options to appear are

> FormView TableView FormToggle

If you want the application to display data on a custom form, select FormView. If you want the application to display data in Table view during data entry, select TableView. If you want the user to be able to switch back and forth between Table and Form views, select the FormToggle option.

In this example, we'll develop a custom form for data entry, so select FormView. The next menu options are

> Design Borrow StandardForm

The Design option lets you design a new form. The Borrow option lets you borrow another form in the table. The StandardForm option displays the Paradox standard form. Select Design in this case to design a new form.

Select option 1 from the forms menu to assign the number 1 to the new form we'll be designing. For the form description, enter **Enter/edit master inventory data**. The screen for designing forms (discussed in Chapter 9) appears on the screen.

Using the usual techniques, design the form to your liking. Figure 20.9 shows an example you might want to follow. All of the field masks are placed on the form using the Field, Place, and Regular options from the menu (accessed by pressing F10).

Press F2 after you've created form. Your next menu options are

> Settings DO-IT! Cancel

```
Changing F1 form for Mastinv                           Form    1/1
<18, 4>
                         ┌─────────────────────────────────────┐
                         │        Master Inventory File        │
                         └─────────────────────────────────────┘
  Part number: ____
  Part name:   _____
        In           Reorder          On              Date
      Stock           Point          Order          Ordered
    _____        _____        _____       _____
                  Purchase price: _____
                  Selling price:  _____
                  Location: _____
```

Figure 20.9: A custom form for the Mastinv table

We'll explore the Settings option later. For now, select DO-IT! to save the current form. You'll be returned to the Action menu, to define an Action for the next Master Inventory submenu option.

Master Inventory Editing

The second item in the Master Inventory submenu is *Change data*. The action you'll want to assign to this item is Edit, so select the Edit option from the Action menu.

Once again, you'll be asked to define tables to use. Select Select-Table, and specify Mastinv as the table to use. Then select DO-IT! to stop selecting tables.

Once again the screen displays the options

   FormView   TableView   FormToggle

and once again, you select FormView to allow editing through a custom form. From the next submenu, select Borrow to borrow an existing form for editing. Select 1 to select the previously defined form for the Mastinv table.

The next menu presents the options

> Settings   InsertDelete   DO-IT!   Cancel

The Settings option lets you change settings, such as validity checks and image settings, on the custom form, which we don't need to do right now. The InsertDelete option lets you decide whether or not the user can insert and/or delete records in this edit mode. There is no need for the user to be able to insert records, as we have a data-entry menu item for that. However, the user must be able to delete a record in this mode. So select InsertDelete, Insert, and No, and then select InsertDelete, Delete, and Yes.

At this point, you are done defining the Change data option on the Master Inventory submenu. Select DO-IT!

Master Inventory Lookup

For the *Look up data* selection, we'll allow the user to look up an item in the master inventory by either part number or name (in case he or she does not know the part number). To define the action for this menu selection, select View from the Action menu. As usual, you'll be prompted to define a table to use. Select the SelectTable option, the Mastinv table, and then select DO-IT!

Next you'll be given the options

> SelectFields   AllFields

The SelectFields option lets you select specific fields to include in the view. The AllFields selection automatically displays all fields in the view. Select AllFields for this example.

The next menu displays the options

> SelectRecords   AllRecords

We want to allow the user to specify a particular record to view. So select the SelectRecords option, and you'll see query form for the Mastinv table.

In this case, we want the user to be able to search by either part number or part name. We do not want to specify a particular record to display right now. Rather, we want to tell the Personal Programmer to allow *users* of the completed application to look up part numbers or names on their own. To do this, you create a query that uses *tilde variables*, temporary placeholders for a later query. A tilde variable must begin with the tilde character (~) followed by a variable name that begins with a letter and contains no blank spaces. In addition, we need to specify an Or search; since we don't know if the user will enter a part name or part number, the query must be able to search for either a part name or a part number. Furthermore, since the part name that the user enters to search for may not exactly match the part name in the table, we need to use the *like* command on the query form.

Figure 20.10 shows how to set up the query form on the screen. Note that both entries use tilde variables. Also notice that each entry is placed on a separate row to specify an OR search. Press F2 after filling in the query form as shown in Figure 20.10.

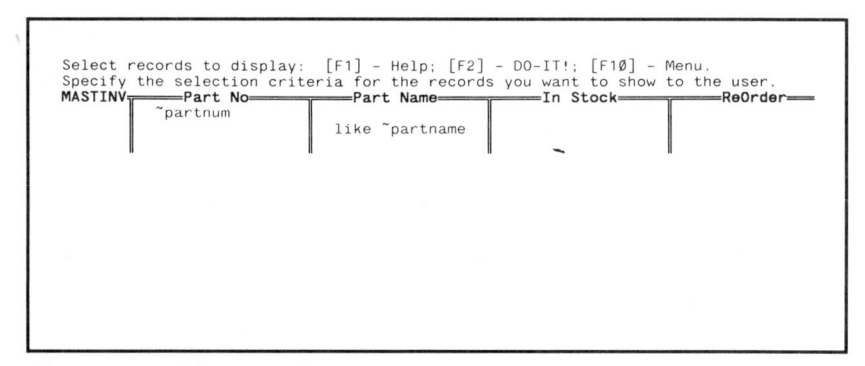

```
Select records to display:  [F1] - Help; [F2] - DO-IT!; [F10] - Menu.
Specify the selection criteria for the records you want to show to the user.
MASTINV      Part No        Part Name         In Stock         ReOrder
             ~partnum
                            like ~partname
```

Figure 20.10: The query form for the Mastinv table look-up

Now the screen asks for prompts for the tilde variables. For the partnum variable, type in the prompt below, then press Enter.

Enter part number to locate, or press Enter:

Press Enter again to accept the suggested data type, A5. For the partname variable, type in the prompt below, and then press Enter.

Optionally, enter the part name to locate:

Press Enter again to accept the suggested data type, A25.

From the next menu, select FormView to display the data on a form. Select Borrow to use an existing form, select 1 to use form number one. That completes the action for the Master Inventory Look up data menu item. Next, you'll want to define an action for the *Reports* menu item.

Master Inventory Reports

When the user selects *Reports* from the Master Inventory submenu, we want to display yet another menu of report options, as shown in Figure 20.2. Therefore, select Menu as the action for the Reports option. Define the first submenu (or, actually sub-submenu) item as **Entire inventory**, and enter the description **Display entire master inventory**. Enter **Reorder report** as the second menu option, and **List items below reorder point** as the description. Press F2 after entering the menu descriptions.

The *Entire inventory* option blinks to tell you that you are ready to work with this menu item. Select SpecifyAction from the top menu to begin. Select Report as the action, select SelectTable, Mastinv, and DO-IT!, and then select AllRecords so the report displays all the records. Select Design to design a report format, and select 1 as the report number.

Enter **Master inventory display** as the description of the form; you can then design the report format to your liking (as discussed in Chapter 8). For this example, I designed a free-form report as shown in Figure 20.11, (though you, of course, can develop a report format to your own liking).

Press F2 after designing your report format. Your next options will be:

    Printer   Screen   File

Select Printer so the report will be displayed on the printer.

Next you'll define an action for the *Reorder report* menu option. Again, select Report, SelectTable, Mastinv, and DO-IT!. Because this report is to display only certain records (those with in-stock and on-order quantities below the reorder point), select the SelectRecords option to specify records to display.

When the first query appears, you'll want to define the search condition, which is records whose reorder point is greater than the sum

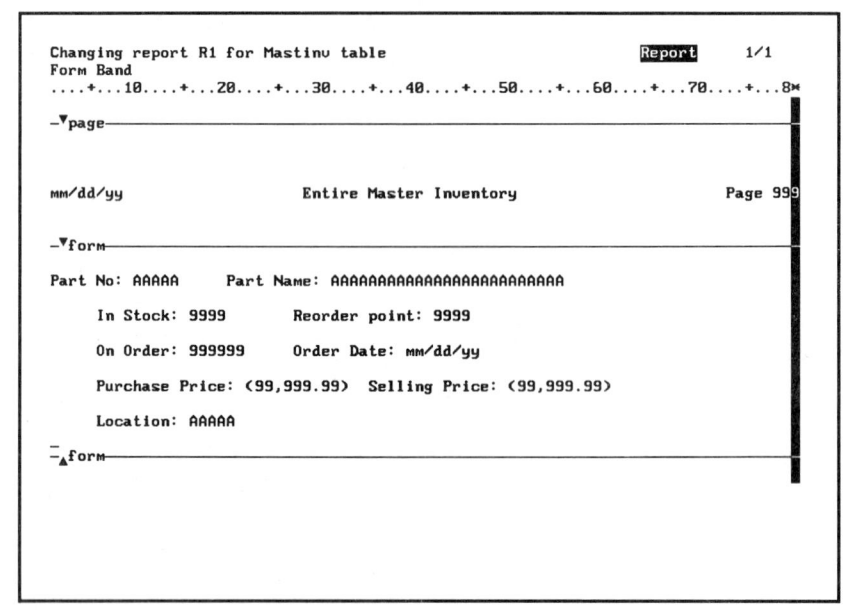

```
Changing report R1 for Mastinv table                    Report    1/1
Form Band
....+...10....+...20....+...30....+...40....+...50....+...60....+...70....+...8»
 -▼page
 
 
 mm/dd/yy                    Entire Master Inventory              Page 999
 -▼form
    Part No: AAAAA     Part Name: AAAAAAAAAAAAAAAAAAAAAAAA
       In Stock: 9999      Reorder point: 9999
       On Order: 999999    Order Date: mm/dd/yy
       Purchase Price: (99,999.99)  Selling Price: (99,999.99)
       Location: AAAAA
 -▲form
```

Figure 20.11: A suggested format for the Entire inventory report

of the in-stock and on-order quantities. You'll need to use some F5 examples to set up the query. This is where we hit our first dead end. This query form does not allow the use of examples. How should we deal with this?

Well, we know that *Paradox* is capable of printing such a report; only the Personal Programmer is having trouble here. The solution will be to create a script (later) that goes through all the necessary steps to print the report we want, and attach that script to this menu item.

For now, we need to back out of our current position. You can always do so using a combination of the Esc key and the Cancel options from the menus until you're back at the Action menu. In this example, press F10 to call up the menu, then select Cancel and Yes. To move up another menu level, press Esc. Select Cancel and Yes again to move back to the Action menu. Select NotDefined to leave this menu option undefined for the time being.

INVENTORY SALES SUBMENU

Now we need to develop the submenu and its actions for the sales system submenu. In this section we'll look at a more advanced feature of the Personal Programmer, called *MultiTable views*. Like the Multitable forms we discussed in Chapter 14, MultiTable views let you view data from two or more tables at once. This can be very handy in the Sales system, because when the user enters the part number for a sales transaction, we can display the part name and other information about the part to provide some feedback to the person at the keyboard.

We'll also see how to use MultiTable views to print reports. Once again, we can display the part name and other information to provide additional information that is available only from the Mastinv table.

The only restriction on MultiTable views within the Personal Programmer is that you cannot use them to edit information, unless all the tables used in the MultiTable edit are keyed. Usually, only one table is keyed, because the two tables are in a one-to-many relationship, and only the table on the "one" side of the relationship has a true key field. Nonetheless, these views are very useful tools when developing applications with multiple tables.

THE SALES SUBMENU

The Sales option on the main menu needs to branch to a submenu of choices for managing the Sales table. Therefore, select Menu from the Action menu. You'll be prompted to type in menu items and descriptions using the same techniques we've used with previous menus. For this example, type in the following menu items and descriptions:

ITEM	*DESCRIPTION*
Add data	Add new sales transactions
Change data	Edit/delete current sales transactions
Look up	Look up a current sales transaction
Report	Print current sales transactions

Press F2 when done entering the menu items and descriptions.

Sales Table Data Entry

After you enter the menu options and descriptions, you are ready to define actions for the *Add data* menu option. *Add data* blinks on the screen. Select SpecifyAction to define an action for the item. We'll develop a custom form for entering data into the Sales table that also displays data from the Mastinv table.

From the Action menu, select DataEntry. To define the tables to use during data entry, select SelectTable, the Sales table, SelectTable again, and then the Mastinv table. Notice that both the Sales and Mastinv tables are listed as selected tables. Select DO-IT! to stop selecting tables for this menu action.

Next, the screen needs to know which fields are involved in the MultiTable view of the inventory data and presents two options to you:

Create   Borrow

As implied, the Create option lets you create a new MultiTable view, while Borrow lets you use a previously defined MultiTable view. You need to select Create to create a new view.

Two query forms will appear on the screen: one for each table in the MultiTable view. Using these query forms, you need to place checkmarks in fields that you want to use in the MultiTable view, and enter an example that links the two tables via a common field.

For this example, press F6 with the cursor in the leftmost column of the Sales query form, so that all the fields have check marks. Move the cursor into the Part No field, and enter the example ABC (by pressing F5 and then typing **ABC**).

Press F4 to move down to the Mastinv query form. Type in the example that links Mastinv to Sales. (In this case, move the cursor to the Part No field, press F5, and type in **ABC**.) Next, place check marks in any fields that you want to display from this table. For this example, place a check mark (using the usual F6 key) in the Part Name and Sel Price fields. Figure 20.12 shows the two query forms on the screen (I've manipulated the image a bit so that you can see all the fields). Press F2 after completing the query forms.

Next you'll see the following familiar menu:

FormView   TableView   FormToggle

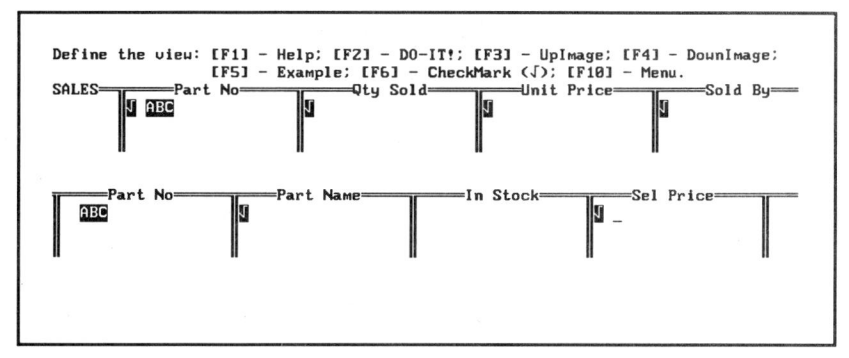

```
Define the view: [F1] - Help; [F2] - DO-IT!; [F3] - UpImage; [F4] - DownImage;
                 [F5] - Example; [F6] - CheckMark (√); [F10] - Menu.
SALES======Part No======T======Qty Sold======T======Unit Price======T======Sold By======
      |√|ABC|          |√|                  |√|                   |√|

      ======Part No======T======Part Name======T======In Stock======T======Sel Price======
      |ABC|              |√|                   |√|                  |√|_
```

Figure 20.12: Query forms completed for the MultiTable view

Once again, select FormView to allow the user to enter data through a custom screen. Select Design and 1 to design form number 1 for the Sales table data entry. Enter **Current sales transactions** as the form description.

The standard screen for developing a custom form will appear. You can use the usual Field and Place options to place fields on the screen, but there is one very important point to keep in mind. When placing fields from the Mastinv table onto the form, use the Field, Place, and DisplayOnly menu options, rather than the Field, Place, and Regular options. This is an important point, because we do not want the user to change information on the Mastinv table while entering Sales transactions. Instead, we want to display this information on the form only to provide feedback.

When developing your own applications, you'll want to do the same. That is, use Field, Place, and Regular to place fields that will be changed, and Field, Place, and DisplayOnly to place fields from the related table.

Figure 20.13 shows a suggested format for the custom Sales form. The fields were placed on the screen as listed below (note that Regular refers to the Field, Place, and Regular menu options; DisplayOnly refers to the Field, Place, and DisplayOnly menu options; and Calculated refers to the Field, Place, and Calculated menu options):

OPTION	LOCATION	FIELD NAME
Regular	< 5,15>	Part No
Regular	<12, 2>	Qty Sold

Regular	<12,13>	Unit Price
Regular	<12,30>	Date Sold
Regular	<12,49>	Sold By
Regular	<16,11>	Remarks
DisplayOnly	< 5,46>	Part Name
DisplayOnly	< 6,46>	Sel Price
Calculated	<12,59>	[Qty Sold] * [Unit Price]

The boxes are drawn using the usual Border and Place options from the menu, and all the rest of the form is simply typed in. When you've finished designing your form, call up the menu and select DO-IT!.

```
Changing F1 form for Invs1                              Form     1/1
<22, 1>
              ┌─────────────────────────────────────────────┐
              │           Current Sales Transactions        │
              └─────────────────────────────────────────────┘
Part Number: ____        ┌─────────────────────────────────┐
                         │ Part name: _____ │
                         │ List price: _____ │
                         └─────────────────────────────────┘

     Qty      Unit Price      Date Sold      Salesperson's        Total
                                                Initials
     ____     _____      _____          ____         _____

Remarks: _____
        ┌──────────────────────────────────────────────────────────────┐
        │ When cursor is in Part Number field, press F1 to view part   │
        │ numbers. When part number table is displayed, press F2 to    │
        │ select current part.                                         │
        └──────────────────────────────────────────────────────────────┘
```

Figure 20.13: The suggested format for the custom Sales form

This selection brings up the options

Settings   DO-IT!   Cancel

Select Settings to add validity checks and HelpAndFill to this form. Note that the cursor is in the Part No field. You can move the cursor to any field and then call up the menu to define a validity check. In this case, leave the cursor in the Part No field, and press F10 to call up the menu. Select ValCheck and Define to define a validity check.

The standard options for validity checks appear on the next menu. Select TableLookup, enter Mastinv as the table to check entries against, then select AllCorrespondingFields and HelpAndFill. This validity check is sufficient for entering Sales data. Press F2 to save the validity check, and you'll see the menu

    Settings   DO-IT!   Cancel

again. Select DO-IT! to save the form.

At this point, you've finished defining the action and the custom form for Sales data entry. You'll be prompted to define an action for the *Change data* submenu item.

Sales Table Editing

The *Change data* menu option should now be blinking on the screen. You cannot use MultiTable view during editing, because the Personal Programmer requires that both tables be keyed for editing (as discussed earlier). Therefore, we'll use a simple TableView to allow edits to the Sales table.

From the Action menu, select Edit, then select SelectTable, Sales, and DO-IT! to define the table to use. Select TableView as the format for editing, and Settings to set up a validity check for editing. Move the cursor to the Part No field, press F10, select ValCheck, Define, TableLookup, and enter Mastinv as the lookup table. Select JustCurrentField and HelpAndFill. These selections will make sure the user enters valid part numbers, and will also help him to look up part numbers and part names. Press F2.

Next you can define whether or not the user can insert and delete records during editing. To limit this menu option to editing and deleting, select InsertDelete, Delete, and Yes. (The default setting for Insert is No, so you need not respecify that option.) Select DO-IT! to save the setting.

This completes the action for the Change data option on the Sales menu. Now the *Look up data* option blinks, and you can define its action.

Sales Table Lookup

For the *Look up data* option on the Sales submenu, we'll display data using the MultiTable view we developed for the data-entry portion of the menu. Rather than recreating the MultiTable view, we'll borrow that existing view and its custom form.

From the Action menu, select View. Then select SelectTable, Sales, SelectTable, Mastinv, and DO-IT! to specify the Sales and Mastinv tables for the Look up data menu option. Once again, your options are

Create   Borrow

To borrow the previously created MultiTable view, select the Borrow option. This brings up the options

Menu   Name

The Name option lets you specify the MultiTable view by name, and is generally used only with MultiTable views you create outside of the Personal Programmer. The Menu option let's you borrow the view from another previously defined menu item. In this example, you want to select Menu.

Recall that the MultiTable view we created earlier was defined under the Add data option from the Sales submenu. You now need to select items that lead to that existing menu choice. In this example, select Sales. When the Add data option is displayed, press F10 to call up the menu. Select BorrowView from the next menu to appear, to indicate that you want to borrow the MultiTable view from the Sales Add data menu action.

After a brief pause while the Personal Programmer copies and validates information, you'll be given the standard menu:

SelectRecords   AllRecords

Again, we want the user to be able to specify a particular record to view, so select the SelectRecords options. A query form will appear on the screen. To help the user locate a particular transaction, we'll have the application prompt him or her for a part number and salesperson's initials. Place the tilde variable

~ partno

in the Part No field, and

~ person

in the Sold By field, as shown in Figure 20.14.

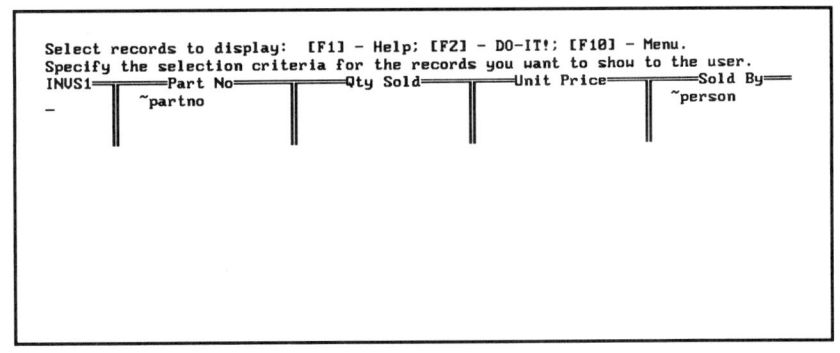

```
Select records to display:  [F1] - Help; [F2] - DO-IT!; [F10] - Menu.
Specify the selection criteria for the records you want to show to the user.
INVS1=======Part No=========Qty Sold========Unit Price=======Sold By==
  _          ~partno                                          ~person
```

Figure 20.14: Tilde variables in the Sales query form

Press F2 after entering the tilde variables. You'll be asked to provide prompts for the tilde variables. For the *partno* variable, enter the prompt

Enter part number to locate:

Press Enter to accept the suggested data type. For the *person* tilde variable, enter the prompt

Enter sales person's initials:

Press Enter to accept the suggested data type, A3.

Now you'll be given the options to display data in FormView, TableView, or FormToggle. Select FormView to use a custom form, select Borrow to use the existing form from the Add data option, and then select 1 to indicate the specific custom form.

This completes the action for the Look up data option from the Sales menu. Now you are ready to define the action for the Sales table Reports option.

Sales Table Reports

Once again, we'll use a MultiTable view to display data from the Sales and Mastinv tables simultaneously, this time using a report format to print the data. While the Report menu item is blinking, select Report from the Action menu. To select tables, select the options SelectTable, Sales, SelectTable, Mastinv, and press DO-IT!

Because you've selected multiple tables, the screen will once again present the options

Create   Borrow

to help you create or borrow a MultiTable view. We can again use the MultiTable view created for the data entry option on the Sales submenu, so select Borrow, Menu, and Sales. With the Add data option highlighted on the submenu, press F10 to call up the menu, and select BorrowView.

The screen asks if the report should print some records (SelectRecords) or all records (AllRecords). For this example, select AllRecords. Now you can define a format for the Sales table report.

Select Design from the report menu, 1 as the report format, and enter the report description as **Current Sales Transactions**. You can next select whether you want your report to be tabular or free-form. For this example, I selected Tabular and designed the format as shown in Figure 20.16. Of course, you may design the report to your own liking.

In Figure 20.15, the TableBand and Erase options are also used to delete the Part No, Part Name, Remarks, and Sel Price columns from the suggested report format.

I've used the Group, Insert, and Field options to define a group band based on the Part No field. Within the group band, but outside

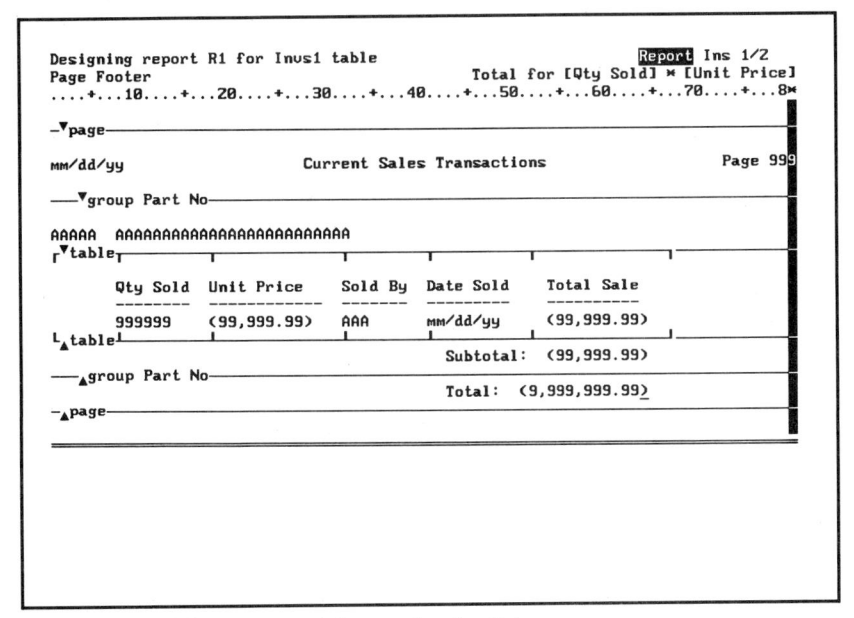

```
Designing report R1 for Invs1 table                    Report  Ins 1/2
Page Footer                              Total for [Qty Sold] * [Unit Price]
....+...10....+...20....+...30....+...40....+...50....+...60....+...70....+...8»
—▼page─────────────────────────────────────────────────────────────────
mm/dd/yy                    Current Sales Transactions          Page 99
──▼group Part No──────────────────────────────────────────────────────
AAAAA   AAAAAAAAAAAAAAAAAAAAAAAA
 ┌▼table┬─────────┬──────────┬────────┬──────────┬─────────────┐
        Qty Sold  Unit Price  Sold By  Date Sold  Total Sale
        ────────  ──────────  ───────  ─────────  ──────────
        999999    (99,999.99)  AAA     mm/dd/yy   (99,999.99)
 └▲table┴─────────┴──────────┴────────┴──────────┴─────────────┘
                                         Subtotal: (99,999.99)
  ──▲group Part No────────────────────────────────────────────
                                         Total:  (9,999,999.99)
—▲page─────────────────────────────────────────────────────────────────
```

Figure 20.15: The suggested format for the Sales report

of the table band, I've placed the Part No and Part Name fields, using the usual Field, Place, and Regular menu options. (These appear as AAA masks in the Part No group heading area.)

The TableBand and Insert options are used to insert the blank column at the left of the table band. This column is then narrowed using TableBand and Resize. This blank column appears as an indentation on the final printed report.

To reduce the size of the Unit Price field, use Field and Erase to erase the current field contents, and then Field, Place, and Regular to put the Unit Price field back. When you place the field back into its column, you'll be given the option to specify the size of the field. (The Field, Reformat, and Comma options do not allow you to resize the field; you need to use this delete-and-replace technique instead.)

The TableBand and Insert options are used to create the Total Sale column at the right of the table band. The heading and underline are typed in as shown, and the Field, Place, and Calculated options are used to place the expression *[Qty Sold] * [Unit Price]* within the report column.

The subtotal calculation is placed using the Field, Place, Summary, and Calculated menu options; these place the expression

[Qty Sold] * *[Unit Price]* beneath the table band (but within the group band). The Sum and PerGroup options are selected to ensure proper subtotaling. The grand total, outside the group band, is placed using the Field, Place, Summary, and Calculated menu options, again using *[Qty Sold]* * *[Unit Price]* as the expression. Then, the Sum and Overall options are selected to ensure a grand total.

After designing the report specification to your liking, press F2, and select Printer as the destination for the report. That concludes the action definition for the Sales menu Reports option, and for the entire Sales submenu as well.

THE PURCHASES SUBMENU

The Purchases section of the inventory system also requires a submenu of options for managing the Purchase table. This submenu uses basically the same techniques that the Sales submenu does to present information from multiple tables, and does not present any new Personal Programmer techniques. Therefore, to help you develop this module quickly, we'll just run through the required entries and menu selections involved in an abbreviated format.

Select Menu to begin defining the submenu. Enter the menu items and descriptions as listed below:

ITEM	DESCRIPTION
Add data	Add new purchases (items received)
Change data	Edit/delete current purchases
Look up data	Look up a current purchase (item received)
Reports	Print current purchases (items received)

Press F2 when done entering the menu items and descriptions.

Purchase Table Data Entry

When the *Add data* option is blinking, select SpecifyAction, DataEntry, SelectTable, Purchase, SelectTable, Mastinv, and DO-IT! to select the tables. Select Create to create a MultiTable view, and fill in the query forms as shown in Figure 20.16. Note that all the

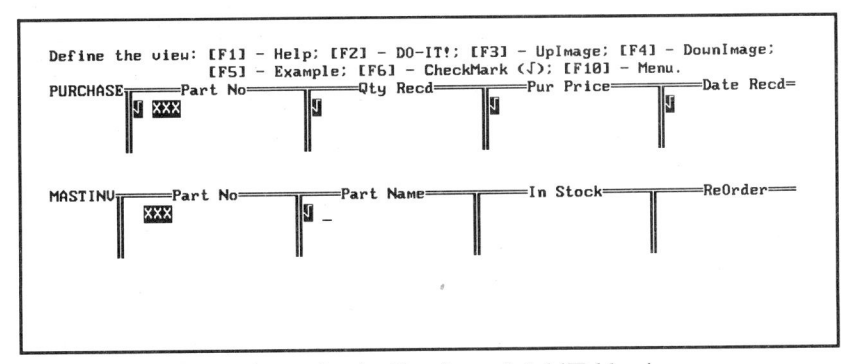

```
Define the view: [F1] - Help; [F2] - DO-IT!; [F3] - UpImage; [F4] - DownImage;
                 [F5] - Example; [F6] - CheckMark (√); [F10] - Menu.
PURCHASE╤═══Part No═══╤═══Qty Recd═══╤═══Pur Price═══╤═══Date Recd═
        │√  XXX       │√             │√              │√
        
        
MASTINV╤═══Part No═══╤═══Part Name═══╤═══In Stock═══╤═══ReOrder═══
       │   XXX       │√  _           │              │
```

Figure 20.16: Query forms for the Purchases MultiTable view

fields in the Purchase query form are checked, and the XXX examples are entered using the F5 key to define an example. Press F2 after filling in the query forms.

Select FormView, Design, and 1, and enter **Current Purchases (items received)** as the form description. You'll be given the standard screen for designing a new form. Once again, when placing the Part Name field from the Mastinv table, be sure to use the Field, Place, and DisplayOnly options (rather than Field, Place, and Regular options) so that the field cannot be changed during data entry. Figure 20.17 shows a sample form. Press F2 after designing the form to your liking.

Select Settings and, with the cursor in the Part No field, press F10. Select ValCheck, Define, and TableLookup, then enter Mastinv as the table name. Select AllCorrespondingFields and HelpAndFill. Press F2 and select DO-IT!.

Purchase Table Editing

When the *Change data* submenu option blinks, select Edit, SelectTable, Purchase, DO-IT!, TableView, and Settings, and make sure the cursor is in the Part No field. Press F10, and select ValCheck, Define, TableLookup, and Mastinv as the look-up table. Select JustCurrentField and HelpAndFill. Press F2. Select InsertDelete, Delete, Yes, and DO-IT!.

Purchase Table Lookup

When the *Look up data* option blinks, select View, SelectTable, Purchase, SelectTable, Mastinv, and DO-IT!. Select Borrow, Menu,

```
           Changing F1 form for Invs2                           Form    1/1
           <21, 1>
                          Current Purchases (Items Received)


           Part Number: _____        Part name: _____


              Date                             Purchase
            Received              Qty           Price
           _____            _____        _____


           Remarks : _____


              When cursor is in the Part Number field, press F1 for part number list.
              When part number list is displayed, press F2 to select part number.
```

Figure 20.17: The Purchases data-entry form

Purchases, and with the highlight on the Add data option, press F10 and select BorrowView.

From the next menu, select SelectRecords, enter ˜**partno** in the Part No field, and press F2 to save the tilde variable. Enter the prompt **Enter part number to locate**, and press Enter to accept the default data type, A5.

Select FormView, Borrow, and 1 to use the current Purchases form, defined earlier.

Purchase Table Reports

When *Reports* is blinking on the Purchases submenu, select Report from the Action menu. Select SelectTable, Purchase, SelectTable, Mastinv, and DO-IT! to specify the Purchase and Mastinv tables for this menu action.

To borrow the existing MultiTable view, select Borrow, Menu, and Purchases, press F10 while *Add data* is highlighted, and select BorrowView.

Select AllRecords to have the report print all records. Select Design and 1, and enter the report description as **Current Purchases**. You can select Tabular to design a tabular report format, and use a format similar to that presented in Figure 20.18. Note that in this format, the TableBand and Erase options are used to remove the Remarks column and the Part Name field is moved using the TableBand and Move options. To ensure sorting by part number, select Group, Insert, Field, and Part No to insert a group band, and use Ctrl-Y with the cursor in the leftmost column to delete any unwanted blank lines between the group and table bands.

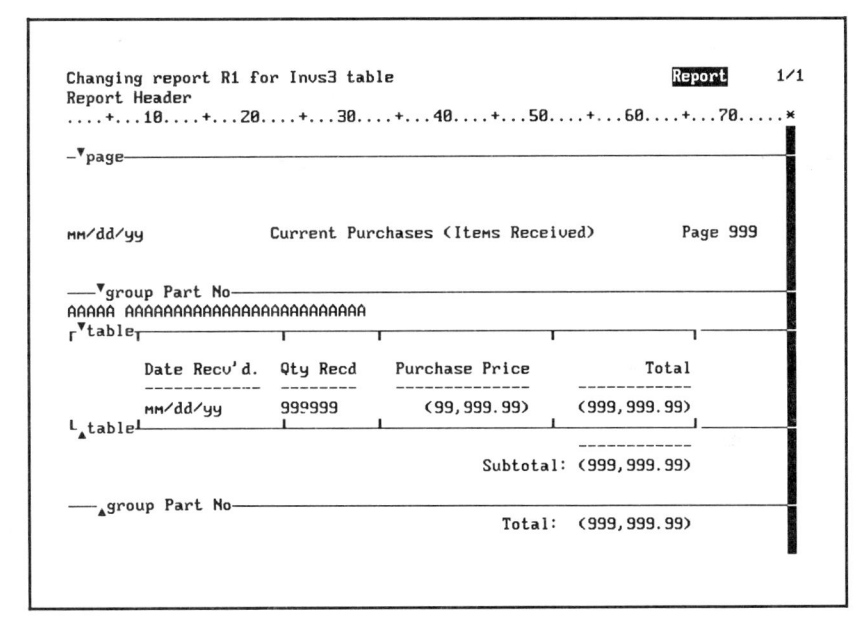

```
Changing report R1 for Invs3 table                        Report    1/1
Report Header
....+...10....+...20....+...30....+...40....+...50....+...60....+...70.....*
—▼page—

MM/dd/yy                  Current Purchases (Items Received)     Page 999

——▼group Part No——
AAAAA AAAAAAAAAAAAAAAAAAAAAA
 ┌▼table┐
         Date Recv'd.  Qty Recd    Purchase Price          Total
         ------------  --------    --------------       -----------
           MM/dd/yy     999999       (99,999.99)         (999,999.99)
 └▲table┘
                                                         -----------
                                             Subtotal:   (999,999.99)

——▲group Part No——
                                                Total:   (999,999.99)
```

Figure 20.18: A sample format for the Current Purchases report

Press F2 after designing your report format, and select Printer to channel the printed report to the printer.

That concludes the submenu for the Purchase table. Now we have two more items to create. First, we still need a script to print the reorder report, and another script to perform updates. (This script will be identical to the recorded script discussed in Chapter 15.) We'll need to put some sample data in the various tables to create these scripts, so now would be a good time to leave the Personal Programmer, and try out some aspects of the application developed so far.

For now, leave the Update option undefined. Select NotDefined, NoSplashScreen, and DO-IT! from the next menus to save your work so far. You'll see the scripts that the Personal Programmer creates whiz by on the screen as it does its work. The Personal Programmer menu will reappear.

TESTING OUR PROGRESS

Let's take a look at our work so far by adding some records to the Mastinv, Sales, and Purchase tables, using the application system developed by the Personal Programmer. To do so, select Play from the Personal Programmer Main menu, and enter **Inv** as the name of the application. Press Enter rather than entering a password. (You could also run the application directly from Paradox, as we'll discuss later.)

You'll see the inventory system main menu appear on the screen, displaying the menu options and option descriptions that you defined within the Personal Programmer, as below:

> Master Inventory   Sales   Purchases   Update   Leave
> Manage the master inventory file.

If you use the arrow keys to scroll around the menu options, you'll see the other descriptions you defined in the Personal Programmer.

First, let's add a couple of records to the Master Inventory (Mastinv) table. Select Master Inventory and Add data from the custom menus, and you'll see the custom form for entering master-inventory records. For the first record, enter the sample data below (of course, you can add some real data from your own inventory if you prefer):

Part number:	1001
Part name:	Artichokes
In stock:	1
Reorder point:	10
On order:	5
Date order:	11/10/90
Purchase price:	100.00
Selling Price:	150.00
Location:	LZ1

As a second sample record, enter the data below:

Part number:	1002
Part name:	Bananas
In stock:	50
Reorder point:	10
On order:	0
Date order:	11/10/90
Purchase price:	20.00
Selling Price:	30.00
Location:	BZ1

Press F2 after entering the second record.

Now let's add a couple of transactions to the Sales table. Select Sales from the main menu, and Add data from the submenu. Enter the information below. (You'll notice that the appropriate information from the Mastinv appears on the screen after you enter the part number):

Part number:	1001
Qty sold:	2
Unit price:	150.00
Sold by:	SAM
Date sold:	10/11/90

Before entering the second record, you might want to try the HelpAndFill feature we added. Press F1 to see a list of part numbers and names. Move the cursor to part number 1002. (You can also use Zoom [Ctrl-Z] to locate information in any field on the look-up table.) Press F2 to copy the selected part number to the current form. Fill in the form with the following sample data:

Part number:	1002
Qty sold:	5
Unit price:	30.00
Sold by:	SAM
Date sold:	10/11/90

Press F2 after entering the second record.

Now we'll add a single record to the Purchase table. Select Purchases from the main menu, and Add data from the submenu.

Again, you can use the F1 and F2 keys to select a part number from the Mastinv table, or just type in the sample record below:

Part no:	1001
Qty received:	100
Purchase price:	110.00
Date received:	12/1/90

Press F2 after entering the sample record.

You might want to take some time now to try out other options from the custom menu (though remember, the reorder report and update options have not been assigned actions yet). When you are done experimenting with the inventory system menus, select Leave and Yes from the submenus that appear.

CUSTOM SCRIPTS FOR THE INVENTORY SYSTEM

We'll need to create a couple of scripts now: one to print the reorder report and one to perform updates. To do so, exit the Personal Programmer by selecting Exit and Yes from its Main menu. The DOS prompt should appear on your screen when you've successfully exited.

The custom scripts that you tie into an application can be either hand-written or recorded. For these examples, we'll use recorded scripts. We'll also need to create a new report format for the reorder report.

First, you'll want to run Paradox in the usual manner, but from the current directory so that it uses the tables on the same directory as the application and stores any files on this same directory. While still logged onto the INVMGR directory, enter the command

    PARADOX3

and press Enter to run Paradox.

THE REORDER REPORT

To create the reorder report format, select Report and Design, and enter Mastinv as the table to use. Select report number 2, and enter the description **Reorder report**. Select Tabular, and design the report to your liking. Figure 20.19 shows a sample format.

In the example, I have shortened the Part Name field slightly by backspacing over some of the hyphens and using the Field and Resize options from the menu to narrow the field. The Location, Sel Price, and Order Date fields are deleted using TableBand and Erase. To reduce the size of the Purchase Price field, I have deleted it and reinserted it using TableBand Erase, TableBand Insert, and Field, Place, and Regular. Press F2 after designing the report format to your liking, and return to the Paradox Main menu.

To begin recording the script, press Alt-F3. Select Ask from the menu, and specify Mastinv as the table to ask about. Press F6 so that all the fields receive a check mark. Move the cursor to the In Stock field, press F5, and type in the example **In**. Move the cursor to the On Order field, press F5, and enter the example **Coming**. Move back to the Reorder field, and enter the expression

```
> In + Coming
```

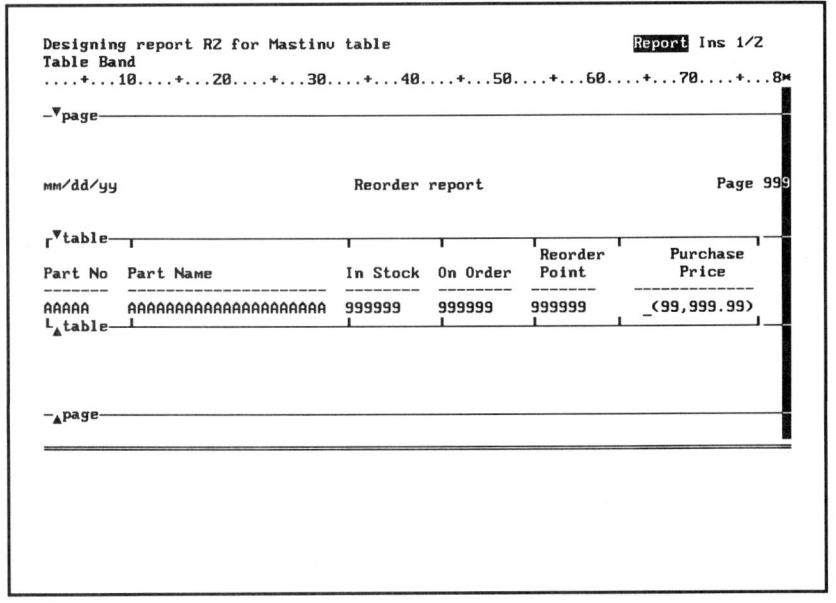

```
Designing report R2 for Mastinv table                      Report  Ins 1/2
Table Band
....+...10....+...20....+...30....+...40....+...50....+...60....+...70....+...8
  page


 mm/dd/yy                              Reorder report                  Page 999

   table
                                                       Reorder      Purchase
  Part No   Part Name              In Stock  On Order  Point         Price
  -------   ---------------------  --------  --------  -------       ---------
  AAAAA     AAAAAAAAAAAAAAAAAAAAA   999999    999999   999999        (99,999.99)
   table


  page
```

Figure 20.19: A sample reorder report format

where *In* and *Coming* are both examples (each preceded by a press on the F5 key before being typed in). This query limits records displayed to those which have Reorder values greater than the sums of the In Stock and On Order quantities. Figure 20.20 shows the completed query form on the screen. Press F2 to perform the completed query.

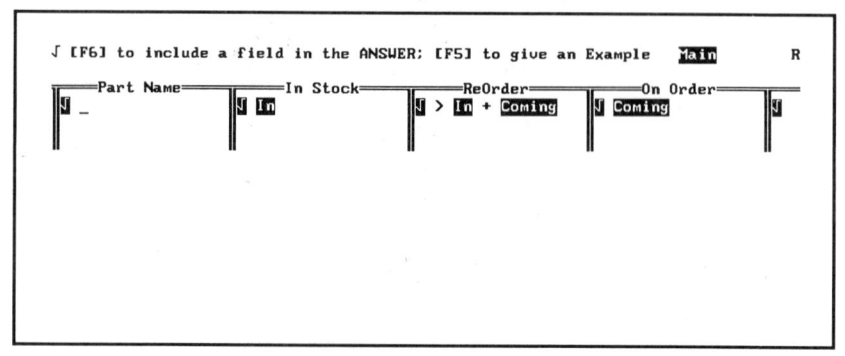

```
√ [F6] to include a field in the ANSWER; [F5] to give an Example   Main        R
 ═Part Name═══╤═══In Stock═══╤══ReOrder═══════╤═══On Order══╤
    √ _       │    √ In      │ √ > In + Coming│ √ Coming    │  √
```

Figure 20.20: The reorder report query

Next, copy the report formats from the Mastinv table to the Answer table. To do so, press Menu (F10), and select Tools, Copy, and JustFamily. Enter Mastinv as the source table to copy from, and Answer as the target table to copy to and select Replace when prompted.

Next, call up the menu, select Report and Output, and specify Answer as the table to print from. Select option 2, and then Printer, and you should see the only item that needs reordering appear on the report.

Clear the screen by pressing Clear All (Alt-F8), and then stop recording the script by typing Alt-F3 again. The completed script is stored as Instant.SC, but you'll want to change its name. To do so, call up the menu, select Tools, Rename, and Scripts, and change the name of the Instant script to Reorder.

To verify that the Reorder script exists, select Scripts, Editor, and Edit, and enter Reorder as the name of the script. It should appear on your screen looking something like Figure 20.21. Then call up the menu, and select Cancel and Yes to return to the Paradox Main menu.

```
Changing script C:\invmgr\reorder                              Script
....+...10....+...20....+...30....+...40....+...50....+...60....+...70....+...80
{Ask} {MastInv} Check Right Right Right Example  "In" Right
"> " Example  "In + " Example  "Coming" Right Example  "Com"
"ing" Do_It! Menu {Tools} {Copy} {JustFamily} {MastInv} {Answer}
{Replace} Menu {Report} {Output} {Answer} {2} {Printer} ClearAll
```

Figure 20.21: The Reorder script

INVENTORY SYSTEM UPDATE SCRIPTS

You can use the InvUpdat script developed back in Chapter 15 for the current inventory application. If you have not already created that script, find the section entitled "Automating an Update Procedure," and follow all the steps presented to create the InvUpdat script. (Note that the sample data in the figures won't match the sample data you see when working with these versions of the Mastinv, Sales, and Purchase tables, but the query forms in the figures will be the same.)

If you have already created the InvUpdat script, you'll need to copy it from the \PARADOX3 directory to the \INVMGR directory. A quick and easy way to accomplish this goal would be to first select the Tools, More, and ToDos options from the Paradox Main menu. Then, when the DOS prompt appears, type in the command

```
COPY C:\PDOX35\INVUPDAT.SC
C:\INVMGR\INVUPDAT.SC
```

and press Enter. (The formula is broken onto two lines only to fit within the margins of this book; when typing it in you would type it as one long line.)

You should see the message *1 file(s) copied* if DOS was able to find and copy the script. To return to Paradox, type in the command **EXIT** and press Enter.

You might also want to provide the option to "back out" from the update procedure in the custom application. To do so, use the Scripts, Edit, and Write options to create a script named Updater. Type in the script exactly as shown in Figure 20.22. Note that this script plays the InvUpdat script only if the user selects Proceed from the submenu. (You could have also used the Personal Programmer to create this same simple Proceed and Cancel menu, but this example will demonstrate how to attach a hand-written script to the inventory application.) Press F10 and select DO-IT! after creating the Updater script.

```
;-------- Double-check on automatic update.
CLEAR
SHOWMENU
    "Proceed" : "Proceed with the update",
    "Cancel"  : "Cancel this selection"
TO UChoice
IF UChoice = "Proceed" THEN
    CLEAR
    STYLE BLINK
    @ 5,10
    ? "Performing the update... Please wait."
    ;---- Play the updating script.
    PLAY "InvUpdat"
ENDIF
RETURN
```

Figure 20.22: The Updater script

After defining the additional scripts for the inventory application, you can exit Paradox and go back to the Personal Programmer to attach them to their menu items; we'll look at this process next.

ATTACHING THE CUSTOM SCRIPTS

To attach custom scripts to the inventory application, run the Personal Programmer from the inventory directory, and select Modify. In this example, first make sure that you are still logged onto the InvMgr directory, and enter the command PPROG to run the Personal Programmer. Select Modify from the Main Menu, and enter the application name **Inv**.

From the Main menu, select NotDefined to move directly to the first undefined menu option, which in this case will be Update. As instructed on the screen, press F10 to call up the menu. Select Action and Define from the next menus to define an action for the item. We want this menu option to play the Updater script developed in the last section, so select Script, and enter **Updater** as the name of the script that this menu option should play.

Next, you'll be instructed to move to the next menu selection you want to modify. In this case, we want to define an action for the Reorder report menu option on the Master Inventory Reports submenu. So, move the highlighter to the *Master Inventory* option, and press Enter to move down to its submenu. On the submenu, move the highlighter to the Reports option, and press Enter to move down another menu level.

Next, move the highlighter to the Reorder report option, and press F10. Select Action and Define from the next menus to define an action for the item. We want this menu option to play the Reorder script developed in the last section, so select Script, and enter **Reorder** as the name of the script that this menu option should play.

Now the new custom scripts are attached to the appropriate application menu items. Save all your work by calling up the menu (F10) and selecting DO-IT! from the remaining menus. Select Exit and Yes from the Personal Programmer Main menu to return to the DOS prompt.

RUNNING THE INVENTORY APPLICATION

Whenever you want to use the completed application, log onto the appropriate directory using the DOS CD command (CD\INVMGR in this example). Run Paradox from that directory by entering the usual PARADOX3 command at the DOS prompt. From the Paradox Main menu, select Scripts, Play, and specify Inv as the script to play.

When instructed to enter a password, you can just press Enter to move directly to the inventory system main menu. This will bring you to the inventory system main menu options shown below:

Master Inventory   Sales   Purchases   Update   Leave

Below are some general tips on using the inventory system.

MANAGING THE MASTER INVENTORY TABLE

Any new item that is to be carried in the inventory system must be added to the Mastinv table before being entered on either the Sales or Purchase tables. Use the Add data option on the Master Inventory submenu to enter these new products. Each item must be assigned a unique part number (or product number). Duplicate part numbers will be rejected into a Keyviol table with the name Kv<number>, where <number> keeps track of multiple tables. For example, the first Keyviol table is named Kv1, the second is named Kv2, and so forth.

The Personal Programmer does not provide any built-in means for managing these Keyviol tables. As an applications developer, you have two choices for dealing with these:

- Teach users how to rectify key violations and use Tools, More, and Add to move the corrected key violations into the Mastinv table.
- Write a custom script to do this automatically.

If you use the second method, you can attach the custom script to the application menu so that users can access it from within the application.

You may enter the new item with an in-stock quantity of zero if you wish to use an entry on the Purchase table as the first items-received transaction for the new item. After updating, the master-inventory table will reflect the correct in-stock quantity.

You may change any information on the Mastinv table using the Change data option from the Master Inventory submenu. However, you should try to avoid changing part numbers once they've been assigned, as the same change will *not* be made on the Sales and Purchase tables. If you *must* change a part number on the Master Inventory table, do so *only* immediately after performing an update (using the Update option from the Inventory system main menu). That way, the Sales and Purchase tables will be empty when you make the change.

To locate information about a particular item in stock, select the Look up data option from the Master Inventory submenu. Enter the part number, or the part name, of the item to look up when instructed on the screen.

To bring the in-stock, on-order, and purchase price quantities up to date in the master inventory, select the Update and Proceed options from the inventory system main menu. Once you select this option, however, you cannot go back and make corrections to the Sales or Purchase table transactions, as those data will have been moved to the history tables. Instead, enter *adjustment transactions* into the Sales or Purchase tables, as discussed later in this section.

To print up-to-date reports of the status of the inventory, select the Reports option from the Master Inventory system submenu. Select either the Entire inventory or the Reorder report option, depending on which report you wish to print.

To leave the Master Inventory submenu and return to the main menu, press the Esc key.

MANAGING THE SALES TABLE

As items are sold, enter a record of the transaction of each sale into the Sales table, using the Add data option from the Sales submenu. You may only enter a part number for parts that have already been entered onto the Mastinv table. Any other part number will be rejected as invalid.

When entering sales transactions, you can press F1 while the cursor is in the Part No field to browse through valid part numbers and part names. You can use Zoom (Ctrl-Z) to look up the information if you wish. When you've located the appropriate part number, press F2 to copy those data to the Sales form. Optionally, press Esc to return to the Sales form without copying.

You can use the Change data option under the Sales submenu to edit or delete any *current* sales transaction (that is, any transaction which has not already been posted to the master inventory). To make corrections to sales transactions that have already been posted, use *adjustment transactions* instead, as discussed later in this section.

During editing of the Sales table, you can use F1 to browse through valid part numbers and names; you can also use the Zoom (Ctrl-Z) and Zoom Next (Alt-Z) keys to locate a particular record. You can, optionally, use the Look up data option under the Sales submenu to locate a particular current sales transaction.

Before performing an update, you should probably print a copy of all current Sales transactions, using the Reports option from the Sales submenu. Check for any obvious errors, and correct them using the Change data option from the Sales submenu, before performing the update.

To leave the Sales submenu and return to the main menu, press the Esc key.

MANAGING THE PURCHASES TABLE

The term "purchases" in this system refers to items that have actually been received. As items are delivered to you, enter transactions into the Purchase table using the Add data option from the Purchases submenu. While the cursor is on the Part No field of the Purchase data entry form, you can use the F1 key and Zoom to browse through part numbers and part names, if necessary.

The Change data, Look up data and Reports options from the Purchases submenu work in the same manner that they do on the Sales submenu. Before performing updates, you should probably print a report of all current purchases, and check it for any obvious errors. Any errors that are found should be corrected before performing an update.

To leave the Purchases menu and return to the main menu, just press Esc.

ENTERING ADJUSTMENT TRANSACTIONS

If an error on the Sales or Purchase table is discovered *after* the update has been performed, you can make corrections by entering adjustment transactions into either table. Use the usual Add Data option from either the Sales or Purchases submenu to enter adjustment transactions, and use the Remarks field to describe the adjustment. Doing so will correct any inaccurate values in the Mastinv table, and also provide an audit trail of the change.

Let's look at an example of an adjustment transaction. Suppose you enter a sales transaction of 100 of part number 1001, but actually only 10 of the items were sold. The Update procedure will delete 100 of part number 1001 from the Mastinv table In Stock quantity (as it should), but this is actually 90 too many items to subtract.

If the transaction has already been posted, you could enter a Sales transaction, using the usual Add data option from the Sales submenu, to enter an adjustment transaction. Enter part number 1001, and the quantity sold as −90. Enter a descriptive remark such as "Adjustment to previous error" (or something more descriptive). Later, when you perform the update, −90 will be subtracted from the In Stock quantity (which, if you remember your basic math, means that 90 will actually be added, because when you subtract a negative number, it actually gets added to the current value).

The same basic technique can be used for returned items. Either enter a Sales transaction with the appropriate part number, a negative quantity, and a remark, or enter a Purchase transaction with a positive quantity and the appropriate remark.

UPDATING

The *Update* option from the inventory main menu updates the in-stock and on-order quantities and the purchase price of the item. You can perform updates as often as you wish. When you opt to update, you'll be given the options to

Proceed   Cancel

Select Proceed to proceed with the update, or Cancel to cancel the update and return to the inventory system main menu.

LEAVING THE INVENTORY SYSTEM

To leave the inventory system and return to the Paradox Main menu, select Leave. Note that you can still use items from the Paradox Main menu to manage data in the Mastinv, Sales, and Purchase tables if you so desire.

MODIFYING AN APPLICATION

Developing an application is usually a trial-and-error process. You will probably find that after you initially create an application, there are more features that you want to add, or existing features that you'd like to change or delete. You can modify your application at any time by using the Personal Programmer. To do so, just log onto the same directory that the application is stored on, run the Personal Programmer in the usual manner, and select Modify from the Personal Programmer Main menu. When prompted, type in the name of the application (Inv in the example) and press Enter.

The Modify menu presents the options below:

```
Tables   MenuAction   NotDefined   SplashScreen   DO-IT!
Cancel
```

> Remember, you might need to enter a DOS PATH command before running the Personal Programmer.

These options can be summarized as follows:

OPTION	EFFECT
Tables	Changes the tables used by the application
MenuAction	Changes a menu item, or the action assigned to an item
NotDefined	Moves directly to the first undefined menu action
SplashScreen	Develops a SplashScreen for the application
DO-IT!	Saves all current modifications
Cancel	Abandons all current modifications

If you are attempting to modify an application that was created with an earlier version of Paradox, you'll be prompted to either convert the old application to Paradox 3 format or cancel the modification. Note that if you do convert an earlier version application to Paradox 3 format, the converted application will no longer run with earlier versions of Paradox. Therefore, before you perform the conversion, you should make a copy of the original application for use with earlier versions of Paradox.

Most of the menus and submenus that appear will be identical to those you used while creating the application, except that the Personal Programmer will provide some additional options for locating specific menu options to work with. Complete instructions appear on the screen as you modify the application.

The inventory application we developed in this chapter is somewhat rudimentary, because space simply does not permit us to develop a huge sample application. But if you are willing to experiment, you can use the Modify option from the Personal Programmer main menu to add new features, reports, tables, and anything else that comes to mind to tailor the inventory system to your own needs.

MORE PERSONAL PROGRAMMER FEATURES

The sample inventory application used in this chapter provided a useful tool for demonstrating some of the major features of the Personal Programmer, as well as some basic techniques for designing and developing applications. In this next section, we'll discuss some features of the Paradox Personal Programmer in a more general context.

ADDING CUSTOM HELP SCREENS

You can add custom help screens to your own applications using the Help option from the Action menu. When you select this option, you'll see a blank screen for designing your own help screen. Designing a help screen is very much like designing a form. You can manipulate the cursor and type in text using the usual arrow, Insert, Delete, and Backspace keys. You can also press F10 to bring up a menu with the following options on it:

OPTION	EFFECT
Area	Moves or deletes an area on the screen
Border	Draws a border on any area of the screen
DO-IT!	Saves the completed help screen
Cancel	Abandons the current help screen

The help screens that you develop for your application are unlike the Paradox help screens in that they do not "pop up" whenever the user presses F1. Instead, the help screen must be attached to a specific menu item. The best way to add help screens to your application is to define an item named Help on the application menu, and to assign Help as the action to that one item.

SPLASH SCREENS

A *splash screen* is an introductory screen that appears whenever a user runs your application. For example, when you first run Paradox itself, you see its splash screen before the Paradox Main menu appears.

Whenever you create or modify an application with the Personal Programmer, you'll be given the options below before the application is created and saved:

SplashScreen   NoSplashScreen

If you select SplashScreen, you can design a splash screen for your own application. The process for designing a splash screen is identical to the process of designing a help screen, as described above. Just design the screen to your liking, call up the menu, and select DO-IT! Then proceed with other menu items, as instructed on the screen, to save your application.

SUMMARIZING AN APPLICATION

The Summarize option from the Personal Programmer prints a report which describes how your application is structured and which files it uses. To use Summarize, you must run the Personal Programmer from the same directory that your application is stored on. Select Summarize from the Personal Programmer Main menu, and enter the application name when prompted. You'll be given the options

Menu   File   Tree   All

These options provide the following reports:

OPTION	REPORT
Menu	The application's menu options and their actions
File	A list of all files used by the application
Tree	A tree-structured diagram of the menus
All	All of the above reports

You'll then be given the option to send the report or reports to the printer, the screen, or a file. If you select File, you'll be prompted to enter a name for the file. Enter a valid DOS file name (eight letters maximum, no spaces or punctuation). The report will be stored with the file-name extension .RPT added to the file name you supply. The report is a standard ASCII file that can be viewed or printed with any word processor or text editor.

Figure 20.23 shows a partial example of the Menu summary for the Inv application. The Selection Name column lists the menu option, and the Selection Action column lists the action assigned to the menu option. The Source Table and Map Table columns show

```
11/11/90                          Inv Menu Structure                              Page 1
Menu Path:
/Main/
  Script containing this menu: Inv1
  Library containing the procedures for this menu: Inv1        Query,
                                                               Help, or
  Selection             Selection      Source    Map      Tables    User
  Name                  Action         Table     Table    Used      Script
  --------------------  -----------    --------  -------- --------  --------
  Master Inventory      Menu
  Sales                 Menu
  Purchases             Menu
  Update                Script                                      Updater
  Leave                 Leave

Menu Path:
/Main/Master Inventory/
  Script containing this menu: Inv2
  Library containing the procedures for this menu: Inv2        Query,
                                                               Help, or
  Selection             Selection      Source    Map      Tables    User
  Name                  Action         Table     Table    Used      Script
  --------------------  -----------    --------  -------- --------  --------
  Add data              DataEntry                          Mastinv
  Change data           Edit                               Mastinv   Invq1
  Look up               View                               Mastinv   Invq2
  Reports               Menu

Menu Path:
/Main/Master Inventory/Reports/
  Script containing this menu: Inv5
  Library containing the procedures for this menu: Inv2        Query,
                                                               Help, or
  Selection             Selection      Source    Map      Tables    User
  Name                  Action         Table     Table    Used      Script
  --------------------  -----------    --------  -------- --------  --------
  Entire inventory      Report                              Mastinv
  Reorder report        Script                              Reorder
```

Figure 20.23: A partial example of a menu summary for the Inv application

the names of any MultiTable views used in the application (the Personal Programmer assigns these names). The Tables Used column lists the names of tables used for the menu option, and the Query, Help, or User Script column lists the names of any of query forms, help screens, or custom scripts (developed outside the Personal Programmer) that the menu item accesses.

Figure 20.24 shows the simple File list for the Inv application. Most of the file names assigned are created by the Personal Programmer, though you should recognize the names of tables and custom scripts within that list. Figure 20.25 shows the menu tree for the Inv application.

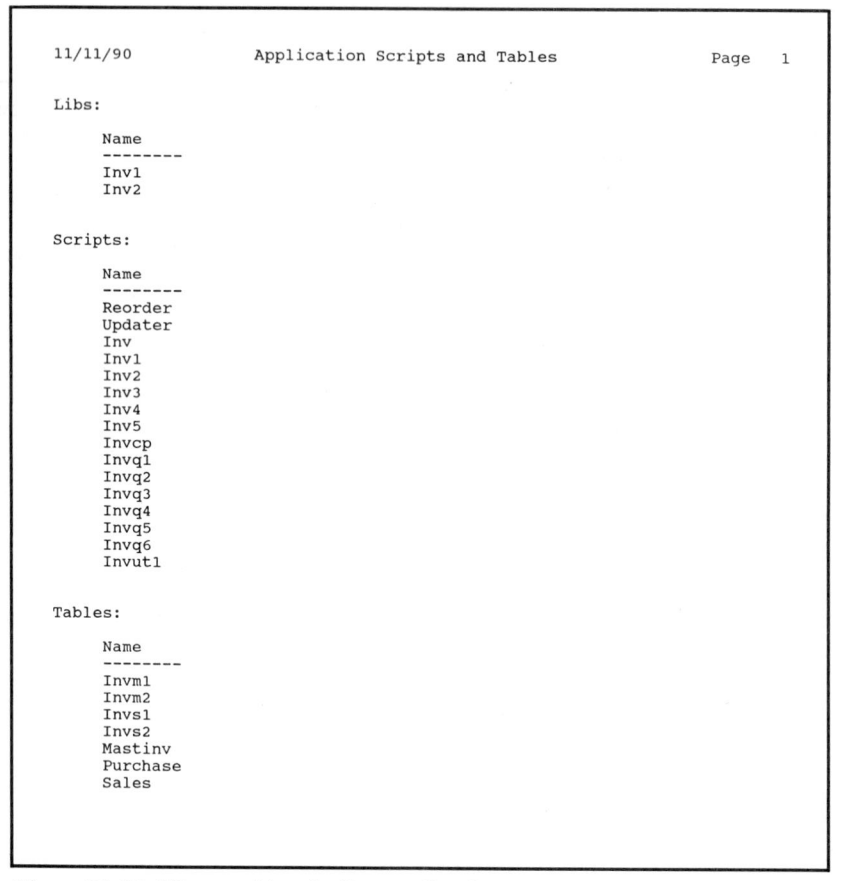

```
11/11/90              Application Scripts and Tables              Page    1

  Libs:

          Name
          --------
          Inv1
          Inv2

  Scripts:

          Name
          --------
          Reorder
          Updater
          Inv
          Inv1
          Inv2
          Inv3
          Inv4
          Inv5
          Invcp
          Invq1
          Invq2
          Invq3
          Invq4
          Invq5
          Invq6
          Invut1

  Tables:

          Name
          --------
          Invm1
          Invm2
          Invs1
          Invs2
          Mastinv
          Purchase
          Sales
```

Figure 20.24: Files used by the Inv application

```
11/12/90              Application Menu Tree:              Page  1.1
                      ======================
   Main --
        |--- Master Inventory --
        |                     |--- Add data    [ DataEntry ]
        |                     |--- Change data [ Edit ]
        |                     |--- Look up     [ View ]
        |                     ---- Reports --
        |                                   |--- Entire inventory [Reports]
        |                                   ---- Reorder report   [Scripts]
        |--- Sales --
        |          |--- Add data    [ DataEntry ]
        |          |--- Change data [ Edit ]
        |          |--- Look up     [ View ]
        |          ---- Reports     [ Report ]
        |--- Purchases --
        |              |--- Add data    [ DataEntry ]
        |              |--- Change data [ Edit ]
        |              |--- Look up     [ View ]
        |              ---- Report      [ Report ]
        |--- Update  [ Script ]
        ---- Leave   [ Leave ]
   Note:  "...<Menu Selection>" means that <Menu Selection> is not defined.
   ====
```

Figure 20.25: The menu tree for the Inv application

TESTING THE MENU STRUCTURE

The Review option on the Personal Programmer allows you to test the menu structure of your application, without actually performing any of the actions associated with each menu item. This feature lets you experiment with your menu structure to decide if there is anything you want to change.

To work backwards through your menu structure at any time, press Esc. To actually modify the menu structure, you'll need to select the Modify option from the Personal Programmer Main menu and MenuAction from the submenu.

GENERAL APPLICATION MANAGEMENT

The Tools option on the Personal Programmer Main menu provides several useful tools for managing an application. These can be summarized as follows:

OPTION	EFFECT
Copy	Copies the entire application from the current directory to another directory or disk

Delete	Deletes the entire application from the current directory
Rename	Changes the name of the application
Settings	Allows you to modify various settings in the application, as discussed below
Directory	Allows you to change to a new directory without exiting to DOS. (Never use this option while actually creating or modifying an application; use it only to switch to a new directory before creating a new application.)

The Settings option on the Tools menu offers the following options:

OPTION	EFFECT
PrinterSetup	Lets you change printer characteristics for the application
HelpMode	Removes or replaces the help screens that the Personal Programmer normally displays. Only old pros will want to switch from the helpful Verbose mode to the Terse mode that this option offers.
LibrariesOnly	Erases the files that allow you to modify an existing application, without erasing the application itself. Again, strictly for old pros.

SUMMARY

- The Personal Programmer lets you develop applications without programming. It asks you questions about the application, and writes programs automatically based on your answers.

- The Personal Programmer requires a hard disk, and must be installed on a subdirectory named \PDOX35\PPROG.

- Before building an application, it is best to create all the tables used in the application, and to draw a diagram of the *menu tree* for the application.

- Each application that you develop should be stored on its own directory.

- To start the Personal Programmer, log onto the directory for the application, and enter the command PPROG at the DOS prompt.

- When the Paradox Personal Programmer Main menu appears, select Create to create a new application, or Modify to modify an existing application.

- Once the Paradox Personal Programmer is running, follow the instructions on the screen, making menu selections to develop the application to your liking.

- To run an completed application, log on to the application directory, run Paradox in the usual manner, and select Scripts, Play, and the application name. (Optionally, just enter the command PARADOX followed by the application name at the DOS prompt.)

APPENDICES

INSTALLING PARADOX

APPENDIX A

BEFORE YOU CAN USE PARADOX ON YOUR COMPUTER, it must be installed. You need only install Paradox once, not each time you wish to use it. If you or somebody else has already installed Paradox on your computer, you can skip this Appendix and go right to Chapter 1.

COMPUTER REQUIREMENTS

For use with Paradox, your computer must be an IBM or 100%-compatible. Also, it must have the following:

1. One hard disk and at least one floppy disk drive.
2. DOS 2.0 or higher.
3. 512 kilobytes of RAM (random access memory).

If you will want to print and distribute copies of your reports, you must also have a printer attached to your computer.

If you want to view graphs, you'll need a graphics monitor and display adapter, such as CGA, VGA, EGA, or Hercules. You'll need a graphics printer to print graphs.

The amount of disk space you'll need to store Paradox depends on how many of the optional programs you want to store. Your basic Paradox package (the part covered in Chapters 1-19 in this book) requires about 3Mb (megabytes) of disk storage. If you want to install all of the optional programs that come with Paradox, you'll need another 3Mb for a total of 6Mb. The DOS DIR command will tell you how much free disk space is available (see your DOS manual if you are unfamiliar with the DIR command).

INSTALLING PARADOX

Before Paradox can be loaded and used, it must be properly *installed*. That means you must tell Paradox what kind of computer you are using by running a program called Install and answering a few questions. If you are going to use Paradox on a Local Area Network (LAN), let your network supervisor install the program.

To install Paradox on your hard disk, follow these steps:

1. Start your computer so that the DOS command prompt (usually A> or C>) appears.

2. Put the Paradox Installation/Sample Tables disk in disk drive A, and close the drive door (if any).

3. Switch to the drive that you want to store Paradox on. For example, type **C:** and press ← to switch to hard disk drive C.

4. Type **A:INSTALL** and press ←.

Some computer monitors may "clip off" a part of the installation screen. If you do not see the message "Press Enter to continue, Esc to Exit" at the bottom of the screen, press the Esc key, then type **Y** and press ←. Then type **A:INSTALL -B&W** and press ←. When you see the full installation screen, proceed with the next steps.

5. Press ← to leave the introductory screen and view the screen with the options (1) Hard Disk Installation, (2) Network Installation, (3) SQL Link Installation, and (4) Optional Software Installation.

This Appendix covers hard disk installation only; Network and SQL Link installations are more complex. You will need to refer to the *Network Administrator's Guide* that came with your Paradox package and/or the *SQL Link User's Guide* that came with SQL Link for information on those installation procedures. You can select option (5), Quit, if you choose not to proceed with the installation now.

6. Type **1** and press ← to select Hard Disk Installation.

INSTALLING PARADOX 623

7. You will see a prompt asking for the SOURCE drive (where the Installation disk is stored). Type **A** and press ↵.

8. When prompted for the DESTINATION drive, type the name of the hard disk where you want to install Paradox (usually **C**) then press ↵.

9. Next, the program asks for the directory to install Paradox on and suggests PDOX35 on the specified drive (e.g. C: \PDOX35). Press ↵ to accept this suggestion unless (for whatever reason) you want to use a different directory name.

10. The installation program then checks your CONFIG.SYS file to ensure that the BUFFERS and FILES settings are sufficient. If they are not, it changes these settings. (This step is automatic, so you can just let the installation program make this change. Just follow any instructions that appear on the screen.)

11. Next you'll be prompted to select a country group to determine how numbers, dates, and sort orders will be presented by Paradox. Select the country that most closely resembles your own by typing its number and pressing ↵.

Paradox will start "unpacking" (decompressing) and copying files from the floppy disk to the hard disk. When it is finished, you will be prompted to change disks. Continue with the steps below when the Copying prompt disappears:

12. If you are using 5¼-inch disks for the installation, remove the disk currently in drive A, put in the Paradox System Disk 1, and press ↵. If you are using 3½-inch disks, do not change disks.

13. Next you will see the Paradox Signature Screen. Carefully type your name, company name, and serial number from the 5¼-inch Installation disk into the designated prompts. You can use the →, ←, ↑, ↓ and Backspace keys to move the cursor and make corrections. (If these keys don't move the cursor, press the NumLock key once, then try again.)

14. At the bottom of the signature screen you'll see the prompt "Access data on a network?" Type **N** and press ⏎ (unless you are the network administrator installing copies of Paradox for network use).

15. Press the F2 key after completing steps 12 and 13 above.

The installation program will now copy some of the files from the remaining disks to your hard disk. Follow the instructions presented on the screen, remembering to remove the disk currently in the drive before inserting the requested disk; and remember to close the drive door after inserting the requested disk.

If a message appears indicating that the installation was not successful, you may need to start over from step 1. Check to make sure there is sufficient space on your hard disk and, if not, erase some unwanted files. (See the DIR and ERASE commands in your computer or DOS manual for information on the appropriate commands to use, or consult someone who knows about these things.)

If the installation is successful, you will see another menu listing optional software that you can install now. Since you are probably learning Paradox as a beginner, you can bypass these for now. Instead, follow these simple steps:

16. Type **7** and press ⏎ to Exit.

17. Press Esc to leave the installation screen and return to DOS.

The installation program may have changed your DOS CONFIG.SYS file. If so, those changes will not take effect until the next time you boot up (start your computer). To activate any changes now, first remove the disk in drive A and store it in a safe place, then reboot by holding down and then releasing the Ctrl, Alt, and Del keys. When the DOS prompt reappears, you can start Paradox, as described at the beginning of Chapter 2.

INSTALLING THE PARADOX PERSONAL PROGRAMMER

Like Paradox itself, the Paradox Personal Programmer must be installed on your computer before you can use it. You can install the

Personal Programmer at any time or choose not to install it at all. Be aware that the Personal Programmer will consume as much as two megabytes of disk space, so you may want to wait and make sure that you want to use the Personal Programmer (discussed in Chapter 20 of this book) before you decide.

If you do decide to install the Personal Programmer after installing and using Paradox for a while, follow the steps below:

1. Start your computer normally and get to the DOS command prompt (usually A> or C>).
2. Switch to the drive that you stored Paradox on (for example, type **C:** and press ← to switch to hard disk drive C).
3. Switch to the directory that you stored Paradox on (e.g. type **CD \PDOX35** and press ←).
4. Put the Paradox Installation/Sample Tables disk in drive A.
5. Type **A:INSTALL** and press ←.
6. Press ← to get past the opening screen.
7. Type **4** and press ← to select Optional Software Installation.
8. Type **A** and press ← to identify the source drive.
9. Type the letter of the destination drive (usually **C**) and press ←.
10. On the next screen, type the drive\directory that you installed Paradox on *only* if it is different from what is shown. Press ← to move to the next screen.
11. Type **3** and press ← to select PPROG, Paradox Personal Programmer Installation.
12. Press ← to accept the suggested subdirectory.
13. Follow the instructions for inserting disks for copying. Whenever you are prompted to insert a new disk, remove the disk currently in drive A, put in the requested disk, then press ← to continue.
14. When you see the message "Paradox Personal Programmer Installation complete," press ← to continue.
15. Type **7** and press ← to return to DOS.

Chapter 20 discusses techniques for starting the Personal Programmer. You can simplify the startup procedure by modifying the DOS path defined in your Autoexec.BAT file, if you wish, by reading the next section.

MODIFYING YOUR AUTOEXEC.BAT FILE

Whenever you first turn on your computer, DOS searches the root directory of the hard disk for a file named AUTOEXEC.BAT, and then automatically executes all the commands in that file. You can include a PATH command in the AUTOEXEC.BAT file to tell DOS to search specific directories for programs. This allows you to start a program, such as Paradox or the Personal Programmer, from any directory on your hard disk.

You can easily view the contents of your AUTOEXEC.BAT (if one exists on your computer). At the DOS C> prompt, type in the command **TYPE C:\AUTOEXEC.BAT** and then press Enter. If there is already an AUTOEXEC.BAT file on your hard disk, it may or may not already have a PATH defined in it (the command will begin with either the word PATH or the words SET PATH).

You can use any text editor or word processor (but *not* the Paradox scripts editor) to create or modify the AUTOEXEC.BAT file. If you use a word processing program, such as WordStar or WordPerfect, to create or modify the file, *make sure that you take the necessary steps to save the file in ASCII text format!* For example, if using WordStar, you must use the nondocument (N) mode rather than the document mode. If you are using WordPerfect version 5, use the DOS Text Retrieval option to read in the file (Ctrl-F5 T R).

Make sure that, no matter what text editor you use, you specify C:\AUTOEXEC.BAT as the file to edit, because DOS can only read the AUTOEXEC.BAT file if it is stored on the root directory of the startup drive (C:\).

If your AUTOEXEC.BAT file already has a PATH or SET PATH command in it, you can add the PDOX35 and PDOX35\PPROG directories to the existing path. For example, if your AUTOEXEC-.BAT file contains

   PATH C:\DOS;C:\WP51

you would want to change that to

   PATH C:\DOS;C:\WP51;C:\PDOX35;C:\PDOX35\PPROG

If your AUTOEXEC.BAT file is empty, or does not already contain a PATH or SET PATH command, you can insert the command

   PATH C:\PDOX35;C:\PDOX35\PPROG

In either case above, be sure to use backslashes (\) rather than forward slashes, and do not include blank spaces except for immediately after the PATH (or SET PATH =) command. Also, if you are using Version 4 or 5 of DOS, the PATH or SET PATH command must be above the DOSSHELL command within the file.

After modifying your AUTOEXEC.BAT file, save it as an ASCII file on the root directory. For example, if you are using WordStar, you can just press Ctrl-KX. If you are using WordPerfect 5, use DOS Text Save (Ctrl-F5 T S) to resave C:\AUTOEXEC.BAT, and answer Yes when asked about replacing the original copy. Do not resave the file when exiting WordPerfect.

After modifying the AUTOEXEC.BAT file, you should enter the command **TYPE C:\AUTOEXEC.BAT** at the DOS prompt to inspect the contents of the file. If you see any odd-looking graphics characters in the file, you have not saved the file in the proper format. You will need to use your word processor to convert the file to ASCII text format.

Any changes that you made to the AUTOEXEC.BAT file will take effect each time you start your computer in the future, or if you reboot (by pressing Ctrl-Alt-Del). When the PATH command is in effect, you can start Paradox, or the Personal Programmer, from any directory on your hard disk. (You can type the command **PATH** at the DOS prompt at any time to see the current path setting.) See your DOS manual if you need additional information about the PATH command.

NETWORKS, SQL LINK, AND MEMORY MANAGEMENT

APPENDIX B

IF YOU ARE USING PARADOX IN AN OFFICE WHERE several people working on separate computers can share the same data, then Paradox will behave slightly differently than described in the main chapters of this book. Throughout the tutorial chapters that precede this appendix, you'll find references indicating where and when differences between single-user and multiuser applications might surface.

ABOUT NETWORKS

A Local Area Network (LAN, often called simply a network) is a collection of interconnected computers on which several users can share files. Installing Paradox on the network is generally the responsibility of the network manager or network administrator (the person in charge of the network). Network installation is covered in the *Network Administrator's Guide* that comes with the Paradox program.

STARTING PARADOX ON A NETWORK

The exact procedures for starting Paradox vary from one network to the next. Therefore, you should consult your network administrator for information on starting Paradox on your system.

LOCKING

One of the key concepts in using Paradox on a network is *locking*. Locking limits access to data to a particular user. Paradox automatically locks tables and other objects, such as reports and forms, on an as-needed basis only. When a particular user no longer needs to have a lock on an object, Paradox automatically clears the lock.

Paradox's automatic locking and unlocking is designed to minimize locking, which in turn maximizes all users' access to all files. However, locking is required from time to time, and in some situations you may not be able to gain access to a file because another user on the network already has that object locked. When this happens, you'll see a message on your screen indicating which user on the network currently has the object locked. You'll need to wait for that user to finish his or her work before you can gain access to the file.

It's important to understand that placing a lock on an object does not place any restrictions on what *you* can do with that object. Rather, it restricts what everyone else on the network can do with that object while you have it locked.

Basically, there are four types of locks that can be placed on Paradox objects:

Full Lock: The person with a full lock has exclusive use of the object; no other user can change or view the object.

Write Lock: The person who has a write lock is the only one who can change the object, but other users can still use and view the object.

Prevent Full Lock: All users can view and change data. No single user can place a full lock on the object, but other users can place a write lock on the file.

Prevent Write Lock: All users can view and change the object; no user can place a full lock or a write lock on the table.

As mentioned, Paradox automatically places and removes locks on an as-needed basis in order to maintain data integrity and maximize access to all users.

Record Locks

The Paradox CoEdit mode lets multiple users make simultaneous changes to the same table. However, whenever you start editing a particular record, Paradox will automatically place a write lock on that single record, preventing others from changing that record at the same time. If you try to edit a record that is currently locked by another user, you'll see a message indicating the name of the user who has the record locked, and you'll need to wait for that user to finish before you can edit the record.

You can explicitly lock a single record by pressing Alt-L while the cursor is in the record. The message "Record is locked" appears at the top of the screen, and the triangular field indicator is highlighted. You can also press Alt-L to explicitly unlock the record. However, the record will be unlocked automatically as soon as you move the cursor to a different record.

Family Locks

Paradox also uses *family locks*. A family lock is automatically placed on all the objects in a family during a Tools, Copy, Table or a Tools, Copy, JustFamily operation. During the operation, other users can still view the contents of the locked objects, but cannot make changes to those objects (like a write lock). The family lock is automatically removed as soon as the copy operation is complete.

Snapshots

When multiple users have access to the same files, there is always the possibility that one user will change data while another user is performing a lengthy operation, such as printing a report or performing a query, with that table. To maximize data integrity, Paradox will take a "snapshot" of the current data and use that snapshot to perform the lengthy operation.

If another user changes data while Paradox is taking the snapshot, Paradox will automatically try to take the snapshot again. You'll see a message each time this happens. If you change your mind and don't want Paradox to continue trying to take the snapshot, press Ctrl-Break.

Paradox's Automatic Locking Scheme

Table B.1 summarizes Paradox's automatic locking scheme by operations selected from the Main (or Edit) menu. Additional details are presented in the section "Using Paradox on a Network" later in this appendix.

Table B.1: Paradox's Automatic Locking Scheme

MENU	OPTION	EFFECT
View	Table view	prevent full lock
	Form view	prevent full lock
Ask	Regular, Find, Set	snapshot at DO-IT!
	Insert, Delete, Changeto	prevent full lock, full lock at DO-IT!
Report	Output, RangeOutput	prevent full lock, snapshot at DO-IT!
	Design or Change	prevent full lock on table, full lock on report design
Create	Create	full lock
	Borrow	full lock on table, prevent full lock on table being borrowed
Modify	Sort, New	write lock on table, full lock on new table
	Sort, Same	full lock
	Edit	full lock
	CoEdit	full lock
	DataEntry	prevent full lock on source, prevent write lock at DO-IT!
	MultiEntry	write lock on source, write lock on map, prevent write lock on all at DO-IT!
	Restructure	full lock
ValCheck	Define or Clear	full lock
	TableLookup	prevent full lock on lookup table

Table B.1: Paradox's Automatic Locking Scheme (continued)

MENU	OPTION	EFFECT
Image	KeepSet	full lock
	Graph, CrossTab	snapshot at DO-IT!
	Graph, View	prevent full lock
Forms	Design or Change	prevent full lock on table, full lock on form
Tools	Rename	full lock on source and target
	QuerySpeed	snapshot at DO-IT!
	ExportImport, Export	write lock on source
	ExportImport, Import	full lock on target
	Copy, Tables	family lock on source, full lock on target
	Copy (object other than table)	write lock on source, full lock on target, prevent full lock on associated table
	JustFamily	prevent full lock on source table, family lock on objects, full lock on target table and objects
	Delete, Table	full lock on table
	Delete, Forms or Reports	full lock on object, prevent full lock on table
	Delete, KeepSet or ValCheck	full lock on object, prevent full lock on table
	Info, Structure	prevent full lock
	Info, Family	family lock
	More, Add	write lock on source, prevent write lock on target

Table B.1: Paradox's Automatic Locking Scheme (continued)

MENU	OPTION	EFFECT
	More, MultiAdd	write locks on source and map, prevent write lock on targets
	More, FormAdd	prevent full lock on targets, prevent full lock on sources at DO-IT!
	More, Subtract	full lock on both source and target
	More, Empty	full lock
	More, Protect	full lock

Explicit Locks

Besides Paradox's automatic locking, it is also possible for any user to place an *explicit* lock on an object by following these steps:

1. Select Tools from the Main menu.
2. Select Net.
3. If you want to set or remove a lock, select Lock. If you want to set or remove a prevent lock, select PreventLock.
4. Select FullLock to set or remove a full lock, or select Write-Lock to set or remove a write lock.
5. Type the name of the table, or press ↵ and select the table name from the menu that appears.
6. Select Set to place the lock or prevent lock, or select Clear to remove the lock or prevent lock.

It's important to remember that if you place an explicit lock on a table, the table remains locked until you explicitly remove the lock (following the same general steps you used to lock it, but selecting Clear rather then Set in the last step). You'll want to keep your explicit locks to a minimum so that other users can have access to the data.

Of course, if another user has already locked a table, or has already placed a prevent lock on a table, you cannot override that lock. For example, if another user has placed a prevent write lock on a table to make sure he or she can keep changing data in a table, you could not place a write lock on that table.

Again, there is rarely a need for individual users to place explicit locks on objects, since Paradox automatically sets and clears locks on an efficient as-needed basis.

USING PARADOX ON A NETWORK

The sections that follow describe specific differences between single-user Paradox, which is the main emphasis throughout the chapters of this book, and Paradox on a network.

REFRESHING THE SCREEN

If several people are working on the same table at once, the data on the various screens may become out-of-sync from time to time. You can bring your own screen up-to-date with other users' screens at any time simply by pressing the Refresh (Alt-R) key.

You can also determine how frequently your screen is automatically refreshed by using the Tools, Net, AutoRefresh options from the Paradox Main menu.

PRIVATE DIRECTORIES

Each user on a network must have his or her own *private directory*. This is where Paradox will store temporary objects, such as the Answer table generated by queries. It will seem as though these objects are stored in your current network directory, because the table names from both the network working directory and the private directory appear in menus of table names (as when you press Enter in response to the request for a table name). However, if you were to list all table names using the Tools, Info, Inventory options, you'd see only the files on the network directory, not the ones from your private directory.

> The network administrator can set the private directory and user name for each workstation by using Scripts, Play to play the Custom script, and selecting Net from the Main menu.

In most cases the network administrator is responsible for setting up the private directory at each workstation, so chances are that you don't need to do anything to declare a private directory when you use Paradox.

If, for whatever reason, you need to manually determine a private directory, you can do so by selecting Tools, SetPrivate and typing in a valid drive and directory (e.g., C:\MYDATA). You must specify a directory that already exists, preferably on your own workstation rather than on the network. (If you declare a network directory as private, other users will lose access to that directory.)

If you try to declare a directory that other people are currently using as private, or if you try to declare somebody else's private directory as your own, your request will be rejected.

NETWORK USER NAMES

Each workstation in a network has a name, commonly referred to as its *user name*. This is the name that appears when you try to use an object that's currently locked by another user (for example, "Names table has been locked by Martha").

There are three ways to enter user names:

- Through the network operating system, if it has the capability. Paradox will use this method of entering the user name if it's available.

- From Paradox at each workstation, using the Scripts, Play, Custom, Net, UserName options in Paradox. This name will then be the default for the workstation, and will override the name defined in the network operating system.

- By selecting Tools, Net, UserName, typing in a name, and pressing Enter. This name will override both of the above for the remainder of the session, or until yet a different user name is entered.

An example of when you might want to change the default user name using Tools, Net, UserName would be when you are working at another person's workstation (for whatever reason), and want to identify yourself as the user at that workstation.

NETWORK INFORMATION

You can get a list of all the users currently on the network by selecting Tools, Info, Who from the Paradox Main menu. You can also see a list of all the locks on a table using the Tools, Info, Lock options from the Main menu. This is particularly handy in a situation where you get a message like "Table is in use by Martha and 2 others" and you want to find out who the others are.

CREATING A TABLE ON A NETWORK

While you are creating a table on a network, Paradox places a full lock on it to prevent other users from creating a table with the same name.

If you want to borrow the structure of an existing table, you will be allowed to do so only if another user has not placed a full lock on that file. When you borrow another table's structure, that table will (briefly) have a full lock placed on it while its structure is copied to the new table.

DATA ENTRY ON A NETWORK

In a multiuser environment, the network manager may implement a protection scheme that limits your access to certain tables and certain fields within those tables. If you are not sure which data you are allowed access to, or the necessary passwords, ask your network administrator.

If you do have the right to add new records to a table, you should be aware that when adding new records with the Modify, DataEntry options, Paradox places a prevent full lock on the table (or tables) so that other users can still access the data currently in the table. However, none of these other users can place a full lock on the table while you are adding records, which in turn means that they cannot perform any operations that require exclusive use of the table, such as deleting all its records or changing the table's structure.

If somebody on the network already has exclusive use of a table when you select the Modify, DataEntry options, you won't be able to start adding data until that other user releases the lock.

Keep in mind that when you add new data to a Paradox table, the records are actually added to temporary *entry* tables; your new records do not become part of the actual table until you press DO-IT! (F2). As soon as you press DO-IT!, Paradox places a prevent write lock on the actual target table so that data from the entry tables can be sent to the target tables.

However, if another user already had the table locked when pressed DO-IT!, you will not be able to get records from the entry table to the target table. In that situation, you can use the KeepEntry option on the DataEntry menu to save the newly added records without passing them to the target table by following these steps:

1. Press F10 and select KeepEntry.

2. Press F10 and select Tools, Rename, Table.

3. Type **Entry** as the name of the table to rename, then press Enter.

4. Enter a unique, valid name for the new name (such as **NEWRECS**), then press Enter.

Later, when the target table is available, you can use the Tools, More, Add options from the Main menu to copy data from the source (i.e., NEWRECS in this example) table to the target table. (For more information, see Chapter 16.)

VIEWING DATA ON A NETWORK

The steps for viewing table data on a network are identical to those for viewing table data on a single-user system. While you have the table in view, Paradox places a prevent full lock on the table to allow other users access to the same table for all operations excluding those that require a full lock.

When you try to view a table on a network, your request might be denied for any of the following reasons:

- Another user has a full lock on the table.

- You are trying to view the table via a custom form, but another user has a full lock on that form.

- You do not have full access rights to that table because of the protection scheme designed by the network administrator.

If either of the first two items prevents your access, you can just wait a few minutes and try to view the table again later. If the network administrator has limited your access to the table (or certain fields in the table), only people who know the password can view the protected data. (When viewing protected fields without access to those fields, they appear as blanks on your screen.)

EDITING ON A NETWORK

When you select the Modify, Edit options or press Edit (F9) to edit a table on a network, Paradox places a full lock on the table, thereby preventing other users from viewing or accessing the table in any way.

In most situations it's preferable to select Modify, CoEdit or to press CoEdit (Alt-F9) to edit a table on a network. This allows other users to view and edit the same table that you are editing.

When you are editing tables, remember that your company's network administrator has the power to decide which users have access to which fields. The restrictions placed on you for editing tables are the same as described above in the section "Data Entry on a Network."

SORTING ON A NETWORK

Using the Modify, Sort options to sort a table on a network requires that you have a write lock on the table. If another user has a full lock or prevent write lock on the table, you will not be able to begin your sort operation until the other user releases the lock. Once you do successfully begin your sort operation, your write lock stays in effect for the duration of the sort, preventing other users from writing to that table.

If you are sorting the contents of your table to another, separate table, Paradox places a full lock on the target table for the duration of the sorting operation.

QUERYING ON A NETWORK

When you access a query form for a particular table on a network, Paradox places a prevent full lock on that table. If another user already has a full lock on the table you want to query, you'll have to wait until that user releases the lock to access the query form.

If other users are editing the table that you are querying, Paradox takes a snapshot of the current data as soon as you press DO-IT! to activate the query, enabling you to perform a query even while other users are modifying data in the table.

If another user happens to change the table data in the small period of time it takes to take the snapshot, Paradox will try to take the snapshot again. If so many changes are taking place that you can no longer wait for Paradox to take the snapshot to complete the query, you can press Ctrl-Break to prevent additional tries.

REPORTS ON A NETWORK

Paradox places a prevent full lock on a table while you are designing, modifying, or printing from a report format. This means that other users can still access the data in the table, but cannot change its structure or delete all of its records. If another user already has a full lock on the table before you begin your report operation, your request will be denied and you'll need to try again later.

Also, while you are designing or changing a report format, the format itself is locked so that other users cannot view, change, or print from that format.

The network administrator can assign passwords to reports, so you may need to enter a password in order to print or view those reports.

If other users are editing a table when you try to use it to print a report, Paradox takes a snapshot of the table in its current state, and prints the data from that snapshot. If another user makes a change to the table while the snapshot is being taken, you'll see a message to this effect, and Paradox will retake the snapshot. If table use is so heavy that you no longer want to keep retrying the automatic snapshot, press Ctrl-Break.

If your network offers several printers, you can use the Report, SetPrinter commands to select a network printer for your report.

FORMS ON A NETWORK

While you are designing or modifying a form, Paradox places a prevent full lock on that form's table, and a full lock on the form itself (as with reports, described in the preceding section). This allows other users the opportunity to continue to edit data in the table (without the form), but prevents their access to the form you are working with at the moment.

If you try to edit a form while another user has a full lock on its associated table, Paradox will reject your request and you'll have to try again later after the lock has been released by the other user. Similarly, if another user is already modifying the form that you want to modify, your request will be denied until the other user is finished with the form.

If the network administrator has placed access limitations on a form, you can access that form only if you know the password.

If one user on a network is coediting a table with a particular form, other users who want to edit that same table must also use the same form.

GRAPHS ON A NETWORK

The only restriction to viewing graphs on a network is the obvious fact that in order to view a graph for a table, you must first be able to view the table. The only situation that would prevent this arises when another user has exclusive use of the table, such as when that user is changing the table's structure or emptying all the records from that table.

Once you gain access to the table to view your graph, Paradox places a prevent full lock on that table to ensure that others can still view and edit the table, but cannot take the table away from you by fully locking it. Similarly, if you graph data based on the results of a query or crosstab, that table is private and cannot be locked by another user.

SCRIPTS ON A NETWORK

Multiple users on a network can play the same script simultaneously, provided that nobody is editing the script. A script that is currently being played by any user cannot be edited and, conversely, a script that is being edited cannot be played by any user.

If you are denied access to a script, Paradox does not tell you which user is currently editing the script, as it does with other network messages. Instead, it simply displays the message "Can't access script."

UPDATE QUERIES ON A NETWORK

When you perform an INSERT, a DELETE, or a CHANGETO query on a network by pressing DO-IT! (F2), Paradox automatically places a full lock on all the tables involved in the query. If another user is already using any table involved in the query, you will not be able to perform the query until the other user has finished his or her operations and the locks have been released.

TOOLS ON A NETWORK

Most Tools operations, such as copying and renaming objects, involve full locks and write locks on the objects being manipulated (see the bottom of Table B.1 presented earlier in this appendix). As usual, when you have these locks in place, other users will have little or no access to the files. When you finish the operation, Paradox will, as usual, release the lock automatically.

If another user already has a lock, or prevent lock, on an object you want to manipulate with a Tools operation, you'll have to wait until that other user releases his or her lock.

SECURITY AND PROTECTION

> Security and protection are generally the responsibility of the network administrator rather than individual users on the network.

One potential problem with networks is the simple fact that everyone on the network has access to all the data. Some of that data, such as employee salaries, might be confidential. Paradox provides two means of protecting data: the Tools, More, Protect options on the Main menu, and the Paradox Protection Generator, which allows the network administrator to define groups of users, each with its own level of access to Paradox objects. The combination of these two tools gives the network administrator control over every item of data that users have access to. You use the Tools, More, Protect options to create *table-level passwords* (that is, passwords for each individual table), then you use the protection generator to develop a protection scheme based on *user passwords*. Each user on the network, then, will need to remember only her or his own single password.

CREATING TABLE LEVEL PASSWORDS

> The Tools, More, Protect options are also covered in Chapter 16.

The owner of a table (typically the network administrator on a network) can define an *owner password*, which provides total access to the table, and *auxiliary passwords*, which provide limited access to the table, for every Paradox table. You can create both owner and auxiliary passwords by following these general steps:

1. From the Paradox Main menu, select Tools.
2. Select More.
3. Select Protect.
4. Select Password.
5. Select Table (or Script, if you want to protect a script).
6. Specify the table you want to protect, either by typing its name and pressing Enter, or by pressing Enter and selecting the name from the menu that appears.

If this is the first time you are assigning passwords to this table, you'll be asked to type an owner password. This is the password that provides unlimited access to the table, and even access to the passwords themselves. Be aware too that passwords are case-sensitive—for example, HONCHO, Honcho, and honcho are three entirely different passwords. Carefully type in your owner password (up to 15 characters in length) and press Enter. You'll be prompted to type it a second time for verification.

One thing you definitely don't want to do is forget the owner password. It's a good idea to write it down (don't forget to use the same upper- and lowercase letters) and store it someplace safe, where you can easily find it but other network users cannot.

After entering the owner password, you'll be taken to a screen for defining auxiliary passwords, shown in Figure B.1. You can define as many auxiliary passwords as you wish for the table, each providing its own level of access.

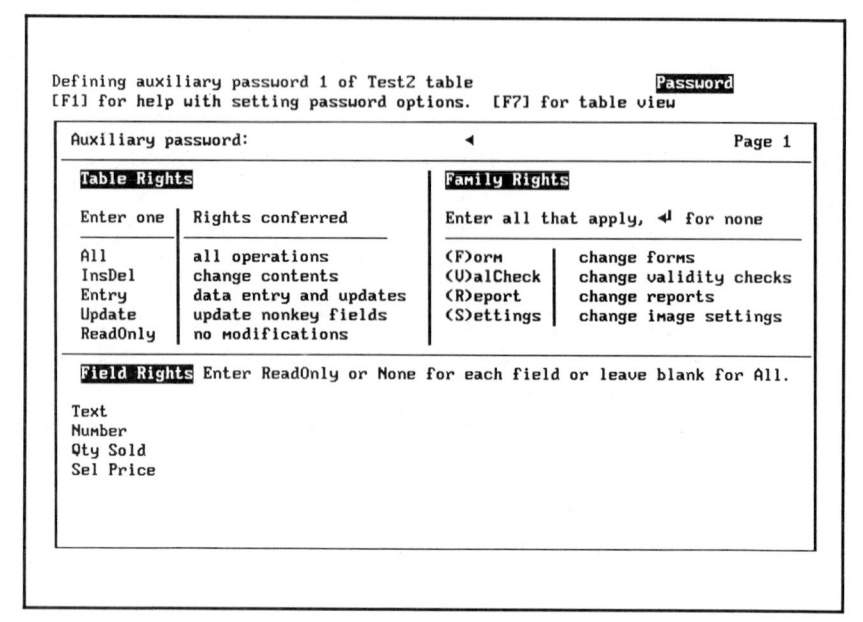

```
Defining auxiliary password 1 of Test2 table              Password
[F1] for help with setting password options.   [F7] for table view

   Auxiliary password:                    ◄                    Page 1
   ┌─────────────────────────────────┬──────────────────────────────────┐
   │ Table Rights                    │ Family Rights                    │
   │ Enter one │ Rights conferred    │ Enter all that apply, ↵ for none │
   │                                 │                                  │
   │ All       │ all operations      │ (F)orm     │ change forms        │
   │ InsDel    │ change contents     │ (V)alCheck │ change validity checks│
   │ Entry     │ data entry and updates│ (R)eport │ change reports      │
   │ Update    │ update nonkey fields│ (S)ettings │ change image settings│
   │ ReadOnly  │ no modifications    │            │                     │
   ├─────────────────────────────────┴──────────────────────────────────┤
   │ Field Rights  Enter ReadOnly or None for each field or leave blank for All.│
   │ Text                                                                       │
   │ Number                                                                     │
   │ Qty Sold                                                                   │
   │ Sel Price                                                                  │
   │                                                                            │
   └────────────────────────────────────────────────────────────────────────────┘
```

Figure B.1: Screen for defining auxiliary passwords

For each auxiliary password you create, you can define table rights, family rights, and field rights, as summarized below:

- **Table Rights**: You can specify the level of access to the overall table by typing the first letter of the options below:

    ReadOnly: User can view the contents of the table, but cannot make any changes.

    Update: User can view data, make changes to nonkey fields, but cannot insert or delete records.

    Entry: User has Update rights, and can also add new records using the Modify, DataEntry and the Tools, More, Add options.

InsDel: In addition to Entry rights, the user can change the contents of any field, insert records, delete records, and empty the table.

All: User has the same rights as the owner of the table: unlimited access to the contents and structure of the table.

- **Family Rights**: You can determine whether or not the user can modify the table's objects: forms, validity checks, reports, and settings. Type the first letter of each option. For example, FR gives the user rights to change forms and reports.

    Form: User can design, change, and delete any form associated with the table.

    Report: User can modify any report associated with the table.

    ValCheck: User can create, change, or delete validity checks for the table.

    Settings: User can create, change, or delete image settings for the table.

- **Field Rights**: At the bottom of the screen you'll see the name of each field in the table, and here you can assign any of three levels of access to each field:

    (blank): User has all rights to the field; he or she can view it and change its contents.

    ReadOnly: User can view the contents of the field, but cannot change the contents.

    None: User can neither view the field nor change its contents.

As an example, suppose you have a table named Payroll that includes employee salaries. While you could set up any number of auxiliary passwords, you might want to set up at least three, one called FULLSALARY that provides the user complete access to the salaries; and second auxiliary password, VIEWSALARY, that allows a user to view the salary but not change it, and a third auxiliary password, HIDESALARY, that does not allow the user to view nor change the salary, but provides some access to other fields.

You can use the following keys while defining your auxiliary passwords:

- **F7**: Switches between form view and table view
- **F10**: Calls up a menu with the following options:

    Undo: Undoes the most recent change to the auxiliary password (same as pressing Ctrl-U).

    Help: Provides help on creating auxiliary passwords (same as pressing F1).

    DO-IT!: Saves all recent changes (same as pressing F2).

    Cancel: Cancels all recent changes and returns you to the Main menu.

Because your passwords are being stored in a Paradox table, you can scroll through fields and records in the usual manner, with the arrow, PgUp, and PgDn keys. If the table you are assigning passwords to has more than 16 fields, there will be multiple pages of field names that you can scroll through with the PgUp and PgDn keys.

After defining the auxiliary passwords for all the protected tables on the network, the next step is to attach various users to various auxiliary passwords using the Paradox Protection Generator. You might want to jot down all your auxiliary passwords or print the completed passwords table as a reference when using the protection generator.

USING THE PROTECTION GENERATOR

The primary purpose of the protection generator is to simplify the overall password system. Basically, you want to give each user a single password, and then have Paradox automatically "know" the correct auxiliary password to use for that user in every table. In other words, when the user logs onto the system and enters his or her user password, Paradox then automatically enters all the appropriate auxiliary passwords for that user.

The Protection Generator comes with the Paradox package, and is installed on a subdirectory named \PROTECT beneath the Paradox directory (e.g. \PDOX35\PROTECT). If the protection generator is not already installed on your hard disk, run the Paradox Install program from drive A, and select Optional Software Installation (option 4) from the Main menu. Follow the prompts on the screen, and select Protect (option 4) when you get to the Optional Software Installation menu.

Linking Logical Drives

Before you run the protection generator, you need to link logical drives to all the directories that contain protected tables. This is a job that's performed at the network operating system level, and different networks use different commands to link directories to logical drives. For example, Novell provides MAP, while 3COM provides LINK. (See your network documentation for additional information.)

It's important to remember that once you add a table to the protection system, the protection generator always identifies the table by its logical drive and path. Therefore, once you've entered a table in the protection system, you need to link it to the same drive and directory any time you modify the protection system in the future. If you already have a protection system in place, and want to add new tables from a new directory, link that directory to a drive that's not already used in the protection system.

Starting the Protection Generator

After you've installed the protection generator and linked logical drives to the directories containing the tables you want to protect, you can follow these steps to start the protection generator:

1. Decide on a directory to store the protection system on, keeping in mind that you must have read/write/create privileges on the directory. Do not use the \PROTECT subdirectory where the protection generator itself is stored.

2. Decide on a password for yourself in your capacity as network administrator, and write it down. The password may be up to 15 characters in length.

3. Run Paradox and Play the Protect script on the \PROTECT directory using the Script, Play options from the Paradox Main menu.

4. When prompted for a network administrator, carefully type in the password, keeping in mind that it is case-sensitive (e.g., TOPDOG, TopDog, and Topdog are three different passwords).

5. If this is the first time you've entered this password, you'll be prompted to type it a second time for verification.

6. When prompted, enter the logical drive and path of the working directory (i.e., the directory that contains the tables you want to protect) and press Enter.

At this point you'll be taken to the Protection Generator main menu, which has the options summarized below:

Create: Builds a new protection system.

Modify: Changes an existing protection system.

NewPassword: Changes the administrator password (the one that provides access to the protection generator).

GenerateLogin: Creates a login script.

Help: Gets help.

Exit: Leaves the protection system and returns you to Paradox.

Once a protection scheme is implemented, only people who know the administrator password can change the scheme.

Creating the MapUsers Table

Once you are in the Protection Generator, you need to create the MapUsers table, which maps individual user names to auxiliary passwords in tables. Select Create, and you will be taken to an empty MapUsers table. This is a normal Paradox table, so you can fill it in and make changes as with any other Paradox table. You can also press F7 to switch between form view and table view.

Each user/table combination should be entered into this table as a single record. For example, if user Wanda has access to tables

Orders, Parts, and Customer, you'll need three records to define these, as below:

User	Table
Wanda	Orders
Wanda	Parts
Wanda	Customer

Each record in the MapUsers table needs to be filled with the following information:

> You can use the Ditto key (Ctrl-D) to repeat the name from the preceding record in the current record.

User: Specify the user's name. For simplicity, you might want to use the person's network name. Names are case-sensitive, so be sure to use upper- and lowercase letters consistently.

Table: Define one table that this user has access to. You can press Help (F1) when the cursor is in the Table field to see a list of tables on the current (working) directory. If the table is on a different directory, specify the logical drive of that table, or wait until you've finished with the tables on the current directory only. Later you'll have an opportunity to switch to another working directory and continue entering records.

TablePassword: Enter the auxiliary password (which you previously defined with Tools, More, Protect) that identifies the level of access you want this user to have for this table. Be sure to use the same upper- and lowercase letters that you used when originally typing the auxiliary passwords. If necessary, you can define a new table-level password now, then later go back to Tools, More, Protect to define the table access for the new password.

Description: This field is optional, and can contain any text you want. A "plain English" description of how much access the table password provides might be useful for future reference.

When you've finished adding records, or want to start assigning users and passwords to tables on a different directory, press DO-IT! (F2).

You'll then be given four choices:

TablePasswords: Lets you define the access rights to any new table-level (auxiliary) passwords (i.e., any auxiliary passwords that you created in the preceding step of filling in the MapUsers table, and did not previously define using Tools, More, Protect). If you are working with a newly created MapUser table, you can modify any existing auxiliary passwords. When you've finished, you'll automatically be taken to the next step in the Protection Generator.

AnotherDirectory: Switches you to another working directory and adds its tables to the MapUsers table.

Save: Saves the MapUsers table and returns you to the Protection Generator Main menu.

Cancel: Cancels current changes to the MapUsers table and returns you to the Protection Generator Main menu.

Assigning User Passwords

After you've filled in the MapUsers table, and assigned access rights to the new table (auxiliary) passwords (if necessary), you can assign passwords to users in the UserPass table. Select the UserPasswords option from the menu that appears after you've changed the table passwords, or select Modify, UserPasswords from the Protection Generator Main menu.

You will see a list of user names that you created in the MapUsers table. Next to each user name in the User Password column, enter the user's password (up to 15 characters in length). This is the one and only password that the user needs to remember to gain access to his or her tables, so you might want to ask each user to invent his or her own password.

Press DO-IT! (F2) to save the user passwords.

Generating a Login Script

The next step in creating a protection system is to generate a login script. To do so, select GenerateLogin from the menu that appears after you save the UserPass table, or select GenerateLogin from the

Protection Generator Main menu. The only feedback you'll receive is the message *Generating Login script* near the lower right corner of the screen. Then the entire Protection Generator script will end and you'll be returned to the Paradox Main menu.

The script created by the GenerateLogin option is named Login.SC. To activate the script you can include the command **PLAY Login** in the Init.SC script (which is executed automatically whenever Paradox is started) or use **PLAY Login** as the first command in an application that runs on the network. Of course, either way, Paradox needs to be able to find the Login.SC script, so be sure to include the drive and directory.

Chapter 17 explains how to create Paradox scripts.

Keep in mind that Paradox looks for the Init.SC script on the current drive and directory of each workstation, so you'll need to put a copy of Init.SC on the Paradox directory of each workstation. The PLAY command within each Init.SC script must clearly identify the location of the Login.SC script.

For example, suppose that Login.SC is stored on the \PDOXDATA\PSCHEME directory, and the \PDOXDATA directory is linked to network logical drive P:. The command used in each Init.SC script to play the Login.SC script in this example would be:

PLAY "P:\\PSCHEME\\Login"

Once this command has been added to the Init.SC script, the user will see the following prompt on the screens whenever he or she starts Paradox:

PARADOX LOGIN
User   :
Password:

Users should type in both their user (network) names and their passwords as they are listed in the UserPass table. (The password does not appear on the screen.) Remind users that they must use exact upper- and lowercase letters when typing in these names. Once the user is logged in, he or she need not enter anymore passwords. The MapUsers table takes care of entering the appropriate auxiliary passwords automatically as the user opens tables.

PARADOX SQL LINK

> SQL is often pronounced *sequel*.

SQL is an acronym for Structured Query Language, and is a standardized technique for accessing data stored in a database, particularly on large mainframe and minicomputers. SQL Link is a package offered by Borland that translates your Paradox query-by-example queries to SQL format so that you can access these databases via Paradox.

Typically, you would use SQL Link to query a *remote* table; that is, one that is not on your computer. The remote database might be on a large mainframe or minicomputer, or on a dedicated microcomputer commonly referred to as the *database server*.

SQL Link is based on *client-server architecture*. The computer that the database is stored on is the server, and acts as an intelligent *back-end* by taking care of security restraints, data integrity, and other database management jobs that normally require substantial computing resources.

Paradox is the client, or *front end*, to the server, and is your interface for querying the remote database. You can query the remote database through your normal Paradox Query-by-Example screen. SQL Link translates that query to SQL (behind the scenes if you wish) and sends the query to the remote database. The remote database then performs the query and sends back only the results. Because the remote database performs all the actions required to complete the query, only data is sent back to the client, which minimizes network traffic and keeps the overall system running more quickly.

Installing SQL Link on the company computers is the responsibility of the person in charge of the overall database (often referred to as the database administrator), and is a topic that goes beyond the scope of this book—space permits us to provide only a brief overview of SQL Link here. If you happen to be the person who is responsible for installing SQL Link, you should note that before you can install that program, one of the following servers must already be installed:

- IBM Extended Edition 1.2 Database Manager
- Microsoft SQL Server Version 1.0 or later
- Oracle Server 6.0

The *SQL Link User's Guide* that comes with the SQL Link package documents the installation procedures.

STARTING PARADOX SQL LINK

Starting Paradox with SQL Link is generally the same as starting single-user Paradox—you switch to the PDOX35 directory and enter the **PARADOX** command as described at the beginning of Chapter 2. This will activate both Paradox and SQL Link.

CONNECTING TO THE SERVER

Your database administrator may have automated the steps required to connect to the server on your workstation already. If not, the manual procedure is quite simple, as listed in the steps below:

1. Press F10 to access the Paradox Main menu.
2. Select Tools, SQL, Connection, Select from the Main menu.
3. Press ↑ and/or ↓ until the highlighter is on the connection you want.
4. Press DO-IT! (F2) to select that connection.
5. Provide any other information as requested (such as user name and/or password).
6. Press DO-IT! (F2).

From this point on, you can perform operations either on local tables (those on your own workstation), or remote tables (those stored on the database server). More specific instructions are provided later in this appendix.

CREATING A REMOTE TABLE WITH SQL LINK

If you are using Paradox in conjunction with SQL Link and are connected to the server, you'll be presented with the following options after selecting Create from the Paradox Main menu to create a table:

```
Local    Remote
Create a local table
```

Choose Local if you want to create a local table, or Remote to create a remote table. If you choose Remote (and enter a valid table name) the screen will display a message reminding you of the name of the currently connected server, and then the usual screen for designing a table structure will return.

When defining the new table structure, be sure to conform to the server's rules for defining the table name, field names, and data types. For example, while Paradox allows you to include blank spaces in field names, your server may not. If this is the case, you can use underlines instead of blank spaces when naming fields in your table. If you use a Paradox data type that is not supported by your server, Paradox will automatically revert to the closest available data type on your server.

ADDING DATA TO A REMOTE TABLE

Once you are connected to the server, adding data to a table is the same as in regular Paradox: you select Modify, DataEntry from the Main menu, then press Enter to see a list of tables. Highlight the name of the table you want (or start typing its name), and press Enter. Fill in your data as normal. Initially, your new entries will be placed in a table named Entry.

When you've finished entering the data, press DO-IT! (F2). The data from the Entry table will be passed to the remote table. If any key violations occur during data entry, Paradox places them in a local KeyViol table (see Chapter 12). Other problems with records will be stored in a Problems table. You can edit the KeyViol and Problems tables to fix the problems, then use Tools, More, Add to send the edited records to the remote table.

If the server connection is broken and the data in the Entry table cannot be sent to the remote table, use the KeepEntry option to rename the Entry table. Then later you can use Tools, More, Add to send data to the remote table.

QUERYING A REMOTE TABLE

To query a remote table with SQL Link, follow these general steps:

1. Select Ask from the Paradox Main menu.
2. Enter (or select) the name of the remote table you wish to query.
3. When prompted, type your remote user name and press Enter.
4. When prompted, type your remote password and press Enter.
5. Fill in the query form in the usual manner, avoiding the restrictions on query options discussed in the section below.
6. Press DO-IT! (F2).
7. A local Answer table displaying the results of your query appears on your screen.

If you wish to work only with the remote Answer table (for example, to create custom forms, graphs, reports, or to perform additional queries), you can use the Tools, Rename options from the Main menu to rename the Answer table.

Restrictions on Querying Remote Tables

You *can* perform a query for all records in a remote table, then use these operators to query the resulting local Answer table.

The following Paradox query operators are not allowed when querying remote tables:

G	FIND
SET	LIKE
!	ONLY
NO	EVERY
EXACTLY	

You can use the summary operators with the CALC operator, such as CALC SUM, but you cannot use restricted aggregation (such as AVERAGE < 5000) or aggregate constants (such as SUM Salary).

You cannot use the @ or .. pattern-matching characters in Date or Numeric fields.

You cannot use either multiline or multitable DELETE or CHANGETO queries.

Your particular server may impose additional limitations (see your database administrator or server documentation for additional information if necessary).

Viewing the SQL Version of your Query

Whenever you query a remote table via SQL Link, Paradox translates your query to SQL syntax (which in turn explains why there are restrictions on the query form—SQL simply does not offer the full range of capabilities that Paradox offers in this arena). If you would like to see how your Paradox query looks when translated to SQL, press Show SQL (Alt-F2). You'll see the SQL query statement in a box at the bottom of the screen. If you are familiar with SQL, this will let you determine whether or not the query to be performed is indeed the query you had in mind at the outset.

When you are through viewing the SQL version of your Paradox query, press any key to clear the SQL Query box and return to the query form.

Saving Remote Queries

You can save a remote SQL query just as you would any other query. However, with SQL Link you have two options: you can select Scripts, QuerySave from the menu in the usual manner to save the query as a PAL QUERY...ENDQUERY command, or you can select Tools, SQL, SQLSave to save the query as a PAL SQL...ENDSQL command.

In either case, you can play back the query in the future by playing the script by itself from the Scripts menu or by embedding the script in a PAL application.

USING REPORTS WITH SQL LINK

You can design and change Paradox reports for remote tables using the usual Reports, Design or Reports, Change options from the Main menu. You cannot design multitable reports from remote tables, but you can query remote tables and use the resulting (local) Answer table to design a multitable report.

USING FORMS WITH SQL LINK

You can use Paradox forms to create custom screens for use with the Modify, DataEntry options on a remote table. Just select the Forms, Design or Forms, Change options from the Main menu as usual.

You cannot create a multitable form for a remote table. But you can query the remote table(s) and use the resulting local Answer table to build a multitable form.

USING TOOLS WITH SQL LINK

When using SQL Link, you can use only the following options on the Tools menu to manipulate remote tables:

Copy: To copy remote or local tables.

Delete: To delete remote or local tables.

More, Add: To copy records from one table to another (any combination of remote/local tables is acceptable).

More, Empty: To remove all the records from a remote or local table.

More, Protect: To password-protect the *replica* (local copy of the table).

These options work as they do in normal Paradox (see Chapter 16) and provide options for managing remote tables as well as manual ones.

When using Paradox SQL Link, the Tools menu also offers the option SQL. This menu offers more advanced SQL options such as transaction processing support. Most likely, if you are a user of Paradox SQL Link, many SQL operations have probably already been automated, so you should see the database administrator for information on using more advanced SQL features. If you are the database administrator, please see the *SQL Link User's Guide* that comes with the Paradox SQL Link package or a more advanced book for additional information on Paradox SQL Link.

MEMORY MANAGEMENT

Paradox 3.5 is designed to take advantage of the sophisticated memory capabilities of modern computers. Like other Borland products, Paradox 3.5 uses Borland's own VROOMM (Virtual Runtime Object-Oriented Memory Manager) technology to manage extended or expanded memory in order to maximize speed. Paradox manages your computer's memory automatically and behind the scenes; so don't feel that you need to understand VROOMM to use Paradox 3.5 effectively.

However, if you are the program installer or network administrator, there are a few things you might want to know about how Paradox 3.5 uses memory. First, in case you are not already fully familiar with things like real and protected mode, we'll discuss those concepts in general.

The original IBM PCs and XTs (as well as DOS) were based on the 8086 (or 8088) microprocessor, which had a limit of 1Mb addressable memory. The first 640K of that was RAM; the rest was used as ROM or other "extra" memory above 640K. Due to the physical design of the 8086 or 8088 processor, it was virtually impossible to address memory beyond 1Mb (because 20 bits were used to address memory, and 2^{20} is 1,048,576—one megabyte).

Later microprocessors, such as the 80286 used in the AT class of computers, the 80386, and the 80486, offered memory well beyond 1Mb. Unfortunately, DOS was never designed to use this extra memory, and so initially it was wasted (though you could use extended memory above 1Mb as a RAM disk or a disk cache to improve the overall performance of the system to some extent, particularly in DOS versions 3.3 and later).

EXPANDED MEMORY

In order to circumvent these limitations, some standardized methods of allowing DOS applications programs to use memory beyond

NETWORKS, SQL LINK, AND MEMORY MANAGEMENT   659

1Mb were devised. Those standards are now known as

- EMS 3.2 or EMS 4.0, the Expanded Memory Specification (also called LIM for Lotus, Intel, and Microsoft, the companies that created it).
- EEMS, the Enhanced Expanded Memory Specification.

or simply as *expanded memory* (not extended memory).

These expanded memory solutions use a 16K "window" of memory above 640K (a 16K page frame to be specific), but below 1Mb, as a "switching area." Excess data is stored above 1Mb, then swapped into and out of the 16K page frame on an as-needed basis. While the expanded memory manager manages all this swapping of memory, the DOS application program runs normally, largely oblivious of all this swapping.

Expanded memory gives DOS application programs access to lots of extra RAM, but one problem remains. All of this swapping takes time and slows things down a bit. Furthermore (with all due respect to the creators of the complex expanded memory model), expanded memory is something of a kludge, and does not really take advantage of two important features of the 80286 and 80386 microprocessors—real mode and protected mode.

Kludge is an electronics term meaning a temporary trick or splint to fix a problem, as opposed to a clean, proper design.

In fact, expanded memory is generally sold as a memory board. To use it, you need to physically place this board in your 8086 or 80286 computer, then use a *device driver* (a DEVICE = command in your CONFIG.SYS file) to activate the board. On an 80386, you can emulate expanded memory with extended memory so that no extra board is required, but let's back up for a moment and discuss extended memory.

EXTENDED MEMORY

Extended memory is memory that can be used directly by the 80286 or 80386 microprocessor (no such memory exists for 8086 processors). There is no need to install an extra board, use a device driver, or do any swapping. Hence, extended memory is preferred because it is a simpler, cleaner, and more straightforward design.

But extended memory is designed with the notion that several programs can be running simultaneously (called *multitasking*), which brings up a new set of memory management problems. If several different programs are running simultaneously, and using the same memory, how do you keep them out of one another's way, and prevent them from trying to use the same chunks of memory?

Well, you cannot expect all of the software manufacturers to "claim rights" to certain parts of memory, so you need some sort of a memory management scheme that protects various running programs from crashing into one another.

That scheme is referred to as running in the *protected mode* (as opposed to *real mode*). No program is allowed direct access to extended memory until it is running in protected mode. Version 3.5 of Paradox is the first version of Paradox that can run in protected mode, and thus is the only version of Paradox that can take direct advantage of the extended memory of your 80286 or 80386 processor, and thereby run at the fastest speeds.

JUDICIOUS USE OF MEMORY

When you first install Paradox, it automatically figures out the best way to use the capabilities, based on the following:

- If you have an 8086 computer without expanded memory, Paradox will run in real mode, and use VROOMM to use the available 512–640K as efficiently as possible.

- If you have an 8086 or an 80286 or higher processor with properly installed expanded memory, Paradox will run in real mode, but use all the available expanded memory as efficiently as possible.

- If you have an 80286 or higher processor with extended memory, Paradox will try to run in protected mode, and use all of the available extended memory to run as quickly and efficiently as possible.

It is quite possible for a single computer to have both extended and expanded memory. For example, with an 80386 computer, you can use a device driver (a DEVICE = command in your CONFIG.SYS file) to emulate expanded memory in a portion of your extended memory. When this is the case, Paradox will still run in protected mode and take advantage of whatever extended memory is available. In fact, the more extended memory available, the better.

WHAT ABOUT YOUR COMPUTER?

You can use the Custom script to find out more about your computer and how Paradox is running on it. Assuming you have already installed Paradox and it is running right now, follow these steps:

1. Press F10 to access the Main menu (if it is not already displayed).
2. Select Scripts, then Play.
3. Type **Custom** and press Enter.
4. Select Tune.
5. Select MachineInfo.

You can then select either Basic or Detailed to see information about your computer (or you might try printing a copy of each). After you make a selection, you'll have the option of displaying the results on the screen, printing, or storing them in a DOS text file for future use. Choose any option and follow the prompts on the screen. You can select Return from the SubMenus at any time to return to the Custom script main menu. Then select DO-IT! (to save any changes) or Cancel (to abandon any changes) to get back to the Paradox Main menu.

COMPATIBILITY ISSUES

Note that even if you have an 80286 or higher processor and plenty of extended memory, Paradox might still be running in real mode.

There could be several reasons for this:

- Another device driver is using memory between 640K and 1Mb as shadow RAM. Paradox cannot use extended memory until you remove the CONFIG.SYS device driver that creates the shadow RAM.
- An incompatible memory manager is in use. For example, if you have used a device driver to convert all extended memory to expanded memory, Paradox won't have any extended memory to work with.

Also note that if you start Paradox from Windows 3.0 (perhaps as a windowed non-Windows Application using a PIF file), the Windows XMS memory manager might force Paradox to run in real mode. However, if you exit Windows 3.0 and start Paradox from the DOS command prompt, it may then run in protected Mode because the XMS memory Manager is not in full control. Again, you can use the MachineInfo option described above at any time to see how Paradox is running at the moment.

Additional information about configuring Paradox 3.5 to run on your computer is included in the *Paradox 3.5 Upgrade Guide* that comes with the Paradox 3.5 package. Also, for late-breaking news on this topic, and current compatibility with other products such as DESQView and Windows 3.0, see the README file on your \PDOX35 directory. To do so, go to the \PDOX35 directory (or wherever you stored Paradox 3.5), and at the DOS command prompt type **README** and press Enter. If you need help in using the README program, press F1.

CUSTOMIZING PARADOX

APPENDIX C

WHEN YOU INSTALL PARADOX, IT AUTOMATICALLY determines numerous default settings for various options, such as screen colors, date formats, and so forth. These defaults are the most commonly used settings, but they are not necessarily the right ones for every user. Therefore, Paradox offers the Custom Configuration Program (abbreviated CCP), which allows you to make changes to these default settings.

You can change the default settings at any time. Once you do change a default setting, the new setting becomes the default for all future Paradox sessions—unless, of course, you change the default again in the future. Remember, changing the default settings is entirely optional. If you are happy with the way Paradox is running on your computer, you can ignore everything in this appendix.

RUNNING THE CUSTOM CONFIGURATION PROGRAM

To run the CCP, follow these basic steps:

1. If you have not already done so, start Paradox in the usual manner (as described in Chapter 2).
2. Press F10 to get to the Main menu.
3. Select Scripts.
4. Select Play.
5. Type **Custom**, or press ⏎ and move the highlighter to Custom.
6. Press ⏎.

As an alternative to the above steps, you can run Paradox and the CCP directly by switching to the directory that Paradox is stored on and typing **PARADOX CUSTOM** at the DOS command prompt (don't forget to press ← after typing the command).

Either method of starting the CCP will bring you to the CCP Main menu, which displays the options listed below:

> Tune Video Reports Graphs Defaults Int'l Net PAL
> Ascii DO-IT! Cancel

You make choices from these menus as you do in all other Paradox menus—either by using the arrow keys to position the highlighter to the option desired and pressing ←, or by typing the first letter of the option you want to select. Either method will typically take you to a submenu. (On all submenus, the Return option takes you back to the CCP Main menu.)

On the CCP Main menu, selecting DO-IT! saves any changes you have made and takes you back to the Paradox Main menu. Selecting Cancel also exits the CCP and returns you to the Paradox Main menu, but without saving any changes or selections you made while in the CCP.

For the remainder of this appendix, we'll discuss what each of the various options on the CCP Main menu lets you do.

FINE TUNING PARADOX FOR YOUR HARDWARE

The Tune option on the CCP Main menu lets you choose how Paradox is executed on your computer, as discussed in Appendix B. When you select Tune, you'll see the options below:

> MachineInfo ProtectedMode Return

Each of these options is summarized in the sections that follow.

MACHINEINFO

Choosing MachineInfo analyzes your computer system and produces a report that includes:

Processor type

Presence of a coprocessor

Amount of conventional memory

Type of monitor

Presence and type of mouse

Presence of EMS or Extended memory

Disk drives available and whether local or shared

Contents of the CONFIG.SYS file

Contents of the AUTOEXEC.BAT file

This report, at your option, can be sent to the screen, printer, or a file. The Basic and Detailed submenu choices determine how much information will be supplied.

PROTECTEDMODE

The ProtectedMode submenu contains the following choices:

Configure   DefaultMode   Return

Each of these is discussed in the sections that follow.

Configure

> If you are using Paradox on a network, the network administrator is usually the only person that can change the Paradox configuration.

The Configure option displays choices only if you have not configured Paradox previously—via the CCP or the Paradox Install program. If Paradox has already been configured for use on your computer, selecting this option simply displays how Paradox is currently configured; it does not let you make any changes.

If Paradox is not already configured to your hardware, you'll see a message to this effect whenever you start Paradox. In that case, you can use the Configure option to let Paradox determine the best way to run on your hardware. However, you need to use this option with caution. You should first make sure that there are no memory-resident (TSR) programs currently in memory. Once you start the CCP, don't perform any operations other than the protected mode configuration.

If you do opt to configure Paradox yourself, selecting this option will take you through a series of tests that help Paradox determine how best to run on your hardware. Follow the instructions that appear on the screen to complete these tests.

If you find that the keyboard becomes locked (i.e., the computer ignores your keypresses), reboot by pressing (and holding down) the Ctrl, Alt, and Delete (Del) keys. After the computer reboots, run Paradox and the CCP again, and select the Tune and Configure options again. The tests will resume where you left off.

DefaultMode

Choosing DefaultMode lets you determine whether Paradox starts in real or protected mode. Protected mode is available only on computers with 80286, 80386, or 80486 microprocessors. If you have one of these processors and at least 1Mb of extended (not total) memory, protected mode is probably the better choice. The aforementioned Configure option automatically determines the best way to run in protected mode on your computer.

The Return option takes you back to the previous menu.

CHANGING THE SCREEN DISPLAY

Choosing Video from the CCP Main menu lets you change the way Paradox appears on your screen. When you select Video, you will see the submenu shown below:

Monitor   Snow   Colors   NegativeColors   FormPalette
Return

Use these choices to determine the appearance of Paradox's displays on your monitor, as described in the sections below.

MONITOR

The Monitor choice permits you to override the type of monitor detected by Paradox. You could use this, for example, if you are using a monochrome monitor with a CGA video adapter. Your choices are:

Mono: Monochrome monitor and monochrome video adapter.

B&W: Monochrome monitor and color video adapter.

Color: Color monitor and color video adapter.

SNOW

If you see "snow" (annoying white dots that appear in bursts) on the screen when the display is altered and you are using an IBM CGA adapter, select this option and respond with Yes. This response will cause information to be changed on the display at a slightly slower rate, so don't use it unless it is necessary.

COLORS

The Colors option lets you change the screen colors that Paradox uses, including the color of the workspace, menu, prompt line, check marks, field values, and so forth. When you select Colors, you'll see a submenu with the following options:

Design   Change   PickSetting   Tools   Help   Return

Each of these options is described in the sections below.

Design

The Design option lets you create up to ten color schemes. The default color scheme is named Standard, but you can define up to nine other color schemes, numbered 1 through 9. For example, if several people share the same computer, each person can set up his or her own color scheme and readjust all the screen colors simply by selecting his or her color scheme rather than going through all the laborious steps of defining individual colors.

When you select Design, your first option will be to select which color scheme you want to define. You must select one of the unused schemes (the Change option described below lets you change an existing color scheme). You'll then be prompted to enter a description for the new color scheme you are creating. This can be any name up to 65 characters long. You will then be taken to the screen for setting up screen colors (See "Selecting Screen Colors" below).

Change

The Change option lets you modify an existing color screen. You can change the description, the color scheme, or both. When you select Change, you'll first be given the option of choosing which color scheme you want to modify, then you will be taken to the screen for selecting screen colors (as discussed below).

Selecting Screen Colors

After you've selected Design or Change from the Colors submenu and determined which color scheme you want to work with, you'll be taken to a screen that shows portions of various screens, as shown in Figure C.1.

You can use the arrow keys to move the blinking cursor to any portion of the sample screen you want to change the color of. A brief description of the current area ("menu background," for example) appears near the upper right corner of the screen.

▰ While at the color selection scheme, you can press F1 to get help.

To change the color of any portion of the screen, move the cursor to that portion and press ↲. This activates the color palette near the upper right corner of the screen. Within the palette, you choose a color combination by moving the blinking cursor with the arrow keys. The colors in the selected area will change as you move through various foreground/background color combinations on the palette. Also, the name of the current color combination ("Yellow on Blue," for example) appears near the upper right corner of the screen.

▰ The colors you specify while designing a custom form will override the default screen colors. If you want to change default graph colors of a graph, see "Changing Graph Defaults" later in this appendix.

When you've found a foreground/background color combination that you like, press ↲ to select it. You'll be returned to the sample screens, where you can select another area to color. You can color as many areas as you wish. When you've finished, press F10 to get to the menu, then select either DO-IT! (to save your work) or Cancel to return to the previous menu.

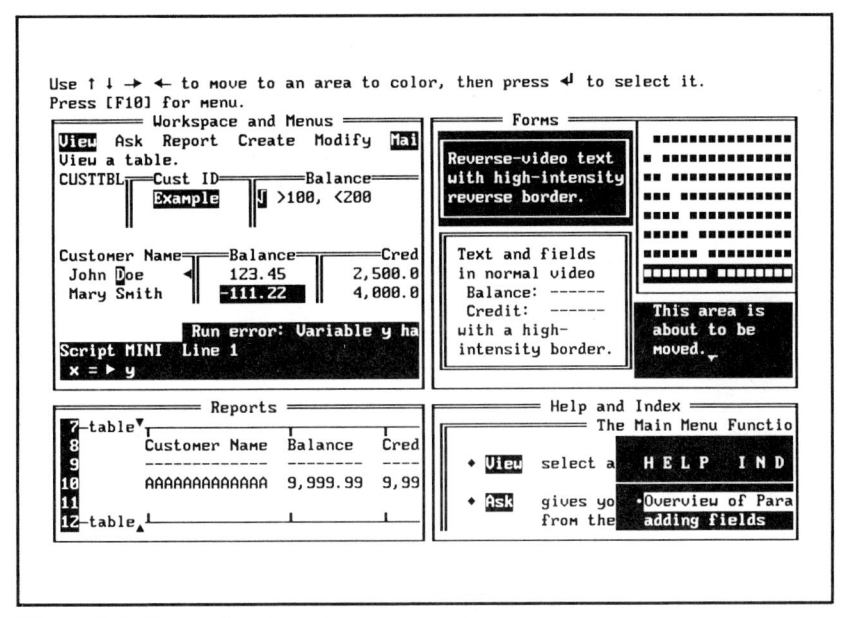

Figure C.1: Screen for changing screen colors.

PickSetting

The PickSetting option lets you determine which color scheme will be the default in future Paradox sessions. Normally the default is Standard color scheme, but the PickSetting option will let you change that to any other existing color scheme.

Tools

The Tools submenu has the following options:

NewName: Changes the letter or number designation of a color setting.

Copy: Lets you copy a color setting from one name (letter or number) to another.

Delete: Deletes a color setting by changing its colors back to the defaults and changing the description to "Unused."

As usual, the Return option takes you back to the previous menu.

NEGATIVECOLORS

The NegativeColors option on the Colors submenu lets you decide how negative numbers (and negative dollar amounts) are displayed. Normally, these are displayed in red, but you can change this by selecting the NegativeColors option. When you select this option, you'll be given the choices summarized below:

BothDifferent: Displays both negative numbers and negative currency amounts in a different color.

Numbers: Displays negative numbers only (not negative currency amounts) in a different color.

Currency: Displays negative currency amounts only (not negative numbers) in a different color.

Same: Does not display negative currency values and negative numbers in a different color.

> If you want to display negative numbers in a color other than red, change the color of −111.22 next to Mary Smith on the screen shown in Figure C.1.

FORMPALETTE

When you design custom forms (Chapter 9) and use the Style, Colors options to color part of a form, a small color palette automatically appears in the upper right hand corner of the screen, from which you can choose your colors. You can turn that palette on and off at any time by pressing Alt-C. This can be useful if you want to turn off the palette to view what's behind it. FormPalette gives you the following options:

Show: The color palette is displayed automatically when coloring a custom form.

Hide: The form color palette is not displayed automatically; the user must press Alt-C to see the palette.

CHANGING THE REPORT DEFAULTS

The Reports option on the CCP Main menu lets you choose default setting for custom reports. Of course, the CCP lets you change only the default settings. When you are designing a specific

CUSTOMIZING PARADOX   673

> To change printing options for graphs, see "Changing Graph Defaults" later in this appendix.

report, you can easily override any defaults for that particular report using options on the Settings menu (Chapter 8).

When you select Reports from the CCP Main menu, you'll see the following submenu:

> PageWidth   LengthOfPage   Margin   Wait   GroupRepeats
> Setups   FormFeed   Return

Each of these options is summarized below.

PAGEWIDTH

Use PageWidth to set the default for the number of columns on a page. The original default is 80 (10 characters to the inch across an 8-inch page). If you were using 11-inch wide paper, you'd want to change this setting to 110.

LENGTHOFPAGE

The LengthOfPage choice is used to set the default for the number of lines per page. The original default is 66; that is, 6 lines per inch on an 11 inch page. You can enter a new page length in the range of 2 to 2000, or you can enter **C** (for continuous) where paper is treated as one long page, as when printing on mailing labels, checks, and other preprinted forms.

MARGIN

Use Margin to set the default width of the left margin. The original default is 0, meaning that Paradox will start printing at the left edge of that page (that is, as far to the left edge of the page as the printer can reach).

To change the margin, select Margin and you will see the current margin setting. You can erase the existing setting by pressing Backspace. Then type in a new setting, measured in characters. For example, if you want a one-inch margin, and your printer prints 10 characters to the inch, you would type in 10, then press ↵.

WAIT

If you want Paradox to pause between printed pages to give you time to insert a new page, select Wait, then Yes. To have Paradox print continuously, select No.

GROUPREPEATS

Paradox lets you decide whether or not you want repetitive group values to be printed (as when printing a detailed report with data, subtotals, and totals). Additionally, you can have only the first of the repetitive values printed (as when printing a summary report with subtotals and totals only).

To change the default setting for this option, select GroupRepeats, then either Retain (to print repeated values) or Suppress (to not print repeated values). As with all report defaults, you can change this setting for an individual report using options in the Settings menu while designing the report.

SETUPS

When you choose Setups you are supplied with the Printer table. You can then add, change, or delete printer assignments.

When you access this table for the first time, you will find a list of printer names. Those names will be consecutively numbered, assigned to the port LPT1, and followed by an optional printer setup string. Table values can be added, modified, or deleted just as you would in any Paradox table. The default printer setup is marked by an asterisk in the table.

You can change the name, default indicator, port, or setup string for any printer. If you wish, you can have several printers in the list with the same name, but different numbers and setup strings—perhaps one for regular sized characters, another with a setup string for condensed mode. (Setup strings for printers vary greatly; see your printer manual for more information.)

The printer name cannot consist of over 20 characters and no spaces are permitted. The valid port designations are LPT1, LPT2, LPT3, COM1, COM2, PRN, and AUX. Setup strings can consist of no more than 50 characters. To indicate the Escape character use \027. Thus for Escape L use \027L. Use this same system for any other unprintable characters. For example, Ctrl-A is \001, Ctrl-B is \002, and so forth up to Ctrl-Z, which is \026.

To choose one of the setup strings as the default for all future printed reports, just type an asterisk at the end of its name. Be sure to also remove any other asterisks, since only one setup string can be designated as the default.

FORMFEED

The FormFeed submenu choices permit using linefeeds (No) or a formfeed to move to the top of the next page (Yes). Generally, the default setting (No) is fine. However, if you have a laser printer and its manufacturer recommends using a formfeed rather than linefeeds to eject pages, you can select this option and change its setting to yes. Future reports will use a formfeed to eject pages.

CHANGING GRAPH DEFAULTS

The CCP lets you change default settings for various aspects of displaying and printing graphs. When you select Graphs from the CCP Main menu, you'll see these options:

> GraphSettings   Printers   Screen   Return

These options are described in the sections that follow.

GRAPHSETTINGS

The GraphSettings option can be used to change the defaults used to display graphs on the screen and to print graphs. See the discussion in Chapter 10 of the various Customize Graph forms for explanations and examples of ways in which you can modify a graph. In the CCP, you'll be changing the default settings for all future graphs, but you can override those defaults for any particular graph using the Image, Graph, Modify options from the Paradox Main menu.

After you select GraphSettings, press F10 to access the submenu of default settings that you can change. The options are summarized in the following list:

Type: Determines the default graph type, and default override graph type.

Overall: Sets the defaults for titles, axes, grids, screen and printer colors, page layout, and output devices. Overall has a submenu of its own consisting of the following options:

Titles: Sets defaults for the font and size of graph titles and axis titles.

Colors: Sets up default colors for graphs displayed on the screen as well as for printed graphs.

Axes: Sets the default scaling values, tick mark measurements, and label formats.

Grids: Sets the default grid line colors and patterns, and also sets the graph frame color (or no frame).

PrinterLayout: Sets the defaults for unit of measurement (inches or centimeters), the graph margins, the graph size, the page orientation as either landscape (sideways) or portrait (vertical), page breaks, and plotter speed.

Device: Sets the default output for graphs to either Printer or File. If you choose Printer, you must then specify which printer to use. If you choose File, you must select one of the following formats: CurrentPrinter (has a .grf format and can usually be sent straight to the printer later using a DOS command like PRINT), EPS (Encapsulated PostScript), or PIC (Lotus 1-2-3 format).

Wait: Determines how long a graph is displayed on the screen and whether a keystroke is necessary to return to the workspace (the default).

Series: Sets the defaults for legends and labels, markers and patterns, and colors that affect series elements. Series also has a submenu, which consists of the options summarized below:

LegendsAndLabels: Sets defaults for displaying graph legends and series.

MarkersAndFills: Designates the markers and fill patterns.

Colors: Sets the screen and printer default colors, and also lets you copy the color scheme from screen to printer and vice versa.

Pies: Determines the default pie label format, fill patterns, colors, and whether or not a slice should be exploded.

Help: Information about graph settings.

Cancel: Cancels current changes and returns you to the previous menu.

As usual, the Return option takes you back to the previous menu.

PRINTERS

The Printers choice from the Graphs submenu lets you define up to four printers for printing graphs. When you first select this option, you'll see the submenu:

    1stPrinter   2ndPrinter   3rdPrinter   4thPrinter

Choose a printer to define, then you'll see the submenu:

    TypeOfPrinter   Settings   Return

These options are discussed in more detail below:

> High resolution produces crisper, finer print but takes much longer than lower resolution.

TypeOfPrinter: Select this option, then select the name of your printer's manufacturer from the list that appears. Next, select the printer model from the list of models that appears. If your printer offers several modes, such as low, medium, and high resolution, you'll also have a chance to select a mode.

Device: Select the port that the current printer is connected to. If it is a serial port, define the baud rate, parity, and stopbits on the next menu to appear (see your printer manual for recommended settings).

PrinterWait: Use this option to determine whether or not the printer pauses for a new page between printed pages.

Note that you can use the same printer, with different settings, for 1stPrinter, 2ndPrinter, and so forth. For example, 1stPrinter might be a laser printer with low resolution mode for quick printing of graphs. 2ndPrinter might be that same printer at high resolution for slower printing of final copies. When it comes time to print a graph in Paradox, you can use the Image, Graph, Modify, (F10), Overall, Device, Printer options to choose a printer just before printing the graph.

SCREEN

The Screen option lets you tell Paradox what kind of screen you have for displaying graphs. Choosing Auto from the submenu lets Paradox automatically detect and use the screen connected to your computer.

If you have more than one screen, or if you have a screen that offers various resolutions, you might want to select a different screen type. If so, select the Screen option to view other available screen types. Highlight the option that defines your screen and, if resolution options appear, select a resolution.

SETTING THE MISCELLANEOUS DEFAULTS

The Defaults selection on the CCP Main menu lets you set a variety of miscellaneous defaults. When you select this option you'll see the menu below:

SetDirectory   QueryOrder   Blank=Zero   AutoSave
DisableBreak   Return

SETDIRECTORY

Use the SetDirectory option to designate the default working subdirectory where Paradox stores and searches for tables, report formats, custom forms, and other files that you create.

Within Paradox, you can override this default using the Tools, More, Directory options from the Main menu.

QUERYORDER

You can make the Answer tables sensitive to rotation with this selection. Your choices are ImageOrder and TableOrder. If you choose ImageOrder, the Answer table fields are displayed in the same order as they are in the Query form; TableOrder arranges them according to their sequence in the underlying table structures. If in doubt try TableOrder. ImageOrder is generally appropriate for graphs and crosstabs.

BLANK=ZERO

Normally, any calculation that attempts to use a blank field value will end up with a blank result. For example, suppose that a table has three fields named Qty, UnitPrice, and Tax (where Tax is a sales tax rate such as 0.065).

Suppose further that you have included a calculated field in a report that uses the expression *[Qty] * [UnitPrice] * (1 + [Tax])* to calculate the total sale. When printing the report, any records that have a blank in the Tax field will not calculate the total sale (even if the Tax field was intentionally left blank to indicate no tax).

If you change the Blank = Zero default option from No to Yes, Paradox will treat blank numeric fields as zero. Thus, in the example just described, total sales would be calculated for all records, even those with blanks in the Tax field.

Treating blanks as zeroes is generally safe in calculations that multiply field values, since any number times zero is just zero. However, when a field is used for addition, subtraction, or division, treating blanks as zeros can lead to errors that are not immediately noticeable. For example, if our total sale formula included a shipping charge, like

([Qty] * [UnitPrice] * (1 + [Tax])) + Shipping, and the Shipping field were left blank (by accident), the formula would still be calculated and its result displayed with the shipping charge assumed to be zero. If, however, Paradox were not treating blanks as zeros, the missing shipping charge would cause the calculation to display a blank result and might thereby call attention to an error or omission.

AUTOSAVE

Paradox automatically saves your new data from time to time to minimize data loss in the event of a power failure or other mishap. The AutoSave option determines how frequently Paradox performs automatic saves. If you set the AutoSave option to Yes, Paradox saves your work frequently, particularly during lulls in your typing. If you change the setting to No, Paradox performs automatic saves less frequently. The original default setting for this option is Yes.

DISABLEBREAK

Whenever you are using Paradox, you can press Ctrl-Break at any time to interrupt a time-consuming process. However, pressing Ctrl-Break can cause other strange behavior on networks and on some nonstandard keyboards.

If you want to disable the interruption capability of the Ctrl-Break key, select DisableBreak, then Disable.

CHANGING INTERNATIONAL DEFAULTS

The Int'l (International) option on the CCP Main menu lets you change several International defaults. When you select Int'l, you will be taken to a submenu displaying the options summarized below:

DateFormat: Lets you choose a format for displaying Paradox dates: mm/dd/yy (e.g., 12/31/90), dd-Mon-yy (e.g., 31-Dec-90), or dd.mm.yy (31.12.90).

NumberFormat: Lets you choose a format for displaying numbers and currency values.

USFormat: Uses periods for decimal points and commas to separate thousands (e.g., 123,456.78).

InternationalFormat: Uses commas for decimal points and periods to separate thousands (e.g., 123.456,78).

CHANGING NETWORK DEFAULTS

The Net option on the CCP Main menu lets you change default settings at the current workstation. When you select this option, you'll see the following submenu:

UserName   SetPrivate   AutoRefresh   Return

Each option is described in more detail below.

USERNAME

The UserName option sets the default network user name for the current workstation. This is the name that other users see if they try to gain access to an object that you've locked.

If your network operating system supports user names, Paradox will use those user names if you do not specify a user name within Paradox, either through the CCP or by using the Tools, Net, UserName options at the Paradox Main menu.

SETPRIVATE

The SetPrivate option, used only on a network, lets you choose a private directory for the current workstation. Each workstation must have its own private directory for storing temporary tables such as Answer and Keyviol. Typically, this is the \PDOX35 directory on the local hard disk.

When specifying a private directory, be sure to include both the drive and directory name, e.g., C:\PDOX35.

AUTOREFRESH

The AutoRefresh option designates the interval between the screen refreshes, which allow all network users to see one another's changes to table data. The default setting for this refresh interval is every three seconds. You can change this to any value from 1 second to 3600 seconds (one hour), or you can leave it blank, which disables the automatic refreshing.

The Return option, as usual, takes you back to the CCP main menu.

SETTING PAL DEFAULTS

The PAL submenu lets you control secondary indexes, change to an external editor, and control the way errors in calculated fields are handled. The submenu looks like this

MaintainIndexes   Editor   CalcDebug   Return

and its options are described below.

MAINTAININDEXES

The MaintainIndexes option lets you choose whether secondary indexes (QuerySpeed files) are adjusted on a record-by-record basis (incrementally), or if the indexes are updated in groups (batch mode) only when they are about to be used. The incremental approach (the preset default) is preferred unless the table is so large that the index updating is slowing down your data entry and editing. If that's the case, you may want to try the batch mode, which will bring your data entry and editing speeds back to normal. You will, however, notice some delays when performing operations that require updated indexes (such as queries), because Paradox will update the indexes at that time.

After selecting MaintainIndexes, select No to switch to batch mode updating, or select Yes to use the incremental approach.

EDITOR

If you prefer to use a word processor or other outside editor rather than the PAL scripts editor, you can use this option to make that change. You can determine the amount of memory to use and pass along the script's name.

When you select the Editor option, you'll be prompted to enter an editor command. Type in the command you usually use to run your editor or word processor from the DOS command prompt. For example, should you wish to use Brief as the external editor (which is activated by the simple command **B**), you'd fill in the prompt as below:

   EDITOR COMMAND: B

Of course, Brief must be located in a directory in the DOS PATH so DOS can find it.

You can also pass along the script name if your editor or word processor has this capability. Just place a blank space and an asterisk next to the editor command, as below:

   EDITOR COMMAND: B *

Later when you use the Script, Edit options from the Paradox Main menu (or the PAL debugger), Paradox will send the name of the script you specify or the one you're debugging to the DOS command line.

If your editor can also accept a line number at the DOS command prompt, you can place double asterisks next to the editor command as below:

   EDITOR COMMAND: B **

When the editor is called from the PAL debugger, the debugger will replace the ** with the name of the script being debugged and the line number of the faulty line.

Normally, your external editor receives the same amount of memory it would receive if you accessed DOS with the Tools, More, ToDOS options. This, however, might not be enough for some large word processors or for editing very large scripts. If you need more memory for your external editor, place an exclamation mark before the editor command as below:

```
EDITOR COMMAND: !B *
```

This supplies the external editor with the larger amount of RAM available when DOS Big (Alt-O) is used (see Chapter 16).

If you use a word processor rather than a text editor, you must remember to save the script as an ASCII file, not as a formatted word processing document. Paradox cannot read the hidden codes that word processors place in their documents. For example, if you use WordPerfect, you must save the script using the Ctrl-F5, Dos Text, Save options, and then make sure not to save the file again while exiting WordPerfect.

Remember to return to Paradox from your editor; don't just turn off the computer when you've finished editing. It is not a good idea to run other programs from your editor while Paradox is suspended. To revert to the built-in editor, run CCP again and remove the editor command line.

CALCDEBUG

The CalcDebug option lets you determine how errors in calculated fields are handled. When selected, it displays the following options:

```
ToggleMessage   ErrorString   Return
```

When an error occurs in a calculated field, no error message is normally displayed and the field is filled with blanks. If you select On from the ToggleMessage option, an error message will be shown when an error occurs in a calculated field.

If you wish the field to be filled with something other than blanks, select ErrorString and provide the character to use.

SETTING ASCII FILE DEFAULTS

When you import or export Paradox tables in ASCII format, you typically use a delimiter and separator to differentiate the fields. The default separator is the comma, placed between fields. The delimiter enclosing non-numeric fields is the quotation mark (''). AscII lets you change these and other settings. The submenu looks like this:

Delimiter   FieldsDelimited   Separator   ZeroFill
ChooseDecimal   Return

Use Delimiter to designate the delimiter character. Use FieldsDelimited to determine which fields are delimited. Separator allows you to change the default separator character. You can choose between Nothing and Zeros when you select ZeroFill. Nothing exports blank numeric fields as blanks (the default); Zeros exports a 0 instead. A decimal point can be imported or exported as a period (the default) or a comma.

SAVING CCP CHANGES

After making your selections and changes in the CCP, you can choose Return from the various submenus until you work your way back up to the CCP Main menu. Then select DO-IT! to save your changes and exit the CCP.

In most cases, you'll be returned all the way to the DOS command prompt, because Paradox can only activate the new defaults when it's first started from DOS. To rerun Paradox, type **PARADOX** and press ↵ as usual. You'll start at a blank workspace, as usual, with your new defaults in effect.

PARADOX COMMAND LINE CONFIGURATION

You can define some default settings at the DOS command prompt and override the defaults for the current session only. These options are sometimes used by advanced programmers to gain more control over how Paradox behaves in a given setting.

Command line options always begin with a space and hyphen followed by a command, and they are always placed to the right of the command used to start Paradox from the DOS command prompt. For example, entering the command

PARADOX -REAL

at the DOS command prompt starts Paradox and runs it in real (rather than protected) mode. You can combine these options as well. For example, the command

PARADOX -REAL -STACK 16

starts Paradox in real mode and sets its internal stack to a size of 16Kb. Command line options are described in more detail in the sections that follow.

COMMAND LINE VIDEO OPTIONS

There are four video options that you can activate at the command line:

-MONO: Notifies Paradox that a monochrome monitor is being used with a monochrome adapter.

-B&W: Tells Paradox that a monochrome monitor is being used with a color adapter or that you want to run Paradox in black and white.

-COLOR: Notifies Paradox that a color adapter and monitor (CGA, EGA, or VGA) are being used.

-SNOW: If you see snow (random white dots that appear in bursts) on the screen when its contents are altered and you are using an IBM CGA adapter, use this option to clear the snow.

EXPANDED MEMORY

The -EMK option is used to tell Paradox to restrict its use of expanded memory to a designated amount. (Normally, all available expanded memory is acquired.) To use it, a numeric value must be included, as below:

PARADOX -EMK 512

This tells Paradox to use only 512K of the available expanded memory. Use a value of 0 to indicate that no expanded memory should be used.

SWAPPING WITH EXTENDED MEMORY

This option is not to be used if Paradox is running in protected mode. You can use the -EXTK option followed by a numeric value to tell Paradox to employ a specific amount of extended memory. (Normally, all available extended memory is acquired.) For example

PARADOX -EXTK 512

tells Paradox to use only 512K of the available extended memory. Use a value of 0 to indicate that no extended memory should be used.

CACHE

Normally Paradox dynamically determines the best cache size to employ. To override this feature you can set the cache size with the -CACHEK option. Thus

PARADOX -CACHEK 64

sets the cache to 64K. However, it is best to let Paradox set the size dynamically.

STACK

It is possible to adjust the size of Paradox's internal stack if your PAL script contains unusually large nested computations. The option is -STACK followed by a numeric value. For example

PARADOX -STACK 16

sets the stack size to 16K. The default and minimum settings are the same—8K; the maximum is 64K.

MODE

To force Paradox to start in real mode, use -REAL. Protected mode is specified with -PROT. See "Fine Tuning Paradox for Your Computer" earlier in this appendix and Appendix B for additional information on real and protected modes.

SQL

If you have the Paradox SQL Link installed, Paradox will normally start with the link active. If you use

PARADOX -SQL ON

Paradox will not run if the link is not installed and operable. Use

PARADOX -SQL OFF

to ensure the link will not be activated, even if it is available. (Paradox handles some table operations more quickly if the link is not active.)

TABLE BUFFERS

Normally, the table's block size determines the table buffer size. The default minimum buffer size is 24K. To alter this minimum value, use -TABLEK followed by a numeric value. Thus

PARADOX -TABLEK 36

sets the minimum buffer size to 36K. A larger buffer size results in better performance. However, once a buffer is allocated the memory is not recovered for reuse by Paradox. Thus a smaller minimum size can tie up less memory. Remember, Paradox can always allocate a larger buffer than the minimum, but never a smaller.

NETWORK

There are three network related options:

-USERNAME: Determines the network user identification. For example, **PARADOX -USERNAME GLENDA** defines the current username as Glenda.

-SHARE: Tells Paradox to emulate network operation on a single machine so you can take advantage of some network features such as table protection or use multitasking to emulate a network.

-NET: Changes the path to the Paradox.NET file. This path is normally found in the Paradox.SOM file. Thus

    PARADOX -NET C:\NETSTUFF

tells Paradox to look for the Paradox.NET file on a directory named Netstuff on local drive C. This might come in handy when you are having low memory problems on a network and want to run Paradox on a single-user computer without loading the network drivers.

INDEX

~ (tilde variable), 582
! (exclamation point)
  as inclusion operator, 304–305
  in Picture formats, 74
" (quotation marks), 127, 345–346, 444, 479
(number symbol), 74–75
& (ampersand), 74–75
( ) (parentheses), 305, 341–343
* (asterisk), 24, 71, 74–75, 280, 435
+ (plus operator), 305, 341–345
, (comma)
  in custom menus, 478–479
  in delimited ASCII files, 444–445
  in group expressions, 382
  in number formatting, 55
  in Picture formats, 74–75
  in queries, 108, 111–112, 124
- (hyphen), 76, 305, 341, 343
.. (periods), 117–118
/ (slash), 305, 341
: (colon), 479
; (semicolon), 74–75
< (less-than operator), 108
< = (less-than-or-equal-to operator), 108
> (greater-than operator), 108
> = (greater-than-or-equal-to operator), 108
? (question mark), 74–75, 435, 464
@ (at symbol), 74–75, 117–118, 464
[ ] (square brackets), 74–75, 341–342
\ (backslash), 176, 345
{ } (curly braces), 74–76

ACCEPT command, 464, 467–468
Action menu, 576–577
Add option, 414, 417, 425–426
adding records
  on networks, 637–638
  to remote tables, 654
  using Edit key (F9), 42–44
  using Form View (F7), 35–38
  using Modify/DataEntry option, 27–35
addition operator (+), 305, 341–345
adjustment transactions, 419, 607–609
AllCorrespondingFields option, 286
alphanumeric data, 18–19
  in calculated fields, 344–347
  formatting, 338
  justifying, 352–353
  range operators with, 108–109
Alt-F3 key (Instant Script Record), 260, 328
Alt-F4 key (Instant Script Play), 260
Alt-F5 key (Field View), 33–34, 65
Alt-F6 key (Check Plus), 103–104
Alt-F7 key (Instant Report), 62, 102
Alt-F8 key (Clear All), 101, 256, 299
Alt-F10 key (PAL menu), 260, 532
Alt-X key (CrossTab shortcut), 250–251
AlwaysSign option, 173
American Standard Code for Information Interchange. *See* ASCII codes; ASCII files
Ampersand (&), 74–75
And/Or searches, 112–116, 302–304
Answer tables, 102–103
  clearing, 103
  copying report formats to, 168–170
  creating graphs from, 204, 208, 213
  printing from, 102, 169
  record numbers in, 102
  sort order in, 102, 104–105
AppendDelimited option, 444–445
applications, 493, 561
area graphs, 209–210
arithmetic operators, 121, 305–306
arrays, 541
arrow keys, 13, 19–20, 49–50
  in designing report formats, 136
  exaggerating movement of, 49–50
  with query forms, 102
ASCII codes, 176
ASCII files, 444–453, 684–685
Ascii option, 444, 446–447, 449
Ask option, 101, 295. *See also* queries
asterisk (*)
  for designating key fields, 24, 280
  multiple (***), 71
  in Picture formats, 74–75
  as wild cards, 435
at symbol (@)
  as PAL command, 464
  in Picture formats, 74–75
  in searches, 117–118
AUTOEXEC.BAT file, 626–627
automatic fill-in, 284–290
automatic scripts, 261, 523–524
automatic updating, 409–421
automatic validation, 72–79

INDEX 691

AutoSave option, 680
auxiliary passwords, 430

backslash (\\), 176, 345
Backspace key, 19-20
bar graphs, 206-208
BEEP command, 477
BeginRecord option, 255-256, 258-259
blank lines
   with BLANKLINE keyword, 355
   deleting. *See* Ctrl-Y key
   inserting, 137, 366-367
blank operator, 117, 120
BLANKLINE keyword, 355
blanks
   calculating as zeros, 347
   deleting, 146-148
   in query calculations, 326
Blank=Zero option, 679-680
borders, 189-190, 197-198
Borrow option, 590-592
Break key, 462, 531. *See also* Ctrl-Break key
bugs. *See* debugging

Calc option, 306-309
calculated fields, 340-347, 386-387
calculations
   crosstab, graphing, 242-251
   in custom forms, 386-387
   in groups of records, 307-308
   handling blanks in, 326
   in many-to-many designs, 314-319
   in queries, 305-327
   in reports, 240-249
Cancel option, 67-68, 147-148, 437
CASE command, 475, 477, 479-480
case sensitivity, 119
CCP. *See* Custom Configuration Program
Changed table, 124-125
changeto operator, 123-125
check marks, 102-103, 307-309
Check Plus key (Alt-F6), 103-104
CHECKPLUS command, 507
Checkprn.SC script, 545-546, 555
Checkprn2.SC script, 555-557
Clear All command (Alt-F8), 101, 256, 299
CLEAR command, 464
Clear Image key (F8), 62, 103, 299
Clear option, 77
CLEARALL command, 493-494
ClearPasswords option, 431
colon (:), 479

colors
   customizing, 669-672
   in forms display, 193-195
   in graphs, 222-224
   using PAL scripts to display, 464-480
Colors option, 669-672
columns, 3-4, 333-336
   aligning, 352-353
   copying, 336
   erasing, 334
   inserting, 333-334
   justifying, 352-353
   moving, 58-60, 335
   multiple, printing, 160
   resizing, 334-335
   width of, 52-54, 334-335
ColumnSize option, 52-54
comma (,)
   in custom menus, 478-479
   in delimited ASCII files, 444-445
   in group expressions, 382
   in number formatting, 55
   in Picture formats, 74-75
   in queries, 108, 111-112, 124
command line options, 685-689
commands, 463-480, 484-485
comments, 488
common fields, 267-271. *See also* key fields
condensed print, 173-176
Configuration option, 449
constant record numbers, 537-541
constants in calculated fields, 342
context-sensitive help system, 15
continuous-feed paper, 159-160, 167
Control (Ctrl) key as Turbo key, 49
copying
   custom forms, 199, 424
   with Ditto command, 35
   objects, 424, 567-568
   records, 425-426
   report formats, 155-156, 424
   scripts using PAL RUN command, 525
   tables, 424
   between tables, 425-426
Create option, 16-23, 570-571
CREATELIB command, 546-547
creating tables, 16-23
cross tabulations, 242-251
CrossTab option, 244-247, 249-251
Crosstab tables
   creating, 245-247
   graphing, 247-248
Ctrl key as Turbo key, 49

Ctrl-Backspace key, 156
Ctrl-Break key, 62, 167
Ctrl-D key (Ditto), 35
Ctrl-F6 key, 105
Ctrl-F7 key (Instant Graph), 202, 205
Ctrl-Pause key, 462
Ctrl-Q key, 463
Ctrl-R key (Rotate), 60, 104, 106, 335
Ctrl-U key (Undelete), 66-68
Ctrl-Y key, 137, 151
Ctrl-Z key (Zoom), 57, 68-69
curly braces ({}), 74-76
currency data, 19, 38, 73, 76, 143, 438
   field size limitation, 54
   formatting, 173, 339-343
   range groupings, 362-363
CurrentPrinter option, 241
Custom Configuration Program, 175-176, 237-238, 445
   ASCII file defaults, 684-685
   graph defaults, 675-678
   international defaults, 680-681
   miscellaneous defaults, 678-680
   network defaults, 681-682
   PAL defaults, 682-684
   printer defaults, 674-675
   report defaults, 672-675
   running, 665-666
   saving of defaults, 685
   screen display defaults, 668-672
custom forms, 181-199
   borders in, 189-190
   calculations in, 386-387
   canceling, 199
   changing, 196-198
   colors in, 193-195
   copying, 199, 424
   creating, 182-183
   cursor in, 184
   erasing parts of, 197-198
   help screens for, 191-193
   keys for, 184
   moving items in, 190-191
   multiple-page, 382-387
   multirecord, 389, 397-399
   multitable, 387-405
   placing fields in, 185-198
   placing text in, 184-185
   saving, 195
   using, 196
custom menus, 477-480
Custom option, 393
Custom script, 661

customizing help screens, 611

data, 3
data entry, 27-38, 42-45, 578-580, 586-589, 594-595, 637-638
Data Interchange Format (DIF), 443-444
data types, 18-19
database design, 265
   many-to-many, 272-277, 312-319
   one-to-many, 266-272
   one-to-one, 265-266
database servers, 652-653
database-management systems, 3
databases, 3-5, 7, 278-280
DataEntry option, 27-41, 44
date fields, 38-39, 54-55
   calculations in, 343-344
   column size limitation, 54
   formatting, 54-55, 170-171, 339
   placing, 350-351
Date option, 170-171, 337, 339
dates, 19
   default format, 681
   searching for, 107, 108-111, 120-121
   translating, 546-549
DAY function, 548
.DB filename extension, 41
dBASE files, 442
.DBF filename extension, 442
DEBUG command, 531
Debugger menu, 532
debugging, 462-463, 531-537
default directory, 432
default settings. *See* Custom Configuration Program
default values, 73
Define option, 72
Del key, 44, 68
Deleted tables, 126
deleting
   globally, 125-126
   objects, 425
   parts of a form, 197-198
   records, 44, 68, 426-427
   single records, 44, 68
   undoing, 68
Delimited option, 444-445
delimiters in WordPerfect, 448-449. *See also* Ascii option
dependencies, 278-279
Design option, 134
DIF (Data Interchange Format), 443-444

INDEX 693

directories
 changing defaults, 679
 on networks, 635–636
 in Personal Programmer, 567
 private, 635–636
 setting, 432
 viewing, 434–435
DisplayOnly option, 384–386
Ditto command (Ctrl-D), 35
DO-IT! key (F2), 22, 41, 44–45, 66. *See also* saving
DO_IT! command, 483–484, 500
dollar amounts, 541–545, 551–557. *See also* currency data
DOS, 453–454, 525–526, 567–568
 AUTOEXEC.BAT file, 626–627
 running scripts from, 523
DOS Big key (Alt-O), 454, 525
DOS text files, 444–453
dots (..), 117–118
Down Image key (F4), 299
duplicate entries, 103–104

ECHO command, 462
Edit key (F9), 42, 65
Edit menu, 67, 71–72
EditDel.SC script, 494, 515–518
editing, 65–72
 calculated fields, 347
 global, 122–126
 menu options for, 67, 71–72
 and MultiTable views, 585, 589–590
 on networks, 639
 PAL programs, 459–460, 463
 in Personal Programmer, 580–581, 589–590, 595
 procedure libraries, 551–557
 scripts, 260, 459–460, 463, 524–525
 from scripts, 513–518
 undoing, 66–68
 using Field View (Alt-F5), 33–34, 65–66
 using Form View (F7), 65
 using queries, 122–126
 using Table View, 42–44, 45
Editor option, 537
ELSE command, 473
Empty option, 414, 417, 427–428
emptying tables, 414, 417, 427–428
End key, 50–51
ENDIF command, 473–474, 511
ENDPROC command, 544, 547, 554
EndRecord option, 256
ENDSCAN command, 545
ENDTEXT command, 494, 495

ENDWHILE command, 469, 471
.EPS filename extension, 241
equal to operator (=), 108
erasing. *See* deleting
error messages, 463, 531
errors. *See* debugging
Escape key, 14
escape sequences, 176
Example key (F5), 297–298
examples, 295–299, 309–312
exclamation point (!)
 as inclusion operator, 304–305
 in Picture formats, 74–75
exiting Paradox, 23, 45
expanded memory, 658–659
exporting files
 in ASCII format, 444
 to dBASE, 442
 to Framework, 443
 to Lotus 1-2-3, 441
 for mailmerge applications, 447–453
 to Symphony, 441
 in VisiCalc format, 443–444
 to WordPerfect, 448–453
 to WordStar, 447–448
extended memory, 659–660, 687
external programs, running, 453–454, 525–526

F1 key (Help), 14–15
F2 key (DO-IT!), 22, 41, 44–45, 66
F3 key (Up Image), 299
F4 key (Down Image), 299
F5 key (Example), 297–298
F6 key (Checkmark), 102
F7 key (Form View), 35, 60–61, 65, 181
F8 key (Clear Image), 62, 102, 299
F9 key (Edit), 42, 65
F10 key (Menu), 14
family locks, 631
Family option, 435
field delimiters in WordPerfect, 448–449
Field Name area, 18
field names, 5–6, 18, 485
Field Type column, 18–19
Field View (Alt-F5), 33–34, 65
 editing from, 66, 102
 keys used, 34
fields, 4. *See also* columns
 calculated, 340–347, 386–387
 changing type of, 438–439
 common, 267–271
 for crosstabs, 248–250

date, 38–41, 54–55, 170–171, 343–344, 350–351
defining, 18–22
deleting, 157, 159, 437
display-only, 383–386
Ditto command in, 35
formatting, 338–340
grouping by, 361–362
key, 24, 267–269, 280–281, 376–377
lengthening, 438
naming, 5–6, 18
numeric, 38, 54–56, 172–173, 339–340
placing, 138–143, 170–172, 185–189, 337–352
rearranging, 437
regular, 340
renaming, 437
shortening, 438
sorting by, 83–84, 87–92
summary, 349–350
in tabular reports, 336–352
FieldSqueeze option, 147–148
File option, 150, 612–614
filename extensions
 .DB, 41
 .EPS, 241
 .GRF, 241
 .LIB, 547
 .PIC, 241
 .RPT, 447, 613
 .SC, 261
 .SET, 61
 .VAL, 78
files, 3. *See also* tables
 listing, 434–435
 printing to, 150
 summary of, in Personal Programmer, 612–614
Files option, 433–434
fill patterns, 231–233
FillNoHelp option, 286
Fillrec.SC script, 538–539
find operator, 122
Fixed option, 147
footers, 366–369
footing margins, 151
form bands, 135–136, 151–152, 159, 161, 171–172
form feeds, 159
form letters, 162–166
 using WordPerfect, 448–453
 using WordStar, 447–448
Form Toggle key (F7), 35, 60–61, 65, 181
Form View, 35–38, 60–61, 181

editing from, 65
keys used, 36–38
FORMAT command (PAL), 470
formatting fields, 54–56, 170–173, 338–340
forms, 181–199
 adding help to, 191–193
 adding records using, 35–38
 borders in, 189–190, 197–198
 calculations in, 386–387
 changing, 196
 copying, 199, 424
 creating, 182–183
 cursor movement in, 184
 description of, 183
 erasing parts of, 197–198
 moving items in, 190–191
 multiple-page, 382–387
 multirecord, 389, 397–399
 multitable, 387–405
 on networks, 641
 placing fields in, 185–189
 placing text in, 184–185
 reformatting fields in, 197
 for remote tables, 657
 removing borders from, 197–198
 saving, 195
 using, 196
Forms option, 181–182
Forms/Area/Erase option, 198
Forms/Area/Move option, 190–191
Forms/Border option, 189–190
Forms/Border/Erase option, 197–198
Forms/Change option, 191–193, 196
Forms/Design option, 182–183
Forms/Field/Erase option, 197
Forms/Field/Place option, 185–189
Forms/Style option, 193–195
FormView option, 579–580
Framework files, 443
Free-form option, 135
free-form reports, 135–173
frequency distribution, 308–310
functions, 484–485, 532–534

GETCHAR function, 464, 467–468, 511–512
global deletions, 125–126
global editing, 122–126
Go option, 460–461, 535
Graph key (Ctrl-F7), 202, 205, 216–218, 220, 232
 using, before printing graphs, 238
 viewing crosstabs with, 247–248

INDEX 695

Graph menu, 215
graphs
   axes in, 221, 224-228
   changing defaults, 675-678
   colors of, 222-224
   creating, from Answer tables, 204, 208, 213
   cross tabulation with, 242-251
   customizing, 214-221
   fill patterns in, 231-233
   grids in, 229-230
   instant, 202-203, 205, 216-218, 220, 232
   labels in, 221, 226-227, 231
   legends in, 221, 230-231
   mixing types of, 211-212, 213-214
   modifying, 220-221
   on networks, 641
   overall option, 222-230, 238-242
   printing, 236-242
   recalling, 219-220
   refining, 221-233
   scaling, 221, 224-226
   series in, 221, 230-233
   tick marks in, 221, 226
   titles in, 215-219
   types of, 204-214
   viewing. *See* Graph key
greater-than operator (>), 108
greater-than-or-equal-to operator (> =), 108
.GRF filename extension, 241
group bands, 357-361
group headings, 370
group keyword, 379, 381-382
Group menu, 361
groupby operator, 325-327
grouping, 356-371
GroupOfTables option, 372, 374
GroupRepeats option, 372-375
groups
   blank lines in, 366-367
   changing, 371
   deleting, 369-370
   footers in, 366-369
   headers in, 366-369
   headings for, 370
   inserting, 361-365
   sorting, 371

headers, 366-369
heading margins, 152
Help key (F1), 14-15
Help option, 71, 98
help screens, 14-15, 611
HelpAndFill option, 285-286, 402-403

HighValue option, 73
history tables, 409-410, 414, 417, 573
Home key, 50-51
hyphen (-)
   as minus operator, 305, 341, 343
   in Picture formats, 76

IBM Filing Assistant format, 443
IF...THEN...ELSE...ENDIF command clause, 472-474
image, 49
Image menu, 51
Image/ColumnSize option, 52-54
Image/Format option, 54-56
Image/Graph/Load option, 219
Image/Graph/Modify option, 215, 220, 222-233, 238-242
Image/Graph/ViewGraph option, 238
Image/KeepSet option, 61
Image/Move option, 58-60
Image/PickForm option, 61
Image/TableSize option, 51-52
Image/Zoom option, 56-58
importing
   ASCII files, 445-446
   dBASE files, 442
   Framework files, 443
   Lotus 1-2-3 files, 441-442
   Pfs files, 443
   Quattro files, 440-441
   Reflex files, 443
   Symphony files, 441-442
   VisiCalc files, 443-444
inclusion operator (!), 304-305
indentations, 488-489
INDEX command, 519-520
infinite loops, 471-472
Info option, 432-435
INFOLIB command, 546, 557
Init.SC script, 261, 523-524
Insert (Ins) key, 137
InsertDelete option, 581
inserting records, 43-44, 71
installing Paradox, 622-627
Instant Graph (Ctrl-F7), 202-203. *See also* Graph key
Instant Report (Alt-F7), 62, 102
Instant Script Play (Alt-F4), 260
Instant Script Record (Alt-F3), 260, 328
International option, 173, 680-681
inventory management system, 563-566, 570-598, 600-609, 613-614

Inventory option, 434–435
ISBLANK function, 516

JustCurrent field option, 285–286
JustFamily option, 170
justifying column data, 352–353

KeepSet option, 61
key fields, 24, 267–269, 280–281, 376–377. *See also* common fields; secondary indexes
key violations, 281–282, 425–426, 606
keyboard macros, 526–531
keys, 19–20
  for accessing menus, 13
  for changing column size, 53
  for custom forms, 184
  for data entry, 31–32
  for defining table structures, 19–20
  in Field View, 34
  in Form View, 36–37
  for keyboard macro codes, 527–528
  for modifying report formats, 136–137
  for multitable forms, 404
  names of, in scripts, 482–484
  for PAL command files, 459–460
  in Table View, 49–51
Keystroke option, 242
keystrokes, literal, 481
Keyviol tables, 281–282, 425–426, 606

labels. *See* graphs, labels on; mailing labels
laser printers, 160, 173, 528–529
leap years, 30
LegendsAndLabels option, 230–231
less-than operator (<), 108
less-than-or-equal-to operator (< =), 108
.LIB filename extension, 547
like operator, 117, 119
line graphs, 210–212
LineSqueeze option, 146–148, 160
linking tables, 272, 274, 276–277
literal data, 467
literal keystrokes, 481
locating records. *See also* queries
  using find operator, 122
  using Image/Zoom option, 56–58
locking objects, 629–635
login script, 650–651
Lookup option, 377–378, 582–583, 590–592, 595–596
loops, 468–472, 511
Lotus 1-2-3, 441–442, 525

lowercase type, 119
LowValue option, 72–73

MachineInfo option, 667
macros, 526–531
mailing labels, 155–161
  on continuous-feed paper, 159–160
  deleting a field from, 157, 159
  fine-tuning, 160–161
  formatting, 156–157
  multicolumn, 160–161
  printing, 159–161
mailing list application, 493–521
  Addnew.SC script for, 494, 498–500
  EditDel.SC script for, 494, 515–518
  Mail.SC script for, 493–497
  RepMenu.SC script for, 494, 504–513
  Sorter.SC script for, 494, 500–502
mailmerge files, 447–453
Mail.SC script, 493–497
Main menu, 12–14. *See also* menus
  defining, in Personal Programmer, 574–576
  sample application, 493–497
mainframe computers, querying, 652–658
Makelib.SC script, 547–549
many-to-many database design, 272–277, 312–319
MapUsers table, 648–650
margins, 151–152, 153–155
markers graphs, 211–212
master-table/transaction-table structure, 271–272
Mastinv table, 280–283, 571–572, 577–584
memory, 454
menu area, 12
menu structure. *See* menu trees
menu trees, 564–566
menus. *See also* Main menu
  assigning actions to, 576–577
  customizing, 574–598
  highlighting, 12–13
  selecting options from, 13
  unselecting options from, 14
  using, with scripts, 481
MESSAGE command, 538
message window, 12
minicomputers, querying, 652–658
MiniScript option, 535–536
minus operator (-), 305, 341, 343
MOD function, 474
Modify option, 27
Modify/DataEntry option, 27–33, 44–45
Modify/Edit/ValCheck option, 72

INDEX 697

Modify/Restructure option, 436
Modify/Sort option, 83
modulus, 474
MONTH function, 548
moving columns, 58-60, 335
multiple tables, 265-293
    many-to-many design, 272-277, 312-319
    one-to-many design, 266-272
    one-to-one design, 265-266
    outer joins in, 304-305
    printing reports from, 376-379
    querying, 295-304
    searching, 295-304
    updating, 409-421
    working inventory example, 280-292
multiple-page forms, 382-387
multirecord forms, 389, 397-399
multitable forms, 387-405
MultiTable views, 585-589

negative numbers, 38, 173
nested loops, 511
networks, 620, 629-635
    changing defaults, 681-682
    limiting access on, 629-635
    protecting data on, 642-651
    starting Paradox on, 629
    using Paradox on, 635-642
New option, 84, 91
NewEntries option, 445-446
Next option, 535
normalization process, 278-280
not blank operator, 121-122
not operator, 110, 117, 121-122
NRECORDS function, 509
number symbol (#), 74-75
numbers
    in Picture formats, 74-77
    translating into words, 541-545, 551-557
numeric fields, 19, 38, 54-56, 339-340
    calculations in, 340-343
    formatting, 54-56, 172-173, 339-340
NumLock key, 13
Numwords.SC script, 541-542, 554

objects, 423-425. *See also* files; reports; scripts; tables
one-to-many database design, 266-272
one-to-one database design, 265-266
Oops! option, 437
operators, 117
    arithmetic, 121, 305-306

range, 108-110
Or searches, 112-116, 302-304
OTHERWISE command, 475, 477
outer joins, 304-305
Output option, 145, 149-150
Overall option, 144, 222-230, 238-242, 349-350, 352

page bands, 135-136, 357-358
page breaks, 164-165
Page field, 351
Page Layout option, 152-153
Page Length option, 152-153
page numbers, placing, 171-172
Page option, 171-172
Page Width option, 153
PAGEBREAK keyword, 164
pages
    ejecting, from printer, 513, 528-529
    multiple, in custom forms, 382-387
    numbering options for, 171-172
    printing, in groups, 167
PAL canvas, 462
PAL menu (Alt-F10), 260, 532
PAL programs. *See also* scripts
    canceling, 462
    changing defaults, 682-684
    creating, 459-460
    debugging, 462-463, 531-537
    editing, 463
    running, 461-462
    sample, 493-521
    saving, 460-461
paper, continuous-feed, 159-160, 167
paper length, 178
Paradox
    exiting, 23, 45
    installing, 11, 622-624
    limitations of, 7-8
    programming in, 459, 488-489, 520
    referential integrity in, 405
    starting, 11-12
    suspending, temporarily, 453-454, 525-526
    system requirements, 621
Paradox Personal Programmer
    adding custom help screens, 611
    attaching custom scripts, 604-605
    copying objects for, 567-568
    creating applications, 570-598
    custom scripts for, 600-605
    entering, 568-570
    exiting, 600
    hardware requirements, 562, 625

installing, 624–625
limitations, 562–563
Main menu in, 569–570
managing key violations, 606
menu structure in, 564–566
modifying applications, 609–611
planning applications, 563–568
scripts for, 600–605
splash screens, 612
starting, 568–570
summarizing applications, 612–615
testing, 598–600
Paradox Runtime package, 561
ParenNegative option, 173
parentheses, 305, 341–343
partial dependencies, 278–279
password protection, 429–431
  on networks, 643–651
  for scripts, 524
  table-level, 643–646
PATH command (DOS), 626–627
pattern-matching searches, 116–122
PerGroup option, 349–350, 352, 369
periods (..), 117–118
Personal Programmer. *See* Paradox Personal Programmer
Pfs files, 443
PgDn key, 49–50
PgUp key, 49–50
.PIC filename extension, 241
PickForm option, 61
Picture formats, 74–77
pie charts, 213, 221, 233–236
Place option, 138–143, 170–172, 185–189, 337–352
PLAY command, 480, 530
Play option, 258, 449, 480
Plus operator (+), 305, 341–345
Pop option, 534, 536–537
power failure, 45
PPROG command, 568, 569
Predefined option, 174–175
preparsed procedure libraries, 545–557
printers
  calculated field codes for, 345–347
  changing defaults, 674–675, 677–678
  configuring, for graphs, 237–238
  escape sequences, 176
  interrupting, 167
  options, 173–176
  redirection, 177
  setup strings for, 174–176, 177
PRINTER.STATUS function, 511

printing, 62, 148–150
  from Answer table, 102
  condensed, 173–176
  continuous-feed, 159–160, 167
  graphs, 236–242
  groups of pages, 167
  instant (Alt-F7), 62, 102
  interrupting, 167
  mailing labels, 159–161
  from multiple tables, 376–379
  options, 149–150
  query answers, 102
  quick images, 62, 102
  sample PAL application, 502–513
  scripts, 524
  single sheets, 165
PrivateLookup option, 285
Problems table, 446
PROC command, 544, 547, 554
procedures, 541–545. *See also* preparsed procedure libraries
Proclib1.LIB program, 551–555
Proclib1.SC script, 551–554
programming, 459, 488–489, 520. *See also* Paradox Personal Programmer
ProtectedMode option, 667–668
protecting data, 428–432
  on networks, 642–651
  during suspended session, 524
Protection Generator, 646–651
Purchases table, 291–292, 571, 573, 594–598

Quattro files, 440–441
queries
  And/Or searches, 112–116, 302–304
  calculations in, 305–327
  clearing, from screen, 103
  creating graphs from, 204, 208, 213
  cursor moves in, 102
  for editing, 122–126
  form for, 101–102
  handling blanks in, 326
  limitations on, 126–127
  in many-to-many designs, 312–314
  of multiple tables, 295–304
  on networks, 640, 642
  outer joins in, 304–305
  pattern-matching, 116–122
  printing, 102
  range operators in, 108–110
  and record numbers, 102
  reports from, 167–170
  sample, 127–130

INDEX 699

saving, 327–328
selecting fields to view, 102
sorting, 104–105
speeding up, 328, 439–440, 519
for updating, 411–417
using commas in, 108, 111–112, 124
using quotation marks in, 127
using SQL Link, 652–658
values in, 107–110
QuerySave option, 259–260, 327–328
QuerySpeed option, 328, 439–440, 519
question mark (?), 74–75, 435, 464
Quit option, 537
QUITLOOP command, 516–517
quotation marks (''), 127, 345–346, 444, 479

range operators, 108–110
RangeOutput option, 160
ranges, 110–112
Read option, 460–461
READLIB command, 546, 549
record numbers, 102, 143–144. *See also*
 #Records field
 constant, 537–541
records, 4
 adding, 27–45
 calculations in, 307–308
 copying, from one table to another, 425–426
 deleting, 44, 68
 grouping, 356–371
 inserting, 43–44, 71
 locating, 56–58, 122
 locking, 630–631
 querying. *See* queries
 sets of, 319–326
#Records field, 352, 386
referential integrity, 405
Reformat option, 172–173
Refresh key (Alt-R), 635
Regroup option, 371
regular fields, 340
Regular option, 138–139, 185–187, 337, 340,
 587–588
remote tables, 652, 653–657
RemoveBlanks option, 146–148, 160
Rename option, 423–424
RepMenu.SC script, 494, 504–513
report bands, 356–357
REPORT command, 512
report generator, 133
Report menu, 138, 332–333
Report option, 134, 331
Report/Change option, 150–155

Report/Design option, 134–147
Report/Field/Erase option, 157, 159
Report/Field/Justify option, 352–353
Report/Field/Place option, 138–143, 170–172,
 337–352
Report/Field/Reformat option, 172–173
Report/Field/WordWrap option, 354
Report/Group option, 361–365, 370–371
Report/Output option, 145, 149–150
Report/SetPrinter option, 177
Report/Setting/Format option, 372–375
Report/Setting/Labels option, 160
Report/Setting/Margin option, 153–155
Report/Setting/PageLayout option, 152–153
Report/Setting/RemoveBlanks option,
 146–148, 160
Report/Setting/Setup option, 174–176
Report/TableBand option, 333–336
reports
 blank lines in, 137, 366–367
 calculations in, 340–350
 canceling formats, 147–148
 changing defaults, 672–675
 column formatting in, 333–336
 column justification in, 352–353
 copying formats of, 155–156
 date and time in, 170–171, 339, 350–351
 deleting columns in, 334
 deleting fields in, 157, 159
 description of, 134–135
 designing, 134–147
 erasing columns in, 334
 exporting, 446–447
 free-form, 135–173
 group headings in, 370
 grouping in, 356–371
 inserting columns in, 333–334
 keys used for, 136–137
 margin setting, 153–155
 margins in, 151–152
 moving columns in, 335
 from multiple tables, 376–379
 on networks, 640
 number formats in, 172–173, 339–340
 page breaks in, 164–165
 page length of, 152–153
 page numbers in, 171–172
 page width of, 153
 in Personal Programmer, 583–584, 592–594,
  596–598
 placing fields in, 138–143, 337–352
 printing, 62, 148–150
 from queries, 167–170

record numbers in, 143-144
from remote tables, 656-657
removing blanks in, 146-148
resizing columns in, 334-335
saving formats of, 147
squeezing out blanks in, 146-148
subtotals in, 350, 366, 368-369
tabular, 331-382
word-wrap in, 354
Reports option, 672-675
Required option, 72, 77
Resize option, 334-335
Restructure option, 436
Retain option, 372-373
RETURN command, 506-507
Rotate command (Ctrl-R), 60, 104, 106, 203-205, 248, 250-255, 335
rotated bar graphs, 206-207
rows, 3-4. *See also* records
.RPT filename extension, 447, 613
RUN BIG command, 525-526
RUN command, 525-526
running external programs, 453-454, 525-526

Sales table, 283-290, 571-572, 585-594
saving
  edits, 66
  graphs, 218-219
  image settings, 61
  new table structures, 22-23
  PAL programs, 460-461
  queries, 327-328
  report formats, 147
  tables, 41, 44
  validity checks, 78
.SC filename extension, 261
SCAN...ENDSCAN loop, 545
Screen option, 145
scripts. *See also* PAL programs
  attaching, to menu applications, 604-605
  autoexecute, 261
  automatic, 523-524
  conventions for, 480-488
  debugging, 462-463, 531-537
  editing, with word processor, 524-525
  encrypting, 429-431, 524
  filename extension (.SC), 261
  instant, 260, 328
  key names in, 482-484
  literal keystrokes, 481
  menu selections, 481
  naming, 255-256
  on networks, 641-642

playing, 258, 449, 480
playing back, 256-257, 259
printing, 524
protecting, 524
recording, 255-256
repeating, 259
running, from DOS, 600, 605
running external programs from, 525-526
saving queries with, 327-328
for updating tables, 410-418
variables in, 466-467, 485-488
viewing, 257-258
Scripts menu, 255, 258-260
Scripts/BeginRecord option, 255-256, 258-259
Scripts/Editor/Edit option, 257-258, 260, 463
Scripts/Editor/Edit/Print option, 524
Scripts/Editor/Write option, 260
Scripts/EndRecord option, 256, 259
Scripts/Play option, 258, 449, 480
Scripts/QuerySave option, 259-260, 327-328
Scripts/RepeatPlay option, 259
Scripts/ShowPlay option, 256-257, 259
searching. *See* queries
secondary indexes, 519. *See also* key fields
SelectFields option, 581
SelectRecords option, 581, 591
SelectTable option, 579
semicolon (;), 74-75
sequential data files, 445. *See also* ASCII files
servers, 652-653
.SET filename extension, 61, 532
set operators, 320
set queries, 319-326
SETKEY command, 526, 529-530
SetPrinter option, 177
Setting option, 174, 176
Setup strings, 174-176
Setups option, 674-675
SHOWMENU command, 477-479
ShowPlay option, 256-257, 259
Sign-Convention option, 172-173
slash (/), 305, 341
SLEEP command, 461
snapshots, 631
social security numbers, 74, 76
SORT command, 501-502
Sort menu, 98
Sort option, 83-84
sort order in Answer tables, 102, 104-105
Sorter.SC script, 494, 500-502
sorting, 83-98
  in descending orders, 84-87
  for editing, 513-518

by groups, 371
for mailing list, 500-502
on networks, 639
on one field, 83-84, 256
sample applications of, 92-98
script for, 500-502
on several fields, 87-97
source table, 414, 417
SpecifyAction option, 576-577
speeding up queries, 328, 439-440, 519
splash screens, 612
SQL Link, 652-658
square brackets ([ ]), 74-75, 341-342
stacked bar graphs, 206. *See also* area graphs
standard bar graphs, 206-207
StandardPrinter* option, 174, 176
Step option, 534-535
structured programming, 488-489
structured query language (SQL), 652-658
STRVAL function, 548-549
STYLE command, 464-467
subtotals in reports, 350, 366, 368-369
Summarize option, 612-615
summary fields, 349-350
summary operators, 324-325, 349-350, 379-382
summary reports, 375-376
summary values in Crosstab tables, 245
Suppress option, 372, 374-375
SWITCH...CASE...OTHERWISE...END-SWITCH command clause, 474-477
Symphony files, 441-442

table bands, 331-332, 357-358
Table View, 30, 49-51
editing from, 42-44, 65
keys used, 31-32
TableBand option, 332-336
table-level passwords, 643-646
TableLookup option, 77, 285-286, 288-289
TableOfGroups option, 372-373
tables, 3
adding fields to, 436
copying, 424
creating, 16-23
deleting, 425
editing, 65-72
filename extension (.DB), 41
linking, 272, 274, 276-277
modifying, 65-72
multiple, 265-293
naming, 16-17
on networks, 637-642

printing. *See* reports
remote, 652-657
restructuring, 435-436
saving, 41, 44
selecting, for Personal Progammer application, 571-574
structuring, 19-23
updating, 271-272, 409-421
viewing, 49-62
Tables option, 434
TableSize option, 51-52
TableView option, 579. *See also* MultiTable views
Tabular option, 331
tabular reports, 331-382
target table, 414, 417
templates, 137-138
Testlib.SC script, 549-551
text files, 444-453
Text option, 446
TEXT...ENDTEXT command clause, 494-495
3-D bar graphs, 206, 208
tilde (~) variable, 582
Time option, 171, 351
TO clause, 502
TO clause, 502
today operator, 117, 120
ToDos option, 453-454
Tools menu, 423
Tools option in Personal Programmer, 615-616
Tools/Copy option, 424
Tools/Copy/Form option, 199
Tools/Copy/JustFamily option, 170, 424
Tools/Copy/Report option, 155-156, 424
Tools/Copy/Table option, 424
Tools/Delete option, 425
Tools/ExportImport option, 440-446
Tools/Info/Family option, 435
Tools/Info/Inventory option, 434-435
Tools/Info/Structure option, 433
Tools/More/Add option, 414, 417, 425-426
Tools/More/Directory option, 432
Tools/More/Empty option, 414, 417, 427-428
Tools/More/Protect option, 428-432, 643-646
Tools/More/Subtract option, 426-427
Tools/More/ToDos option, 453-454
Tools/QuerySpeedup option, 328, 439-440
Tools/Rename option, 423-424
transaction-table structure, 271-272
transitive dependencies, 279
translating numbers into words, 541-545
Translat.SC script, 541, 543, 544-545, 554
Tune option, 666-668

Turbo key (Ctrl key), 49
.TXT filename extension, 443-444
TYPEIN command, 538

undeleting records, 68
Undo option, 67-68
Up Image key (F3), 299
UpDate option, 445-446
updating, 271-272
   automatic, 409-421
   queries for, 411-417, 642
   scripts for, 410-418, 603-604
UPPER function, 510
uppercase type, 119
U.S.Convention option, 173
user names, 636, 681-682

.VAL filename extension, 78
ValCheck option, 72
validity checks, 72-79
   clearing, 77
   filename extension (.VAL), 78
   saving, 78
   TableLookup option, 77, 285-286
Value option, 532-534
Variable option, 147
variables, 466-467, 485-488
Video option, 668-672
View option, 49-50
viewing tables, 49-62, 638-639
VisiCalc file format, 443-444

WAIT command, 462, 499
Wait option, 242
Where? option, 536
WHILE...ENDWHILE loop, 469, 471
wild-card characters, 58, 435
Windows 3.0, 662
.WK1 filename extension, 441
.WKS filename extension, 441
word processors
   editing scripts in, 524-525
   exporting files to, 446-453
WordPerfect, exporting files to, 448-453
WordStar, exporting files to, 447-448
word-wrap, 353-356
workspace, 12, 65
.WR1 filename extension, 441
WRITELIB command, 546, 549
write-protecting data, 431-432
.WRK filename extension, 441

x-y graphs, 209

YEAR function, 548

zeros, calculating blanks as, 347
zip codes, 75
   in PAL application, 500-501, 503
   sorting by, 161
Zoom key (Ctrl-Z), 57, 68-69
Zoom Next key (Alt-Z), 57
Zoom option, 56-58

SYBEX®

TO JOIN THE SYBEX MAILING LIST OR ORDER BOOKS PLEASE COMPLETE THIS FORM

NAME _____ COMPANY _____

STREET _____ CITY _____

STATE _____ ZIP _____

☐ PLEASE MAIL ME MORE INFORMATION ABOUT **SYBEX** TITLES

ORDER FORM (There is no obligation to order)

PLEASE SEND ME THE FOLLOWING:

TITLE	QTY	PRICE
_____	___	___
_____	___	___
_____	___	___
_____	___	___

TOTAL BOOK ORDER _____ $_____

SHIPPING AND HANDLING PLEASE ADD $2.00 PER BOOK VIA UPS _____

FOR OVERSEAS SURFACE ADD $5.25 PER BOOK PLUS $4.40 REGISTRATION FEE _____

FOR OVERSEAS AIRMAIL ADD $18.25 PER BOOK PLUS $4.40 REGISTRATION FEE _____

CALIFORNIA RESIDENTS PLEASE ADD APPLICABLE SALES TAX _____

TOTAL AMOUNT PAYABLE _____

☐ CHECK ENCLOSED ☐ VISA
☐ MASTERCARD ☐ AMERICAN EXPRESS

ACCOUNT NUMBER _____

EXPIR. DATE _____ DAYTIME PHONE _____

CUSTOMER SIGNATURE _____

CHECK AREA OF COMPUTER INTEREST:

☐ BUSINESS SOFTWARE
☐ TECHNICAL PROGRAMMING
☐ OTHER: _____

THE FACTOR THAT WAS MOST IMPORTANT IN YOUR SELECTION:

☐ THE SYBEX NAME
☐ QUALITY
☐ PRICE
☐ EXTRA FEATURES
☐ COMPREHENSIVENESS
☐ CLEAR WRITING
☐ OTHER _____

OTHER COMPUTER TITLES YOU WOULD LIKE TO SEE IN PRINT:

_____
_____

OCCUPATION

☐ PROGRAMMER ☐ TEACHER
☐ SENIOR EXECUTIVE ☐ HOMEMAKER
☐ COMPUTER CONSULTANT ☐ RETIRED
☐ SUPERVISOR ☐ STUDENT
☐ MIDDLE MANAGEMENT ☐ OTHER: _____
☐ ENGINEER/TECHNICAL
☐ CLERICAL/SERVICE
☐ BUSINESS OWNER/SELF EMPLOYED

CHECK YOUR LEVEL OF COMPUTER USE

☐ NEW TO COMPUTERS

☐ INFREQUENT COMPUTER USER

☐ FREQUENT USER OF ONE SOFTWARE
   PACKAGE:
   NAME _____

☐ FREQUENT USER OF MANY SOFTWARE
   PACKAGES

☐ PROFESSIONAL PROGRAMMER

OTHER COMMENTS:

_____
_____
_____
_____
_____
_____
_____
_____

PLEASE FOLD, SEAL, AND MAIL TO SYBEX

SYBEX, INC.
2021 CHALLENGER DR. #100
ALAMEDA, CALIFORNIA USA
94501

SEAL

SYBEX Computer Books are different.

Here is why . . .

At SYBEX, each book is designed with you in mind. Every manuscript is carefully selected and supervised by our editors, who are themselves computer experts. We publish the best authors, whose technical expertise is matched by an ability to write clearly and to communicate effectively. Programs are thoroughly tested for accuracy by our technical staff. Our computerized production department goes to great lengths to make sure that each book is well-designed.

In the pursuit of timeliness, SYBEX has achieved many publishing firsts. SYBEX was among the first to integrate personal computers used by authors and staff into the publishing process. SYBEX was the first to publish books on the CP/M operating system, microprocessor interfacing techniques, word processing, and many more topics.

Expertise in computers and dedication to the highest quality product have made SYBEX a world leader in computer book publishing. Translated into fourteen languages, SYBEX books have helped millions of people around the world to get the most from their computers. We hope we have helped you, too.

For a complete catalog of our publications:

SYBEX, Inc. 2021 Challenger Drive, #100, Alameda, CA 94501
Tel: (415) 523-8233/(800) 227-2346   Telex: 336311
Fax: (415) 523-2373

KEYS USED IN FIELD VIEW

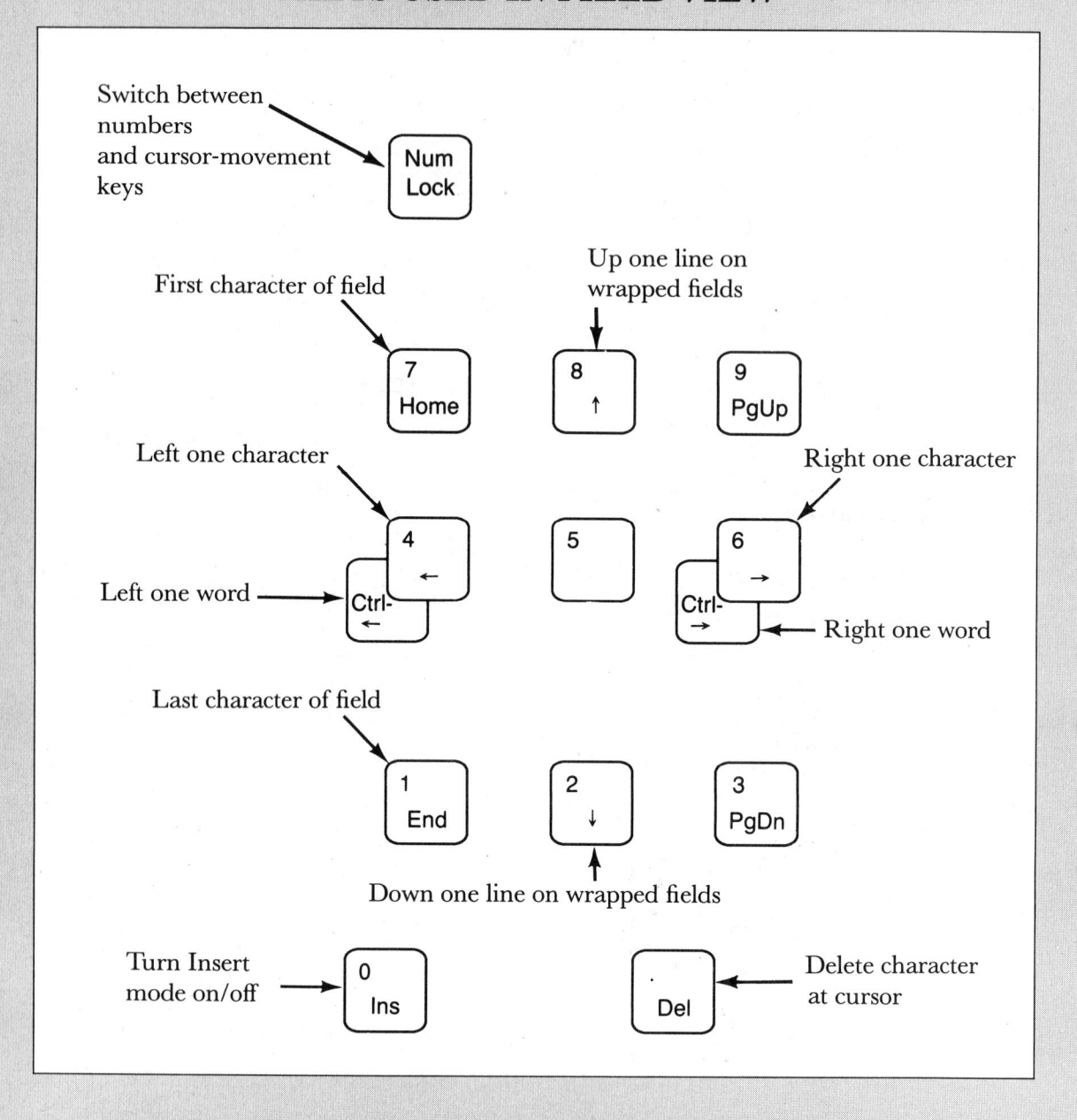

Switch between numbers and cursor-movement keys → [Num Lock]

First character of field ↓ [7 Home]

Up one line on wrapped fields ↓ [8 ↑]

[9 PgUp]

Left one character ↓ [4 ←]

Right one character ↓ [6 →]

Left one word → [Ctrl-←]

[5]

[Ctrl-→] ← Right one word

Last character of field ↓ [1 End]

[2 ↓]
↑
Down one line on wrapped fields

[3 PgDn]

Turn Insert mode on/off → [0 Ins]

[. Del] ← Delete character at cursor